Introducing UNIX Syste

Introducing UNIX System V

Rachel Morgan

Henry McGilton

McGraw-Hill Book Company

New York St. Louis San Francisco Au
Hamburg London Madrid Mexico
Milan Montreal New Delhi Panama
Paris São Paulo Singapore
Sydney Tokyo Toronto

INTRODUCING UNIX SYSTEM V
INTERNATIONAL EDITION

8 9 0 CMO 9 4 3

When ordering this title use ISBN 0-07-100210-3

Printed in Singapore

Contents

Preface

It is probably true that the UNIX† System V operating system has extensive documentation, since most things are written down somewhere. The problem is that an inexperienced user usually does not know where to look for a particular subject, and even when the requisite subject matter has been found, it is sometimes hard to understand.

This book sets out to lead the beginner by the hand, to show how to use System V in a simple fashion, and how to gain more information by reading the available documentation. For the user with some experience, this book shows how to use some of the more sophisticated programs provided on System V.

Caveat

This book is not a substitute for the existing System V documentation — it is a supplement to it.

Before you dip into the body of this book, you are encouraged to read through the table of contents. Although reading the table of contents is not normally the first thing you might think of doing with a book, the table of contents in this book is arranged such that it represents an overview of the topics and materials discussed herein.

Who Should Read This Book

This book is an introductory guide for users who are new to System V. Although the system and its myriad utilities are comprehensively documented, that documentation is mostly in the form of reference materials, 'memory joggers', and 'cheat sheets'.

Additionally the commands for handling files, getting information, and processing text, tend to have short and sometimes cryptic names such as `ls`, `grep`, `rm`, and so on. The system itself, and its many utilities, are often terse in their interactions with users. This book provides a bridge for users who have never used System V before, to help them over the initial hurdles of learning this new and powerful computer tool.

† UNIX is a trademark of AT&T Bell Laboratories.

Readers with some experience of System V can gain a better understanding of the system and its extensive but sometimes cryptic documentation. Experienced users will probably find that the logical arrangement of subject matter in this book is useful.

Educators should find this book suitable for course material, either about System V itself, or when using System V as a vehicle for other topics.

We have tried to show not only the facilities, commands, and utilities of System V, but what they might be used for. We use the examples to illustrate how the various utilities can be applied to transform text files in useful ways. We illustrate using System V by successively introducing more of the system's capabilities on a chapter-by-chapter basis. Each set of new capabilities uses material which has gone before. This ordering of material is part of the philosophy behind System V: to build upon what went before.

We have also tried to show areas where the misspelling of a command or a filename, or the misuse of a command, might give rise to error responses from the system. Therefore, as you read through the examples, you will find many illustrations of the form:

If you do *this*, you will get *that* result, and here is a possible reason

We believe that this is a positive approach to learning a new system. Many beginners get discouraged when the results of a command are not what they expected, and they have no idea why, or what to do next. In this book we have tried to remedy that situation.

Acknowledgements

There are many people we wish to thank for all their help.

- **Dual Systems** of Berkeley, California, sold us the computer system — a System 83/80 running System V — used to develop and check out the examples you will read in these pages.
- **Sun Microsystems** of Mountain View, California, provided the computer systems to format and print the camera-ready copy for this book.
- **Ken Greer** of the **Elan Computer Group**, Los Altos, California, provided use of his A. T. and T. 7300 system running System V, where we were able to cross check some of the examples.
- **Earl Stahl** acted as general purpose system wizard and troubleshooter.
- **J. D. Cloer** provided book-design, graphics advice, and aesthetics, while **Sean Browne** provided some last-minute crisis management.
- Most deserving of our thanks are the many friends and colleagues who encouraged us, proof-read for us, and corrected our blunders.

Colophon

This book was completely typed and checked out using UNIX-based and System V-based computers.

The text was typed using the `vi` and `ex` editors which we discuss in chapters 7 and 8 — *The Visual Text Editor* **`vi`** and *The* **`ex`** *and* **`ed`** *Line Editors*.

The manuscript was formatted using the System V tools `pic` (for drawing pictures), `tbl` (for laying out tables), `eqn` (for describing mathematical equations), and device-independent `troff` (that did the actual page layout). We discuss these tools in chapters 9, 10, and 11 — *Document Preparation Using System V*, *Document Formatting Packages*, and *Typesetting with* **`troff`** *and* **`nroff`**.

Table of contents and index were generated by home-grown software packages.

The formatting tools were run on a Sun Microsystems Sun-2/120 system running Sun's version of the 4.2 BSD operating system. The camera-ready manuscript was printed on Sun Microsystems' LaserWriters.

1 Introduction

Welcome to System V. System V represents a major step in the evolution of the powerful UNIX† system.

When we wrote our first book about the UNIX system[1], the UNIX system was a *phenomenon* rather than a commercial reality. Up until 1981, the UNIX system was confined mostly to University computer science departments and to research institutions. Now, the UNIX system, backed by A. T. & T's push to establish UNIX *System V* as a commercial standard, plus the marketplace acceptance of the UNIX System as a vehicle upon which to build and sell applications software, has gained widespread acceptance.

System V represents a point in an evolution of the UNIX system. System V retains most of the major characteristics of its predecessors. System V is 'lean and clean', built around a small but powerful set of mechanisms which can be combined to provide a working environment of considerable power and effectiveness. This working environment, System V, has proved itself to be of great convenience to people from fields as diverse as publishing, word processing, aerospace, computer science, and software development.

System V developed from the Computing Science Research Group at Bell Laboratories in New Jersey. It is said that the creators of the original UNIX system had this objective in mind:

> *'to create a computing environment where they themselves [the staff of the Computing Science Research Group] could comfortably and effectively pursue their own work — programming research'*[2].

Because of the direction of the work at Bell Laboratories, the UNIX system turned out to be particularly useful both for developing computer software, and for producing documents. Both of these applications need many and varied tools for processing files of text and numbers, and the UNIX system is particularly rich in this area. the UNIX system comes equipped with text manipulation tools, documentation processing utilities, an electronic mail system, and a flexible file system to

---

† UNIX is a trademark of AT&T Bell Laboratories.

1 *Introducing the UNIX System*, Morgan and McGilton, McGraw-Hill, 1983.

2 Bell System Technical Journal, July-August 1978

hold everything together.

Until 1981, the UNIX system was mostly confined to an environment consisting of university computer science departments, research laboratories connected with the Department of Defense Advanced Research Projects Agency (ARPA), and various industrial research and development organizations. With the widening of the installed base of the UNIX system to small machines such as those using the Motorola MC68000 microprocessors, the market for this popular operating system now extends to the small business, office, and home environments.

As the UNIX system spread out into the commercial marketplace, A. T. & T. in conjunction with various user groups set out to establish standards, starting with System III, and evolving to System V — the current commercial standard version.

This book is an introductory guide for users who are new to System V. The remainder of this chapter discusses the overall organization of a computer, the need for software to run that computer, and describes the way in which System V meets those needs.

Why have an Operating System?

On its own, a computer system is just a collection of metal, silicon, communications equipment, and magnetic media. It is the application programs which make a computer system useful to its users. Applications can range from word processing, through writing compilers, to generating new operating systems.

To exploit the communications, data storage, and information processing capabilities of the computer hardware, the applications software requires some form of overseer, which can handle the details of managing the hardware resources, accessing the files, and interacting with the users. These supervisory functions are the job of the 'operating system', which in this case, is System V.

Operating systems come in many shapes, sizes and guises. All operating systems have more or less the same function, namely to hold the ring between all the different hardware resources of a computer system in such a way that users can get work done. After all, getting the job done faster, or easier, or cheaper, is the putative reason we use computers in the first place.

System V is a relatively 'small' operating system. This is not to say that System V is poor in capability. On the contrary, it is constructed from a few basic ideas, which can be combined to form a user environment of considerable power. System V manages the resources of your computer system to perform useful work on your behalf. It is composed of three major parts. Two of these parts — the *File System* and the *Shell* — are visible to the users. The other major part — the *Kernel* — is not really visible but is equally important in the great scheme of things. Here is a brief summary of these three parts of the system:

the Kernel is that part of the system which manages the resources of whatever computer system it lives on, to keep track of the disks, tapes, printers, terminals, communication lines, and any other devices.

the File System is the organizing structure for data. The file system is perhaps the most important part of System V. Chapter 3 discusses the directory structure and the file system. The file system goes beyond being a simple repository for data, and provides the means of organizing the layout of the data storage in complex ways.

the Shell is the command interpreter. Although the Shell is just a utility program, and is not properly a part of the system, it is the part that the user sees. The Shell listens to your terminal, and translates your requests into actions on the part of the kernel and the many utility programs.

Main Features of UNIX System V

System V is an *interactive* operating system. This means that you type commands, the system obeys the commands and displays appropriate responses, you type some more commands, the system does the work and responds, and so on.

System V is a *multi-tasking* operating system. This means that the system can perform several tasks — called *processes* — at the same time. The multi-tasking feature means that you can give the system one or more tasks to be done 'in the background', and then you can get on with something else without having to wait for the task to finish.

System V is also a *multi-user* operating system. This means that more than one person can use the system at the same time. The multi-user aspect comes as a natural consequence of the multi-tasking feature just described: the system can attend to more than one user at a time just as easily as it can do more than one job at a time for one user. The multi-user facet means that groups of people can easily work together, sharing information and common utilities through the file system. With the trend away from large time-sharing systems and more towards one computer per person, the multi-user facilities are being deemphasized. If you run System V on a small personal computer you might be the only user, but the multi-tasking feature means that you can have more than one job going concurrently.

The File System

System V maintains a *file system* where users can store and retrieve information in named chunks called *files*. The organization of System V's file system is a *hierarchical* file system, sometimes called a tree-structured file system.

A hierarchical organization means that there is a special kind of file called a *directory*. Instead of holding users' data, a directory actually contains lists of file names, and signposts to where the files can be found in the file system. On System V this process can be carried to arbitrary limits, so that a directory can have sub-directories which in turn can have more sub-directories, and so on.

Understanding how to use the capabilities that the file system offers is perhaps the most important part of using System V effectively.

The Shell

The *Shell* is a program that listens to your terminal and accepts and interprets the commands you type. The Shell interprets the commands and turns them into requests to the underlying kernel, to perform the work you want. Not all versions of System V have the same Shell. There are several popular Shells in existence. Some installations support more than one Shell, and users can select which Shell they want to use.

System V Utility Software

In addition to the 'core' of System V described above (the kernel, Shell, and file system), System V comes equipped with a large number of utilities (tools) to help users get started with useful applications right away.

A large proportion of the utilities are devoted to manipulating text files in one form or another. There are text manipulation tools such as `grep` for selecting lines from a file according to specific criteria; tools like `ed`, `sed`, `tr`, and `awk` for selectively changing the contents of a file; there are tools such as `sort` and `uniq` for rearranging the order of lines in a file.

Then there are utilities for formatting documents, such as `nroff` (a text formatter), `troff` (a version of `nroff` oriented towards a phototypesetter), `eqn` (for setting mathematical equations), and `tbl` (for laying out tabular material).

There are various programming languages such as C, Pascal, FORTRAN, SNOBOL, BASIC and others. There are interactive arithmetic 'calculators', `bc` and `dc`.

Then, as befits a system geared up for programming research, there are tools such as `make` for managing large amounts of program source-text, and advanced aids such as `lex` and `yacc` for building compilers and other language products.

The above is by no means an exhaustive list of the facilities available. There are also aids to using System V itself, such as `who`, to find out who is using the system, `mail`, for user to user communication, and lots more.

All these utilities and tools comprise what is collectively called System V. In addition, by using the facilities which the Shell provides, it is very easy to tailor tools to fit your own special requirements.

1.1. UNIX System V Documentation

System V is extensively documented with ten or more thick books. The physical bulk of System V manuals is not an indication of complexity. System V is in fact a fairly simple and elegant system, on which there exist many things which must be documented.

Any given user will probably only use a small fraction of the total collection of available utilities. The problem is to find the ones that will be useful to you. This can sometimes be a big job, because the utilities are documented in alphabetical order, by name rather than by function. Therefore, this book sets out to guide you through what is in System V, and show you the more useful commands.

Chapter 2 of this book — *Getting Started on UNIX System V*, has some discussion on how to read the System V manuals, and how to get more information.

This book is not intended to replace the existing System V manuals. It is a guide to the basics of the system, and how to find your way through the manuals that come with System V. Because of this, you will frequently find the phrase:

Refer to the System V Manuals

to remind you that this book is a supplement to the existing documentation, not a replacement for it.

1.2. Evolution of the UNIX System

System V is an evolving system. As it got distributed out into the world, various groups of people made changes. The major core is more or less the same wherever you go, but there are cultural differences.

The picture below shows (some of) the evolutionary paths:

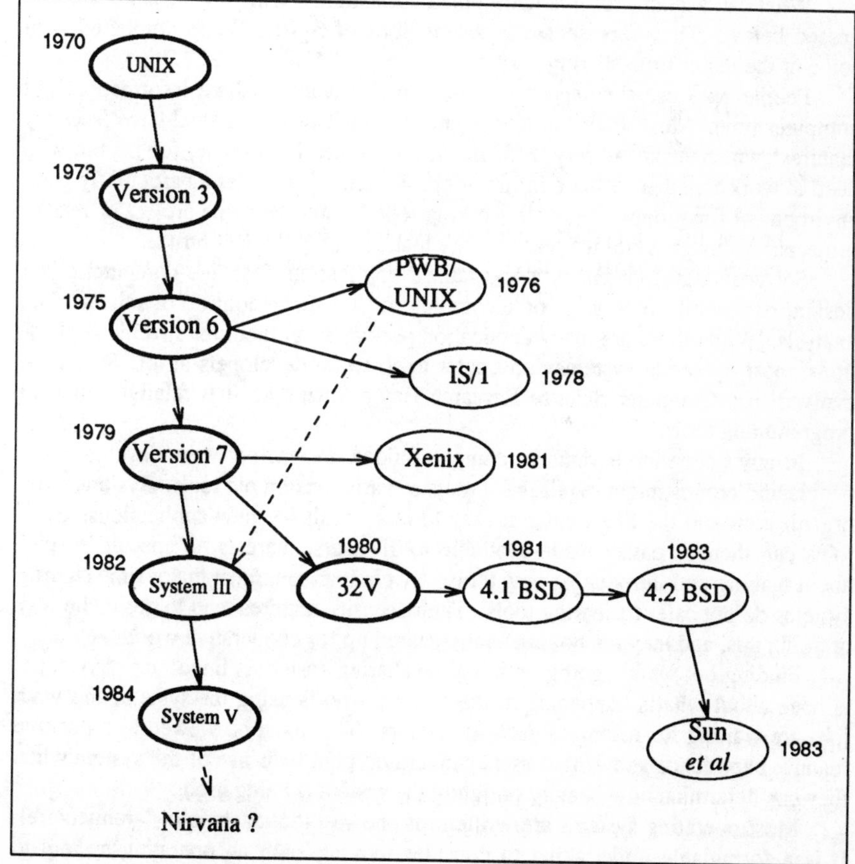

The dates are approximate. In addition, we haven't showed all the manufacturers that have jumped on the UNIX system bandwagon — there are just too many of them. The main diagonal on the left of the picture shows the main line of evolution.

The first few versions of the UNIX System were internal to Bell Laboratories. But in the early 1970's, Bell Laboratories began distributing the system to universities. The result of that move is that a whole generation of Computer Science graduates moved into the industrial sector as UNIX evangelists.

In the mid-1970's, *Interactive System One* (IS/1) was an important milestone — it was the first *commercial* implementation of the UNIX System. The Xenix System from Microsoft represented the next major commercial implementation.

In the academic/military world, the 4.1 and 4.2 Berkeley Software Distributions were the standards for the DEC VAX line of computers. From this implementation derived many of the microprocessor-based version of the UNIX System that are commercially available today.

What can account for this widespread acceptance? The key elements are discussed below. They represent our observations of System V, as compared with some of the major time-sharing systems.

People who use time-sharing systems really want to share information, not computer time. Most time-sharing systems overlook this point, and have 'security features' which make it very difficult, or sometimes impossible, for people who need to work together to share information. System V provides a particularly good environment for groups of people working together on the same project or related projects. Although System V has security features, they do not obtrude.

Software development is a specialized application, just like computer-aided design, or payroll processing, or accounting, or inventory control, or seismic data analysis. While there are many application packages out there for specific applications, most operating systems don't cater to software developers at all. System V evolved in a Computer Science Research Environment, so it is relatively rich in programming tools.

In any cooperative venture (computer-aided design, software development), people and groups might require new tools or variations on old tools. System V file organization and the Shell make it easy to tailor tools for new applications. Such tools can then be easily made available to all users; there is no special 'magic' about making and introducing new tools. By comparison, most major time-sharing systems do not cater to sharing tools. Their security features tend to get in the way of doing this, and they are not especially geared up for cooperative work.

Finding out what's going on in a time-sharing system is important. System V is open about what's happening in the system, who is using the system, and what jobs are waiting for resources such as printers. This must be viewed as a positive feature: experience shows that users can and do plan their use of the system when they can determine how heavily or lightly the system is being used.

Most operating systems are written for one specific machine or 'architecture'. It is a formidable undertaking to consider moving such an operating system to another computer. By contrast, System V is highly portable, because it is written in the C programming language.

Compared with other time-sharing systems, System V is an easy one to work on, and to get work done on. Nothing is perfect, and System V has its faults, but getting in the way of the user is not one of them. Some people even think that the system takes the policy of self-effacement too far, since it does nothing to stop the user from doing stupid things. In general, though, the features that make System V unique are a help rather than a hindrance. Above all, System V provides an environment for tool-using and tool-building. No matter what the application — documentation, business, or software development — System V supplies an extensive set of tools to assist these processes. Just about any tool you need is there. If it isn't, you will find that it is very easy to construct the process you want by connecting together existing tools.

This then, is System V. We hope that you will enjoy using System V, and gain as much from reading this book as we did from writing it.

1.3. Conventions

In this book we've made heavy use of `different` *fonts* to indicate different things. In addition, we've used grayscale to show examples of computer screens. Here are the general conventions:

- The regular text is set in Times Roman just as you are reading it now.
- We use this `typewriter font` to indicate the names of System V commands, and to show what the system displays to you when you are interacting with it.
- We use this **`bold typewriter font`** to indicate stuff that *you* type at the system when you are interacting with it.
- We use *italic font* for two purposes — for emphasis, and to show the names of files in the running text.
- We use a **helvetica bold** font to show special keys — that is, the convention **CNTRL-A** means 'press the **CONTROL** key while at the same time press the letter **A**.

Here is an example of an interactive dialog surrounded by a gray scale box. You should notice the use of the different typewriter fonts to indicate what you type and what the system displays in response.

```
$ who                                          you type in bold typewriter font
sally      tty00      Apr  9 08:30
peter      tty02      Apr  9 08:32             system displays in
henry      tty03      Apr  9 09:04             typewriter font
maryann    tty08      Apr  9 10:34
$
```

- *When you see a large black bullet at the start of a whole paragraph of text set all in italic font just like this paragraph, it's a sign that we're introducing something you should take special note of — that is, some kind of note or caution that demands special attention.*
- When you see an example of interactive dialog and part of the text is surrounded by a little lozenge:

  ```
  password: wizard
  ```

  it means that the text in the lozenge will not actually appear on your terminal on a real system — we show what the user types as if it was actually echoed.
- The chapter on `vi` relies heavily on the use of a small rectangle to show the position of the cursor on the screen:

  ```
  Use not vain repetition, as the heathen do.
  ```

1.4. How This Book Is Organized

Describing an operating system such as System V brings you, the reader, the problem of trying to learn everything at once; it brings us, the writers, the problem of trying to tell you everything at the same time. There is a certain core of knowledge which you must grasp, before the rest becomes clear.

Essential Core Ideas

For this reason, this book is really in two major parts. The essential knowledge is contained in chapters 2, 3, and 4. These chapters describe the key concepts behind System V. You should read these introductory chapters on the basics of System V, and learn how to log on (gain access to the system), learn about the directory structure and the file system, and the ideas of standard files and processes. Since there is no substitute for hands-on experience we suggest you should, if possible, follow the examples given while at a terminal connected to a real System V operating system.

- *Gaining Access to the System* is covered in chapter 2 — *Getting Started on UNIX System V* — where we introduce the basic notions of System V, such as how to gain access to the system, the notions of passwords, correcting typing errors, the format of commands, and how to find your way around the System V documentation.
- *The Hierarchical File System* is described in chapter 3 — *Directories and Files*. Chapter 3 covers the way in which you can move around in the file system, get information about directories, and how to create and remove directories. It discusses the rules for assigning names to files and directories. The basic commands needed to create, copy, rename, and remove files are covered in this chapter.

- Chapter 4 — *Processes and Standard Files* — covers the ways in which System V and its utilities communicate with your terminal and handle files. In this chapter you can learn how input to and output from a utility can be '*redirected*' to somewhere other than its standard places. You can also learn the way in which utilities can be hooked together, one after the other, in the form of a '*pipeline*'.

Once you have explored the ideas presented in those three chapters, the rest is relatively easy going, for everything else in System V operating is built upon those concepts.

System V Utilities

The remainder of the book discusses the utilities available, and the kinds of things you can do with them. We describe System V and its capabilities by means of a coherent thread of examples. The examples are introduced in a semi-tutorial fashion, starting with simple examples, and working to more complicated ones.

- *Communications facilities* are described in chapter 5 — *User to User Communication* — which covers the facilities by which users can communicate with each other using the system's electronic mail utilities.

Text Processing and Text Editing

Text Processing is one of the strong areas of System V, evolving as it did in the computer science research area where statistical text processing was a major application.

- Chapter 6 — *Text Manipulation* — introduces some of the powerful tools for looking at files of text in various ways. In this chapter you can find out how to print a file, how to select lines from a file, and how to sort a file in any way you want, and more.
- Chapter 12 — *Advanced Text Manipulation* — appears later in the book and covers the `sed` *stream editor* and the `awk` 'programmable report generator'.
- *Text Editing* is described in chapter 7 — *The Visual Text Editor* **`vi`** and in chapter 8 — *The* **`ex`** *and* **`ed`** *Line Editors*. The `vi` editor and the `ex` editor derive from the Berkeley version of the UNIX system, but are also available on System V. The `vi` editor provides on-screen editing capabilities; `ex` is a part of `vi` that provides line oriented editing. The `ed` editor, which was available with the original versions of UNIX systems, also provides line oriented editing.

Document Preparation

Document Preparation is another area of strength in System V. Although the document preparation facilities are 'batch' oriented, they provide extremely powerful tools for generating documentation. The document preparation facilities are described in three separate chapters:

- Chapter 9 — *Document Preparation Using System V* — introduces the capabilities of the `-mm` *macro package* — a (relatively) 'high-level' set of commands to get the formatting tools processing documents.
- Chapter 10 — *Document Formatting Packages* — discusses *preprocessors* that enhance on the capabilities of `troff` (the document formatting software). The three tools described here are `tbl` (a tool and a language for describing *tables*), `eqn` (for describing *mathematical equations*), and `pic` (for describing *pictures*).
- Finally, chapter 11 — *Typesetting with* **`troff`** *and* **`nroff`** — is a simple introduction to the `troff` text formatter — the underlying core of the document formatting system.

Note that the document preparation facilities we describe in this book are part of a separately licensed software package called the *Documentor's Workbench*.

Software Development Tools

Software development is another major area where System V is rich. The system evolved in the computer science research field where the ability to create and evaluate software quickly and easily is of paramount importance.

- The first line of attack in creating tools is to use the *Shell* — the programmable command language interpreter. In chapter 13 — *Using the Shell as a Programming Language* — we describe how you can easily create your own commands, by using other commands in combination. This chapter covers the concepts of programming the Shell, to create new commands and tools.
- Chapter 14 — *Programming Tools in System V* — provides a summary of programming tools available to the programmer, to aid the software development process. We provide a quick run-down of C language development aids. We discuss performance monitoring tools. We also cover (briefly) two main development tools — `make` (for assisting building large programs out of many interdependent pieces), and SCCS (the Source Code Control System) which assists in maintaining history in a project.

System Administration

System administration is covered in chapter 15 — *System Administration* — which describes subjects of interest to anyone who might have to do the day-to-day job of caring for and feeding System V.

2 Getting Started on UNIX System V

This chapter covers some of the most basic issues on how to get to grips with UNIX System V. First we show you how to get signed on (gain access) to the system. This topic includes the philosophies of user name and password. Then we follow with a section concerned with correcting typing mistakes. After that there are examples of some simple commands, which we use to introduce the basic format of System V commands. In this section we also introduce the idea of arguments to commands, and options which modify the behavior of commands. Finally, we give guidelines to help you find your way around the System V Manuals.

It is hard for anyone to learn about a new computer system in the abstract. The best way to learn how to use System V is to relax in front of a terminal connected to a *real* system, armed with a copy of this book, a glass of champagne, and the System V Manuals close at hand.

2.1. User Names and Passwords

Everyone who uses System V is given a special 'user name' to use when signing on to the system. A user name is also quite often called an 'account', since in many installations someone is keeping an account of usage by different people and groups.

In practice, one person might have several user names; different names would be used when using the system for different purposes. For example, if Joe Mugg is responsible for payroll, he would probably use the user name 'joe' while developing new accounting programs; but for running the finished programs to compute people's take-home pay he would use a different user name, say 'payroll'.

Several people working on related things can be grouped together on the system, and the group can be allocated a group name or group identity.

One of the users on any given System V is called the 'super-user'. This is the person who has the administrative duties of assigning new user names, and generally looking after the system. The super-user has the name 'root' as the user name[1].

---

[1] There can be several kinds of super-user, each with different administrative duties, and each with different user-names. But, 'root' is the 'super'-est of the super-users.

In addition to your user name, you can also have a password. This is a string of characters which you type to gain access to the system. But, whereas your user name is assigned by the super-user, your password is your own choice entirely. You can change your password at any time and nobody, not even the super-user, can figure out what it is.

2.2. Signing On to the UNIX System

To gain access to System V so that you can use its facilities, you must go through a 'sign-on' process. This process is usually known as 'logging in', or sometimes 'logging on'.

In the discussion to follow, we assume that the terminal which you are using is connected directly ('hard-wired') to the system in question. On some installations, you have to dial up over a telephone line, via a modem, to gain access. We ignore this aspect for the time being, and assume that the terminal is already connected and ready to go.

When you approach a terminal connected to System V, it should be displaying a message which looks something like this one show here[2]:

```
Dual 83/80 68000 System V UNIX

login:
```

Some System V installations don't have any initial display to indicate whose company it is, they just show 'login'. The exact details of this message differ from one System V installation to another, but this does not affect the actions you have to perform.

To log in to the system you simply type your user name, and then press the carriage-return key (labelled **RETURN**, or **ENTER**, or **NEWLINE**). Notice that as you type in your user name, what you type is displayed on the terminal screen. With very few exceptions, System V generally echoes (plays back to you) what you type. In all the examples in this book, what you type is shown in **`bold typewriter print`**. When you have typed your user name, the system responds by asking you for your password, thus:

```
Dual 83/80 68000 System V UNIX

login: maryann
password: wizard
```

---

2 This is what our Dual Systems machine displays — your system will probably display something entirely different.

Type in your password, then press the RETURN key. If you don't have a password, simply press the RETURN key. We show the password typed in surrounded with the little lozenge:

`wizard`

because on a real system, your password is not echoed as you type it — nothing appears on the screen as you are typing. This is because your password is private and anyone who might happen to be looking over your shoulder should not be able to see it.

If you don't know, or have forgotten, your password, find a 'super-user'. A System V administrator can make your password anything you like. You can change your password later for privacy.

When you have typed in your user name and password, the system checks that you are indeed a known user of the system, and that you have given the correct password. If for any reason your login is not correct, the system displays a message to that effect:

```
Dual 83/80 68000 System V UNIX

login: maryan
password: wizard
Login incorrect
login:
```

Getting a 'Login incorrect' message can happen for a number of reasons. One way to get it wrong is to misspell either your user name or your password. In the example above, one 'n' was left out of the user name.

Another possibility is that you might not even have an account on that particular System V installation. This sometimes happens when you try to log in before the super-user has had time to assign your user name and password.

It might also happen that you log in correctly, but a different problem arises:

```
Dual 83/80 68000 System V UNIX

login: maryann
password: wizard
No directory
login:
```

As we shall explain in chapter 3 — *Directories and Files*, there is a 'home' directory associated with every user name on the system. If you get the response as above, it might be because the super-user did not assign a directory for you. Or the super-user might have misspelled the name of your login directory[3]. In this case,

---

[3] Don't be misled by the term 'super-user'. These beings are in fact as human as you or I, and they do occasionally make mistakes.

you will have to go and see the super-user to have things set up correctly.

But let's be cheerful about this whole process and assume that you have logged in successfully. After you have logged in the system displays a prompt, which indicates that it is ready to do your bidding. Your terminal screen looks something like this:

```
Dual 83/80 68000 System V UNIX

login: maryann
password: wizard
Last login: Fri Apr 4 08:05

$
```

The 'Last login' message indicates the last time that your account was used. At some installations this message is not displayed, so don't worry if you don't see it. The presence or otherwise of the message is controlled by the System Administrator. If this is your first login session, the message displayed probably shows when the System Administrator set up your account. It is a good idea to check the message when you log in; if the date and time displayed are not in accord with your memory of when you last logged in, it could be that someone else is using your account.

Now that you've successfully logged in, you might want to know how to log out again. There is a short section, called '*Signing Off*', later in this chapter.

The UNIX System Prompt

The `$` shown at the end of the above example is the system prompt. It tells you that System V is waiting for you to type a command. Every time the system has finished running a command and is listening to your terminal, it replies with the `$` prompt.

System V has the capability to let you choose your own prompt. If you have several different login-names on your system, you might want to set up your prompt so that it reminds you which user name you are currently logged in as.

In the examples we give in this book, we use the `$` prompt. We generally show the prompt before what you type, and after the system's response. Also, we will show what you type in **`bold typewriter text like this`**, and what the system displays in `typewriter text like this`.

Remember that, at the end of every line you type to System V, you have to press the RETURN key before the system sees that input. We do not explicitly show the RETURN at the end of the lines in our examples.

Notes and Cautions on Login

Be aware that System V distinguishes between upper and lower case, so do not type your user name in upper case — not even the initial letter. If you do, the system might not recognize you as a valid user and you will get the 'Login incorrect' message. In some cases the system might even assume that you are using a terminal that only has upper case, and henceforth talks to you only in CAPITAL LETTERS.

Because your password doesn't appear on the terminal as you type it, make sure that your password is easy to type. It is very frustrating to have to make several attempts at logging in simply because you can't get your password right. You can change your password using the `passwd` command. We show you how to do this later in this chapter.

Certain characters have special meaning to System V. You should avoid using these characters in both you user name and your password. A fuller discussion of these special characters is given later in this chapter, and also in chapter chapter 3. Most important to avoid are # and `@`. You are unlikely to be allocated a user-name that contains these characters, but be careful when choosing your password. If you are feeling angry, do not succumb to the temptation to make your password something like `@$#!!` — you will have trouble logging in.

On most System V installations there is a predefined limit on the number of times that you can attempt to log in without getting it right. The actions taken if this limit (usually five) is exceeded vary depending on the installation. If you are accessing System V through a telephone modem, the system may well disconnect ('hang up on you'), and you have to dial again to get a connection.

Initial Password

Depending on the bureaucracy at your System V installation, you might or might not have a password already assigned to you when you first get an account on the system.

In some installations you are not assigned a password, and you can set your own with the `passwd` command the first time you log in. Of course you can continue without a password if that suits you.

At other sites, the super-user assigns your password (sometimes of your choice, sometimes not) and it is up to you to change it if you want to.

Login Messages from the UNIX System

When you have typed your password, the system might well type out some messages before the `$` prompt. These messages are usually information about the system: maybe some added features, or notification of planned maintenance shutdowns. Here is an example:

```
Dual 83/80 68000 System V UNIX

login: maryann
password: wizard
Last login: Fri Apr 4 08:05

D U A L   8 3 / 8 0   6 8 0 0 0   S Y S T E M   V   U N I X

The system will be down this Saturday from 8am to 2pm
while we are doing Preventive Maintenance.

Filesystem /aa is VERY low on space !!!
Please inspect your files and remove moldy oldies.

$
```

This message is often called the message of the day. It appears every time you log in to System V.

Another form of initial message is concerned with the `mail` facility for inter-user communication.

```
Dual 83/80 68000 System V UNIX

login: maryann
password: wizard
Last login: Fri Apr 4 08:05

You have mail.
$
```

This message means that someone has sent you mail through the `mail` facility. If there is a login message, it appears before any notification of mail. We cover the `mail` facility in chapter 5 — *User to User Communication.*

2.3. Correcting Typing Mistakes

What do you do when you make a mistake when typing a command? For instance, suppose you wanted to use the `date` command to find the current date and time, and you typed this:

```
$ dste
```

Normally, to complete the command you would press RETURN, but in this case you realize that you have a spelling mistake. The easiest thing to do is to press RETURN anyway, and let the system try to run this mysterious `dste` command:

```
$ dste
dste: not found
$
```

However, if there really was a dste command, you could be in trouble. It would be better to correct your command line, or tell the system to ignore it.

There are two characters you can use to tell System V you've made a mistake. The *erase character* erases the previously typed character. The *kill character* tells System V to ignore ('kill') the entire line typed so far. A more detailed discussion of these characters follows.

As an aside: The original UNIX system began its life on systems where the terminals were Teletypes (slow hard-copy devices). Since a lot of these devices do not have a backspace key or any other form of control key, the system pre-empted some of the printing characters for control purposes. And so the *erase* and *kill* characters were selected as # and @ respectively. Although most systems today work on terminals with all the required controls, the legacy of the early days is still with us on some installations.

The Erase Character

On most System V installations, the character for erasing the previous character is the backspace character. This is labelled BACKSPACE or BS on some terminals. Other terminals label it as a left pointing arrow (a cursor control). On some primitive terminals, you have to type 'control-H'.

To get a control character, you hold down the control key (marked CTRL on most terminals) while typing the character you want. For example, to get 'control-H', you hold down the key marked CTRL while you type 'h'. The 'control-H' combination usually backspaces the cursor position on a terminal, but in general the other control characters are non-printing characters. The control key is often marked CNTR, CNTRL, or sometimes even CONTROL. On most terminals, it is located somewhere on the left-hand side of the keyboard.

In printed documentation, it is conventional to use the 'hat' (or 'caret' or circumflex) character, ^, followed by a 'whatever' character to mean 'control-whatever'. For example ^H means you should type 'control-H' (hold down the CTRL key while pressing the h key). It doesn't mean type the separate characters ^ and H. In the examples in this book, we follow the convention of using the circumflex character ^ in examples, and we use the symbol CTRL- when talking about the examples.

Every time you type CTRL-H the cursor moves one position to the left on the terminal screen. The erase character tells the system to ignore the last character you typed, two erases mean ignore the last two characters, and so on. So you could have corrected the misspelling:

```
$ dste^H^H^Hate
Wed Apr  9 09:12:34 PST 1986
$
```

The three CTRL-H characters erase the 'e', the 't', and the incorrect 's'. The rest of the line is what should have been typed in the first place. As you type each CTRL-H the cursor backspaces (moves to the left) one character on the screen. This can't be shown on a static display such as a page in a book, so the above example shows what you type, not what you see on your terminal screen.

If you should happen to be working on a system where the erase character is #, this character does not backspace over previous characters. So on your terminal screen you would actually see:

```
$ dste###ate
Wed Apr  9 09:13:04 PST 1986
$
```

When using # as the erase character you have to count the number of characters to be corrected, something that is unnecessary when you use backspace or CTRL-H.

If the erase character is # and you need to enter a # literally, you have to tell System V that this is really what you want, that you haven't made a mistake this time. This is achieved by preceding the # by a \. So to actually get # you have to type \#.

The \ is the 'escape' character. It is used to remove any special meaning that the system might attach to the character following it.

The Line Kill Character

The line kill character at the end of a line means 'kill', or 'ignore the line typed so far'. It tells System V that you didn't want it to obey the command line you have just typed.

On many systems the line kill character is left as `@`, on others it could have been changed to a control character. Two popular choices are CTRL-X and CTRL-U. In this book we use CTRL-U as the kill character.

You don't have to type RETURN after the kill character. The system just ignores everything on that line so you can straight away type another command line. You do not get the `$` sign prompt after typing the kill, unless you press the RETURN key. So, for example:

```
$ dste^U date
Wed Apr  9 09:13:19 PST 1986
$
```

Although there is a command `stty` that purports to display the current erase and kill characters (among other things), interpretation of the output of this command is not easy. So the best way to determine your line kill character is by experiment: type some garbage command (`gmph`, say) followed by the presumed kill character, followed by **RETURN**. If you get a message 'gmph not found', then that wasn't your kill character. If you get the system prompt you have found your kill character.

As in the case of #, if the kill character is an @ sign and you really want a @, you have to escape it by typing \@.

Changing the Erase and Kill Characters with `stty`

You can change the erase and kill characters to anything you like using the `stty` command. This is especially valuable if you are on a system where the erase and kill characters are # and @. We do not go into all the details of `stty` at this point. We just show you how to change erase and kill characters.

To change the erase character to **CTRL-H** you say:

```
$ stty erase ^H
$
```

If you wanted to change it back to #, you would say:

```
$ stty erase #
$
```

To change the kill character to **CTRL-U** you could say:

```
$ stty kill ^U
$
```

Now, when you type **CTRL-U**, the system ignores everything on that command line.

You can change both characters in the same command:

```
$ stty erase ^H kill ^U
$
```

If you change the erase and kill characters during a login session, they only remain in effect until you log off System V. They then revert to whatever the system default is. Next time you log in you will have to give the `stty` command again. There is a way of getting commands executed automatically when you log in. This capability is exploited through a file called your 'login profile', and is described in chapter 13 — *Using the Shell as a Programming Language.*

stty also accepts the literal characters '^' (caret), followed by 'H', to mean CTRL-H. This means that you type the stty command like this:

```
$ stty erase '^H'
$
```

Note that there are single quote signs around the argument. This is one of the places where you must use single quotes, and double quotes will not do.

If you make any mistakes while typing your user name or password at login time, you have to use whatever the system default erase and kill characters are to correct the errors, even if your erase and kill characters are automatically set up in a login profile. This is because the system doesn't see the profile until after you have logged in.

2.4. Some Simple Commands

Let's start with a very simple command, one we have already seen. Just one word to System V:

```
$ date
Wed Apr  9 09:19:41 PST 1986
$
```

Type the word date, followed by the RETURN key. All System V command lines are terminated by pressing the RETURN key. The system displays the current date and time (or, since the date and time can be changed by the super-user, what System V thinks is the current date and time). In fact you can tell the date command the format in which you wish to see the date, but the above is the default layout, and it is good enough for most purposes.

Another simple one-word command — who — tells you who is using the system. The information that who displays is: who is logged on to the system, the system's name for the terminal they are logged on at, and the time they logged on. Here is an example of who:

```
$ who
sally      tty00      Apr  9 08:30
peter      tty02      Apr  9 08:32
henry      tty03      Apr  9 09:04
maryann    tty08      Apr  9 10:34
$
```

A variation of the who command is who am i as shown below.

```
$ who am i
maryann    tty08        Apr  9 10:34
$
```

Here, we typed three words. The first word is the command who. The remaining words are *arguments* to that command. Arguments are separated from the command, and from each other, by one or more spaces. Arguments to commands are mostly names of files to be manipulated but, since we haven't described files yet, we are giving examples of those commands which don't use filenames.

At first sight, wanting to know who you are might seem like a dumb thing to do. But if you have to share a terminal with other users, and a previous user has not logged out, you can use who in this way to find out who has abandoned the terminal. Also, you sometimes need to know your terminal identity to do other checks on the progress of jobs running on your behalf, who am i provides a way of finding that.

2.5. Format of UNIX System Commands

We have seen the general format of commands in the above example. It is a sequence of words (by which we mean non-blank characters), each word being separated from its neighbors by one or more spaces (blanks). The entire command is terminated by a newline character, which is produced when you press the **RETURN** key (the key marked **LINEFEED** or **NL** does it too).

The first word is the command itself, the remaining words are *arguments* to the command. There can be spaces before the command, and there can be spaces after the last argument, before the newline. Since spaces are used to separate the arguments, the arguments themselves must not contain spaces. If for some reason you have to give an argument containing a space, the entire argument should be surrounded with double quotes ("), or with single quotes or apostrophes ('). Do not use the grave accent (`) for this purpose. Apostrophe and grave are not the same character. Make sure that you know which is which. We show an example of this in chapter 6, when we describe the pr command.

Several commands can be put on the same line by typing a semicolon (;) between them, thus:

```
$ who am i; date
maryann    tty08        Apr  9 10:34
Wed Apr  9 11:19:41 PST 1986
$
```

There can be spaces on either side of the ; or not, it doesn't matter. System V obeys the who command first, then the date command. Notice that the system doesn't respond with its prompt character, $, until it has completed all the commands on that line.

Arguments to commands

For the most part, arguments to System V commands are one of three things:

filename the name of a file which the command is to manipulate in some way. Filenames can be up to fourteen characters long, and can consist of just about any characters. In practice, however, most file names are shorter and consist only of letters a-z, numbers 0-9 and some other characters such as underscore (_), period (.) and minus sign (-). On System V, uppercase letters and lowercase letters are considered different in filenames.

The system provides special 'metacharacters' or 'wild card characters' for filename matching, so that you can use a shorthand notation for working on groups of files at a time. The topics of filenames, file naming conventions, and wild-card matching, are covered in chapter 3 — *Directories and Files*.

option this is a literal, usually introduced by a minus sign, for example `-al`. An option modifies the action of the command in some way, or gives details of exactly how the command is to operate. The exact effect of the option is different for each command. Some options are introduced by a plus sign rather than a minus, and some are not preceded by anything.

expression an expression describing a character string which is to be used as input to the command. In the simplest case the expression is the string itself. We describe string-matching expressions later, when we talk about the `grep` command.

Although we just described the types of arguments in the order: files, options, and expressions, generally the order of the arguments following the command is:

```
command options expression filename(s)
```

However, different commands can have different requirements; the exact order required for each command should be found by referring to the documentation for the specific command.

Here are some typical System V commands to give you the flavors of the arguments. Don't bother about what the commands and their options actually do, just take note of the layout of the commands.

`rm old.news bad.news`

a typical `rm` (remove files) command with two filename arguments. It removes the two files called *old.news* and *bad.news* from the file system.

`rm -fr goodies.c baddies.o`

another `rm` command with two options (f and r), and two filename arguments.

`grep "Sally Smith" people`

a fairly typical use of the `grep` command, (look for patterns in a file) where the first argument is an expression, and the second argument is a filename.

The first argument is two words, so it is enclosed in quotes.

`grep -v "Sally Smith" people`
the same `grep` command, except this time the first argument is an option.

As you read through the book, there are many examples of the different commands and their arguments.

Quoting Arguments to Commands

You will notice that the argument, `Sally Smith`, on the **grep** command, above, is contained in quote signs, ("). Arguments to commands can be enclosed either in double quotes, or within single quote signs, ('). The single quote sign is the same character as the apostrophe.

In general, it usually doesn't matter which kinds of quotes you use. You could type the `grep` command either as:

```
$ grep  "Sally Smith"  people
```

with the argument in double quotes, or you could type it like this:

```
$ grep 'Sally Smith' people
```

with single quotes (apostrophes). Of course, if the argument already contains one kind of quote, (an apostrophe in the next example) you have to enclose the string in the other kind, like this:

```
$ grep "Sally Smith's Project" people
```

There are cases, however, when the Shell (the command-line interpreter) places some special interpretation on certain characters in arguments. For instance, when you get to chapter 3, you will see that the Shell uses some characters to provide the means to work with whole groups of files.

There are other cases where the Shell assigns special meanings to characters even when they are enclosed in double quotes. The most likely
cial treatment is the dollar sign, $. If your argument contains a $
enclose it in single quotes.

Some general 'rules of thumb':

- If a command doesn't work with an unquoted argument,
ment within quote signs, (").
- If that doesn't work either, use the single quote signs, ('
- If that still doesn't work, 'escape' any special charact
them with the reverse slash character, (\ ).

- If this still doesn't work, you should go find a System V wizard who can help.

2.6. Changing Your Password with passwd

Everyone should have a password, and should change passwords at reasonably frequent intervals for security reasons. The command that changes your password (or installs one for you if you don't already have one) is `passwd`.

The `passwd` command is a little different from the ones we have been discussing, in that it is interactive. You simply type the command and `passwd` tells you what input it wants. A conversation with `passwd` goes something like this:

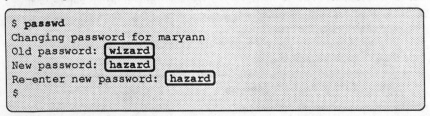

```
$ passwd
Changing password for maryann
Old password: wizard
New password: hazard
Re-enter new password: hazard
$
```

Notice that you have to type your new password twice. Because the system does not echo the passwords as you type them (illustrated by the lozenged[4] print in the example), it asks for confirmation. If the second time you type your new password, it differs from the first, no action is taken. This prevents fumble-finger accidents getting into your password, which would make it difficult for you to log in next time.

There is a file called the password file, which contains an entry for each user of System V. Each entry consists of the user name, password and other interesting information about the user. The file can be accessed by all users so, to preserve the security of passwords, the passwords are encrypted (enciphered). This means that your password as it appears in the file looks nothing like what you type in response to the prompt 'Password'. The encryption of the password means that no one, not even the super-user, can figure out what it is by looking at the encrypted version, so you should not forget your password. It is recommended that you write your password on a piece of paper, then eat it with a champagne chaser — you shouldn't leave the piece of paper lying around where anyone could find it.

A description of the encryption process can be found under the command `crypt` in the *System V User's Manual*.

When changing your password, there are a couple of things which can go wrong. The first is that your old password doesn't match what the system thinks it should be:

---

[4] You can *verb* anything!

```
$ passwd
Changing password for maryann
Old password: blizzard
Sorry.
$
```

Here, Maryann typed the wrong password, and got the indicated response. It is also possible that you type a different new password on the first and second tries:

```
$ passwd
Changing password for maryann
Old password: hazard
New password: blizzard
Re-enter new password: blizzadr
They don't match; try again
Re-enter new password:
```

If you keep on getting mismatches on your password (3 or more), the command exits with the message

```
Too many tries; try again later
$
```

This is probably a good thing because, if you can't get it right while trying to install it you're almost certain to have trouble when you try to log in!

In general, System V doesn't like short passwords (they might be too easy for someone to guess at), so the `passwd` command rejects passwords that are too short. Here's what happens when you try a password that the system doesn't like:

```
$ passwd
Changing password for maryann
Old password: wiz
Too short. Password unchanged.
$
```

2.7. The Shell's Use of Special Characters

We have briefly stated that the Shell interprets some characters in special ways. Some of these characters are used for filename expansion, some are used inside the Shell itself for substitution of arguments, and some are used to stop and start any display coming from a running program. We will just list these special characters here. The full discussions are to be found in chapters 3 and 13.

- The backslash character \ is used everywhere, and is interpreted as an 'escape' character. The backslash character nullifies the special meaning of any character which immediately follows it.
- The Shell interprets the characters:

  ***** (*asterisk*), **?** (*question mark*), **[** (*left bracket*), **]** (*right bracket*), and **–** (*hyphen*)

  as abbreviations for filename expansion. Chapter 3 covers this subject in more detail.
- The Shell uses the dollar sign character $ for argument substitution. We discuss this in chapter 13.
- The CTRL-D character is used as a 'log-out' signal to the Shell, and is an 'end-of-text' signal to programs requesting input from the terminal.
- The CTRL-S and CTRL-Q characters are used for stopping and re-starting output to the terminal. The DELETE or RUBOUT character is used for stopping a running command. These topics are discussed just below.

The moral of this section is: the special characters should be used with caution.

Halting Output Temporarily

The commands we have seen so far have produced very little in the way of output on the terminal, not more than a few lines. Quite frequently, the output of a command is very long — much more than will fit on a terminal screen, which holds only 24 lines. Unless you have a terminal that is slow enough for you to read things before they disappear off the top of the screen, you will want to stop the display temporarily, then continue when you've seen what you wanted.

Stopping the display temporarily is done by typing CTRL-S (hold down the CTRL key while typing 's'). CTRL-S suspends the screen scrolling process. Whatever command is displaying to the screen is still running, only the display of the output to the screen is halted temporarily.

To resume displaying the command's output, you type CTRL-Q. Output to the screen then continues until you type another CTRL-S, or until the command is finished.

Stopping a Command

If the output of a command is very long, you may not want to see it all. For instance, if you simply want to check what the first few lines of a file look like, there is no need to display the entire file; and if the file is a long one it will take too much precious time to do so.

To completely stop (abandon) the command, you can hit the key marked BREAK (if there is one), or the RUBOUT key, or the DEL key. The command is interrupted and the system requests another command, so you see the system prompt $.

The character which interrupts a command can be set with `stty`, in much the same way as we could set CTRL-H as the erase character. If you have this feature, we recommend you use it to change the interrupt character to CTRL-C:

```
$ stty intr ^C
$
```

```
$ stty intr '^C'
$
```

This is particularly important if you are working over a phone line. On a bad line many spurious 'delete' characters appear — each of these will interrupt the command you are currently running, so it's better to change to CTRL-C if you can.

2.8. Signing Off

When you have finished working with System V, you can sign off ('logout', or 'log off') simply by typing CTRL-D when you see the $ sign. CTRL-D, at the start of a line of input, is the 'end of text' character, and is used in many ways throughout the system, usually to indicate the end of something. A special use of it is in response to the system prompt $. Under those conditions, CTRL-D has the effect of logging you off the system.

The only indication that you have logged off is a new request for a log in:

```
$ ^D
Dual 83/80 68000 System V UNIX

login:
```

If you are dialling into System V over a telephone line, it is possible that the logout will hang up the telephone, in which case you don't get any further requests for login.

2.9. How to Read the UNIX System Manuals

Documentation for UNIX System V consists of many, many manuals.

Historically, the UNIX system was documented in a large volume known as the *UNIX Programmer's Manual*, which was divided into eight sections. Each section represented a different category of the system, of interest to different people. Here are the traditional eight sections:

1. Commands

2. System calls
3. Subroutines
4. Special files
5. File formats and conventions
6. Games
7. Macro packages and language conventions
8. Maintenance commands and procedures

Section 1 (commands) often has a special suffix of '1M' for maintenance commands.

In general, each command or subroutine or file format was documented in as few pages as possible — they are supposed to be *reference* material. These pages are referred to as the 'man' (manual) pages.

Within each section the entries are arranged in alphabetical order. There is a table of contents which lists alphabetically the names of the commands in each section, and there is a 'Permuted Index' which gives you a limited capability to look up commands by function rather than by name.

With the advent of System V, the man-pages have been rearranged.

In general, the only section needed by most users is the first one, 'Commands', although the section on 'Games' is interesting too. And so, Sections 1 and 6 of the 'man pages' form the *User's Manual*.

Sections 2, 3, 4, and 5 are mostly required by people who are involved in writing programs to run under System V, so these sections are grouped together in the *Programmers Manual*.

People concerned with the care and feeding of System V will need to refer to the last section: 'Maintenance commands and procedures' (many commands in this section are only available to the super-user); sections 1M, 7, and 8 of the 'man-pages' form the *Administrators Manual*.

For each area you will often find a guide, containing tutorials that expand upon the various commands that are too complex to be described in a single page.

An example of a typical 'man-page' from the *System V User's Manual* is shown in figure 2.1 on the next page. It describes the `date` command, which you have already seen an example of.

Each entry for a command in the 'man_pages' is described under these headings:

`NAME`

gives the name of the command and a brief description of what it does. Where there are alternative names for the command, these are listed.

`SYNOPSIS`

shows how the command is to be used. Possible options to the command and the type of expected argument(s) is indicated.

`DESCRIPTION`

gives more detail of what the command does, and how its action is modified by the options.

date(1) date(1)

Version 1.1

NAME

date – print and set the date

SYNOPSIS

date [yymmddhhmm[.ss]]

DESCRIPTION

If no argument is given, the current date and time are printed. If an argument is given, the current date is set. *yy* is the last two digits of the year; the first *mm* is the month number; *dd* is the day number in the month; *hh* is the hour number (24 hour system); the second *mm* is the minute number; *ss* is optional and is the seconds. For example:

date 10080045

sets the date to Oct 8, 12:45 AM. The year, month and day may be omitted, the current values being the defaults. The system operates in GMT. *Date* takes care of the conversion to and from local standard and daylight time.

FILES

/usr/adm/wtmpto record time setting

SEE ALSO

utmp(5)

DIAGNOSTICS

'No permission' if you aren't the super-user and you try to change the date; 'bad conversion' if the date set is syntactically incorrect.

Figure 2.1 Example Manual Page[5]

[5] The discerning reader will compare this with the actual page in the *System V User's Manual*, and will find it different. Do not write in to complain, this is a deliberate mistake. Since the purpose of the example is illustrative, and it is not intended as reference material, we have used an older (and simpler) version of `date` than is currently available.

`FILES`
gives the names of any files which are important to the command.

`SEE ALSO`
refers to related commands or other documentation which could be useful to the reader.

`DIAGNOSTICS`
gives explanations of cryptic error messages which might occur if the command is misused.

`BUGS`
gives details of errors known to exist in the command, and sometimes tells you how to overcome these.

The NAME, SYNOPSIS, and DESCRIPTION headings are present for all commands. The other headings might or might not be present, depending on whether there is any subject matter for that particular heading.

Perhaps the most important heading is SYNOPSIS, which shows how the command is to be used. Here is the synopsis for the `date` command shown in the example:

> SYNOPSIS
> **date** [yymmddhhmm[.ss]]

Under the SYNOPSIS heading, all command documentation uses these conventions:

- Words in **boldface** are considered to be literal and are typed exactly as shown. Options are usually literal. The command name is always shown as a literal.
- Square brackets around an argument indicate that it is optional and need not appear when the command is used.
- Where the word 'file' appears in the SYNOPSIS, it always means a filename.
- Ellipses '. . . .' following an argument indicate that that type of argument may be repeated any number of times.

These conventions make it fairly easy to see the correct usage for each command. For example, if the SYNOPSIS of the `rm` (remove files) command is:

```
rm  [-fri]  file ...
```

it means that `rm` accepts three options (`f`, `r`, and `i`), which may be combined, and the command accepts any number of filenames. All of the following are acceptable uses of the `rm` command:

```
rm  file1
rm file2 file3 file4 file5
rm -f file6 file7
rm -ri file8 file9 file10
```

An unacceptable form of the `rm` command would be

```
rm -i -i
```

where the same option — the `-i` option — is specified twice, and no file names are given.

The above descriptions of the command documentation appears in the Introduction to the *System V User's Manual*. However, experience has shown that very few people take the trouble to read that bit of the manual, so we are repeating it here for good measure.

Print Manual Sections with `man`

The *System V User's Manual* itself may be kept on the system. It is possible to get the documentation for any given command by using the `man` command.

`man` has many options to direct the results to various kinds of printers or phototypesetters. The normal action, in the absence of any option, is to display the specified page on the terminal. For example, figure 2.2 on the next page shows how to get the manual page for the `date` command that we showed you in figure 2.1 earlier. Words enclosed in the small boxes represent words that were in *italic* in figure 2.1. On most terminals, such words are highlighted in some way.

For a full-blown description of `man`, refer to the *System V User's Manual* or, alternatively, type:

```
$ man man
```

Be aware that if your System V is running on a small computer system which has a limited amount of disk space, the documentation might not be on-line.

Table of contents and the Permuted Index

At the front of the *System V User's Manual* there is a table of contents, which shows every command and the entry under the `NAME` heading. An example of a table of contents entry is:

rm ....remove (unlink) files

The *System V User's Manual* also has an index. Unlike the index to (say) this book, the *System V User's Manual* index is not necessarily in a form you might be familiar with. It is based upon an indexing strategy called Key-Word-In-Context, or KWIC. This index is often at the front of the *System V User's Manual*, but is sometimes found at the back. System V documentation calls the KWIC index a 'Permuted Index'.

```
$ man date
date(1)                                                   date(1)
                        Version 1.1


NAME
     date - print and set the date

SYNOPSIS
     date [yymmddhhmm[.ss]]

DESCRIPTION
     If no argument is given, the current date and time are printed.
     If an argument is given, the current date is set. yy is the
     last two digits of the year; the first mm is the month number;
     dd is the day number in the month; hh is the hour number (24
     hour system); the second mm is the minute number; ss is optional
     and is the seconds.  For example:

             date 10080045

     sets the date to Oct 8, 12:45 AM.  The year, month and day may
     be omitted, the current values being the defaults.  The system
     operates in GMT. Date takes care of the conversion to and from
     local standard and daylight time.

FILES
     /usr/adm/wtmp to record time setting

SEE ALSO
     utmp(5)

DIAGNOSTICS
     'No permission' if you aren't the super-user and you try to change
     the date; 'bad conversion' if the date set is syntactically incorrect.
                                    . . . . .
$
```

Figure 2.2 Using the man Command

The Permuted Index is obtained by taking the one-line descriptions found under the NAME headings for the commands, and duplicating each line for each keyword in the line. All the lines are then sorted.

To give an example of the Permuted Index: suppose you wish to delete some files, and you need to find the name of the command to use. The way to do this is to look for a 'keyword'. In the Permuted Index, all the keywords appear just to the right of the centerline of the page. If you look up the keyword 'files' in the Permuted Index, you will find the entry:

rm,rmdir – remove (unlink) `files` .... rm (1)

There will also be an entry under 'remove':

rm,rmdir – `remove` (unlink) files .... rm(1)

These entries tell you that the command you want to use is `rm`, and that it is documented in Section 1 of the manual. There is no entry for this command under the keyword 'delete', because that word doesn't appear in the NAME entry. Sometimes you need to use a Thesaurus in conjunction with the Permuted Index. The Permuted Index is constructed with the command `ptx` — if you want to know more detail, look up that command in Section 1 of the manual.

2.10. Summary

This chapter should have got you started with the basic ideas of accessing System V, how to correct typing mistakes, change your password, and the ideas of some simple commands. See if you can find out what the erase and kill characters normally are on your system. If you don't like them, see how you can get them changed. Try to find out the rules for user names and passwords on your system.

Now you should try exploring parts of the *System V User's Manual* and any other documentation you have about your system. Look up `date`, `who`, and the other commands that we described.

Read some of the manual pages for commands other than those we described so far, and make sure you understand the conventions. Delve into the permuted index at random to see what's there. Look in the table of contents.

The next chapter tells you about files, directories, the file system, and what you can do with it. A reasonable grasp of command syntax and the ideas of options will be helpful when you are exploring the file system.

3 Directories and Files

This chapter describes (rather than defines) the UNIX System V file and directory structures, in terms of how you use it and the things you can do with it. We take the approach of first examining those files and directories already in the system before taking the step of creating new files and directories.

UNIX System V knows about three kinds of files:

- directories,
- ordinary files,
- special files.

This chapter is concerned only with ordinary files and directories. Special files are mentioned in chapter 15.

In the most basic terms, an *ordinary file* is simply a container into which you can put data. The most important thing about a file is that it has a name by which you can refer to it. It is the container that has the name, not the data in the container. By using the container's name, commands work on the whole collection of data contained therein. The contents of a file can be displayed, files can be copied, they can be removed from file system, or they can be moved around in the file system.

A *directory* is a file containing information about other files and directories. It is probably easiest to think of a directory as a thing which 'contains' files and other directories. A directory 'contained' within another directory is called a subdirectory. The subdirectories can themselves contain files and more subdirectories. Directories in System V supply the glue or matrix which superimposes a structure on the file system as a whole. In this chapter we also discuss the commands that work with directories.

In everyday terms, a directory has been compared to a filing cabinet, its subdirectories to the drawers in the cabinet, and files to the actual files held in the filing drawers. This analogy is incomplete, since a filing cabinet is a much more limited filing system than the one that System V provides. In the System V scheme of things, an index entry in a drawer of the filing cabinet could contain a reference (a pointer) to another entire filing cabinet. Nevertheless, the filing cabinet analogy is useful, as long as you realize that System V file structure can handle arbitrary depths of directories and subdirectories.

Let us start off by examining those files and directories that already exist on System V. This achieves two things: it shows the overall system file structure, and introduces the commands available for using that structure.

3.1. Print Current or Working Directory with pwd

When you are assigned a user name so that you can log in to System V, you are also assigned a directory. This directory is your 'home' directory. Every time you log in, you will find yourself positioned in this directory.

After you have logged in and seen the system prompt $, type the command pwd, which is a request to print the working directory.

```
$ pwd
/aa/widget/maryann
$
```

In practice, the response you get might look more like:

```
$ pwd
/usr/maryann
$
```

or even:

```
$ pwd
/users/widget/maryann
$
```

The allocation of directories for users is under control of the System Administrator, and thus will vary at each installation. For the purposes of showing examples in this book we have assumed a certain layout of the users directories. You will need to translate this into the directory structure that actually exists at your installation.

To repeat our original example, in our assumed directory structure the response to the pwd command is:

```
$ pwd
/aa/widget/maryann
$
```

The response from the system is the name of the directory you are working in at the moment. This directory is called the 'current directory', or 'working directory', or (in full) 'current working directory'.

This is what the example of pwd above shows you; since you have just logged in, it is your 'home' directory. It is yours to do what you will: create files, make subdirectories, remove files, or rename files and directories.

The name of the directory, as the pwd command displays it, is the *full pathname* to your directory. The full pathname is a complete specification of where that directory is in relation to the total file system.

There are three directories shown in the example above, namely, *aa*, *widget*, and *maryann*. There is in fact a fourth directory which is implicit. That directory is the 'root' of the file system, and it is represented by the initial slash character in the example above. We will see this in more detail when we examine the system directories.

You can move to another directory in the system (that is the current working directory can be changed) by using the change directory command, cd. But, before you start using cd to move around to different places in the directory structure, let's see what you have in your own directory.

3.2. List Directory Contents with ls

The ls command is a request to the system to 'list the contents of a directory'. If no directory is specified on the ls command line, you get a list of files in the current directory, which is the one you are working in:

```
$ ls
$
```

The response here is simply the prompt; this means that there are no files to list. This is hardly surprising, since you only just logged in and have not yet created any files or subdirectories. Of course if you had inherited someone else's user name, there might be some files left over, which would show up on the display.

But let's assume that this is a new user name, and there are no files or subdirectories in this directory. So, let us have a closer look at this directory, using some of the options to the ls command.

```
$ ls -al
total 547
drwxr-xr-x   2 maryann widget        32 Apr 10 10:31 .
drwxrwxr-x  12 widget  widget       240 Jan  4 15:22 ..
$
```

The -a (all) option to ls asks that all files and subdirectories are listed. Some files are 'hidden' — more on that later. The -l (long) option asks for a long listing; without it only the names of the files and subdirectories are shown.

ls now shows two directories. The letter d in the first column indicates that they are directories. We won't bother with what the rest of the line means right now; we'll just note that the third field of the line shows the owner of the directories, and the last field shows the names of the directories, '.' and '..'.

The period character '.' (usually called 'dot') is ubiquitous in System V, and means different things in different places. In this particular case, '.' means 'the current directory'. The two periods '..' (pronounced 'dot dot') means 'the parent directory', that is, the directory that this directory ').' is a subdirectory of. No matter which directory you are working in at any time, '.' always stands for the current directory, and '..' is the one 'above' it.

Figure 3.1 shows the relationship between the current directory and the parent directory.

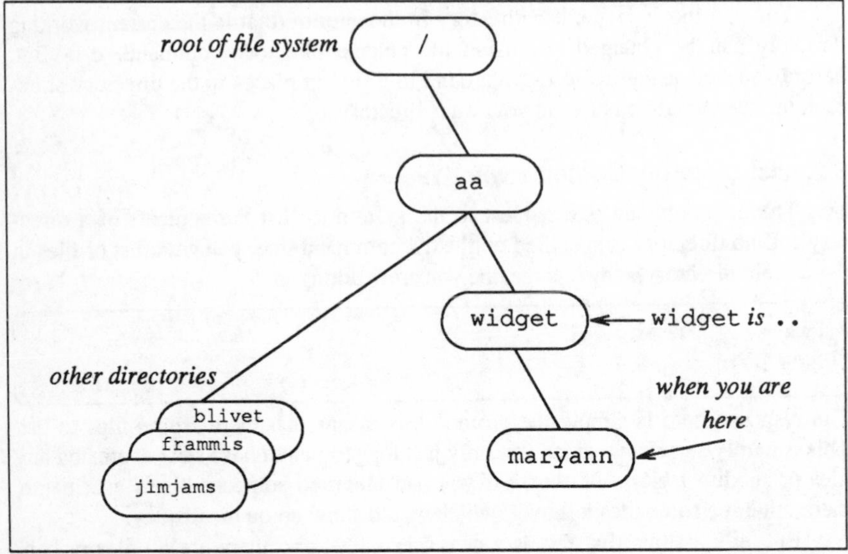

Figure 3.1 Relationship Between Parent Directory and Current Directory

Although you are the owner of your own 'home' directory, you are not necessarily the owner of the parent directory. In our example, the parent directory is owned by 'widget'.

Now let us look at some more of the file system. The full pathname to your home directory starts with the / character. In addition to separating directory names from each other when a pathname is given, the initial slash character, /, is called the 'root' of the file system. A slash on its own means the root of the file system. The example on the following page is a display of the root file susyem in response to an `ls` command.

```
$ ls /
aa
ab
bin
dev
etc
lib
lost+found
tmp
usr
$
```

Don't be surprised if what you see on your system doesn't look exactly like the above example. There are two ways in which your system might be different. One is that the names displayed will not be the same. As we said earlier, the allocation of directories is at the discretion of the System Administrator for each installation, and so some of the names shown above might not exist on your system. Also you might have other, different, names. But there should be some commonality — certainly you should see *bin*, *dev*, *etc*, *usr*.

Another difference could be that you see the names listed, not one per line as in the example, but several on one line. Although the standard version of `ls` produces names one per line as shown, there are options to the command that allow you to list several names per line. Since these options use the space on your terminal screen more efficiently, some System Administrators make one of these optional versions available to the users by default.

If your default `ls` command does list the names one per line, and you would like to see them listed differently, you can use one of the options `-x` or `-C`:

```
$ ls -x /
aa      ab      bin     dev     etc     lib     lost+found
tmp     usr
$ ls -C /
aa        bin       etc       lost+found  usr
ab        dev       lib       tmp
$
```

As you can see, an `ls` command with the `-x` option displays the contents of the directory with several names per line. The names are sorted alphabetically across the lines. The `-C` option also displays several names per line, but this time the names are sorted alphabetically down the columns of names.

Notice that in the `ls` display above, there is no indication whether the names displayed are files or subdirectories. To discover that information, you can use the `-l` option to get the long list.

```
$ ls -l /
total 10
drwxr-xr-x   3 root     root         112 Jan 10 10:41 aa
drwxr-xr-x   3 root     root          96 Jan 14 08:55 ab
drwxr-xr-x   2 bin      bin         1216 Nov 25 10:42 bin
drwxr-xr-x   2 root     root         960 Nov 25 10:41 dev
drwxr-xr-x   2 root     root         512 Nov 25 11:02 etc
drwxr-xr-x   2 root     root          32 Apr 10 19:35 lib
drwxr-xr-x   2 root     root          32 Apr 10 19:31 lost+found
drwxrwxrwx   8 root     root         734 Feb 14 09:02 tmp
drwxr-xr-x  19 bin      bin          368 Nov 25 12:14 usr
$
```

The letter 'd' in the very first column of each line of the display means that the entry is a directory. If an entry is a file, it is indicated by the presence of a hyphen character, '-', instead of the letter 'd'.

Another way to see whether the names displayed represent files or directories is to use the -p option to ls, possibly in conjunction with the -x option:

```
$ ls  -xp  /
aa/           ab/          bin/         dev/         etc/         lib/
lost+found/   tmp/         usr/
$
```

The -p option asks the ls command to indicate which of the listed names represent directories by showing a slash / after the name. Notice that the / character is an indicator only — it does not form part of the name.

A similar option to ls that you might try is the -F option. This option also marks directories with a trailing / character. In addition it marks executable files (that is, commands) with a trailing asterisk (*). Again, be aware that the * is an indicator only, and is not part of the file name. An interesting directory to try this on is */etc*.

As you can see, all of the entries displayed in the above example are directories. Some of these directories might contain files, some might contain subdirectories, and some might contain both. To avoid having very long examples in future, we will only indicate some of the directory contents, and we use '*<etcetera . . .>*' to mean that we have left out stuff.

Notice that all the directories under root / are owned either by 'root', or by 'bin'; these are two special user names that are used exclusively for maintaining System V.

Let's look at figure 3.2 on the following page to see a diagram of the root file system.

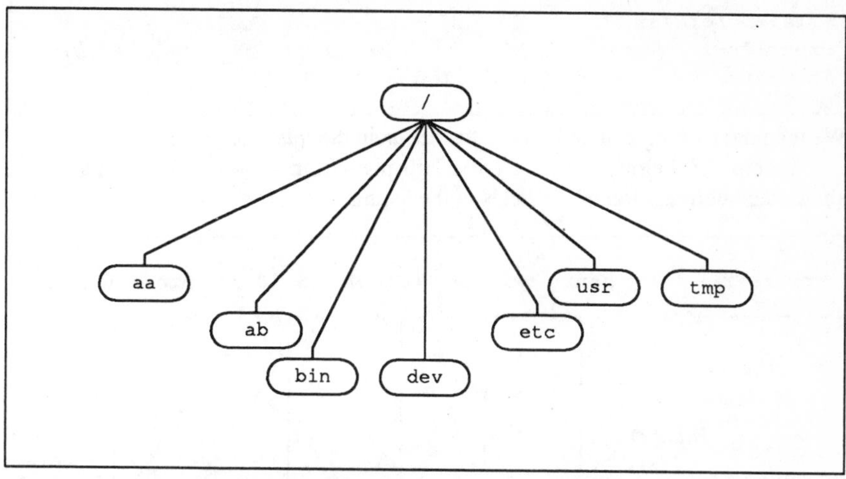

Figure 3.2 A Typical Root File System

Now let's explore a little further and look at one of the system directories:

```
$ ls -l /bin
-r-xr-xr-x   1 bin     bin       21428 Sep 24  1983 ar
-r-xr-xr-x   1 bin     bin       47528 Mar 20  1984 as
             <etcetera . . .>
-r-sr-xr-x   3 root    daemon    15464 Feb 15  1984 cp
             <etcetera . . .>
-r-xr-xr-x   4 bin     bin       23988 Feb 15  1984 ls
             <etcetera . . .>
-r-sr-xr-x   3 root    daemon    15464 Feb 15  1984 mv
             <etcetera . . .>
-r-xr-xr-x   1 bin     bin       14916 Jul 18  1983 uniq
-r-xr-xr-x   1 bin     bin       24696 Feb 15  1984 who
$
```

All the entries in this display are files, indicated by the '–' in the first column of the display. There are no subdirectories in the */bin* directory. Also, don't the names look familiar? They are the names that appear on the commands documented in the *System V User's Manual*. 'bin' is short for 'binary', and the */bin* directory is where most (but not necessarily all) of the binary (executable) versions of System V commands are kept.

At this point, let's take time out to have a closer look at what we get when we use the `-l` option on `ls`. We don't have to show an entire directory with `ls`. We can see details of one file (or a group of files) by specifying the names of the files we are interested in, for example:

```
$ ls -l /bin/ar
-r-xr-xr-x   1 bin      bin         21428 Sep 24  1983 /bin/ar
$
```

We are now looking at details about the file *ar* in the */bin* directory.

Figure 3.3 below shows a typical display from an `ls -l` command and shows the interpretation of the fields in the listing.

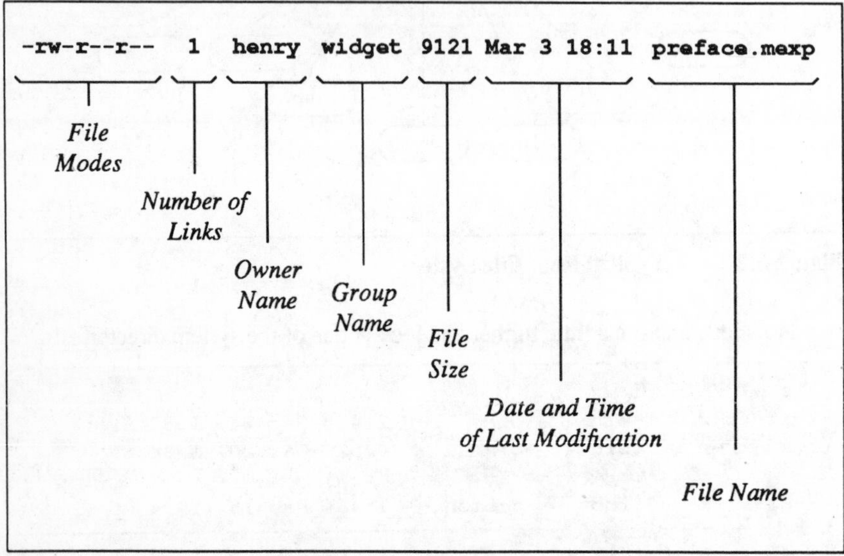

Figure 3.3 Details of Fields in a File Display

Here is a detailed explanation of the fields in the above diagram:

- The very first column in the *File Modes* field tells us that we have an ordinary file, indicated by the '–' (remember that '`d`' in the first column means an entry is a directory). The remainder of the *File Modes* field (the `r-xr-xr-x`) tells us about permissions on that file. Permissions are described in section 3.17 later in this chapter.
- *Number of Links* For files the number of links is usually 1. If the number of links is more than 1, it shows that a number of identical copies of the file exist in different places on the system. For directories, the number of links is an indication of the number of subdirectories in that directory.
- *Name of Owner* shows the owner of the directory or file. In this case the user's name is '*henry*'.
- *Name of Group* shows the group of users that the owner is part of. In this case the user '*henry*' belongs to the group called '*widget*'.

- *Size of File* shows the size of the file in bytes. For text files the size of file is the number of characters in the file.
- *Date and Time of Last Modification* is a date entry. It shows when the file was last modified, or when it was created. The format of this field depends on how old the file is. If the file is less than one year old, then both the date (month and day) and the time are shown. If the file is older than that, no time is shown but the year is added to the date. If you wish to see the time a file was last accessed rather than its modification date, you can use the `-u` option in conjunction with the `-l` option (that is, say `ls -ul`) to get that information.

  If you are mainly interested in dates, you might wish to use the `-t` option in conjunction with the `-l` and `-u` options. When you use the `-t` option, the files are displayed in order of their modification times (or access times if you also use `-u`) instead of being shown in alphabetical order. Normally the latest (newest) files are shown first — if you wish to show the oldest files first you also need to use the `-r` option[1].
- *Name of File* is the actual name of the file or directory.

Sometimes you want to find out information about the directory itself, rather than about the contents of a directory. Just giving the name of the directory to `ls` shows the files and subdirectories, as we have seen. To force `ls` to show information about the directory, we have to use the `-d` option. Used on its own, the -d option does no more than confirm the existence of the directory. Usually we want to check things like ownership and write permissions, so the `-d` option is most often used in conjunction with the `-l` option:

```
$ ls -ld /bin
drwxr-xr-x   2 bin      bin          3744 Aug  1  1985 /bin
$
```

Here we can see that the */bin* directory is owned by the user 'bin'.

If you use this option on your own home directory:

```
$ ls -ld .
drwxr-xr-x   2 maryann widget         32 Apr 10 10:31 .
$
```

you get the same information as shown previously using the `-a` option.

---

[1] You can also use the `-r` option to reverse the order on an alphabetic display.

3.3. Changing Working Directory with `cd`

Now let's continue looking at the other system directories. We'll look at the directory */etc*, but this time we'll do it slightly differently:

```
$ cd /etc
$ ls -l
-rw-r--r--    1 bin     bin          962 Apr 10 08:10 motd
              <etcetera . . .>
-r--r--r--    1 root    root         680 Apr  8 15:26 passwd
              <etcetera . . .>
-rw-r--r--    1 adm     adm        46296 Apr 10 19:07 wtmp
$
```

First of all, we've used two commands instead of one. The `cd` command stands for change working directory (or more simply change directory). After the `cd`, we are 'positioned' in the */etc* directory, so that it is now our working directory. Having got to the */etc* directory, which is the one we want to examine, we need not tell `ls` which directory we want. We can just let it show the current working directory.

The */etc* directory contains a mixture of files and subdirectories. The contents are probably different for each System V, but just about all will have the files *motd* and *passwd*.

The file *motd* is the message-of-the-day file, which is displayed every time you log in.

The file *passwd* is the password file that we described in chapter 2 — *Getting Started on UNIX System V*. The password file contains one entry for each person who can use the system. Each entry contains the user's login-name, group, encrypted password and other interesting information about the user.

Now let's look at another directory:

```
$ cd /usr; ls -l
total 22
drwxr-xr-x    2 bin     bin          656 Aug  1  1985 bin
drwxr-xr-x    2 bin     bin           48 Aug  1  1985 dict
drwxr-xr-x    3 bin     bin          528 Aug  1  1985 games
drwxr-xr-x    3 bin     bin          832 Aug  1  1985 include
drwxr-xr-x   17 bin     bin          960 Dec 31 14:25 lib
drwxrwxrwx    2 bin     bin           64 Feb  6 21:00 mail
drwxr-xr-x    4 bin     bin           64 Aug  1  1985 man
drwxrwxrwx    2 bin     bin           48 Apr  9 16:59 news
drwxr-xr-x    2 bin     bin          112 Aug  1  1985 pub
$
```

Notice that this time we put our two commands on the same line, separated with the semicolon *;*. There can be spaces on either or both sides of the *;* command separator — it doesn't matter.

The */usr* directory has more subdirectories, so we can expand our diagram to a bigger tree as shown in figure 3.4.

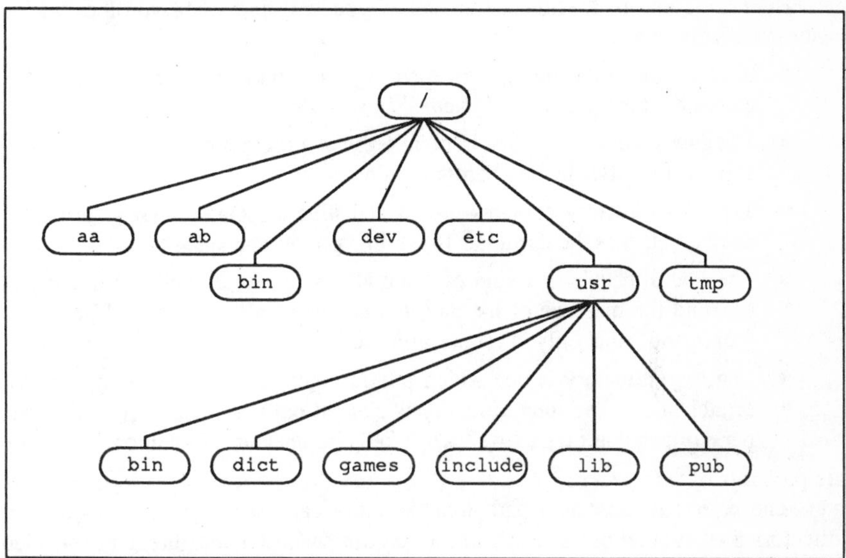

Figure 3.4 Expanding the File System Map

You can see from this diagram that there are two directories named *bin*. There is no confusion between them because they are on different paths; one is */bin*, the other is */usr/bin*.

The contents of */bin* we have already seen. To see the contents of */usr/bin* we can say:

```
$ ls -l bin
-r-xr-xr-x   1 bin    bin      42148 Dec 12  1983 /bin/adb
-r-xr-xr-x   1 bin    bin      11660 Jun  9  1983 /bin/cal
          <etcetera . . .>
-r-xr-xr-x   1 bin    bin      20200 Jun  9  1983 /bin/write
-r-xr-xr-x   1 bin    bin      44324 Nov 28  1983 /bin/yacc
$
```

We saw earlier that many of the commands documented in the *System V User's Manual* are to be found in the directory */bin*. This directory */usr/bin*, is where the rest of them live. This is not always true, however. Some installations put everything in the */bin* directory, and there is no */usr/bin* directory at all.

We leave it as an exercise for the reader to examine the other system directories, using combinations of `cd` and `ls`, and checking your position in the file system hierarchy with `pwd`. Remember that if you get lost you can always return to your home directory by typing the `cd` command with no argument.

Here are some of the interesting things you will find when you look in the other system directories:

- If you look in the */usr/games* directory, you will see that it contains the games documented in the *System V User's Manual*.
- The */usr/include* directory is of interest to programmers, because it contains include files in the C programming language.
- The */dev* directory contains the special files associated with input/output devices, such as the terminals (ttys), line printer and such.
- The */etc* directory is a kind of catch-all, as its name implies. In */etc* you can find the message-of-the-day, the password file, and several programs (commands) that only the super-user can access.
- The */tmp* directory is one which programmers use to create temporary or scratch files. The */tmp* directory is cleared out periodically (usually once per day), so don't try to use */tmp* to keep permanent information.

The person who owns a particular directory can set the permissions on that directory so that other users cannot use a `cd` command with that directory specified as a destination. If you try to `cd` to a directory to which you do not have access, you get an error response:

```
$ cd /aa/widget/kingsland
/aa/widget/kingsland: bad directory
$
```

This doesn't tell you much. You get the same response if you try to `cd` to a file instead of a directory, and also if you try to change to a directory that does not exist. In none of those cases is it clear why the directory or file is 'bad', so you might have to look at the destination directory with the `ls` command to find out what the problem really is. You have probably misspelled the name, or got the path wrong. Check carefully what you typed to see if it is either of these problems.

Notes and Cautions on Changing Directory

It is a good idea to use `pwd` whenever you change directories, to verify that you are where you expect to be in the directory structure. Of course, if the first thing you do when you arrive at the destination directory is an `ls` command, an unfamiliar list of files will alert you that you aren't where you thought you were.

However, if you were to do a `cd`, and then full of confidence in your own infallibility, immediately issue a 'remove files' command, the result might be to wipe out valuable files which you (or worse, someone else) want to keep. So get into the habit of typing a `pwd` command whenever you change directories. You will save yourself much grief in the long run.

3.4. Full Pathnames and Relative Pathnames

In our last `ls` example above, we specified simply *bin* as the directory we wanted to list, we didn't say */usr/bin*. This is because we were already in the directory */usr*. We just gave the *relative pathname* of the directory we wished to see. Had we been in a directory other than */usr* we would have had to specify the full pathname — */usr/bin*.

Consider that our diagram is a map of the file system, and imagine an arrow with the words 'you are here' pointing to the current working directory (at the moment, */usr*). To get to any other directory, or any file in any directory, you can give a command either a relative pathname (or 'how to get there from here'), or a full pathname (or 'how to get there from the system root'). Using the `cd` command changes the position of the 'you are here' arrow.

Regardless of where you are currently positioned in the file system hierarchy, when you want to either move somewhere else, or refer to a file or directory at another place in the hierarchy, there are two basic ways of specifying the destination.

One way is to start from where you are and give a pathname corresponding to the move you want to make. This is called a 'relative pathname', because it is relative to (starts from) your current directory.

Sometimes, when you are a long way down some path, an old country folks' adage applies:

■ *if you want to get there, you shouldn't start from here!*

In this case, it's best to use a full pathname, starting from the 'root' of the file system.

Another way is to revert to your home directory, by typing a `cd` command with no pathname, and then moving on from there. A plain `cd` command with no arguments always takes you back to your home directory, which is a known place.

A pathname, whether a full pathname or a relative pathname, can be given anywhere the name of a file or directory can appear on System V commands.

Let us illustrate the ways which full and relative pathnames are used with a couple of examples. Each example shows how to do the job in these different ways:

- using a relative pathname,
- using a full pathname,
- changing directory first.

In the following examples we use the cat command to look at a file. The derivation of this odd name is given later; right now the important things are full and relative pathnames. Suppose you have the directory structure shown in figure 3.5 below.

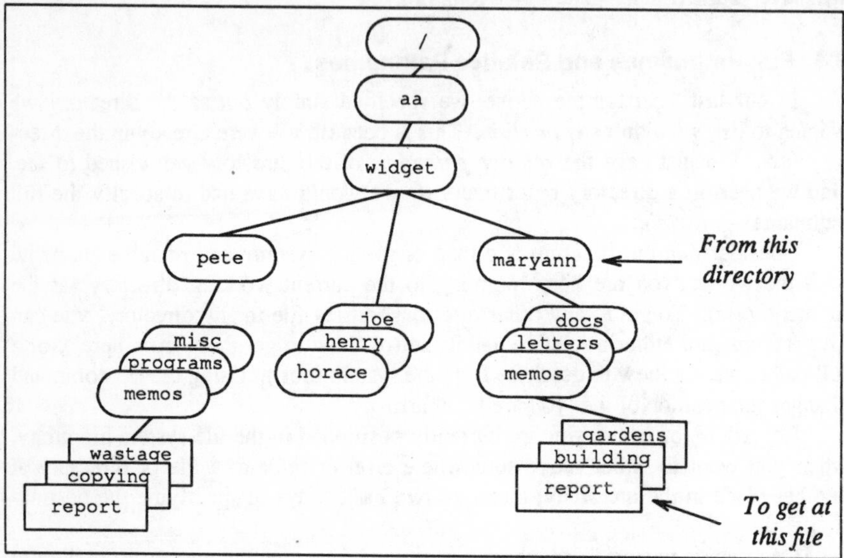

Figure 3.5 Full and Relative Pathnames

To view the *report* file with the cat command, here is how it is done with a relative pathname:

```
$ cat memos/report
```

and here is how to do it using the full pathname:

```
$ cat /aa/widget/maryann/memos/report
```

and finally, you can change directory before you do the cat command:

```
$ cd memos; cat report
```

The next example is slightly more complex, because you are looking at a file in another part of the hierarchy, as shown in figure 3.6 on the next page.

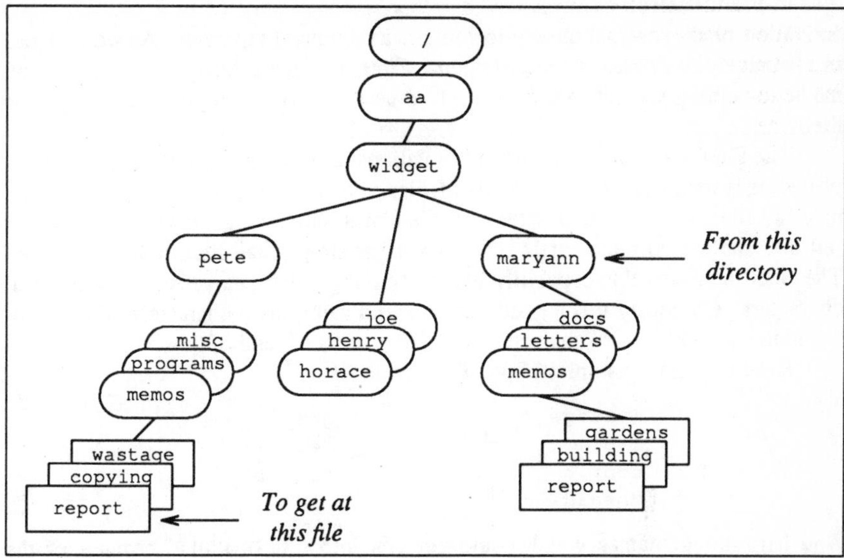

Figure 3.6 More Full and Relative Pathnames

You get at Pete's copy of *report* with a relative pathname like this:

```
$ cat ../pete/memos/report
```

with a full pathname like this:

```
$ cat /aa/widget/pete/memos/report
```

and then there are two ways you might use when changing directory first:

```
$ cd ../pete/memos; cat report
$ cd /aa/widget/pete/memos; cat report
```

3.5. Rules for Names of Files and Directories

So far, although we have been dealing with named files and directories, we have not specified what a filename (or a directory name) can consist of.

Filenames can be up to fourteen characters long and, at least in theory, can consist of any characters whatsoever. In practice, however, many characters in the ASCII character set can mean something special to the Shell (the part of the system that decodes your commands), and so these special characters should be avoided in filenames and directory names.

We already saw that the semicolon ; is a command separator. As we shall see in chapter 4 — *Processes and Standard Files*, the characters >, <, |, and & all mean something special to the Shell. It is best to avoid using these characters in filenames.

The Shell has certain 'shorthand' notations, or character matching capabilities providing a means to refer to groups of files. For instance, it is possible to designate 'all files starting with a letter', or 'filenames with a single digit at the end', or 'all files starting with the letters I through N', or simply, 'all files in this directory'. The Shell achieves this capability by pre-empting some characters as 'wild-card' characters. Obviously it is a good idea to avoid using these characters when forming filenames. Wild card characters are discussed at the end of this chapter.

Here are some examples of possible filenames:

```
message          joe_muggs
1982             .errors
conv.c           old-mesg
Message
```

And here are filenames which could get you into BIG TROUBLE, because of the Shell's special characters:

```
>5lines          4or<lines
4|5words         ?words
?WORDS           $junk
[Aix-Ghent]      morejunk**
```

When choosing filenames, as a general rule it is best to restrict yourself to names consisting of letters, digits, the underscore character, (_), and the period character, (.). The period can be used safely in the middle of a filename, but do not use the period at the beginning of a filename unless you want the files hidden.

Uppercase letters and lowercase letters are significant in filenames on System V. The filenames:

```
POT_OF_MESSAGE       pot_of_message
Pot_of_message       Pot_Of_Message
```

represent four entirely different files. In this respect, UNIX System V is different from most other operating systems.

File Naming Conventions

There are certain file naming conventions followed on System V, mostly connected with the various programming languages available.

A filename ending in *.c* is usually taken to be a file containing a program written in the C programming language; a filename ending in *.h* is an include file (containing 'header' data) for the C programming language. Similarly, a filename ending in *.f* is taken to be a program written in FORTRAN, one ending in *.p* is assumed to be a Pascal program, and a filename ending in *.s* usually means a program written in assembly language. A filename ending in *.o* is the object code produced by any of the compilers.

Some of the other conventions used are: *.y* for `yacc` source; *.r* for `ratfor` source, *.l* for `lex` source, *.e* for `efl` source, and so on.

When creating programs these conventions should be followed; your program probably won't compile if you don't. If you are not writing programs, try to name your files in such a way that there is no confusion with the conventions.

There are other conventions that are not associated with programming languages. Source Code Control System (SCCS) files all begin with the characters '*s.*', and various of SCCS commands produce files beginning with *p.* *g.* *x.* and *z.* If you use SCCS, try to avoid using this type of name for non-SCCS files.

It should be emphasized that these are file naming conventions, not rules imposed by System V. Some commands, that deal with certain types of files, expect the names of those files to have a particular format; but the Shell, and the system in general, doesn't care.

3.6. Looking at the Contents of a File with `cat`

One command that can be used to look at the contents of a file is the `cat` command. `cat` is so named because, if more than one filename is specified, all files are concatenated (joined end to end) and copied to the Standard Output (usually your terminal screen). You should be aware that `cat`'s main purpose is to concatenate files. It just so happens that its action of copying the result to the Standard Output is a side effect, which we can use to look at a text file. Note that the command can only be used meaningfully with text files — if you `cat` a non-text file to your terminal screen, the results are generally unreadable.

`cat` is a simple command. Suppose that you forgot to read the message of the day when you logged in; to examine the message of the day file, you just type:

```
$ cat /etc/motd
The system will be down this Saturday from 8am to 2pm
while we are doing Preventive Maintenance.

Filesystem /aa is VERY low on space !!!
Please inspect your files and remove moldy oldies.
$
```

Since we've mentioned the ASCII character set several times, an interesting file to look at is a chart of the ASCII character-set, which lives in */usr/pub/ascii*[2]:

---

2 /usr/pub/ascii reproduced with permission from Bell Laboratories.

```
$ cat /usr/pub/ascii
|000 nul|001 soh|002 stx|003 etx|004 eot|005 enq|006 ack|007 bel|
|010 bs |011 ht |012 nl |013 vt |014 np |015 cr |016 so |017 si |
|020 dle|021 dc1|022 dc2|023 dc3|024 dc4|025 nak|026 syn|027 etb|
|030 can|031 em |032 sub|033 esc|034 fs |035 gs |036 rs |037 us |
|040 sp |041 ! |042 " |043 # |044 $ |045 % |046 & |047 ' |
|050 ( |051 ) |052 * |053 + |054 , |055 - |056 . |057 / |
|060 0 |061 1 |062 2 |063 3 |064 4 |065 5 |066 6 |067 7 |
|070 8 |071 9 |072 : |073 ; |074 < |075 = |076 > |077 ? |
|100 @ |101 A |102 B |103 C |104 D |105 E |106 F |107 G |
|110 H |111 I |112 J |113 K |114 L |115 M |116 N |117 O |
|120 P |121 Q |122 R |123 S |124 T |125 U |126 V |127 W |
|130 X |131 Y |132 Z |133 [ |134 \ |135 ] |136 ^ |137 _ |
|140 ` |141 a |142 b |143 c |144 d |145 e |146 f |147 g |
|150 h |151 i |152 j |153 k |154 l |155 m |156 n |157 o |
|160 p |161 q |162 r |163 s |164 t |165 u |166 v |167 w |
|170 x |171 y |172 z |173 { |174 | |175 } |176 ~ |177 del|
$
```

This file gives the character values, in octal notation, of all the characters in the ASCII character set.[3]

The first four lines show all the non-printing characters. Those are the characters obtained when you hold down the control key and type another character (for example, the character value 010 is CTRL-H or backspace, abbreviated to 'bs' in the table above). Although it isn't needed very often, the ASCII chart is a useful file to have on the system.

If you try to `cat` a file which doesn't exist, or a file for which you don't have read permission, `cat` displays an error response:

```
$ cat jambly
cat: cannot open jambly
$
```

You usually get this message if you have misspelled the filename, or if you are not in the directory you thought you were in. It is a good idea to do an `ls` of the directory first, to make sure you get the correct filenames, or maybe a `pwd` to find out where you actually are.

If the file you are `cat`-ing is large, you might want to suspend the output so you can look at it easily. Remember you can stop and start output with the CTRL-S and CTRL-Q keys, as we described in chapter 2.

[3] In fact we have only shown the first part of the */usr/pub/ascii* file. The second part is similar, but it shows the character values in hexadecimal (base 16) notation instead of octal (base 8).

3.7. Looking at the contents of a file with `pg`

If you have a large file to look at, you might prefer to use `pg` instead of `cat`. This command gives paged output — the page in this case being your terminal screen.

If you have a 24-line screen, the command:

```
$ pg bigfile
```

will show the first 23 lines of *bigfile*, and will display a : prompt on the last line of the screen.

At this point you can type **RETURN** to display the next screen-full, or a space followed by a **RETURN** will do it too.

When you have seen as much of the file as you want you can type `q`, or `Q`, followed by a **RETURN**, to exit from `pg` without displaying the rest of the file.

There are other things that you can type in response to the : prompt that `pg` gives you. We don't cover them here, but we'll just mention that if you type `h` (followed by **RETURN**) you will see a list of all the other things you can do.

`pg` is actually quite a sophisticated program, unlike `cat`, and has many options to change the way the user interacts with it. We'll just show a couple of them here.

If you give a number preceded by a – sign:

```
$ pg -20 bigfile
```

this alters the number of lines appearing on each 'page', or screen-full. In this case, when you move on to the next page, the last 3 lines of this page become the first 3 lines of the next page — this gives you some continuity, so you can keep things in context.

If you precede the number with a + instead of a – sign :

```
$ pg +20 bigfile
```

you get a completely different effect. `pg` doesn't show the very beginning of the file, but starts the display of the file at the 20th line.

We leave it as an exercise for the reader to explore the other capabilities of this command.

3.8. Looking at the End of a File with `tail`

If what you want to see in a file is towards the end of the file, a useful command is `tail`, which simply shows the tail-end of the file. If you don't specify how much you want, `tail` gives you the last 10 lines of the file, but you can tell it to give more or less, for example: [4]

[4] /usr/pub/greek reproduced with permission from Bell Laboratories.

```
$ tail -3 /usr/pub/greek
psi      V  V  |  PSI       H  H  |  omega    C  C
OMEGA    Z  Z  |  nabla     [  [  |  not      _  _
partial  ]  ]  |  integral  ^  ^
$
```

This is a display of the last three lines of the file which gives information to the text formatters about how Greek symbols can be printed on certain terminals. The number we give to `tail` is preceded by a minus sign to indicate that the last 3 lines of the file are to be displayed.

If you precede the number of lines with a plus sign, `tail` starts at the specified line number and displays all lines from there to the end of the file, so:

```
$ tail +7 /usr/pub/greek
rho      K  K  |  sigma     Y  Y  |  SIGMA    R  R
tau      I  I  |  phi       U  U  |  PHI      F  F
psi      V  V  |  PSI       H  H  |  omega    C  C
OMEGA    Z  Z  |  nabla     [  [  |  not      _  _
partial  ]  ]  |  integral  ^  ^
$
```

displays all lines from line 6 to the end of */usr/pub/greek*.

If you use the + option to `tail`, and give a number greater than the number of lines in the file, `tail` does not display anything.

If you try to `tail` a file that doesn't exist, or for which you don't have read permission, you get an error message:

```
$ tail spurious
tail: Can't open input
$
```

3.9. Determining the Type of a File with `file`

`cat` and `tail` are really only useful for displaying text files. If you try to look at something which is not a text file, they do not warn you (they don't care what is in the file), but what you see displayed will look like complete garbage.

To find out whether it makes sense to display a file on the terminal screen using `cat` or `tail`, you can use the `file` command, which determines the type of data which is in a file. If it finds the file is ASCII, `file` even tries to identify the language (in programming terms) of the file:

```
$ file /bin/ls /usr/bin /etc/passwd /usr/include/stdio.h
/bin/ls:          pure executable
/usr/bin:         directory
/etc/passwd:      ascii text
/usr/include/stdio.h:   c program text
$
```

If you try to use `file` on a non-existent file, you will get an error message to tell you that the `file` command cannot do its thing on that file:

```
$ file illusory
illusory: cannot open
$
```

And, if you try to use the `file` command on a file for which you don't have read permission, you'll get a slightly different error response:

```
$ file closedown
closedown: cannot open for reading
$
```

3.10. Creating User Directories with `mkdir`

Having shown the simple commands for working with files, we now continue with more information on directories. We describe how to make your own directories.

In the discussion and examples at the start of this chapter, we showed the layout of the directory structure for a typical file system. In those diagrams and examples there are two directories, called */aa*and */ab*, that are not system directories. They are user directories, and might be called anything on your system, */u0* and */u1*, for instance[5]. We just picked some arbitrary names. The number of user directories also varies from one system to another — it depends on how big each system is, and how many people can use it.

Each person who has a user-name has a directory somewhere in the system. It could be immediately under the */aa* directory, for example */aa/maryann*, or there could be other directories in between. In our earlier example, we assumed that there was a group of users in the 'widget' project, and that there was a directory for the group, so pictorially, we have something like the tree shown in figure 3.7.

---

[5] On some smaller installations the System Administrator does not set aside special filesystems for users' directories — users have their home directories directly under the */usr* system directory.

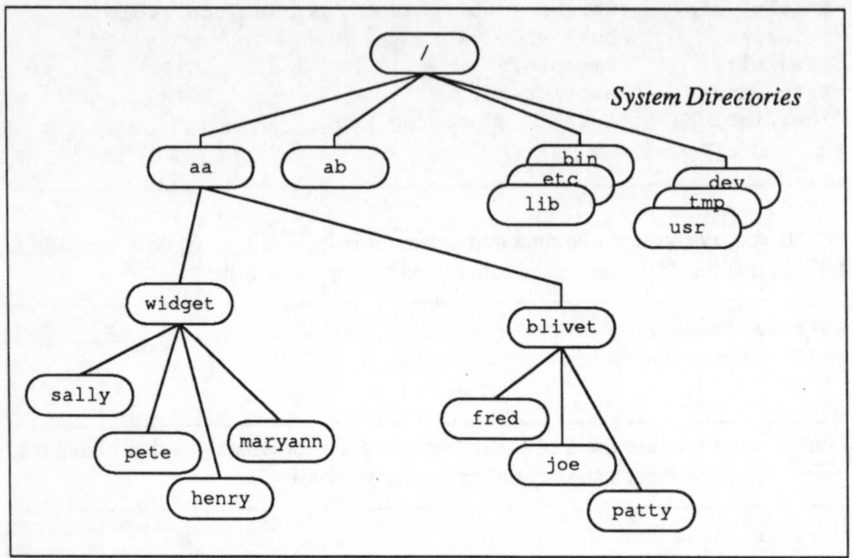

Figure 3.7 Projects and Groups

We showed another group of people in the 'blivet' project, who share the */aa* directory, so there are user directories under both */aa/widget* and */aa/blivet*. Each user has control over the contents of his own directory, and can create as many subdirectories and files as required. This is not necessarily a typical file structure for user directories, it merely illustrates what is possible with the file system structure.

The `mkdir` command makes (or creates) directories. Suppose that you are going to write some programs, some in the C programming language and some in Pascal; and there will be documentation: specifications, memos, letters. You might want to create separate subdirectories for all these things:

```
$ cd
$ mkdir progs docs
$ cd progs
$ mkdir c pascal
```

The first `cd` command is to make sure that you are positioned at your own login or 'home' directory, the place where the `cd` command takes you if you don't specify anywhere.

The example on the next page shows what you've got after you created those subdirectories.

```
$ ls -l
total 2
drwxrwxrwx   2 maryann widget        32 Apr 10 10:28 c
drwxrwxrwx   2 maryann widget        32 Apr 10 10:28 pascal
```

And now we'll create subdirectories for our documents and take a look at those:

```
$ cd ../docs
$ mkdir memos specs letters
$ ls  -l
total 3
drwxrwxrwx   2 maryann widget        32 Apr 10 10:28 letters
drwxrwxrwx   2 maryann widget        32 Apr 10 10:28 memos
drwxrwxrwx   2 maryann widget        32 Apr 10 10:28 specs
$ cd
$
```

Observe the use of '..' in specifying the relative pathname to *docs* from *progs*. The hierarchy of directories we have created now looks like the one shown in figure 3.8.

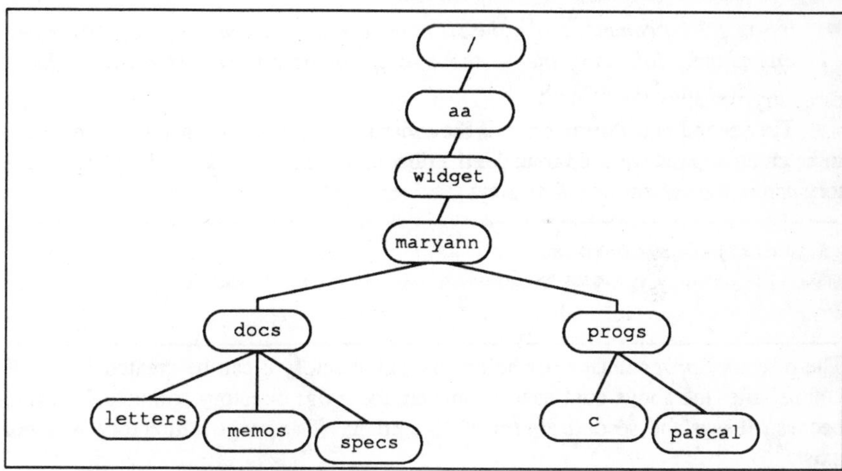

Figure 3.8 User Subdirectories

We could, in fact have created all these directories at the same time, as we show next.

```
$ mkdir progs progs/c progs/pascal \
      docs docs/letters docs/memos docs/specs
$ ls -l
total 2
drwxrwxrwx   5 maryann widget       80 Apr 10 10:28 docs
drwxrwxrwx   4 maryann widget       64 Apr 10 10:28 progs
$
```

There are several points of interest in this example. First of all, we've split the command over two lines. Remember back in chapter 2 we said that the reverse slash character \ is an 'escape' character, and removes any special meaning from the character immediately following it. We've used the \ character in this case to remove the special meaning of command terminator from the newline character (obtained when we typed **RETURN** at the end of the first line). So the Shell doesn't do anything until it sees the newline at the end of the second line.

We needn't, in fact, have split the command line this. The system will accept a very long command line, much longer than will fit on a terminal screen, and we could have just kept typing. But many people find it disconcerting to do that, they prefer to split the command as we've shown.

■ *If you split a command like this, it is important that you type the* **RETURN** *key immediately following the* *; there must not be any spaces between the* \ *character and the* **RETURN**.

The second noteworthy thing is the order in which we specified the directories to be created. Had we tried to make the directory *progs/c* before making the directory *progs*, the system would display:

```
$ mkdir progs/c progs
mkdir: cannot access progs/.
$
```

The directory *progs* must exist before the subdirectory *c* can be created in it. Of course, after the above command is obeyed, the *progs* directory will actually exist, because it was the second argument to `mkdir`. The *progs/c* directory will not exist.

Having tried to make the directories in the wrong order (as shown above), you might then try to start over, and make them in the right order. But now you are trying to make a directory (*progs*) which already exists, in which case you would get these results:

```
$ mkdir  progs  progs/c
mkdir: cannot make directory progs
$
```

By this time, things are so confused that might be better to remove the directories with the `rmdir` command described below, and start again.

The third point about the above example is that an `ls` of the current directory only shows the subdirectories *progs* and *docs*. To see the subdirectories of those directories we have to say:

```
$ ls -l docs progs

docs:
total 3
drwxrwxrwx   2 maryann widget          32 Apr 10 10:28 letters
drwxrwxrwx   2 maryann widget          32 Apr 10 10:28 memos
drwxrwxrwx   2 maryann widget          32 Apr 10 10:28 specs

progs:
total 2
drwxrwxrwx   2 maryann widget          32 Apr 10 10:28 c
drwxrwxrwx   2 maryann widget          32 Apr 10 10:28 pascal
$
```

The `ls` command above requests a 'long' display of the two directories *docs* and *progs*. This form of `ls` places the name of each directory before the information for its subdirectories.

You can also display the contents of subdirectories by using the `-R` (recursive) option to the `ls` command. Figure 3.9 on the next page shows an example of its use.

The `-R` option means that `ls` should display the contents of the directory and, recursively, all its subdirectories.

At this point the alert reader will have noticed a subtle difference in the above examples, compared with those we gave earlier in this chapter. The first line of each long listing shows 'total *N*', where *N* is some number. In fact, this appears on all long directory listings, we simply didn't show it on the earlier examples. The number shown as the total gives a count of the number of disk blocks that the directory occupies, so if you are concerned about disk space you should pay heed to this number. When a directory has subdirectories, the block total includes the blocks used up by the existence of the subdirectories. However, it does not include the blocks used up by any files that are in the subdirectories. So to compute the total amount of disk space you are using, you must add together the totals shown by `ls` for this directory and all subdirectories.

```
$ ls -lR
total 2
drwxrwxrwx   5 maryann widget        80 Apr 10 10:28 docs
drwxrwxrwx   4 maryann widget        64 Apr 10 10:28 progs

docs:
total 3
drwxrwxrwx   2 maryann widget        32 Apr 10 10:28 letters
drwxrwxrwx   2 maryann widget        32 Apr 10 10:28 memos
drwxrwxrwx   2 maryann widget        32 Apr 10 10:28 specs

progs:
total 2
drwxrwxrwx   2 maryann widget        32 Apr 10 10:28 c
drwxrwxrwx   2 maryann widget        32 Apr 10 10:28 pascal

docs/letters:
total 0

docs/memos:
total 0

docs/specs:
total 0

progs/c:
total 0

progs/pascal:
total 0
```

Figure 3.9 Using `ls` with the `-R` Option

If you are a new user, you are probably not concerned about disk usage at this stage. But something you might want to watch out for is:

```
$ ls -l docs/letters
$ docs/letters
total 6
$
```

Here we have an apparently empty directory, no filenames are shown, but it occupies 6 blocks. This probably means there is a hidden file (one whose name starts with a period) in that directory, it could bear investigation.

Now that we have made some directories, we resume the discussion on working with files within those directories.

3.11. Copying Files with cp

The easiest way to get a file of your own is to take a copy of someone else's. This is achieved using the copy command, cp:

```
$ cp /etc/motd message
$
```

copies the message of the day file into a file named *message* in your current working directory. You can make yet another copy of that file with another cp command:

```
$ cp message message_too
$
```

Assuming that you are in your login directory, an ls command should show a directory which looks like this.

```
$ ls -l
total 4
drwxrwxrwx   5 maryann widget       80 Apr 10 10:28 docs
-rw-r--r--   1 maryann widget      189 Apr 12 18:06 message
-rw-r--r--   1 maryann widget      189 Apr 12 18:06 message_too
drwxrwxrwx   4 maryann widget       80 Apr 12 18:22 progs
$
```

In brief, cp takes two arguments, the names of files, or pathnames to files. The first argument is the name of the file we want to copy from, and the second argument is the name of the file that we want to be the copy. It is important to remember this order, since every operating system seems to have its own ideas about file copying.

■ *On System V, a* cp *command which looks like this:*

```
    cp here there
```

means 'copy from here *to* there'.

To get the same named file in your own directory, the filename is mentioned twice:

```
$ cp /etc/motd motd
$
```

puts a copy of the file called *motd* into the current directory.

However, there is another way of using cp. If the second argument you give it is an existing directory, cp copies the file named as the first argument into that directory, and retains the filename. So, we could have got our own copy of *motd* by saying:

```
$ cp /etc/motd .
$
```

Remember that . ('dot') stands for current directory.

Similarly, you could put it in one of your subdirectories:

```
$ cp /etc/motd docs/memos
$
```

When we use cp in this way, we are not restricted to copying one file, we can copy many files into a directory:

```
$ cp /usr/include/stdio.h /usr/include/time.h progs/c
$ ls  -l  progs/c
-r--r--r--  1  maryann  1544  Feb 14 12:40  stdio.h
-r--r--r--  1  maryann   286  Feb 14 12:40  time.h
$
```

Now the directory *progs/c* contains copies of the C programming language include files *stdio.h* and *time.h*[6].

Here are some things which might go wrong when using cp, and what they mean. If a file of the name you are trying to copy *to* already exists, there is no warning unless the file is write protected; the old version of the file is simply overwritten. If you try to copy to a file which is write-protected, or if you try to copy into a directory which does not exist, you get this result:

```
$ cp goodies no_holds/barred
cp: cannot create no_holds/barred
$
```

[6] This example should not be interpreted as a suggestion that it is a good idea for a user to have private copies of these files. It is in fact a very bad idea; the example is purely intended to demonstrate the use of cp.

Remember, the second argument is the destination of the copy. If you do not have read permission on the source file (the file you are trying to copy from) cp gives you this answer:

```
$ cp unreadable/file mine_all_mine
cp: cannot open unreadable/file
$
```

If the file you are trying to copy does not exist, you get a different message:

```
$ cp no_such/file mine_all_mine
cp: cannot access no_such/file
$
```

In figure 3.10 on page 64 we show some 'before and after' pictures of a directory structure, and how it changes when you use the cp command to copy files.

In the top left hand corner is a picture of part of a simple directory structure. It shows two directories: one contains two files, the other is empty. There is an arrow pointing to the current working directory. Beneath that picture are four cp commands; to the right of each command is a picture of the new directory structure which results from applying that cp command to the original structure.

One final note on cp: after you have made a copy of a file, the modes for that file are the same as the original version of the file. So if you copied a read-only file from somewhere else, you have to change the mode of your copy if you want to alter the file in any way.

3.12. Moving and Renaming Files with mv

The mv command moves files and directories around in the filesystem. In the process of moving a file or a directory, mv can rename the file or directory. The process of renaming a file or a directory is considered as a side effect of the move function.

Many people new to System V are baffled by this aspect of mv: 'why does move rename a file?' The principal function of mv is to move a file or directory from one place in the file system to another. The file name in the destination directory does not have to be the same as it was in the original directory. If the starting directory and the destination directory happen to be the same, the effect of specifying a different origin and destination name for the file is simply to rename the file; the file has been 'moved' within the same directory.

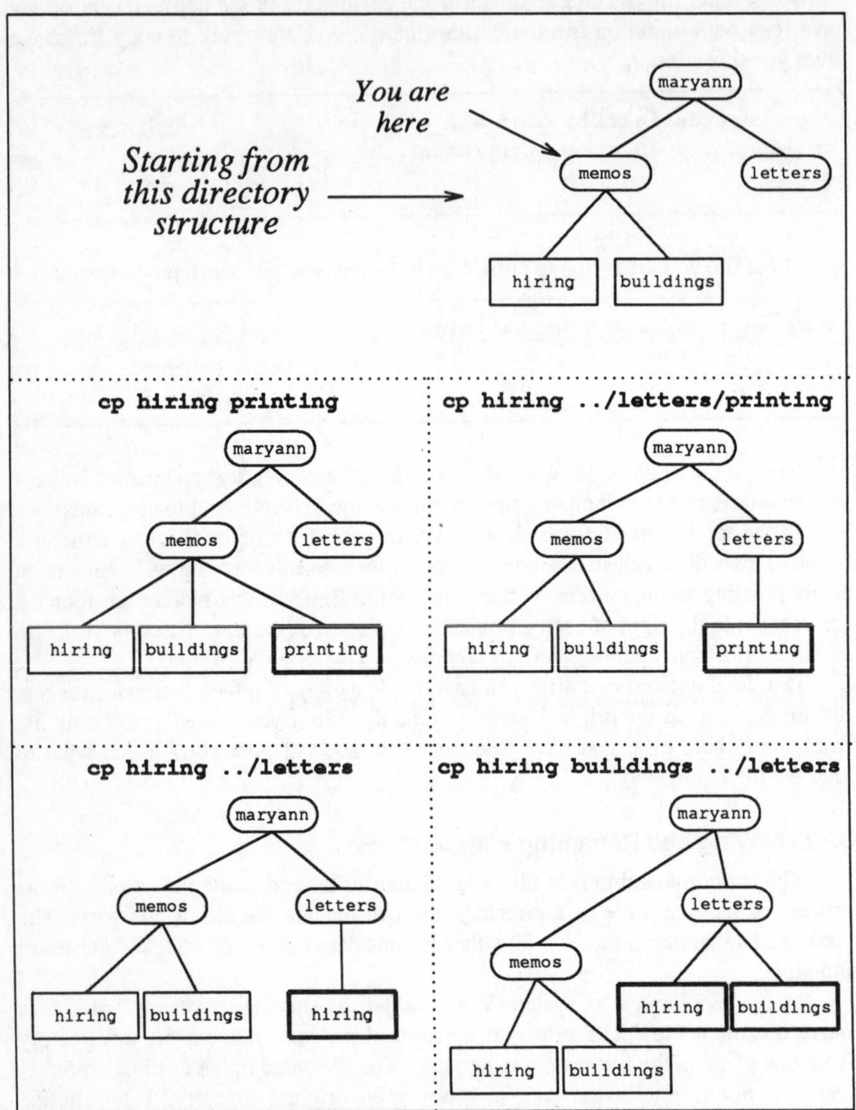

Figure 3.10 Effects of Copying Files with the cp Command

Obviously, a move differs from a copy operation in that the original of the file disappears. For example, after we had copied the file */etc/motd* into the current directory as the file *message*, the original file still existed. Had we used the mv command, */etc/motd* would have disappeared, and would have appeared as *message* in the current directory.

Here is an example of renaming files, with before and after displays of the filenames:

```
$ ls -l
total 4
drwxrwxrwx   5 maryann widget      80 Apr 10 10:28 docs
-rw-r--r--   1 maryann widget     189 Apr 12 18:06 message
-rw-r--r--   1 maryann widget     189 Apr 12 18:06 message_too
drwxrwxrwx   4 maryann widget      80 Apr 12 18:22 progs
$ mv message_too mesg
$ ls  -l
total 4
drwxrwxrwx   5 maryann widget      80 Apr 10 10:28 docs
-rw-r--r--   1 maryann widget     189 Apr 12 18:06 mesg
-rw-r--r--   1 maryann widget     189 Apr 12 18:06 message
drwxrwxrwx   4 maryann widget      80 Apr 12 18:22 progs
$
```

The file *message_too* has been renamed *mesg*. If a file already exists whose name is that of the second argument to mv, that file is removed.

Now we move the file *mesg* to *message*:

```
$ mv mesg message
$ ls  -l
total 3
drwxrwxrwx   5 maryann widget      80 Apr 10 10:28 docs
-rw-r--r--   1 maryann widget     189 Apr 12 18:06 message
drwxrwxrwx   4 maryann widget      80 Apr 12 18:22 progs
$
```

If the target file is write protected, mv checks with you before removing the file. mv prints out the mode of the target file and waits for your response. If your answer begins with the letter y (yes) the move is carried out, otherwise no action is taken, as shown in the example on the following page.

```
$ cp message mesg
$ chmod 444 message
$ ls  -l
total 4
drwxrwxrwx   5 maryann widget       80 Apr 10 10:28 docs
-rw-r--r--   1 maryann widget      189 Apr 12 18:06 mesg
-r--r--r--   1 maryann widget      189 Apr 12 18:06 message
drwxrwxrwx   4 maryann widget       80 Apr 12 18:22 progs
$ mv  mesg  message
message: mode 444 ?
y
$
```

The chmod command in the above example shows a way of making a file read-only (no write permission). The subject of file modes and protection is covered in detail later in this chapter.

A file can be moved from one directory to another by making the second argument to mv the name of the target directory. Here is a list of files and directories:

```
$ ls -l
total 3
drwxrwxrwx   5 maryann widget       80 Apr 10 10:28 docs
-rw-r--r--   1 maryann widget      189 Apr 12 18:06 message
drwxrwxrwx   4 maryann widget       80 Apr 12 18:22 progs
$
```

and then we move some files and look at what we have:

```
$ mv message docs/memos
$ ls  -l
total 2
drwxrwxrwx   5 maryann widget       80 Apr 10 10:28 docs
drwxrwxrwx   4 maryann widget       80 Apr 12 18:22 progs
$
```

the *message* file has gone and has been moved into the *docs/memos* directory:

```
$ ls  -l docs/memos
total 2
-rw-r--r--   1 maryann widget      189 Apr 12 18:06 message
-rw-r--r--   1 maryann widget      189 Apr 12 12:06 motd
$
```

As was the case for cp, we are not restricted to moving one file at a time, we can move several:

```
$ cd progs/c
$ ls -l
total 5
-r--r--r--   1 maryann widget      1814 Apr 12 18:08 stdio.h
-r--r--r--   1 maryann widget       362 Apr 12 18:08 time.h
$ mv stdio.h time.h ..
$ ls
$ cd ..
$ ls -l
total 7
drwxrwxrwx   2 maryann widget        64 Apr 12 19:47 c
drwxrwxrwx   2 maryann widget        32 Apr 10 10:28 pascal
-r--r--r--   1 maryann widget      1814 Apr 12 18:08 stdio.h
-r--r--r--   1 maryann widget       362 Apr 12 18:08 time.h
$
```

Remember that '..' ('dot dot') means the parent directory, so the include files have been moved from the directory */aa/widget/maryann/progs/c* to */aa/widget/maryann/progs*.

If you try to move or rename a file that doesn't exist, mv displays an error response:

```
$ mv chimera reality
mv: cannot access chimera
$
```

Figure 3.11 on page 68 shows some 'before and after' pictures of a directory structure showing what happens when you use mv to move files around.

These are laid out in a manner similar to those showing the cp command. Compare diagrams 3.10 and 3.11 — they should give you a clear picture of the difference between the two commands.

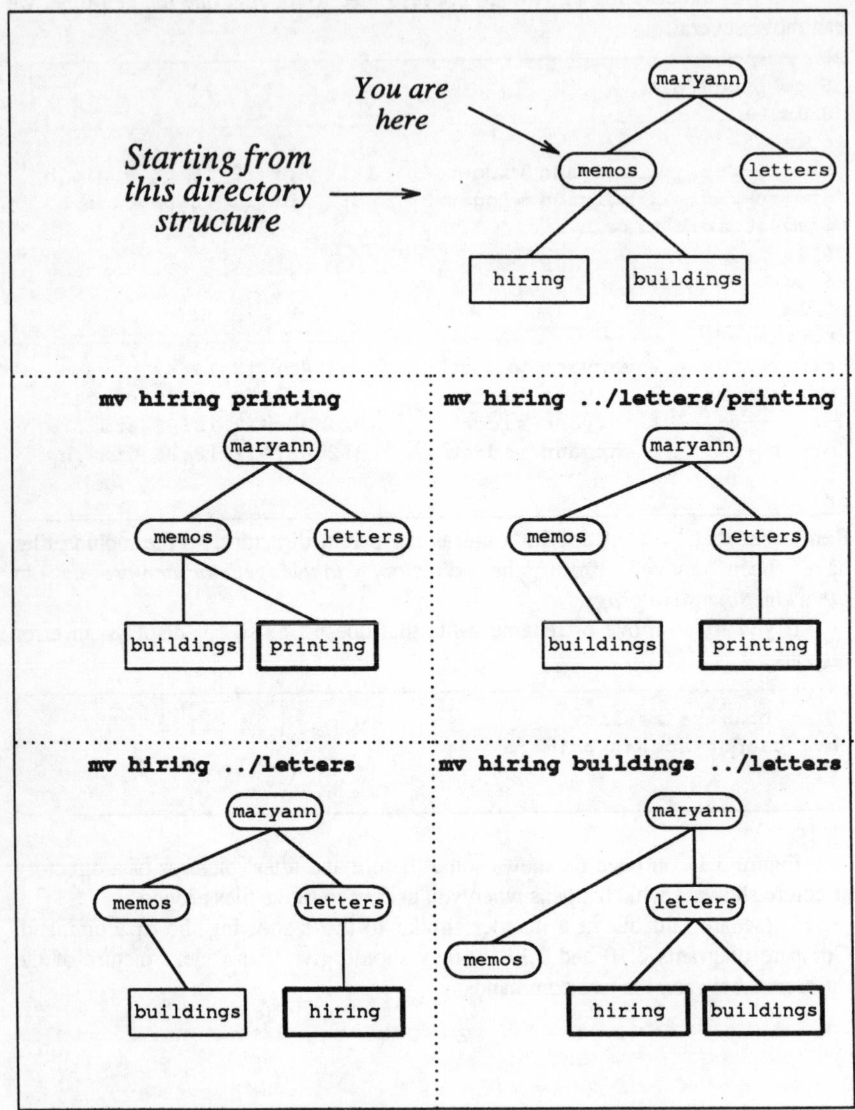

Figure 3.11 Effects of Moving Files with the mv Command

3.13. Removing Files with `rm`

The `rm` command deletes or removes files from a directory. For example, remember that we copied the message-of-the-day file into our local directory *docs/memos*. We can now remove that file like this:

```
$ cd
$ rm docs/memos/motd
$ ls -l docs/memos
total 1
-rw-r--r--   1 maryann widget       189 Apr 12 18:06 message
$
```

`rm` can remove more than one file at a time. If any file is write protected, `rm` checks whether you really want to remove it by informing you of the actual mode of the file, and waiting for confirmation. If you type anything which begins with a `y` (yes), `rm` accepts that as confirmation that the file is to be removed. If you type anything which does not start with `y`, `rm` does not remove the file:

```
$ cd progs
$ rm stdio.h time.h
rm: stdio.h 444 mode
rm: time.h 444 mode y
$ ls  -l
total 7
drwxrwxrwx   2 maryann widget        64 Apr 12 19:47 c
drwxrwxrwx   2 maryann widget        32 Apr 10 10:28 pascal
-r--r--r--   1 maryann widget      1814 Apr 12 18:08 stdio.h
$
```

The first file, *stdio.h*, was not removed because the reply to the check did not begin with `y`. A similar check happens when you have write permission on a directory, but try to remove a file that you don't own.

If you use the `-i` (interactive) option, `rm` checks with you before removing each file, regardless of whether it is write protected. This is a very wise precaution against accidentally removing a file you really want to keep. When you use the `-i` option `rm` doesn't print the mode of the file, it just prints the filename and waits for an answer:

```
$ rm -i frammis whammo
frammis: n
whammo: y
$
```

This example succeeds in removing *whammo*, but leaves *frammis* intact.

■ *Remember that typing a* **y** *in answer to* `rm`*'s query means 'Yes, go ahead and remove the file'!!*

The `-f` (force) option is the inverse of the `-i` option — it forces removal of the files without question, even if they are write protected:

```
$ rm -f c stdio.h
rm: c directory
$ ls -l
total 2
drwxrwxrwx   2 maryann widget         64 Apr 12 19:47 c
drwxrwxrwx   2 maryann widget         32 Apr 10 10:28 pascal
$
```

This example also shows what happens if you try to remove a directory: you get a message to tell you that it is a directory, and the directory is left alone.

The `-i` option and the `-f` option are mutually exclusive. If you use both of them, the `-i` option takes precedence and the `-f` option is ignored.

Normally, `rm` is for removing files rather than directories, as illustrated in the example above. But `rm` can be made to remove directories and, recursively, files and subdirectories by giving the `-r` (recursive) option:

```
$ rm -r progs docs
$ ls
$
```

When used with the `-r` option, `rm` searches down the directory tree, removing all files it finds. When a subdirectory is empty, `rm` then removes that subdirectory. The command does this for every file in every subdirectory (and so on) that it finds in the specified directory. As we shall show in the discussion on wild-card characters which follows, the `*` character means 'everything'; so, if you were to type the command:

```
$ rm -r *
```

every file and subdirectory (and all their subdirectories) from the current directory on down, would get removed. You had better be sure that this is what you really wanted. When used with the recursive option, `rm` is a very powerful command; use it with care and caution, and much trepidation.

If you try to remove a file which does not exist, `rm` informs you in no uncertain terms:

```
$ rm nonesuch
rm: nonesuch non-existent
$
```

3.14. Deleting Directories with `rmdir`

The command to delete (or remove) a directory is `rmdir`. To remove a directory with `rmdir` the directory must be empty, that is it must not contain any files or subdirectories. So if you decided you weren't going to write any programs and tried to use the `rmdir` command get rid of the *progs* directory, you would get this result:

```
$ rmdir progs
rmdir: progs not empty
$
```

You get this response because *progs* still contains two subdirectories, even though there are no files. You have to get rid of the subdirectories first:

```
$ rmdir progs/pascal progs/c progs
$
```

Had there been any files in any of the directories, you would have to remove them before you could remove the directories. Alternatively, you could use `rm` with the `-r` option.

If you try to remove a directory that does not exist, the system responds with an error message:

```
$ rmdir nonesuch
rmdir: nonesuch non-existent
$
```

3.15. Wild-card Characters or Metacharacters

You have seen some of the commands for working with files and directories in UNIX System V. Now we describe one of the most powerful features of the Shell, the capability to use a 'shorthand' notation for operating upon whole aggregates of files and directories in a single command. Using the Shell's shorthand notation, you can refer to filenames such as 'all files consisting of the letter `c` followed by a digit', or 'all four letter filenames', or 'all filenames containing the letters `a` through g', or 'every file in this directory', and so on.

The Shell achieves this capability by using some characters to represent things other than themselves. These special characters are often called 'wild-card' characters, taken from the analogy with card games, where (for instance) a Joker can be any card. In the Shell, the wild-card characters are called metacharacters. These special characters are used to 'match' filenames or parts of filenames. They ease the job of specifying particular files or whole groups of files.

- The asterisk character * represents any arbitrary character string, including an empty (null) string.
- The question-mark character ? represents any single character.
- Brackets, [and] enclose a list of characters where the match is on 'any single character enclosed in the brackets'. The hyphen character - used inside the brackets indicates a range of characters, for instance

  ```
  [a-z]
  ```

  is a shorthand notation for every lowercase letter in the alphabet. An exclamation mark ! used inside brackets inverts the match.

To illustrate the use of these characters, let's assume we have a directory containing files relating to some document. There are chapters (abbreviated to *c*), appendices (abbreviated to *a*), some figures and some tables (abbreviations *f* and *t*). Then there are some miscellaneous files. Let us say here that these are very bad file names. It would be much better to call the files *chapter1*, or at least *chap1*, *fig1* and so on. The names have been chosen with a view to illustrating the use of wild-card characters, rather than making them decently mnemonic.

```
$ ls -x
a          aA         aB         aC         c1
c10        c11        c12        c13        c2
c3         c4         c5         c6         c7
c8         c9         contents   f1-1       f10-1
f11-1      f11-2      f2-1       f2-2       f2-3
f7-1       f8-1       f8-2       t3-1       t3-2
t6-1       t8-1       temp       zonk8
$
```

We use ls to show the Shell's file matching capabilities because ls simply prints the names of the files matched, but the special characters can be used to specify filenames in *any* command.

Match any Single Character with ?

The question-mark character ? matches any single character:

```
$ ls -x c?
c1      c2      c3      c4      c5      c6      c7      c8      c9
$
```

This command finds all files that have names consisting of the letter c followed by a single character, which in this case happens to be numbers.

```
$ ls -x  a?
aA          aB          aC
$
```

Similarly, this command finds all files whose names start with a and are followed by one other character (here, they are uppercase letters). Notice that the file *a* was not found because the initial a isn't followed by any other character.

```
$ ls -x  ?
a
$
```

However, this command does find *a*, and only *a* — it is the only single-character filename.

```
$ ls -x  f?
f? not found
$
```

There are no filenames which consist of f followed by a single character; all the files beginning with the letter f are four or more characters long. And so we get the 'not found' message.

```
$ ls -x  c??
c10       c11       c12       c13
$
```

This last command prints the names of all files which consist of a c followed by two more characters.

Match String of Characters with *

The asterisk character * matches any string of characters, including a string of zero length (also called a null string):

```
$ ls -x  c*
c1        c10       c11       c12       c13
c2        c3        c4        c5        c6
c7        c8        c9        contents
$
```

This command finds all filenames that begin with c, regardless of how long the filename is.

```
$ ls -x  f*
f1-1     f10-1    f11-1    f11-2    f2-1
f2-2     f2-3     f7-1     f8-1     f8-2
$
```

Here we find all filenames that begin with f. The next example finds all those files that begin with a:

```
$ ls a*
a        aA       aB       aC
$
```

The string a* finds the file *a* even though there are no following characters in the name. This is because the * matches a null string as well as any other string.

Any number of * and ? can be used in conjunction with each other to specify the files you want, for example:

```
$ ls -x  ?8*
c8       f8-1     f8-2     t8-1
$ ls -x  ?11*
c11      f11-1    f11-2
$ ls -x  ?1*
c1       c10      c11      c12      c13
f1-1     f10-1    f11-1    f11-2
$ ls -x  *8*
c8       f8-1     f8-2     t8-1     zonk8
$
```

The first ls in the above example finds all files relating to chapter 8, including figures and tables; the second does the same thing for chapter 11. The third ls attempts to do the same for chapter 1, but this time we have also found files pertaining to chapters 10 through 13 too, because they all contain 1 as the second character.

The character * on its own matches *all* filenames, so be wary of it. Also be careful when typing commands containing *, since an extraneous space can do much harm. For example, supposing we had mistyped the `ls` command from the example above, and inadvertently placed a space between the letter `c` and the `*` character:

```
$ ls -x  c *
c not found
a           aA          aB          aC          c1
c10         c11         c12         c13         c2
c3          c4          c5          c6          c7
c8          c9          contents    f1-1        f10-1
f11-1       f11-2       f2-1        f2-2        f2-3
f7-1        f8-1        f8-2        t3-1        t3-2
t6-1        t8-1        temp        zonk8
$
```

Given such a command, `ls` first tries to list the file `c` (which doesn't exist, hence the error message), then proceeds to list everything else.

Since we are using `ls` no harm is done, BUT:

■ *If the command had been the remove files command,* `rm`, *we would have just wiped out our entire directory!!*

Here are some simple rules to follow to avoid this type of accident:

- Always use `ls` before `rm` with wild-cards. Then you can check that what you are actually going to remove is what you really want to remove.
- After you have typed the `rm` command line, study it and make sure there are no mistakes *before* you type **RETURN**.
- Get into the habit of using the `-i` (interactive) option on `rm`.
- Always keep your important files write-protected. This way, `rm` checks with you before it destroys them. You are also protecting them from being overwritten by `cp` and `mv`. This can be a bit of a nuisance, because now you have to change the mode of a file to make it writeable before you can alter it, and then change the mode back again. However, in the long run this can be less work than having to recreate a file (even from a backup tape) because you accidentally destroyed it.

Classes of Characters with [and] and -

A string of characters enclosed in the [and] brackets is known as a 'character-class'. The meaning of this construct is 'match any single character which appears within the brackets'. For example:

```
$ ls -x  c[12684xyz]
c1          c2          c4          c6          c8
$
```

This command lists all filenames which begin with c and are followed by one of 1 or 2 or 6 or 8 or 4 or x or y or z.

As it happens, we don't have files *cx*, *cy* or *cz*, but the system is happy as long as it can find some files that match the wild-cards. However, if the system can't find any files:

```
$ ls -x  c[xyz]
c[xyz] not found
$
```

you get a message as shown above.

```
$ ls -x  c1[0123]
c10      c11      c12      c13
$
```

Here we find files starting with c1 and followed by a digit in the range 0 through 3.

```
$ ls -x   [tf]*
f1-1     f10-1    f11-1    f11-2    f2-1
f2-2     f2-3     f7-1     f8-1     f8-2
t3-1     t3-2     t6-1     t8-1     temp
$
```

This last example finds all files which begin with the letter t or the letter f. The filenames are still shown in alphabetical order, even though you didn't specify your character class in that order.

Within brackets, the minus sign – can be used to denote a range of characters:

```
$ ls -x  c1[0-3]
c10      c11      c12      c13
$
```

This ls command reproduces the third example in the previous set of examples. It finds all files starting with c1 and followed by a digit in the range 0 through 3.

```
$ ls -x  a[A-Z]
aA       aB       aC
$
```

This command finds all filenames consisting of a followed by an uppercase letter.

It should be emphasized that the ends of the range are actually the values of the characters as they are represented in the ASCII character code. So the range

•

```
[A-z]
```

(capital A through lowercase z) not only gets all lower and upper case letters, but all other characters whose values fall in the range between. You can see what those are by looking at the cat example earlier in this chapter, where the file */usr/pub/ascii* appears.

This aspect of character classes can be particularly confusing when dealing with filenames with digits in them. For instance:

```
$ ls -x  c[10-13]
c1       c3
$
```

This ls command does *not* find files beginning with c and followed by a number 10 through 13. It finds files beginning with c and followed by a character which is either 1, or lies in the range 0 through 1, or is a 3.

The same is true of this next example. In fact here, since 6 is greater in the ASCII ordering than 1 it doesn't recognize a range at all:

```
$ ls -x  c[6-12]
c1       c2       c6
$
```

An exclamation mark as the first character within brackets has a special meaning. It inverts the character match, for example:

```
$ ls -x  c[!456]
c1    c2    c3    c7    c8    c9
$
```

In this case we found files that began with the letter c and had one more character, which was *not* 4, nor 5, nor 6.

```
$ ls -x  f[!1-7]*
f8-1     f8-2
$
```

In this case we found all filenames beginning with f, followed by a character that was not 1 through 7, followed by anything else.

In all the above, notice that 'hidden' files (those whose names start with a .) don't get found by the wild-cards. For example, if we had had a file called *.trouble*, it would not show up in any of the examples, not even in

```
ls  *
```

It could have been explicitly found by using

```
ls  .*
```

but that is the equivalent of the command line:

```
ls  .trouble  .  ..
```

so, as well as seeing the file *.trouble*, you also get an `ls` of both the current directory and its parent directory. In general, these hidden files are not much used. To see them it is best to use the `-a` option of `ls` to find the proper names, then use the full names, rather than trying to short-cut using the wild-card characters.

3.16. Non-Printing Characters in Filenames

Because a System V filename system can consist of *any* characters, it sometimes happens that you accidentally create a file whose name contains a non-printing character, or a control character. **CTRL-A** seems to be a common culprit, and so is the **ESCAPE** key which produces the same character as (**CTRL-[**). These characters are almost always inserted by 'fat-fingering' two keys at a time when typing a filename. The **CONTROL** key is often just to the left of the `a` on most terminal keyboards, and you often hit the two keys together when you are typing the `a`.

When this has happened, the file will show on a directory listing like this:

```
$ ls -x
arrow       circle      squ?are     triangle
$
```

You can see that there is a character between the `u` and the `a` of the file we wanted to call *square*. However, in this case the `?` is merely `ls`'s way of telling you there is a non-printing character in the filename, it does not mean that the extra character is really a question mark.

To some extent this is irrelevant. Because `?` is the metacharacter that matches *any* single character, you can use that to correct the situation:

```
$ mv squ?are square
$ ls -x
arrow       circle      square      triangle
$
```

But, suppose you had managed to do a similar dumb thing twice. You might get the situation where you have two files of apparently the same name:

```
$ ls -x
arrow       circle      squ?are      squ?are      triangle
$
```

Using ? to match any character will give you various error messages if you try to correct the situation using mv or cp, although you should be able to remove both files with rm.

You can get ls to show exactly what the non-printing character is by using the -b option:

```
$ ls -xb
arrow     circle    squ\001are        squ\033are        triangle
$
```

The non-printing character are shown by their octal values, preceded by a reverse slash (\). So you can use the ASCII character table, as found in */usr/pub/ascii*, to figure out what you really have to type in order to specify the correct file. In the example above, one mistake was made by adding an extra **CTRL-A**, the other was made by hitting the **ESCAPE** key at an inappropriate point. To rename the first file, and remove the second we would type:

```
$  mv squ^Aare square
$ rm squ?are
$ ls -x
arrow       circle      square      triangle
$
```

Remember that in our examples, the two characters ^A mean you are actually to type **CTRL-A**, not the two separate characters ^ and A.

3.17. Ownership and Protection

UNIX System V provides a means to assign permissions for files and directories, such that the range of users who can access those files and directories is constrained. Here, we discuss the ideas behind access rights to files and directories.

Every file or directory anyone creates on System V has an owner, usually the person who created the file or directory in the first place. The owner of a file or directory can then assign various permissions (or protections), allowing or prohibiting access to that directory or file.

For every file and every directory in the file system, there are three classes of users who may have access:

Owner The owner is the user who initially created it. It is possible for the creator of a file to give it to somebody else (the chown command changes ownership of a file). In general, the super-user is the only person who uses the `chown` command. For this reason, we do not discuss `chown` here; it is covered in chapter 15 — *System Administration.*

Group Several users can be combined into a user group, and so there is a group ownership associated with each file and directory.

Public All other users of System V. That is, anyone who has a user-name and can gain access to the system.

Every file and every directory on System V has three types of permission, which describe what kinds of things can be done with the directory or file. Because directories and files are slightly different entities, the interpretation of the permissions also differs slightly. The meanings assigned to the permissions are:

Read A user who has read permission for a file can look at the contents of that file.

A user who has read permission for a directory can find out what files there are in that directory. If detailed information about the files in the directory is required (the `-l` option to `ls`), the directory must have execute permission for that user. Whether the user can see the contents of the files in the directory, depends on the read permissions for the files themselves.

Write A user who has write permission for a file can change the contents of that file.

A user who has write permission for a directory can change the contents of the directory — she can create new files and remove existing files. Whether she can change existing files in the directory depends on the write permission for the files themselves.

Execute A user who has execute permission for a file can use that filename as a UNIX System V command.

A user who has execute permission for a directory can change directory to that directory, and can copy files from that directory, providing she also has read permission for the directory. The `x` permission for a directory is often called a 'search' permission.

By combining the three types of permissions and the three types of user, we can come up with a total of nine sets of permissions:

- `read`, write, and execute permission for the *owner* (user who created the file)
- `read`, write, and execute permission for the *group*
- `read`, write, and execute permission for the *public* (others)

These nine permissions are usually written:

```
rwxrwxrwx
```

As we show in figure 3.12 below,

- the leftmost three letters refer to the permission that the owner (user) has;
- the middle three refer to the group permissions;
- the rightmost three letters refer to the permissions that other users of the system (the public) have.

These permissions appear on the long directory listing (`ls -l`) in the first field, adjacent to the directory or file indication ('d' or '-').

A missing permission is indicated by a '-' and is called a 'protection' (hence the title of this section). The nine permissions, or protections, are collectively known as the 'mode' of the file or directory, and can be changed with the `chmod` command, which is described below.

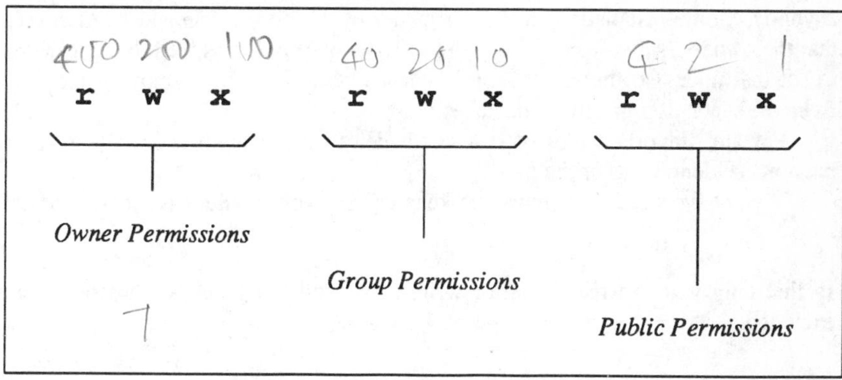

Figure 3.12 Permissions for Files and Directories

A 'read-only mode' file has these permissions:

```
r--r--r--
```

A file with this mode can be read by the owner, the group, and the public. It is protected from being written (modified) or executed by anybody: the public, the group, or the owner.

When we were exploring the system directories we looked at the contents of */bin* and */usr/bin*, where the system commands are held. Files in those directories usually have entries that should look like this:

```
$ ls -l /bin
-r-xr-xr-x   1 bin      bin         21428 Sep 24  1983 ar
-r-xr-xr-x   1 bin      bin         47528 Mar 20  1984 as
             <etcetera . . .>
-r-xr-xr-x   4 bin      bin         23988 Feb 15  1984 ls
             <etcetera . . .>
-r-xr-xr-x   1 bin      bin         14916 Jul 18  1983 uniq
-r-xr-xr-x   1 bin      bin         24696 Feb 15  1984 who
$
```

The important thing about these files is that the mode is (or should be):

```
r-xr-xr-x
```

That is, they can be read and executed by everybody, but cannot be written over by anybody. Some installations make the modes of the files in */bin* and */usr/bin* such that the owners (super-user, or 'bin') have write permission as well, but it is better to set the modes so that there is little chance of accidentally removing the files. Even the super-user can make mistakes.

For any important files, it is a good idea to make them read-only mode to prevent accidental loss of the files.

If you have any files you want to keep private, you should make them mode:

```
rw-------
```

so that only you can read them or write them, and the group and all others are excluded.

Changing Permissions with `chmod`

The command `chmod` changes the mode of a file or directory. The mode can only be changed by the owner (that is the user who first created the file or directory), or by the super-user.

Newcomers to UNIX System V are sometimes confused about the directory/file indication, and the directory or file modes in the display from `ls`. Although the permissions appear on the output of '`ls -l`' next to the directory indication, these two things have nothing to do with each other. In other words:

- *you cannot convert a file into a directory, or change a directory into a file, by changing its mode!!*

`chmod` accepts specification of the required mode in one of two different ways:

- As an absolute value given as an octal number
- As what is termed a 'symbolic mode', described below.

The format of the chmod command is:

chmod *mode file* . . . .

Let's deal with the numerical specification first, although it is not the easiest to use unless you are familiar with binary arithmetic. For users who know binary arithmetic it's easy — each permission in the group of nine is represented by a one, each protection (lack of permission) is represented by a zero. So rw-r--r--'' translates to '110100100', or '644' in octal notation.

Users not familiar with binary notation can use the translation diagram shown in figure 3.13 below.

To translate the mode you require to a number, simply add up the numbers corresponding to the individual permissions you want.

Owner (user) *Group* *Public (others)*

```
r w x   r w x   r w x

400 ........ r (owner)
200 ........ w (owner)
100 ........ x (owner)

40 ......... r (group)
20 ......... w (group)
10 ......... x (group)

4 .......... r (public)
2 .......... w (public)
1 .......... x (public)
```

Figure 3.13 Translation Diagram for Permissions

So, if you want the files to be readable and writeable by the owner (that is, you), readable by the group, and readable by all the other users of the system, you perform the addition:

```
400
200
 40
  4
---
644
```

So your chmod command will look like:

```
$ chmod 644 this that theother
$
```

If you try to change the mode of a file or directory that doesn't exist, you will get an error message:

```
$ chmod 444 nonesuch
chmod: can't access nonesuch
$
```

If you should get this response, check that you have spelled the filename correctly.

If you try to change the mode of a file or directory that you don't own, you will get the message:

```
$ chmod 644 notmine
chmod: can't change notmine
$
```

In this case, use **ls -l** to check ownership of the file.

Remember that the mode must be the first argument to chmod:

```
$ chmod filefirst 644
chmod: invalid mode
$
```

will not work because *filefirst* was taken to be the mode.

Using octal numbers to specify the mode may seem cumbersome at first, but you soon get to know the numbers corresponding to the most common permissions attached to files. When you have reached this stage this is the easiest method to use. The table on the following page shows a few of the more common ones.

Octal Code	*Permissions*	*Meaning*
644	rw-r--r--	the owner can read and write the file or directory, everybody else can only read it.
755	rwxr-xr-x	the owner can read, write, and execute the file, everybody else can read or execute it. For a directory, this mode is equivalent to 644 for a file.
711	rwx--x--x	the owner can read, write, and execute the file, everybody else can only execute it.
444	r--r--r--	this permission implies read-only for everybody.

The second method of specifying the modes is the 'symbolic mode', and is rather more complex. You have the choice of saying what you want the mode to be, or of saying how you want the existing permissions to be modified. To do this, the following abbreviations are used:

- `u` user (owner) permissions
- `g` group permissions
- `o` others (public) permissions
- `a` all of user, group and others permissions
- `=` assign a permission absolutely
- `+` add a permission
- `-` take away a permission.

The types of permission are, as usual `r`, `w`, and `x`.

Let us look at a few examples of this method of changing mode, with 'before and after' directory listings. Here is how to assign read/write permission for user, read for group, and read for others:

```
$ ls -l
total 3
-r--------   1 maryann widget        5 Apr 13 19:12 that
-r--------   1 maryann widget        5 Apr 13 19:12 theother
-r--------   1 maryann widget        5 Apr 13 19:12 this
$ chmod a=r,u+w this that theother
$ ls  -l
total 3
-rw-r--r--   1 maryann widget        5 Apr 13 19:12 that
-rw-r--r--   1 maryann widget        5 Apr 13 19:12 theother
-rw-r--r--   1 maryann widget        5 Apr 13 19:12 this
$
```

The first symbolic mode allocates read permission for everybody, the second adds write permission for the user. If we had said 'u=w' instead of 'u+w', we would have allocated write permission but removed the read permission for the user.

■ *The new mode you require must form a single argument to* chmod. *That means there must not be any spaces in it. So if there is more than one change to be specified, they are separated by commas but no spaces — though that is unusual in the System V way of things.*

Another way of achieving the required permissions would be:

```
$ chmod u=rw,go=r this that theother
$
```

If the directory was already readable and writeable by everybody:

```
$ ls -l
total 3
-rwxrwxrwx   1 maryann widget        5 Apr 13 19:12 that
-rwxrwxrwx   1 maryann widget        5 Apr 13 19:12 theother
-rwxrwxrwx   1 maryann widget        5 Apr 13 19:12 this
$
```

we could have simply removed the write permissions for group and others:

```
$ chmod go-w this that theother
$ ls -l
total 3
-rwxr-xr-x   1 maryann widget        5 Apr 13 19:12 that
-rwxr-xr-x   1 maryann widget        5 Apr 13 19:12 theother
-rwxr-xr-x   1 maryann widget        5 Apr 13 19:12 this
$
```

As another example, if you want a file to be executable by everybody, but you want to leave the read/write permissions as they are:

```
$ chmod a+x file
$
```

If you don't specify any of user, group or others, it is taken to be everybody. So, the following chmod command:

```
$ chmod +x file
$
```

does exactly the same thing as the previous example.

There are other protections described under chmod in the *System V User's Manual*. These additional protections are not used by most users; they are primarily used by the system administrator or super-user. Some of them are concerned with making a file accessible only via a command or program. Another gets the system to treat an executable program file in a special way, this can only be set by the super-user. If these additional protections apply to a file, you see the letter 's' or the letter 't' in the place where you normally see the letter 'x'.

Initial Permissions — the User Mask

The permissions assigned when a file or directory is created are under the control of something called the 'user mask', or umask for short. You can display the current value of the user mask by giving the command umask without any arguments:

```
$ umask
0000
$
```

On most installations it is zero as shown in the above example. This means that when you create a file its permissions will by default be set to rw-rw-rw- (mode 666). Also every directory your make will have default permissions rwxrwxrwx (mode 777). If you don't like these defaults you can change the value of the user mask by giving the umask command with an argument.

The value of the argument can be calculated by subtracting the mode you want as default from the current default mode. For instance, suppose you want your default mode to be 644 (rw-r--r--) for files:

```
 666   (The current default)
-644   (The default you want)
 ---
 022
```

When typing the umask command, leading zeros can be ignored, so:

```
$ umask 22
$
```

Now your files are automatically created with rw-r--r-- permissions, and your directories are rwxr-xr-x.

If you want your files to be mode 644 by default, but your directories to default to 777, you have a problem. It is probably better to concentrate on the file permissions you want when setting the default — you can `chmod` your directories as you create them.

The effect of the `umask` command only lasts for your current login session. After you log out, the defaults revert to the system defaults next time you log in. So if you always want a default mode that is different from the system default, you should put the `umask` command in your login profile.

3.18. Summary

By now, you should be comfortable with the commands for displaying the contents of a directory (`ls`), for moving around in the directory structure (`cd`), for making and removing directories (`mkdir` and `rmdir`), those for copying and renaming files (`cp` and `mv`), for removing files (`rm`), and some of the commands (such as `cat` and `file`) for examining what is in a file.

Once you are at ease with the notions of directories and files in System V, you are in a position to use the system effectively. Experiment with making your own directories and creating files in those directories. Play with full pathnames and relative pathnames to gain facility in their use.

Also try using `chmod` to change permissions on your own files and directories. See what happens when you can write files but not directories, and vice versa. It is important to explore the different effects of permissions for files and directories, and their interactions.

Used effectively, the UNIX System V file structure is a powerful tool in its own right; experienced users can exploit the capabilities of the file system to organize their data in efficient structures.

4 Processes and Standard Files

When a program runs on UNIX System V, it usually expects some input (data) and it usually produces some output (results). With very few exceptions, most System V commands (programs) have three 'standard' files.

- 'Standard Input' — the place from which a program expects to read its input.
- 'Standard Output' — the file to which the program writes its results.
- 'Diagnostic Output' — the file to which the program writes any error responses.

In general, if a command expects input and no file is specified, the Standard Input for that command is taken to be the user's terminal keyboard. Most commands are geared up to display their results on the Standard Output, which is usually the user's terminal screen. Lastly, the diagnostic output is also usually sent to the terminal screen.

System V provides a simple but very powerful capability to change the default cases listed above. You can tell the Shell that the Standard Input for a command is to be taken from a file. You can also have the Standard Output of a command written to a file. This process is called *redirecting Input and Output.*

The Diagnostic Output can be redirected just as can the Standard Output. You can arrange that any error messages from a command go to a file other than the one where the Standard Output is going, so that error messages do not clutter up the results.

You can also take the Standard Input of a command directly from the Standard Output of another command, and similarly you can direct the Standard Output of one command straight to the Standard Input of the next command. This feature is called *piping*, and a string of commands hooked together in this way is called a *pipeline.*

There are a few minor exceptions to these rules. These exceptions constitute end cases, where reading input from the terminal, or writing output to the terminal, does not make sense. For instance: the `ls` command takes its 'input' as the name of a directory whose contents are to be displayed; the `lp` command sends its output to a line printer; the `rm` command has no output.

4.1. Redirecting the Standard Output

If a filename argument to a command is prefixed by the > character, the Standard Output of that command is *redirected* so that it is placed in that file instead of going to the terminal screen. For example, the straight `ls` command displays a list of the contents of a directory on your terminal screen:

```
$ ls -l
total 3
drwxrwxrwx   5 maryann widget       80 Apr 10 10:28 docs
-rw-r--r--   1 maryann widget      189 Apr 12 15:06 message
-rw-r--r--   1 maryann widget      189 Apr 12 15:26 message_too
drwxrwxrwx   4 maryann widget       96 Apr 10 10:28 progs
$
```

But if we use the > sign as a redirection indicator, the command line:

```
$ ls -l > dirconts
$
```

puts the contents listing of the current working directory into a file called *dirconts* in the current directory. You can now view the file at your leisure, or change it around for any useful purposes of your own.

You don't *have* to surround the > character with spaces, so the commands:

```
$ date > today
$ date >today
$ date>today
$
```

are all correct and all do the same thing, namely direct the output of the `date` command into a file called *today*.

If the named file to which output is redirected doesn't already exist, it is created.

■ *If the file to which the Standard Output is redirected* **does** *already exist, the previous contents of the file are lost!! This is because the first thing the Shell does when it sees the redirection mark (>), is to create an empty file to hold the results of the command.*

Now, if you look in the *dirconts* file with the `cat` command, you should see a regular directory listing, as shown below.

```
$ cat dirconts
total 4
-rw-rw-rw-   1 maryann widget        0 Apr 15 15:27 dirconts
drwxrwxrwx   5 maryann widget       80 Apr 10 10:28 docs
-rw-rw-rw-   1 maryann widget      189 Apr 12 15:06 message
-rw-rw-rw-   1 maryann widget      189 Apr 12 15:26 message_too
drwxrwxrwx   4 maryann widget       96 Apr 10 10:28 progs
$
```

You see that *dirconts* itself appears in the directory listing as a zero-length file. The reason for this is that it is the Shell which creates the file to receive the command's output, and it does this before the command runs. So, at the instant the `ls` command starts, there is an empty file, called *dirconts*, in the directory. Here is a case where you might want to use one of those 'hidden' files whose names start with a period:

```
$ ls -l > .dirconts
$
```

Redirecting and Appending the Standard Output

If you don't want to lose the contents of an existing file, but want the output of a command appended to the end of it, you can do this by prefixing the file name with two right chevron signs >>. For example:

```
$ pwd  >> dirconts
$
```

prints the name of the current working directory at the end of the contents listing of the directory that we obtained above.

If the file to which the Standard Output is being redirected via the >> sign doesn't exist, it is created. So if we hadn't done the previous

```
ls -l > dirconts
```

the *dirconts* file would contain only the name of the current working directory. In many ways >> is safer to use than >, because it doesn't destroy previous information.

4.2. Redirecting the Standard Input

Just as the > character or the >> sign redirects the Standard Output of a command to a file, so we can redirect the Standard Input for a command to come from a file, instead of the terminal keyboard, by prefixing the file name with a left chevron sign <.

An example of the use of this redirection is with the `mail` facility:

```
$ mail
```

enters the `mail` utility, and expects mail messages from the terminal keyboard, while:

```
$ mail  <message
$
```

enters `mail`, and takes mail messages from the file *messages*, created previously by means of (say) an editor. The `mail` command is discussed in more detail in chapter 5 — *User to User Communication*.

In general, redirecting Input is not used as often as redirecting Output, because most commands are designed to take their input from files anyway.

If no files are specified, commands use the Standard Input. Let us show this with an example of using the `cat` command:

```
$ cat
So the IRS said to us:
So the IRS said to us:
hold out your wallets and repeat after me:
hold out your wallets and repeat after me:
Help yourself.
Help yourself.
^D
$
```

Having typed the `cat` command as shown above, the system responds with a glassy-eyed stare. There is no indication that `cat` wants anything. But if you start typing, `cat` echoes each line that you type, after each **RETURN**. We indicated the end of the data by typing a **CTRL-D** character, (`^D`) in the example.

Now talking to yourself with the `cat` command is an exercise in futility. The really useful aspect of `cat` is to concatenate files, and copy the result onto the Standard Output. So, the more appropriate use of `cat` is like this:

```
$ cat <  thisfile
```

which concatenates the contents of the file called *thisfile* to the Standard Output. As it happens, `cat` is one of the many commands which accept filenames as arguments, and as such, `cat` does not actually need the redirection marker:

```
$ cat  thisfile
```

has just the same effect as does the example above.

However, there are many commands which only act on the Standard Input. If you want these to work on a file you have to redirect the input to be from that file. An example of this is the command `tr` (translate characters), which we show you how to use in chapter 6.

4.3. Notes and Cautions on Redirection

You must take special care if you are redirecting both Standard Input and Standard Output, for example:

```
$ cat < left > right
$
```

Don't use the same filename in both places. A `cat` command which looks like this:

```
$ cat < thisfile  > thisfile
$
```

is a sure way to lose *thisfile*. This is because, when the Shell sees the redirection character (>), it creates an empty file ready to hold your output. If the output file happens to be the same name as the input file, the command just empties your input file!!

By the same token:

```
$ cat thisfile > thisfile
$
```

is no good either, but:

```
$ cat thatfile >> thatfile
$
```

is OK — you just copy *thatfile* onto the end of itself. This might not be what you want, but at least you haven't lost any information.

4.4. Creating a File the Easy Way with `cat`

We have said that commands which are not given a file name take the Standard Input, which is usually the terminal keyboard. Thus if you simply say:

```
$ cat
```

everything you type is transferred to the Standard Output. Under normal circumstances this means that whatever you type is echoed on the screen. But, supposing you redirect the Standard Output, like this:

```
$ cat > newfile
```

everything you type (including your mistakes) gets put in the file called *newfile*. `cat` holds a certain amount of data (usually 512 characters) before producing any output — this process is called 'buffering'. So nothing appears in the file until you have typed that amount. If you accidentally interrupted the process, or if the system crashed while you were typing, you would lose a lot of work. It is best to use the `-u` (unbuffered) option:

```
$ cat -u > newfile
```

so that each line goes into *newfile* as it is typed. Now if you accidentally interrupt the process, the only thing you will lose is any partial line that you were typing when the interrupt occurred.

To stop input and revert to the Shell, you type the 'end of text' character (CTRL-D) after your last line. At that point you will again see the system prompt `$`. So, using `cat` is a way to create files without having to learn how to use the text editor. Of course, if you make mistakes you will have to use the editor, or some other means, to correct them.

For instance, suppose you want to make a list of the people in your project, with their phone numbers:

```
$ cat -u >people
Maryann Clark    101
Sally Smith      113
Jane Bailey      121
Jack Austen      120
Steve Daniels    111
Sylvia Dawson    110
Henry Morgan     112
^D
$
```

You can also use `cat` to modify the file by adding things to the end of it:

```
$ cat -u >>people
Hank Parker        114
Charlie Smith      122
Bill Williams      100
^D
$
```

Remember to type the end-of-file character, CTRL-D, to terminate input to the `cat` command, as we have shown in the examples.

Now, of course, we can use `cat` to play back what we just created:

```
$ cat  people
Maryann Clark      101
Sally Smith        113
          . . . .
<and so on and so on>
             . . . .
Charlie Smith      122
Bill Williams      100
$
```

4.5. Connecting Commands with Pipelines

We have said that the Standard Output of one process (or program) can be the Standard Input of another process. When this is done a *pipeline* is formed.

We already showed the `who` command back in chapter 2. `who` displays a list of users on the system. There is another command called `wc`, which counts things. Using these two utilities, we can find out how many people are logged in:

```
$ who | wc  -l
     9
$
```

This simple example shows the Standard Output of the `who` command feeding to the Standard Input of the `wc` command (which we told to count lines with the `-l` option). The result is a count of the number of users on the system.

Pipelines provide a flexible and powerful mechanism for doing jobs easily and quickly, without the need to construct special purpose tools. Existing tools can be combined to do those one-off jobs that crop up so often.

To explain pipelines it is often easier to think of this as a flow of data that is operated on by several programs (or processes) in turn. Consider a number of operations being performed on a set of data, as shown in the diagram in figure 4.1.

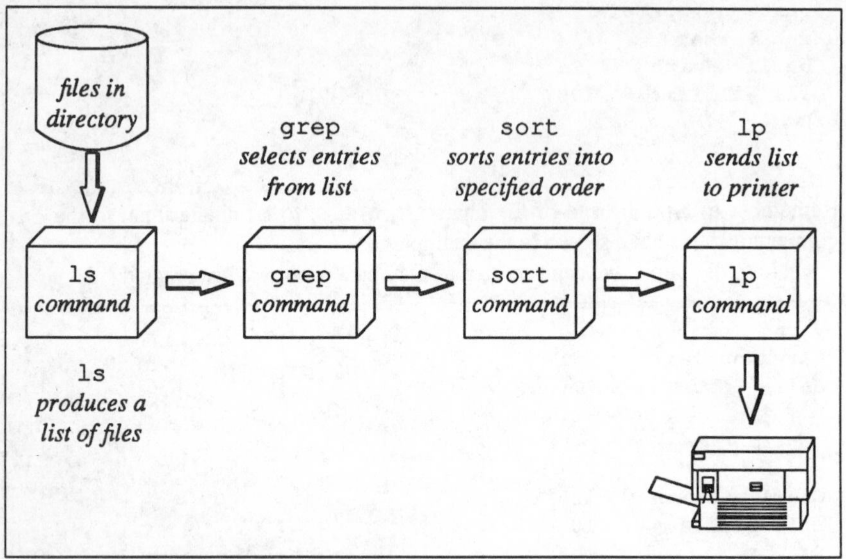

Figure 4.1 A Pipeline of Commands

```
$ ls -l /tmp | grep maryann | sort +4nr | lp
$
```

The symbol | (vertical bar) is known as the 'pipe' symbol. The Standard Output of the command to the left of the | becomes the Standard Input to the command on the right of |.

The output of the above `ls` command is a 'long' listing of all files and sub-directories in the system directory */tmp*. Instead of being written to the terminal (the default Standard Output), it is passed to the `grep` command.

`grep` and `sort` are two utility programs which find all kinds of uses. In this particular example, `grep` is selecting all lines containing the string 'maryann' from its Standard Input, and `sort` is sorting the fifth field of all those selected lines in reverse numerical order. We explain `grep` and `sort` in some detail in chapter 6 — *Text Manipulation*. What is important is to understand the concept of taking the results of one command, and passing it through various operations which modify it in some way, before the final result is seen. This string of connected commands is a pipeline.

The final stage of our pipeline is the command `lp`, which routes its input to a printer, so we get a print-out instead of seeing the results on the terminal screen. This, in fact, is the most common use of *piping*. Since all commands except `lp` provide output to the Standard Output (normally the terminal screen), the only way to get a hard copy (print-out) of anything is to pipe it to `lp` (covered in chapter 6).

The effect of the above pipeline could be achieved by typing the commands one at a time and using temporary files, in a sequence like this:

```
$ ls -l /tmp >temp1
$ grep maryann temp1 >temp2
$ sort +4nr temp2 >temp3
$ lp temp3
$ rm temp[123]
$
```

Note the use of temporary files. Although we used three, we could have got away with two by re-using *temp1* for the output of `sort`. For tidiness, and to avoid eating up space, these files should be removed. *But*, we must be careful not to remove *temp3* before it has finished printing.

This is one of the major advantages of pipes: the system does all the intermediate work for you. Were you to use temporary files instead of pipelines, you burden yourself with unnecessary work; you have to keep track of which temporary files you use; then you must ensure they get removed when you have finished with them. All this adds up to boring busy-work that a computer is better fitted to take care of.

Another point to note is that piping is quicker. With redirecting output, each command must be completed before the next one begins to work on the data. In a pipeline, each process starts executing as soon as there is some data for it to work on.

Filters

A command which accepts its input from the Standard Input, and produces its output on the Standard Output, is known as a 'filter'. The word 'filter' is derived from the analogy with the kinds of filters used in plumbing or electronics. A command which is a filter takes some input, performs some filtering action (weeding out blank lines, for instance), and finally generates some output.

There are some commands (`tr` for example) which can *only* be used as filters. If you want to apply them to files you have to redirect the Standard Input.

Most commands on UNIX System V can be used as filters. Commands which are filters can be used as intermediate operations in a pipeline (between two | symbols). In our examples above, `grep` and `sort` are filters, and can be used at intermediate places in the pipe.

Some commands are not filters because either their input does not come from the Standard Input, or they do not produce their output on the Standard Output.

The `ls` command is not a filter since it does not accept the Standard Input — its 'input' is a directory whose contents are to be listed. `ls` can only be the first command in a pipeline.

Similarly, the `lp` command cannot be used as a filter because it does not write to the Standard Output — its 'output' is to a printer somewhere. `lp` can only be used as the last command in a pipeline.

Redirecting input and output can be used in conjunction with pipelines, but:

- It makes no sense to redirect input in any of the commands in the pipeline other than the first.
- It is nonsense to redirect output on any command in a pipeline except the last.

4.6. To See and to Save with `tee`

Sometimes, although you want to save the output of a command in a file, you would also like to see it on the terminal as it is being produced. Then, if you see that the output looks wrong, you can stop the command. A useful command which helps you achieve this is `tee`, which acts like a T-junction, as shown in figure 4.2.

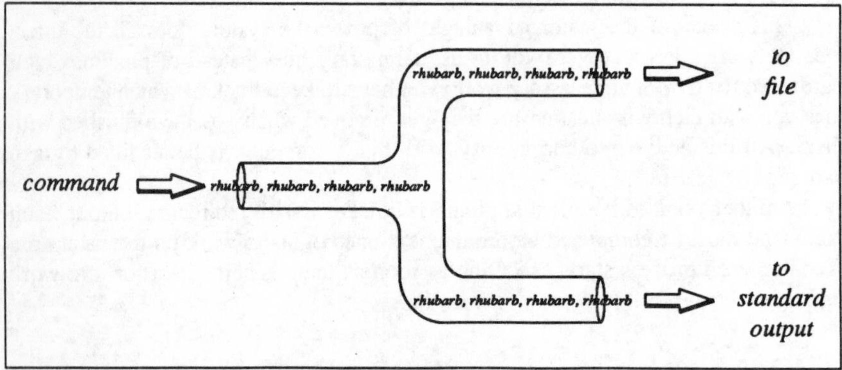

Figure 4.2 Operation of the `tee` Command

The command:

```
$ ls -l | tee dirconts
```

shows a full listing of the contents of the current directory on the terminal screen, and also puts it in the file *dirconts*.

4.7. Diagnostic Output

The output from most commands is written to the Standard Output, but if errors occur when the command is executed, the error messages produced are not necessarily written to the Standard Output. There is another type of output that commands can generate: this is called the Diagnostic Output.

Like the Standard Output, the Diagnostic Output is the user's terminal screen by default. Also like the Standard Output, the Diagnostic Output may be redirected to a file. Redirecting the Diagnostic Output is not quite such a straightforward matter as redirecting the Standard Output, before we can do it we must know about File Descriptors.

A File Descriptor is simply a number associated with a file of data. Three such numbers are assigned by default on System V:

0 file descriptor for the Standard Input,

1 file descriptor for the Standard Output,

2 file descriptor for the Diagnostic Output.

When you redirect the Standard Output to a file by using the notation

```
> outfile
```

the Diagnostic Output is not redirected. So error messages still appear on the terminal screen. In order to put the error messages into a file it is also necessary to redirect the Diagnostic Output.

The Diagnostic Output can be redirected by preceding the usual redirection sign > with the file descriptor number associated with the Diagnostic Output:

```
$ cat somefile nofile 2> errfile
```

redirects the error messages to the file *errfile*. The normal output of the command still appears on the terminal screen. If you wish to redirect both Standard and Diagnostic Outputs, you have to give two redirection signs:

```
$ cat somefile nofile > outfile 2> errfile
$
```

The simple > sign, which redirects the Standard Output, is merely the default case of the more general:

file_descriptor_number > *filename*

so that the command:

```
$ cat somefile nofile 1> outfile 2> errfile
$
```

has exactly the same effect as the previous example.

If you want to redirect both the Standard Output and the Diagnostic Output to the same place, the format of the command is like this:

```
$ cat firsthalf secondhalf > composite 2>&1
```

The construct 2>&1 means 'redirect the Diagnostic output to the same place as the Standard Output'.

If you don't want to see error messages appearing anywhere, they can be effectively thrown away by redirecting the Diagnostic Output to the device called */dev/null*:

```
$ cat somefile nofile > outfile 2> /dev/null
$
```

/dev/null is a special file which acts just like an end-of-file when a program tries to read it, and is an infinite sink when a command writes to it.

4.8. Background Processing

In the introduction, we said that UNIX System V is a multi-tasking system. This means that the system can attend to more than one job at a time, for any given user. In System V terminology, each one of these multiple tasks is called a 'process'. A process is a running program with some specific job to do. For example there is a process, which happens to be the Shell, doing the job of listening to your terminal. Every time you ask the Shell to run a command, the Shell runs that command as a separate process. For historical reasons, the process which converses with your terminal is called a 'foreground' process, so called because it is in the foreground of your attention. Normally, each command you type, or each pipeline of commands, is a foreground process. As such they run 'while you wait', at the terminal.

It is possible, however, to run commands in the 'background'. This means that the system prompt re-appears immediately after you type the command. The command has not completed, it is still running; but you can use the system to do other things while the background command proceeds. If you want to run a command which takes a long time to complete, you can run that command in the background.

The way in which you ask System V to run a command in the background, is by ending the command with the ampersand character &, for example:

```
$ troff doc &
179
$
```

The command troff is the text formatting command described in chapter 11 — *Typesetting with* **troff** *and* **nroff**. Text formatting is a time-consuming process, so it is a good candidate for background processing. We put a space between the last argument and the &, but a space is not necessary:

```
troff doc&
```

would do just as well.

When you ask System V to run a command in the background, it replies with a number ('179' in our example above). This is the process number (or process identity, abbreviated PID) that the operating system associates with the command you typed. Sometimes the command (process) you put in the background calls up other commands (processes) which you don't know about, but only the number for the primary (parent) process is shown when you type the command.

When you put a command in the background, make a note of the process number which System V displays — it is useful when you want to see what's going on, or if you decide to stop the background process.

After displaying the process number associated with the background task, the system displays its prompt sign. You can then type another command, so you are actually having System V doing two things for you at the same time. Alternatively, you can log off. The background command continues running, even while you are not using the system.

In fact, you can have several commands running in the background if you want to. But avoid having too many things going on at the same time: it slows the system down considerably, and you might end up taking just as long to complete all your tasks as if you had done them one by one at the terminal keyboard waiting for the prompt each time (in the foreground). The definition of 'too many things going on' depends on the size of the machine and the number of other users. You have to guess at it.

■ *One word of caution: if your background process is taking input from a file, don't start another command, either in the background or in the foreground, which will modify the contents of that file. If, in our example*

```
troff doc&
```

we had immediately called up a text editor and used it to modify the file doc, the results of the text formatting operation would be unpredictable.

What happens to the output from a background task? The answer is, nothing out of the ordinary. The output of the command:

```
troff doc&
```

goes to the Standard Output as usual. So if, while you are formatting a file in the background, you type:

```
ls -l
```

the results of both commands will be mixed up together on the screen. Even worse, if you have logged off, the output of the formatter will be completely lost. Perhaps the very worst is when someone has put a process in the background, then logged off, then you log on at the same terminal: you get the output of someone else's command on your screen!

Obviously, the thing to do is to redirect the output of the background command to a file:

```
$ troff doc > doc.format &
179
$
```

Now the output of your background command will not disturb you, or anyone else who is executing commands in the foreground.

Alternatively, you could pipe the results to the printer:

```
$ troff doc | lp &
179
$
```

In practice, you may want to redirect the Diagnostic Output as well as the Standard Output. This is especially true if you are going to log off: if your command fails for some reason, you still want to see what error messages were produced.

Finding out What is Going On with ps

When you are executing commands in the background, how can you check whether they are still running or have finished?

There is a command called ps which displays the status of active processes. If you simply type the ps command on its own, you will see something like this:

```
$ ps
  PID TTY TIME CMD
   89 02  0:05 sh
  102 02  0:01 ps
$
```

These are the processes belonging to (activated by) the user who typed the ps command. As you can see, there are two — the login process shown by sh (the Shell), and the ps process itself.

The information given is the process identification number (PID), the terminal that the process was started from (TTY), the amount of time (computer time, not wall-clock time) that the process has taken to execute so far (TIME), and the command line that was typed to initiate the process (CMD). The CMD information is not always exact. ps comes up with the nearest approximation it can to the typed command line.

If you type a ps command, and you see something like this:

```
$ ps
  PID TTY TIME CMD
   70 08  0:20 sh
   89 02  0:05 sh
  102 02  0:01 ps
$
```

it means you are logged on twice, once on tty02 and once on tty08. This illustrates that ps displays all processes associated with the user, not those associated with a particular terminal.

Now suppose you put a command to be processed in the background:

```
$ troff doc &
182
$ ps
  PID TTY TIME CMD
   89 02  0:05 sh
  182 02  0:02 troff doc
  183 02  0:01 ps
$
```

you can see that the troff command is running. If a ps sometime after this doesn't show troff running, it means that formatting is complete, or has failed for some reason.

Here is a general rule on how to misuse System V:

■ *If you put a command to be executed in the background, then do nothing but sit at your terminal typing* ps *commands until you see that it is complete — there was no point in putting it in the background in the first place!!*

You might just as well have run the command in the foreground, and waited for the system prompt to tell you it was finished. This may seem obvious, but it quite commonly happens with fairly new users of the system when they first 'discover' background processing.

Nevertheless there are still a couple of advantages to using background processing. One is that you can decide to do something else at any time while background job is running. The other advantage is that you are not likely to interrupt the job accidentally by hitting the interrupt key on the keyboard.

There are various options to the ps command, one is the -l option, which gives a 'long' listing of the processes statuses.

```
$ ps -l
F S UID   PID  PPID CPU PRI NICE  ADDR  SZ  WCHAN TTY  TIME CMD
1 S 101    89     1   3  30   20  5512  12  50602 02   0:02 sh
1 R 101   183    89  52  53   20  6021  20        02   0:02 ps l
$
```

Much of the information here is concerned with details of what the operating system does when it is processing your commands. We refer you to the description of ps in the *System V User's Manual* if you want to know about this. However, some of the columns are of interest:

- The column headed S displays the state of the process. There are many different values that can appear in this place, the interesting ones are R, which means that the process is running; S, which means that the process is sleeping (while the system is doing something else); W, which means that the process is waiting for some other process to finish before it can proceed.
- UID is the user identity number of the user who started the process.
- PPID is the name of the parent process, in our example the PID of the login process (sh) is the PPID of the other commands.
- PRI shows the priority allocated to the process — the user has no control over this. However, one of the factors that System V uses to compute the priority of a process is the figure given under the next column, NICE, and the user can control this to some extent by using the nice command. In both the PRI and NICE columns, a high number means a low priority.

Another option to ps is -a (all). Normally ps only displays the processes activated by the user who types the ps command. When the a option is given, the processes activated by all users are displayed. Both the a and l options can be given together:

```
$ ps -al
F S UID   PID  PPID CPU PRI NICE  ADDR  SZ  WCHAN TTY  TIME CMD
1 S 102    66     1   0  30   20  6203  12  50762 03   0.15 sh
1 S 105    71     1   0  30   20  4732  12  51266 06   0.03 sh
1 S 102    74    66   0  29   20  4454  13  51356 03   0.10 ed conv.c
1 S 105    75    71   0  28   20 10244  12   7102 06   0.03 troff spec
1 S 101    89     1   3  30   20  5512  12  50602 02   0:02 sh
1 S 105    81    71   2  29   20  7756  02   2722 06   0.01 ls
1 R 101   183    89  52  53   20  6021  20        02   0:02 ps l
```

We can see that users number 102 and 105 are logged on, as well as number 101. Number 102 is using the editor ed and number 105 is formatting a file called *spec* (probably in the background) and using ls.

Running Low Priority Commands with `nice`

If you are not in a hurry for the results of the command you put in the background, you can tell the operating system that this is not of high priority by using the `nice` command:

```
$ nice troff doc > doc.fmat &
103
$
```

This is a nice thing to do, because then System V can give more attention to things that require quick response (an `ls` command typed at a terminal, for instance). Here are some illustrations of the effects of using `nice`. First, we simply put a `troff` command in the background:

```
$ troff doc > doc.fmat &
115
$ ps -l
F S UID   PID  PPID CPU PRI NICE  ADDR  SZ  WCHAN TTY  TIME CMD
1 S 101    89     1   3  30   20  5512  12  50602 02   0:02 sh
1 R 101   115    89 111  56   20 10244  34        02   0.15 troff doc
1 R 101   116    89  39  52   20  6021  20        02   0:02 ps l
$
```

You can see that all the processes have the same value of 20 in the column headed `NICE`. The system uses this value to calculate the priority it attaches to each process; the priority value is shown in the column headed `PRI`. As you can see, the `troff` command and the `ps` command have very similar priority values. This means that the system is giving more or less equal time to both commands, with the foreground `ps` getting slightly more than the background `troff`. Highest priority is given to the `sh` command which is watching what you type at your terminal, indicated by its having the lowest number under PRI.

Now we will put the same command 'nicely' in the background.

```
$ nice troff doc > doc.fmat &
118
$ ps -l
F S UID   PID  PPID CPU PRI NICE  ADDR  SZ  WCHAN TTY  TIME CMD
1 S 101    89     1   3  30   20  5512  12  50602 02   0:02 sh
1 R 101   118    89 160  70   30 10244  34        02   0.03 troff doc
1 R 101   119    89  36  52   20  6021  20        02   0:02 ps l
$
```

You can see that the `NICE` value is now 30, and the priority value is up to 70. Now the `troff` command will take longer to complete, but you are not hogging the system to the possible detriment of the other users, or your own foreground processes.

You can control the amount of 'niceness' by giving a number:

```
$ nice -5 troff doc > doc.fmat &
121
$ ps -l
F S UID   PID  PPID CPU PRI NICE  ADDR  SZ  WCHAN TTY  TIME CMD
1 S 101    89     1   3  30   20  5512  12  50602 02   0:02 sh
1 R 101   121    89 160  64   25 10244  34        02   0.03 troff doc
1 R 101   123    89  36  52   20  6021  20        02   0:02 ps l
$
```

As you can see from the above ps, this adds a 'niceness' value of 5 to the 'not nice' number of 20. The troff command runs at a higher priority than it would with a straight nice, but not so high as it would without any nice command at all. The highest niceness (lowest priority) that can be called for is 39, this is achieved by putting a value of 20, or higher, on the nice command.

The super-user can use nice to execute high priority commands by giving a negative niceness; for example, -10 runs a command at a very high priority.

Immunity from Disconnects with nohup

Another command which can be used in connection with background processes is nohup. The name of this command is derived from 'no hang-up', and has nothing to do with the state of one's psyche.

nohup makes a command immune from a telephone line connection getting disconnected. However it can be interrupted by the DEL key, so the command should be put in the background:

```
$ nohup  troff doc&
129
$ Sending output to nohup.out
```

If you don't redirect the output of your command, the system will automatically re-direct it to a file called *nohup.out*, as indicated by the message in the example above. You can use both nohup and nice together, for example:

```
$ nice -5 nohup troff doc > doc.fmat&
131
$
```

Stopping Background Processes with `kill`

If you start a command running in the background, and then change your mind for some reason, you can stop the process with the `kill` command. To do this you need to know the process identification number (PID). For instance, in the very first example we gave of a command put in the background, we showed a process identification number of 179. To stop that command running, we say:

```
$ kill 179
$
```

If the process you put in the background started lots of other sub-processes (called children), they will all eventually die. However, this may take some time. You might want to find the PID numbers of these child processes using `ps`, then kill them all with the same `kill` command. You can put more than one process identification number on the `kill` command line.

Processes are usually stopped when System V sends them a certain *signal*. Signals are numbered 1 through 15, signal number 15 being the usual termination signal that the `kill` command sends. However, some processes are clever enough to be able to ignore that signal, so they cannot be stopped in this fashion. You can send a different signal if you wish, by specifying the signal number as an option to the `kill` command. Signal number 9 is a sure kill signal, so if your process refuses to die in the normal manner, you can zap it with:

```
$ kill -9 179
$
```

A final word of caution. We saw in `ps` that your login is a process and has a process identification number. If you `kill` that process, you will log yourself off of System V. Luckily, the login process avoids a normal `kill`, but

```
kill -9 89
```

is a sure way to suicide. You will be logged off the system, and you will see the usual request for login.

4.9. Summary

If you have made it this far, you have covered the essential core ideas behind UNIX System V. Now is probably a good time to take a rest, lie back with a glass of champagne, and mull over what you have learned so far.

The power of System V derives from the synergism of the concepts we have discussed: the hierarchical directory and file system; redirecting input and output; pipes, and filters. The combinations of all these facilities is what makes System V a benign environment for the software developer, and for the serious technical writer.

The remainder of this book describes individual utilities in some detail, and illustrates their use in processing textual data.

5 User to User Communication

Part of the philosophy behind UNIX System V is that of cooperation between the people who are using it for their day to day work. Cooperation and working together imply good facilities for communications.

This chapter covers those facilities whereby users can communicate via the computer system, without the need to telephone each other or walk around to find each other.

The main UNIX System V features which facilitate communication are:

- the `write` command, which enables a message to be sent directly to another user;
- the `mail` facility, for 'electronic mail'.
- There is also a 'timed delivery' command called `at`, which has many applications when combined with the electronic mail facilities.
- The `news` system for keeping up to date with current events.

5.1. Sending Messages with `write`

The `write` command sends a message to a specified user right at the time when you type the message, provided that the recipient is logged in to the system. `write` should really only be used when you are in a panic and wish to talk at somebody right away. Some people get very distracted and annoyed when messages start appearing at random intervals while they're trying to type at the terminal. For this reason, you should be circumspect in your use of `write`.

If someone is logged in over a phone line, their phone will be continuously busy, and `write` is the handiest way to get in touch with them. Here is a typical example of how to use the `write` command:

```
$ write henry
Flee, all is discovered!!!!!!
^D
$
```

Since `write` takes the message from the Standard Input, there is nothing to indicate that the command is waiting for input after you have typed `write` and the login name. You simply type in the message you want to send, as many lines as you like, and you terminate the message with the end-of-text character, **CTRL-D**. You don't get any indication that your message has actually been received anywhere.

What the recipient, in our case the user 'henry', sees is:

```
Message from maryann tty08 [Wed Jun 11 14:15:09] ...
Flee, all is discovered!!!!!!
EOF
```

The `EOF` indicates the the message is finished, and Maryann has quit writing.

In this example we have shown a simple one-line message. If the message is more than one line, the recipient doesn't receive it all in one fell swoop. Rather, he sees each line as it is typed, so he has no indication that the message is complete other than the EOF. When conducting a two-way 'conversation' this can be a problem, as we discuss below.

Considering the content of the message in the above example, the one-way nature of the communication may be justified. But under normal circumstances, you would expect the 'conversation' to be two-sided. For example, suppose Maryann tries to get in touch with Steve:

```
$ write steve
```

she doesn't immediately enter the message, but waits to see if Steve responds. Steve receives a message that says:

```
Message from maryann tty08 [Wed Jun 11 15:14:06] ...
```

At this point Steve gives his own `write` command:

```
$ write maryann
Hi.  What?
```

Steve doesn't type **CTRL-D**, so now we have two people 'talking' to each other, until one of them types **CTRL-D** to drop out of the conversation.

At the end of the conversation, Maryann's screen might look as shown in the example on the next page. What Maryann has typed is shown in the **`bold face text`**. Steve's replies are in normal `typewriter font`, as we show in the next example.

```
$ write steve
Message from steve tty04 [Wed Jun 11 15:15:07] ...
Hi. What?
How about dinner tonight?
I have to wash my socks, how about tomorrow?
I must take the cat to the vet. Friday?
chess club.  Next week?
^D
$
```

Steve's side of the conversation would leave his screen looking like:

```
$ Message from maryann tty08 [Wed Jun 11 15:15:06] ...
write maryann
Hi. What?
How about dinner tonight?
I have to wash my socks, how about tomorrow?
I must take the cat to the vet. Friday?
chess club.  Next week?
EOF
^D
$
```

Here we have shown what Steve typed boldface, and Maryann's contributions in normal type.

There are two points to notice about this conversation. One is that Maryann 'hung up' on Steve — that is she terminated her part of the conversation without warning, which is rather rude. Another point is that on each side the dialogue consisted of one-line questions. But this is not always going to be the case. You are often going to convey information rather than ask questions, and the information may well take more than one line. How does each party know when the other has finished and is waiting for a reply? There is no easy way, the people concerned must set up some protocol so that they understand each other.

The protocol suggested in the *System V User's Manual* is that each message is terminated by the character 'o' ('over') and when one party is about to quit the conversation they type 'oo' ('over and out'). Another way is to set up the signals when you first invoke the `write` command, for instance:

```
$ write henry
I will signal the end of each message with '->' are you
receiving me ? ->
```

and then Henry would write back with a reply that looks like:

```
Message from henry tty03 [Wed Jun 11 15:57:03] ...
receiving you loud and clear ->
    .
      <etcetera...>
                .
That's all. Bye
^D
$
```

If you try to write to someone who is not logged in, you get a message:

```
$ write sylvia
sylvia is not logged on.
$
```

and the `write` command terminates. If you try to write to someone who is not a user,

```
$ write percival
percival is not logged on.
$
```

you get the same message, because `write` doesn't check for known system users, only for users logged in. Before writing, you could check to see who is logged in with:

```
$ who
sally    tty00   08:30
henry    tty03   08:31
steve    tty04   09:05
sally    tty06   09:15
hank     tty07   09:15
maryann  tty08   09:10
$
```

It takes the system a while to check if the user you wish to communicate with is logged in. You may have already started typing your message before the system finds the user is not logged in and decides to ignore your command. If this happens, it is a good idea to cancel what you have typed using your line kill character. If you don't, then the next time you type RETURN, the system will try and interpret your partial message as a command. This is unlikely to do any damage, but can be disconcerting.

There are some System V system commands that 'lock out' the `write` command for potential recipients. These are commands designed to produce a nicely formatted output, which would be really messed up if messages were received in the middle of it. If you try to `write` to someone who is using one of these commands, you get a message:

```
$ write  hank
Permission denied.
$
```

and the command terminates. You also get this message if you try to write to a user who has used `mesg` to prevent you writing to his terminal.

Although we have been talking about writing messages to a user, we are really writing to that user's terminal. When we say

```
$ write henry
```

we are really writing to the terminal `tty03`, where our `who` example shows Henry logged in.

The example of the `who` command shows that the user 'sally' is logged in to the system twice, once on `tty00`, and again on `tty06`. You cannot write to both terminals, you have to choose one. If you get no response, you can quit that `write` command, and try to get the user on the other terminal:

```
$ write sally tty06
Are you there?
^D
$ write sally tty00
Are you there?
Message from sally tty00 [Wed Jun 11 16:05:23] ...
yup. que pasa?
tennis saturday 10am - OK?
ok. bye
EOF
^D
$
```

If you don't specify a terminal, `write` chooses one for you:

```
$ write sally
sally logged more than once
writing to tty00
```

The `write` command always chooses the lowest number terminal that the user is logged in at. If you get no response there, you will have to specify the tty number to get messages sent to the other terminal.

In all the examples so far the messages have been short. If you have a long message to communicate, you may wish to use a text editor to prepare the message in a file, so that you can correct any mistakes you make before anyone else sees them. You can then send this message by redirecting the Standard Input:

```
$ write steve < message
$
```

The recipient receives the message all at once. There is no waiting between lines, as there is when the message is typed following the `write` command. To send a long message with `write` is not a very polite thing to do. It is better to use `mail` for long messages. That means the recipient can choose his own time to read the message.

Another feature of `write` is that lines starting with the exclamation mark character `!` are interpreted as UNIX system commands, and are obeyed. As an instance of how this can be useful, let's suppose you have had a query as to the location of some files. You roam around the system using `cd` and `ls` commands until you find them, and now you want to answer the enquirer. However, half way through your message, you realize that you've forgotten the pathname to the current directory. You can find out in the middle of writing by saying `!pwd`, thus:

```
$ write hank
The files you want are in the directory:
!pwd
/aa/widget/maryann/docs/specs/thing
!
/aa/widget/maryann/docs/specs/thing
^D
$
```

The output of the command called up via `!` does not form part of the message being sent. You still have to type the information. Of course, the command you give following `!` may have nothing to do with the message you are sending. You may even redirect the Standard Output of the command, so that you see no output on the screen. That is why, when the command has terminated, `write` signals that termination by the second `!` sign.

This use of `!` to access system commands from within another command is quite common in those commands which are interactive in nature.

5.2. Controlling Messages with `mesg`

When you are working at your terminal it can be very annoying to be interrupted with messages. This is especially true when you are using an editor to enter text to create new files. Novice users have been known to re-do hours of work, because they mistakenly thought a received message had destroyed their text input.

You can stop these rude interruptions by using the `mesg` command to prevent other users writing to your terminal.

```
$ mesg n
$
```

The 'n' (no) tells the system that you don't want to be interrupted — if anyone tries to `write` to you, they will get the message

```
Permission denied
```

The argument to `mesg` can be a full word if you like. So long as it begins with the letter 'n', the write permission is denied. So `mesg` followed by any of 'no', 'none', or 'nyet' will do just as well.

If you decide to `write` to somebody, and expect to get a reply, you must allow (permit) messages again by typing:

```
$ mesg y
$
```

The 'y' means 'yes', which allows messages to come through again. Again, you can give a whole word like 'yes', or 'yeah ', or 'yoiks'. Provided that it starts with the letter 'y', you will be able to receive messages.

If you just type the `mesg` command on its own, it tells you the current state of things:

```
$ mesg
is y
$
```

As you can see, the `mesg` command confirmed that messages are enabled. This is not surprising, since we just turned them on.

The default state of the write permission to your terminal is 'y'. If you use `mesg` to deny access to your terminal, that denial only lasts for your current login session. After you have logged out, it reverts to 'y'.

5.3. The Electronic Mail System using `mail`

`mail` is the UNIX facility where users can send messages to each other, such that the messages pile up in a 'mailbox' somewhere in the system.

If the user you are mailing to is logged in to the system, they are notified of the arrival of mail when they have completed whatever command they are using at the time. If the user is not currently logged in, the mail remains in the mailbox file, and they are notified of its delivery next time they log in:

```
Dual 83/80 68000 System V UNIX

login: maryann
password: wizard
you have mail
```

Unlike the `write` command, which interrupts whatever you are doing to display the message on your screen, `mail` waits until you have finished what you are doing before telling you there is mail waiting.

The system informs you of waiting mail at two different times: one time is just after you log in, as shown in the example above; the other time is when mail arrives while you are using some System V command. After you have finished whatever you are doing, you get the message that says

```
you have mail
```

You do not have to look at your mail immediately. You can simply ignore the messages and carry on with whatever you are doing. However, it is easy to get engrossed in the job at hand, so that you forget all about your pending mail, and eventually log out and head home. System V does not remind you that there are messages waiting. The next time you log in, the '`You have mail`' message will appear again. By this time, the mail might have gone stale and be of little use. For this reason it usually pays to inspect your mail as soon as possible after you get it.

Sending Mail

To send mail to somebody, you simply type the `mail` command, followed by the user name of the person you want to send the mail to:

```
$ mail henry
```

Like `write`, `mail` takes the message from the Standard Input, so at this point you see nothing — `mail` is waiting for you to type in your message. The full process of sending mail looks like this:

```
$ mail henry
It's our turn to play tennis for the league.
I've booked a court for 4:30 on Saturday afternoon.
Maybe we could have dinner together afterward?
^D
$
```

As usual, `^D` means that you type CTRL-D at the end of your message. The `mail` command will also take the period character `.` on a line by itself, as a signal meaning end of the message. We show this in some of the following examples.

You can send mail to several people by giving more than one user name on the command line:

```
$ mail maryann sylvia jack bill
There will be a meeting at 3:30 Friday, to
discuss staff relocation to our new offices.
The meeting will be held in my office.
      Bill
.
$
```

In this case, Bill sent notification of a meeting to Maryann, Sylvia and Jack. He also sent a copy to himself — this is a good idea, especially if you are expecting an answer to your mail and want to remember exactly what you said.

If you have a long message to send, you might wish to prepare it before-hand using a text editor, so that you can correct any mistakes before anyone else sees them. In this case, you can send the message by redirecting the Standard Input:

```
$ mail bill sylvia jack < memo
$
```

The `mail` command does not check that the recipient is a known user of the system until it tries to deliver your message. If you try to send mail to someone who is not a user of the system (for example, you might misspell the name), you see something like this:

```
$ mail sulvia
The files you are interested in are in the
directory /aa/widget/maryann/docs/specs/thing.
^D
mail: can't send to sulvia
Mail saved in dead.letter
$
```

So that you won't have to type your message all over again, the `mail` command saves it in a file called *dead.letter* in the current directory. So you can send it to the correct recipient by:

```
$ mail sylvia < dead.letter
$ rm dead.letter
$
```

When sending mail to more than one person, if any one of them is not a known user, the message is saved as shown in the above example. If you don't have write permission on the current working directory at the time you send the mail, the mail is saved in a *dead.letter* file in your home directory.

As a general rule, it is a good idea to make sure that you are in your own user directories, rather than in the system directories, when you send mail.

Reading Your Mail

When you get the message:

```
You have mail
```

it indicates that there is a new message in your 'mailbox' since you last looked there. In order to read it, you simply type the command `mail`, on its own. The command does have some options, which we describe later. For the moment we won't bother with them.

Before we show how to read your mail, we'll show one way that things can go wrong. Suppose you had the message to tell you that you had mail, but when you try to read it you get the response:

```
$ mail
No mail.
$
```

These conflicting responses can sometimes happen if you are a new user, and have never received any mail before. The cause is that the permissions on your 'mailbox' file are wrong. You should ask your System Administrator to correct them, but you could also try to do it yourself. Your 'mailbox' is a file that has a name the same as your login (user) name; it is located in the directory */usr/mail*. You could use `ls -l` to check the ownership and permissions on your mailbox file and, if necessary, use `chmod` to set them to what you want.

But let's assume you do have some mail, and your mailbox file is set up properly. If you only have one message, it is printed out. If you have several messages, the last one that was received is printed. Your other messages are not lost, but will be printed later. `mail` just happens to show you your mail in the order last delivered, first 'opened'.

After showing you one message, `mail` waits for you to type in something to say what shall be done with the message. As you see in the example on the next page, `mail` prompts you for input with the `?` character.

```
$ You have mail.
$ mail
From henry Wed Jun 11 13:58:23 1986
Saturday at 4:30 is fine for tennis.
Dinner sounds good, too.  Where?
?
```

If you respond with another ?, `mail` shows you what choices you have. You can also get this list by typing an asterisk, (*) in response to the ? prompt:

```
? ?
q               quit
x               exit without changing mail
p               print
s [file]        save (default mbox)
w [file]        same without header
-               print previous
d               delete
+               next (no delete)
m user          mail to user
! cmd           execute cmd
?
```

There are ten actions you can take listed above. There are also two other responses that are not listed, you can type **RETURN**, or you can type **CTRL-D**. For the most part, these responses achieve some combination of four basic operations:

- print (show, display) a message
- save the message
- delete the message
- get out of the `mail` command

As you saw in the last example, simply invoking the `mail` command displays the first of your messages:

```
$ mail
From henry Wed Jun 11 13:58:23 1986
Saturday at 4:30 is fine for tennis.
Dinner sounds good, too.  Where?
?
```

If you wanted to save that message you could respond as follows:

```
? s from_henry
From steve Wed Jun 11 16:29:02 1986
A gang of us are going for Sunday brunch
would you like to join us?
?
```

We show the mail from Henry being saved with the command

```
s from_henry
```

This does three things:

- If the file *from_henry* does not exist, it is created and the entire message, including the header line '`From henry....`' is placed in it.
- If the file already exists, the message is appended to the end of the file. The message is then deleted from the mail and the next message in the mail is displayed.
- If there are no other messages, `mail` quits and you see the System V prompt `$`.

Another way of saving mail is using the `w` operation. For example, to save the next message from Steve:

```
From steve Wed Jun 11 16:29:02 1986
A gang of us are going for Sunday brunch
would you like to join us?
? w from_steve
From bill  Wed Jun 11 18:54:32 1986
There will be a meeting at 3:30 Friday, to
discuss staff relocation to our new offices.
The meeting will be held in my office.
      Bill
?
```

The only difference is that, with `w`, the header line '`From steve...`' does not get saved in the file. As with `s`, the message is deleted and the next message, if any, is displayed.

If you don't give any filename to the `s` and `w` operations they create, or append to, a file called *mbox* in your home directory. It is usually a good idea to be in your home directory when you read your mail.

If you don't have write permission on the current directory when you save your mail, or if you try to save mail in a file which is write protected, the `mail` command displays an error response:

```
? s  some_mail
mail: cannot append to some_mail
?
```

You can repeat the s or w operation and give a pathname to a file that is in a directory you do have write permission on. Alternatively, you could

```
? !chmod  644  some_mail
```

and then repeat the s command. This is another good reason for being in your own home directory when you read your mail.

The above example illustrates a feature of the `mail` command which can be useful when saving messages. Everything following ! on the line is passed to the Shell and executed. So you could use it to check which directory you are in before saving any mail:

```
? !pwd
/aa/widget/maryann
!
?
```

This example shows that we are in an appropriate directory. Had we not been, we could have exited from `mail` without disturbing anything, as we describe later. Then we could have changed directory to a good one, and re-entered the mail command. You cannot change directory from within `mail`. Another good use is to type `!ls` to check the spelling of a file for appending saved mail to.

Suppose you got this mail message:

```
From bill  Wed Jun 11 18:54:32 1986
There will be a meeting at 3:30 Friday, to
discuss staff relocation to our new offices.
The meeting will be held in my office.
      Bill
?
```

As we show in the example on the next page, you could then also use ! to answer messages as you read them, without exiting from the `mail` command.

```
? !mail bill
I'm sorry, I can't make it to Friday's meeting,
I have a dental appointment at 3.
^D
!
?
```

If you don't want to save a message, but want to get rid of it when you have seen it, you must give the d operation to delete it. If you don't do this, the message will appear again next time you read your mail. Messages are not deleted immediately. They are only removed when you exit from the mail command.

If you just want to leave a message in your mail file, you can display the next message by typing the + operation, or simply by typing RETURN. If there is no other message, the mail command is terminated.

If your message is a very long one, by the time you get to the end the first part of it might have scrolled off the top of the screen. If you want to see the first part a second time, you can display the same message again by typing p for print. When you have seen enough, you can stop the rest of that message printing by pressing the 'Interrupt' key. This is usually the BREAK key, or the key marked DEL or RUBOUT, unless you have changed it as we described in chapter 2.

If you want to go back and re-examine a previous message, you type a minus sign - in response to the ? prompt. This will show you the message immediately before the one you've just seen. If you want to see the message before that, you can type - again when you get the prompt. You cannot go directly back to any specific previous message; you have to examine each message in between, but you can always interrupt the messages that you are not interested in.

Forwarding Mail to other Users

In the above paragraphs, we didn't cover the m operator. m stands for 'mail', and it can be used to forward mail you have received on to other users. For instance:

```
$ mail
From sally Tue Jun 10 10:24:16 1986
We're having a party Friday night, pass this
invite on to anyone else you'd like to be there.
Show up around 8.
? m henry steve
?
```

The message is deleted from your mail file after it has been sent to the named users.

When they receive the mail they can see that it is forwarded mail, and also they can see the name of the original sender. For example, Steve will get mail:

```
You have mail.
$ mail
From maryann Tue Jun 10 12:38:01 1986
>From sally Tue Jun 10 10:24:16 1986 forwarded
We're having a party Friday night, pass this
invite on to anyone else you'd like to be there.
Show up around 8.
```

Steve can forward the mail again, by doing this:

```
? m jane
?
```

and what Jane will see is:

```
$ mail
From steve Wed Jun 11 07:15:23 1986
>From maryann Tue Jun 10 12:38:01 1986 forwarded
>From sally Tue Jun 10 10:24:16 1986 forwarded
We're having a party Friday night, pass this
invite on to anyone else you'd like to be there.
Show up around 8.
?
```

If you type `m` on its own, without any following user name, the message is left alone.

Exiting from `mail`

You will exit from the `mail` command automatically after you have responded to the prompt ?

following the last message. Deleted messages are removed from the mail file, and the rest are put back. You see the UNIX system prompt `$`.

However, you can quit reading your mail at any time, in one of three ways:

- by typing **CTRL-D**
- by typing the `q` for quit operation
- by typing the `x` for exit operation

The `q` operation and **CTRL-D** do the same thing. Deleted messages are removed from the mail file; undeleted and unread messages are put back. You see the UNIX system prompt `$`.

If you use `x` to exit from `mail`, the mail file is left unchanged. That is messages are not deleted, even though you did something that would normally delete them. So if you delete a message, then change your mind, you can exit safely with `x`. As usual, you then see the `$` system prompt.

When you quit reading your mail, you might get the message:

```
? q
you have mail
$
```

This doesn't necessarily mean that you have any new mail that you haven't seen. If you exit from `mail` with some, but not all, messages deleted, the system can get confused. Because your mail file is not empty (there are some messages you didn't delete), but has changed since you last looked at it (because some messages got deleted), the system reminds you that you still have mail.

If new mail arrives while you are reading existing mail, then you see:

```
? q
new mail arrived
you have mail
$
```

when you get out of the `mail` command.

Options to the `mail` Command

We have shown that when you read your mail, the latest received message is displayed first. You can change that if you want. For instance, suppose someone has sent you two messages on the same subject, and has referenced the first message in the second. It can be confusing to find a reference to an as yet unread message.

You might prefer to read your mail in the order it was delivered. You can call up the `mail` command with the `-r` (reverse) option:

```
$ mail -r
From bill ......
        <etcetera...>
?
```

Usually `mail` pauses after each message, and asks you what action to take. If you don't want `mail` to ask you what to do, but simply to print all your messages in turn, you should use the `-p` (print) option.

If you give the `-q` (quit) option to `mail`, and happen to interrupt the printing of any of the messages, `mail` exits without updating the mail file (that is, as if you had done a x operation).

The `-f` option tells `mail` to look at a file other than the mail file. For example, to look at all the mail saved in the file *from_henry*:

```
$ mail  -f from_henry
```

When you look at a file of saved mail, what you see depends on how the messages were written onto the file. If they were saved using `s`, which saves the message headers too, you see the messages one at a time, just as if you were reading your mail file. However, if the messages were written onto the file with w, the headers are not in the file, and the messages are displayed one after the other without pause. If you have a mixture of 'saved' and 'written' messages, the output could be very confusing.

If you give more than one option to `mail`, all the options can be given separately:

```
$ mail  -r -p -q -f from_henry
```

or they can be combined:

```
$ mail -rqpf mbox
```

5.4. The Electronic Mail System using `mailx`

Most System V installations have another command, called `mailx`, for sending and reading electronic mail. `mailx` is more complex than is `mail` — it gives you more capabilities.

The `mailx` command can be tailored to suit the specific requirements of any installation, and also to meet the requirements of each individual user. This makes it difficult to describe its detailed operation in general terms, and we make no attempt to do so. We just give a quick overview, so that you get the general idea and so that you can see some of the advantages it has over `mail`.

Sending mail with `mailx`

At first glance this is very similar to using `mail`, you just give the command and a list of the usernames of people who are to receive the mail:

```
$ mailx maryann sylvia jack bill
Subject:
```

The first thing that is different from `mail` is that you get prompted for a 'Subject'.[1]

[1] Whether or not you get this prompt, and what form it actually takes, is one of the things

Anything you type up to the next **RETURN** becomes the message header. This header is displayed when the mail is read.

After this, `mailx` behaves very much like `mail` — you type in the message, and terminate it by **CTRL-D**:

```
$ mailx maryann sylvia jack bill
Subject: Staff Meeting
There will be a meeting at 3:30 Friday, to
discuss staff relocation to our new offices.
The meeting will be held in my office.
^D
$
```

However, you can give commands to `mailx` while you are typing in your message. `mailx` commands start with the tilde character (~). Typing `~?` displays a list of all the `mailx` commands.

As you can see from the example on the next page, there are quite a lot of things you can do while sending mail. We do not describe all the `mailx` commands, or 'escapes' as they are called. But here are some of the really useful ones.

If you make a mistake while you are entering your message, you can call up a text editor so that you can correct your errors. `~e` calls up the `ex` line editor, and `~v` calls up the `vi` screen editor. `ex` is described in chapter 8 and `vi` is described in chapter 7.

If, while you are composing your message, you suddenly realize that there are more people who should receive it, you can add them to the list of recipients using the `~t` escape.

You can take part or all of your message from a previously prepared file using `~r`; you can save your message in a file using `~w`.

The `~m` and `~f` escapes can be used to read an old message into the message you are currently sending. These find most use when you want to reply to mail you have received, or when you want to forward mail (possibly with additional comments) to another user.

The `~!` escape can be used to run a System V command, for instance to check your working directory and the files it contains.

The `~|` escape can be used to pipe your message through a command. You might want to get your message nicely laid out by running it through the `nroff` text formatter.

---

that can be tailored for each installation. Be aware that on your installation the prompt might be 'Header', or there might not be a prompt at all.

```
$ mailx maryann sylvia jack bill
Subject: Staff meeting
~?
 ------------------ ~ ESCAPES --------------------------
~~                   Quote a single tilde
~a,~A                Autograph (insert 'sign' variable)
~b users             Add users to Bcc list
~c users             Add users to Cc list
~d                   Read in dead.letter file
~e                   Edit the message buffer
~m messages          Read in messages, right-shifted by a tab
~f messages          Read in messages, do not right-shift
~h                   Prompt for To list, Subject and Cc list
~p                   Print the message buffer
~q,~Q                Quit, save letter in $HOME/dead.letter
~x                   Quit, do not save letter
~r file              Read a file into the message buffer
~s subject           Set subject
~t users             Add users to To list
~v                   Invoke display editor on message
~w file              Write message onto file
~.                   End of input
~!command            Run a shell command
~|command            Pipe the message through the command
--------------------------------------------------------
```

Reading mail with `mailx`

You type the `mailx` command, without any usernames, to read your own mail. You are first shown a list of the various messages in your mailbox, each message is preceded by a status letter.

```
"/usr/mail/maryann": 4 messages 1 new 4 unread
 U  1 henry     Wed Jun 11 13:58  6/64
 U  2 steve     Wed Jun 11 16:29  6/71   Sunday Brunch
 U  3 bill      Wed Jun 11 18:54  6/67   Staff Meeting
>N  4 henry     Thu Jun 12 17:38  5/67   Re: tennis
?
```

Each item in the list (called the header) shows who the message is from, when it was sent, and how long it is in lines and characters. The last thing on each header is the line that was typed in response to the 'Subject' prompt when the mail was sent.

The status of each message is indicated by a single uppercase letter at the beginning of the line. In our example we have one new message — that is to say it arrived in the mailbox since the last time the `mailx` command was used. We also have three old messages that haven't yet been read. The first new message is pointed at by the > character.

After showing you the message headers, `mailx` waits for you to type in something to say which message you want to read, or to do something with. `mailx` prompts you for input with the `?` character. If you respond with another `?`, `mailx` shows you what choices you have. As you can see from the display on the next page, there are many choices.

You can display a message using the `t` command. If you don't give a message number, `mailx` displays the message pointed at by the > marker.

You can use `r` or `R` to answer messages, or you could use `m` to send mail in response to a message. You could also use `m`, in conjunction with the `~m` or `~f` escapes, to forward mail to other users.

```
? ?
                    mailx commands
type [msglist]              print messages
next                        goto and type next message
edit [msglist]              edit messages
from [msglist]              give header lines of messages
delete [msglist]            delete messages
undelete [msglist]          restore deleted messages
save [msglist] file         append messages to file
reply [message]             reply to message, including all recipients
Reply [msglist]             reply to the authors of the messages
preserve [msglist]          preserve messages in mailbox
mail user                   mail to specific user
quit                        quit, preserving unread messages
xit                         quit, preserving all messages
header                      print page of active message headers
!                           shell escape
cd [directory]              chdir to directory or home if none given
list                        list all commands (no explanations)
top [msglist]               print top 5 lines of messages
z [-]                       display next [last] page of 10 headers

[msglist] is optional and specifies messages by number, author,
subject or type.  The default is the current message.
?
```

To delete a message you must give the `d` command, if you later change your mind you can use `u` to undelete it. Deleted messages aren't deleted straight away, they get deleted when you exit from the `mailx` command.

You exit from `mailx` using `q`; any messages that you have read, but neither deleted nor saved, will automatically be saved in a file called *mbox* in your home directory. Unread messages remain in your mailbox file. If you use `x` to exit, all messages remain in your mailbox file.

You can read messages in a file other than your mailbox file by using the `-f` option on the `mailx` command line:

```
$ mailx -f from_henry
```

will read the messages saved in the file *from_henry*. If you don't specify a filename when you use the option, the file *mbox* will be read by default.

This has been a very brief overview of the `mailx` command. As for all complex commands, especially interactive ones, the best way to learn about it is to use it. Look at the write-up in the *System V User's Manual* and experiment.

5.5. Keeping an Engagement Diary with `calendar`

The `calendar` command is not concerned with communicating with other users, but is more a means of reminding yourself of things to do. In order to use this facility you must set up a file, called *calendar*, in one of your directories. It is best if this is set up in your home (or login) directory, for reasons which we'll explain later.

Let's look at an example of a calendar file:

```
$ cat calendar
June 16th - Dad's birthday (Monday)
Thurs Jun 12 - shop for present for Dad
6/12 classes start, 7-10pm.
Friday 6/13 - dentist 3pm
Saturday at 4:30 is fine for tennis.  henry, jun 14
Dinner sounds good, too.  Where ?
A gang of us are going for Sunday brunch - steve, Jun 15
would you like to join us?
There will be a meeting at 3:30 Friday, to - bill, June 13
discuss staff relocation to our new offices.
The meeting will be held in my office.
          Bill
Mon june 16 lunch Jane
We're having a party Friday night, pass this - sally, 6/13
invite on to anyone else you'd like to be there.
Show up around 8.
16th June, collect cleaning.
$
```

The first few entries in the file are simple enough, they are just one-line reminders of what's happening, or what has to be done, on a particular date. The next entry is a bit more subtle: it is what you would get if you saved your mail with

```
w calendar
```

Unfortunately, that isn't quite good enough. For the `calendar` command to be of any use, it must contain dates. So we have added the date on the end of the first line of the message from Henry, and the following messages from Steve, Bill, and Sally. We used a text editor to do this — text editors are explained in chapters 7 and 8.

If people put the date in the mail they send you, you won't have to add it yourself. If you save your mail with the `s` operation the dates do get saved. Unfortunately the date is the date it was sent, not the date on which something is happening. Also the line that contains the date simply says '`From henry...`', which doesn't tell you what is happening. As we shall see in the following examples, `calendar` strips out lines that don't contain a date, so using `s` to save mail in your *calendar* file is no help.

Notice that the dates are given in a variety of styles: some are in number only form, some give the month in words. When the month is given as a word, it is sometimes given in full, sometimes abbreviated, sometimes it has a capital initial letter, and sometimes not.

If we run the `calendar` command on a particular date, we get:

```
$ date
Thu Jun 12 08:29:32 1982
$ calendar
Thurs Jun 12 - shop for present for Dad
6/12 classes start, 7-10pm.
Friday 6/13 - dentist 3pm
There will be a meeting at 3:30 Friday, to - bill, June 13
We're having a party Friday night, pass this - sally, 6/13
$
```

The `date` command is not necessary here, we have only given it to show that we gave the command on a Thursday, and that the date was June 12th. The output of the `calendar` command consists of selected lines from the *calendar* file. The lines selected are those which contain dates representing today (June 12th), and tomorrow (June 13th). Lines which contain other dates, and lines which do not contain dates, are not shown.

On a weekend, `calendar`'s idea of 'tomorrow' covers the whole weekend through to Monday. So if we give the `calendar` command on Friday, June 13th, we see all the engagements for the weekend, and the following Monday. The example on the following page illustrates this.

```
$ calendar
June 16th - Dad's birthday (Monday)
Friday 6/13 - dentist 3pm
Saturday at 4:30 is fine for tennis.  henry, jun 14
A gang of us are going for Sunday brunch - steve, Jun 15
There will be a meeting at 3:30 Friday, to - bill, June 13
Mon june 16 lunch Jane
We're having a party Friday night, pass this - sally, 6/13
$
```

There was one reminder in the *calendar* file that did not get shown. This is the reminder to collect cleaning on Monday. `calendar` doesn't show this entry because the date is given as `16th June`. `calendar` only recognizes dates in the form month followed by day, although it is pretty elastic about how you specify the month. If you give the date entirely in numbers, it must be in the form '`6/11`'. `calendar` will not recognize '`6-11`', for example.

The *calendar* file can be in any of your directories; as long as you are in that directory when you give the `calendar` command, you will see your daily engagements. However, many installations have an automatic reminder service. What happens is that sometime during the night, the `calendar` command is run on every user's *calendar* file, and the results are mailed to each user. In order to get this reminder service, your *calendar* file must be in your login or home directory.

If your system doesn't have a reminder service, you might be able to achieve a similar effect using the `at` command.

5.6. Timed Delivery Messages with `at`

The `at` command is not specifically concerned with communication. It provides the facility to perform System V commands at some time in the future. One of its applications, however, is to arrange for messages to be delivered at a specific time, which is the reason it is discussed here.

The `at` command can be set up so that only certain users can use it. The easiest way to find out whether you can use it, is to try it. If you get this response:

```
$ at 0130
at: you are not authorized to use at.  Sorry.
$
```

then you are out of luck. Who can use `at` is controlled by two files that only the super-user can modify, so you should ask your System Administrator to set things up such that you can use the command. Some System Administrators like to keep `at` for their own exclusive use; if that is your situation you might as well skip the rest of this section.

But let's assume you are authorized to use the command. Suppose that you wanted to run the `calendar` program at sometime during the night. You could say:

```
$ at 0130
calendar
^D
520763400.a     at Thu Jun 12 01:30:00 1986
$
```

As usual, `^D` indicates that you should type CTRL-D. This command says 'run the `calendar` command at 1:30 in the morning'. The output of the command will automatically be mailed to you. However, the mail you get from `at` contains lots of extraneous verbiage, so you might prefer to redirect the output of `calendar`:

```
$ at 0130
calendar > do_today
^D
520763400.a     at Thu Jun 12 01:30:00 1986
$
```

or, better still, pipe it to the `mail` command:

```
$ at 0130
calendar | mail maryann
^D
520763400.a     at Thu Jun 12 01:30:00 1986
$
```

If you redirect the Standard Output yourself, `at` will not send mail to you unless there are errors. In that case you will get mail containing the error messages.

In the above examples you will notice that `at` responds to your request with confirmation of the time at which your commands will run, preceded by an identification number. If you change your mind, and want to cancel your request, you will need to know that number.

There are various ways of specifying the time at which you want your commands to run. You can give the time in terms of the 24-hour clock, where 0130 is 1:30am, and 1330 is 1:30pm. If you are only interested in the hour, you can simply leave out the minutes, 8 is 8 o'clock in the morning, and 20 is 8 o'clock in the evening. Alternatively, you can add `am` or `pm` to the specified time. In this case the hours and minutes must be separated by a colon (`:`). 12 o'clock noon and midnight are distinguished by following the time by the words `noon` or `midnight`. We show some of these different time specifications in the following examples.

The way we called the `at` command in the previous example shows that it takes the Standard Input, up until a CTRL-D, and executes that command at the specified time. You are not limited to one command, for example:

```
$ at  10pm
troff -mm -t doc1  >doc1.fmt
troff -mm -t doc2  >doc2.fmt
troff -mm -t doc3  >doc3.fmt
^D
520750800.a      at Wed Jun 11 22:00:00 1986
$
```

We have used the `troff` command, which formats documents (see chapter 11). Because formatting is a lengthy process, it is a good candidate for execution late at night, when you don't expect the system to be busy.

Another way of using `at` is to create a file containing the commands that you want executed, then tell `at` the name of the file:

```
$ cat > format
troff -mm -t doc1 >>doc.fmt
troff -mm -t doc2 >>doc.fmt
troff -mm -t doc3 >>doc.fmt
^D
$ chmod 755 format
$ at 10pm
format
^D
520750800.a      at Wed Jun 11 22:00:00 1986
$
```

If you do this, you must change the mode of the file to make it executable, as we show in the above example.[2] The advantage of doing this is that if you think of something else to be done at the same time, you only have to add the additional commands to the *format* file.

A word of warning: `at` doesn't check for the existence of any files at the time you make the request for later execution. But when the commands are executed, the current directory is made the same as the working directory at the time the request was made. If, in the above example, the file *doc3* didn't exist, or you removed it later — you would not know about it until `at` mailed you the Diagnostic Output from `troff`.

You can use `at` to send yourself a reminder:

---

[2] What you are actually doing here is creating a very simple shell procedure. We describe shell procedures in a lot more detail in Chapter 13.

```
$ cat > reminder
time to go to dentist
^D
$ at 2:30pm
mail maryann < reminder
^D
520740000.a     at Wed Jun 11 14:30:00 1986
$
```

Now, if you are logged on to the system at 2:30 in the afternoon, you will get mail reminding yourself that it's time to leave for your dental appointment.

You could keep a general purpose 'reminder' file for occasions like this, but if you don't want to have such a file, you can use the `echo` command. The `echo` command simply echoes its arguments on the Standard Output:

```
$ echo time to go
time to go
$
```

you can pipe the Standard Output to the `mail` command:

```
$ at  1430
echo time to go | mail maryann
^D
520740000.a     at Wed Jun 11 14:30:00 1986
$
```

With `at` you are not restricted to scheduling things by time alone. You can give a day of the week, or a date. The day of the week can be abbreviated. For example, to remind Jane about a lunch date,

```
$ at 11am  Mon
echo  lunch in 30 mins | mail  jane
^D
521143200.a     Mon Jun 16 11:00:00 1986
$
```

Jane will get the message at 11 o'clock on the Monday following the day on which you gave the `at` command.

You can also give an increment consisting of a plus sign, a number, and one of the words: `minutes`, `hours`, `days`, `weeks`, `months`, or `years`. For example, if on Wednesday June 11th, you give the command:

```
$ at 4am Fri +1week
echo happy birthday | mail steve
^D
521463600.a     at Fri Jun 20 04:00:00 1986
$
```

the message will be delivered, not two days later, but on Friday June 20th. In this case we were not especially interested in what time the message was delivered, only in the day, but we always have to specify a time.

Another word that can be used in specifying the time is `now`. If we want to do something in exactly one years time, we can say:

```
$  at now + 1 year
echo 'The year is up! you owe me $10' | mail sylvia
^D
552273840.a     at Wed Jun 11 15:24:00 1987
$
```

You can also give `at` a date in the form month-name followed by day of the month. The month name can be abbreviated. For instance, you could send Steve birthday greetings by:

```
$ at 4 jun 20
echo happy birthday | mail steve
^D
521463601.a     Fri Jun 20 04:00:01 1986
$
```

When you give `at` a date, if the date is earlier than today, 'next year' is assumed. You can also specify a year, for instance:

```
$ at 12noon jul 4,1987
mail hank < greetings
^D
552423600.a     at Sat Jul  4 12:00:00 1987
$
```

Two more words that can be used when scheduling commands with `at` are `today` and `tomorrow`, for instance:

```
$ at 7:30pm today
echo "isn't it time you went home" | mail maryann
^D
520741800.a      Wed Jun 11 19:30:00 1986
$ at 9:30 tomorrow
echo "time for staff meeting" | write sylvia bill jack
^D
520792200.a      Thu Jun 12 09:30:00 1986
$
```

Looking at requested `at` jobs

You can see what jobs you have requested to run later by using the `-l` option to `at`:

```
$ at -l
520763400.a      Thu Jun 12 01:30:00 1986
520750800.a      Wed Jun 11 22:00:00 1986
520740000.a      Wed Jun 11 14:30:00 1986
521143200.a      Mon Jun 16 11:00:00 1986
521463600.a      Fri Jun 20 04:00:00 1986
552273840.a      Wed Jun 11 15:24:00 1987
521463601.a      Fri Jun 20 04:00:01 1986
552423600.a      Sat Jul  4 12:00:00 1987
520741800.a      Wed Jun 11 19:30:00 1986
520792200.a      Thu Jun 12 09:30:00 1986
$
```

This shows all the jobs you have requested, and that have not yet been completed. It doesn't show jobs that have been requested by other users.

Unfortunately, it only shows the times at which things are scheduled to happen. It doesn't show what is going to be executed at what time, you have to remember that for yourself.

We scheduled two different things to happen at 4:00am on June 20th. Both were birthday greetings to Steve. If you look closely at the above list, you will see that they are actually scheduled 1 second apart. You cannot guarantee a time exact to the second with `at`, if someone has already booked that time slot your job will be scheduled for the next available second.

Cancelling requests scheduled with `at`

If you change your mind about a job you have scheduled with `at`, you can cancel the request by using the `-r` (remove) option.

To remove the request you have to give the job identification number. If you didn't note it down at the time you made the request, you can probably find it by using `at -l` as we described above. Of course, if you requested several different jobs to run at the same time, you will have to take a guess at which number applies to which job.

The command line:

```
$ at -r 521463600.a 521463601.a
```

removes both the jobs scheduled to send birthday greetings to Steve.

5.7. Reading current events with `news`

Another means of communication between various users of System V is via a news system. News items are stored in files on one of the system directories; these could be about system upgrades, or they could be more personal matters. The items can be read by issuing the command `news`:

```
$ news
printer (root)  Wed Jun 18  08:29:26 1982
A new printer will be installed next week.
It will be capable of producing high quality
text, and will have 14 different fonts.
Details can be obtained from the System Administrator.
picnic (maryann)  Tue Jun 17 17:05:14 1986
The company picnic will be held this year on
         Saturday June 28th
         11:30am - 6:30pm
at
     Stevenson Park.
To make your reservations, call Maryann at ext 101
$
```

The most recent news item is displayed first.

The `news` command only prints those news items that have been added, or have changed, since you last issued the command. This is controlled by a file called *.news_time* in your home directory. Note that this is a 'hidden' file (it begins with the '`.`' character), so it will not normally show up on an `ls` directory listing. Every time `news` is called, the date of this file is checked and only those news items having more recent modification dates are displayed. The date of *.news_time* is then updated.

A new user will not normally have this file, so the first time ever that the `news` command is issued, *all* news items will be shown. If old news items are not deleted, this could be a lot of old news. You could get round this by creating an empty *.news_time* file in your home directory, but before that you might want to look at what items there are to be read.

Before reading the news items in detail, you can check to see what news items there are by using the -n option:

```
$ news -n
news:  picnic   leaving
$
```

With this option only the names of the items are displayed. Again, only the names of those items that have been updated, or added, since you last read the news are displayed. This can be a useful command to put in your login profile.

Once you know the names of the items, you can selectively display them. For example:

```
$ news leaving
leaving  (patty)  Thu Jun 19 12:31:03 1986
Joe Knudsen is leaving the company, his last
day is Friday 27th.  we are planning a farewell
lunch on Thursday 26th.  If you're interested
in attending, see Patty Hughes.
$
```

displays only the item *leaving*. More than one item can be put on the same `news` command, so you can display several items at once.

If you think you have missed some news, you can use the -a option to print all available news items, regardless of how old they are.

Adding a news item

The news items themselves are kept in the system directory */usr/news*. Each file in this directory is a news item, the name of the file is the name of the news item.

Whether or not you can insert new items will depend on the write permissions of the */usr/news* directory at your installation, you can examine these with `ls`. If, for instance, the permissions look like this:

```
$ ls -ld /usr/news
drwxr-xr-x   2 bin      bin           80 Jun 18 20:41 /usr/news
$
```

then only the super-user can write in the directory, and you will have to ask your System Administrator to insert the item for you.

But if the permissions look as shown below,

```
$ ls -ld /usr/news
drwxrwxrwx   2 bin      bin          80 Jun 18 20:41 /usr/news
$
```

the directory is open for anyone to create files in it. Choose a news item name that is short (14 characters or less), but is descriptive of the item — remember that it will appear on the list produced by `news -n`. Then create a file of that name in the */usr/news* directory, using the text editor of your choice, or simply using `cat`. The file can be updated if ever you have more information on the subject.

■ *Remember to remove the file when the news becomes stale.*

5.8. Summary

You have seen here that the UNIX operating system has facilities for users to communicate with each other electronically, either directly using `write`, or indirectly via `mail`. You should try using these facilities initially to write messages to yourself, and to send mail to yourself. When you think you understand these things, find a kindred spirit (another Sytem V user) and write messages to each other, and send mail to each other.

In addition, System V provides convenient mechanisms to keep an electronic datebook, via `calendar`, and also to perform pre-scheduled tasks by the `at` command. Try out these capabilities: set up an engagement diary, send yourself reminders of things to do, read the news.

In this chapter we have outlined the facilities provided on UNIX System V. As always, you should be aware that on your own particular installation the system may be a little different. Experiment to find out just what facilities you have.

At many sites, there are multiple systems connected via networks, so users at remote locations can communicate easily, avoiding the hazards of human-carried mail.

We now leave the communication capabilities, and go on to describe some of the power tools available on System V for manipulating text files.

6 Text Manipulation

An amazing amount of the day-to-day work on a computer system is concerned with very simple processing of text in some form or another. The job of computer programming might seem to involve analysis, design, verification, redesign, and so on but, if you actually analyze the situation, you will find that computer programmers also spend a major portion of their time editing and rearranging text in various forms. This is especially true now that computers are used to support the entire design and documentation process, as well as the programming. As the customer base and applications areas for UNIX System V move into the office environment, the requirements for text processing will expand.

There are many utilities on System V which provide ways of manipulating files of text. We cover some of the more useful commands in this chapter.

- *Print* the contents of a file using the `pr` and `lp` commands;
- *sort* lines in a file into alphabetic or numeric order, using the `sort` utility;
- *count* lines, words, and characters in a file with the `wc` command;
- *select* lines from a file for inspection or further processing according to quite complex criteria with the `grep`, `fgrep`, and `egrep` facilities;
- *selectively change* individual characters with the `tr` command.
- *selectively change* character strings with the `sed` stream editor.
- *cut and paste* columns of text from files, and join them together again, with the `cut` and `paste` commands.
- *track differences or commonality* of files using the `diff` and `comm` programs.

These text processing utilities, in conjunction with redirection of Standard Output and/or piping, make it possible to select parts of files for display, or make selective changes to text files without having recourse to a text editor; and indeed, sometimes perform jobs that are difficult or impossible with a text editor.

One of the first questions most newcomers to any system have is: "How do I print a file?" So before we get into any other form of text manipulation, let's see how to get a hard-copy (printout) of a file.

6.1. Printing a File

A printout of a file, with ink marks on paper, is often called a 'hard-copy'. This is because you can see it, touch it, feel it, crumple it up and throw it in the wastebasket, or even eat it if you wish. You can do none of these things with a copy of a file that is stored on a disk somewhere in the filesystem — this is known as a soft-copy. This distinction is analogous to the difference between hardware (which exists in the real world) and software (which only exists as electronic or magnetic patterns somewhere in the computer system).

One easy way of getting a hard-copy of a file is to log in to System V using a hard-copy terminal (one that produces a paper printout of command and responses, rather than displaying them on a screen) then `cat` the file. However, few installations have such terminals, and sometimes there are none. Where there are some hard-copy terminals, a method that could be used is to `cat` the file, and redirect the output to the hard-copy device, for example:

```
$ cat file >/dev/tty10
$
```

Problems arise if someone is already using the hard-copy device when the output of `cat` is redirected there, or when more than one user tries to redirect output to that device at the same time.

For this reason, most installations have a 'spooled' printing device. The term 'spool' is an acronym for Simultaneous Peripheral Output On-Line, and it provides a mechanism whereby several people can use an output device, such as a printer, without conflict.

The printing device driven by such a spooling mechanism is very often a line printer (which prints an entire line in one fell swoop, rather than typing each character separately). For this reason, the spooler on System V is called the line printer spooler, and the command to use it is `lp`. If printout is requested while the printer is in use, the request is queued. Queued requests are usually serviced on a first in, first out basis. Depending on the installation, there may be several printers of different types and capabilities.

The Line Printer Spooler — `lp`

`lp` is the command to route files to the printer, and is used this way:

```
$ lp thisfile thatfile theotherfile
request id is 175 (3 files)
$
```

The command responds with a line of text which tells you what identity number has been allocated to your print request. You will need to know this number if you later decide that you don't want the printout after all.

The exact workings of the `lp` command vary from one installation to another, since they largely depend on the number and the types of printers available. For this reason we cannot give too many details of the operation of `lp` in this book. We refer you to your local System V wizard.

All that `lp` does is route the named file(s), or the Standard Input if there are no named files, to the printer. It does nothing else, so your file is printed beginning at the very top of the page. Also, if your file takes more than one page, the printing carries over the perforations (assuming you are using fan-fold paper) without a break. This isn't very readable — it is usual to have a few blank lines at the top and bottom of each page. The program which achieves this is `pr`, the next command we describe.

We can point out a few of the useful options to `lp`. The `-c` (copy) option makes a copy of the file, so that you are sheltered from any changes that might get made before the file is actually printed.

The `-m` (mail) option indicates that `lp` should notify you by mail when the file has been printed. This, and the `-c` option, are useful on busy systems, where files might lie in the printer queue for ages before printing.

The `-w` option is similar to `-m`, but a message is sent to your terminal using the `write` command when the file has been printed. If you are not logged on at that time, you will be sent mail instead.

The `-n` option lets you request that more than one copy of the file should be printed. You give the number of copies immediately following the `n`, for instance:

```
$ lp -n3 myfile
request id is 182 (1 file)
$
```

prints three copies of *myfile*.

There are two other commands connected with the line printer spooler, these are `lpstat` and `cancel`. If you want to know whether your files have printed, or where they stand in the queue of files waiting to be printed, you can find out with `lpstat`. Without any arguments this command shows information about all jobs waiting to be printed on all available printers. There are several options that can be used to restrict the amount of information you are shown, but in general it's easier to use the command on its own.

If you request a printout of a file, then decide you don't want it, you can use `cancel` to remove the request. `cancel` requires that you give it the 'request id' of the job you want cancelled — that is the number indicated by the system when you used `lp` to make the request.

Preparing a File for Printing with `pr`

The description of `pr` in *System V User's Manual* is 'print file', but this is misleading since the 'printing' is done to the Standard Output, which is normally your terminal screen. Really what `pr` does is prepare a file for printing, or make a file pretty for printing. Mostly you will use `pr` in conjunction with the `lp` command, thus:

```
$ pr myfile | lp
request id is 195 (standard input)
$
```

The output of `pr` is separated into pages and normally each page has a five-line header at the top and a five-line trailer at the foot. The trailer at the foot of the page consists of blank lines. In the header, one of the lines forms a title consisting of a date, the file name and a page number. The date shown in the header is the date the file was last modified. The header can be changed by various options to the `pr` command. Here is an example of the results of running a `pr` command on the *people* file which we created in chapter 4:

```
$ pr people


Apr 27 13:33 1986  people Page 1


Maryann Clark    101
Sally Smith      113
Jane Bailey      121
Jack Austen      120
Steve Daniels    111
Sylvia Dawson    110
Henry Morgan     112
Hank Parker      114
Charlie Smith    122
Bill Williams    100

$
```

There are more blank lines at the end of the printout than we have shown, There are enough to make the entire output fill an 11-inch long page. The value of the page-length can be adjusted by the `-l` option, as we describe in a little while.

If you want the title line in the header to contain something other than the file name, you can use the `-h` (header) option:

```
$ pr -h Distribution people | lp
request id is 196 (standard input)
$
```

Now the printout, instead of having the file name *people* in the page header, has the word 'Distribution'. The -h option tells pr to take the very next argument as the required header. If the header you want has spaces in it, you must put quotes (") around it:

```
$ pr -h "Distribution List" people | lp
request id is 197 (standard input)
$
```

otherwise pr tries to interpret everything except the first word as a file name.

If you want to retain the page numbers, but without any title in the header, you can give a blank string on the -h option:

```
$ pr -h "" myfile | lp
request id is 199 (standard input)
$
```

Even so, when using a blank header field, you still get the date printed on the output.

pr assumes that the page you are printing on has enough room for 72 characters across the page and 66 lines down the page. This is a normal U. S. A. letter size page (8½ inches by 11 inches).

If the length of the page you are using is not 66 lines, use the -l (length) option to adjust it.

```
$ pr -l25 -t addresses | lp
request id is 200 (standard input)
$
```

The option takes a trailing number to say how many lines fit on the paper currently in the printer.

The -t option in the above example asks pr to omit the usual 5-line header and trailer that it produces. There are times when these headers get in the way — for instance when you are trying to print address labels from a file of addresses.

The metric paper size A4 (the standard in European countries) has room for 72 lines on a page, you can specify this by:

```
$ pr -l72 myfile | lp
request id is 201 (standard input)
$
```

Be careful when adjusting the page length — if the number of lines you give to pr doesn't match the physical size of the paper you are printing on, the results are probably not going to be what you expect. This is because pr uses blank lines to skip over page breaks. If the page breaks are not where pr thinks they are, there will be a misalignment of the printing on the paper. One possible way round this is use the -f option to tell pr to use form feeds instead of blank lines.

The output of pr is usually scrunched up at the left hand side of the page when the output is routed to the printer. Some printers are clever enough to provide a left margin for you, but if you don't have one of those you can ask pr to give you such a margin by using the -o (offset) option. This option takes a trailing number to say how wide the margin should be, so:

```
$ pr -o8 myfile | lp
request id is 203 (standard input)
$
```

asks for a left-hand margin of 8 spaces (columns).

If the printout you are requesting is a draft of some document, you might want to see the output double spaced. You can ask pr to produce double spaced output by using the -d option.

Another option that is sometimes useful is -n. This precedes each line of the output by a line number. Most compilers give messages referring to line numbers when they encounter an error. Having a printout of your program that shows these line numbers can help you clean up your errors.

This has been a brief description of the pr command, showing how it can help you get a readable printout of your file. In fact there is a lot more to the command than this. However, for the moment we put aside the more complex capabilities of pr, and look at some of the other available utilities for text manipulation. Later in the chapter we show more of the wonderful things that pr can do for you.

6.2. Splitting a File Apart with split

Many commands are limited in the size of file which they can digest. For example the text editor, ed, reads the text file to be edited into an internal 'buffer', and works on that, rather than the actual contents of the file itself. This means that there are times when a file might be too large to fit in the buffer. In these cases we use the 'divide and conquer' principle, and split the file into smaller and more manageable chunks. The split utility performs this task. Having split a file into smaller pieces, the pieces can be edited singly, then the pieces can be concatenated into one whole file again with the cat command.

You can split a mammoth-sized file into smaller pieces with a split command, like this:

```
$ split mammoth
$
```

The file *mammoth* is split into 1000-line pieces. Each piece gets put into a different file in the current directory. The names of the output files are generated by using the letter *x*, followed by two more letters.

The first output filename in this example is called *xaa*, the second is called *xab*, the third, *xac*, and so on through *xaz* and then *xba*, and so on right through *xzz*. Each of the files produced, except the last, will contain 1000 lines. The number of lines in the last file will be whatever was left over a multiple of 1000.

The number of lines in each output file can be controlled via an option to `split`, so this version of the command:

```
$ split -500 mammoth
$
```

carves our *mammoth* file into 500-line pieces.

■ *Note that the number given is the number of lines per chunk, not the number of separate chunks.*

`split` can also take a second, optional, filename on the command line. This governs the names of the files containing the separate chunks of the original file:

```
$ split mammoth ribs
$
```

Now the output files are named *ribsaa*, *ribsab*, and so on.

Having done whatever you want to do with the smaller files, you can put the whole lot back together again, using a `cat` command that looks like this:

```
$ cat ribs?? >mammoth.new
$
```

And having done that, you get rid of all the *ribs* files, using an `rm` command like this:

```
$ rm ribs??
$
```

but it would be wise to do an `ls ribs??` first.

One very useful application of `split` is to print individual pages of a file. Suppose you had obtained a printout of a large file, say 100 pages or so, then discovered some minor errors in the sixth and tenth pages. After correcting the file, you don't necessarily want to print the whole thing again, just the pages with errors. You can achieve this with `split` as we show on the next page.

We use 66 lines because that is the default page size used by `pr`. The sixth page is the file *xaf*, and the tenth page is the file *xaj*.

```
$ pr infile >outfile
$ split -66 outfile
$ lp xaf xaj
request id is 211 (2 files)
$
```

Remember to remove the *x??* files when they have finished printing; *outfile* can be removed immediately following the `split`.

6.3. Sorting Text Files with `sort`

`sort` is a utility program which sorts the contents of a file into alphabetic or numeric order. There are many options which control the sort order. We make no attempt to cover all the intricacies of `sort`, but in the next few paragraphs we show some of the more useful options and suggest ways in which you might want to use the program. For more detail refer to the description of the `sort` utility in the *System V User's Manual.*

We must point out here that the `sort` utility on UNIX System V is different from the sort/merge utilities found on other systems. In common with the majority of UNIX System V text-processing software, `sort` does not expect fields on a line to appear in a fixed columnar layout. The `sort` utility just works on fields that are normally separated by spaces or tabs (you can specify any field-separator you want). If you come from the punched card orientation which most of the computer industry forces on its users, you might at first find `sort` odd, but after a while, the typewriter oriented approach becomes much more natural.

Sorting into Alphabetical Order

Let's take our *people* file and see what happens when we sort it.

```
$ sort people
Bill Williams   100
Charlie Smith   122
Hank Parker     114
Henry Morgan    112
Jack Austen     120
Jane Bailey     121
Maryann Clark   101
Sally Smith     113
Steve Daniels   111
Sylvia Dawson   110
$
```

The output of `sort` is a list of people sorted into alphabetical order by their first names. This is unusual, since it's more common to find lists of people sorted on last name. We could have entered the names in the form `Smith, Sally`, then the result would have been in order of last name. But we can tell `sort` to sort on last name.

Each line in the file is considered to consist of fields, the fields being separated by spaces. To get our file in order of last name, we tell the program to skip one field (the first names) before it starts the sorting process, thus: Last Names

```
$ sort +1 people
Jack Austen      120
Jane Bailey      121
Maryann Clark    101
Steve Daniels    111
Sylvia Dawson    110
Henry Morgan     112
Hank Parker      114
Sally Smith      113
Charlie Smith    122
Bill Williams    100
$
```

Of course this method breaks down if someone has a middle initial which they insist on using, because that would give an extra field on that line. So you might find that you have to hold people as `Parker, Hank J.` after all. However, if everybody had a middle initial, and only one, that would be OK. In that case, you just ask `sort` to skip two fields before starting the sort process.

Notice that Sally Smith comes before Charlie Smith, which is not in the true spirit of alphabetical order. This is because, once you have told `sort` which field to start on, it sorts from that field on to the end of the line. To get true alphabetical order you have to say:

```
$ sort +1 -2 people
```

that is, skip one field before you start sorting (first names), then stop sorting after the second field (last names). When `sort` stops sorting after the second field, it then resumes sorting from the beginning of the line again, so it will sort on first names. This gives us the result we want.

Sorting Into Numerical Order

Suppose we wanted to show our list of people in order of phone numbers. We want to skip two fields before we start sorting, as we show in the next example.

```
$ sort +2 people
Sally Smith        113
Hank Parker        114
Jack Austen        120
Jane Bailey        121
Henry Morgan       112
Bill Williams      100
Maryann Clark      101
Sylvia Dawson      110
Steve Daniels      111
Charlie Smith      122
$
```

This is obviously not correct. Notice that all the shorter names appear first, followed by the longer ones. This is because of two things: firstly, each field is considered to start immediately after the end of the previous field, so the spaces between the last name and the phone number count as part of the phone number; secondly, `sort` is really sorting on ASCII characters, and the character for space has a lower value than any of the characters for the digits 0 through 9.

We can tell `sort` to ignore leading spaces (blanks) in the fields by using the `-b` option:

```
$ sort -b +2 people
Bill Williams    100
Maryann Clark    101
Sylvia Dawson    110
Steve Daniels    111
Henry Morgan     112
Sally Smith      113
Hank Parker      114
Jack Austen      120
Jane Bailey      121
Charlie Smith    122
$
```

Using the `-b` option in this way tells `sort` to ignore blanks in *all* fields on the line. If we want to restrict the effect of ignoring blanks to *only* the numeric field, we append the `b` option to the field number as shown in the example on the next page.

When you attach the `b` to one of the fields like this, it is called a 'flag', rather than an option. In our example we get the same results either way, but there will be cases where the different ways of specifying that blanks are to be ignored will produce different results.

```
$ sort +2b people
Bill Williams   100
Maryann Clark   101
     <etcetera . . .>
Charlie Smith   122
$
```

We have got what we wanted, but this is not *really* numeric sorting. We got there more or less by accident. The ASCII characters for the digits 0 through 9 are in ascending order and, because all our numbers have exactly the same number of digits, we have the appearance of numerical order.

But suppose our file holds, not phone numbers, but some other numbers which don't all have the same number of digits. Take the example of a tennis league, where we want to keep track of the number of games that each person has won. The file we create in this case looks something like:

```
$ cat >tennis
Maryann Clark    18
Sally Smith      14
Jane Bailey       2
Jack Austen       3
Steve Daniels    11
Sylvia Dawson     7
Henry Morgan      5
Hank Parker      18
Charlie Smith     9
Bill Williams     2
$
```

If we merely sort the file by skipping two fields, and ignoring blanks in the third, we get the sorted file shown in the example on the next page.

This is obviously not the right order. We have to tell `sort` that the characters in the field we are sorting on are to be treated as numbers, and to sort according to the arithmetic values of those numbers.

```
$ sort +2b tennis
Steve Daniels    11
Sally Smith      14
Hank Parker      18
Maryann Clark    18
Bill Williams     2
Jane Bailey       2
Jack Austen       3
Henry Morgan      5
Sylvia Dawson     7
Charlie Smith     9
$
```

To treat the fields as numbers, and to sort according to the arithmetic values of those numbers, you add the letter `n` (numeric) as a flag:

```
$ sort +2n +1 tennis
Jane Bailey       2
Bill Williams     2
Jack Austen       3
Henry Morgan      5
Sylvia Dawson     7
Charlie Smith     9
Steve Daniels    11
Sally Smith      14
Maryann Clark    18
Hank Parker      18
$
```

We don't have to use the `b` option in this case, because using the `n` for numeric sorting implies that spaces are ignored. People having the same scores should be shown in alphabetical order, so we need to say `+1` to specify the ordering of that field too.

We could specify that we want numerical order like this:

```
$ sort -n +2 +1 tennis
Bill Williams     2
Jane Bailey       2
Jack Austen       3
     <etcetera . . .>
Hank Parker      18
Maryann Clark    18
$
```

Specifying `-n` in this way tells `sort` to treat *all* fields as numeric. As you can see, this doesn't give quite the right answer, because people with the same scores are no longer in alphabetical order.

In a list of scores like this, it is more usual to see the winners listed first. We can tell `sort` to reverse the order of sorting by adding the letter `r` (reverse) as a flag after the field that we want reversed:

```
$ sort +2nr +1 tennis
Maryann Clark      18
Hank Parker        18
Sally Smith        14
Steve Daniels      11
Charlie Smith       9
Sylvia Dawson       7
Henry Morgan        5
Jack Austen         3
Jane Bailey         2
Bill Williams       2
$
```

The use of `r` to reverse the order of the sort is not restricted to numeric sorting, although that is where it is most commonly found. We could, for example, have used `+1r` and `+0r` to produce the names in reverse alphabetic order.

Again, we could have used `-r` as an option instead of a flag, to tell `sort` to reverse the sort order on all fields. Interestingly, in our particular example, using both options `-nr` will produce the results we want. The wrongness introduced by trying to numerically sort non-numeric fields, is cancelled by the 'wrongness' of reversing the order of all fields. However, be aware that this is just a lucky coincidence, don't rely on it happening in your files.

Saving Sorted Output

So far, the output of `sort` has been displayed on the terminal screen. You might want to save the output in a file — you can do this with the `-o` (output) option. When you give the `-o` option, the very next argument to `sort` must be the name of a file that is to contain the output. For example:

```
$ sort -o speople +1 -2 people
$ cat speople
Jack Austen      120
Jane Bailey      121
    <etcetera . . .>
$
```

Because `sort` normally sends its results to the Standard Output you can achieve the same effect by redirecting the Standard Output to a file:

```
$ sort +1 -2 people >speople
$
```

Merging Already Sorted Files

So far we have only shown `sort` operating on one file. If we give more than one filename, the contents of all the files named are considered to be joined together, end to end, and the composite is then sorted.

Suppose that instead of one file of people we had several. Perhaps your project has two types of people — some are concerned with designing hardware, those names go into one file:

```
$ cat hardpeople
Jack Austen    120
Charlie Smith  122
Jane Bailey    121
$
```

and some are involved with software development, those names go in another file:

```
$ cat softpeople
Sylvia Dawson  110
Sally Smith    113
Steve Daniels  111
Henry Morgan   112
Hank Parker    114
$
```

Then there will be some administrative people like the manager and the secretary, whose names will be in yet another file:

```
$ cat adminpeople
Bill Williams  100
Maryann Clark  101
$
```

We can produce a distribution list of software developers by sorting *softpeople*, and one for hardware designers by sorting *hardpeople*, but what about a distribution list that includes everybody? We simply give all the filenames to the `sort` command:

```
$ sort +1 -2 adminpeople hardpeople softpeople >everybody
$
```

or we could make use of the Shell's file matching capabilities and say:

```
$ sort +1 -2  *people >everybody
$
```

If your input files are already sorted you can simply merge them by using the -m (merge) option:

```
$ sort +1 -2 adminpeople >sadmin
$ sort +1 -2 hardpeople >shard
$ sort +1 -2 softpeople >ssoft
$ sort -m +1 -2 sadmin shard ssoft >everybody
$
```

The -m option tells sort that the files are already sorted, and need only be merged, thereby saving sort some work.

Note that the final sort can *not* be replaced by a simple cat command — that wouldn't give a fully sorted output. What you would get with cat would be *adminpeople* sorted into order, followed by *hardpeople* sorted into order, followed by *softpeople* sorted into order. With sort you get *adminpeople*, *hardpeople*, and *softpeople* all together sorted into order.

If you use the -m option to sort, your input files had really better be sorted. If they are not already sorted, the final result is not properly sorted:

```
$ sort -m +1 -2 *people
Jack Austen      120
Jane Bailey      121
Sylvia Dawson    110
Charlie Smith    122
Sally Smith      113
Steve Daniels    111
Henry Morgan     112
Hank Parker      114
Bill Williams    100
Maryann Clark    101
$
```

Duplicated Lines in Sorted Files

Suppose that instead of having a separate file for the administrative people, we had put them in both the other files. For this example we're going to forget about phone numbers, so we assume our *hardpeople* file contains:

```
$ cat hardpeople
Bill Williams
Maryann Clark
Jane Bailey
Jack Austen
Charlie Smith
$
```

and the *softpeople* file looks like this:

```
$ cat softpeople
Bill Williams
Maryann Clark
Sylvia Dawson
Sally Smith
Steve Daniels
Henry Morgan
Hank Parker
$
```

Further suppose that we had a file which contained only the managers:

```
$ cat managers
Bill Williams
Jack Austen
Sylvia Dawson
$
```

Now if we sort and merge the three files as shown in the next example on the next page, we will get duplicate lines. Lines that are the same but in different files get sorted together and will appear duplicated in the output.

```
$ sort +1 managers hardpeople softpeople
Jack Austen
Jack Austen
Jane Bailey
Maryann Clark
Maryann Clark
Steve Daniels
Sylvia Dawson
Sylvia Dawson
Henry Morgan
Hank Parker
Charlie Smith
Sally Smith
Bill Williams
Bill Williams
Bill Williams
$
```

This duplication won't do at all. To get rid of the duplications we use the `-u` (unique) option, thus:

```
$ sort -u +1 managers hardpeople softpeople >everybody
$
```

We could also do it by using another utility program called `uniq`, whose purpose is to remove adjacent duplicate lines from a sorted file. We take the output of `sort` and pipe it to `uniq`:

```
$ sort +1 managers hardpeople softpeople | uniq >everybody
$
```

Duplicate lines must be adjacent to one another for `uniq` to find them, so you must use `sort`, then `uniq`, not the other way around.

Field Separators for Sorting

Normally `sort` assumes fields are separated by spaces or tabs. However some files may have a format where the fields are separated by something else. To tell `sort` this, we use the `-t` option.

A file that does not use spaces as field separators is the password file */etc/passwd*. This file uses the colon character `:` as its field separator. We can sort on the sixth field of each line (the users' home directory names) by typing this command:

```
$ sort -t: +5 /etc/passwd
```

It is unfortunate that many of the characters that are most likely to be used as field separators mean something special to the Shell. For example, if you have a file with the fields separated by |, and you try:

```
$ sort -t| myfile
```

you will have problems, because the system will try to take the output of the (incomplete) `sort` command on the left of the | and pipe it to the (unknown) command `myfile`. In this situation you have to remove the special meaning of | by preceding it with the Shell 'escape' character \, thus:

```
$ sort -t\| myfile
```

or we could use quotes:

```
$ sort -t"|" myfile
```

6.4. Counting Things in a File with wc

The `wc` command counts the number of lines, words, and characters in a file. It is used heavily for things such as counting the number of lines of source code in a program, the number of words in a document, and other ostensibly useful statistics so dear to the hearts of project management.

We can count what is in our *people* file with a `wc` command like this:

```
$ wc people
      10      30      200 people
$
```

The first number is the number of lines in the file. The second number is the number of words in the file. The third number is the number of characters (including newlines) in the file. Finally, `wc` displays the name of the file it counted.

A 'word' in the context of `wc` is a string of characters delimited by spaces, tabs, or newlines.

`wc` can accept any combination of three options. The options restrict the counting process to the indicated object. The `-l` option means that only lines are to be counted. The `-w` option indicates that `wc` should only count words. The `-c` option implies that characters are the only things to be counted.

We can count just the number of lines in the *people* file with a wc command line like this:

```
$ wc -l people
     10 people
$
```

The options can be combined, so the number of lines and characters in *people* can be counted this way:

```
$ wc -lc people
     10      200 people
$
```

Of course, using all three options together is a complicated way to get wc's normal behavior, namely, count everything. However, the order of the combination of options affects the order in which the counts are printed, so

```
$ wc -wcl people
     30     200       10 people
$
```

counts the same things as a straight wc without any options, but the values of the counts are shown in a different order.

If wc counts its Standard Input, it does not, obviously, display the name of the file which was counted. This is what happens when you count lines in the Standard Input, redirected from the *people* file:

```
$ wc -l < people
     10
$
```

Here, there is no filename to display, and all we get is the count of the number of lines in the Standard Input.

You can count more than one file at a time with wc. In this case, you get the counts for the individual files and, as a bonus, wc prints the total for all the files. So suppose we had three small files of people, instead of one big people file, as we show below.

```
$ wc *people
       2       6      40 adminpeople
       3       9      60 hardpeople
       5      15     100 softpeople
      10      30     200 total
$
```

Do not confuse the last line designated 'total' with a file called *total*. It really is the totals of the previous files. This can be done in a different way, using the `cat` command piped to the `wc` utility:

```
$ cat  *people | wc
      10      30     200
$
```

Although the `wc` command seems trivial, it finds application in scores of mundane tasks in the system every day. Perhaps the canonical example of `wc` is finding out how many users are logged on to the system:

```
$ who | wc
      17      34     510
$
```

This display tells us that there are 17 users on the system. With that many people sharing a $1,000 microprocessor, it is time to have lunch.

6.5. Finding Text Patterns in a File with `grep`

`grep` is a utility program that searches a file, or more than one file, for lines which contain strings of a certain pattern. Such lines are said to match the pattern. Lines which match the specified pattern are printed on the Standard Output.

In its simplest use, `grep` just looks for a pattern which consists of a fixed character string. It is possible, however, to describe more complex patterns, called 'regular expressions'. We start off the examples showing simple fixed strings, then later we move on to regular expressions.

Searching for Character Strings

The simplest pattern to give to `grep` is a fixed character string. For example, suppose we want to find the phone number of Sally Smith. We simply use `grep` to find the string `Sally` in the file *people*, which contains the phone numbers:

```
$ grep Sally people
Sally Smith      113
$
```

With the people arranged in three files, as we used in examples for `sort`, we can tell `grep` to scan all three files at the same time:

```
$ grep Sally adminpeople hardpeople softpeople
softpeople: Sally Smith   113
$
```

Now we have the name of the file in which Sally was found — this could be useful, depending on how well we had named our files. If we don't want to see the filename, we can suppress it with the `-h` (omit file header) option. Assuming a judicious choice of filenames in the first place, the above example could also be written as:

```
$ grep Sally *people
softpeople: Sally Smith   113
$
```

We used the word `Sally` to search for the phone number, but we could equally well have used `Smith`:

```
$ grep Smith people
Sally Smith      113
Charlie Smith    122
$
```

There are two lines containing `Smith` in the file *people*, and both are printed.

If we are interested only in Sally Smith, and don't want to see anything about any other Smith, or any other Sally, we have to use both names in the search string:

```
$ grep "Sally Smith" people
Sally Smith      113
$
```

Note that the name is surrounded by quote signs ("). This is because the pattern you're looking for must form one argument to `grep`. Since a space is used to separate arguments, a pattern which also contains spaces must be enclosed in quotes.

If we leave out the quotes and say:

```
$ grep Sally Smith people
grep: can't open Smith
people: Sally Smith    113
$
```

we get an error message as you can see, because the program is trying to look for 'Sally' in the files *Smith* and *people*.

Inverting the Search with the v Option

So far we have seen how `grep` prints all lines which contain the given character string. The `-v` (invert) option instructs `grep` to print all lines *except* those which match the string.

As an example of how this can be useful, suppose Henry Morgan leaves the group and his place is taken by James Walker. We now have to update our list of people. James Walker can easily be added to the file using `cat`, as we showed in the last chapter, but to eliminate Henry we will have to use `grep` with the `-v` option.

The entire sequence of commands to do the update job is:

```
$ grep Henry people
Henry Morgan    112
$ grep -v "Henry Morgan" people >people.new
$ cat >>people.new
James Walker    112
^D
$ mv people people.old
$ mv people.new people
$ chmod 444 people
$
```

The first `grep` of the sequence is simply to find Henry's phone number so that we can allocate it to James. In fact, there is only one Henry in our file, so we could also have used this in the second `grep` command to delete him from the file.

Note that we did *not* say:

```
grep -v "Henry Morgan" people >people
```

That would destroy our original *people* file (unless we had protected it by making it read-only mode). Instead we did all the changes into new file called *people.new*, and when we were finished we renamed the files.

The final stage in the process is to use the `chmod` command to make the new *people* file read-only mode as a protection against accidental loss.

Regular Expressions in Text Patterns

So far we have only given grep a fixed character string to look for, but it is capable of more complex searches. We can give grep a pattern (or template) of the text we want to search for. We can ask for things like

> find all four-letter words beginning with d,
>
> *or*
>
> all words ending in able,
>
> *or*
>
> all 6-digit numbers appearing at the end of a line.

Such a pattern or template is called a 'regular expression' and the name of the command derives from that. grep stands for 'Global Regular Expression Printer'. When we get to chapter 8 on the text editor ed, the derivation of this apparently odd name will be made clear.

Regular expressions work in a way similar to the Shell's file-matching capability that we discussed in chapter 3 — *Directories and Files.* Certain characters have a special meaning. These special characters are called 'metacharacters' because they represent something other than themselves.

Unfortunately, the metacharacters used in grep (and incidentally, in the editor ed and many other utilities) are not quite the same as those that the Shell uses for matching filenames. This can cause confusion, especially if you are using both in the same command, so be careful about how you specify your text-patterns.

Because many of the characters which have special meanings in regular expressions also have special meaning to the System V Shell, it is best to enclose the regular expression in quotes. Single quotes (') are safest, but often double quotes (") are sufficient.

Match Beginning and End of Line with ^ and $ Two of the simplest metacharacters to use are the circumflex (^) and the dollar sign ($), which match the beginning of a line and the end of a line, respectively.

A (^) appearing at the beginning of a string matches the beginning of a line. So, whereas the string:

```
"Genesis"
```

finds any line containing the word Genesis, preceding it with the circumflex (^) character like this:

```
"^Genesis"
```

only finds lines starting with the word Genesis.

Similarly ($) appearing at the end of a string matches the end of a line, so:

```
"eschatus$"
```

selects only those lines ending with the word eschatus.

An expression preceded by (^) and followed with ($), for instance:

```
"^Out in the cold$"
```

selects only those lines consisting of the phrase `Out in the cold`, and nothing else.

A text pattern which matches at a specific place on a line is called an 'anchored match', because it is 'anchored' to a particular position.

The (^) and ($) characters lose their special meaning if they appear in places other than the beginning of the pattern, or the end of the pattern, respectively.

Blank lines in a file can be found with the expression (^$). This pattern finds lines which have only a newline, and no other text. If there are spaces or tabs or other non-printing characters on the line, the pattern (^$) will not find them.

Match Any Character with . The period (or **dot** as it's usually known in System V) is a metacharacter which matches any character at all.

So the string

```
" d... "
```

selects all words starting with the letter `d`, and having three more characters, provided they are preceded and followed by a space. To find such words at the beginning of a line we need to use

```
"^d... "
```

To find such words at the end of a line we would use the expression

```
" d...$"
```

However, following the word with a period

```
" d...."
```

won't only find four-letter '`d`'-words at the end of a sentence: it will find all sequences of five characters starting with the letter `d`. To tell `grep` that you want that final dot to really be a period character, you have to remove its special significance by preceding it with the escape character \, and use the expression

```
" d...\."
```

We said that `grep` will find words starting with `d` with this expression, but we lied a little. What `grep` actually finds is any string of four characters starting with the letter `d`. So

```
" d... "
```

finds any of the patterns:

```
dc13                                drat
dr-x          as well as            dumb
dry!                                dogs
```

To specify that we only want letters in the 'word', we have to give a different expression, and this is discussed below.

The period metacharacter never matches the newline at the end of a line. A consequence of this is that text patterns never match across lines, they only match within a line. There is a good practical reason for this apparently antisocial behavior.

Character Classes with `[` and `]` and `-` Characters enclosed in brackets, `[ ]`, specify a set of characters that are to be searched for. The match is on any one of the characters inside the brackets. For example, the expression:

```
[Gg]enesis
```

finds both `genesis` and `Genesis`. The expression:

```
^[abcxyz]
```

finds all lines beginning with `a` or `b` or `c` or `x` or `y` or `z`.

Inside `[ ]`, the hyphen character (`-`) specifies a range of characters, so

```
^[abcxyz]
```

can also be expressed in the shorthand notation as:

```
^[a-cx-z]
```

The patterns:

`[a-z]`	*all lowercase letters*
`[A-Z]`	*all uppercase letters*
`[0-9]`	*all digits*

are very common regular expressions. So, for our previous example of '`d`'-words, to really limit it to letters only, we should use the pattern:

```
" [Dd][a-z][a-z][a-z] "
```

assuming that only the initial letter can be in uppercase.

In the example

```
^[a-cx-z]
```

you should note that the `^` metacharacter (match the beginning of the line) is *outside* the brackets. When the circumflex appears *inside* the brackets it has a different meaning. If the character `^` is the first character inside `[ ]` it doesn't mean 'beginning of line'. Instead it inverts the selection process. So the expression:

```
" [^Dd][a-z][a-z][a-z] "
```

specifies all four letter words that begin with something other than D or d, and the pattern:

```
^[^a-z]
```

finds all lines except those that begin with lowercase letters.

It should be emphasized that ranges of characters pertain to the ASCII character set, so that the pattern:

```
[A-z]
```

not only gets you all upper and lowercase letters, but all the other characters that fall in that range of ASCII character values, namely:

```
[ \ ] ^ _ `
```

This sort of confusion occurs most often when dealing with digits. The pattern:

```
[1-30]
```

does *not* mean 'numbers in the range one through 30', it means 'digits in the range 1 through 3, or 0'. It is the same as a pattern that looks like:

`[1230]` *or* `[0-3]`

If you really wish to include - in the class of characters, it isn't necessary to escape it so long as it is positioned such that it won't be confused with a range specification. For example, a hyphen at the beginning of the pattern stands for itself:

```
[-ab]
```

means the pattern - or a or b. The same is true for the characters [and] themselves.

Closures — Repeated Pattern Matches A number enclosed in braces { } following an expression specifies the number of times that the preceding expression is to be repeated. So our search for four letter words could be expressed:

```
" [Dd][a-z]{3} "
```

This repeat number specification is known as a 'closure'.

The general format of the closure is { *n*, *m* }, where *n* is the minimum number of repeats and *m* is the maximum number of repeats. A missing *n* is assumed to be one, and a missing *m* is assumed to be infinity (or at least huge).

There are shorthand ways of expressing some closures:

- * (asterisk) is equivalent to {0,}, meaning that the preceding pattern is to be repeated *zero or more* times.

\+ (plus sign) is equivalent to {1,}, meaning that the preceding pattern is to be repeated *one or more* times.

? (question mark) is the same as {0,1}, which means that the preceding pattern can be repeated *zero or once only*.

Closures are the reason why text patterns do not span across lines. If you just type a grep command like this:

```
$ grep '.*'  people
```

you are using a pattern which says:

'match zero to infinity amounts of any character'

If patterns could span lines, this would (try to) eat up an entire file. Like any other utility, grep has some limit to the size of the pattern which it can hold internally, and a whole file probably is too big for it to digest.

Since there is a restriction which says that patterns do not match a line boundary, the command:

```
$ grep '.*' people
```

simply finds (and displays) every line in the *people* file. This is the same as saying:

```
$ cat people
```

but cat is a lot easier and faster.

Subsets of Regular Expressions

At this point we must confess that we have been lying to you in the previous paragraphs. What we have described is the full set of regular expression metacharacters. In practice, many of the System V utilities do not support this full set, and grep is one of them.

One of the things that are missing are the full format of closures {*n*,*m*}. However, all of the closures +, ?, and * are available.

Regular expressions are used by many other commands in the system, most notably the text editors. The range of metacharacters available varies from one System V command to the next, Always consult your *System V User's Manual* to find out what you have available.

Examples of Regular Expressions

Regular expressions are a powerful tool, but they can be very complex and they need practice in using them. To an inexperienced user, it often seems that figuring out a regular expression to find a number of character strings takes longer than doing things the hard way and finding each string one at a time.

It is difficult to give examples covering all possible combinations of metacharacters, but here are some situations where you will find regular expressions useful.

You can delete all blank lines from a file by:

```
$ grep -v "^$" file > newfile
$
```

The regular expression `^$` finds all the blank lines, and the `-v` option tells `grep` to save all the other lines and ignore the blank lines.

This only gets rid of lines that are really blank. Lines that appear blank, but actually contain spaces, will remain in `newfile`. To delete the apparently blank lines as well, we should say:

```
$ grep -v "^ *$" file > newfile
$
```

The regular expression says, in effect, 'look for a beginning of line, followed by any number of spaces (including no spaces), followed by an end of line'.

But what if the apparently empty line contains tabs as well as spaces? You must replace the simple space in the above regular expression with an expression that says 'space or tab':

```
$ grep "^[ ^I]*$" file > newfile
$
```

The `^I` in the above example doesn't mean the characters `^` and `I`. It indicates that you should type CTRL-I, which is the tab character. When you type the tab character the cursor will move to the next tab position, so what you will see on the screen is:

```
"^[         ]*$"
```

Many keyboards have a separate 'tab' key, marked TAB, so you don't actually have to type CTRL-I.

Suppose we want to find the person or persons having the initials 'SD', we can use `grep` for this:

```
$ grep "S.* D.*" people
Steve Daniels   111
Sylvia Dawson   110
$
```

The regular expression looks for an initial 'S' followed by some characters, followed by a space, followed by a 'D' followed by some more characters. This is a fairly sloppy pattern, we could have made it tighter by introducing lowercase letters:

```
"S[a-z]* D[a-z]*"
```

but we are relying on our knowledge of the format of the file.

There is no point in making a regular expression more complex than it need be. However, be aware that a regular expression will find the longest string of characters which matches the pattern — this often causes grief.

Other Options to grep

Earlier we showed the use of the -v option to grep, to invert the search. There are other options which can be given to the command.

-n (number) option asks grep to show the line numbers of lines that match the string or pattern, for example:

```
$ grep -n Smith *people
hardpeople:3:Charlie Smith   122
softpeople:2:Sally Smith     113
$
```

This can be sometimes be useful when you intend to use an editor, or some other command, to process the file using line numbers.

When you give the -c (count) option, lines that match the pattern are not displayed. Instead, a count of the number of lines that match the pattern in each file is shown:

```
$ grep -c "S.* D.*" *people
adminpeople:0
hardpeople:0
softpeople:2
$
```

This is useful when you want to see the distribution of a string throughout a set of files.

-l (list) option is usually only used when you give multiple filenames to the grep command. Instead of showing every line in every file that matches the pattern, grep simply displays the name of each file that contains at least one line that matches the pattern:

```
$ grep -l Smith *people
hardpeople
softpeople
$
```

This is used when you are only interested in which of a set of files contains a particular string.

A useful option, which is unfortunately not available on some older versions of `grep`, is the `-i` (ignore case) option. When you use this option `grep` makes no distinction between uppercase and lowercase letters when trying to match patterns. So the command

```
$ grep -i Smith *people
```

will find lines that contain any of the strings `Smith`, `smith`. `SMITH`, or even `sMITH`. This can be a lot easier than typing a regular expression to do the same job.

6.6. Fast Searching for Fixed Strings with `fgrep`

The `fgrep` command is another text processing utility in the same family as `grep` (described above), and `egrep` (described below). The `fgrep` command only handles fixed character strings as text patterns. `fgrep` stands for 'fast `grep`', or maybe, 'fixed `grep`'. The `fgrep` command cannot process wild-card matches, character classes, anchored matches, or closures. For these reasons, `fgrep` is considerably faster than `grep`, when all you want to look for is a fixed text string.

`fgrep` is typically used as in our `grep` examples above:

```
$ fgrep Sylvia *people
softpeople: Sylvia Dawson   110
$
```

As we said, `fgrep` cannot cope with anchored matches. So you cannot give an expression like

```
"^Out in the cold$"
```

to find lines that consist only of that phrase. However there is a `-x` option which finds lines that are an exact match of the given string. So that the command:

```
$ grep -x "Out in the cold" somefile
```

will only find lines that contain the given character string, and nothing else.

Although you can't give `fgrep` a regular expression such as `[Hh]is`, there is a `-i` option that tells `fgrep` to ignore the case of letters when matching the patterns. Unfortunately, as we stated for `grep`, some older versions of the command do not support this option.

You can also feed `fgrep` a file of fixed strings. Each string appears on a line by itself, but the newline characters have to be escaped with the \ character.

6.7. Finding Full Regular Expressions with `egrep`

Another variation on the basic `grep` utility is `egrep`. `egrep` stands for 'extended `grep`'. The `egrep` command is an extension to the basic `grep`, such that it can handle full regular expressions. For example, `egrep` can handle complex regular expressions, of the form:

> 'find a pattern, followed by a this or a that or one of those, followed by something else'.

Alternative patterns are specified by separating the alternatives with the `|` (vertical bar) character. This form of regular expression is technically called 'alternation'.

Alternate patterns within regular expressions can be grouped by enclosing the patterns within parentheses `( )`.

To give a simple example, let us revert to our original `people` file. Let's assume that Sally Smith married someone called White, but we are unsure whether she changed her name, or whether the file has been updated to reflect such a change. To find her in the *people* file we can use `egrep` like this:

```
$ egrep 'Sally (White|Smith)' *people
Sally Smith     113
$
```

What we are searching for here is an occurrence of either `Sally White`, or `Sally Smith`. Using the alternation capability of full regular expressions makes this easy to express. The regular expression above asks to match a line containing the string `Sally`, followed by either of the strings `White` or `Smith`.

Notice that the alternatives are in parentheses. If we had typed it as:

```
$ egrep 'Sally White|Smith' *people
```

the result would be to look for a line containing `Sally White`, or a line containing `Smith`, which is not what we wanted.

6.8. Replacing Character Strings with `sed`

`sed` is the stream editor. This is quite a complex program, to use all of its features you really need to be familiar with the line editor `ed`. We describe the command in detail later in the book, in chapter 12 — *Advanced Text Manipulation*. In this chapter we just show a very simple use of `sed` to change character strings in a file.

To replace a character string with a different string, the format of the `sed` command is:

sed **s/** *string* **/** *newstring* **/** *file*

The s stands for substitute. It is followed by the string to be substituted, then the string to be put in its place. Both the strings are separated from each other, and from the initial s, by a slash character /. In fact the separator need not be a /, it can be any character that is not in either of the strings.

To give an example using our *people* file, let's assume that when Sally Smith married she changed her name. We can modify our file:

```
$ mv people people.old
$ sed s/Smith/White/ people.old >people
$
```

We have changed the string 'Smith' to 'White'.

Unfortunately in this case, sed does the change to every applicable line in the file. So we have also changed Charlie Smith's name to Charlie White. To change Sally Smith's name without affecting any other Smith, we have to say:

```
$ sed "s/Sally Smith/Sally White/" people.old >people
$
```

Now that our strings contain spaces we have to surround the entire substitute expression with quotes, because the substitute expression must form one argument to sed.

The string that is to be replaced can also be a regular expression, for instance we can put a left margin of 5 spaces on our *people* file like this:

```
$ sed "s/^/     /" people
     Maryann Clark  101
     Sally Smith    113
     Jane Bailey    121
         <etcetera . . .>
     Bill Williams  100
$
```

The new string that is to be substituted for the existing string can be null, in which case the original string is, effectively, deleted. To remove the phone numbers from the *people* file we could use this command:

```
$ sed "s/ [0-9]*$//" people
Maryann Clark
Sally Smith
Jane Bailey
    <etcetera . . .>
Bill Williams
$
```

There are a lot more things that you can do with the stream editor, but it is not the easiest program to drive. If you are interested in playing with it further, refer to chapter 12.

6.9. Translating Characters with `tr`

The utility program `tr` translates (or transliterates) characters in a file. `tr` works on the Standard Input. If you want to take input from a file, you have to redirect the Standard Input so that it comes from that file.

`tr` can take two arguments which specify character sets. Each member of the first set is replaced by the equivalent member of the second set. To give a crazy example:

```
$ tr abcdefghijklmnopqrstuvwxyz  \
    zyxwvutsrqponmlkjihgfedcba  <people
Mzibzmm Cozip    101
Szoob Snrgs      113
Jzmv Bzrovb      121
    <etcetera . . .>
Broo Wroorznh    100
$
```

We have reversed the alphabet for lowercase letters, uppercase letters are not affected because we didn't include them in our character set.

We could have stated the first character set by giving a range `a-z`, but not the second since it is not in ascending order of ASCII character values.

If the second character set doesn't contain as many characters as the first, the remaining characters in the first set are simply left alone. Had we left out the `ba` at the end of the second argument in the above example, both `y` and `z` would have been remained untranslated.

Suppose we want our file of *people* to be printed all in capital letters. We can get our file ready for the printer like this:

```
$ tr "[a-z]" "[A-Z]" <people
MARYANN CLARK    101
SALLY SMITH      113
JANE BAILEY      120
    <etcetera . . .>
BILL WILLIAMS    100
$
```

All characters in the range `a` through `z` are replaced by the corresponding character in the range `A` through `Z`. Everything can be turned into lower case by reversing the strings `a-z` and `A-Z`.

The quotes in the above example are necessary to prevent the Shell trying to interpret the square brackets as a wild-card characters for filenames. The square brackets are necessary to tell `tr` that you mean a range of characters. If you leave them out, you get this result:

```
$ tr a-z A-Z <people
MAryAnn ClArk   101
SAlly Smith     113
JAne BAiley     121
    <etcetera . . .>
Bill WilliAms   100
$
```

`tr` is seeing `a-z` as a set of the three characters `a`, `-` and `z`.

A different way of escaping the square brackets is by using the reverse slash character, \:

```
$ tr \[a-z\] \[A-Z\] <people >u-people
$
```

We can get rid of the phone numbers in our *people* file by using the `-d` (delete) option of `tr`:

```
$ tr -d "[0-9]" <people
Maryann Clark
Sally Smith
Jane Bailey
   <etcetera . . .>
Bill Williams
$
```

In this case we only give `tr` one set of characters, the `-d` option tells `tr` to delete all characters in that set. Since the only digits we have are those in the phone numbers, `tr` has the effect of removing the phone numbers. There are still spaces at the end of the line. It would be dangerous to use this technique to remove numbers from the end of a line if the file might contain digits elsewhere.

`-s` (squeeze) option has the effect of squeezing, or collapsing, multiple consecutive occurrences of a character in the set into a single occurrence. For example, to replace multiple spaces by one space, you use the `-s` option with a space as the first string and nothing as the second string. We show an example below.

```
$ tr -s " " <people
Maryann Clark 101
Sally Smith 113
Jane Bailey 121
    <etcetera . . .>
Bill Williams 100
$
```

The -s option can also be used to get rid of blank lines in a file:

```
$ tr -s "\012" <file >newfile
$
```

'\012' is the value of the ASCII character for newline. This will only get rid of really blank lines. Lines that are apparently blank, but contain spaces and tabs, are still around.

The -c option complements (inverts) the set of characters given in the first string. For example, to delete everything except digits from the people file:

```
$ tr -cd "[0-9]"
101113121120111110112114122100$
```

Notice that even newline characters have been deleted. The System V prompt appears at the end of the output line. To preserve the newlines we need to say:

```
$ tr -cd "\012[0-9]" <people
101
113
<etcetera . . .>
100
$
```

6.10. Rearranging Files with cut and paste

Earlier in this chapter we showed how you could use grep to select specific lines from a file. Lines selected from several different files can then be joined together using cat, to form an entirely new file. If you translate this into manual terms, you can think of it as a horizontal cut and paste procedure. You would make cuts across the paper to select the lines you wanted, then you would paste these cut-outs onto a new piece of paper to get the new layout.

Sometimes you want to do the same thing in a vertical direction — you want to cut specific columns or fields out of all lines on a page, then rearrange them in a different order. System V has two commands that help you do this to files, they are called `cut` and `paste`.

Cutting Out Columns with `cut`

`cut` has two ways of specifying what you want to cut out of a file. You can say something like 'columns 3 through 5', or you can specify 'the second and sixth fields'.

Remember that in `cut` the phrase 'cut out' doesn't mean the same as 'delete'. What you get as your output is the bit you cut out — it's the same principle as cutting something out of a newspaper to keep for future reference.

In our file of people and phone numbers, the numbers are all lined up in specific columns. So we can cut out the phone numbers with this command:

```
$ cut -c17,18,19 people
101
113
<etcetera . . .>
100
$
```

The `-c` option tells `cut` that you want to cut out columns. It is immediately followed by a list of the numbers of the columns that you want. Each number in the list is separated by a comma.

If you want several consecutive columns (which is usually the case), you can give them as a range. We could have cut out the phone numbers like this:

```
$ cut -c17-19 people
101
113
<etcetera . . .>
100
$
```

In our case the columns we want are the last columns on the line, so we could leave out the end of the range and simply say:

```
$ cut -c17- people >phones
$
```

If we want to delete the phone numbers from the file, we have to cut out all the other columns:

```
$ cut -c1-16 people >names
$
```

The lines in the *names* file will have trailing spaces, since we cut out all of columns 1 through 16. In fact the names are not arranged in neat columns, they are fields separated by spaces. We would be better off telling `cut` about this.

Cutting Out Fields with `cut`

To tell `cut` to work on fields instead of columns we use the `-f` option in place of `-c`. Again the option is followed by a list of numbers — these are the numbers of the fields we want, the first field on the line being field number 1.

The names are the first two fields in the *people* file, so to cut them out we could say:

```
$ cut -f1,2 people
Maryann Clark   101
Sally Smith     113
<etcetera . . .>
Bill Williams   100
$
```

This doesn't seem to have done anything — the file is unchanged. The reason is that `cut` expects fields to be separated by tabs by default. We don't have tabs in our file, our field separator is a space.

To tell `cut` that our field separator (or delimiter) is a space we use the `-d` option. This option is immediately followed by the character that is the field separator. If this character is one of those that mean something special to the Shell, then it must be surrounded by quotes. So let's try again:

```
$ cut -d" " -f1,2 people
Maryann Clark
Sally Smith
  <etcetera . . .>
Bill Williams
$
```

We already created a file called *phones* that contains only the phone numbers. let's split up our *people* file some more:

```
$ cut -d" " -f1  people >firstnames
$ cut -d" " -f2  people >lastnames
$
```

Now we show how you can use paste to put them all back together again.

Joining Lines using paste

The paste command takes input from several files. It takes the first line form each file and combines them to form one line of the output. Then it forms the next line of output from the second line of each input file, and so on. By default, the lines from the input file are separated by tab characters in the output.

Let's see what happens when we try to recreate our *people* file from the separate files *firstnames*, *lastnames*, and *phones*:

```
$ paste firstnames lastnames phones
Maryann Clark   101
Sally   Smith   113
    <etcetera . . .>
Charlie Smith   122
Bill    Williams        100
```

As you can see, all the last names are lined up because of the tabs that paste inserted. The output mostly looks good, except for the last line. Bill's last name is longer than the others, so the following tab puts his phone number 8 spaces further over than the rest. This is one of the problems with using tabs.

If you want paste to use some character other than a tab for separating the fields, you use the -d option. For instance, to separate the fields by a space:

```
$ paste -d" " firstnames lastnames phones
Maryann Clark 101
Sally Smith 113
   <etcetera . . .>
Charlie Smith 122
Bill Williams 100
$
```

Now there is just one space between the fields on each line, so the phone numbers are not aligned as they were in our original *people* file.

You can give paste more than one field separator. It uses the first separator after the first field, the second after the second field, and so on. For example, we can change the appearance of our phone list by using paste as shown in the example on the next page.

```
$ paste -d", " lastnames firstnames phones
Clark,Maryann 101
Smith,Sally 113
Bailey,Jane 121
Austen,Jack 120
Daniels,Steve 111
Dawson,Sylvia 110
Morgan,Henry 112
Parker,Hank 114
Smith,Charlie 122
Williams,Bill 100
$
```

If you want some, but not all, of the field separators to be tabs you must use the `-d` option, but one of the field separators you give can be a tab. Here is a slightly different version of the last example:

```
$ paste -d",^I" lastnames firstnames phones
Clark,Maryann   101
Smith,Sally     113
Bailey,Jane     121
Austen,Jack     120
Daniels,Steve   111
Dawson,Sylvia   110
Morgan,Henry    112
Parker,Hank     114
Smith,Charlie   122
Williams,Bill   100
$
```

As usual, the character `^I` means you type CTRL-I, or TAB, not the separate characters `^` and `I`. This output has a fairly reasonable layout.

Using `cut` and `paste` in a Pipeline

Both `cut` and `paste` are filters, and so can be used in a pipeline. `paste` expects several filenames, so somehow you have to tell it where the Standard Input is to be used. In common with other System V commands that accept multiple filenames, you use the minus sign, `-`, to indicate that the Standard Input is to be used at that point.

To show an example of this, lets use a file that we showed in our `sort` examples. This is a file called *tennis* that holds the scores from a tennis league, and we show how it could be created from the *people* file without re-typing all the names again. First we assume you create a file (called *scores*, say) that contains all the league scores. The scores are arranged one per line, in the same order as names are listed in the *people* file. We can now create the *tennis* file by the following pipeline:

```
$ cut -d" " -f1,2 people | paste - scores >tennis
$ cat tennis
Maryann Clark   18
Sally Smith     14
     <etcetera . . .>
Charlie Smith   9
Bill Williams   2
```

The `cut` command cuts out just the names of people, the `paste` command takes that output (indicated by the -) and tacks the tennis scores on the end.

6.11. The `pr` Command Revisited

Earlier in this chapter we showed you how to use the `pr` command to produce a reasonably good-looking printout of a file. In fact, `pr` can do much more than this — it can be used to do some of the text manipulation we have been showing you using other commands.

Mostly, when you use `pr` for text manipulation, you use the `-t` option to suppress the header and trailer normally produced for hard-copy output. For instance, if you want to create a file that is like the *people* file, but with spaces at the beginning of each line, you can say

```
$ pr -t -o5 people >people.spaced
$
```

In particular, `pr` can sometimes be used in place of `paste`, with better results. But before we show some examples of this, we must introduce the multi-column features of `pr`.

Multi Column Printing with `pr`

Earlier we showed you how to produce a distribution list from the *people* file:

```
$ pr h "Distribution List" people

Apr 27 13:33 1986  Distribution List Page 1

Maryann Clark  101
Sally Smith    113
    <etcetera . . .>
Charlie Smith  122
Bill Williams  100
$
```

There are only ten names in the file, so the list is quite short.

But suppose that your list of people contains 70 or 80 names, obviously when this is printed it will take more than one page. Apart from wasting paper, this is awkward to handle. It would be better if there were only one page with several columns of names on it. To achieve this, we tell `pr` how many columns we want by preceding the number of columns with the - character which usually introduces options:

```
$ pr -3 people
Jun 30 20:56 1986  people Page 1
Maryann Clark  101    Steve Daniels  111    Hank Parker    114
Sally Smith    113    Sylvia Dawson  110    Charlie Smith  122
Jane Bailey    121    Henry Morgan   112    Bill Williams  100
Jack Austen    120
$
```

This produces three columns of names.

Another option that can be used in conjunction with multi-column printing is `-w`, which is used to adjust the total width of the printout. For instance, we can bring the columns closer together by saying:

```
$ pr -3 -w65 people
Jun 30 20:56 1986  people Page 1
Maryann Clark  101   Steve Daniels  111   Hank Parker    114
Sally Smith    113   Sylvia Dawson  110   Charlie Smith  122
Jane Bailey    121   Henry Morgan   112   Bill Williams  100
Jack Austen    120
$
```

If you make the total width too small, the various columns will overlap:

```
$ pr -3 -w40 people
Jun 30 20:56 1986  people Page 1
Maryann Clar Steve Daniel Hank Parker
Sally Smith  Sylvia Dawso Charlie Smit
Jane Bailey  Henry Morgan Bill William
Jack Austen
$
```

If you have a printer that uses wide paper, as most line printers do, you have to give the -w option to tell pr to use the full width of the paper:

```
$ pr -w132 -8 lotsofpeople | lp
request id is 214 (standard input)
$
```

In all the above examples, the lines in the original file are printed down each column. We can ask pr to print the lines of the original file across the page by using the -a option:

```
$ pr -3 -a -w65 people

Jun 30 20:56 1986  people Page 1

Maryann Clark  101   Sally Smith    113   Jane Bailey     121
Jack Austen    120   Steve Daniels  111   Sylvia Dawson   110
Henry Morgan   112   Hank Parker    114   Charlie Smith   122
Bill Williams  100
$
```

Printing Files in Columns using pr

When you give pr several files to work on it will process the files in turn, starting each file on a new page. Even if you ask for multiple column output, pr will print the first file in the number of columns you asked for, then on the next page it will print the next file in multiple columns, and so on. However, if you use the -m option, pr will merge the files and print them simultaneously, one file per column.

To give an example of this, let's say you had your lists of names and phone numbers in three separate files, as we showed for our sort examples. We can get a multiple column output like this:

```
$ pr -m -w65 adminpeople hardpeople softpeople

Jun 30 20:34 1986   Page 1

Bill Williams  100   Jane Bailey    121   Sylvia Dawson  110
Maryann Clark  101   Jack Austen    120   Sally Smith    113
                     Charlie Smith  122   Steve Daniels  111
                                          Henry Morgan   112
                                          Hank Parker    114
$
```

As you can see, the file *adminpeople* is printed in the first column, *hardpeople* in the second, and *softpeople* in the third column.

Joining Lines using pr

You can see that the -m option, used in conjunction with the -t option, gives us the capability to use pr in much the same way as we can use paste. For example, having cut the people file up into *firstnames*, *lastnames* and *phones* we can put them all back together using this pr command:

```
$ pr -m -t firstnames lastnames phones
Maryann                 Clark                   101
Sally                   Smith                   113
        <etcetera . . .>
Charlie                 Smith                   122
Bill                    Williams                100
$
```

The spacing isn't too good, but we can adjust that by using the -w option as well:

```
$ pr -m -t -w30 firstnames lastnames phones
Maryann   Clark     101
Sally     Smith     113
    <etcetera . . .>
Charlie   Smith     122
Bill      Williams  100
$
```

This output looks much better than that produced by paste.

You can also tell pr to separate the columns using a specific character, instead of just spacing things out to take up the full page width. This is done with the -s option:

```
$ pr -m -t -s, lastnames firstnames phones
Clark,Maryann,101
Smith,Sally,113
   <etcetera . . .>
Smith,Charlie,122
Williams,Bill,100
$
```

The character to be used to separate the columns must immediately follow the -s. If the character can mean something special to the Shell it must be escaped, using either quotes or a reverse slash. Unfortunately you can only give one separator to pr, all columns are separated using the same character. This output doesn't look too good.

If you use the `-s` option, but don't give a character to use as separator, the default separator is the tab character. The command:

```
$ pr -m -t -s firstnames lastnames phones
Maryann Clark   101
Sally   Smith   113
     <etcetera . . .>
Charlie Smith   122
Bill    Williams        100
$
```

gives output that is identical to that given by `paste`.

Incidentally, in all our examples we have shown the different options to `pr` each as a separate argument. But they don't have to be that way, you can run them all together as a single argument. In this case you only need one - sign to introduce the options. However, we feel that with a command line like this:

```
$ pr -3aw65l20h Distribution people >list.people
$
```

it's not easy to see what is meant,

```
$ pr -3 -a -w65 -l20 -h Distribution  people >list.people
$
```

is much easier to interpret, so that's why we used this form.

Viewing a File with pr

In chapter 3 (*Directories and Files*) we described the `pg` command, which displays a file one screen-full at a time. If it should happen that this command (or an equivalent command 'borrowed' from some other flavor of a UNIX system) is not available at your installation, don't despair — you can achieve the same thing using `pr`.

First of all, we use the `-l` option to set the page length equal to the length of your terminal screen, usually 23 lines. Then we use the `-t` option to suppress the page headers and footers that `pr` usually gives. Lastly, we use the `-p` option. So we give a command that looks like this:

```
$ pr -tl23p longfile
```

or like this:

```
$ pr -t -l23 -p longfile
```

The `-p` option tells `pr` to pause at the beginning of each page if the output is to a terminal. The terminal bell will sound, and `pr` will wait for a **RETURN** character to be typed before proceeding. So, when you type one of the commands above, there will at first be no output except a 'beep' sound. When you type **RETURN** the first 23 lines of the file will be displayed, then there will be a pause and another 'beep'. You can go on to the next screen-full by typing another **RETURN**, and so on through the file. When you have seen as much as you want you can interrupt the command with **CTRL-C**, or **BREAK**, or **DEL**.

You might want to make your page length a little shorter, say 20 or 21 lines. That way the last few lines on one screen become the first few lines of the next, thus providing some continuity of context.

You might want to create your own command for this function, using a shell procedure — we show you how in chapter 13, Using the Shell as a Programming Language.

6.12. Tracking Differences Between Files with `diff`

A fairly common state of affairs is that there are several different versions of a file around, at various stages of development. When that situation arises, it is important to be able, at any time, to get an answer to the question "How does the latest version of this file differ from the previous version?" The `diff` utility is intended to answer just that question. `diff` can display the differences between two text files. The name `diff` comes from 'differential file comparator'.

To illustrate `diff`'s usage, let us revisit our *people* file. We did various changes to that file, and we kept our original version in *people.old*:

```
$ cat people.old
Maryann Clark     101
Sally Smith       113
Jane Bailey       121
Jack Austen       120
Steve Daniels     111
Sylvia Dawson     110
Henry Morgan      112
Hank Parker       114
Charlie Smith     122
Bill Williams     100
```

The latest version, including the changes we made, looks as shown in the example on the next page.

You can see by visual inspection that there are a few changes between these two files. But using a computer utility to track the changes gives us a mechanical and more reliable indication.

```
$ cat people
Maryann Clark     101
Sally White       113
Jane Bailey       121
Jack Austen       120
Steve Daniels     111
Sylvia Dawson     110
Hank Parker       114
Charlie Smith     122
Bill Williams     100
James Walker      112
$
```

You can run the `diff` utility to tell what lines are different in the two files:

```
$ diff people.old people
2c2
< Sally Smith      113
---
> Sally White      113
7d6
< Henry Morgan     112
10a10
> James Walker     112
$
```

This tells us that there are three changes to the file.

To start with, the second line of the file has changed, but it is still line number two (indicated by `2c2`). We then see the old version of the line, preceded by <, and the new version of the line preceded by >.

The next change to the file is that line 7 of the original file has been deleted. This is indicated by the `7d6`.

The third and last change is that a new line has been added after line 10 of the original file. The new line is still line 10 in the new file, because we deleted the original line 7.

Of course, if we specify the files the other way round on the command line, the results from `diff` will look different, as we show in the next example.

When looking at `diff` output, be sure you know which way round you specified the filenames, or you could misinterpret it. Lines starting with < show lines which are in the first file, but do not appear in the second of the two files you specify. Lines starting with > show new lines that appear in the second file you specify. Lines changed between the two files show as both < and >.

```
$ diff people people.old
2c2
< Sally White     113
---
> Sally Smith     113
6a7
> Henry Morgan    112
10d10
< James Walker    112
$
```

■ *The order of filename arguments on the* `diff` *command line is important. The* `diff` *command line is like:*

```
diff  oldfile  newfile
```

Here is a short summary of the meaning of `diff`'s results. There are only three ways in which `diff` indicates changes to a file:

- `a` means that lines are added, or appended, to the first file, in order to obtain the result shown in the second file.
- `d` means that lines have been deleted from the second file.
- `c` means that lines have been changed between the first file and the second file.

`diff` finds *all* differences, so if you change the spacing on a line, or remove spaces from the end of a line, these will show up as differences:

```
$ diff oldfile newfile
4,5c4,5
< There once was a lady from Maine
< Whose name was thought to be Jane,
---
> There  once  was  a  lady  from  Maine
> Whose name was thought to be Jane,
$
```

You can see that the difference in line 4 is that there are two spaces between each word in *newfile*. It is not so obvious that there are spaces at the end of line 5 in one of the files.

Much of the time you are not really interested in a difference in spacing. You can suppress these differences with the `-b` (blanks) option. The `-b` option tells `diff` to ignore trailing space and tab characters, and differences in spacing between words:

```
$ diff -b oldfile newfile
$
```

This time there are no apparent differences between the two files, as shown by the fact that there is no output from `diff`.

The `-b` option does not ignore spaces appearing at the beginning of a line. If you use the `-b` option and a line has leading spaces in one file but not in the other file, it will still show as a difference.

There is a `-e` option to `diff`, which makes it display the differences between the files in a different way:

```
$ diff -e people.old people
10a
James Walker    112
.
7d
2c
Sally White     113
.
$
```

This format represents the editor commands we would have to give if we were using the `ed` text editor to change *people.old* to look like *people*. You will learn just what these commands do when you get to chapter 8 but here is a brief rundown: first we add a new line after the line number 10 in the old file; then we delete line 7 of the old file; lastly we change line 2 of the old file to be the new line given.

You will notice that the differences are shown starting at the end of the file and working backwards towards the beginning. This is necessary when using line numbers in the editor. The `ed` text editor numbers its lines relative to the start of the file. So if you add or delete lines at the beginning of the file, the location of the rest of the lines in the file changes. For this reason, `diff` generates its `ed` commands to start editing at the end of the file, and work towards the start of the file.

You can keep a permanent record of the differences between two files by redirecting the output from `diff` into a file:

```
$ diff -e people.old people > changes
$
```

Now, to change the old version of the file into the new version, you simply run the `ed` text editor, with the *changes* file as input:

```
$ ed - people.old < changes
$
```

This tells ed to edit the file called *people.old*, using the editing commands contained in the file called *changes*. The - option on the ed command line suppresses messages which ed usually prints when used interactively.

We end up with a file which looks just like the new file *people*:

```
$ cat people.old
Maryann Clark     101
Sally White       113
Jane Bailey       121
Jack Austen       120
Steve Daniels     111
Sylvia Dawson     110
Hank Parker       114
Charlie Smith     122
Bill Williams     100
James Walker      112
$
```

In practice, things aren't quite this easy. Before you can edit the file in this way you have to add two lines to the end of the *changes* file. One contains the letter w, which tells the editor to write away the changed file; the other says q which tells the editor to quit the editing job. These are described in more detail in chapter 8.

The burning question is: why would you want to do this? Consider the following scenario. You start off with a program (or it could be a document, but we're going to talk about a program) which initially exists as Version 0, say. Then it gets changed and becomes Version 1, then it gets changed again to be Version 2, and so on, until it's changed so many times that it's at version 10.

Now suppose you want to be able to get at any one of these versions. When a bug[1] is found in the program, it's sometimes nice to know if it was always there, or if it was introduced by some other change made during the program's history.

One way to achieve this is to keep every version of the program, so you have all these files:

prog.v0 prog.v1 prog.v2 .... prog.v9 prog.v10

Unless you have a very small program, keeping multiple versions is going to consume massive amounts of space.

---

1 a euphemism for mistake.

Also, if you want to know just what changes were introduced in each different version, you have to run `diff` on each pair:

```
$ diff  prog.v0  prog.v1  > changes1
$ diff  prog.v1  prog.v2  > changes2
            <etcetera . . .>
$ diff  prog.v8  prog.v9  > changes9
$ diff  prog.v9  prog.v10 > changes10
$
```

A different way to achieve the objective is to keep only the first version of the program, but keep all the changes files too:

prog.v0 changes1 changes2 .... changes9 changes10

Now you can see what changes were made for each new version of the program just by looking at the changes files.

To get any version of the program, you simply apply all the changes in turn. For example, to get *prog.v3*, you use this sequence of commands:

```
$ cp prog.v0 prog.v3
$ ed prog.v3 < changes1
$ ed prog.v3 < changes2
$ ed prog.v3 < changes3
$
```

In practice, the process may be a bit more awkward than shown above, but this is enough to give you the idea. This is the basic method used by the Source Code Control System (abbreviated SCCS), which we describe in chapter 14.

The size of file that `diff` can handle is limited, and so is the number of differences that it can cope with. Should you get a message indicating that `diff` is out of space, you can try using the `-h` option:

```
$ diff -h oldfile newfile > changes
$
```

This tells `diff` to do a half-hearted job, and it only works when the changed portions of the file are short and far apart. You can't use the `-e` option when you use the `-h` option.

Another solution to lack of space is to do a judicious `split` on your files, then apply `diff` to the pieces. This is not always satisfactory, because if the changed portions of the file cross the boundary of the `split` files it can be difficult to see the exact differences.

Tracking Differences with `bdiff`

System V also has a command called `bdiff` (big `diff`) which can handle larger files than `diff`. However, `bdiff` works by splitting the files and then finding the differences in the pieces, so it's better to use `diff` if you can.

Because `bdiff` works by splitting the files into chunks and comparing the chunks, it doesn't always find the smallest set of differences. This means that some of the reported differences might not, in fact, really be differences in the files. By default `bdiff` splits the files into 3500-line chunks, this figure can be changed by giving a different value on the command line.

The main reason for `bdiff`'s existence is the Source Code Control System (SCCS), in fact `bdiff` is really a SCCS command. Because of this you can use the SCCS `help` command to interpret any error messages.

Displaying Differences with `sdiff`

Another command that can be used to show differences between two text files is `sdiff`. This works the same as `diff`, but the two files are displayed side-by-side with the differences marked. To show how this works on our *people* and *people.old* files:

```
$ sdiff -w 55 people.old people
Maryann Clark    101          Maryann Clark    101
Sally Smith      113      |   Sally White      113
Jane Bailey      121          Jane Bailey      121
Jack Austen      120          Jack Austen      120
Steve Daniels    111          Steve Daniels    111
Sylvia Dawson    110          Sylvia Dawson    110
Henry Morgan     112      <
Hank Parker      114          Hank Parker      114
Charlie Smith    122          Charlie Smith    122
Bill Williams    100          Bill Williams    100
                          >   James Walker     112
$
```

As you can see, the files are shown with the first file on the command line at the left, the second file is shown at the right. Lines that are different are marked with a vertical bar, |. Lines that are in one file but not the other are marked with either a > or a <.

We used the `-w` option in the above example to make the display narrower than the default, we can do this because our file contains short lines. Normally you wouldn't be able to make the display this narrow. The default width provided by `sdiff` is 130 columns, this is just about the right size for printing on a wide line printer.

Lines that are unchanged appear on both sides of the display. The `-l` option changes the display so that unchanged lines only appear on the left side:

```
$ sdiff -w 55 -l people.old people
Maryann Clark   101
Sally Smith     113      | Sally White     113
Jane Bailey     121
Jack Austen     120
Steve Daniels   111
Sylvia Dawson   110
Henry Morgan    112      <
Hank Parker     114
Charlie Smith   122
Bill Williams   100
                         > James Walker    112
$
```

If you don't want to see the unchanged lines at all, they can be suppressed using the `-s` option:

```
$ sdiff -w 55 -s people.old people
2c2
Sally Smith     113      | Sally White     113
7d6
Henry Morgan    112      <
10a10
                         > James Walker    112
$
```

If you have a file that has been changed in two different ways, `sdiff` can also be used to merge the two different files into one file that contains both sets of changes.

Let's say that we had done our changes to the original *people* file separately. First we change Smith to White, and put the output into a file called *people1*:

```
$ sed s/Smith/White/ people >people1
$
```

Then suppose we had changed Henry to James and put the result in *people2*:

```
$ grep -v Henry people >people2
$ cat >> people2
James Walker   112
^D
$
```

The differences between the files are now:

```
$ sdiff -w 55 -s people1 people2
2c2
Sally White      113       | Sally Smith      113
7d6
Henry Morgan     112       <
9c8
Charlie White    122       | Charlie Smith    122
10a10
                           > James Walker     112
$
```

Notice that we made a change we didn't want to make, we changed Charlie's last name.

We can use `sdiff` to combine these changes into a new file by using the `-o` option, followed by the name of the new file we want to create. When `sdiff` is used in this way it works interactively — it prompts you for input with the `%` character. Here's what a session might look like:

```
$  sdiff -w 55 -s -o people.new people1 people2
2c2
Sally White      113       | Sally Smith      113
% l
7d6
Henry Morgan     112       <
% r
9c8
Charlie White    122       | Charlie Smith    122
% r
10a10
                           > James Walker     112
% r
$
```

Each time we were prompted for input we responded with either a `l` or a `r`, to say whether we wanted the left side of the display, or the right side, to go into the file being created.

The new file looks as shown on the next page. As you can see, it contains both sets of changes.

There are other responses you can give to `sdiff`'s prompt. You can say `s`, this will suppress display of unchanged lines if you didn't already say it on the calling command line. Lines are only suppressed from the display, they are copied over to the output file. The `v` response is the inverse of `s` — it displays unchanged lines.

```
$ cat people.new
Maryann Clark   101
Sally White     113
Jane Bailey     121
Jack Austen     120
Steve Daniels   111
Sylvia Dawson   110
Hank Parker     114
Charlie Smith   122
Bill Williams   100
James Walker    112
$
```

If you want a line in the output file that is unlike either of the lines on the display you can call up the line editor, `ed`, to make up the new lines. We suggest you play with this after you've learned how to use that editor.

Usually you automatically exit from `sdiff` when all the lines in the two input files have been processed. However, if you respond to the `%` prompt with a `q` you exit immediately, any remaining lines in the input files will not be copied over to the output file.

6.13. Comparing Files with `cmp`

Another utility program which can be used to find differences between two files is `cmp`, for compare. While `diff` looks for lines that are different, `cmp` just does a byte-by-byte (character-by-character for text files) comparison of the two files you specify:

```
$ cmp people.old people
people.old, people differ: char 26, line 2
$
```

As soon as `cmp` finds one byte that is different between the two files, it displays a message as shown in the example, and stops.

If you want to see all the differences in the files, you need to use the `-l` (long) option, in which case `cmp` now displays every byte that is different in the two files. For each difference, it displays the position of the byte in the file (in decimal), the octal value of the byte in the first file, and the octal value of the byte in the second file.

For text files, these values are the octal values of the characters as they are represented by the ASCII character set.

```
$ cmp -l people.old people
26 123 127
27 155 150
30 150 155
121 145 141
123 162 153
  <etcetera . . .>
192 163  40
197  60  61
198  60  62
$
```

In our example, bytes 26, 27 and 30 are different because we changed `Smith` to `White`. The fact that we deleted a line from *people.old* (the line containing `Henry`) makes all the remaining bytes in the file different, except when both files coincidentally contain the same character.

As you can see, `cmp` is not very usable for showing the differences between text files, it is more suited for program object and data files. However, it does provide a quick way to find out whether files are different or not. If the files are different, you can then use `diff` to get details of the differences.

6.14. Finding Commonality Between Files with `comm`

The `diff` and `cmp` commands answer the question "what is different about these two files?". We now discuss a command that answers the question "what is the same about these two files?".

`comm` prints lines that are common to two files. To give an example of this command, we are going to revert to the files we used in some of the `sort` examples. Instead of having everybody in the group in one *people* file, suppose you have separate files for the software development people and the hardware designers, with the administrative people appearing in both, so one of the files looks like this:

```
$ cat softpeople
Bill Williams
Maryann Clark
Sylvia Dawson
Sally Smith
Steve Daniels
Henry Morgan
Hank Parker
$
```

Then you also have a file containing only the managers:

```
$ cat managers
Bill Williams
Jack Austen
Sylvia Dawson
$
```

In this example we leave out the phone numbers, just as we did in `sort`.

Now we run the `comm` command on these two files:

```
$ comm managers softpeople
                Bill Williams
Jack Austen
        Maryann Clark
                Sylvia Dawson
        Sally Smith
        Steve Daniels
        Henry Morgan
        Hank Parker
$
```

The `comm` utility produces three columns. Unfortunately they overlap, so they aren't too easy to read.

- The first column shows lines that are in the first of the files you specified, but not in the second.
- The second column shows lines that are in the second file, but not in the first.
- The third column shows lines that appear in both files.

So, Jack Austen is a manager but not a software person. Hank, Henry, Steve *et al.*, are software people, but not managers. Sylvia and Bill are both software people and managers.

If you don't want to see all this information, some of it can be suppressed by giving `comm` an option stating which column or columns you don't want to see. To see columns 1 and 3 only, you tell `comm` to suppress column 2:

```
$ comm -2 managers softpeople
        Bill Williams
Jack Austen
        Sylvia Dawson
```

Just to confuse you, column 3 has shifted over to the left, so that it occupies the space normally taken by column 2.

To see only those lines which appear in both files, that is column 3, you need to suppress both columns 1 and 2:

```
$ comm -12 managers softpeople
Bill Williams
Sylvia Dawson
$
```

For comm to be really useful, lines in the two files being compared should be in the same order. Notice that in our example, Bill appeared before Sylvia in both files. To show what happens if lines in the files are not in the same order, let's take our original *people* file and sort it two different ways, then compare the results:

```
$ sort people > people1
$ sort +1 people > people2
$ comm people1 people2
Bill Williams   100
Charlie Smith   122
Hank Parker     114
Henry Morgan    112
                Jack Austen     120
                Jane Bailey     121
                Maryann Clark   101
Sally Smith     113
                Steve Daniels   111
                Sylvia Dawson   110
        Henry Morgan    112
        Hank Parker     114
        Sally Smith     113
        Charlie Smith   122
        Bill Williams   100
$
```

After the two sort commands, *people1* contains lines sorted by first-name order, and *people2* contains lines sorted by second-name order. The result of trying to find the common lines is hopelessly confused. First we see that Bill is in *people1*, but not *people2*. But then the last line of the results show that Bill is in *people2*, but not in *people1*. In fact comm only recognizes five lines as being common to the two files. The moral is: make sure that lines in your files are in the same order, before you try to use comm.

6.15. Summary

We have covered a lot in this chapter. The text processing utilities are some of the things which make UNIX System V such a powerful tool.

You should use grep and its variations to study and thoroughly understand the ideas of regular expressions, since many of System V utilities revolve around their use.

Try playing with options to `pr` so that you can get multiple columns of stuff on a terminal screen, with no headers, trailers, or any extraneous data.

Experiment with `sort`, to determine the kinds of things you can do with it. Although there is a spelling checker available on System V, you can construct your own using `tr`, `sort`, `uniq`, and `comm`, in a pipeline. See if you can do this, or find out how to do it.

The next two chapters describe text editors. The concepts of regular expressions are deeply entwined in the capabilities of those editors, so it is essential that you are comfortable with regular expressions and their use.

7 The Visual Text Editor `vi`

An *editor* is a utility program that you use to make modifications to the contents of a file. When we talk about an editor, we usually mean a *text* editor. That is, an editor designed to deal with files containing strings of characters in a particular character set. Additionally, an editor usually means an *interactive* utility, where you can view what you have already, before deciding to make changes. There are exceptions to the interactive editors, such as the `sed` stream editor, discussed in the chapter 6.

Utilities such as `grep`, `tr`, `awk` and others, have two characteristics which differentiate them from text editors. First, they do not change the original file in any way. They simply modify the data contained in the file, on its way from one place (the original file) to another (another file, the line-printer, or the terminal screen). Second, those commands select and alter things on a global basis. That means that the things to be selected or altered must conform to regular patterns.

But there are times when you want to make selective and detailed changes to specific lines, or parts of lines, and also make those changes permanent. With a text editor you can interactively browse through a file, inspecting things and deciding if you want to change them. When you have finished the process of inspection and modification, you can instruct the text editor to make the changes permanent. Again, the `sed` stream editor is an exception, since it is more often used for making transient changes.

In general, editors fall into two categories, namely *line* editors, and *screen* editors. By a *line* editor, we mean one in which the basic unit for change is a line (a string of characters terminated by a newline character). You can give commands to the editor to perform various operations on the lines: lines can be printed (displayed); lines can be changed; new lines can be inserted, existing lines can be deleted; lines can be moved or copied to a different place within the file; substitutions of character strings can be made within a line or group of lines. Two line editors that are available on System V are discussed in the next chapter.

In this chapter we describe `vi` the screen editor that runs on System V. A *screen* editor is one where a portion of the file is displayed on the terminal screen, and the cursor can be moved around the screen to indicate where you want to make changes. You can select which part of the file you want to have displayed. Screen editors are also called *display* editors, or *visual* editors.

Most editors, both line editors and screen editors, have one thing in common, namely that they do not change the file *in situ.* The file is first copied into a temporary scratch-pad area, called a 'buffer', and changes are made in that buffer. When the changes are complete (or at some convenient point in the editing session), the file must be 'saved' (or 'written') back onto the original file. Any changes you have made during the editing session do not appear in the original file until you have done this save operation.

In some ways this is a good thing. If you really make a mess of things, as you are apt to do when you're just learning, you can easily get back to square one.

However, there is a disadvantage, in that should your system 'crash' before you have saved your file, you have lost all your changes. So if you have a fragile system, we recommend that you save your file often during a heavy editing session. It's a good idea even if your system seems fairly robust — disease can strike rapidly at times. This is particularly important when using the editor to create a new file, and is a reason for using `cat` (as we showed earlier) to create a new file by entering text directly, without an editor. If the system goes down while you're using `cat` you still have all lines that you have typed so far[1].

Another possible disadvantage to the use of an editor which uses a buffer, is that the buffer might not be big enough to hold the file you wish to modify. In general the buffer size can accommodate most files, but there could be occasions when you want to modify a very large file, one that contains more text than the buffer can hold. If this is the case you must `split` the file into pieces. We described the `split` command in chapter 3. Having `split` the file, you can then edit the pieces one at a time using the editor of your choice, then use `cat` to put them back together again.

7.1. The `vi` Text Editor

The screen editor available on System V is called `vi` (visual). What happens is that a portion of the file you wish to modify is displayed on your terminal screen. This is often termed a window on the file[2]. Within that window you can move the cursor around to control where changes are to be made, and then you can make changes by replacing text, adding text or deleting text. The portion of the file displayed in the window can be changed, so you have access to the whole file.

The behavior of the different screen editors varies widely in the way in which they handle text that you just type then and there. Some screen editors (such as the RAND editor) replace what is already on the screen with what you type, and you have to tell them something special when you want to insert new text. Other screen editors (such as EMACS) insert new text by default, and you have to do something

---

[1] Provided that you use the `-u` option to `cat`, described in chapter 4 — Processes and Standard Files.

[2] In fact, `vi` uses an edit buffer, so what you see is actually a window on the buffer. But in this chapter we use the more common term 'window on the file'.

different to change or replace text. Unlike these other editors, `vi` has no default mode. Everything you want to change, insert, replace, or delete, you have to tell `vi` explicitly what to do.

One of the things that makes `vi` a very powerful editor is the fact that you have access to the `ex` line editor's commands too. To fully use the power of the editor, the user is advised to get familiar with `ex` (described in the next chapter), particularly with the global commands such as substitution.

`vi` has a wide range of commands for positioning the cursor at the spot you want changed — too many to learn them all easily. We introduce the most generally useful ones first. You should practice using these until you are thoroughly familiar with them, before advancing to the more specialized ones.

Practice is the key to using a display editor. You must become so familiar with the commands that you don't have to think about them: they just flow out of your fingertips.

It is difficult to learn how to use a display editor by reading a book, you really need to get on a terminal and *use* the editor. It is also difficult to give examples of a screen oriented editor on paper, but we will do so as far as possible.

We don't cover all the features of `vi` in this chapter. As is our wont, we only show you how to perform the more common useful functions. More details of using `vi` can be found in the paper *An Introduction to Display Editing with Vi* by William Joy. There is also a *Ex/Vi Quick Reference* card, which is useful for the experienced user who needs a memory-jogger.

7.2. Calling up vi

In common with most screen editors, `vi` needs to know the type of terminal you are using in order to work properly. In general you don't have to worry too much about this, your System Administrator should have set things up so that `vi` knows your terminal type. However you should be aware that, if the editor does unexpected things, one possibility is that it thinks you have a terminal of a different type from the one you are actually using.

The editor is called up by the `vi` command:

```
$ vi myfile
```

After you have typed this command, your file is read into the edit buffer, the terminal screen is cleared, the window is set at the first lines of the buffer, and the cursor is initially set at the first character of the first line in the window.

You can specify multiple file names on the command line:

```
$ vi thisfile thatfile theotherfile
```

The first file is read into the edit buffer, and the first lines of it are displayed in the window.

The size of the window is dependent on two things, namely the speed of your terminal, and the setting of the window option. For slow speeds (600 baud or less) the default window is 8 lines; for medium speed (1200 baud) it is 16 lines; for higher speeds the window is the full screen size, less one line (this usually works out to be 23 lines).

The name of the file, and its length in characters and lines, is shown on the last (bottom) line of the screen.

The default window size can be changed by using the set command to set the required window size, for example:

```
: set window=12
```

Editor options, and how to change them using the set editor command, are described in more detail later in this chapter.

In all the examples we give, we assume a window of 8 lines, although usually you would use the full screenfull. Use of an 8-line window is only a device to make our examples fairly short, and in fact we show them as though the screen itself were only 9 lines long — an 8 line window on a standard 24 line screen would not behave exactly like we've shown. So, if we have an 8-line window and we call up vi:

```
$ vi  omarkhayyam
```

what we see is:

```
How long, how long, in infinite Pursuit
    Of This and That endeavour and dispute?
    Better be merry with the fruitful Grape
    Than sadden after none, or bitter, fruit.

You know, my Friends, how long since in my House
    For a new Marriage I did make Carouse:
    Divorced old barren Reason from my Bed,
"omarkhayyam" 19 lines, 715 characters
```

The bottom line of the screen shows statistics about the file we are editing, the first eight lines of the file are shown in the window. The cursor is sitting at the very first character in the file.

The width of the window is always the full width of the screen (80 columns). If you have a file with lines that are longer than 80 characters, they can still be edited. The characters over 80 look as though they were another line because the display wraps round. This can be a little confusing, but isn't as bad as it sounds. It is relatively easy to tell when you have a wrapped line by the way the cursor moves.

The file statistics at the bottom of the screen disappear when the window on the file is moved. Some vi commands also use this space, and the file statistics go away if one of these commands is typed.

Another way of invoking vi is with the + flag:

```
$ vi + omarkhayyam
```

When you call vi this way, the last part of the file is displayed on the screen, and the cursor is positioned at the beginning of the last line.

A variation of this is:

```
$ vi +10 omarkhayyam
```

which displays the initial window such that line 10 (or whatever number you specify) is in the middle of the screen, and the cursor is positioned at the beginning of that line.

When you call up vi with more than one file name, you first get a '*n* files to edit' message (useful if you have said something like vi *.c), then the first of the *n* files is read into the buffer, with the same effect as if it were the only file.

Recovery from system Crashes

If the system should crash, or if you accidentally get disconnected, while you are in the middle of editing a file, there is the possibility of recovering form this, even if you hadn't saved your file.

When you next log in, you will have mail from the super-user 'root' which says something like:

```
A copy of an editor buffer of your file "omarkhayyam"
was saved when the system went down.
This buffer can be retrieved using the "recover" command to the editor.
An easy way to do this is to give the command "vi -r omarkhayyam".
```

As you can see from the mail, this tells you to use the -r option to the command:

```
$ vi -r omarkhayyam
```

once you have positioned yourself in the same working directory as you were before the crash.

Even if you don't get mail, it is worth trying the recovery procedure.

7.3. Getting out of `vi`

As usual, we're putting this information first, because getting out of the editor, especially when you have made many mistakes and want to start over, is very important.

There are many different ways of getting out of `vi`. Which one you use depends, in part, on whether you want to save the changes you have already made.

If you want to save your changes, you can exit the editor by typing any of the following:

```
:wq<CR>
```

or

```
:x<CR>
```

or

```
ZZ
```

The notation <CR> indicates that you have to press the key marked **RETURN**. You have to do it in the first two cases (the reason for this will become clear in the next paragraph), but not in the third.

If you do not want to save your changes, you exit the editor by typing:

```
:q!<CR>
```

Again, the <CR> indicates that you have to press the key marked **RETURN**.

7.4. Command Structure

We said earlier that `vi` has no default mode, you have to give it specific commands. Just about every key on the keyboard is some command to `vi`. So are combinations of the **SHIFT** key and the other keys, and combinations of the **CONTROL** key and the other keys. This is particularly important in the case of the **SHIFT** key. In the following paragraphs, when we talk about the **W** command, we really do mean uppercase '**W**'. Lowercase '**w**' is another command, and does something different.

`vi` commands are mnemonic for the most part. There are some exceptions, and in some cases the mnemonic is a little strained.

There are some keys for which there is no function. If you type one of these, `vi` will 'beep' at you; that is, it will ring the terminal bell. The 'beep' is not restricted to this error, it is `vi`'s general signal that you are doing something wrong, like trying to move the cursor further than it can go.

The general structure of most `vi` commands is:

[*count*] *operator* [*count*] *object*

The distinction between operators and objects is sometimes blurred, because an object can also be a command. For example, the command **w** moves the cursor forward one word of text, while the command **dw** deletes the next word of text. The **w** acts as the operator in the first case, and as the object in the second.

The optional count can appear in either place in the command, either before the operator, or after the operator and before the object. For instance, to delete three words we could say either **3dw** or **d3w**.

■ *You can also place the count in both places, before the operator **and** before the object. If you place the count in both places, the effect is multiplicative. In other words, the command* **3d3w** *deletes nine words.*

With a few exceptions, `vi` commands are not echoed to the screen, but are simply obeyed. You see the result of them by either a movement of the cursor, or a change in the text that appears on the screen.

A very important key is the escape key. On most terminals it is labelled **ESC**, but on some it is marked **ALT**. For any commands which require text to be entered, you tell `vi` when you have finished entering text by pressing the **ESC** (or **ALT**) key. Also, if you start to type a `vi` command, and then change your mind before you finish, you cancel the partial command by pressing **ESC**. There is no command associated with the **ESC** key, so it is the safest key to press. If you are not sure what state you are in, press **ESC** until `vi` beeps. You then know that `vi` is listening for your commands. The combination **CTRL-[** is the equivalent of **ESC**, and performs the same function. However, it is a lot easier to use the **ESC** key.

7.5. Accessing ex Commands

One command that deserves special attention right now is the colon : character. When you type : the character is echoed at the beginning of the bottom line of the screen. Whatever you now type, up to **RETURN**, is interpreted as a command to the `ex` line editor, and is acted upon accordingly. The command you type is echoed on the last line of the screen as you type it. This is how `vi` has access to all of `ex`'s powerful features, like global substitution. It is also the way in which many `vi` features are implemented. For example, to save your file you say:

```
:w<CR>
```

the '`w`' in this case is the `ex` write operation, and has no connection with `vi`'s **w** operator which moves the cursor a word. Similarly, to exit from `vi` you can say:

```
:q<CR>
```

which is the same as giving the quit command in `ex`.

The line editor `ex` and its commands are described in detail in the next chapter. In this chapter we will only mention those cases where using an `ex` command affects the way `vi` works.

7.6. Basic Cursor Movements

You can move the position of the cursor in a variety of different ways:

- It can be moved left and right along the screen a character at a time, a word at a time, or directly to the beginning or end of a line.
- It can be moved up and down the screen.
- You can specify a line number to go to, or a string to search for. Sometimes this may change the window on the file.

In this section we only describe the most basic cursor movements. You should practice these for a while. When you find your impatience growing at the slowness of them, it is time to move on to more sophisticated commands.

The simplest way to position the cursor is a character at a time. How you do this depends somewhat on the type of terminal you are using. Some terminals have four keys marked with arrows, usually on the right with a numeric keypad, sometimes elsewhere. These four 'arrow' keys should do this:

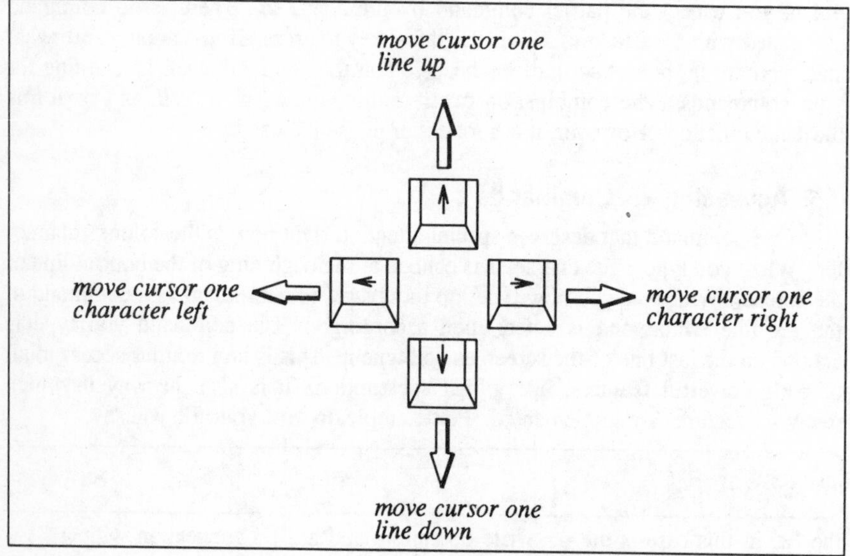

If you *don't* have keys with arrows on them, the four keys `h`, `j`, `k`, and `l` should be capable of being used instead, as we show in the illustration on page 207.

We suggest you mark arrows on these keys.

Investigate your terminal and find out which keys you use to perform these cursor moving functions before you proceed any further. They are the most basic commands in the editor, and you won't become proficient until you are thoroughly familiar with them.

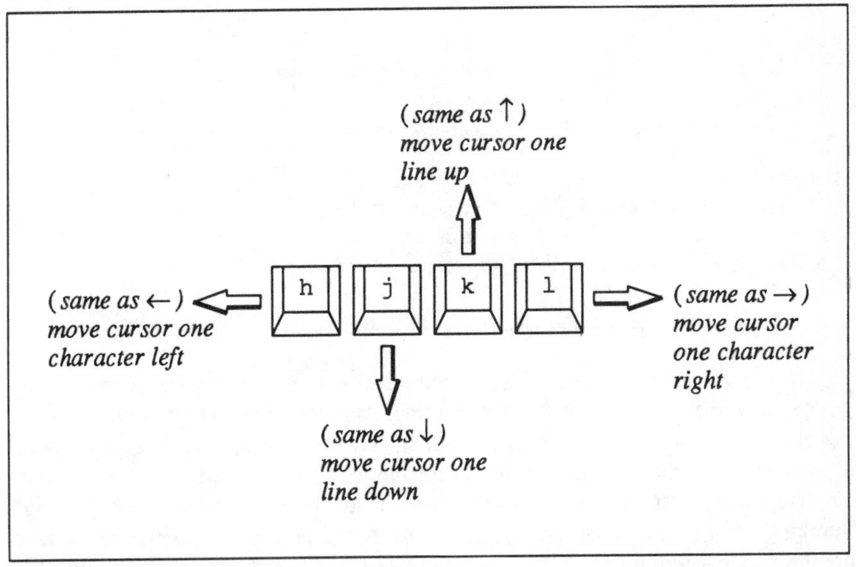

Each time you press one of these four keys, the cursor moves one unit in the required direction. You can move several lines or characters by pressing the key repeatedly. Most terminals have an automatic repeat function, so that if you hold a key down it will repeat until you let go. Other terminals have a key marked **REPEAT**, if you hold this key down while typing some other character, that character is repeated until you let go. These features can be used when you have long distances to move the cursor, but be careful if you are working at a low baud rate — it's very easy to go too far.

The cursor positioning commands can be given a preceding count, the cursor will move the specified number of characters or lines. For instance, **8**→ moves the cursor eight characters to the right; **4**↑ moves it up four lines.

When you are moving the cursor in a horizontal direction, it will not go beyond the end of the line when you're moving it to the right, or beyond the beginning of line when you are moving it to the left. This is how you can tell that you have a long line that is wrapped round the display, the cursor keeps moving beyond the apparent end of line.

When you are moving the cursor vertically up or down, the horizontal position of the cursor is unchanged, as far as possible. If the cursor is towards the end of a line, and you move it down to a shorter line, then the cursor is placed at the end of that shorter line. However it will revert to its original horizontal position on any line that is long enough. The following diagram illustrates the position of the cursor on three successive ↓ movements.

```
How long, how long, in infinite Pursuit
    Of This and That endeavour and dispute?
    Better be merry with the fruitful Grape
    Than sadden after none, or bitter, fruit.
█
You know, my Friends, how long since in█my House
    For a new Marriage I did make Carouse:
    Divorced old barren Reason from my Bed,
"omarkhayyam" 19 lines, 715 characters
```

If you are on the last line of the window and you try to move the cursor down, the window will move down the file one line. An alternative way of saying this is that the lines on the screen scroll up one line. That is, the top line disappears from the display, and the next line in the buffer appears at the bottom of the display. You cannot go past the end of the file, there is no wrap around to the beginning. Similarly, if you are on the top line of the window and you try to move the cursor up, the window will move up the file 5 lines (the lines on the screen scroll down 5 lines). Again, there is no wrap around from beginning to end of file, you cannot move past the first line of the file.

When you do something that changes the window on the file, the bottom line of the screen, which initially shows the filename and length, goes blank. Some of the `vi` commands use this space, and we'll describe these in the next few paragraphs.

There are a few other basic cursor positioning keys. For horizontal motions along the lines, two useful functions are:

`^`	move cursor to beginning of line
`$`	move cursor to end of line

For those who are used to using regular expressions, these should be easy to remember. When moving the cursor vertically up and down the screen,

RETURN	move to beginning of next line
`-`	move to beginning of previous line

The key combination **CTRL-M** is the equivalent of **RETURN**, and has the same effect.

'Beginning of line' is not always the real beginning of line. Leading spaces and tabs are ignored, so the cursor moves to the first non-blank character. Most of the time this is where you really want to be; but if it isn't, you can get to the very first character on the line by using ←. Alternatively, the **0** (that's the figure zero) command puts the cursor on the very first character of the line.

Three more basic cursor movements are:

`H` home — move the cursor to the first character on the first line of the screen.

`M` middle — move the cursor to the first character on the middle line of the screen.

`L` last — move the cursor to the first character on the last line of the screen.

The **H** command homes the cursor onto the top line of the screen, **M** moves the cursor to the middle line of the screen, and **L** moves it to the last line of the screen. Note that these commands must be uppercase letters. All three commands position the cursor at the 'beginning of line' (that is, at the first non blank character). **H** and **L** take preceding counts — **3H** moves to the 3rd line on the screen, **2L** moves to the second line from the bottom. If you have a key marked **HOME** on your terminal, this will probably achieve the same as the **H** command.

Once you know these basic cursor positioning commands, you can use `vi` to change existing files. It is probably a good idea at this stage to move on to learning how to do simple text changes, and to use the editor for a while, before progressing to the other types of cursor movements.

7.7. Changing the Window

So far, all the cursor movements we have shown you have been within the current window on the file, or have adjusted it by only one line. There are commands which affect the window without changing the position of the cursor on the line.

The **z** command redraws the screen with the current line positioned at the top, or in the middle, or at the bottom of the screen:

z<CR>	current line is at the top of the screen
`z.`	current line is in the middle
`z-`	current line is at the bottom

So, if our screen initially looked like this:

```
How long, how long, in infinite Pursuit
    Of This and That endeavour and dispute?
    Better be merry with the fruitful Grape
    Than sadden after none, or bitter, fruit.

You know, my Friends, how long since in my House
    For a new Marriage I did make Carouse:
    Divorced old barren Reason from my Bed,
"omarkhayyam" 19 lines, 715 characters
```

and we typed the command **z** the screen would be changed to look like:

```
    Than sadden after none, or bitter, fruit.

You know, my Friends, how long since in my House
    For a new Marriage I did make Carouse:
    Divorced old barren Reason from my Bed,
    And took the Daughter of the Vine to Spouse.

For 'Is' and 'Is-not' though with Rule and Line,
```

Two control characters scroll the screen by one line at a time:

CTRL-E scroll up one line. Show one more line at the end of the screen.

CTRL-Y scroll down one line. Show one more line at the top of the screen.

Both CTRL-E and CTRL-Y leave the cursor on the same line.

There are other commands which change the window on the file, they also change the cursor position with respect to the line (it stays constant with respect to the window):

CTRL-D scroll down half window

CTRL-U scroll up half window

If you type CTRL-D, the top half of the text in your window moves off the screen, the bottom half moves into the top half, and the next lines in the buffer are displayed in the bottom half. The cursor stays in the same position on the screen. So if we typed a CTRL-D command from the position shown in the previous example, the result would be:

```
    Divorced old barren Reason from my Bed,
    And took the Daughter of the Vine to Spouse.

For 'Is' and 'Is-not' though with Rule and Line,
    And "Up-and-Down" without, I could define,
    I yet in all I cared to know,
    Was never deep in anything but - Wine.
```

In other words, the window has moved down the file.

CTRL-U has the same effect in the reverse direction — it moves the window up the file.

The window can be also be moved up and down the file with:

`CTRL-F`	move the window forward through the file
`CTRL-B`	move the window backward through the file

If you type CTRL-F the whole window moves forward (down) in the file, apart from 2 lines retained for continuity. So the last two lines of the screen become the first two lines. The cursor is placed at the beginning of the first line on the new screen display. CTRL-B does the same thing in the reverse direction, the two top lines become the bottom lines and the cursor is placed on the bottom line of the screen.

7.8. The `undo` and `.` Commands

We have now shown you some of the ways to get the cursor to the position in the file where you want to make changes. But we haven't yet shown you how to make any changes. Before we do that, we're going to tell you about the 'undo' commands, so that if you make any mistakes while doing the changes, you can take corrective action.

There are two 'undo' commands, namely **u** and **U**. The lowercase **u** simply undoes the last change you made. If you have moved the cursor away from the position at which you did the change, the cursor is repositioned to its original place after the change has been undone. Similarly, if the window has been moved since you did the change, it is moved back to its original display. The **u** command undoes any change to the edit buffer, even if that change affected many lines.

Another **u** command *does not* undo the change before the last one: it undoes the original 'undo' command, thus applying the change all over again.

The uppercase **U** command is different: it can undo several changes, but only those made on the same line. **U** undoes all the changes you have made to the current line, that is, the line the cursor is currently sitting on. If you move the cursor away from that line, **U** doesn't do anything. **U** will not undo itself, so typing a second **U** has no effect.

In general, **u** is more useful than **U**. However, there are cases where you need **U**, and we show an example of the different actions of the two in the next paragraph. Beware of using **u** and **U** in succession, the one will not undo the effects of the other.

Another special command is **.** the period character, called 'dot'. While **u** says 'undo that which I just did', **.** says 'do it again'. Regardless of the change you made, whether it changed a word, added a new sentence, or deleted two lines, if you change the position of the cursor and say **.** the same change will be done at the new position. Again, we show some examples in the next paragraph.

7.9. Simple Text Additions, Changes, and Deletions

In this paragraph, we talk about making changes at a character level. We introduce commands for deleting characters, changing characters, and adding new text. Since these commands are often used to alter only a single line, most of the examples given only show one line of text. Your imagination will have to supply the rest of the window.

Deleting Text with x and X

The simplest command to use is the 'delete character' command **x**. This command is sometimes called 'x-out' or 'gobble'. If you have a line, with the cursor positioned like this:

```
Use not vain repetition, as the heathen do.
```

and you 'gobble' a character, the result is:

```
Use not ain repetition, as the heathen do.
```

If you want to gobble five characters, you can do it in two different ways. You can either repeat the **x** five times (so you say **xxxxx**), or you give the command a leading count and say **5x**. In either case, the result is the same (assuming you started with the cursor placed on the 'v' of 'vain' as in the last example):

```
Use not repetition, as the heathen do.
```

However, if you change your mind, and want the characters replaced, the command you gave in the first place matters a lot. If you gave the **5x** command, you can get them all back with an undo command of **u**. However, if you said **xxxxx** the **u** command will undo only the last **x** command:

```
Use not  repetition, as the heathen do.
```

To restore the line to its original state, you have to use **U**.

The difference between **xxxxx** and **5x** is also important if you use **.** to repeat changes. If you said **xxxxx** to start with, typing **.** gives you:

```
Use not epetition, as the heathen do.
```

that is, one more character has been deleted. But, if you initially said **5x** and now say **.** the result is:

```
Use not ition, as the heathen do.
```

another 5 characters have been deleted.

The **x** command will not gobble characters beyond the end of a line. Normally, after a character has been deleted, the cursor is left sitting on top of the character after (that is, to the right of) the deleted character, this is illustrated by the examples above. However if you use **x** to gobble the last character on a line:

```
Use not vain repetition, as the heathen do.
```

the cursor is left sitting on the new last character on the line:

```
Use not vain repetition, as the heathen do
```

So another **x** command would gobble that one:

```
Use not vain repetition, as the heathen d
```

This has the effect of making **x** gobble characters backward along the line, rather than forward in its usual fashion. If you use repeated **x**'s (either with the **REPEAT** key, or with the automatic repeat feature of your terminal) be careful, because it's very easy to gobble up an entire line without meaning to. However, things are not too bad — **x** will not go past the beginning of the line, and the entire line can be restored using **U**.

Another command which deletes characters is **X** (uppercase 'X'). This is similar to the lowercase **x** command that we have been discussing. Instead of deleting the character under the cursor (and moving the cursor to the right), it deletes the character to the left of the cursor. The cursor is left sitting over the same character. It can therefore be considered the reverse of **x**, deleting characters backward along the line instead of forward. **X** can also be given a preceding count, for example **3X** deletes three characters to the left of the cursor. The 'reverse gobble' command **X** will not go further back than the beginning of the line, neither will it reverse direction like **x** does.

Replacing Characters with r and R

The command to replace (change) a single character is **r**. You first position the cursor on top of the character you want to replace, then you type **r** followed by the character you want at that position. So if you started out with the cursor positioned:

```
Use not vain repetition, as the heathen do.
```

and typed the command **rV**, the result would be:

```
Use not Vain repetition, as the heathen do.
```

The cursor remains over the same character, so if you want to replace it by something else again, all you have to do is type another **r** command.

The character you put in place of the one under the cursor can be a newline character. So if you want to split a line, you can first position the cursor:

```
Use not vain repetition, as the heathen do.
```

then type **r** followed by the **RETURN** key. The result is:

```
Use not vain repetition,
as the heathen do.
```

The **r** command can be given a preceding count. For example, if we started with our cursor on the 'v' of 'vain', and typed **4r**V, the result would be:

```
Use not VVVV repetition, as the heathen do.
```

This is not a very useful feature, except under some specialized circumstances.

More useful is a variation of the **r** command: the uppercase **R** replaces characters until you tell it to stop. You tell it to stop by pressing the **ESC** (escape — labelled **ALT** on some terminals) key. So if you started with the cursor:

```
Use not vain repetition, as the heathen do.
```

and typed '**R**You use <ESC>', the result would be:

```
You use vain repetition, as the heathen do.
```

The cursor is left sitting on top of the last character which was replaced. We have just used **R** to change two words. We were lucky, in that the total length of the new words we wanted was the same as the total length of the words we were replacing. A better way of changing words is described in the next section. The **R** command is useful when you have a fixed format, where you want to preserve column alignment for example.

Another useful command is ~, the tilde character. This command has the effect of changing the case of the letter under the cursor. For example, if the character under the cursor is 'V', the ~ command will change it to 'v', and will move the cursor to the right one position. If the character under the cursor is 'a', then ~ changes it to 'A' and moves the cursor one character to the right. The command does not take a preceding count, but because the cursor is moved one place to the right after the command is executed, it is easy to change a whole word to upper or lower case by giving repeated ~'s.

Entering new text with a, i, and s

There are two basic commands that can be used to enter new text into a file, They are **a**, which appends text after the current cursor position, and **i** which inserts text before the current cursor position. The **a** command is the equivalent of →**i**: when you give the command, the first thing that happens is that the cursor moves one place to the right, then text gets inserted before it.

When you give either of these commands, any following text you type gets put in the file. To stop text entry you press the ESC key. So, for example, if you had a line:

```
The good, and the ugly
```

with the cursor positioned on the ',' as shown, if you type '**a** and the bad<ESC>', the result is:

```
The good, and the bad and the ugly
```

Whereas, if you start from the same position and type '**i** and the bad<ESC>', what you get is:

```
The good and the bad, and the ugly
```

If you are using what is called a dumb terminal, when you type in the additional text, it might look as if you are over-typing the existing text. However, as soon as you press ESC, it all gets straightened out.

What you see when you are inserting new text on a dumb terminal depends on an option called `redraw`. If this option is set, then as you type in new text, the rest of the line gets shuffled along to the right, and you can see exactly where you are. If the redraw option is not set, the text you insert gets displayed on top of the original display, and it looks like you are overwriting it. So when we did the insert in the previous example, just before we pressed ESC, the text would look like this:

```
The good and the badly
```

but as soon as we typed ESC, the line would show in its final form. The redraw option makes `vi` do a lot of work, and slows down the editor quite a bit. For this reason, the default value of the option is `noredraw`. We tell you how to alter the setting of this option in the next section.

If you make a mistake while entering new text, you can backspace to correct it in the usual way, by typing CTRL-H (assuming that you have made this your erase character). Another correction feature, only usable in the editor, is CTRL-W. This backspaces over and erases a whole word, so you can correct it. The erased characters don't disappear from the screen at the time you backspace, but your corrections over-type them. This feature is independent of the `redraw` option.

Both the **a** and **i** commands can take a preceding count. In this case, whatever gets typed between the command and **ESC** is entered into the text the specified number of times.

So if we take the result of the last example, and place the cursor at the beginning of 'bad':

```
The good and the bad, and the ugly
```

If we then type the command '**2i**`very <ESC>`', the result is:

```
The good and the very very bad, and the ugly
```

This does not appear to be a very useful feature, but it makes for a certain amount of consistency in the editor commands.

Another command which can be used to enter new text is **s**. There are two ways of looking at this command. In the `vi` documents the **s** command is described with the **r** and **R** commands. The '**s**' stands for substitute — it replaces a single character with lots of characters until you type **ESC**. Another, but less mnemonic, way of describing it, is as a 'gobble' followed by an insert. Typing '**s***text*' has the same effect as typing '**xi***text*'. So if we start with our original line:

```
The good, and the ugly
```

with the cursor over the ',' as usual, and type '**s** `and the bad<ESC>`', the result is:

```
The good and the bad and the ugly
```

The comma has been deleted and the new text inserted in its place. Or, if you prefer, the text 'and the bad' has been substituted for the comma.

All the commands used for text entry consider the newline character as part of the text being entered. So you can split a line simply by typing **RETURN** at the appropriate point. If we start, as usual with:

```
The good, and the ugly
```

and type '**a**`<CR>and the bad,<CR><ESC>`' we end up with three lines:

```
The good,
and the bad,
and the ugly
```

If you want to insert completely new lines of text, all you have to do is position the cursor to the end of the line they have to go after, give the **a** command, then type RETURN as the first character of the new text you want to put in.

There are two other simple commands for entering additional text:

I insert text at the beginning of the line

A append text at the end of the line

Regardless of where the cursor is positioned on a line, the **I** command inserts text at the beginning of that line. It is as if you had typed **^i** (we don't mean CTRL-I — we mean the two characters '`^`' and '`i`'). Similarly, **A** has the same effect as typing **$a** — text is added at the end of the line, regardless of the cursor position.

New lines of text can be inserted by using the **A** command and making the first character you enter a RETURN. The picture on the next page contains a summary of the append and insert commands.

There are also two other commands that can be used to add new lines of text. These are the 'open lines' commands, **o** and **O**. When you give the **o** command, regardless of the position of the cursor on the line, a blank line is opened up following the current line, and the cursor is placed at the beginning of the new line. Anything you type from now on, until you type ESC, becomes the new line or lines.

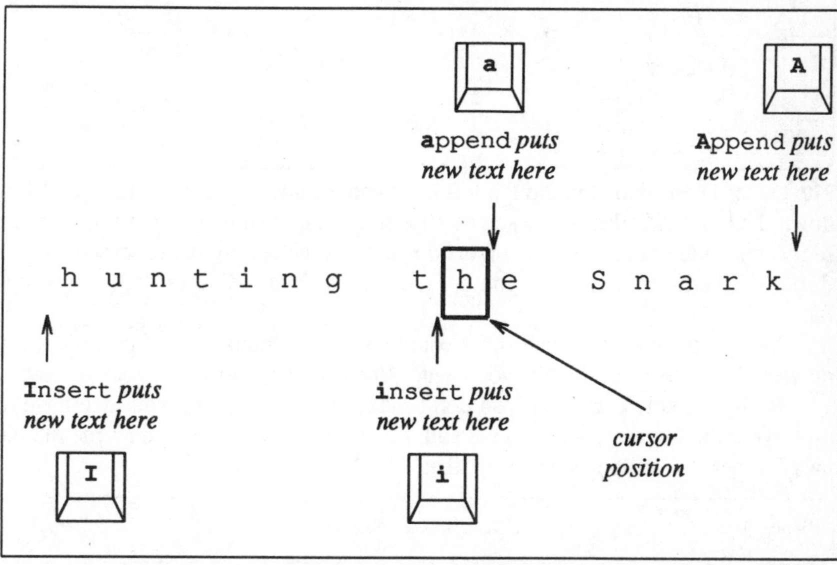

When you use o or O, you don't have to enter any text; if all you want is a blank line, you can type **ESC** immediately following the **o**. It is a fairly simple process to make a file double spaced. Simply place the cursor at the beginning of the file and type o<ESC> then type a sequence of repeated '<CR>.' to apply the same change to the rest of the file. If the file is a long one, this method is not recommended. It is better to use : to access ex's global command to add the blank lines.

The **O** command is similar to the **o** command, except that it opens a line above the current one, instead of below.

7.10. Creating a New File

You can now see that it is quite a simple matter to create a new file. You simply call up vi with the name of the file you want to create:

```
$ vi somejunk
```

The screen goes almost completely blank:

```
~
~
~
~
~
~
~
~
~
~
~
"somejunk" [New File]
```

The cursor is positioned in the top left hand corner; there are a row of ~ characters down the left hand edge of the screen. These indicate that there are no lines in the file corresponding to these lines on the display. At the bottom of the screen there is displayed the name of the file you are creating, and an indication that it is a new file.

You give the **a** command (or it could be the **i** command — it doesn't really matter), then type in all the text you want. When you have finished, you type **ESC**.

In the unlikely event that you don't make any mistakes, all you then have to do is write the file away and quit the editor by typing :wq. When you write the file away, a message looking something like:

```
"somejunk" 50 lines, 3172 characters
```

appears at the bottom of the screen. After you have quit the editor, you see System

V prompt again.

If you make mistakes while entering text, you can correct them at any time. Remember to type **ESC** to stop the current text addition, before moving the cursor to the place where the correction is needed. When you have made the corrections, to continue adding more text you simply put the cursor at the end of your previous text, type another **a** command, and repeat the whole process. When all is to your satisfaction, write the file away and quit the editor as we described above. It is a good idea to save the file periodically with the `:w` command — you have less to recover if the system crashes when you are creating a new file, or even editing an old one.

If you want to enter a control character in the file (for example, you might want to put **CTRL-L**, which is the form feed character, at strategic places) you have to escape it by preceding it by the `vi` escape character **CTRL-V**. In other words, to get **CTRL-L** into the file you have to type **CTRL-V** first, then immediately follow it by **CTRL-L**. Control characters in the file are displayed by the notation `^L`, for example. They look like two characters, but you can tell that they are only one because the cursor moves over them as one unit, never coming to rest on the `^`.

7.11. Setting Editor Options

At this point let's take time out to discuss `vi` options, which we have briefly mentioned a couple of times. Options can be set or unset to affect the overall operation of the editor. The command that is used to change the options is an `ex` command, so to use it from `vi` you first give the colon character `:`, then the `set` command.

Each option usually has an abbreviation which is used with the `set` command. For instance, the `autoindent` option, which requests automatic indentation of lines during text entry, is abbreviated to `ai`. To set it you use the command:

```
:set ai
```

The meaning of automatic indentation is described in the paragraphs below.

Options are unset, or nullified, by preceding the abbreviation with the letters `no`. For example, to request 'no automatic indentation' you say:

```
:set noai
```

Some options have values or strings associated with them. In this case they follow the option name, separated by an equals sign:

```
:set sw=4
```

More than one option can be set or unset by the same `set` operation, the different options are separated by spaces. Setting and unsetting can be mixed, for example:

```
:set ai noopen sw=8 nowarn
```

All options have some default setting. The `:set` command on its own displays the current state of those options that have been changed from the default. To examine the state of any one option, you follow `set` with a question mark:

```
:set magic ?
nomagic
```

The answer to the query replaces the query itself on the bottom line of the screen. The command '`set all`' displays the settings of all the possible options that can be set or unset.

In the following paragraphs we discuss some of the options that are useful when you are doing a lot of text entry, as when creating a new document or program. Other options will be discussed along with those editor functions where the options are applicable.

The `wrapmargin` Option

When you are entering a great deal of text, you can get `vi` to insert newline (RETURN) characters automatically. This provides for fast text entry, since you don't have to watch the screen and type **RETURN** at the appropriate places. This feature is controlled by an option called `wrapmargin`, which has a value associated with it. If the value is zero, the feature is turned off (this is the default case). If the value is set to some value other than zero, for example:

```
:set wrapmargin=8
```

then every time a space is typed at a position less than 8 places from the right hand edge of the screen, the previous space is converted into a newline character. The result is that you can just keep typing, and your file will be such that none of the lines exceed 72 characters. So you only need to type **RETURN** when you deliberately want to start a new line. This feature is useful when typing text for document preparation, it is not so useful when typing computer programs.

The `beautify` Option

The `beautify` option (`bf`), when set, instructs `vi` to clean up any text that you input, by discarding all unimportant control characters. Significant control characters, such as CTRL-I (tab), CTRL-L (form feed) and newline are not discarded.

This is a useful option, because some programs (like the `nroff` text formatter) don't behave properly if their input text contains funny characters like CTRL-A. The default setting for this option is `nobf` which puts everything you type (including the garbage) into the edit buffer.

The `autoindent` and `shiftwidth` Options

A useful option when you are typing programs is `autoindent`, abbreviated to `ai`. The `ai` option can be set with the command:

```
:set ai
```

Because the feature is not generally useful for text other than program source, the default case is no auto-indentation (`noai`).

When `ai` is set, each new line of text inserted is automatically started at the same indentation depth as the previous line. So for example, if you start your second line of text spaced in 4 spaces from the first, then when you type the RETURN for that line, the cursor will not appear in column 1 of the screen, but directly in line with the start of the second line. Thus, once you have indented one line, all succeeding lines are indented by the same amount. This continues until you either cancel the indentation, or change the indentation by putting spaces or tabs at the beginning of the next line.

To back up (outdent, if you like) you type CTRL-D. The number of columns that CTRL-D backs up is controlled by the `shiftwidth` option, so it pays to use a uniform depth of indentation and to set the shiftwidth to that number.

The `shiftwidth` option has a value associated with it. If you are using auto-indent, and not using shiftwidth, you are going to experience problems unless you always have your indentation depths at TAB (CTRL-I) positions. The auto-indentation, as far as positioning the cursor for indents (that is, to the right) is concerned, always works. But the outdent function of CTRL-D always moves leftwards by `shiftwidth` spaces.

By default, `shiftwidth` is set to 8 spaces, the same as the system tab stops as produced by CTRL-I or the TAB key. So if you always indent 8 spaces, everything goes smoothly. However, 8 spaces is a lot of indent on a program, 4 is more reasonable, and even 2 is enough for program readability. If you try to do this without adjusting your shiftwidth, what will happen is that all your indents will be OK, but your outdents won't take you to the right place — you will have to indent again in most cases.

If you want to use an indentation depth of 4 spaces, the correct thing to do is set the shiftwidth option:

```
:set shiftwidth=4
```

or it can be abbreviated:

```
:set sw=4
```

Now the CTRL-D will only take you 4 spaces back to the left.

The `showmatch` Option

Another option which can be useful when entering program source code is `showmatch`. When this option is set, each time a closing parenthesis `)`, closing bracket `]`, or closing brace `}` is typed, the cursor moves to the matching `(`, `[`, or `{` for one second, if the matching character is on the screen. The abbreviation for the `showmatch` option is `sm`, and it can be set by typing:

```
:set sm
```

The default is to not show matches (`nosm`).

Even if you don't have the `showmatch` option set, you can show matching pairs of parentheses, brackets, or braces with the `%` command. If you place the cursor over any of `(`, `[`, or `{`, and then type `%`, the cursor will move to the matching `)`, `]`, or `}`. Similarly if the cursor is placed on the closing character of such a pair, the `%` command moves the cursor to the corresponding opening character. Remember to type ESC to stop text entry before using this command.

7.12. Dealing with Words

So far we have seen how to get to the beginning and end of line quickly, but otherwise movements are mostly a character at a time. Also the changes we have shown have been based on a character position, and character replacement. In practice, especially when dealing with documentation, it is more usual to think of changing text by word — for instance 'delete the third word on this line', or 'replace that phrase by this word'. `vi` accommodates this way of thinking by giving the capability to move over, delete, and replace text objects. The most commonly used text object is a word.

Cursor Positioning over Words

You can tell `vi` to move over the text a word at a time by using the commands:

- **w** move forward to beginning of next word
- **e** move to end of this word
- **b** move back to beginning of word

If you are already at the beginning of a word when you type the **b** command, the cursor will go to the beginning of the previous word. If you are at the end of a word when you give a **e** command, the cursor will move to the end of the next word.

The definition of a 'word' is:

- *Anything consisting of letters, digits and underscores; surrounded by anything which is not a letter, a digit or an underscore.*

This definition covers variable identifiers in most programming languages, so the commands are useful for editing both programs and documentation.

The following picture shows the position of the cursor on several successive **w** commands:

```
The source code for the program is in the file
/aa/widget/henry/progs/c/thingummy.c.  Documentation
is in directory /aa/widget/henry/docs -  thingspec
is the specification, it needs to be formatted
using -mm; thinguser is the user's guide, it also
requires -mm.
~
~
"thinginfo", 6 lines, 251 characters
```

In the above example the file is shorter than the window. Lines in the window that are in excess are indicated by the tilde character ~ to avoid confusion with blank lines in the file.

You can also move the cursor forward a word by the command **W**. When you use **W** instead of **w**, a word is any sequence of characters surrounded by spaces. So if we had started with the cursor in the same position as in our previous example, the position of the cursor on the same number of successive **W** commands is:

```
The source code for the program is in the file
/aa/widget/henry/progs/c/thingummy.c.  Documentation
is in directory /aa/widget/henry/docs -  thingspec
is the specification, it needs to be formatted
using -mm; thinguser is the user's guide, it also
requires -mm.
~
~
"thinginfo", 6 lines, 251 characters
```

There are commands **B** and **E** which are similarly related to **b** and **e**.

All the commands **w**, **b**, **e**, **W**, **B** and **E** move past the end of a line, as is demonstrated in the above examples. If you use them to move past the upper or lower limits of the window, the lines scroll up the screen accordingly.

The picture below summarizes the effects of the word movement commands[3].

[3] Thanks to Bill Tuthill for suggesting this title for the seventh book in the *Dune* trilogy.

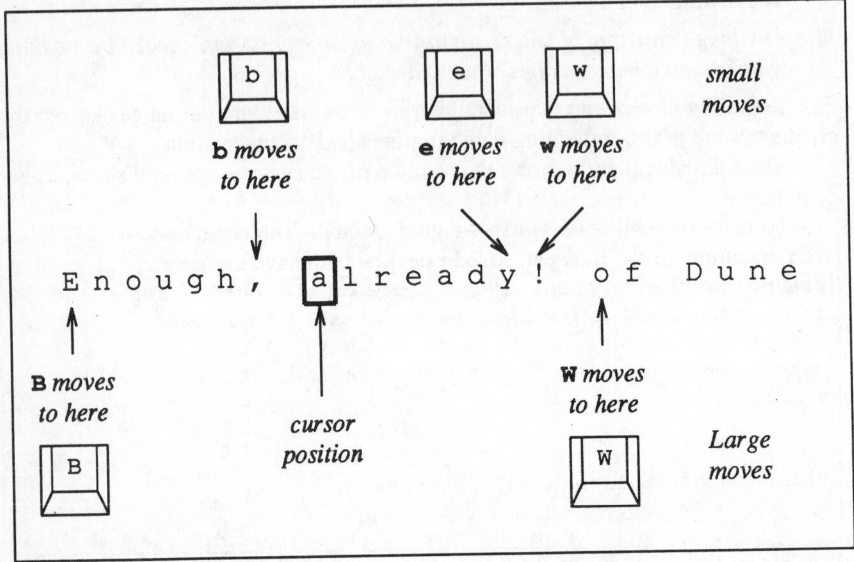

These commands can take a preceding count, so the command **5w** moves the cursor forward five words, as if you had typed five separate **w** commands. This means you have to count the number of words to move. The easiest way of doing this is to mark each one by placing the cursor over it. The net result is that this is not a particularly useful feature under most circumstances. It is useful if you are working in what is termed 'slow open' mode, which is what you get if you call up `vi` on a dumb terminal.

Operating on Words

In the previous paragraph we showed you how you could move the cursor whole words by typing the commands **w** or **W** to go forward, or the commands **b** or **B** to go backward. These 'commands' are actually descriptions of text objects, and they can be affected by various `vi` operators, which can in themselves be considered 'commands'. The operators are:

- `d` delete
- `c` change
- `y` yank

The **y** operator is covered later — we deal with **d** and **c** here.

Deleting Words

To delete a word, you just place the cursor at the beginning of it and type the **dw** command (delete word). `vi` takes care of spacing, so you don't get left with a double space where you only want one. For example:

```
Use not vain repetition, as the heathen do
```

after a **dw** command, looks like:

```
Use not repetition, as the heathen do
```

To delete a number of words, we give a count. The count can precede either the **d** operation, or the **w** object, so **2dw** or **d2w** both have the same effect, namely, delete two words:

```
It was a dark and stormy night
```

becomes:

```
It was a stormy night
```

If the words you want to delete are not all on the same line, `vi` joins the lines together. For example, suppose you want to delete three words starting from:

```
It was a dark and stormy night;
the young boy said to his
uncle 'Tell me a story, Uncle'
```

the result would be:

```
It was a dark and stormy night;
the young boy said 'Tell me a story, Uncle'
```

This might result in a very long line. To split it you would have to move the cursor to some suitable place and insert a RETURN character.

If the cursor is not at the beginning of a word when you type the **dw** command, the partial word from the cursor position to the end of the word is deleted. For example:

```
With all due pomposity and circumstance
```

after a **dw** command, becomes:

```
With all due pompand circumstance
```

This unfortunately deletes the space between words as well, however the cursor is left in just the right position for inserting a space by typing '`i` <ESC>'.

In the same way you can delete 'Words' — objects found by the **W** command rather than the **w** command. You can also delete words to the left of the cursor, by saying **db** or **dB**.

Changing Words

If you want to replace one word by a different word, or by several words, you move the cursor to the start of the word, then give the **cw** command. At this point, the symbol `$` appears to mark the extent of the change. In the case of **cw**, it appears over the last character of the word. You then type in the new word or words that you want, then press the escape key (**ESC**) to finish text entry. Suppose we wanted to change:

```
It was a dark and stormy night
```

to:

```
It was a dark and turbulent night
```

we would have to type '**cw**`turbulent<ESC>`'.

If you want to replace more than one word, you give a count: **3cw** or **c3w** for example. The `$` sign appears to mark the end of the text you are going to replace by the text you enter. If we have this:

```
It was a dark and stormy night
```

to get this:

```
It was an inky and stormy night
```

type '**c2w**`an inky<ESC>`'.

So far we have replaced words with the same number of words, but it doesn't have to be that way. You can replace one word with many or many words with one. You can get:

```
It was an incredibly inky, black, rain-filled,
wind-blown, and stormy night
```

from:

```
It was a dark and stormy night
```

simply by typing the **cw** command then typing the text

```
an incredibly inky, black, rain-filled,<CR>
wind-blown,
```

followed by **ESC**. Or you can change

```
It was a dark and stormy night
```

to

```
It was raining
```

by typing '**c5w**raining<ESC>'.

As is the case when deleting words, the words we want to change don't have to be all on the same line. So to change:

```
It was an incredibly inky, black, rain-filled,
wind-blown, and stormy night
```

to something simpler, we can type '**c2W**rainy', to get

```
It was an incredibly inky, black, rainy and stormy night
```

The action taken by vi is a little different in this case. Before you start entering the replacement text, the words that will be replaced disappear from the display, and the remaining parts of the two lines are joined together on the display. There is no $ sign to indicate the end of the replacement. This is exactly as if you had typed the commands **d2wi**

Notice that in the last example we used **W** rather than **w**. If we had used **w** instead of **W**, the result would have been:

```
It was an incredibly inky, black, rainyfilled,
wind-blown, and stormy night
```

because according to the definition of **w** words 'rain' is a word, so is '–', so is 'filled', so is ',' and so on. To use **w**, we would have had to give a count of 8.

This is the sort of situation where that $-sign comes in handy. As soon as you have typed the command, before you enter text, look for that $ sign. If it isn't sitting on top of the last character you want to replace, you need to take some sort of corrective action. In our example, after typing **c2w** we would see the $ sign sitting on the '–' of 'rain-filled'. If we now type **ESC**, we effectively delete those two words (replace them with nothing). Since a word is a subset of a Word, we can still use the same count and say **c2W**, which is the correct command.

The command **cw** doesn't have to be used to change whole words, it can change partial words. Given the phrase:

```
with all due pomposity and circumstance
```

by typing '`cw`locution<ESC>', we get a different phrase:

```
with all due pomposity and circumlocution
```

In a similar way the change operator can be applied to the objects **b** and **B**, although these are not so commonly useful, since it's not easy to envision changes backward along a line. The command **cb** changes the word before the cursor, **cB** changes the Word before the cursor. Both can be given counts. The extent of the text that will be replaced is indicated by the cursor moving to the leftmost character that will be replaced, and the `$` sign sitting over the rightmost character (actually the one just to the left of where the cursor was when you gave the command). When changing words in this way, if you start with the cursor at the beginning of a word, you will have to supply the space between that word and the one before it as part of the text you enter.

7.13. Dealing with Sentences and Paragraphs

With `vi` you are not restricted to moving forward or backward a word, or groups of words, at a time. You can move forward whole sentences. A sentence is defined as string of words ending with one of the characters '`.`', '`!`' or '`?`' followed by two spaces, or occurring at the end of a line. The commands which move the the cursor over sentences are **(** and **)**. Typing **)** moves the cursor to the beginning of the next sentence, and **(** moves the cursor to the beginning of the previous sentence[4]. The commands can be given counts, so **2)** moves forward 2 sentences; **3(** moves back three sentences.

You can also move the cursor whole paragraphs at a time by the commands **}** (beginning of next paragraph) and **{** (beginning of previous paragraph). Every time there is a blank line, the next line is considered to be the start of a new paragraph. However, if your file is text to be input to the text formatter using the `-ms` or `-mm` macro packages, `vi` recognizes the 'start of paragraph' macros available in these packages, and positions the cursor accordingly.

If the file you are editing contains text to be formatted using one of the formatting macro packages, you can also tell `vi` to move forward or backward whole sections. The command to move forward a section is **]]**, to move back a section you type **[[**. `vi` makes you type the double character in each case, because it is not so easy to type two **]**'s or **[**'s by accident. In the case of sentences or paragraphs, you will not move very far, so if you move by accident it is not too difficult to get

---

4 If the file you are editing contains a LISP program, you may want to change the meaning of these commands by setting the `lisp` option When this option is set, **(** and **)** move backward and forward over s-expressions. The meaning of **{** and **}** is changed too.

back to where you started. But sections can be huge, and it would be easy to get completely lost by mistake, hence the precaution of double characters.

If the text you are editing is source text in the C programming language, the section positioning commands `[[` and `]]` move forward or backward over whole procedures.

`vi` recognizes the paragraph and section macros provided by the `-ms` and `-mm` macro packages, but if you want to provide your own definitions, you can do it with the `para` and `sect` options.

Deleting Sentences and Paragraphs

Using `vi` you can easily delete whole sentences, or parts of sentences. This works in much the same way as it does for words. To delete a whole sentence, first move your cursor to the beginning of the first word of the sentence, then type the **`d)`** command. `vi` joins the sentences on either side of the deleted sentence. To delete several consecutive sentences you give a count, in the same way as you do for words: **`2d)`** or **`d2)`** for instance.

Exactly what you see displayed when you delete large amounts of text depends on the type of terminal you are using. On an an intelligent terminal, the undeleted text is rearranged. However, if you are using a dumb terminal, this does not happen unless you have the 'redraw' option set. Instead, whole lines that get deleted are indicated by a `@` in the first column, the remainder of the line is blank. These lines are blank on the screen, but there is no corresponding blank line in the edit buffer. If you get too many of these lines, it is hard to see what you are doing. At this point, you can ask `vi` to redraw the screen by typing `^R` (CTRL-R). This redraws the screen beyond the current cursor position, the entire screen can be redrawn by typing CTRL-L.

You can delete parts of sentences by placing the cursor part way through the sentence before giving the command, but you will probably have to do other small cosmetic changes too.

The command **`d(`** deletes the sentence before the cursor, or several sentences if a count is given. It can also be used to delete part of a sentence, but again you will probably have to make some cosmetic changes to repair punctuation and initial capital letters on sentences.

After deleting large portions of text you might wish to make further changes to adjust the length of the lines so that they are all more or less the same. However, if the text you are entering is to be passed through the `nroff` text formatter it is a waste of time and effort to do this. Adjusting the line lengths so that they are all much the same is one of the formatter's most basic functions.

Paragraphs and larger text objects can also be deleted. The **`d}`** command deletes the following paragraph, **`d{`** deletes the preceding one. Similarly, sections can be deleted by **`d]]`** and **`d[[`**.

Changing Sentences and Paragraphs

Just as the change operator can be applied to words in either direction from the cursor, it can be applied to sentences. The **c)** command, followed by some text and the ESC character, changes the next sentence, or the last part of the current sentence. **2c)** or **c2)** changes the next two sentences. When changing sentences, the old sentences are deleted from the display, a blank line is opened up, and you start typing the new sentences in that line. In a like manner, **c(** will change the previous sentence, or the first part of the current sentence.

For those brave enough to try it, the **c** operator can also be applied to paragraphs and sections.

7.14. Dealing with Lines of Text

So far we have been dealing with language constructs, such as words and sentences. Sometimes it is inconvenient to consider things in this way, it is easier to work simply with lines of text. This is especially true when the text you are editing is not documentation, but program source code. However, even during document preparation, it is often convenient to be able to say 'delete the rest of this line', rather than 'delete the next 4 words', or 'delete the rest of the sentence'. `vi` has commands for dealing with partial lines, and also for dealing with whole lines, in blocks if necessary.

Moving to Specific Characters or Columns

Suppose that you have the cursor positioned at the beginning of a line, and you want to position the cursor to the character 'n'. This can be done by saying 'find n' — the `f` command followed by the character you want to find, in other words `fn`. This command positions the cursor to the first character 'n' following the current cursor position. The following example shows the different cursor positions from initial beginning of line to after the `fn` command:

```
How long, how long, in infinite Pursuit
    Of This and That endeavour and dispute?
    Better be merry with the fruitful Grape
    Than sadden after none, or bitter, fruit.
```

If you then want to find the next 'n' character, you can repeat the `fn` command. However, you can use the semicolon character (`;`) as a shorthand command which says, in effect, 'search forward for the same character as you looked forward for before'. So, having found the first 'n', giving four `;` commands will position the cursor at the following points in turn:

```
How long, how long, ininfinite Pursuit
    Of This and That endeavour and dispute?
    Better be merry with the fruitful Grape
    Than sadden after none, or bitter, fruit.
```

If you go too far, and want to go back one or more 'n's, the comma character (`,`) is another shorthand command which says, effectively, 'look for the same character as you did last time, but in the other direction'.

The 'find' command **`f`** will not go past the end of line. To find the same characters on the next line you have to first type the **RETURN** key to get you to the beginning of the next line, then you can type more `;` commands to find the character.

The reverse of the **`f`** command is **`F`**, which searches the line backwards for the specified character. Again, there is a shorthand form `;` which continues the search for the same character. So if we started off with the cursor positioned as at the end of our last example, then gave a **`Fo`** command followed by three `;` commands, the positions taken by the cursor at each step would be:

```
How long, how long, in infinite Pursuit
    Of This and That endeavour and dispute?
    Better be merry with the fruitful Grape
    Than sadden after none, or bitter, fruit.
```

The `,` command can be used to reverse the direction of the search. As for **`f`**, the **`F`** command will not move past the beginning of line.

To summarize these commands:

`f`*a* search forward on line for character *a*

`F`*a* search backward on line for character *a*

`;` search for same character in same direction

`,` search for same character in opposite direction

You will notice that, if you start off with a **`f`** then `;` goes forwards whereas `,` goes backwards. However, if you start off with **`F`** then `,` goes forwards and `;` goes backwards. Try not to let this confuse you[5]. All the commands can be given leading counts. If the cursor is sitting at the beginning of a line, you can find the fourth 'c' character by the command **`4fc`**. However you can't say **`f4c`** — that is looking for a character `4`. If you use a simple **`fc`** to get to the first, you can get to the third next 'c' by the command **`3;`**. If this takes you two 'c's beyond where you want to be, you can say **`2,`** Similarly for moving in the other direction with **`F`**

---

[5] Those who have used the screen editor in the UCSD P-system can probably cope with this.

Even with the count, the commands will not go beyond the end of line. If you ask to move **4;** and there are only two of them on the line, the cursor will not move and `vi` will beep at you.

These commands are useful for positioning yourself at punctuation marks, or at some unusual characters in the line. The best way to use them when giving letters to look for, is to give the initial letter of the word you want, then use **e** to get to the end of that word, or → to get to somewhere in the middle of it.

There are two other commands that are similar to **f** and **F**, these are **t** and **T**. Lowercase **t** is similar to **f**, but instead of placing the cursor on top of the specified character, the cursor is placed on the character just to the left of the specified character. In a similar way, **T** is like **F**, but puts the cursor over the character immediately to the right of the specified character. The reason for having these two commands, in addition to **f** and **F**, will be made plain when we talk about deleting and changing partial lines.

Yet another way to move the cursor to a point on the line, is to move it to a specified column number. To position the cursor at a particular column in a file, you use the vertical bar (|) command. For example, to place the cursor in column 40, you give the command **40|**.

Changing and Deleting Parts of Lines

We previously saw that to delete a word, we simply applied the delete operator to the cursor positioning command **w**. The same principle applies to the commands used to delete parts of lines. For example, **d$** deletes all characters from the current cursor position to the end of line,

```
#define  LINES  66   /* number of lines on each page */
```

becomes

```
#define  LINES  66 
```

There is also a **D** command which does the same thing, that is, deletes to end of line. The character that is under the cursor is included in the definition of 'here to end of line'.

In the same way, the **d^** command means 'delete from beginning of line to here'. For example:

```
#define  LINES  66   /* number of lines on each page */
```

ends up as:

```
/* number of lines on each page */
```

In this case the character under the cursor does *not* get deleted, but becomes the first character of the new line.

Changing parts of lines is similar — the **c** operator is applied to $ and ^. There is also a **C** command which is identical to **c$**. After the command is given, the last character that will be replaced is indicated by a $ sign (in the case of **c^** the cursor position is adjusted too). The new text you type in can be shorter than or longer than the text you are replacing. It can contain **RETURN** characters, in which case you create new lines of text. You signal the end of text entry by typing **ESC**, as usual.

Another cursor positioning command that the **d** and **c** operators can be applied to is the 'find character' command. There are actually four of these, as we discussed earlier. **f** and **t** find characters forward, **F** and **T** find characters backward on the line. Let's take an example from way back:

```
The source code for the program is in the file
/aa/widget/henry/progs/c/thingummy.c.  Documentation
is in directory /aa/widget/henry/docs -  thingspec
is the specification, it needs to be formatted
using -mm; thinguser is the user's guide, it also
requires -mm.
```

If we want to change the full pathname of the program into a simple filename, we can do this with a **d5f/** command; this deletes everything from the current cursor position, up to and including the fifth / character. So the second line looks like this:

```
thingummy.c.  Documentation
```

We could also have put the count in front of the **d** operator: **5df/** does the same thing. **df5/** will not work, however, because that is telling `vi` to delete characters up to '5'. There is no character '5' on that line, so `vi` beeps at you before you get a chance to type the '/'.

The difference between **f** and **t** becomes important when applying the **d** and **c** operators. Suppose that we decided to use this method of deleting the remainder of the sentence containing the full pathname. If we say **dfD** what we end up with is:

```
ocumentation.
```

We should in fact have used a **dtD** command. The **f** and **F** commands include the character they find. The **t** and **T** commands are exclusive (in either direction) of the character specified.

Changing things is similar. For example, to change the full pathname of the program, we would say something like

c5t//ab/blivet/joe/c-progs<ESC>

We used **t** rather than **f** for the change, it saves us one keystroke (big deal) because we don't have to enter the final '/'. As usual, the last character that will be replaced is marked with a $ sign, and in the case of **F** and **T** the position of the cursor is adjusted.

7.15. Operating on Whole Lines

You can delete or change whole lines by the simple expedient of typing the **d** or **c** operator twice. Thus the command **dd** deletes one line, the line that the cursor is positioned on. The cursor is left sitting at the beginning of the line after the deleted line. Several lines can be deleted by giving a count, for example **10dd** deletes the current line and the following nine lines.

If you are working on an intelligent terminal, or if you have the 'redraw' option set, the lines following the deleted lines will shuffle up the screen to take the place of the deleted ones. However, if you are using a dumb terminal without the 'redraw' option set, this does not happen. Instead, the deleted lines are displayed as lines consisting only of the @ character in the first column. So that if you have:

```
He served out some grog with a liberal hand,
 And bade them sit down on the beach:
And they could not but own that their Captain looked grand,
 As he stood and delivered his speech.
```

then after typing a command of **2dd** the screen will look like this:

```
He served out some grog with a liberal hand,
@
@
 As he stood and delivered his speech.
```

Mostly this is no inconvenience but, if you have done many deletions in the same window of text, the remaining text may become rather sparse on the screen. At this point you may wish to redraw the screen, this can be done by typing CTRL-R or CTRL-L.

Changing lines is similar — **cc** changes one line, while **5cc** changes five lines. The effect of a **5cc** command is the same as that of the commands **5ddO**, that is, 5 lines are deleted, then a line is opened up with the cursor at the beginning of it. At this point, you type the text for the new line or lines, text entry is stopped in the usual fashion by typing ESC. As with delete, exactly what you see on the display depends on your terminal type and the setting of the 'redraw' option.

Joining Lines Together

In an earlier paragraph we told you that the 'gobble' command **x** would not gobble characters beyond the end of line. Although you can split one line into two by finding a suitable space character and replacing it with a carriage-return, you can't reverse the process and join two lines together by **x**-ing out the carriage-return.

There is a special command for joining lines together. It is the **J** (Join) command. This is an uppercase **J**; lowercase **j** moves the cursor down one line, on most terminals. When you type the **J** command, the cursor can be anywhere on the line. The effect of the command is that two lines, the one the cursor is sitting on and the one following it, are joined together to form one line. So if you have:

```
The good,
and the bad,
and the ugly
```

the result of the command will be:

```
The good, and the bad,
and the ugly
```

Notice that vi automatically provides the necessary space between the last word on the first line and the first word on the second line. If the end of the first line is an end of sentence indicator, such as . or ! or ?, vi will provide two spaces. In some contexts, the spaces provided by vi is inappropriate. In this case you have to get rid of them by using the **x** command; the cursor is left in just the correct place for issuing this command.

The **J** command can be given a preceding count, in this case the specified number of lines is joined together, instead of just two. So if our command had been **3J** rather than simply **J**, we would have got:

```
The good, and the bad, and the ugly
```

All three lines are joined together to make one line.

7.16. Line Numbers, Search Strings and Marking

If you are aware of the line numbers of the lines in the file you are editing, you may wish to position the cursor at some specific line. The command you use to do this is **G**, the 'go to' command. This is uppercase 'G' — there is no command for lowercase 'g'. For example, to go to line number 432 you type **432G**. The cursor is moved to the beginning of the requested line. If necessary the window on the file is changed, so that the requested line appears in the middle of the screen.

Typing the **G** command with no preceding line number moves the cursor to the last line of the file.

Another way of going to a specific numbered line, is to use **:** to call up the ex command. Typing **:432** followed by the **RETURN** key also moves the cursor to the beginning of line 432. The legend ':432' appears at the bottom of the screen while you are typing it. To get to the last line by this method, you would use the ex notation $ for last line and you would type **:$** followed by **RETURN**.

To find a particular character string anywhere in the file, you use the **/** command. When you type **/** it is echoed at the bottom line of the screen. You then type the string you want to search for either as a fixed character string, or as a regular expression. Regular expressions, and the magic option which affects them, are described in detail in the next chapter about the ex and ed line editors. To signal the end of the character string, you type either **ESC**, or **RETURN**. This one place where typing **ESC** can't be used to cancel a partial command, you have to backspace over whatever string you have typed so far.

vi places the cursor at the start of the next string that matches what you typed, going forward through the file. The following example shows the starting and ending positions of the cursor, for the search indicated at the bottom of the screen:

```
How long, how long, in infinite Pursuit
    Of This and That endeavour and dispute?
    Better be merry with the fruitful Grape
    Than sadden after none, or bitter, fruit.

You know, my Friends, how long since in my House
    For a new Marriage I did make Carouse:
    Divorced old barren Reason from my Bed,
/fruit
```

If the string is not in the current window, the window is changed to display that part of the file which contains the string. If we entered the search command /though from the position shown in the previous example, the window when the search was completed would look as shown below.

```
    For a new Marriage I did make Carouse:
    Divorced old barren Reason from my Bed,
    And took the Daughter of the Vine to Spouse.

For 'Is' and 'Is-not' though with Rule and Line,
    And "Up-and-Down" without, I could define,
    I yet in all I cared to know,
    Was never deep in anything but - Wine.
```

The search wraps around the file. That is, if the string isn't found between the current position and the end of the file, the file is searched from the beginning up to the current position. This feature is under control of the `wrapscan` option, and is described in more detail under `ex`. If the string doesn't exist in the file at all, the message

```
Pattern not Found
```

is displayed on the bottom line of the screen.

A search forward through the file can also be accomplished by giving the `:` command, and then using `ex`'s search commands. These also start with the `/` character, so you type `:/`, followed by the string or pattern you want to search for, followed by **RETURN**. The difference between this and using `/` on its own is illustrated by the following example, which repeats one of the previous searches, but using `:/` instead of `/` on its own:

```
How long, how long, in infinite Pursuit
    Of This and That endeavour and dispute?
    Better be merry with the fruitful Grape
    Than sadden after none, or bitter, fruit.

You know, my Friends, how long since in my House
    For a new Marriage I did make Carouse:
    Divorced old barren Reason from my Bed,
:/fruit
```

You can see that whereas `:/` places the cursor at the beginning of the line containing the string, `/` on its own places the cursor at the start of the string itself. Both functions are useful under different circumstances.

If you want to search backward through the file instead of forward, you can do this by typing the `?` command, followed by the string (or pattern) you want, terminated by either **ESC** or **RETURN**. Again, what you type is echoed on the bottom line of the screen. Alternatively, you can use `:?` to find the beginning of the line containing the string. Both `?` and `:?` act in a similar manner to `/` and `:/`, the only thing different is the direction of the search.

If you want to search forward again for the same string, you can do it by typing `//` (or `://<CR>`). Similarly, if you want to search backward for the same string, you use `??` or `:??<CR>` However there are two other commands you can use:

- **n** find next occurrence of same string in same direction
- **N** find next occurrence of same string in reverse direction

If you did your initial search with `/`, the **n** command will do the next search forward, and **N** will search backward. On the other hand, if you did your initial search with `?`, **N** will go forward and **n** will search backward. You might find it less confusing to use `//`, which always goes forward, and `??` which always goes backward.

Search Strings

The **df** command deleted parts of lines between the cursor and a specified character. An extension of that is the ability to delete lines up to a specified character string (which may be expressed as a pattern, or regular expression). If we have the text:

```
He served out some grog with a liberal hand,
 And bade them sit down on the beach:
And they could not but own that their Captain looked grand,
 As he stood and delivered his speech.

'Friends, Romans, and countrymen, lend me your ears!'
 (They were all of them fond of quotations:
So they drank to his health, and they gave him three cheers,
  While he served out additional rations.)
```

and we type the command '`d/he <ESC>`',[6] the text between the current cursor position and the next word 'he' is deleted to give:

```
He served out some grog with a liberal hand,
 And bade them sit down on the beach:
And they could not but own that their Captain looked grand,
 While he served out additional rations.)
```

[6] Notice that there is a space at the end of the search string. If this were not the case the first occurrence of the string 'he' would occur as part of the word 'They'.

After you have typed the **d/**, the '/' character appears on the last line of the screen. The search string is echoed as you type it, so you can check it and correct it if necessary. You can do the same thing with a backward search:

```
He served out some grog with a liberal hand,
 And bade them sit down on the beach:
And they could not but own that their Captain looked grand,
 As he stood and delivered his speech.

'Friends, Romans, and countrymen, lend me your ears!'
 (They were all of them fond of quotations:
So they drank to his health, and they gave him three cheers,
  While he served out additional rations.)
```

After typing the command '**d?**they <ESC>' the result is:

```
He served out some grog with a liberal hand,
 And bade them sit down on the beach:
And they drank to his health, and they gave him three cheers,
  While he served out additional rations.)
```

Notice that the deletion is always to the start of the string that is found. So the specified string is not included in the deleted material for forward searches, but is deleted on backward searches.

Changes can also be made with a **c/** (or **c?**) command, followed by a search string. When you do this, you have to type **ESC** twice, once to terminate the search string, and again to finish text input.

Position Markers

You can mark a place in the file using the **m** (mark) command. The command is followed by a single letter, which is the mark or label. For example **mz** marks the character under the current cursor position with the label 'z'. If you move away from that position, you can return to it with the command **`z**. The **`** character is a grave accent, on most terminals it is **SHIFT-@**.

A special case of the **`** command is **``**. This returns you to the place you were at before the last search or 'goto' command.

Another way of returning to the marked place is by using the **'** command, that is the apostrophe character. The difference between **'** and **`** is that **`** places the cursor exactly over the marked position, while **'** puts the cursor at the beginning of the line containing the marked position.

You can also specify changes or deletions that can cover many lines by using character positions previously marked with the **m** command. As we have seen, there are two ways of getting at these positions: with **`** (the grave accent) and with

' (apostrophe). The difference is shown in the following examples. Suppose we have the text:

```
They sought it with thimbles, they sought it with care;
They pursued it with forks and hope;
They threatened its life with a railway share;
They charmed it with smiles and soap.
```

and that we mark the 'w' of 'with' on the third line with the letter **z**. We do this by placing the cursor over that letter and typing **mz**. If we move the cursor over the 'w' of 'with' on the second line, and give the command **d`z** (using the grave accent) the result is:

```
They sought it with thimbles, they sought it with care;
They pursued it with a railway share;
They charmed it with smiles and soap.
```

whereas if we used the command **d'z** (using the apostrophe) from the same position, we would get:

```
They sought it with thimbles, they sought it with care;
  They charmed it with smiles and soap.
```

The ` deletes from the current cursor position up to, but not including, the marked position. The partial lines left by this are joined together. The ' command deletes whole lines from the current line up to and including the line containing the marked position.

In these examples we have deleted text when the cursor has been before the marked position. Deletions can also be done when the cursor is after the marked position. If we marked the 's' of the *second* 'sought' on line 1 with the letter 'x', then moved the cursor on to the beginning of 'charmed' in the last line, the command **d`x** would produce:

```
They sought it with thimbles, they charmed it with smiles and soap.
```

The change operator can also be applied to the ` and ' commands. **c`x** means 'change all text between here and the place marked x', if the cursor is before the marked place. If the marked place is before the cursor position, the meaning becomes 'change all text between the place marked x and here'. In either event, the new text to replace the old text is then typed, terminated by **ESC** as usual.

The use of marks is very useful when you have large amounts of text to delete or change. It is relatively simple to find the beginning of the text you want deleted, mark it, find the end of the text, then type the delete command. This is especially so when the text to be deleted or changed covers many windows on the file. It is less prone to error than using search strings, since you can pin-point exactly where you want the limits of the action, and don't have to rely on correctly specifying a character string or regular expression.

7.17. Cut and Paste and Copy Operations

Very often updating text, whether it be documentation or program, involves more than simple changes, additions, and deletions. Text needs to be rearranged, chunks of it need to be moved from one place to another.

When you have lots of text which is very much repetitive, with only minor changes in each repetition, it is nice to be able to just copy the first line or two and then make those minor changes.

Both of these things can be achieved in `vi` by using the delete operator, which we have already described, and two new commands 'yank' and 'put'. Another feature of `vi` that aids cut and paste operations is the presence of named buffers.

Moving Text with `delete` and `put`

Let's start off with an example. Suppose we take the first two verses of Robert Herrick's poem[7]:

```
The glorious lamp of heaven, the sun,
The higher he's a-getting,
The sooner will his race be run,
And nearer he's to setting.

Gather ye rosebuds wihle ye may,
Old Time still is a-flying:
And this same flower that smiles to-day
To-morrow will be dying.
```

If you check with your poetry book, you will see that we have put these verses in the wrong order. The problem is to correct this situation.

Obviously we can remove the 'first' verse and the following blank line by the command **5dd**, but do we have to retype them after the last blank line? The answer is no.

When you delete something in `vi` it doesn't go away completely, at least not immediately. It goes into a buffer, from which it can be retrieved by a 'put' command. This buffer is called the 'un-named' buffer in order to distinguish it from the 'named' buffers which we discuss below. It behaves in a different manner

---

7 For the unliterary, the title of this poem is 'To the Virgins, to make much of Time'

from the named buffers, as we shall show.

What the 'put' commands do depends on the way the text was placed into the un-named buffer. If the text was deleted as whole lines, it is put back as whole lines. The lowercase **p** command puts the lines back after the current line. Upper-case **P** puts the lines before the current line.

In our example, we deleted five whole lines. To get them to the place we want them, we must move the cursor down to the last line (which is a blank line), then give the command **p**:

```
Gather ye rosebuds wihle ye may,
Old Time still is a-flying:
And this same flower that smiles to-day
To-morrow will be dying.

The glorious lamp of heaven, the sun,
The higher he's a-getting,
The sooner will his race be run,
And nearer he's to setting.
```

When we deleted the first five lines, the cursor was placed on the line starting 'Gather'. There is a spelling mistake in that line. Suppose that we had at that point corrected the mistake, by moving the cursor forward three words and then retyping the word correctly with the command 'cwwhile<ESC>'. Then, when we moved the cursor to the last line and gave the **p** command, what we would have got is:

```
The glorious lamp of heaven, the sun,
The higher he's a-getting,
The sooner will his race be run,
And nearer he's to setting.
wihle
```

which is not what we wanted. The cause of the trouble is that the **cw** command that we did, is the equivalent of a **dw** command followed by some text entry. The un-named buffer always contains the last thing that was deleted. So the 'put' commands always put the last thing that was deleted, in this case the incorrectly spelled word 'wihle'.

The moral is: once you have deleted something, always put it in its new place immediately, ignoring all distractions. This is not easy to achieve unless new place is in the same window. As you are scrolling through the file, you are very likely to notice typos and we all know that it's best to correct a typo as soon as you see it (you might not notice it a second time). If you are moving text a long way from its original place, it is best to use the named buffers, which we describe below.

The word we put appeared, not on the line following the last blank line, but on the blank line itself. This is because it was a word deletion. When dealing with text objects, rather than whole lines, the actions of the put commands are different. In this case, **p** puts the objects back after the cursor, **P** puts them back before the cursor.

Let's illustrate this by correcting yet another error in the poem as we have typed it. We have the line:

```
Old Time still is a-flying:
```

The words 'still' and 'is' are in the wrong order. We can correct this by placing the cursor at the beginning of the first misordered word, as shown, and typing the sequence of commands **dwwP** to give the result:

```
Old Time is still a-flying:
```

The **dw** deletes 'still' and the space following it, the cursor is left at the beginning of the second word, **w** moves to the next word, and **P** puts the deleted text before the cursor. We use **P** rather than **p** because **p** wouldn't give the right spacing.

Character Transposition

This is really just a special case of delete and put, we are putting it in a separate paragraph for emphasis.

In the example in the last paragraph, we had misspelled 'while' as 'wihle'. Character transposition is a very common form of typing error, and the simplest way of correcting it is not obvious. The obvious way is to replace (or Replace) the two characters in the right order. However, unless you have a long word, it's almost as easy to retype the whole thing, as we did in the example.

The easy way to make the correction, is to place the cursor over the first of the two transposed characters, then give the command **xp**. The **x** deletes the first character, and leaves cursor sitting on the second character. The deleted character has gone into the un-named buffer, the **p** puts it back in the word after the second character, so reversing the order of the two characters.

Simple, once you know how.

Copying Text with yank and put

Some documents have the same text appearing in many places. For instance, if you are writing a user guide to a text editor, you might use the same text in all, or most, of your examples. Suppose you were given the task of entering the following verses:

```
Old McDonald had a farm,
and on that farm he had some cows.
With a moo-moo here and a moo-moo there,
here a moo, there a moo, everywhere a moo-moo....

Old McDonald had a farm,
and on that farm he had some ducks.
With a quack-quack here and a quack-quack there,
here a quack, there a quack, everywhere a quack-quack,
here a moo, there a moo, everywhere a moo-moo....
```

and so on for all umpty-ump verses.

Obviously, you wouldn't want to type every character, because the stuff is repetitive with only minor changes. So you start off by typing just the first verse. Now you want to copy it. We know that if you move the cursor to the end and 'put', you will get the contents of the buffer appended to the file. But how do you get things into the buffer without deleting them? The answer lies in the 'yank' command.

'Yank' is actually an operator. Like **d** and **c** it can be applied to text objects and other things. So for example, **yw** yanks the following word into the un-named buffer. We can make use of that when were constructing the first verse. If we enter the first three lines and just a part of the last:

```
Old McDonald had a farm,
and on that farm he had some cows.
With a moo-moo here and a moo-moo there,
here a moo,
```

we can now move to the beginning of that last line and yank three words with **y3W** (or **3yW**), then move to the end of the line and repeat those three words twice with **pp**. The last line now looks like:

```
here a moo,here a moo,here a moo,
```

The first 'put' command didn't destroy the contents of the buffer, so that we can put them again with another **p** command. In fact we can repeat them as many times as we like by issuing the appropriate number of **p**'s (or **P**'s). After the initial put command, we can't repeat it with the **.** command. When used after **p** or **P**, the 'repeat last change' command works differently from usual, and doesn't simply put the same thing again.

It is an easy matter to use **i** to insert ' everyw' before the last 'here', and ' t' before the middle 'here', and **s** to add the other bits at the end of the line, to give the final line of the verse:

```
Old McDonald had a farm,
and on that farm he had some cows.
With a moo-moo here and a moo-moo there,
here a moo, there a moo, everywhere a moo-moo...
```

Now that we have the first verse, we can get the second verse by making a copy of it and making some minor modifications to the copy.

As with the other operators, doubling **y** makes it affect lines, so **yy** yanks the whole of the current line. In addition, there is a command **Y** which is the equivalent of **yy**. So, after we position the cursor to the start of the first line, we can yank the first verse, plus the following blank line, into the buffer with the command **5yy** or with **5Y**. Then we can move to the last line and make a copy of the verse, to give:

```
Old McDonald had a farm,
and on that farm he had some cows.
With a moo-moo here and a moo-moo there,
here a moo, there a moo, everywhere a moo-moo...

Old McDonald had a farm,
and on that farm he had some cows.
With a moo-moo here and a moo-moo there,
here a moo, there a moo, everywhere a moo-moo...
```

It is a relatively simple matter to do the changes necessary to turn 'cows' into 'ducks' and 'moo' into 'quack'. The second verse also repeats a line of the first verse, so we go back and yank it, then put it in the appropriate place in the second verse.

To get the third verse, we yank the first one again, put it at the end of the file, make the necessary changes, and so on ad nauseam. We have to go back and yank the first verse again, because the changes we did in the meantime have destroyed the buffer that it was yanked into.

An alternative approach would have been to make as many copies of the first verse as were required in total in the first place, then go back and alter them, instead of altering them on the fly as we did.

Of course, if you used a named buffer for the initial yank, you could put it again at any time, regardless of any changes you had done in the meantime. In our particular example, to get the third verse, it probably makes more sense to take a copy of the second verse, and alter that to form the third.

Although we have only shown examples of the yank operator used for words and whole lines, it works on other things too, just like the the delete and change operators. For example, **y)** yanks all text to the end of sentence; **y^** yanks everything from the beginning of line to the current cursor position; **y2f;** yanks everything from the cursor position to the second following semicolon.

Named Buffers

We have seen that the un-named buffer always contains the last text that was deleted, or changed, or yanked. In order to copy text once it has been placed in the buffer, it must be put immediately, there must be no other changes in between. Also, you cannot transfer text from one file to another in this way, because each time you call up a new file into the edit buffer, the un-named buffer gets cleared. Both these shortcomings can be circumvented by using named buffers.

There are 26 named buffers, with allocated single-character names *a* through *z*. The buffers are accessed by the notation "*x*, where *x* is the name of the buffer to be addressed.

For example, to yank 3 lines into the buffer named *a*, we type the command **"a3yy**. We can them make a copy of those lines by moving the cursor to the appropriate position and typing **"ap**. Any number of other changes can intervene, so long as they don't affect the buffer named *a*.

The notation "*X*, where *X* is an uppercase letter, has the effect of appending deleted or yanked text to one of the named buffers. For example **"Add** deletes a line of text from the file being edited, and appends it to the text already in the buffer named *A*. Using uppercase letters only has meaning when getting text into the named buffers. When putting the text, *A* is the same as *a*.

The contents of the named buffers are preserved when you change the file you are editing. So you can copy lines from one file to another by yanking them into one of the named buffers, then changing the file by ':e otherfile', then putting the lines from the named buffer in the appropriate place.

7.18. Accessing `ex` from within `vi`

Throughout the chapter we have at times talked about calling up some `ex` commands by starting a command with a colon, `:`. `vi` and `ex` are in fact the same editor — one that can be used either in visual mode or in line mode. Although the visual mode is convenient, it is the line mode that provides a lot of the more powerful capabilities.

Here are the `ex` capabilities that you are most likely to want to use from within `vi`.

- Although there are several ways to exit from `vi`, using the `ex` write (`w`) and quit (`q`) operations are probably the easiest. If you wish to write the edit buffer to a file other than the one you are editing, you will have to use the `ex` write operation.
- If you wish to read some text into the buffer, either from another file or from a UNIX System V command, you will need to use the `ex` read (`r`) operation.

- When you wish to start editing a different file you need to use the ex edit (e) or next (n) operations.
- Setting or unsetting options can only be done by using the set operation of ex.
- If you want to run a UNIX System V command, this is done via ex as we explain in more detail in the next section.
- The ability to apply a change throughout a file using the ex global change facility is a very useful feature to use from within vi.

As we have seen in some examples in this chapter, you can call up a ex command by typing the colon character. This, and the following editor command is echoed at the bottom of the screen.

However, if you want to execute several successive ex commands, it might be easier to exit from visual mode and start using the editor in line mode. This can be done by the vi command Q (that's uppercase Q).

You are now effectively using the line editor ex, rather than the display editor vi.

You can return from line mode to visual mode by typing the ex command vi, this is explained in the next chapter on the line editors.

There is one situation where you must exit from visual mode to do some changes. As we explain in the next chapter, an ex command can span more than one line (for instance, we show how a file can be made double spaced by adding a blank line after every line). This is achieved by escaping all newline characters, except the last, with a reverse slash character. From vi you can only call up a single line ex command. If you try to call up a multiple line command, vi will hang when you escape the newline character. You can only get out of this by using the interrupt key — RETURN or ESC will not do it.

7.19. Accessing UNIX System V commands from within vi

If you wish to run a system command from within vi, you can do it via ex by typing the usual colon (:), followed by an exclamation mark (!), followed by the command you want to run.

If there are several such commands in a row, you might prefer to fork out of vi into the Shell. You can so this by typing either :!sh or just :sh. At this point you see the system prompt ($) and you can type as many commands as you wish.

When you are ready to return to your edit session, you type CTRL-D, just as though you were logging out. You will return to the editor at the same point in the file as you left it.

Be aware that any change directory (cd) commands that yo give are only temporary — as soon as you return to the editor the working directory reverts to what it was when you originally called up vi.

7.20. Summary

Although you can change files without using a text editor, as we showed in the previous chapter, knowledge of a text editor is vital if you are to make use of UNIX System V efficiently. Regardless of whether your job is primarily programming, documentation, or administrative, the ability to create new files and modify existing ones is an essential skill.

A nice thing about using the display editor is that you see things in context because they are displayed a chunk at a time. This helps guard against making changes in the wrong place. It also makes a good facility for just browsing through a file.

As we said earlier, the key to using a screen editor is practice — you need to be so thoroughly familiar with it that you don't even have to think about what you are doing. There is a lot to learn in the `vi` editor, so take it easy — learn it one step at a time.

Much of the power of `vi` comes from its ability to use various features of the `ex` line editor, described in the next chapter, so you should learn (at least in part) how to use that too.

8 The ex and ed Line Editors

On UNIX System V there are two *line editors* — ed and ex. Line editors can in some ways considered rather primitive, which is why there are screen editors around. However, circumstances could arise when using a screen editor is difficult, if not impossible, so a working knowledge of the System V line editors is desirable.

ed is the interactive text editor which forms part of basic System V. It will work on any type of terminal (remember that to use the screen editor vi you have to be using a terminal that the system knows about). ed is not exactly the most talkative text editor in this world — its messages are terse at best, and sometimes downright cryptic. For this reason you will probably find it easier to learn to use ex. A working knowledge of ex will enable to use ed if you find you have to — just remember that some things that you can do with ex cannot be done using ed.

The ex text editor is based on ed, but has many extensions and improvements to that editor. The experienced ed user can use ex quite happily. However, unless the additional features provided are used, using ex like ed will not be as efficient as it could be. In general, ex is somewhat easier to use than ed. This is mostly because ex is more communicative; it tells you what you've done wrong, and in many cases tells you how to correct your error.

Both ed and ex use an *edit buffer*. That is to say your changes do not directly affect the file you are editing. When you first invoke the editor, the file to be changed is copied into a temporary location — this is called the 'edit buffer', or simply the 'buffer'. Changes are made to this temporary copy. To make the changes permanent you have to write the changed copy over the original file.

Both ed and ex are line editors — whatever operation you want to perform, you specify what line or lines on which to perform that operation.

Lines can be accessed (addressed, in ed terminology) in several ways, but the most easily understood way of addressing lines is by line number. In practice, addressing lines by number proves to be the most awkward to use, and there are other mechanisms (by the line's textual contents, for instance) for addressing lines.

This description of the editors is not to be considered as a full tutorial. We try here to give you a quick tour through the main features. We introduce the capabilities of the editors by showing how to add some new text to the edit buffer, and how to change text around in various ways, using different editor commands.

In this chapter we describe ed and ex together. First we show how something can be done using ed. This will also be valid for ex. Then we show, where appropriate, the additional capabilities that are available when using ex. The examples we give are in terms of some of our earlier examples introduced in chapter 6 — *Text Manipulation*. We show you how similar manipulations can be achieved using the editors.

If you want more detail on ed, refer to the description in the System V Manuals, or to *A Tutorial Introduction to the UNIX Text Editor*, or to *Advanced Editing on UNIX*, both by Brian W. Kernighan.

For more information on ex, again refer to the description in the System V Manuals, or to *Ex Reference Manual*, by William Joy and Mark Horton.

8.1. Getting Started with ed

To edit a file using ed, type the command ed followed by the name of the file you wish to make changes to. If you are creating a completely new file (one that does not exist already), you can still put the filename on the command line. For instance, to look at or make changes to a file called *nonesuch*, you start ed like this:

```
$ ed nonesuch
?nonesuch
```

This example shows how uncommunicative ed normally is — whenever ed doesn't understand something, it responds with a ?. Here, we asked ed to work on a file called *nonesuch*. ed's response is just a question mark ? followed by the file name. This we take to mean that the file called *nonesuch* doesn't exist. If this is a new file you are creating, that's fine. But if you are trying to modify an existing file, then either you have misspelled its name, or you are not in the directory you thought you were. Later in this chapter we show you how you can check on both these things without exiting from the editor.

ed has a help feature, whereby you can force it to tell you what's wrong, instead of just saying '?'. This feature is invoked by using one of the commands h or H once you have got into the editor. Applying this to our previous example:

```
$ ed nonesuch
?nonesuch
h
cannot open input file
```

ed now explains what the error actually is. If you use the lowercase h command, as we have shown, then ed explains only the last question mark it printed, all future mistakes will result in another '?'. The uppercase H command forces ed to explain all subsequent errors. A second H will turn off this feature.

Now let us try editing a file which does exist:

```
$ ed myfile
1083
```

This time, the file is there, and ed didn't start with just a query. The number '1083' (or whatever the number is) is a count of the number of *characters* in the file you are editing.

One of the things that makes ed awkward to learn to use is the fact that it normally doesn't prompt you for input. This can be very disconcerting, you can never be quite sure that it has done what you requested, or even whether it is 'listening' to you.

There is an option that instructs ed to give you a prompt. When you use the -p option, the very next argument on the command line is taken to be the character string you want to see as the prompt. The filename is the last argument. So, you could call ed like this:

```
$ ed -p go myfile
1083
go
```

The word 'go' is your prompt. It tells you that the editor is waiting for you to tell it what to do.

Your prompt could be a single character, for instance:

```
$ ed -p : myfile
1083
:
```

Now your prompt is the colon, :, which is the same as the ex prompt. This is probably not a good idea — you might forget that you were using ed and try to do something that is only possible in ex.

In this chapter we assume that you are using a prompt, and that it is the asterisk (*) character. Because * means something special to the Shell, we have to type the ed command line like this:

```
$ ed -p '*' myfile
1083
*
```

The quotes around the `*` ensure that the Shell doesn't try to do anything with it (like match all files in the directory), but passes it on to `ed` to use as the prompt.

If you have to use `ed` often, you might want to create your own version, which always calls the editor with your required prompt. We show you how to do this in Chapter 13 — *Using the Shell as a Programming Language*.

If you really want to use `ed` with a prompt, but forgot to put it on the command line, don't despair. You don't have to exit from the editor and invoke it all over again. There is an editor command `P` (note this is uppercase '`P`' — lowercase '`p`' does something different) that tells `ed` to give you a prompt:

```
$ ed myfile
1083
P
*
```

The prompt you get is an asterisk '*', you will continue to be prompted in this way until you give another `P` command.

You get out of `ed`, and back to the System V Shell, by typing a `q` (quit) command:

```
* q
$
```

There is more information on the quit command later, and a discussion on quit's interactions with the write command.

8.2. Getting Started with `ex`

To edit a text file using `ex`, you just type the command:

```
$ ex myfile
"myfile" 15 lines, 1083 characters
:
```

As `ex` reads your file into the editing buffer, it tells you how long the file is, both in lines and characters. The `ex` prompt is the colon character, ':'.

You can also give `ex` more than one filename when invoking it:

```
$ ex thisfile thatfile theotherfile
3 files to edit
"thisfile" 280 lines, 10994 characters
:
```

ex first tells you how many files you are going to edit (this is useful if you've used a command line like ex c*), then reads the first of the files into the editing buffer. ex tells you how long the file is, then responds with its prompt character, ':'. The next file on the command line can be accessed from within ex by using the n (next) command, described in more detail later.

If you have the terse option set (options are explained below), the message giving the count of lines and characters is abbreviated:

```
$ ex myfile
"myfile" 15/1083
:
```

If you ask ex to edit a non-existent file it assumes you are trying to create a new one, and gives you a message to that effect:

```
$ ex nonesuch
"nonesuch" [New file]
:
```

If you are not creating a new file, then you have probably misspelled the name of the file, or you are not in the correct directory.

8.3. Running System V Commands from Inside the Editors

There are times when you might want to run a UNIX system command, but would really prefer not to get out of the editor and re-enter it. In common with many other System V utilities, you can give both ed and ex a Shell command preceded with an exclamation mark ! When ed sees a line beginning with ! it passes the whole line to the Shell. The Shell runs that command, and then returns to the editor.

Running System commands from ed

Suppose you get the '?myfile' message when you weren't expecting it, but you think you have spelled the filename correctly. By typing

```
* !pwd
/aa/widget/maryann/work
*
```

you can check that you are in the correct directory, and

```
* !ls
Myfile   doc.hdrs   junk      staffmemo
*
```

shows you a list of the files in that directory. In this case you can see that the file is called *Myfile*, not *myfile* (remember that the UNIX system differentiates between upper and lowercase in filenames). In this case we can correct the error without quitting out of the editor:

```
* e Myfile
1083
*
```

The e (edit new file) command is explained later.

If there are several UNIX system commands you wish to run, you don't have to type them individually from within the editor, each preceded by a !. You can call up a new invocation of the Shell using !sh. This temporarily suspends your edit session and puts you at System V command level. You see the system prompt, and can execute any commands you want, including another ed (or ex) to edit another file. When you have finished you type CTRL-D, just as if you were logging out. You then return to your suspended edit session, where you see the editor prompt once more. This is called 'forking out of the editor'. An example is given below.

```
$ ed -p '*' myfile
?
* !sh
$ pwd
/aa/widget/maryann/work
$ ls
doc.hdrs   junk  staffmemo
$ ^D
*
```

Be aware that one thing you cannot achieve using this feature is a change of working directory. While at the UNIX system level you can change working directory, and do whatever you want in that directory. But as soon as you revert to the editor, your working directory also reverts to what it was at the time you invoked the editor.

So, if ed cannot find a file because you are in the wrong directory, you must exit from the editor, then change to the correct directory, and then invoke the editor again. Alternatively you can use the editor e command and give the full (or relative) pathname to the file you want.

When running a system command from within the editor, there a shorthand notation whereby % means 'the current file' — that is, the file you are editing. For instance, if you are editing a file containing a C program, you can check that the program compiles by:

```
* !cc %
```

or you can format your document for proof reading by:

```
* !nroff %
```

Another useful shorthand notation is the double !!, which means 'repeat the last system command'. So when you have corrected your compilation errors, you can recompile your program simply by saying !!.

A point to note is that the last command includes the expanded filename. So if you edit *program1*, and compile it with `!cc %`, then switch to editing `program2`, the !! still refers to *program1*.

Running System commands from ex

If you want to use a System V command while you are in `ex`, you can also use the `!`.

Another instance of the Shell can be invoked by using `!sh`, it can also be invoked by using the `ex` command `sh` (without the leading `!`). The convention of % for 'the current file' also applies, as does the notation !! for 'repeat the last system command'.

When you run a command in this fashion, `ex` warns you if you have changed the buffer since you last wrote it away. In the examples we have been discussing, this is very useful. There is no point in re-formatting your document if the changes you have made haven't been saved in the file yet. However, this warning is under control of the `warn` option, so if you don't want it you can turn it off by:

```
: set nowarn
```

The default setting of the option is `warn`.

8.4. Setting ex Options

The `ex` editor has a feature that is not available in `ed` — editor *options*. Options can be set or unset to affect the overall operation of the editor. The command that is used to change the options is the `set` command.

Each option usually has an abbreviation which is used with the `set` command. For instance, the `autoindent` option, which requests automatic indentation of lines during text entry, is abbreviated to `ai`. To set it you use the command:

```
:set ai
:
```

Options are unset, or nullified, by preceding the abbreviation by the letters no. For example, to request 'no automatic indentation' you say:

```
:set noai
:
```

Some options have values or strings associated with them. In this case they follow the option name, separated by an equals sign:

```
:set sw=4
:
```

More than one option can be set or unset by the same 'set' operation, the different options are separated by spaces. Setting and unsetting can be mixed, for example:

```
:set ai noopen sw=8 nowarn
:
```

All options have some default setting. The set command on its own displays the current state of those options that have been changed from the default. To examine the state of any one option, you follow set with a question mark:

```
:set magic ?
nomagic
:
```

The command 'set all' displays the settings of all the possible options that can be set or unset.

There are many, many options — we do not attempt to cover them all in this book. In general the options modify the way in which the editor commands work. We will explain the effects of the more interesting options along with the description of the commands.

Two of the options affect the messages you get from ex, these are the terse and report options. The terse option is concerned with reducing the length of messages from ex. The messages produced by ex are fairly lengthy. In many instances error messages include statements as to how to override the error condition. The experienced user might grow impatient with all this verbiage, and the person using a slow terminal will probably be upset by it. The messages can be shortened by setting the `terse` option. One instance is the message about the size of the file you are editing, we showed you above how that is shortened when the `terse` option is set. We will be showing other instances later in the chapter. The default setting is `noterse`.

When a command changes a large number of lines, `ex` reports this fact. The value of the `report` number determines what `ex` considers a large change to the buffer. The default definition of 'large' is 5. When you are doing an extensive 'cut-and-paste' operation on a file, you will probably consider 5 lines a small change rather than a large one. The command:

```
: set report=20
:
```

changes things so that `ex` only reports when 20 lines or more are affected by an edit command.

ex Editor Profile

Just as you can have a login profile, into which you put commands that the Shell obeys at login time, so you can have an `ex` profile containing editor commands that are obeyed each time `ex` is invoked.

Each time you use `ex` it looks in your home directory for a file called *.exrc*. If there is such a file, the `ex` commands in it are executed before you are prompted for the usual interactive edit commands.

If there are any `ex` options which you wish to use on a regular basis, the `set` operations for these can be placed in that `ex` profile, *.exrc*. An example of an `ex` profile is:

```
$ cat .exrc
set ai nomagic sw=4 term=adm3a
$
```

which sets the `autoindent` option, makes the `shiftwidth` 4 spaces, unsets the `magic` option, and sets the terminal type for an ADM-3a.

Again, editor options and editor profile are `ex` features, they are not available in `ed`.

8.5. Getting Out of the Editor

Although we haven't yet told you how to make any changes to your file, we are telling you how to get out of the editor first. There is nothing more frustrating than to be in an editor, and want to get out (maybe because you've tried to edit the wrong file), and not know how.

Basically, the same method is used to quit both editors — you save any changes using the w (write) command, then use the q (quit) command to return to the Shell. However, the detailed behavior of ed and ex is slightly different.

Quitting ed with q

To quit the edit session, just type a q command:

```
* q
$
```

You can see that we got out of ed and reverted to the Shell, where we once more got the $ sign system prompt.

Note that the quit command does not automatically write the edited buffer onto the file. To capture any changes made during the editing session, an explicit write command must be given.

```
* w
1205
* q
$
```

The write command in the above example overwrites the contents of the file that was given on the ed command line with the contents of the edit buffer, thus making any changes permanent.

The changes could also be written to a different file by naming a file on the w command:

```
* w myfile.new
1205
* q
$
```

ed makes a note of whether the editing session to date has changed the buffer in any way. If a quit command is given without having previously written the buffer to a file, and the buffer has been changed, ed responds with its usual question mark:

```
* q
?
* h
warning: expecting 'w'
*
```

as a reminder that the buffer has been changed but not written to any file. You can use h to find out what the question mark means, as we show in the above example. A second quit command forces an exit back to the Shell with no further comment, so if you have really made a mess of things you can get out of the editor without affecting your original file. If the buffer has not been changed during the edit session, one q command is enough to get back to the Shell.

ed's memory of the buffer contents is fallible. If you change a line, then change it back to what it was originally, there is no change as far as you are concerned. But ed really has no way to know what you actually did, so the buffer is marked as changed.

If you give the uppercase Q command to get out of the editor, ed doesn't check to see whether the buffer has changed before putting you back at the UNIX system command level.

Quitting ex with q

As with ed, the command to exit from ex is q, for quit. If you try to exit without having written your changes away to a file, ex warns you:

```
: q
No write since last change (quit! overrides)
:
```

If you really don't want your changes saved, you can use the command variant q! (or you can spell out in full quit!) to exit.

If you specified several files on the calling ex command, and try to quit before you have dealt with them all, you get:

```
: q
2 more files to edit
:
```

Again, the q! command variant will get you out.

For convenience, the write and quit operations can be combined:

```
: wq
"myfile" 18 lines, 1205 characters
$
```

If you wish to save your changes in a different file from the one you originally asked to edit, this can be done by putting the new filename on the w command, the same as in ed. In this case, the write and quit commands must be given separately.

8.6. Format of Editor Commands

There is a general format of editor commands. It is not necessary to formally learn this format but we tell you about it so that, as you go through the examples, you will notice that they fit a pattern.

The format of an editor command, using the convention followed by the System V manuals, is:

[*line* [, *line*]] *operation* [*parameter*]

Here is a picture of the situation:

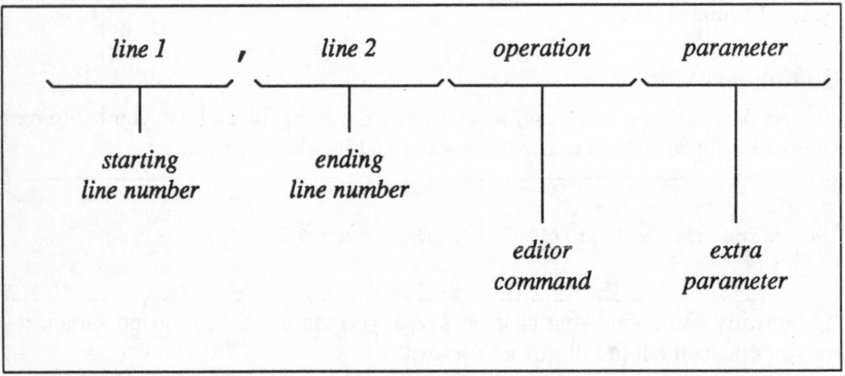

In words: an ed command consists of:

- *one* optional line-address, *or*
- *two* optional line-addresses separated by a comma,
- then a single letter operation,
- optionally followed by some other parameter.

Commands to ex follow the same layout, but the operation is not restricted to a single letter.

The form of the mysterious 'other' parameter varies for each operation, it is mostly obvious what it should be for any specific operation. For the move and transpose operations it is the line that the addressed lines are to be moved or transposed after. These operations actually have three line-addresses. For the read operation, the extra parameter specifies the name of the file that is to be read. For many operations there is no extra parameter, supplying one on a command is invalid and results in an error message.

The substitute operation is an exception to the format described above, because between the operation and the optional parameter you also have to specify the string you want to have substituted, and what you want in its place. Substitution is the most powerful feature of the editors and we cover it in detail later in this chapter.

In general, editor command lines tend to be short. However, if you do have a long command, such as a substitute operation, it can be split over two or more lines. This is done in the same way as for UNIX system commands — the newline characters on all except the last line are escaped by preceding them with a reverse slash character, `\`.

Line Addressing

The format of commands above showed that a command can be preceded by one or two line-addresses. Both of the line-addresses are optional. The line addresses can take several forms, here are some examples of editor commands using the different types of line addressing:

`1,10p`	*using line numbers*
`.,$w partfile`	*current line and last line*
`/Sally/d`	*search strings*
`'a,'zm$`	*marked lines*

The first command uses line numbers; the second uses the 'current line' and the last line in the buffer. The third command uses search strings and the last shows the use of marked lines. These different types of line addressing are discussed below.

If only one line-address is specified, the command is performed on that specific line. If two line-addresses are supplied, the command is done on all lines in the range between them.

The Current Line in the Buffer

While `ed` (or `ex`) is working on the buffer, it keeps track of which line is the one on which you last performed some operation. This line is called the *current line*. You can indicate the current line by typing a period character `.` (**dot** again), and so the word **dot** is used to mean the current line. If you don't specify a line for a command to operate on, most `ed` operations work on the line addressed by **dot**.

When `ed` starts working on a file, **dot** is positioned at the last line in the buffer. Thereafter, **dot** usually changes when any operation is performed. In general, **dot** sits at the last line affected by whatever editor command you used. For instance, if you print lines 1 through 10 of the buffer, after the lines are displayed **dot** will be positioned at line 10.

The Last Line in the Buffer

To get at the last line in the buffer you don't have to know how many lines are in the file you are changing, or how many lines you have added or deleted. The last line in the buffer can always be accessed using the notation '`$`', regardless of whether it's the tenth line or line 2001.

Thus the notation `1,$` stands for the entire buffer. This is the default for the write operation, as we have already seen. The notation `.,$` means 'everything from the current line to the end'.

Line Numbers

The simplest form of line-address is a line number. For example, a straight 4 means line 4 in the buffer. The range 1,10 means lines 1 through 10 in the buffer.

It should be clearly understood that, unlike some other editors, the line numbers that ed knows about are not physically a part of the text in the lines. Also, it is important to understand that the line numbers in the buffer are relative to the start of the buffer. This means that if you delete line 1, the line which was line 2 now becomes the new line 1, and all the other lines move up by one. Similarly, if you append two new lines after line 3, the two new lines become the new lines 4 and 5, and all the other lines move down by two.

If you are doing changes and deletes by line number, it is wise to start at the end of the buffer. That way, you don't have to re-compute all the line numbers on the fly. The diff program, which we saw back in chapter 6, generates its ed commands in this back to front manner.

Line Zero in the Buffer

One important thing to remember is that there is a zero'th line in the buffer. Line 0 never has any text associated with it. It is an 'imaginary' line which is useful when you want to put stuff before the first real line in the buffer. Line 0 is used solely as a crutch to enable operations that are clumsy or impossible in other editors, for instance inserting text before the first line in the buffer.

Text Patterns

Lines can be addressed by their textual contents as well as by line numbers. Line numbers are convenient, but it is even more convenient to be able to locate an arbitrary line in the buffer based on the actual text in the line. The pattern-matching facility in both ed and ex makes this easy. You simply give the editor the text string you want to find surrounded either by slashes (/) or by question marks (?), for instance:

```
/this string/
?that string?
```

Text patterns are also referred to as 'search strings', because that is what the editor does with them. It searches through the file for a line containing the text string specified. When it finds one it stops, and that line becomes the current line (**dot**). If you surround the string with slashes, the editor searches forward through the file. If the string is surrounded by ?'s the editor searches backwards through the file. If the string is not found, **dot** is left unchanged.

The search wraps around the file. That is to say: if you request a forward search it starts at the current line and goes towards the end of the file, then starts back at the beginning of the file and continues searching until the current line is reached once more (or a line containing the string is found). Similarly on a backward search — if the string is not found between the current line and the beginning of the file, the search continues by searching from the end of the file back to the current line. In the `ex` editor this wraparound feature can be turned off.

The simplest text patterns are fixed character strings, but you are not restricted to this. Line-addresses in `ed` can be specified as regular expressions, just like those we described for the `grep` command in chapter 6.

We go into more detail of text patterns and search strings later in this chapter, this is just a quick overview so that you will understand some of the examples of editor commands.

The Remembered Pattern

When you try to find a line of text by specifying a text pattern, the editor will search until it finds the first line containing that pattern. This might not be the line you want, especially if the pattern you gave occurs many times in the file. It is a good idea to display the line that was found, if it is not the right one you must repeat the search until you get to the line you want.

When a text pattern is used to specify a forward or backward search, it is stored away as the 'remembered pattern'. This means that having found a particular line, the next line containing that pattern can be found just by typing two slashes `//` or two question marks `??`.

Marking Lines

Another way of specifying the line you want is by addressing a marked line. This is useful when you have large amounts of text to delete, or move around in a file. We describe the procedure in detail in section 8.15 — *Cut and Paste Operations.* For now we'll just give the bare outline.

Having found the line you want by whatever means (line number or string search) you can mark that line with a label, which is a single lowercase letter. Any line so marked or labelled can be addressed using the notation `'`*z*,where *z* is the label previously attached to the line.

Line Addressing Expressions

You can combine patterns with numbers to form line-addressing expressions. The following are examples of valid expressions:

`$-1`	addresses the penultimate line of the buffer.
`$-10`	addresses the line 10 lines before the end of the buffer.
`/blurb/+`	addresses the line after the one containing '`blurb`'.
`?burble?-2`	addresses the line that is 2 lines before the one containing '`burble`'.

'a+5 addresses the 5th line after the line marked *a*.

If you use a range of line-addresses in a command, the two parts of the range do not have to be the same. One could be formed as a simple line number, and the other could well be formed as a text pattern. For instance

```
1,/Char/
```

addresses all lines from line 1 through to the line containing the character string 'Char'.

8.7. Displaying the Contents of the Buffer

Before we show you how to make changes (have patience, we'll get there) we show you how to display what's currently in the buffer. It is usually a good idea to look at what you intend to change, then look again after you have done the change to verify that what you did was correct. This is especially true when you are learning to use the editor, as you gain confidence you might skip some of the process.

In order to look at the buffer contents you will need to invoke the editor on an existing file. This could be a file you have previously created using `cat`, as we showed in Chapter 4 , or it could be a file you have copied from someone else.

Displaying the Buffer with `ed`

There are two different `ed` commands to display the buffer contents. The most widely used is the `p` (print) command. The `l` (list, or maybe look) command functions just like print, but displays non-printing characters as well. There is also a `n` command which displays lines with line numbers prepended.

The usual way of displaying lines from the buffer is to use the `p` command. Just typing a plain `p` displays the current line:

```
* p
Bill Williams   100
*
```

The third line in the buffer can be printed with this command:

```
* 3p
Jane Bailey     121
*
```

In fact, if you give `ed` a line address without any operation, it assumes you want to print the line or lines. So we could have said simply `3`. The first three lines can be displayed by typing:

```
* 1,3
Maryann Clark   101
Sally Smith     113
Jane Bailey     121
*
```

and the contents of the entire buffer can be displayed by typing the command:

```
* 1,$
Maryann Clark   101
Sally Smith     113
Jane Bailey     121
Jack Austen     120
Steve Daniels   111
Sylvia Dawson   110
Henry Morgan    112
Hank Parker     114
Charlie Smith   122
Bill Williams   100
*
```

The `l` command displays non-printing characters as well as the printable characters. For example, if there are tabs, bell characters, and other control characters in the buffer, list displays them in a special form. Some of the special characters are displayed this way:

> tab character,

< backspace character,

$ newline character.

Other 'funny' characters show up as the octal value of their ASCII representation, preceded by the backslash character \. For example, CTRL-A appears as `\01`, the 'bell' character shows as `\07`.

The `n` command shows lines with line numbers prepended. This can be extremely useful when you have made changes that have altered the original line number. An example of its use is:

```
* /Jane/,/Steve/n
3       Jane Bailey     121
4       Jack Austen     120
5       Steve Daniels   111
```

Note that the line numbers do not form part of the file, they are simply displayed by ed. As with the print command, **dot** is left at the last line displayed.

Stepping Forward and Backward in the Buffer Just entering a plain RETURN is an ed command. A RETURN advances **dot** to the next line in the buffer, then prints that line. This is a convenient way to 'step' through the buffer, printing lines one at a time.

Typing a plus sign + is the same as a single RETURN. The plus sign advances **dot** to the next line in the buffer, then prints that line. Plus signs are cumulative, so typing five of them in a row:

```
+++++
```

advances **dot** by five lines, then prints that line.

It is not possible to step past the end of the buffer. When the end of the buffer is reached, ed displays its usual question mark for a response.

It is also possible to step backwards through the buffer one line at a time in the same way that a RETURN steps forwards through the buffer. Typing a minus sign moves **dot** to the previous line and then displays that line. Minus signs are cumulative, so typing several in a row moves **dot** back that number of lines. When stepping backwards through the buffer, it is not possible to step before line 1 in the buffer. An attempt to do so results in a question mark response from ed.

Both the plus signs and the minus signs may be followed by a decimal number. Typing

```
+7
```

moves **dot** ahead seven lines, then displays that line. Similarly, typing

```
-19
```

moves **dot** back by 19 lines, then displays the addressed line.

Showing a Line Number An equals sign, =, as a command simply prints the line number of the addressed line. This can be used when you want to find the line number of a line containing a particular character string, for instance:

```
* /Maryann/=
6
*
```

This is especially useful when you have been moving text around in the buffer, thereby altering line numbers from their original values. If you want to deal with a large block of text (delete it, or move it to a different place) you could find the first line using a search string and make a note of the number using =. Then, when you find the last line of the block, you know the line numbers you need to specify on your ed command (providing you haven't done any other changes between the two searches).

The = command defaults to the last line in the buffer, so you can see how many lines you have in total by typing = on its own.

There are two ways in which this is different from using the n to display line numbers. One is that n displays the entire line with the number tacked on at the front, whereas = simply displays the number of the line, not its contents. In many ways using n is safer. The other important difference is that n changes the value of **dot** to be the last displayed line. When you use = the value of **dot** is not changed — you are still at the same place in the edit buffer.

Displaying the Buffer with ex

The ex editor has the print and list commands the same as ed, and you can step through the buffer forward or backwards. ex also has other commands that can be used to display the buffer contents in different ways. In addition, there a couple of options that modify ex's behavior when displaying text.

The autoprint option (abbreviated ap) ensures that lines are always printed after they have addressed or changed, so you don't specifically have to use the p command:

```
: 1,5
Bacchus must now his power resign -
I am the only God of Wine!
It is not fit the wretch should be
In competition set with me,
Who can drink ten times more than he.
:
```

However, the p command still exists, and must be used if you have noap (no automatic printing of lines) set. The default setting of this option is autoprint (ap).

The l command shows you all the control characters, which are normally non-printing. In ex the control characters are displayed using the abbreviation '^' for control. So a tab appears as '^I' and CTRL-A appears as '^A'. This is great improvement, since you can see what crazy key you typed, without having to look it up in the */usr/pub/ascii* file.

You can see line numbers by displaying lines with the command # (n is used for a different purpose in ex), as shown in the next example.

This is useful if you like to specify line addresses as line numbers. Note that the numbers only appear on the display — they are not put into the buffer. If you have the number option (abbreviated nu) set, lines are always displayed with numbers prepended, even with the p and l commands. The default setting is nonu. Numbers are not normally displayed.

```
: 6,$#
     6  Make a new world, ye powers divine!
     7  Stock'd with nothing else but Wine:
     8  Let Wine its only product be,
     9  Let Wine be earth, and air, and sea -
    10  And let that Wine be all for me!
:
```

A very useful feature of `ex` is the context display. A screen-full adjacent to the specified line is displayed. If you are using a terminal which doesn't have a screen, the display is 8 lines. The display may be specified in different ways. A plain `z` command displays the addressed line at the top of the screen, `z-` shows the addressed line at the bottom of the screen, and `z.` puts the addressed line in the middle of the screen. In any case, **dot** is set to the last line displayed, that is, the last line displayed becomes the new current line.

Another variation of the context display is `z=`, which is like `z.` in that the current line is at the center of the display. But the current line is marked on the display:

```
: 6z=
In competition set with me,
Who can drink ten times more than he.
----------------------------------------
Make a new world, ye powers divine!
----------------------------------------
Stock'd with nothing else but Wine:
Let Wine its only product be,
:
```

and **dot** is not changed — the current line is still the one marked by the `---`'s on the display.

If the `number` option is set, the lines are displayed with line numbers prepended. If the `number` option is not set (the default), you can combine the `z` and # commands, and say something like '`z.#`'. The `z` and `l` commands can be combined in a similar way.

8.8. The undo command

A very useful command is `u` — the undo command. This is available in both `ed` and `ex`, and works in a similar manner in both of them. The undo command undoes the last change made to the edit buffer, and repositions the current line to where it was before the undone change was made.

This is very handy if you make a mistake while doing some changes. Notice that only the last change is undone, so if you do something wrong you must recover by typing u *immediately*, before you make any further changes.

A second u command will not go back to undo the previous change — it will undo the last u command, thus applying the (presumably wrong) changes all over again.

If the last command was a global operation, all changes made by that command are reversed.

Only changes affecting the edit buffer can be undone. If you write the contents of the buffer to a file using w, you cannot 'unwrite' them by using the u command.

8.9. Adding New Text with a and i

At last we tell you how to make changes to the edit buffer, and we start by showing you how to add new text. Since ed and ex are *line* editors, when we talk about adding text we really mean adding *lines* of text. If you wish to simply add one word into an existing line, you must either change the entire line as described later in section 8.11, or else use the substitute command to replace one word with two as described later in section 8.13. For now we are talking about adding completely new lines of text.

There are two editor operations that can be used: a (append) and i (insert). The difference is that a inserts the new lines of text after the addressed line, while i puts the new text before the addressed line. A useful mnemonic is a for after, i for in front of.

Once you have given the appropriate command the editor is in 'text input mode'. You see no prompt, and every line you type is placed in the editor buffer. To terminate text input mode, and return to the point where you are issuing editor commands, you type a **dot** on a line *on its own*. This is very important. To stop text input mode, the **dot** must be the first thing on the line (no spaces, or even non-printing characters), and there must be nothing between it and the following RETURN.

Adding New Text in ed

To illustrate the append command, we start an editing session with a completely blank file, and add text into it. We use our file of people from earlier chapters, but this time we use ed to create the file, and change it around.

Let us start a new file called *people*:

```
$ ed -p '*' people
?people
*
```

Here, we asked ed to edit a file called *people*, and to prompt us using the character *. The file doesn't exist, so ed's response is just a query of the filename. Since there is nothing in the buffer (because this is a new file), we don't have to bother with line-addressing. We can just type an append command to get into 'text input mode':

```
$ ed -p '*' people
?people
* a
Maryann Clark    101
Sally Smith      113
Jane Bailey      121
Jack Austen      120
Steve Daniels    111
Sylvia Dawson    110
Henry Morgan     112
.
* p
Henry Morgan     112
* w
140
* q
$
```

Having added the new text into the buffer, we terminate the text insertion by typing a period character **.** (**dot**) at the beginning of a line, immediately followed by a carriage-return. This gets you back to the 'command mode', where you can type `ed` commands again. In our example, this is indicated by the prompt, `*`.

After an `a` or `i` command, **dot** stands at the last line of text typed into the buffer. This is illustrated in the example by the fact that the print command (with no specified line address) displayed the last line we entered.

Remember that the text we inserted only goes into the edit buffer at this time. It does not appear in the original file until the buffer is saved away with a write command.

The `i` (insert) command functions just the same as the append command, except that insert places the new text before the specified line. In our example above there were no previously existing lines in the buffer, so we could have equally well have used insert to create the new file.

As in our examples in the earlier chapters, we now wish to complete the *people* file by adding more names and telephone numbers to the list. To do this, simply edit the file again. When `ed` reads the file into the edit buffer, **dot** is left standing at the last line read in. So you can add new text by just typing an append command right away, as we show in the example on the following page.

Since **dot** is positioned at the end of the buffer when `ed` reads the file, we don't have to specify a line number for the append command. New text is automatically placed at the end of the buffer. To place new text somewhere else in the buffer, we would have to supply a line address on the command.

```
$ ed people
140
* a
Hank Parker      114
Charlie Smith    122
Bill Williams    100
.
* w
200
*
```

Possible Problems When Inserting New Text Text input mode is the one that causes most problems, especially when you use ed without asking it to prompt you. It is not always easy to tell when you have really ended text input mode and are back at the stage of typing ed commands. The trouble is that text input must be terminated by a dot **.** at the very beginning of a line, and immediately followed by a carriage-return. It is important that there be no spaces or any other characters (including non-printing characters) on the line, either before or after the period. If you accidentally get some non-printing characters in the line because of 'fat-fingering' (CTRL-A is a common offender), you do not terminate text input mode. Yet there is nothing to indicate that on your terminal.

If you have asked ed to display a prompt when it is ready to accept commands, the matter is straightforward. If you don't see a * (or whatever), you are still in text insertion mode. In this case type, very carefully, a period character **.** followed by RETURN. You should now see the ed prompt. At this point it is a good idea to check that what you have appended (or inserted) is what you thought it was. You may find that you have some garbage lines which need to be deleted.

If you are using ed without a prompt, things are not so easy. One way of finding whether you are still in text input mode is to type a print command, followed by RETURN. It might be better to type 1,$p (print every line in the buffer) in case the last line you appended was a blank line. Whichever method you choose, if you are not in text input mode, ed will print whatever it was you asked for.

If ed's response is still a glassy-eyed stare, not even a blank line, you are still in text input mode. To get out of text input mode, carefully type the period character **.** followed by RETURN. Then type a p command again. This time ed should reply with the last line you appended (or inserted), which should be the letter 'p', or '1,$p'. Now you should check what you actually did. You will have at least one garbage line (the 'p' or '1,$p' you used to determine whether you were still in text input mode) to delete.

Adding New Text in ex

ex also has commands to append text after a given line and to insert text before a given line. Just as in ed these commands are a and i, and text insertion is terminated by a **dot**, or period character, on a line by itself.

There are also variants of these commands, `a!` and `i!`. The action of these variants is tied in with the idea of automatic indentation of lines, as provided by the `ex` option `autoindent`, usually abbreviated `ai`.

This feature of `ex` is handy when the text you are entering is program source, although it is not very useful for documentation text. The `ai` option of `ex` is the same as we have previously described for the `vi` editor, so we refer you to chapter 7 for a full explanation.

The variants of the text insertion commands have the effect of toggling the auto-indentation feature. So if `ai` is set the `a` operator will give you automatic indentation, but if you use `a!`, you will not get automatic indentation. However, if you have set `noai`, `a` will not give you automatic indentation but `a!` will. The effect of `i!` is similar.

There are other options that affect what happens in text input mode. These options are `beautify` and `wrapmargin`. They are also the same as in the `vi` editor, so once again we refer you to chapter 7 for a full description.

8.10. Deleting Lines with `d`

Deleting lines is the easiest change to make in a file. It is done using the `d` operator with line addresses specifying the line or lines you want to get rid of. This command is available in both `ed` and `ex`.

Deleting Lines using `ed`

The delete command removes selected lines from the buffer. A plain:

```
* d
*
```

deletes the current line,

```
* 10,20d
*
```

deletes lines 10 through 20 inclusive,

```
* .,$d
*
```

deletes all lines from the current line through to the end of the buffer and:

```
* /Clark/,/Clark/+3d
*
```

deletes four lines from the buffer, beginning with the line that contains the string 'Clark'.

In the description of grep in chapter 6, we showed the way to remove Henry Morgan from the *people* file, and replace him with James Walker. You can do this with the delete and append commands of ed:

```
* /Henry/
Henry Morgan     112
* dp
Hank Parker      114
* $a
James Walker     112
.
* p
James Walker     112
*
```

The delete command leaves **dot** standing at the first undeleted line. It is possible to append a p suffix after the delete command, as we showed in the example above.

The above example is an exact repetition of the example we gave in chapter 6, where we deleted a line from the middle of the file then added another line to the end of it. In practice, when using ed, it is simpler to replace the line containing Henry with one containing James, in the same place in the file. This would be done using the c (change) operator, described in the next section.

Deleting Lines using ex

The delete command works the same as in ed, but in some cases the definition of the lines you want to delete can be expressed more simply.

You can give an initial line address, then give d a trailing count. For instance, the last example we gave for ed above showed deleting four lines starting with the line that contained the string 'Clark'. This involved computing the address of the last line, it turned out to be 3 more than the first line. We can state this more simply in ex by saying:

```
: /Clark/d 4
:
```

which is easier to type, and less prone to error, than the ed way. The space following the command is not significant. A delete command of the form /Clark/d4 will do the job just as well.

Another difference in ex is that deleted lines don't immediately disappear completely. The go into a buffer (separate from the main editor buffer) and can be retrieved from there. This is the same as the un-named buffer that we talked about in vi. We describe the process of using this buffer in more detail in section 8.15 later on.

8.11. Changing Whole Lines with c

Lines of text can be replaced with new ones using the c (change) operator. Strictly speaking, the change command is redundant. If you want to change some lines in the buffer you can first delete the lines, then insert the replacement text. The change command is simply an extra convenience.

The change command changes entire lines in the buffer. Changed lines are deleted from the buffer, and new lines typed in to replace them. After you have given the change command, the editor is in text input mode, the same as for the append and insert commands. All the same rules apply.

Changing Lines using ed

We can apply the change command to the same example as before, that is removing Henry Morgan from the *people* file, and adding James Walker instead. Here is how to do the job using change:

```
$ ed - p '*' people
200
* /Henry/p
Henry Morgan     112
* c
James Walker     112
.
* p
James Walker     112
*
```

A period at the beginning of the line, followed by a **RETURN**, terminates the insertion of new text, just as it does for the append and insert commands.

dot is left standing at the last line of inserted text, as it is for the append and insert commands.

The number of lines that you type in following the c command need not be the same as the number of lines you are replacing. You can ask to change one line, and then type in several lines. Or you can ask to change a range of lines and only replace them with one (or even none) line.

Changing Lines using ex

As in ed, lines of text can be changed using the c command and the usual rules for text insertion described above apply. Also all the options, such as autoindent, are effective while you are typing in the replacement text. There is a variant of the command c! that toggles the effect of the autoindent (ai) option, just as for append and insert.

When you want to change several lines of text, there are two ways that you can express this — as two line addresses, or as a starting line address and a trailing count. This is the same as the delete operator described above.

For example, suppose you wish to change the four lines starting at line number 9 to something different. You can use the c command in the same way that you would use it in ed:

```
: 9,12c
something different
.
:
```

Or you can use the other, slightly easier, way of specifying the change command with a trailing count:

```
: 9c 4
something different
.
:
```

As with delete, the space following the command is not significant. A change command of the form 9c4 will do the job just as well.

8.12. Global Commands

A text pattern can be used with a *global prefix* to perform an operation on all lines that contain, or do not contain, a specified pattern. There are two global prefixes — g and v. The g prefix operates on all lines that contain the specific pattern. The v prefix inverts the search, just as the -v option did on grep, so commands preceded with the v prefix operate on all lines that do *not* contain the pattern.

The basic form of the global prefixes in both the ed and ex editors is like this:

line_1 , *line_2* g/ *text_pattern* / *command parameters*

where:

- *text_pattern* is the text pattern to search for in the buffer.
- *command* is the command to be performed on all lines that match the pattern (in the case of the g prefix), or on all lines that do not match the pattern (in the case of the v prefix).
- The text pattern matching is attempted on all lines between *line_1* and *line_2* inclusive. If you don't specify any line numbers before the g or v, the pattern match is attempted on all lines in the edit buffer.

The picture on the next page shows the format of the global prefix commands.

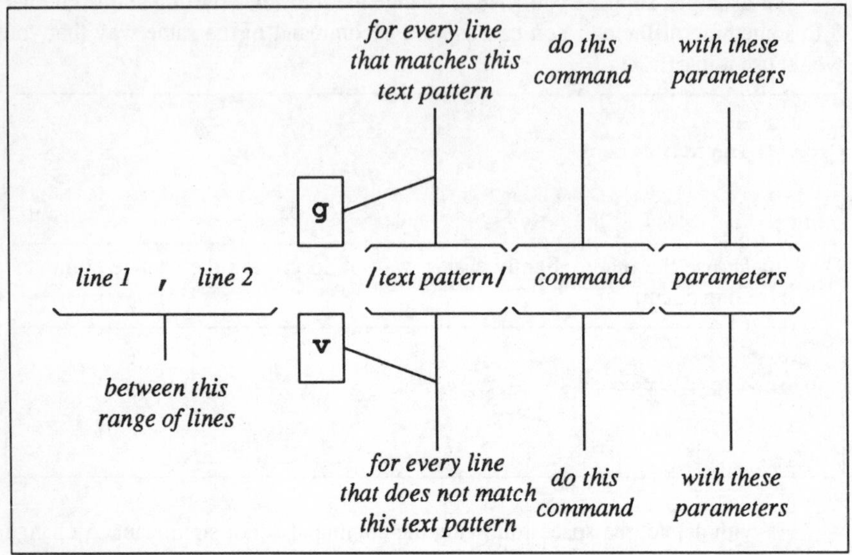

Global Commands in ed

Referring to our *people* example from above, we can find all the 'Smith's in the buffer in one go with a global command like this:

```
* g/Smith/p
Sally Smith      113
Charlie Smith    122
*
```

The command says to print every line containing the word 'Smith'. The pattern that you give to the global commands can be a regular expression, for example

```
v/^$/p
```

displays all non-blank lines in the edit buffer.

As we promised back in chapter 6 — *Text Manipulation*, here is the derivation of the `grep` command name. `grep` simply stands for:

```
g/re/p
```

which is to say: globally search for a regular expression and print every line which contains it. In other words, `grep` is a global regular expression printer.

In fact we can be lazy and not give the full command. The trailing / can be left off the search string unless the last character of the search string is a space. And `ed` command lines that don't specify an operation default to print. So we could have found all 'Smith's in the *people* file with a shorter command:

```
* g/Smith
Sally Smith     113
Charlie Smith   122
*
```

The global prefixes usually find most use in connection with the substitute command described in the next section, but any command can be done globally. For instance, to delete all blank lines, whether really blank or only apparently blank, we can use the global prefix with the delete operation:

```
$ ed -p '*' file
* 1234
* g/^[ ^I]*$/d
* w newfile
* 1221
* q
$
```

As usual `^I` indicates CTRL-I or TAB. The `g` prefix finds only lines consisting of nothing or spaces or tabs, the `d` operation gets applied only to those lines found by the global prefix.

We can make the file double spaced by using the `v` operation in combination with the transpose command:

```
$ ed -p '*' file
* 200
* 1i

.
* v/^$/1t.
* 1d
* w newfile
* 210
* q
$
```

First we inserted a blank line at the beginning of the file, so that it is line number 1, and this will not change. Then we used the `v` operation to find all non-blank lines. You can find details of the transpose (or copy) command later in section 8.15. In this example, the `t` operation copies line 1 (our blank line) after each line found by `v`. Finally we removed the (now redundant) blank line at the beginning of the file.

We could achieve the same thing by using the append command instead of transposing a blank line:

```
$ ed -p '*' file
* 200
* g/^.*$/a\

.
* w newfile
* 210
* q
$
```

We leave it as an exercise for the reader to look at the ed write-up in the System V Manuals and figure this one out, but you can see that we have used the reverse slash character to escape the newline, thus making the command extend over two lines.

ed has two other global commands, uppercase G and V. These are called interactive global commands. Each time ed finds a line containing the pattern (in the case of G), or not containing the pattern (in the case of V), after printing the line it waits for you to type in the operation you want to perform on this line. There is no prompt. You can type any ed command except another global command, or one of the commands that use 'text input mode' (append, insert, change) — this doesn't leave very much. If you just type RETURN no changes are made, the next line containing the pattern is printed. If the change you want to make is the same as the last change you made, you can repeat that by simply typing the ampersand (&) character.

Global commands in ex

The ex editor has the global commands g and v, just like ed. There is also a variant of the g command, g!. The g! variant inverts the meaning of the search, for example:

```
: g!/Wine
Bacchus must now his power resign -
It is not fit the wretch should be
In competition set with me,
Who can drink ten times more than he.
Make a new world, ye powers divine!
:
```

finds all lines that do *not* contain the word 'Wine'. The g! variant is exactly the same as the v command.

ex does not have the G and V commands, but it does have a useful flag that can be put at the end of a global substitution command, the c (confirmation) flag.

This is described in the next section on text substitution.

8.13. Text Searching, and Substitution using s

The substitute command, s, is probably the most useful command in the line editors. Substitution works on character strings within individual lines, instead of entire lines. This obviates re-typing entire lines of text when you only want to change a small part of the line.

Search and Substitution in ed

A substitution command looks like this:

```
* /bread/s/wheat/rye/
```

which means: in the next line containing 'bread' replace 'wheat' with 'rye'.

The remembered pattern applies in the s command as well as everywhere else. So if your search string and the string you want to substitute for are the same, the s command can be shortened:

```
* /wheat/s//rye/
```

means: in the next line containing 'wheat', replace that string with 'rye'. The use of the remembered pattern works even if the searching and substitution are done separately:

```
* /wheat/
* s//rye/
*
```

The substitution only affects the first occurrence of the string on the line. Suppose we print the current line of this imaginary buffer:

```
* p
wheat bread is my favorite, please make my sandwich on wheat
```

we can substitute the first occurrence of the word 'wheat', like this:

```
* s/wheat/rye/
* p
rye bread is my favorite, please make my sandwich on wheat
```

To change the second occurrence of 'wheat' we would have to repeat the substitute command.

However, there is a way to change *all* occurrences of a string on any line in one fell swoop, by adding the global flag at the end of the substitute command. To illustrate this, let us go back to the original example:

```
* p
wheat bread is my favorite, please make my sandwich on wheat
* s/wheat/rye/g
* p
rye bread is my favorite, please make my sandwich on rye
*
```

You can see that this time, the substitute command got them all at the same time.

The other optional extra parameter on the substitute command is the p (print) flag. This can be combined with the g flag if needed, so our previous example could be done like this:

```
* p
wheat bread is my favorite, please make my sandwich on wheat
* s/wheat/rye/gp
rye bread is my favorite, please make my sandwich on rye
*
```

Now you can see that the substitute command is considerably more compact than in some of the earlier examples.

To make substitutions on more than on line, the s can be preceded by a range of lines, for example:

```
1,10s/water/wine/
```

changes 'water' into 'wine' in the first 10 lines of the buffer, and the command:

```
1,$s/water/wine/
```

does the change in all lines in the buffer.

If either of the above substitute commands were to be typed with the p option after it:

```
1,$s/water/wine/p
```

the last line affected by the substitute is the one that is printed.

In all cases, if substitution is done on more than one line, **dot** is left standing at the last line on which a substitute took place.

Global Substitution Substitution on a range of lines can also be achieved by using the global prefix as shown on the next page.

```
* g/water/s//wine/
*
```

finds all lines containing 'water' and changes it to 'wine'. This still only changes the first occurrence of 'water' on each line; to change 'water' to 'wine' *everywhere* we have to use both the global prefix (to find all lines containing the pattern), and the global suffix (to do the substitute on all occurrences in each line).

```
* g/water/s//wine/g
*
```

There is an important distinction between the g at the beginning of the above command, and the g at the end of it. The initial g is the global command prefix, and can be applied to any command. The final g is the global flag suffix, and only applies to the substitute command.

The examples which follow repeat some of the examples of chapter 6, to illustrate how to achieve the same results with ed's global substitution feature.

We can compress a file by changing all sequences of 8 spaces to tabs by using the following global command:

```
$ ed -p '*' file
* 769
* g/        /s//^I/g
* w newfile
* 629
* q
$
```

ed does not support the '{8}' type of closure, so we have to spell out the 8 spaces. This doesn't necessarily achieve what you want, because the alignment of words in the file may be altered.

We can also use the g and s operations to remove the phone numbers from our *people* file:

```
$ ed -p '*' people
* 200
* g/[0-9]*$/s///
* w nophone
* 170
* q
$
```

We still have some spaces at the end of each line, to remove those too we should have used the regular expression

```
/ *[0-9]*$/
```

We can apply the substitute command to our file of people, to do the same job as in the delete and change commands, namely to replace `Henry Morgan` with `James Walker`:

```
* /Henry Morgan/s//James Walker/p
James Walker  112
*
```

We are lucky that the name `James Walker` has the same number of characters as does `Henry Morgan`. If this were not the case, we would have to put extra spaces in one place or the other to preserve the alignment of the telephone numbers.

In the above example, we just did the substitution on the addressed line. In practice, we would be wise to display the line we are about to operate on. Our next example illustrates this.

We want to change Sally's last name from Smith to White. Again, we use the substitute command:

```
* /Smith/s//White/p
Charlie White  122
*
```

Unfortunately, we changed the wrong Smith. This is because, after we had changed Henry to James, **dot** was left standing at that line. The next occurrence of Smith in the buffer is `Charlie Smith`. This demonstrates that it is safer to display the line before you change it.

It also illustrates the usefulness of the undo command, `u`. We can retrieve the original line with `u`, then we can then carry on as before:

```
* u
Charlie Smith   122
* //
Sally Smith     113
* s//White/p
Sally White     113
* w
* 200
*
```

The Remembered Text A special character that can be used in the substitution string is the ampersand character, `&`. It stands for 'whatever text you are replacing'. For example, to replace 'bread' by 'wheat bread', we can say:

```
* /bread/s//wheat &/
```

Here, the `&` simply serves as a shorthand notation, because we searched for a fixed string and could have said:

```
* s/bread//wheat bread/
```

But when the search pattern is a regular expression we don't know exactly what we're going to find, so it is important to have a way of referring to the string that matched the expression on the left hand side.

Grouping Regular Expressions in the `s` Command Within the left-hand side of a substitute command, it is possible to delineate parts of the regular expression, in such a way that they can be referred to in the right-hand side. On the left-hand side, a part of a regular expression can be marked by enclosing it between `\(` and `\)`. You can mark up to nine chunks of a pattern in this way.

Then, on the right-hand side, the delimited groups can be retrieved by using the notation *n*, where *n* is the *n*'th group, numbered from 1 to 9, left to right.

We can illustrate this process by using our *people* file again. In chapter 6 we use the `cut` and `paste` utilities to reverse the first and last names in the *people* file as a sop to a bureaucracy which cannot handle peoples' names in the right order. Here is how we do the same job using `ed`:

```
$ ed people
200
* 1,$/s/\([A-Za-z]*\) \([A-Za-z]*\)/\2, \1/
* 1,$p
Clark, Maryann   101
Smith, Sally     113
Bailey, Jane     121
Austen, Jack     120
Daniels, Steve   111
Dawson, Sylvia   110
Morgan, Henry    112
Parker, Hank     114
Smith, Charlie   122
Williams, Bill   100
*
```

This is not the world's most readable edit command. But take it one thing at a time:

- We want to operate on every line in the file, so the `1,$` addresses every line.
- On every line, we look for two groups of alphabetic characters (either uppercase or lowercase), separated by a space. Each group is represented by the pattern

  ```
  [A-Za-z]*
  ```

  and each group is then enclosed in the `\(` and `\)` delimiters.
- On the right hand side of the substitute, those groups are simply accessed by the `\2` and the `\1` markers, with a comma separating them. The effect is to reverse the names on each line.

Some Notes on Searching and Substitution We have seen that when searching for a string it is not always necessary to give an entire word that you really want to find, but be careful how you abbreviate. For example, suppose you wanted to find the word 'mankind'. If you specify:

```
/man/
```

as your search string, not only will you find 'mankind', but also 'womankind' (which may be OK) and 'manumission' (which probably isn't OK) plus a lot of other words like 'man', 'manual', 'emancipate', and so on. In this case,

```
/mank/
```

is probably a good abbreviation, or

```
/anki/
```

though that's not so easy to think of.

Another thing to beware of is a whole word which can also form part of another, longer, word. For example, suppose you want to find all instances of the word 'his', maybe because you want to replace it by 'her'. Using

```
/his/
```

may also get you 'history', 'histogram' and 'this'. So if you tried to do your change by the command:

```
* g/his/s//her/g
```

you would end up with words like 'hertory' and 'ther', which is not what you want. Using

```
/his /
```

avoids 'history', 'histogram', and 'antihistamine', but you still find 'this'. Using

```
/ his /
```

solves that one, but now we can think of another problem. What happens if 'his' is at the start of a sentence and therefore is actually 'His'?

This is where regular expressions can help us out:

```
/ [Hh]is /
```

finds the word starting with either an uppercase or a lowercase letter, as long as it has a space before it and a space after it. [1] Fine, what about 'his' (or 'His') at the beginning of a line?

```
/^[Hh]is /
```

takes care of that, and likewise:

```
/ [Hh]is$/
```

looks after the case where the word is at the end of a line. In fact, all these can be combined and we can use the search string

```
/[ ^][Hh]is[ $]/
```

We still haven't accounted for the case where the word may be at the end of a sentence and therefore is followed, not by a space or newline, but by a period.

The moral is: if you are doing extensive changes by search and substitution, be careful how you specify your strings. A good practice is to display what the search finds before actually making any substitutions, otherwise the results can be disastrous (though sometimes hilarious).

Search and Substitution in ex

Searching for character strings is similar to ed. In ex you can be lazy: you don't have to put the final / or ? at the end of your character string or regular expression, unless the final character is a space. Also, if you have the default value of the autoprint option, you don't have to specify the print command. Each line that matches the text pattern will automatically be printed. So you can simply say:

```
:/Smith
Charlie Smith   122
:
```

[1] In the ex editor this can be made easier by using the ignorecase option.

In ex there is a useful flag that can be put at the end of a global substitution command. This is the c (confirmation) flag. When the c flag is used, substitution does not happen automatically. Instead, each time the search string is found, ex prints it out and waits for input, which must be terminated by a carriage return. If the input begins with **y**, the substitution occurs, otherwise the string is left as it is. Here is an example:

```
: g/ine/s//ater/gc
I am the only God of Wine!
                      ^^^y
Make a new world, ye powers divine!
                               ^^^
Stock'd with nothing else but Wine:
                               ^^^y
Let Wine its only product be,
     ^^^y
Let Wine be earth, and air, and sea -
     ^^^y
And let that Wine be all for me!
              ^^^y
:
```

Each time ex found the string 'ine' as part of the word 'Wine', we typed y for 'yes'; but when the word 'divine' was selected, we didn't respond with anything other than carriage return. The result is that 'Wine' is changed to 'Water' everywhere, but 'divine' is left intact, it doesn't get changed into 'divater'. If you are not sure how good your search string or regular expression is, this is a good flag to use for safety. However, if you have a big file, giving all the responses can be a tedious business.

ex provides some additional metacharacters that are not found in other System V commands that use regular expressions:

- `\<` The two characters mean beginning of word, in the same way as ^ means beginning of line. So the string '\<d' would only find lines containing a word, or some words, beginning with 'd'. A 'word' is a string consisting of letters, numbers or underscore '_', surrounded by characters which are not letters, numbers or '_'.
- `\>` These two characters mean end of word, so 'y\>' will find lines that contain words ending in 'y'.
- `~` The tilde character ~ used in a regular expression matches the replacement text specified in the last substitute command.

Let's see some examples of these in action, using the verse of Henry Carey's drinking song in the example on the next page.

```
: g/\<m
Bacchus must now his power resign -
In competition set with me,
Who can drink ten times more than he.
And let that Wine be all for me!
: g/s\>
Bacchus must now his power resign -
It is not fit the wretch should be
Who can drink ten times more than he.
Make a new world, ye powers divine!
Let Wine its only product be,
:
```

The first global search finds all lines that contain words starting with 'm'; The second finds all lines containing words that have 's' at the end.

Here is an example of the use of the ~ character:

```
: /Bacch/s/must/should
Bacchus should now his power resign -
:/~
It is not fit the wretch should be
:
```

In this example, we first substitute 'should' for 'must'; the metacharacter ~ then searches for 'should'.

ex has two shorthand forms of substitute operation, namely & and ~. The ampersand operation & repeats the last substitute operation exactly. The tilde ~ replaces the last search or substitute regular expression with the replacement string specified in the last substitute operation. The difference is illustrated by the following examples:

```
: /power
Bacchus must now his power resign -
: s//crown
Bacchus must now his crown resign -
: /world
Make a new world, ye powers divine!
: &
Make a new world, ye crowns divine!
:
```

Although we have changed our search string from 'power' to 'world', the & still substitutes for 'power' — it repeats the last substitute command. However, if at that point we had used ~ instead, the result would be different:

```
: /world
Make a new world, ye powers divine!
: ~
Make a new crown, ye powers divine!
:
```

In this case, the last replacement string 'crown' is put in place of the last search string 'world'.

Although these two shorthand forms are useful, it is easy to confuse them and use the wrong one. In this case, it is tempting to use `u` to undo the substitution, then use the other. Unfortunately, this doesn't work, because the first use of `&` changes the effect of a following `~`. Similarly, if you use `~` first, a following `&` only repeats what you did with the original `~`. This is because `&` and `~` are expanded to full `ex` commands at the time they are typed, and the patterns remembered. The `u` command only undoes the *effect* of the command, it doesn't undo the remembrance of patterns.

`ex` has two other special character sequences which can be used in the replacement text.

`\u` and `\l` the first character of the replacement string (which immediately follows `\u` or `\l`) is converted to upper or lower case respectively.

`\U` and `\L` are similar, but all characters are converted to upper or lower case until the end of the replacement string or `\e` or `\E` is reached. If there is no `\e` or `\E`, all characters of the replacement text are made upper (or lower) case.

These last two can be used to change the case of individual characters, or whole words, or groups of words. For example, let's assume we are editing our *people* file:

```
: /Jane
Jane Bailey     121
: s/Jane/\U&
JANE Bailey     121
:
```

We used the special character sequence `\U` to change 'Jane' to uppercase. Also notice that we used the special character `&` to mean 'the string that was found'. We can change it back to lower case by:

```
: s/JANE/\L&
jane Bailey     121
:
```

We have to give the string 'JANE' to be replaced — we can't use the remembered pattern because our original string ('Jane') no longer exists.

The initial capital 'J' can be restored using the character sequence \u:

```
: s/jane/\u&
Jane Bailey     121
:
```

Again we have to respecify the string to be replaced because our previous one no longer exists.

An entire file can be made uppercase by the ex command:

```
: g/./s//\u&/g
```

There are several ex options which are connected with searching and substitution. These are ignorecase, magic, and wrapscan.

The ignorecase Option When the ignorecase option is set, uppercase letters and lowercase letters are considered to be the same for string searching operations. If the option is not set, uppercase letters are distinct from lowercase letters in a string or regular expression. The option is abbreviated ic; the default setting is noic.

Let's set the option, and repeat one of our searches from the previous examples:

```
: set ic
: g/\<m
Bacchus must now his power resign -
In competition set with me,
Who can drink ten times more than he.
Make a new world, ye powers divine!
And let that Wine be all for me!
:
```

this time the search has found one more line, that containing 'Make'.

The ignorecase option is useful, because you don't have to use regular expressions like

```
/[Hh]is /
```

to ensure you find words at the start of sentences as well as elsewhere.

In the example of changing lower case to upper, we would not have had to keep respecifying our search string, we could have said:

```
: /Jane
Jane Bailey      121
: set ic
: s//\U&
JANE Bailey      121
: s//\L&
jane Bailey      121
: /s//\u&
Jane Bailey      121
:
```

The `magic` Option The `magic` option is concerned with the metacharacters used in regular expressions. When `magic` is set, you have the full range of metacharacters in regular expressions used for searching and substitution. This means that if you really want to search for a character which acts as a metacharacter (for example '.'), you need to escape it by preceding it with a reverse slash \. The default in `ex` is for magic to be set.

If you do not, as a general rule, use regular expressions very often you may wish to set `nomagic`. This removes the special meaning from all characters except `^` and `$`, which still mean beginning and end of line respectively.

If you find that you need a regular expression now and again, you can still use them without turning `magic` on again. This is done by preceding the metacharacters you want to use with a \. The \ character 'toggles' the effect of the metacharacters. When magic is set, \ removes the special meaning from the following character. When magic is not set, \ makes the following character behave magically, if it can.

We previously showed you how an entire file can be made uppercase by the `ex` command:

```
: g/./s//\u&/g
```

This assumes that **.** has its magic meaning of 'match any character'. If `nomagic` is set, the above command has a very different effect — all period characters are changed to ampersands!

We can restore the magical effects to both **.** and `&` by preceding them with a reverse slash:

```
: g/\./s//\u\&/g
```

This temporary restoration of metacharacters is often quicker than setting `magic` and then unsetting it again.

The reverse slash's capability to control another character's magic makes it the most magical character of all. Regardless of whether the `magic` option is set or not, if you want to find a \ you have to give two of them (\\) to achieve it.

The wrapscan Option The wrapscan option controls the extent of a search. The wrapscan option is abbreviated ws. Normally, when searching for a string with

```
/string/
```

ex searches forward from the current line to the end of the buffer, and if the string hasn't been found, proceeds to search from the beginning of the buffer to the current line. A similar action occurs when searching backwards with '?*string*?'.

If you want ex to stop searching when it hits the end (or beginning) of the buffer, you can set no wrapscan option:

```
: .p
Make a new world, ye powers divine!
: /power
Bacchus must now his power resign -
: /
Make a new world, ye powers divine!
: set nows
: /
Address search hit BOTTOM without matching pattern
:
```

The search no longer wraps round the buffer, and you get a message if the pattern is not found before the end of the buffer is reached.

If you have the terse option set, the message is shorter:

```
No match to BOTTOM
```

The default setting is ws, or wrapscan on.

8.14. Reading, Writing, and Editing Files

Both ed and ex have read, write, and enter (or edit) commands that interact with the file system. Using these commands you can:

- read a file into the buffer,
- write the contents of the buffer to a file,
- replace the contents of the editing buffer with a new file so that you can edit a different file from the one you started with.

ex has some additional commands to deal with multiple filename arguments, and also to deal with the remembered file and an alternate editing file.

Read a File using `ed`

The `r` command reads the contents of a specified file into the buffer after a specified line. The basic form of the read command is:

line `r` *filename*

where *line* is the number of the line after which to read the file contents, and *filename* is the name of the file whose contents are to be read. Here is an example of where line zero is useful for editing. The command:

```
* 0r /aa/widget/steve/old.mail
```

reads the contents of the *old.mail* file from the */aa/widget/steve* directory, and places it before the first line in the buffer.

If no line is specified the read command, by default, reads the file in at the end of the buffer.

You can also get `ed` to place the output of a UNIX system command in the buffer. This is done by putting the command, preceded by a `!` in place of the filename. For example:

```
* r !pwd
```

puts the pathname of the current working directory as the last line in the buffer.

Write a File using `ed`

At the end of an edit session, `ed` does not automatically write the buffer onto the original file. An explicit `w` command must be used to write out the contents of the buffer. Of course, you don't have to wait until the end of your edit session before doing a write, you can save the current state of the buffer at any time. In fact, it is a good idea to do so — that way, if the system should crash while you are in the middle of an edit session, you won't have so much to recover.

If you just type a plain `w` command, the entire contents of the buffer are written either onto the file specified on the `ed` command line, or onto any subsequent file you have edited using the `e` operation. That is, if a filename is not explicitly stated in the write command, the buffer contents overwrite the file currently being edited.

The `w` command can be prefixed with a line-address range, to write selected portions of the buffer to the file. It is also possible to specify the name of the file onto which the contents of the buffer are to be written:

```
* 100,200w wurzel
4538
*
```

writes a copy of lines 100 through 200 onto a file called *wurzel*. Lines 100 through

200 remain in the buffer — the write command does not delete them.

When a write command is performed, ed displays a message stating the number of characters written to the file.

The write command can also be used to pass the contents of the buffer to a UNIX system command, without saving the buffer in a file. This is done by putting the command, preceded by a !, in place of the filename.

```
* 1,100w !lp
```

will get a hard-copy printout of the first 100 lines in the buffer.

Enter New File using ed

The e (enter) command enters (starts editing) a completely new file into the buffer, discarding the previous contents of the buffer. The command:

```
* e filename
```

reads the contents of *filename* into the buffer. The original contents of the buffer are discarded. The remembered file name (see the file command) is set to the filename given on the enter command, so that next time you do a write operation that is the default filename that will be used. **dot** is set to the last line in the buffer.

You use the enter command in situations such as getting a '?filename' response from ed, indicating that you probably misspelled the filename. In this case, you simply use the e command to start on the correct file.

The e command can also be used as a quick way to edit a new file after you have saved the changes to another file, or as a way to abandon one file and start work on a new one.

Let's see an example of how you can use these operations. Suppose that you have two files, *widget.spec* and *blivet.spec*. The first 30 lines of *widget.spec* need to be copied, with minor modifications, to the start of *blivet.spec*. The example on the following page shows how to achieve this.

First you use ed to write the first 30 lines of *widget.spec* to a temporary file. Then you edit that file to make the necessary minor modifications, and save them. Next you edit *blivet.spec* to place the lines from the temporary file right at the start of it. Finally, you use the ! feature to remove the temporary file. You are still in the editor, so you can proceed to make any further changes that might be required to *blivet.spec*.

```
$ ed -p '*' widget.spec
23748
* 1,30w temp
1754
* e temp
1754
* g/widget/s//blivet/g
* w
1754
* e blivet.spec
18921
* 0r temp
1754
* w
20675
* !rm temp
*
```

The Remembered File in ed

When an editing session is started on an already existing file with a command of the form:

```
$ ed garfield
```

ed 'remembers' the name of the file that was originally entered. Thus, a subsequent w command to write out the buffer contents will write to the remembered file. The e operation causes the new file to become the remembered file, so again a w command will write to the file that is being edited.

The f (file) command has two flavors. Just typing a plain f displays the current file name:

```
* f
garfield
*
```

This can be useful when you are manipulating several files. When you are using read, edit and write operations to transfer text from one file to another it is easy to lose track of where you are — especially if you go away for a coffee break (even more so if you take a champagne break).

You can also use the file command to set the remembered filename to something else by supplying the name you want:

```
* f something.else
* f
something.else
*
```

From here on, the remembered file name is *something.else*, and if a write command is issued at this time, the buffer is written to that file.

Read a File using ex

The r command reads the contents of a file into the edit buffer after the specified line. If no line is specified, the file is read in *after the current line.*

■ *This is an important difference from* ed, *where the default is to read in the file at the end of the edit buffer.*

Line 0 is a valid line number for the read operation:

```
: 0r preface
```

reads the contents of the file *preface* and places them at the beginning of the edit buffer. The last line of the file read in to the buffer becomes the current line.

The read command can also be used to get the results of a System V command entered into the edit buffer. This is done by giving the command to be executed, preceded by a ! character, in place of the file name. For instance, supposing you are composing a memo and you want to be sure you get today's date on it. You can use the date command:

```
$ ex memo
"memo" [New file]
: a
From: Bill Williams

To: Fred Bloggs

.
: r !date
!
Wed Mar 17 09:33 PST 1982
: 1,$p
From: Bill Williams

To: Fred Bloggs

Sat Apr 26 16:52:32 PST 1986
:
```

Unfortunately, the default format of the date produced by the date command is not the way that you usually see it written in memos, but a small editing change will fix that.

ex displays a ! character to indicate that it is executing the System V command that you have specified. This is displayed on the screen only, it does not get entered into the buffer. When the command has finished running, the last line brought into the buffer is printed. In the example above, only one line was brought into the buffer, and that line was printed. The last line brought into the buffer becomes the current line, **dot**.

Write the Buffer using ex

The w command writes the buffer, or part of the buffer, to a file. This works the same as for ed. A plain w on its own writes the buffer back onto the file you asked to edit, which is the most common use of the write command. In ex the write and quit operations can be combined, and you can save your file and exit from the editor by typing wq.

w followed by a filename writes the contents of the buffer to that specified file. If the file exists already, you get a message:

```
: w oldfile
"oldfile" File exists - use "w! oldfile" to overwrite
:
```

If the terse option is set, the message is simply 'File exists', and the conditions for overriding the situation are not detailed. If the w operation is preceded by a line address, or range of lines, only those lines are written to the specified file.

As indicated in the example above, the w! variant of the w command forces a write over an existing file. Another thing which affects overwriting of existing files is the writeany option, which is abbreviated wa. If this option is set, ex does not check to see if the file already exists when you type a w command.

All write operations to existing files are dependent on the mode of the file. If you don't have write permission, you will get a 'Permission denied' message.

The edit buffer can be appended to the end of an existing file using the notation:

```
: w >>oldfile
```

The edit buffer, or a part of it, can be made the input to a System V command. This is achieved by specifying the command, preceded by a ! character, in place of the filename. For instance, if you want to print the first 100 lines of the buffer on the line printer:

```
: 1,100w !lp
!
:
```

ex tells you when it's finished by repeating the ! character.

Beware of confusion between w! filename and w !command — spacing is very important.

Editing a New File using ex

When you call up ex with a specified filename, you usually get a message telling you how long the file is, in lines and characters:

```
$ ex song
: "song" 10 lines, 337 characters
:
```

If the file you specify doesn't exist, the message is:

```
: "sing" [New File]
:
```

If you see this message when you are not expecting it, you have probably spelled the filename wrongly. You can get at the correct file using the e command:

```
: e song
```

When you have finished editing a file, you can bring another file into the edit buffer with the e command. If you haven't written away the first file, ex warns you in no uncertain terms:

```
: e another
No write since last change (edit! overrides)
:
```

If you have the terse option set, the message is simply 'No write'.

As the non-terse message implies, you can use a variant of the command to force the new file to be brought into the buffer. However, you don't have to spell out in full edit!, e! is sufficient. All changes made to the file currently in the buffer are lost.

Editing Multiple Files using ex

We showed earlier that you can give several files as arguments when calling up ex, for example:

```
$ ex thisfile thatfile theotherfile
3 files to edit
"thisfile" 280 lines, 10994 characters
:
```

There are editor commands to access these files. The n (next) command brings in the next file specified in the argument list when ex was invoked:

```
: n
"thatfile"  120 lines, 7156 characters
:
```

If the current file has been modified but not written, you get a message:

```
: n
No write since last change (next! overrides)
:
```

The n! command variant forces the next file into the buffer, and changes made to the current file are lost. If the current file you are editing is the last file in the argument list, so that there are no more files left to edit, you get a message to that effect.

The args (arguments) command displays the argument list and indicates the file currently being edited:

```
: args
thisfile [thatfile] theotherfile
:
```

By using the rew (rewind) command, the argument list is 'rewound' and ex starts editing the first file all over again. You get the 'N files to edit' message, then the first file in the list is read into the buffer. If the current file has been modified but not written, you get the usual error message, and there is the usual command variant (rew!) that overrides it.

The Remembered and Alternate Files in ex

We described how ed remembers the name of the file you are editing, so that when you issue a write command you don't have to specify the filename. ex does the same thing, and the remembered file name can be accessed using the percent sign % as a shorthand notation. So, if you want to create a backup file before you make any changes, you can make your first command inside the editor a write operation:

```
$ ex myfile
"myfile" 698 lines, 24113 characters
: w %.old
"myfile.old" 698 lines, 24113 characters
:
```

The use of % as an abbreviation for the current file is extremely useful when you are obeying System V commands from within the editor.

The current file name can be displayed with the f (file) command:

```
: f
"myfile" [Modified] line 465 of 698 --66%--
:
```

As you can see, ex tells you more than the file name. It tells you where you are in the file, and whether the buffer has been modified since the last write operation.

The f command can also be used to change the remembered filename:

```
: f otherfile
"otherfile" [Not Edited] [Modified] line 465 of 698 --66%--
:
```

The new state of affairs is displayed automatically. The file is considered to be 'not edited' because there is no request to edit the file. This only becomes important when you try to write the file away. If there is no existing file of the remembered name, everything is fine. But if a file of the same name already exists, ex warns you about it, and you must use the w! command variant to write the file.

Whenever you ask to edit another file, by giving the e, n or rew operations, the new file name becomes the remembered filename. The new file is considered to be 'edited' (as is the file you call up on the ex command line), and you have no problem writing the file away.

There is another file that ex remembers the name of, called the 'alternate file'. When you change the remembered file name, the previous file becomes the alternate file. The alternate file can be accessed with the shorthand notation #. If there are two files you want to edit, you can easily swap from one to another by using the command 'e #'. An advantage of using this, instead of specifying the alternate file in full, is that you get back into the file at the same point you were at when you left it — if you specify the full filename you enter the file at the end again.

If your request to edit a new file is unsuccessful because you haven't written out the current file, then the file name you specify on the `e` command becomes the alternate filename. This means that after writing the current file, you don't have to specify the new file name in full, but you can simply say '`e #`'.

When you specify a file name on a read or write operation, that file becomes the alternate file too.

8.15. Cut and Paste Operations

In the previous section we showed how you could copy lines of text from one file to another by writing to a temporary file, then reading that file into the buffer. The same technique could be used to copy lines within the same file, and if the original lines were deleted the copy operation would become a move.

This procedure is rather cumbersome, and can be extremely tedious when the text to be moved or copied consists of many small blocks. Both `ed` and `ex` have operators that allow you to move and copy lines of text without having recourse to intermediate files.

Cut and Paste with `ed`

`ed` has commands to move and copy (or transpose) lines of text from one place to another in the edit buffer. There is also a command that can be used to mark lines that form the beginning and end of a block of text that is to be moved.

However, in `ed` these commands only work in the edit buffer — that is within the file you are currently editing. They cannot be used to move or copy lines of text from one file to another. For that you have to use the write and read operations and some temporary files, as we showed earlier[2].

Moving Lines in `ed` The basic form of move is:

line_1 , *line_2* `m` *line_3*

This means: 'move all lines between *line_1* and *line_2* inclusive, and place them after *line_3*', as shown in the picture on the following page.

---

2 The same is not true for `ex`. In that editor you can move text to a different file without using temporary files.

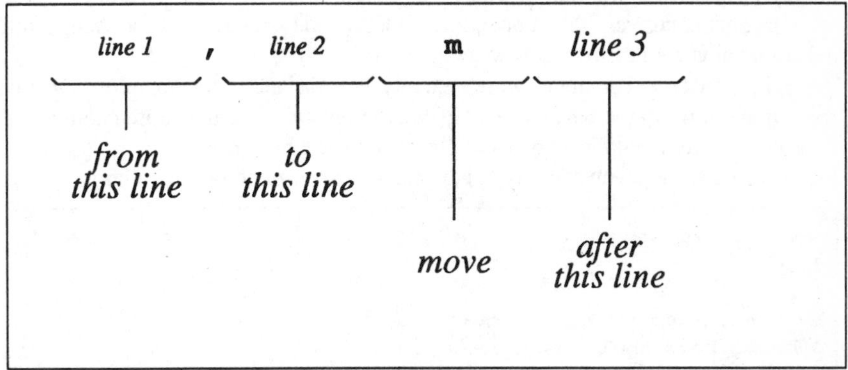

We will demonstrate the move operation by using it to sort our file *people* into alphabetical order:

```
$ ed -p '*' people
* 200
* /Austen/m0
* /Bailey/m/Austen/
* /Clark/m/Bailey/
     <etcetera . . .>
* 1,$p
Jack Austen     120
Jane Bailey     121
Maryann Clark   101
Steve Daniels   111
Sylvia Dawson   110
Henry Morgan    112
Hank Parker     114
Charlie Smith   122
Sally Smith     113
Bill Williams   100
* w
* 200
* q
$
```

In practice, it doesn't make much sense to use an editor to arrange a file into alphabetical order. Either you are going to `sort` the file, or you are going to keep the file in order, in which case you would have created it that way in the first place.

Copying Lines in `ed` The `ed` operation to copy lines is called `t` (transpose). This is not very mnemonic, but the letter `c` is already used for change, and `ed` commands are limited to single letters.

The transpose command works exactly like the move command except that the original lines in the buffer also stay where they are. The transpose command is thus a good way to duplicate blocks of text within the buffer.

It can also save you some typing, if much of your material is similar:

```
$ ed -p '*' song
?song
* a
My bonny lies over the ocean,
O bring back my bonny to me!
.
* 1t1
* 2s/ocean/sea/
* 1t2
* 1,$p
My bonny lies over the ocean,
My bonny lies over the sea,
My bonny lies over the ocean,
O bring back my bonny to me!
*
```

Marking Lines in `ed` The `ed` operation used to mark a line is `k`. Operations are single letters, and `m` is already used for move, so we are left with using the last letter instead of the first. It finds most use when you have large chunks of text, more than can be displayed on the screen at one time, to move or copy to another place. There are of course other ways of doing the job, but it is safest to use the `k` command in conjunction with one of the other commands.

The example on the next pages shows how to move the lines between 'Maryann' and 'Steve' in our *people* file so that those lines appear after `Bill Williams`.

Another marked advantage of the `k` command is that the marks stay with the lines if you move them. If you transpose a block of marked lines, the marks stay with the last copy that was made. The marks on the originals go away. If you delete or change a marked line, the mark also goes away, but if you substitute within a marked line, the mark stays with the line.

```
$ ed -p '*' people
200
* 1,$p
Maryann Clark   101
Sally Smith     113
Jane Bailey     121
Jack Austen     120
Steve Daniels   111
Sylvia Dawson   110
Henry Morgan    112
Hank Parker     114
Charlie Smith   122
Bill Williams   100
```

Here's how to get the lines 'Maryann' and 'Steve' to appear after Bill Williams:

```
* /Maryann/ka
* /Steve/kb
* 'a,'bm/Bill Williams/
* 1,$p
Sylvia Dawson   110
Henry Morgan    112
Hank Parker     114
Charlie Smith   122
Bill Williams   100
Maryann Clark   101
Sally Smith     113
Jane Bailey     121
Jack Austen     120
Steve Daniels   111
*
```

Joining Lines in ed The j operation takes the addressed lines and joins them together to form one line. The example on the next page shows how you join some lines using ed.

Unfortunately, ed just jams the lines together without any intervening spaces.

If no line addresses are given, the current line and the next line are joined. If only one line address is given no action is taken.

```
$ ed -p '*' song
song 117
* 1,$p
My bonny lies over the ocean,
My bonny lies over the sea,
My bonny lies over the ocean,
O bring back my bonny to me!
* 3,4j
* 1,2j
* 1,$p
My bonny lies over the ocean,My bonny lies over the sea,
My bonny lies over the ocean,O bring back my bonny to me!
*
```

Cut and Paste Operations in ex

The move, transpose and mark operations are also available in ex, they work in exactly the same way as for ed. However, operations in ex are not limited to single letters, so there are some additional operations:

co can copy lines from one place to another. It is simply a more mnemonic name for transpose, so it is used in exactly the same way. Saying 1,10co$ does the same thing as 1,10t$.

ma is used to mark a line, it is easier to remember than k. /Maryann/maz has the same effect as /Maryann/kz — the next line containing 'Maryann' is marked with the letter *z*.

These commands are not really new commands — they are simply aliases for old ed commands. But there are some truly new commands, and also some variations of old commands, which make it easier to do cut and paste editing.

Joining Lines in ex The j operation takes the addressed lines and joins them together to form one line. If only one line address is given, then that line and the one following it are joined (this is different from ed). If no line addresses are given, the current line and the next line are joined.

To show an example of this, let's go back to the memo we were writing,

```
$ ex memo
"memo" [New file]
a
From: Bill Williams

To: Fred Bloggs

Date:
.
: r !date
!
Sat Apr 26 16:52:32 PST 1986
-j
Date: Sat Apr 26 16:52:32 PST 1986
:
```

We added the text 'Date:', then used `r` to get the current date as the next line. We then used `j` to get these two things together on the same line.

The join operation in `ex` automatically provides a reasonable amount of space. Usually this is one space, but if one of the lines joined together ends with a period (or any other end of sentence character), then two spaces are provided. Also, if one of the lines to be joined starts with an opening parenthesis '(', no spaces are left.

There is a variant of this command, `j!`. When you use the variant, no spaces are left between the joined lines.

The join command can also be given a trailing count, for instance:

```
: 12j3
```

joins together 3 lines, starting at line 12, to form one line.

Copying Text in `ex` with `yank` and `put` `ex` has two commands which be used to copy text from one place to another in the edit buffer. They can also be used to copy text from one file to another.

The `ya` (yank) command copies the specified lines into a buffer area. This buffer is separate from the buffer area where the file is being edited. The lines are not deleted from the 'main' buffer where the file is being edited. The `pu` (put) command puts the lines in the separate buffer into the file after the specified line.

For instance, if you wanted the last two lines of a file to be a copy of the first two, you would use the commands:

```
: 1,2ya
: $pu
I am the only God of Wine
:
```

The yank command can also be given a starting line and a trailing count, so that:

```
: 1ya 2
```

is another way to get the first two lines into the buffer.

With the `autoprint` option set, the last line put from the buffer is printed. The lines are not printed when they are yanked into the buffer. If a large number of lines is yanked, `ex` reports the number of lines. The exact number considered 'large' is dependent on the setting of the `report` option, the default is 5.

The contents of the buffer are affected by other `ex` commands, so no other changes should be made between the yank and the put. However, there are other buffers which are not affected by `ex` commands unless specifically requested. These are called the 'named buffers', and there are 26 of them named *a* through *z*. To use one of these buffers, you simply tack the name on the end of the yank and put commands:

```
: 1,2ya g
: $pu g
I am the only God of Wine
:
```

The above example uses the buffer *g*. If you specify an uppercase letter in a yank command:

```
: 3ya G
:
```

the specified lines are appended to anything that might already be in the buffer, in our case buffer *g*.

When you use the format of `ya` which takes a trailing count to put lines in a named buffer, the name of the buffer must precede the count:

```
: 1ya g 3
:
```

If you put things in the wrong order you get a message:

```
: 1ya 3 g
Extra characters at end of command
:
```

When a named buffer is used, the contents are not affected by other ex commands, so you can do other changes between the yank and put. In particular, the contents of named buffers are not affected by edit or next operations, so you can copy lines from one file to another without writing temporary files.

Transposing Lines in ex with delete and put In ex, when you delete some lines, they don't disappear completely. They are placed in the same buffer that lines get yanked into, and they can be retrieved with the put operation. Again, there should be no other changes between the d and the pu, unless you use a named buffer. You can use these operations to move stuff around in a file or, if you use named buffers, to transfer lines from one file to another.

Reverting to our files containing names and phone numbers, let's suppose we want to transfer Maryann from *adminpeople* to *softpeople*, and put someone else in her place. Here's how we can use ex to do it:

```
$ ex adminpeople softpeople
"adminpeople" 2 lines, 40 characters
: /Maryann
Maryann Clark   101
: d m
Bill Williams   100
: a
Ethel Snerge    101
.
: w
"adminpeople" 2 lines, 40 characters
: n
"softpeople" 5 lines, 100 characters
: pu m
Maryann Clark   101
: s/01/15
Maryann Clark   115
: wq
"softpeople" 6 lines, 120 characters
$
```

First we dealt with the *adminpeople* file; we deleted the line containing Maryann into the buffer named *m*, then we added a new line for Ethel. After saving the changes, we moved to the *softpeople* file; we put the line containing Maryann, then changed her phone number.

8.16. Extra Goodies in `ex`

The `ex` editor has some features that have no counterpart in `ed`. These extra goodies are described in the following paragraphs.

We have seen that you can get the result of a command into the edit buffer using a variation of the `r` operation. Also we saw that you can pass lines from the buffer as input to a command with a variation of the `w` operation. But the buffer itself is unaffected by the write operation. For instance, suppose we were editing our *people* file, and we gave the command:

```
: 1,$w !sort
```

The sorted names appear on the terminal screen, but the lines in the buffer are in their original unsorted order.

However, there is a way of telling `ex` to use a System V command to transform the contents of the edit buffer. To illustrate this let's continue our earlier example of the memo:

```
$ ex memo
: a
cc:
    Sylvia Dawson
    Jack Austen
    Joe Mugg
    Pat Manders
.
: ?Sylvia?,.  !sort +1
!
Joe Mugg
: ?cc?j
cc: Jack Austen
: 1,$p
From: Bill Williams
To: Fred Bloggs
Date: Sat Apr 26 16:52:32 PST 1986
cc: Jack Austen
    Sylvia Dawson
    Pat Manders
    Joe Mugg
:
```

We wanted the 'copies to' list to be alphabetical order by last name, so we entered them on separate lines from the 'cc:' heading. Then we used the `sort` command to get them into alphabetical order, by giving the range of lines and preceding the `sort` command with `!`. The output of `sort` replaced the original lines in the buffer. Finally we got everything together by using the `j` operation to put the first name on the same line as 'cc:'

Open and Visual Modes

All the commands we have talked about so far deal with lines. The only way to affect parts of a line is with the substitute command. This is because `ex`, like `ed`, is basically a line oriented editor. However, `ex` has two commands which provide intraline editing. This means that you can add characters in the middle of a line, or delete characters from a line.

The `vi` editor command switches `ex` into visual mode. While in visual mode, `ex` is identical with the `vi` editor described in the last chapter. In fact, `ex` and `vi` are one and the same editor — an editor that can be used in either line mode or visual mode.

When `vi` is entered from `ex` the screen of text displayed usually starts at the line specified, for example `10vi` displays a screen which starts at line 10. However the screen display can also be specified backwards from the specified line or on either side of it. This is achieved by following the `vi` command with a `-`, or with a period character `.`, similar to the context display command `z`. To exit from visual mode and revert to the line oriented mode, you type `Q` (uppercase Q).

Open mode gives the same capabilities as visual mode, but only one line is displayed at a time. To enter open mode you use the `o` command. The specified line is displayed, and you can use any command that is available in visual mode. Open mode is useful for 'dumb' terminals, or hard copy terminals, such as the TI-700.

Be careful of using the undo command after you have been using open or visual modes. If the last command was a global operation, all changes made by that command are reversed when you type `u`. The 'visual' and 'open' modes are considered to be global. If you enter visual mode, do a lot of changes, exit from visual mode back to line mode, then a `u` command will undo *all* the changes you made while you were in visual mode.

Recovery from System Crashes

One of the most annoying things that can happen when you are using an editor, is for the system to crash before you have had a chance to write away your modified (or new) file. Just as bad from the user's point of view, is an accidental disconnection from the system. In either case, there is the possibility of hours of work being wasted because a modified file was not saved.

`ex` provides a means of recovering from this situation. When your system recovers, and when you get reconnected, you may have mail telling you that files have been saved to help you recover your changes. Even if you don't get mail, it is worth trying the recovery operation.

Change directory into the same directory you were in when the interruption occurred, and give the command:

```
$ ex -r myfile
"myfile" [Dated: Sat Apr 26 09:41:23] 10 lines, 135 characters
:
```

The filename you specify must obviously be the name of the file you were editing when the interruption occurred.

You will not necessarily recover all the changes you had made, but you will get most of them. In particular, if you had yanked or deleted stuff into a buffer (even a named buffer), those buffer contents are lost.

Different Versions of ex

The ex editor has been around for some time, and over the years various changes and improvements have been made. So there are different versions of ex around, and some of the older version do not have all the features that we have described, or that are described in the document 'Ex Reference Manual'. You can use the editor command ve:

```
: ve
Version 3.7, 10/31/81.
:
```

to check which version of ex you are using.

8.17. Summary

This chapter has given you a basic idea of how to use the line editors, ed and ex. Although the line editors ar not at first sight as easy to use as a screen editor, they have a lot more power.

The main advantage to using a screen editor is that you always see a block of text all at once, and thus you can see the text you are changing in context. The combination of the vi screen editor and the ex line editor gives you the best of both worlds. You can see things in context, but you also have immediate access to the powerful global facilities of ex. It is worthwhile learning how to use the line editor, if only to enable you to use vi more efficiently.

Although the ed line editor has been around for a long time, and so can be considered rather primitive, it too is worthwhile learning about. There are some utility programs that interface with an editor (for example sdiff, which we discussed in chapter 6) and the editor they use is ed. A knowledge of ed will help you to use these utilities more proficiently.

9 Document Preparation Using System V

UNIX System V evolved with a battery of powerful tools for generating neatly formatted documents, often containing complex tabular and mathematical material.

The `troff` and `nroff` programs are the *text formatters* available in System V. `troff` is geared up for typesetter-like devices. `nroff` is oriented towards letter-quality printers and other non-typesetter devices.

Neither `troff` nor `nroff` provide 'what you see is what you get' formatting — instead, you must supply the formatters one or more files containing the text you want formatted, and in general, the text contains embedded formatting *requests* to indicate *how* you want the text laid out.

You don't normally want to use the raw formatting requests at the `troff` or `nroff` level, but rather you use a *macro package* that contains 'high-level' formatting constructs.

This chapter contains an overview of the -mm macro package — the standard macro package supplied with System V.

■ *We assume throughout this chapter and the two following chapters that you will be using the* `troff` *formatter —* `nroff` *is mentioned in passing where applicable.*

Topics covered in this chapter are:

- How to get started with `troff` and the mm macro package.
- Filled text structures — covers textual structures that are filled and optionally hyphenated and justified, such as paragraphs, lists, and quotations.
- Unfilled text structures — covers textual structures that are not filled, but simply laid out the way that you typed them.
- Keeping blocks of text together — discusses the mechanism available to ensure that parts of textual structures are held together without page breaks.
- Documents with sections, titles, and tables of contents — describes how to obtain structure in your document — chapters, sections, and so on, and how to obtain tables of contents.
- Special layout capabilities — discusses the macros needed to lay out tables, pictures, and equations.

- In-line effects in text — how to change fonts and sizes of text.

The next chapter discusses the powerful *preprocessors* available for performing really complex feats of formatting. Chapter 11 discusses the low level `troff` formatting program itself.

9.1. Document Formatters — What They Are

Most people who use personal computers probably use some form of *word processor*. Word processors in general provide for 'what you see is what you get' editing.

The document preparation facilities of UNIX System V evolved from a need to drive sophisticated printing engines such as typesetters, which can do things like:

- set type in a variety of typefaces such as *italic text*, **bold face text**, Helvetica, and *Helvetica italic*,
- provide for making text larger and smaller
- obtain a variety of special symbols such as a complete Greek (Eλλνας) alphabet
- mathematical symbols such as the ∫ (integration sign) and ∞ (infinity) and ∇ (nabla) and so on.

Such printing devices go beyond the capabilities of the average word processing system which evolved to driver 'letter quality' printers at best.

As you might expect, a complex printing device requires a complex collection of software to drive it. The program called `troff` is the System V utility that provides for formatting documents. It is true that `troff` could be simpler, but it gets the job done.

9.2. Getting Started with `troff`

This section shows you how to use `troff` in the most basic way. We assume that you just have a document (say a short memo) that contains no `troff` requests at all.

`troff` was originally designed to drive a second-generation typesetter called a C/A/T. The C/A/T is practically defunct now, and so `troff` has been adapted for other kinds of devices such as laser printers. There have been two separate lines of development:

- Some people have written postprocessing software that converts `troff`'s C/A/T-oriented output codes into codes suitable for driving other devices.
- Brian Kernighan at Bell Laboratories made extensive revisions to `troff` to create a new version called Device Independent `troff` (*ditroff*).

We assume that you either have old-style `troff` with some software package for driving other devices from `troff`'s output codes (most likely), or that you're using device-independent `troff`.

`troff` reads an input file containing unformatted text which is to be formatted so as to produce a neatly laid out document. First you prepare the input file, using the editor of your choice, then you format that text using `troff`, then you apply whatever postprocessing software is necessary to get the `troff` output converted for your printing device. The process is shown in figure 9.1 below.

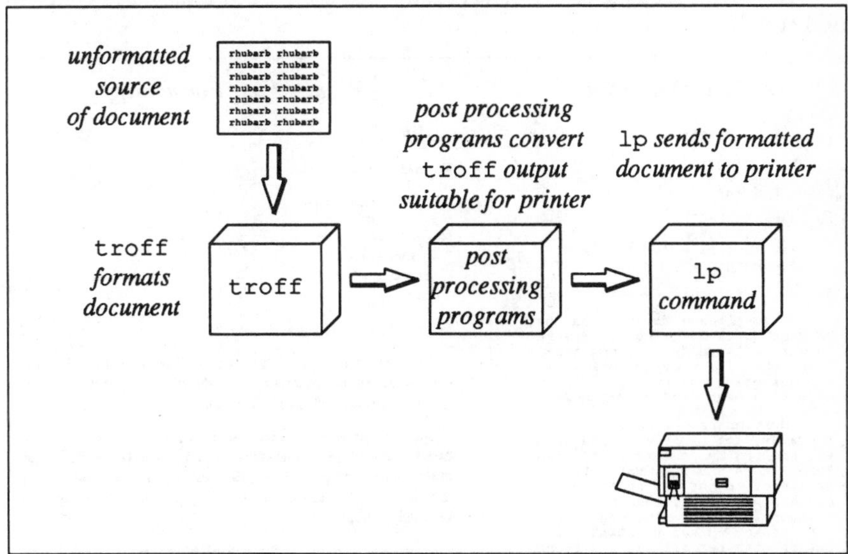

Figure 9.1 Basic Use of `troff`

This process shows `troff` formatting a document that contains no *macro references* at all — the -mm macro package is not used. Later on we'll show how to get the -mm macro package called into play.

You format your document using a `troff` command line that looks like this:

```
$ troff -t manuscript | postprocessing software | printer command
$
```

`troff` formats the document in the file *manuscript*, ready for driving the typesetter. You must use the `-t` option to direct the output to the Standard Output, else `troff` tries to drive the typesetter device. If you omit the `-t` option from the command line and you get a message that reads:

```
Typesetter busy.
```

you're using old-style C/A/T-oriented `troff`.

We have to be deliberately vague here about the nature of the *postprocessing software*, as we do also about the nature of the *printer command* — both areas are very dependent on the particular flavors of `troff` and friends that your installation has. In addition, there is also the possibility of special printer commands for special kinds of printers — such as `lsr` to route output to a laser printer.

Here is an example of a document formatted using `troff` without any macro package:

What You Type

```
From: Bill Williams

To: Fred Bloggs

Date: Wed Mar 17

cc: Jack Austen
    Sylvia Dawson
    Pat Manders
    Joe Mugg

Subject: Personnel Changes

        I am pleased to announce that
Maryann Clark is being transferred
to our software development team,
where she will take up duties as
a programming assistant,
effective next Monday, March 22nd.

        Maryann has been our department
secretary for two years, and we have
all admired her cheerful efficiency.
I feel sure she will carry these
qualities to her new position.
Maryann will be attending outside
classes in programming concurrent
with taking up her new tasks,
please give her all the assistance
you can.

        Maryann's secretarial duties will
be taken over by Ethel Snerge.  Ethel
brings considerable experience to the
job, please join me in welcoming her
to our department.

                        Bill Williams
```

Results After Formatting

From: Bill Williams

To: Fred Bloggs

Date: Wed Mar 17

cc: Jack Austen
Sylvia Dawson
Pat Manders
Joe Mugg

Subject: Personnel Changes

I am pleased to announce that Maryann Clark is being transferred to our software development team, where she will take up duties as a programming assistant, effective next Monday, March 22nd.

Maryann has been our department secretary for two years, and we have all admired her cheerful efficiency. I feel sure she will carry these qualities to her new position. Maryann will be attending outside classes in programming concurrent with taking up her new tasks, please give her all the assistance you can.

Maryann's secretarial duties will be taken over by Ethel Snerge. Ethel brings considerable experience to the job, please join me in welcoming her to our department.

Bill Williams

Figure 9.2 Document Formatted Without Macros

You should note several things about the 'what you type' versus the 'results after formatting':

- Blank lines on the input result in blank lines on the output. This is how you can get formatted paragraphs without any `troff` commands being present in your document.
- The formatting system *filled* and *justified* the lines you typed so that they fill whole lines on the printed copy. *Filling* means that `troff` packs words from the input lines onto the output lines until there's no more room on the line for another word. *Justifying* then means that `troff` pads out the spaces between words so that the right margin is straight.
- Finally, note that the output is in a *proportionally spaced font*. Each character takes up a different amount of horizontal space on the line.

Proportionally spaced characters give a more pleasing appearance to the finished result and are easier to read. However, proportionally spaced characters create problems if you try to line things up in columns by just inserting spaces — in a word processing system, all characters and spaces are the same width, but in a typesetting oriented system, they are of different widths.

9.3. Using `troff` with Preprocessors

Neither `troff` nor the `-mm` macro package alone can cater to all the kinds of complex formatting jobs required. As described in the next chapter, three of the more time-consuming activities in traditional typography are tabular layout, mathematical typesetting, and graphics. Instead of placing all these functions inside `troff`, there are separate software packages that do these specialized functions. These packages interpret specialized languages that describe these different functions and generate `troff` code sequences that do the correct thing. These programs are called *preprocessors*.

The main three preprocessors available for `troff` are:

`pic` a program that interprets a language for describing *pictures*. All the graphical elements in this book were drawn using `pic`.

`tbl` a program that interprets a language for describing *tables*. All the tabular material in this book was generated using `tbl`.

`eqn` a program that interprets a language for describing *equations*. All the mathematical examples in this chapter and the next chapter were generated using `eqn`.

When you use any or all of these preprocessors with `troff`, the interface becomes yet more complex. Figure 9.3 on the next page shows the process flow.

Let's suppose that you have a *manuscript* file like this chapter that contains all three kinds of material. You would use a command line that looks like this:

```
$ pic manuscript | tbl | eqn | troff -mm -t ... | \
    postprocessing software | printer command
$
```

Not always mentioned very clearly in the System V manuals is that the order in which you run these preprocessors is important:

- Always run `pic` before `tbl` or `eqn`.
- Always run `tbl` before `eqn`.

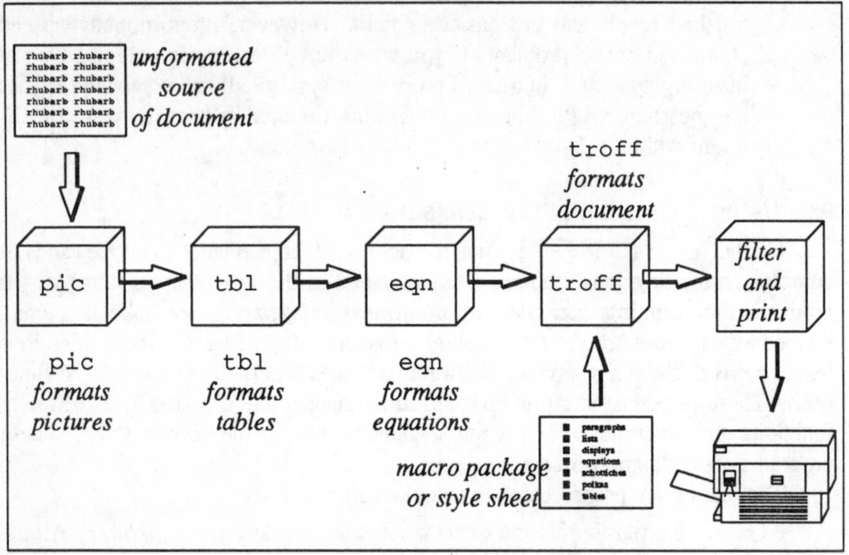

Figure 9.3 Using `troff` with Preprocessors

9.4. Macro Packages — What They Are

Using raw `troff` directly has been likened to programming a typesetter. Most typesetting systems have coding conventions that are arcane beyond belief, and unfortunately `troff` is just one of many packages that reflect this.

When you use `troff` to format a document, you must supply *what* you want formatted — this is the actual text of your document, and you must also supply *how* you want the text formatted — this takes the form of `troff` *requests*. In general, the `troff` requests are very low level, reflecting what the formatter thinks the printing engine is doing. What you really need is some formatting commands that are defined in terms of the document you are formatting.

A `troff` *macro* is a collection of `troff` requests that are given a name by which that collection of requests can be used (referenced, in the jargon). Each macro is a shorthand form for a bunch of `troff` requests that would involve much repetition and error-prone drudge work to type correctly. For example, the `.P` (start new paragraph) macro in the -mm macro package performs all the spadework needed to correctly start a new paragraph. Any given macro can have *arguments* (parameters) that further modify its behavior. For example, the `.P` macro just mentioned can have an argument that determines whether the paragraph is left-flushed or indented.

Macro Packages are a complete collection of macros — they evolved to provide a layer of abstraction above the detailed programming required of `troff`. A macro package is a set of predefined 'high level[1]' commands that perform much of the drudge work for you in laying out documents. A macro package provides your 'style sheet' for a document. When you want to change the appearance of a document, you can alter parameters to the macro package instead of making extensive changes to your document. Figure 9.4 below shows the addition of the macro package to the process of preparing a document.

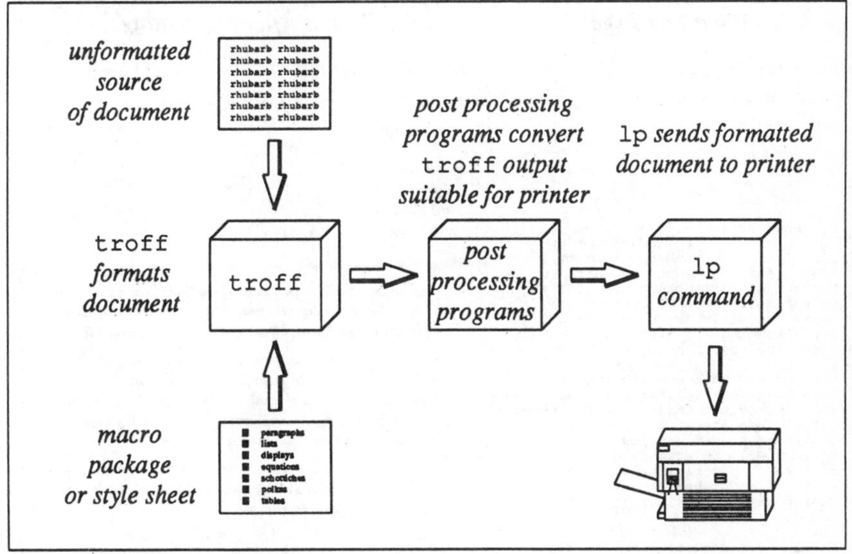

Figure 9.4 `troff` **In Conjunction with the** `-mm` **Macro Package**

The document contains *what* you want formatted — the text of the manuscript embedded with requests of the macro package. The macro package defines *how* to lay out the document.

The `-mm` macro package is the principal means of interfacing with `troff` in System V.

Now that we've introduced the idea of using the macro package, you would format your document using a `troff` command line that looks like this:

```
$ troff -mm -t manuscript | postprocessing software | printer command
$
```

1 at least higher level than raw `troff`.

The example below is somewhat contrived — it shows the example from before, but we've used the -mm macro package *list generating macros* as described in section 9.7 to format the paragraphs. The list macros take care of placing the bullets in the correct place, and adjusting the line length and indentation and so on. We've put comments in the left hand side in italics to show where the list macros are.

What You Type

```
From: Bill Williams

To: Fred Bloggs

Date: Wed Mar 17

cc: Jack Austen
    Sylvia Dawson
    Pat Manders
    Joe Mugg

Subject: Personnel Changes
.BL             ( Initialize a bullet list )
.LI             ( Start a new list item )
I am pleased to announce that
Maryann Clark is being transferred
to our software development team,
where she will take up duties as
a programming assistant,
effective next Monday, March 22nd.
.LI             ( Start a new list item )
Maryann has been our department
secretary for two years, and we have
all admired her cheerful efficiency.
I feel sure she will carry these
qualities to her new position.
Maryann will be attending outside
classes in programming concurrent
with taking up her new tasks,
please give her all the assistance
you can.
.LI             ( Start a new list item )
Maryann's secretarial duties will
be taken over by Ethel Snerge.  Ethel
brings considerable experience to the
job, please join me in welcoming her
to our department.
.LE             ( End of the list )
                              Bill Williams
```

Results After Formatting

From: Bill Williams

To: Fred Bloggs

Date: Wed Mar 17

cc: Jack Austen
Sylvia Dawson
Pat Manders
Joe Mugg

Subject: Personnel Changes

- **I am pleased to announce that Maryann Clark is being transferred to our software development team, where she will take up duties as a programming assistant, effective next Monday, March 22nd.**
- **Maryann has been our department secretary for two years, and we have all admired her cheerful efficiency. I feel sure she will carry these qualities to her new position. Maryann will be attending outside classes in programming concurrent with taking up her new tasks, please give her all the assistance you can.**
- **Maryann's secretarial duties will be taken over by Ethel Snerge. Ethel brings considerable experience to the job, please join me in welcoming her to our department.**

9.5. Using `troff` with the -mm Macro Package

The -mm macro package is the major interface to the System V document preparation system. Although we don't cover the entire -mm macro package here, we show enough of the highlights to get you started.

-mm was designed to be more flexible and easy to parameterize than earlier macro packages (such as -ms).

Now the -mm macro package was designed for the Bell Laboratories environment where writers produce 'Technical Memoranda'. Because of this evolution, -mm contains many macros that are fairly useless to the average person. According to the -mm documentation, a document consists of four parts:

- *Parameter Setting* — this is where you set up the general style and layout of your document, if you don't care for -mm's choices. You can leave this section out if you want to and -mm sets up default styles for you.

- *Beginning Segment* — this part is mostly applicable to the 'Technical Memoranda' papers we mentioned above. The kinds of things that go here are title of document, name of author, and so on. The average user doesn't need all this stuff, and can probably leave it out.
- *Body* — this part is the actual material of your document. In here are the paragraphs and lists and numbered headings and pictures, equations, tables, and footnotes that go to make a document. This is the part that is of the most interest, and the part we discuss in the remalhder of this chapter.
- *Ending Segment* — this part is also mostly applicable to the 'Technical Memoranda' papers. The kinds of things that go here are signatures and 'copies to' lists and so on. The average user doesn't need all this stuff, either, and can probably leave it out.

As you can see, the most interesting part of the four (and usually the only one you need worry about) is part three — the *body* of the document. The other parts are mostly fluff and can be ignored.

The best way to get started with -mm is to start with a very simple document and see what happens. Then as you get to want more (`troff` tends to be somewhat addictive in this regard) you can delve deeper into the System V *Document Processing Guide* itself, to discover how to change the appearance of your document.

Style Parameters for the -mm Macro Package

Although the -mm macro package sets up a standard style for a document, you have control over many of its choices. You control the style with parameters you set in *number registers.*

A number register is a placeholder for a numeric value that -mm uses to modify the behavior of its formatting choices. Number registers have two-character names — most of them of the form *Xy* — that is, an uppercase letter followed by a lowercase letter.

You place a value into a number register with the `.nr` request:

```
.nr Pt 1
```

sets the `Pt` number register to the value 1, so that -mm henceforth generates indented paragraphs.

-mm uses many such number registers. As you read the descriptions of the different macros, you will see some of the more important number registers described.

9.6. Text Structures — Paragraphs and Such

Paragraphs of the type you are reading right now are probably one of the most basic objects in a document. The other basic objects are lists and displays (discussed later in this chapter). Here is a picture of different kinds of paragraphs and textual structures:

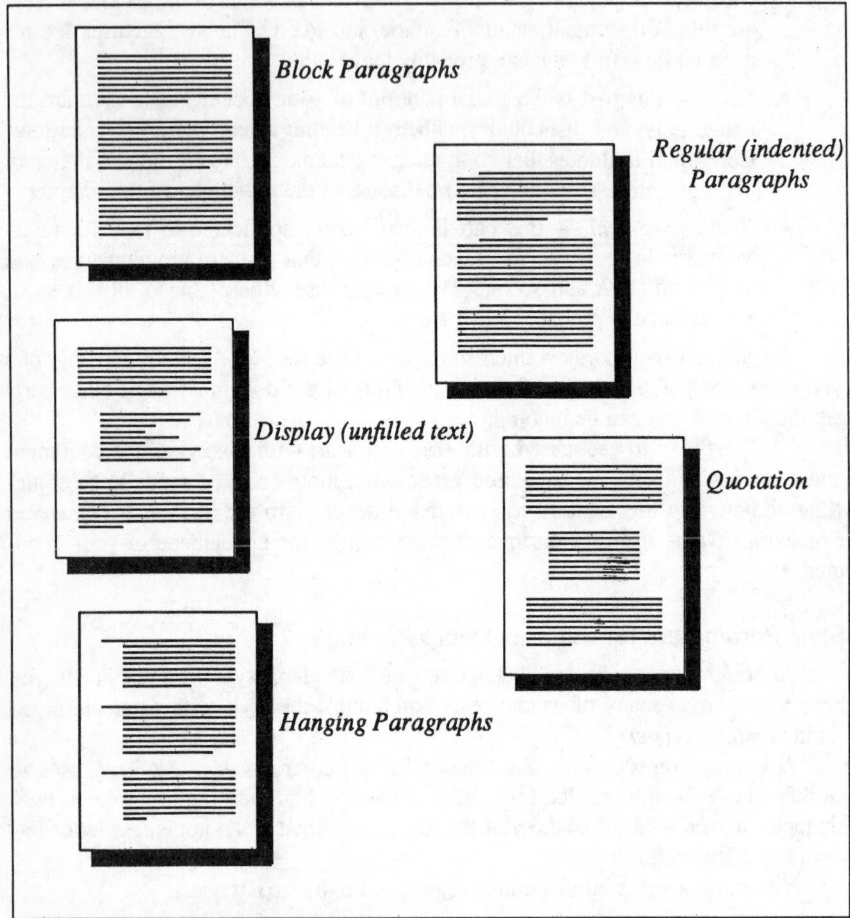

Figure 9.5 Types of Paragraphs

Here is a brief summary of the different paragraph types and where they are discussed:

- *blocked paragraphs* and *regular (indented) paragraphs* are introduced with the .P macro and are discussed below.
- *Hanging Paragraphs* are one of the various forms of *lists* that -mm supports. Lists are discussed in section 9.7 later on.
- *Displays* are regions of text that are not filled or justified. Displays are described in section 9.10 later.

- *Quotations* are simply a different form of paragraph. Quotations have their left and right margins made wider so as to set the material off from the surrounding paragraphs. Although it may seem odd, you use a special form of display to obtain a quotation, and so this is also described in section 9.10.

You use the `.P` macro to indicate the start of a new paragraph. In the absence of any other controlling information, the `.P` macro just gives you straight old left-blocked, filled, justified, and hyphenated paragraphs — nothing fancy there at all. Here are some paragraphs using the `.P` macro:

What You Type	***Results After Formatting***

`.P` *(start paragraph)*
`These people are most excellent`
`mathematicians, and arrived to`
`great perfection in mechanicks,`
`by the countenance and`
`encouragement of the emperor,`
`who is a renowned patron`
`of learning.`
`.P` *(start paragraph)*
`This prince hath several machines`
`fixed on wheels, for the carriage`
`of trees and other great weights.`
`He often buildeth his largest men`
`of war, whereof some are nine foot`
`long, in the woods where the timber`
`grows, and has them carried on`
`these engines three or four`
`hundred yards to the sea.`
`.P` *(start paragraph)*
`Five hundred carpenters and engineers`
`were immediately set to work to`
`prepare the greatest engine they had.`
	These people are most excellent mathematicians, and arrived to great perfection in mechanicks, by the countenance and encouragement of the emperor, who is a renowned patron of learning.
	This prince hath several machines fixed on wheels, for the carriage of trees and other great weights. He often buildeth his largest men of war, whereof some are nine foot long, in the woods where the timber grows, and has them carried on these engines three or four hundred yards to the sea.
	Five hundred carpenters and engineers were immediately set to work to prepare the greatest engine they had.

You can also have the first line of the paragraphs indented as they are in this book. To get this effect you code the `.P` macro with an argument of `1` — as in `.P 1`. The figure below shows a some paragraphs using the `.P` macro to generate indented paragraphs:

What You Type	***Results After Formatting***

`.P 1` *(start indented paragraph)*
`These people are most excellent`
`mathematicians, and arrived to`
`great perfection in mechanicks,`
`by the countenance and`
`encouragement of the emperor,`
`who is a renowned patron`
`of learning.`
`.P 1` *(start indented paragraph)*
`This prince hath several machines`
`fixed on wheels, for the carriage`
`of trees and other great weights.`
`He often buildeth his largest men`
`of war, whereof some are nine foot`
`long, in the woods where the timber`
`grows, and has them carried on`
`these engines three or four`
`hundred yards to the sea.`
`.P 1` *(start indented paragraph)*
`Five hundred carpenters and engineers`
`were immediately set to work to`
`prepare the greatest engine they had.`
	These people are most excellent mathematicians, and arrived to great perfection in mechanicks, by the countenance and encouragement of the emperor, who is a renowned patron of learning.
	This prince hath several machines fixed on wheels, for the carriage of trees and other great weights. He often buildeth his largest men of war, whereof some are nine foot long, in the woods where the timber grows, and has them carried on these engines three or four hundred yards to the sea.
	Five hundred carpenters and engineers were immediately set to work to prepare the greatest engine they had.

9.7. Text Structures — Lists

Lists are another basic object found in documents. This section describes the -mm macros to assist in making lists of various types. In particular, -mm provides facilities to assist with automatically numbered lists, where the numbers are adjusted for you if you add or delete items in the list.

Lists may be nested up to six levels deep, and the -mm macro package keeps track of the types of lists and the nesting for you.

A list has a simple structure, consisting of a start, a body, and an end. These three parts correspond to different -mm macros to do these functions:

- *Initialize* the list. The list initialization macro specifies the *type* of list you will be generating (numbers, bullets, and so on). The macros used here are described in the next section below.
- *Make a new list item.* Generates a new list item of the type specified in the initialization. You use the `.LI` (List Item) macro to indicate the start of each new item in the list.
- *End of list.* Signals that you've reached the end of the list of the type specified in the initialization. You use the `.LE` (List End) macro to indicate the end of the list.

The reason that -mm needs a start and an end for a list is that lists may be nested, and -mm needs to keep track of the type of the list at each level of nesting.

Initializing a List

The -mm macro package provides six off-the-shelf flavors of list macros. Here are the names of the macros that initialize such lists, plus a brief summary of what you get:

`.AL` Automatically numbered or alphabetized list — 1, 2, 3,..., a, b, c,..., i, ii, iii, iv,..., and so on.

`.BL` Bullet list. Items in the list are marked with a bullet (•).

`.DL` Dashed list. Items in the list are marked with dashes (–).

`.ML` Marked list. Items in the list are marked with arbitrary marks of your choice.

`.RL` Reference list. Items in the list are marked as references, like [1], [2], [3], and so on.

`.VL` Variable-item list. Items in the list are marked with variable-text tags. This is called a 'description list' in some circles.

If none of these types of list are what you want, you can use the `.LB` macro to roll your own kind of list. Since this chapter is simply an overview of the document preparation facilities, we suggest you read the System V *Document Processing Guide* for a complete description of the `.LB` macro.

In general, all the list macros look more or less alike. They all have more or less the same parameters. Two parameters that are common to all the list macros are the *text indent* and the *no space* indicator:

The *text indent* is a value that specifies the distance from the position of the current indent (the left margin of the surrounding text paragraphs) to the edge of the *text* in the list. Here's a picture of the relationships between the left margin, the current indent, and the text indent:

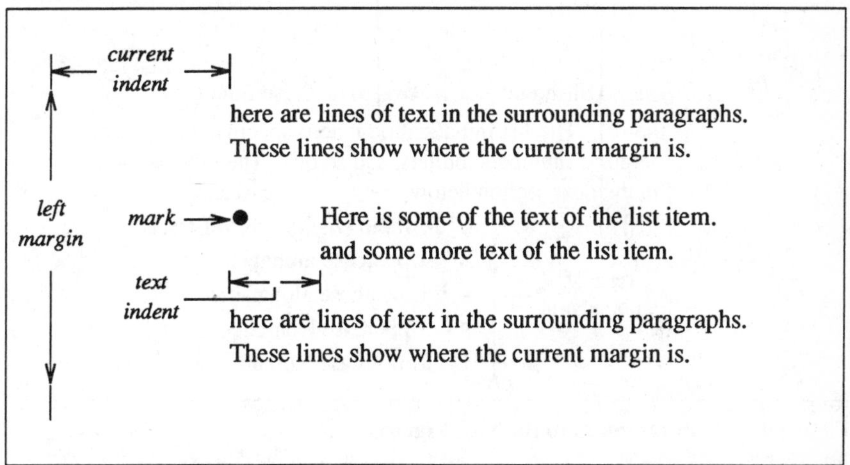

The *no space* indicator is a single value (1) that indicates that items in the list are not to have any vertical space between them. Normally, items are separated vertically by half a vertical line spacing (when using `troff`) or by one line (when using `nroff`). The no space indicator, when specified, makes the list items bunch up closer together. This is often of value when there are several very short items in the list — they would otherwise look too spread out.

Automatically Numbered Lists

The `.AL` macro signals `-mm` to start an automatically numbered list. The normal numbering scheme is for the items in the list to be numbered 1, 2, 3, . . ., but you can change the style of numbering.

Figure 9.6 on the next page is a diagram of the `.AL` macro and the parameters that control its operation.

Figure 9.7 on the next page is an example of using the `.AL` macro to generate a short list of three items. All parameters take on their standard values.

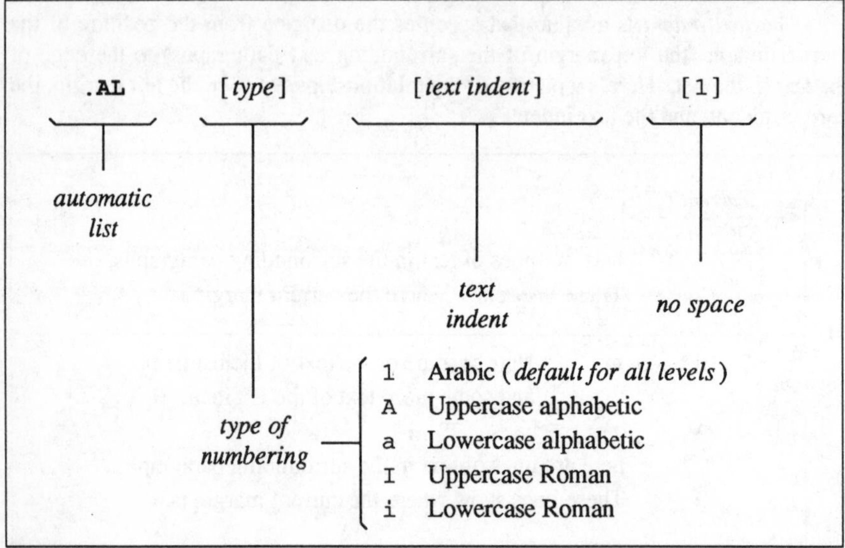

Figure 9.6 Parameters to the .AL Macro

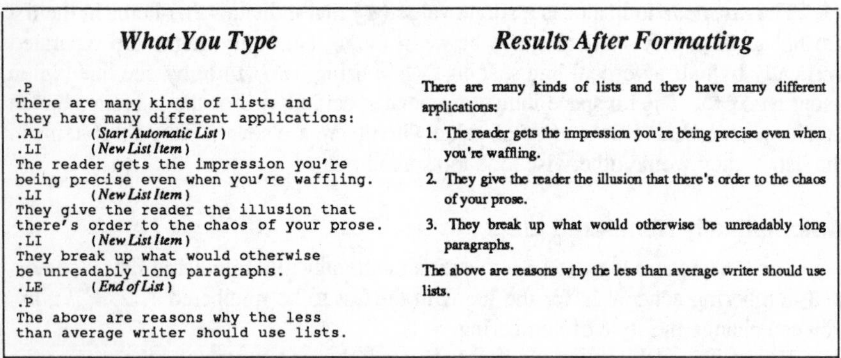

Figure 9.7 Using the .AL Macro

The example above showed an automatically numbered list, using all the default values. Now the example below shows how you can get an automatically numbered list with the numbering changed from Arabic numbers to lowercase Roman numerals:

What You Type	*Results After Formatting*
.P There are many kinds of lists and they have many different applications: .AL i (*Start Automatic List—Roman Numbering*) .LI The reader gets the impression you're being precise even when you're waffling. .LI They give the reader the illusion that there's order to the chaos of your prose. .LI They break up what would otherwise be unreadably long paragraphs. .LE (*End of List*) .P The above are reasons why the less than average writer should use lists.	There are many kinds of lists and they have many different applications: i. The reader gets the impression you're being precise even when you're waffling. ii. They give the reader the illusion that there's order to the chaos of your prose. iii. They break up what would otherwise be unreadably long paragraphs. The above are reasons why the less than average writer should use lists.

Bullet Lists

The `.BL` macro signals `-mm` to start a *bullet list.* Each list item is preceded by a black round bullet (•) character.

The parameters for the `.BL` macro are very simple:

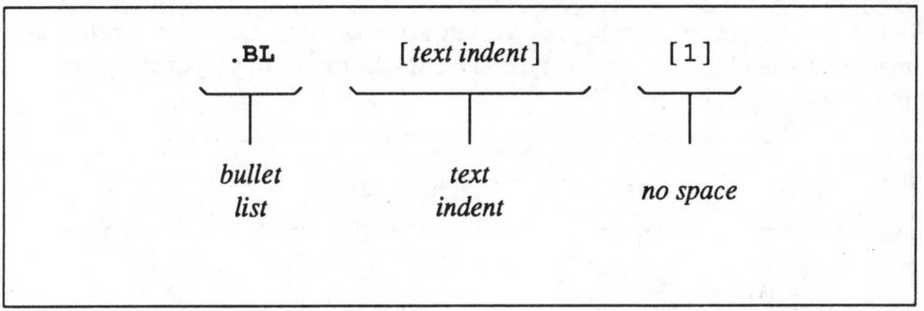

Here's a short example of using the `.BL` macro:

What You Type	*Results After Formatting*
.P Bullets of the world: .BL (*Start Bullet List*) .LI 0.45 caliber bullets were said to have won the West. .LI Square bullets are a new Russian invention. .LI Typographers' bullets are used to set things off in lists. .LE (*End of List*) .P These are just a few of the many bullets that you can find in the armory.	Bullets of the world: • 0.45 caliber bullets were said to have won the West. • Square bullets are a new Russian invention. • Typographers' bullets are used to set things off in lists. These are just a few of the many bullets that you can find in the armory.

Dashed Lists

The `.DL` macro signals `-mm` to start a *dashed list*. Each item in the list is preceded by an *em-dash* (—) character. The layout of the `.DL` macro and its parameters is the same as that of the bullet list. Here's an example:

What You Type	***Results After Formatting***

`.P`
`There are many kinds of lists and`
`they have many different applications:`
`.DL` *(Start Dashed List)*
`.LI`
`The reader gets the impression you're`
`being precise even when you're waffling.`
`.LI`
`They give the reader the illusion that`
`there's order to the chaos of your prose.`
`.LI`
`They break up what would otherwise`
`be unreadably long paragraphs.`
`.LE` *(End of List)*
`.P`
`The above are reasons why the less`
`than average writer should use lists.`
	There are many kinds of lists and they have many different applications:
	— The reader gets the impression you're being precise even when you're waffling.
	— They give the reader the illusion that there's order to the chaos of your prose.
	— They break up what would otherwise be unreadably long paragraphs.
	The above are reasons why the less than average writer should use lists.

Marked Lists

The `.ML` macro signals `-mm` to start a *marked list*. Each item starts with a mark that you choose when you type the `.ML` macro. Here's a picture of the `.ML` macro and its parameters:

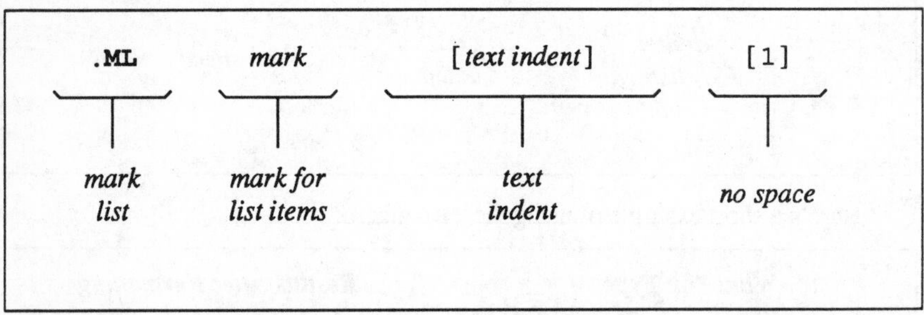

You use the `.ML` macro when you want a mark that isn't covered by the other list macros. The bullet (•) is already covered by the `.BL` macro and the dash (—) is already provided by the `.DL` macro. Common other choices are the open square (□) and the black square (■). You obtain the □ by typing the `troff` `\(sq` escape sequence and you get the ■ by typing the `troff` `\(bx` escape sequence.

■ Note that the `.ML` macro doesn't choose a mark for you — you have to specify it. If you omit the mark, the `.ML` macro displays an error message.

Here's an example of a marked list:

What You Type	Results After Formatting

`.P`
`There are many kinds of lists and`
`they have many different applications:`
`.ML \(sq` *(Start Marked List — Use a Square)*
`.LI`
`The reader gets the impression you're`
`being precise even when you're waffling.`
`.LI`
`They give the reader the illusion that`
`there's order to the chaos of your prose.`
`.LI`
`They break up what would otherwise`
`be unreadably long paragraphs.`
`.LE` *(End of List)*
`.P`
`The above are reasons why the less`
`than average writer should use lists.`
	There are many kinds of lists and they have many different applications:
	□ The reader gets the impression you're being precise even when you're waffling.
	□ They give the reader the illusion that there's order to the chaos of your prose.
	□ They break up what would otherwise be unreadably long paragraphs.
	The above are reasons why the less than average writer should use lists.

Reference Lists

The `.RL` macro signals `-mm` to start a *reference list*. Each new item in the list has an automatically numbered reference enclosed in brackets — like [5]. This style of list finds most of its application in bibliographies and in what are often called 'end notes', where you place what would otherwise be footnotes at the end of the document.

The `.RL` macro is very simple — its parameters are the same as for the `.BL` and `.DL` macros:

Here's an example of the `.RL` macro in action:

What You Type	Results After Formatting

`.P`
`Here are just a few titles of interest`
`to the jaded reader:`
`.RL` *(Start Reference List)*
`.LI`
`Chen-Pi Wong \(em The Fine Points`
`of Acupuncture.`
`.LI`
`Asimov, A. \(em On the Sublime`
`Properties of Endochronic Thiotimoline.`
`.LI`
`Dijkstra, E. \(em Computer Programming`
`Considered Harmful.`
`.LE` *(End of List)*
	Here are just a few titles of interest to the jaded reader:
	[1] Chen-Pi Wong — The Fine Points of Acupuncture.
	[2] Asimov, A. — On the Sublime Properties of Endochronic Thiotimoline.
	[3] Dijkstra, E. — Computer Programming Considered Harmful.

Variable Lists

The `.VL` macro signals `-mm` to start a *variable list*. The mark that precedes each new item is *not* supplied by the macro package — you supply your own information at this point. The mark in each new variable list item is of variable length. Some people call this a 'description list', because you typically use this kind of list to provide descriptions or definitions of things.

The parameters for the `.VL` macro are similar to the other list macros, but not exactly the same:

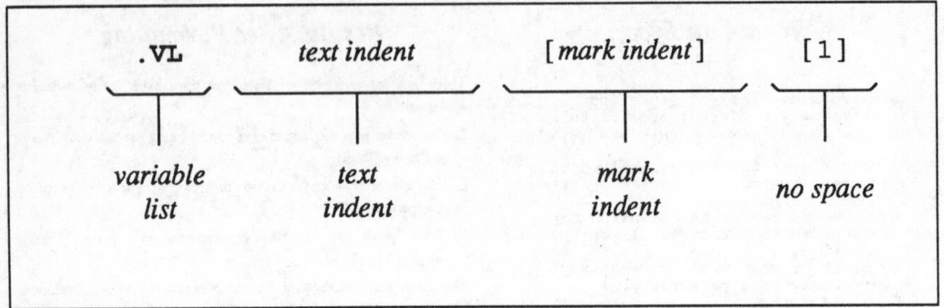

- *text indent* is just like the other list macros — it is the distance from the current indent to the edge of the *text*.
- *mark indent* is the distance from the current indent to the edge of the *mark*. This distance is normally 0.

Here's an example of the .VL macro:

What You Type

```
.P
For the discerning diner, the restaurant
selection in Sierra Park is eclectic:
.VL 15 2        ( start Variable List )
.LI "\fILe Crock Monsieur\fP"
Those who like the flavor of rotted milk
will find that every dish has at least
two kinds of melted cheese.
.LI "\fIDown to Earth\fP"
Favorite eating place of the Sierra
Park set.  Guaranteed protein-free eating.
.LI "\fINsi Han (the Huge)\fP"
All the AI researchers gather
here to zorch their brains.
.LE        ( End of List )
.P
Many more delights can be found within
a ten block area of University.
```

Results After Formatting

For the discerning diner, the restaurant selection in Sierra Park is eclectic:

Le Crock Monsieur Those who like the flavor of rotted milk will find that every dish has at least two kinds of melted cheese.

Down to Earth Favorite eating place of the Sierra Park set. Guaranteed protein-free eating.

Nsi Han (the Huge) All the AI researchers gather here to zorch their brains.

Many more delights can be found within a ten block area of University.

Nested Lists

The -mm macro package can deal with lists nested within lists, to a depth of six. As you nest one kind of list within another, the macro package takes care of indenting the different lists so that the indentation shows structure.

Figure 9.8 on the following page shows an example of lists nested inside lists.

What You Type	***Results After Formatting***

<pre>.P
We have much interesting fauna in
this zoo:
.VL 5
.LI ANIMALS
.AL A
.LI
Aardvarks and Aardwolves
.LI
Bandicoots and Bison
.LI
Camels
.AL 1 "" 1
.LI
Dromedaries
.LI
Bactrian
.LE
.LI
Duck-billed Platypus and Dobermans
.LE
.LI BIRDS
.AL A
.LI
Auks and Albatrosses
.LI
Bobolinks and Bobwhite Quail
.LI
Cassowarys and Cormorants
.LI
Dodos
.LE
.LE
.P
Now that you've seen our zoo,
you should visit the aquarium.</pre>
	We have much interesting fauna in this zoo:
	ANIMALS
	A. Aardvarks and Aardwolves
	B. Bandicoots and Bison
	C. Camels
	1. Dromedaries
	2. Bactrian
	D. Duck-billed Platypus and Dobermans
	BIRDS
	A. Auks and Albatrosses
	B. Bobolinks and Bobwhite Quail
	C. Cassowarys and Cormorants
	D. Dodos
	Now that you've seen our zoo, you should visit the aquarium.

Figure 9.8 Nested Lists

More on List Items

As you've seen from the previous examples, you use the `.LI` macro in all lists to generate the list items.

The `.LI` macro itself has some controlling parameters that you can use. The layout of the `.LI` macro is like:

`.LI [`*mark*`] [1]`

Here is how the controlling parameters operate:

- If you just type a `.LI` macro with no arguments, the list item gets labelled with whatever mark was specified by the last list initialization macro — numbers of some kind for the `.AL` macro, bullets (•) for the `.BL` macro, dashes (—) for the `.DL` macro, whatever mark you specified for the `.ML` macro, and numbers in brackets for the `.RL` macro. You must specify your own mark for the `.VL` macro list.
- If you specify just the *mark* parameter above, you get that mark printed in place of the mark that goes with whatever kind of list you asked for.
- If you specify both the *mark* parameter and the `1` as shown above, the mark you specify gets printed as a *prefix* to the mark that goes with

whatever kind of list you asked for. One space goes between the prefix and the standard mark.

Note that this discussion doesn't apply to variable list items because you already have to specify the mark for those items anyway.

Here's an example of using a marked list, showing the effects of the mark replacing the standard mark, and acting as a prefix to the standard mark:

What You Type	*Results After Formatting*
.P Here is an example of using the list item macro with controls. .ML \(sq .LI This item uses the standard supplied mark. .LI \(bx This item uses the \(bx in place of the standard supplied mark. .LI \(bx 1 This item uses the \(bx as a prefix to the standard supplied mark. .LI This item uses the standard supplied mark. .LE (*End of List*) .P Here is some more text to show the position of the margins.	**Here is an example of using the list item macro with controls.** **□ This item uses the standard supplied mark.** **■ This item uses the ■ in place of the standard supplied mark.** **■ □ This item uses the ■ as a prefix to the standard supplied mark.** **□ This item uses the standard supplied mark.** **Here is some more text to show the position of the margins.**

List Items Without Tags Another feature that you often need in lists is to have a 'list item' that has no tag. You often need one or more extra paragraphs that all belong to the same list item.

You obtain this effect by typing a `.LI` macro with a non-printing string as the mark:

```
.LI   "\ "
```

The backslash followed by the space is an 'unpaddable space' — it is printed in the document, but of course it's not visible.

The End of List Macro

There are two minor items of interest about the `.LE` macro:

You can supply an optional parameter to the `.LE` macro. If you specify such a parameter, the `.LE` macro leaves some blank space after the last item in the list. You should only use this feature when the following text is not preceded by some other form of paragraph or list macro that already generates space.

Any kind of header macros automatically clear all the list nesting information. The philosophy here is that lists don't in general span across headers in a document. You should not take advantage of this feature, however, because if at some time in the future you place more material after the unterminated list, you will get error messages from the macro package telling you that there are unterminated lists.

9.8. Text Structures — Footnotes

Footnotes are a common textual structure[2] that appear in documents. A footnote is used to interject some material that the reader might find useful, but you don't put the parenthetical material right there in the text where it interrupts the flow.

There are two elements in a footnote:

The footnote *reference* that appears in the running text to indicate to the reader that there's a footnote (or an endnote) somewhere.

The *body* of the footnote — usually at the bottom of the page. The body of the footnote is preceded by a copy of the footnote reference so that the reference in the running text is tied to the footnote proper.

There are two methods of getting footnote references using the -mm macro package:

Automatically numbered references are a valuable service that the macro package provides for you. If you add or delete or move footnotes around, they all get renumbered for you automatically.

Labelled references, where you choose your own label or tag for the footnote. Common tags (other than numbers) are asterisk (*), dagger (†), double dagger (‡), and more infrequently, paragraph (¶) and section (§).

You indicate the start of a footnote with the `.FS` (Footnote Start) macro. Then comes the text of the footnote, and finally you end the footnote with the `.FE` (Footnote End) macro.

You get the automatically numbered reference in the running text by using the special -mm string `\*F`. For example, the footnote you see at the bottom of this page was created using this fragment of text in the document:

```
.I Footnotes
are a common textual structure\*F that appear in documents.
.FS
Especially in the legal profession and in the
diaries of Samuel Pepys.
.FE
A footnote is . . .
```

If you want your own labelling instead of automatically numbered references, you have to supply it manually:

[2] Especially in the legal profession and in the diaries of Samuel Pepys.

Place the label of your choice in the running text. Let's say you use the asterisk (*) character.

Then use that same character as an argument to the .FS macro.

Here's an example of rolling your own footnote label:

```
.I Footnotes
are a common textual structure* that appear in documents.
.FS *
Especially in the legal profession and in the
diaries of Samuel Pepys.
.FE
A footnote is . . .
```

There's not much else to say about footnotes. The -mm macro package supplies a .FD macro that controls the *style* of footnotes. You can adjust aspects such as indentation, hyphenation, and where the footnote label appears. The .FD macro takes two arguments:

.FD *style renumber*

The *style* argument is a number between 0 and 11. The useful argument[3] is the *renumber* argument — if you set *renumber* to 1 (one), footnote numbering starts afresh at 1 every time a first level header is encountered[4].

9.9. Numbered Headings

One of the major services that the computer provides for you is numbering things automatically so that all the numbering gets updated when you add new stuff, delete stuff, or move material around.

Numbered headings are introduced in -mm using the .H (heading) macro.

You can have headings numbered up to seven levels deep. Level 1 is the highest level and level 7 is the lowest level. Level 1 headings correspond roughly to chapters or major sections.

You can specify the style of the headings — the fonts, underlining, and standalone or run in style.

In addition to getting numbered headings, you can have the paragraphs following the headings numbered also.

The format of a numbered heading is like this

.H *heading level text of heading suffix*

---

3 The main reason we're telling you about the .FD macro at all.

4 This is the style we use in this book.

The `.H` macro introduces the heading.

The *heading level* specifies the numbering level — from 1 through 7.

The *text of heading* is the text that will be printed in the document, and will also make an entry in the table of contents. The text of the heading is optional. If you omit the text, you just get the numbers.

The *suffix* can be used to append a mark to a heading (such as a footnote callout). The suffix does not appear in the table of contents.

The level of the heading controls to some extent how the text of the heading will be laid out. Here are the standard settings:

Level	*Effects*
1	Heading text is printed in **bold face text**. The heading is standalone — that is, it occupies a line on its own.
2	Heading text is printed in **bold face text**. The heading is standalone — that is, it occupies a line on its own. The heading is printed in a point size that is one point smaller than the regular text (`troff` only).
3 thru 7	Heading text is printed in *italic face text* (underlined in `nroff`). Heading levels 3 through 7 are *run in* headings — the text that follows the heading appears on the same line as the heading.

9.10. Text Structures — Displays and Such

This section describes *displays*, otherwise called *unfilled text structures*. What is a display? It's simply a block of text, set off from the surrounding paragraphs, that's printed just the way you typed it. The most common use of a display in this book (for example) is the examples of what you type and what the system types back at you. We want those examples to appear exactly the way they do on the screen of the terminal. We do not want the formatter to fill up the lines and justify and hyphenate and so on — that would defeat the purpose of the examples. Traditional typesetting systems are excruciatingly hard to use when you want displays — the machines are geared up to justify text, and anything that doesn't fall into this model becomes difficult.

Displays are relatively easy to specify with the `-mm` macro package. The `-mm` macro package defines four kinds of displays:

- *Static Displays* keep the text together in a block and print it on the current page if the display will fit. If the contents of the display won't fit on the current page, it is printed on the next page.
- *Floating Displays* keep the text together in a block and 'float' it until such time as there's enough room to print it. In the case where the display gets floated to another page, the text *following* the display gets printed on the current page.

- *Tables* are special forms of displays used for laying out material in columns. The `tbl` preprocessor is used to process the contents of tables.
- *Equations* are special forms of displays used for laying out mathematical material. The `eqn` preprocessor is used to process the contents of equations.

Static Displays

A *static display* places text on the page the way you typed it — the text is not filled or justified. The text in the display appears on the printed page in the same order relative to the surrounding text as you typed it — the formatter does not rearrange the order of the surrounding text and the display.

Static displays are introduced with the `.DS` macro. The display is ended with the `.DE` macro. Lines of text to be displayed appear between the macros.

The `.DS` macro can accept arguments that control various aspects of its behavior. Here are the parameters to the `.DS` macro:

`.DS` *optional format* *fill* *right indent*

optional format is a letter that controls the left margin and the ultimate layout of the display:

If the optional format is omitted or null, the display is not indented.

`L` This means a left flush display — same as if you omit the argument.

`C` Center every line in the display.

`CB` Center the entire display as a block.

The diagram below shows the effects of the three different kinds of displays as they appear within blocks of surrounding text. Notice that the left display just has all its lines lined up against the left margin. The centered display has each line centered. The center block display has its lines left flushed, but the whole block is centered around the width of the longest line.

Left Display	*Center Lines*	*Center Block*
I am the voice of today, the herald of tomorrow. I am the leaden army that conquers the world. I am type! Of my earliest ancestry neither history nor relics remain.	I am the voice of today, the herald of tomorrow. I am the leaden army that conquers the world. I am type! Of my earliest ancestry neither history nor relics remain.	I am the voice of today, the herald of tomorrow. I am the leaden army that conquers the world. I am type! Of my earliest ancestry neither history nor relics remain.
first line of text	first line of text	first line of text
second line of more text	second line of more text	second line of more text
third line of even more text	third line of even more text	third line of even more text
fourth line of text	fourth line of text	fourth line of text
fifth and last line of text	fifth and last line of text	fifth and last line of text
I am the voice of today, the herald of tomorrow. I am the leaden army that conquers the world. I am type! Of my earliest ancestry neither history nor relics remain.	I am the voice of today, the herald of tomorrow. I am the leaden army that conquers the world. I am type! Of my earliest ancestry neither history nor relics remain.	I am the voice of today, the herald of tomorrow. I am the leaden army that conquers the world. I am type! Of my earliest ancestry neither history nor relics remain.

fill is a letter that controls whether the display is filled:

If *fill* is omitted or null, the display is not filled.

`N` The display is not filled.

`F` Text is filled. This is the way to get a quotation form of paragraph where both the left and the right margins are indented from the surrounding text.

right indent is the amount that the right margin should be indented. Using the `F` fill parameter as described above, plus a right indent is how to get quotations.

Floating Displays

A *floating display* places text on the page the way you typed it — the text is not filled or justified. The formatter makes a decision as to what happens to the contents of the display. If there's enough room on the current page for the display to fit, it is printed on the current page. However, if there's not enough room for the display to fit on the current page, the display is 'floated' to the next page. Text that follows the display in the input file is printed on the current page.

Floating displays provide a means to avoid large blocks of whitespace at the bottom of a page that would normally be generated by the page breaking of static displays.

Floating displays are introduced with the `.DF` macro. The display is ended with the `.DE` macro, just as for the static displays. Lines of text to be displayed appear between the macros.

The format of the `.DF` macro is the same as for the `.DS` macro described above.

Laying Out Tables

Tables are special forms of displays used for laying out material in columns. The `tbl` preprocessor described in chapter 10 is used to process the contents of tables. In this chapter we simply describe the macros you use — the detailed description of the `tbl` preprocessor appears in chapter 10.

There are three macros used in conjunction with laying out tables. The most important are the `.TS` (Table Start) and the `.TE` (Table End) macros.

Of lesser importance is the `.TH` (Table Heading) macro described below.

The basic form of a table is shown in figure 9.9 on the next page.

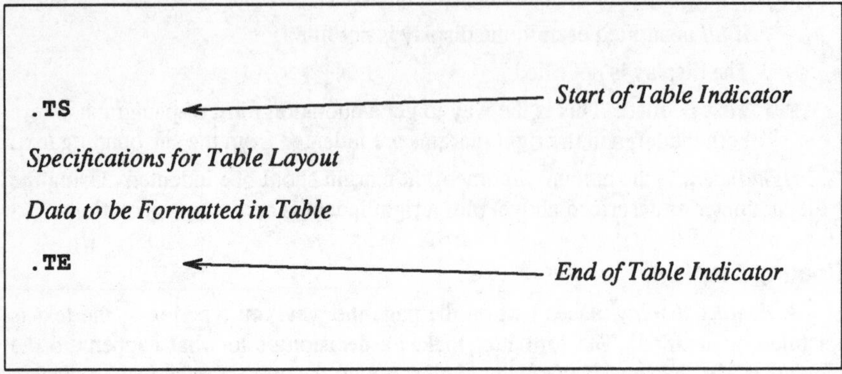

Figure 9.9 Basic Layout of a Table

The .TH macro is used in those cases where you want to have the head of a table placed at the top of every page if a table spans across pages. In this case, the table layout looks like this:

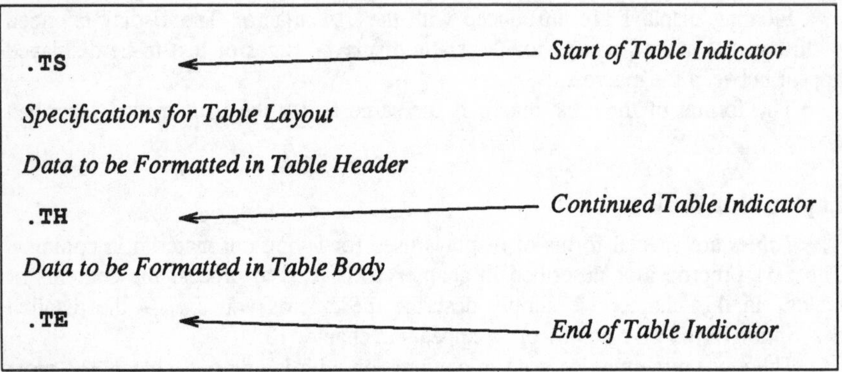

Equation Displays

Equations are special forms of displays used for laying out mathematical material. The eqn preprocessor is used to process the contents of equations. In this chapter we only describe the macros you use for laying out equations. The eqn preprocessor is described in detail in chapter 10.

Equations are laid out between the .EQ (start of equation) and the .EN (end of equation) macros.

The .EQ and .EN macro pair must appear inside of .DS and .DE macro pairs in the -mm macro package, with two exceptions:

- If the equation is being used only for specifying delimiters for in-line equations. We describe this topic in chapter 10.
- If the equation is being used only for defining `eqn` macros.

Here is a picture of the basic equation layout macros:

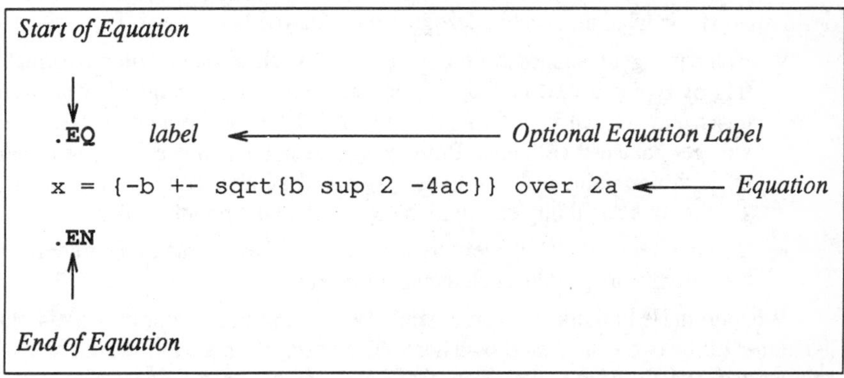

The `.EQ` macro has an optional argument that is the label for the equation. The label is placed in the right margin of the document, centered vertically within the height of the equation, as shown here.

$$x = \frac{-b \pm \sqrt{b^2 - 4ac}}{2a} \qquad (9.1)$$

Describing Pictures

Pictures are another form of display available with the System V document preparation tools. The `pic` picture processing language is described in more detail in section 10. In this section we simply discuss the macros that you use to delimit pictures in a document.

Pictures are laid out between the `.PS` (start of picture) and the `.PE` (end of picture) macros.

9.11. Formatting Text in Two Columns

Textual material formatted in the standard U.S.A. letter size paper (8½×11) is normally laid up in a 6½ inch wide single column. When there's a lot of dense text without any intervening graphics or other material to break it up, this can get hard to read. The solution might well be to format the text in two columns.

The -mm macro package provides for formatting text in two columns on a page. You type a `.2C` macro at the point where you want to start formatting in two columns. Formatting continues in two columns until you type a `.1C` macro to revert to single-column formatting.

Now note that the double-column formatting capabilities of `-mm` are really a kludge — the macro package thinks of each physical page as being composed of two 'pages' that are narrower. Formatting takes place in the first (left-hand) 'page' until that 'page' is full, at which time formatting then continues into the second (right-hand) 'page'. When that 'page' is full, a new real page is started.

Two column formatting being a kludge as we said earlier, there are some serious limitations on what the macro package can do for you here:

- You can't get balanced columns. If you go back to single-column formatting by typing a `.1C` macro, the formatter *starts a new page.* If you were lucky enough that your two-column text fills the last column exactly, you will get balanced columns. But if your text column was short, you'll end up with one column that fills the page, and another column that's short. This is considered unpleasing to the eye in the typographic trade.
- You can't get effects like text 'runarounds' — leave a gap in the middle of the columns for graphical elements for instance.

What do these limitations mean to you? Well, you can get your pages laid out like either of the two examples shown here. The example on the left shows the two column part exactly fitting onto the pages. The example on the right shows what happens when a new page is started — the second column finishes but the columns aren't then balanced to look good.

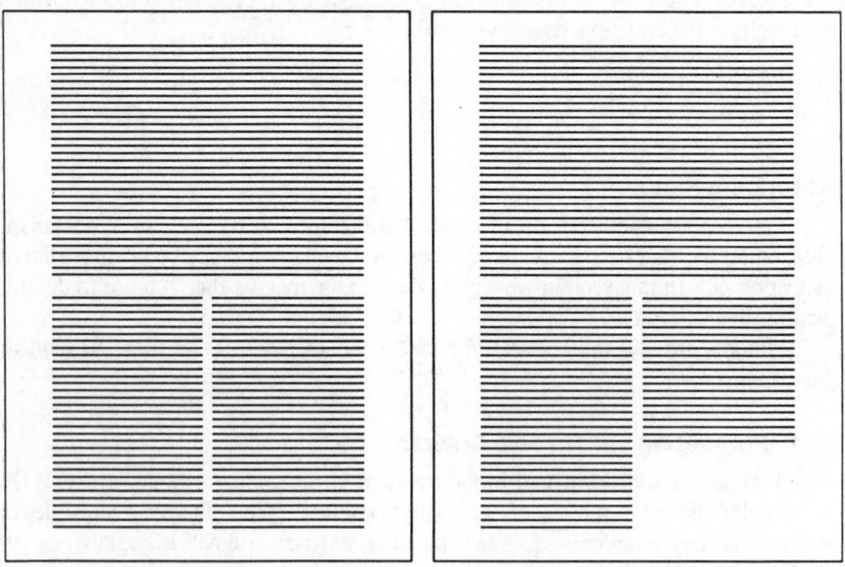

But unfortunately you can *not* get your pages laid out like either of the examples shown below. The example on the left shows a one-column page changed to two-column formatting, and then back to one-column formatting all on the same page — we've already said that the `.2C` and `.1C` macro combination can't do that.

The example on the right shows a two-column block with some kind of graphic in the middle — the macros aren't clever enough to handle that situation. You *can* write incredibly complicated `troff` macros to do this kind of thing, but it's very difficult indeed, and this might be a place where manual pasteup gets the job done quicker.

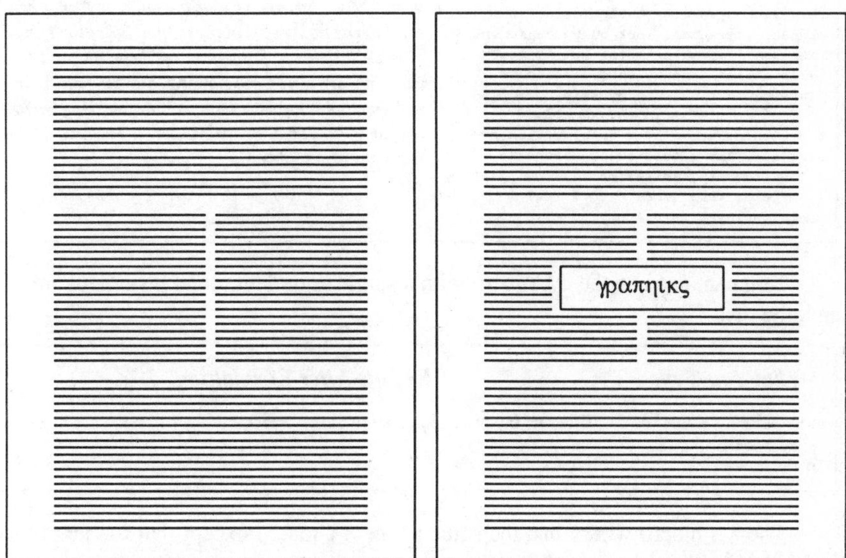

9.12. Changing Fonts and Sizes of Text

This section covers two topics of interest to the document writer: How to change fonts to obtain *italic* and **bold** effects. How to change the size of the text as you go.

Changing Fonts

There are macros to assist in changing fonts. The `.I` macro introduces italic text, the `.B` macro introduces bold text, and the `.R` macro is for Roman text.

To set a block of text in bold or italic, you use the `.B` or `.I` macro without arguments. The block of text to be treated specially follows the macro. Finally, a `.R` macro makes the text revert to the Roman font.

The example on the next page is a 'before and after' example of setting a block of text in italic font using the `.I` and `.R` macros.

What You Type	*Results After Formatting*

`Equal to the gods seems to me that man`
`who sits facing you and hears you nearby`
`sweetly speaking and softly laughing.`
`.I` *(set in italic font)*
`This sets my heart to fluttering in my`
`breast, for when I look on you a moment,`
`then can I speak no more, but my tongue`
`falls silent, and at once a delicate`
`flame courses beneath my skin,`
`.R` *(revert to Roman font)*
`and with my eyes I see nothing, and my`
`ears hum, and a cold sweat bathes me,`
`and a trembling seizes me all over, and`
`I am paler than grass, and I feel`
`that I am near to death.`
	Equal to the gods seems to me that man who sits facing you and hears you nearby sweetly speaking and softly laughing. *This sets my heart to fluttering in my breast, for when I look on you a moment, then can I speak no more, but my tongue falls silent, and at once a delicate flame courses beneath my skin,* and with my eyes I see nothing, and my ears hum, and a cold sweat bathes me, and a trembling seizes me all over, and I am paler than grass, and I feel that I am near to death.

You can also use the `.I` macro with a single argument to get a single word set in italic text.

What You Type	*Results After Formatting*

`This sets my heart to`
`.I fluttering`
`in my breast,`
	This sets my heart to *fluttering* in my breast,

The `.B` macro works just the same as the `.I` macro except that the text is set in **bold face like this** instead of italics.

You can supply up to a maximum of six arguments to the `.I` or `.B` macros. The odd-numbered arguments are set in the italic or bold typeface, and the even-numbered arguments are set in the font that was in effect at the time the macro was used. The arguments are all joined together. So, if you type:

```
.B first  second  third  fourth  fifth  sixth
```

what you get is: **first**second**third**fourth**fifth**sixth.

Finally, there are macros for getting specific *pairs* of fonts joined together. Each of these macros accepts a maximum of six arguments. These macros are:

`.IB`	Join arguments together alternating in *italic* and **bold**.
`.BI`	Join arguments together alternating in **bold** and *italic*.
`.IR`	Join arguments together alternating in *italic* Roman.
`.RI`	Join arguments together alternating in Roman and *italic*.
`.RB`	Join arguments together alternating in Roman and and **bold**.
`.BR`	Join arguments together alternating in **bold**. and Roman.

Now you've seen the *macros* for changing fonts. There are times, however, when the macros can't be used to do the job, and then you must use raw `troff` *escape sequences* to do the job.

A `troff` escape sequence is something that you can type in-line in the input text instead of having to type a macro or request on a line all of its own.

All `troff` escape sequences are introduced with a backslash (`\`) character. There are a multitude of these sequences. the `\f` sequence changes the font. The `\f` is followed by the name of the font. For example, to get **bold font** you'd type `\fB` in the running text. Things are more complicated if the name of the font is a two-character name like `HB` for Helvetica Bold — then you must use the form `\f(HB` to get the font name. This syntax is one of the reasons why people get into a love-hate relationship with `troff`.

To revert to the previous font, you type the `\fP` escape sequence. The `P` is reserved for the *previous font.*

So a one-word change typed in-line would look something like this:

```
. . .This sets my heart to \fIfluttering\fP in my . . .
```

Note that `troff` maintains a *one level deep stack* of font changes — they *do not nest*! That means that were you to type:

```
. . .This sets my \fBheart to \fIfluttering\fP in my . . .
```

you won't get back to Roman font when the `\fP` is seen — you'll get back to bold font — the previous font.

Changing Sizes

Another topic of interest is how to change the size of the type as it is printed. The most frequent need for doing this is when you have text that is typed in ALL CAPITAL LETTERS. The text seems to loom large over the surrounding type — the document 'shouts' at you. The `.SM` macro makes its text argument slightly smaller, so that the text would contain ALL CAPITAL LETTERS as you see here, where it doesn't look quite so bad.

The `.SM` macro accepts up to three arguments. If there are only two arguments, the second argument appears in the normal type size and is then concatenated to the end of the first argument. If there are three arguments, the second and third arguments appear in the normal type size with the second argument concatenated to the start of the first argument and the third argument concatenated to the end of the first argument. These facilities provide for adding punctuation in the normal type size at the start and end of the argument that is set in smaller type.

Here are some input lines using the .SM macro and the results you get when the text is printed.

What You Type	*Results After Formatting*

`Line containing`
`.SM CAPITAL`
`letters`
	Line containing CAPITAL letters

`Line containing`
`.SM CAPITAL )`
`letters`
	Line containing CAPITAL) letters

`Line containing`
`.SM CAPITAL ( )`
`letters`
	Line containing (CAPITAL) letters

`Line containing`
`.SM CAPITAL ( ""`
`letters`
	Line containing (CAPITAL letters

Just as there are escape sequences to change fonts, there are also escape sequences to change point sizes. You use the `\s` escape sequence to call out a size. Type `\s10` (for instance) to get 10-point type. At the end of the size change, the `\s0` escape sequence reverts to the previous size.

Note that `troff` only recognizes some fixed table of point sizes and these are wired right into its brain. The sizes that `troff` recognizes are: 6, 7, 8, 9, 10, 11, 12,14, 16, 18, 22, 24, 28, and 36. This means that if you try to set something in 144-point type using the `\s144` escape sequence, you won't get 144-point type, but instead you'll get a 14-point numeral 4 as shown here.

Instead of using absolute sizes it's usually desirable to change the size by a *relative* amount. You can do this by coding the escape sequence as `\s`±*n* where *n* is the amount of change. The value *n* is limited to a single digit. So, you could type a size change like this:

```
. . .  type the \s-2CAPITALS\s+2 in smaller size . . .
```

Accent Marks

Accent marks are of use when typing foreign words into documents. The -mm macro package contains some predefined *strings* that generate the correct motions to obtain accents for various characters.

The accent marks are defined in terms of `troff` *strings*. There is yet another escape sequence to obtain the value of a string. You type the `\*` escape sequence followed by the (in this case) one-character name of the string.

Here are the accent marks that the -mm macro package provides:

Accent	*What You Type*	*Results After Formatting*
Accent Grave	`dela*``	delà
Accent Grave	`verite\*'`	verité
Circumflex	`fene\*^tre`	fenêtre
Tilde	`pin\*~a colada`	piña colada
Cedilla	`dec\*,a`	deça
Umlaut	`Mu\*:nsterberg`	Münsterberg

9.13. Basic Ideas of Typography

The typography business can trace its evolution in a direct line from the mediaeval scribes, through the Gutenberg press, through the Monotype and Linotype machines of the 20th century. Unfortunately, a lot of baggage that should have been discarded 200 years ago is still around, and when you get to talking with typesetting people, you have to know some of their methods and jargon.

In this section we introduce some ideas of typography that are important in high-quality manuscript production, and we show how these ideas are implemented using `troff` commands and escape sequences. The information contained here should be useful to you if your prior experience is with word processing systems.

Point Size and Leading

Your average word processing system is often fairly limited to a single size of characters (Titan-10 or Ps-Bold, for instance), and also can't make major adjustments to the spacing between lines.

High-quality typographic systems can vary the size of the text and also control very finely the distance between the lines.

Punctuation Marks

One of the biggest differences between word processing and typography is in the available punctuation marks.

Quote Signs On the average word processing keyboard, you have three different quote signs — a double quote ("), a single quote or apostrophe ('), and an accent grave or back quote (`). Word processing systems tend to quote material using the double quote signs as in "Stop that!" she said. Typographically, you should use 'printer's quotes' instead, as in ``Stop that!'' she said.

To get printer's quotes using `troff`, you use two accent grave marks (``) as the opening quote and two apostrophes ('') as the closing quote. `troff` converts those marks into the correct characters when the document is finally printed.

You can get the single printer's quotes simply by opening with one accent grave mark (` ) and closing with one apostrophe ( ' ), and again, `troff` produces the correct characters when the document is finally printed.

Dashes On the average word processing keyboard, you have a minus sign (-) that you use as a minus sign and a hyphen. Typography usually has three different kinds of dashes.

A *hyphen* is a very short (-) dash that is placed in between words to hyphenate them, and is also placed in between compound adjectives such as left-handed.

An *en-dash* is a dash the width of a letter **n** in the current point size.

An *em-dash* is a dash the width of a letter **m** in the current point size. An em-dash is used as a parenthetical construct. In commercial word processing systems, you often use two minus signs (--) as a form of parenthesis. Typographically this is incorrect — you should use an *em-dash* instead. An em-dash (—) is a dash the width of the letter **m** in the current point size. You type the `troff` escape sequence `\(em` to get an em-dash.

9.14. Summary

This chapter was a quick 'show and tell' of the basic elements of the -mm macro package. -mm has many more features, many of dubious worth. -mm evolved in an environment where people write 'technical memoranda', and it's not entirely clear that many of the features of -mm are of use to the average person in the average office.

10 Document Formatting Packages

The previous chapter described the -mm macro package in conjunction with the troff document formatter. This chapter discusses some of the *preprocessors* that work with troff to perform complex feats of formatting. The three major preprocessors covered here are

- tbl — a tool to assist in laying out textual material in tabular (columnar) fashion.
- eqn — a tool and a language for describing mathematical equations.
- pic — a tool and a language for describing pictures.

In the traditional typesetting trade, tabular layout and mathematical typesetting are known as 'penalty copy' — you pay (a lot) more for getting these tasks done because they are very difficult for the typesetting systems to perform. In addition, graphical material is traditionally done by having illustrators draw the material using pen and ink, and then the final copy is produced using manual pasteup.

In this chapter we provide the highlights of using these languages — you get enough information to get started and be a danger to yourself. Once you're past the novice stage, read the *System V Document Processing Guide* for excruciating details on these languages.

10.1. Tabular Layout with tbl

There is a frequent need in document processing for laying out material in tabular format. There may be rows and columns of text. Some of the text might be captions, headers, and such. If the material is numeric, the requirements for how the columns are aligned might be different, because columns of figures are usually lined up differently from alphabetic material.

The tbl utility is intended to assist with the layout of tabular material. tbl is a pre-processor for troff (and for nroff). The tbl command interprets special table layout commands and translates them into streams of detailed commands for troff or nroff.

In this section, we explore some of tbl's capabilities. In general, those capabilities can only be fully exploited when used in conjunction with troff. When used with nroff, tbl's capabilities are somewhat restricted.

We start off with some very simple examples, then gradually expand on them in order to show `tbl`'s abilities.

Basic Concepts of `tbl`

Within a document, you must place your `tbl` layout requests between a 'table-start' indicator and a 'table-end' indicator:

```
.TS
Description of the Table Layout
Data to be Laid Out
.TE
```

In addition to telling `tbl` where the table starts and ends, the `.TS` and `.TE` macros are also used to indicate to `troff` where the streams of table layout commands are.

Do not forget the `.TS` and `.TE` macros in your document file. They are very important, and you get all sorts of weird results if you leave them out.

The `tbl` processor sees a table in terms of three distinct parts:

1. The overall layout or form of the table. For instance, whether the table is centered on the page, or whether the table is to be enclosed in a box.
2. The layout of each line of data in the table. This part determines how each column in the table is laid out — for instance, whether it is left adjusted, or centered, or numeric data which must be aligned on the decimal point.
3. The actual data (the textual material) of the table itself.

Let us start off with a fairly simple example. Here is a small file of wine information, with `tbl` requests in it:

```
$ cat cabernet
.TS
tab (/) ;
l l l .
Sterling Vineyards/1974/20.00
Joseph Phelps Vineyard/1975/8.75
Carneros Creek Winery/1976/8.50
Chateau Montelena/1973/8.50
Diamond Creek Vineyards/1976/10.00
Dehlinger/1976/5.00
Chateau Chevalier/1976/10.00
Trefethen/1974/6.50
Mayacamas/1974/9.50
Silver Oak/1973/7.50
.TE
$
```

Here's a picture with the salient points of the table noted:

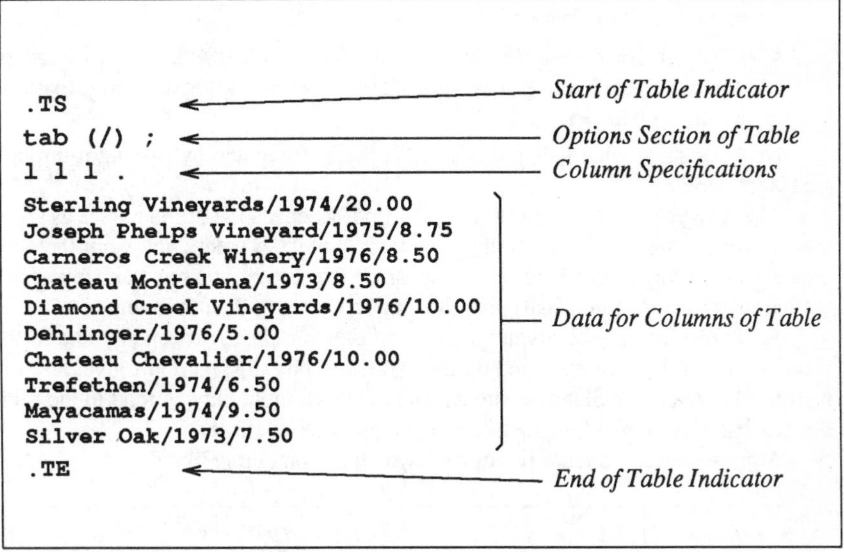

```
.TS
tab (/) ;
l l l .
Sterling Vineyards/1974/20.00
Joseph Phelps Vineyard/1975/8.75
Carneros Creek Winery/1976/8.50
Chateau Montelena/1973/8.50
Diamond Creek Vineyards/1976/10.00
Dehlinger/1976/5.00
Chateau Chevalier/1976/10.00
Trefethen/1974/6.50
Mayacamas/1974/9.50
Silver Oak/1973/7.50
.TE
```


Let us now explain what these bits mean.

- Firstly, there is the `.TS` line to tell `tbl` that there is a table to follow.
- The line with the

  ```
  tab (/) ;
  ```

  on it is the so called 'options' part of the table. This is part (1) from the list above. In this particular case, the only option to `tbl` is to tell it that the 'tab' character is to be a slash character. Normally, `tbl` expects to see the columns of *data* in the data part of a table separated by real tab (CTRL-I) characters. It is usually easier to see what is going on if you use a visible character which is not part of the data. In this case we used the slash character, `/`. The options part of the table is terminated by a semicolon, as shown in the example.
- The next part of the table header is the description of how the actual columns of data are to be laid out. This is part (2) from the list above. In this case, what we have said is that there are three left adjusted columns, indicated by the `l` format letters.

  As we shall illustrate soon, there can be many lines of format descriptions. Each line of format description in part (2) of the table corresponds to a single data line in part (3), the data part of the table. If, however, there are more lines of data in the data part of the table than there are format description lines, the *last* line of the format description part applies to all the remaining lines of the data.

In this example, the three letter l format letters apply to every line in the data part of the table. The format descriptions are terminated with a period at the end of the last one.

- Lastly, there comes the actual data of the table itself. It is the list of wineries, years, and prices. Each of the fields is separated from the next by the / character.

Now we show what happens when this list is formatted by passing it through tbl and troff.

The way you use tbl is very simple. tbl accepts a list of file names as arguments. tbl writes its results to the Standard Output, so unless you want the generated nroff formatting requests to appear on the screen, you must either redirect the output, or (as is more usual) pipe the output of tbl to the formatter.

A list of files may be given to tbl, and they are processed one by one in the order in which they are specified on the command line. If you don't give any file names, tbl reads the Standard Input. The Standard Input may be read in the middle of a list of files, by typing a minus sign at the desired place.

A more-or-less standard use of tbl would be something like

```
$ tbl files... | other preprocessors | troff troff options
$
```

Here is what tbl and troff did to the table above:

Sterling Vineyards	1974	20.00
Joseph Phelps Vineyard	1975	8.75
Carneros Creek Winery	1976	8.50
Chateau Montelena	1973	8.50
Diamond Creek Vineyards	1976	10.00
Dehlinger	1976	5.00
Chateau Chevalier	1976	10.00
Trefethen	1974	6.50
Mayacamas	1974	9.50
Silver Oak	1973	7.50

After formatting, the table appears on the left hand side of the page. The chances are, such a table is part of a larger document. Tables which appear in running text usually look better if they are centered on the page. To achieve that, we specify the requirement for centering in part (1), the 'options' part of the table, which affects the overall layout:

```
$ cat cabernet
.TS
center tab (/) ;
l l l .
Sterling Vineyards/1974/20.00
            <etcetera . . .>
Silver Oak/1973/7.50
.TE
$
```

All we have done here is add a `center` request in the options part of the table. When formatted, this looks much better:

Sterling Vineyards	1974	20.00
Joseph Phelps Vineyard	1975	8.75
Carneros Creek Winery	1976	8.50
Chateau Montelena	1973	8.50
Diamond Creek Vineyards	1976	10.00
Dehlinger	1976	5.00
Chateau Chevalier	1976	10.00
Trefethen	1974	6.50
Mayacamas	1974	9.50
Silver Oak	1973	7.50

`tbl/troff` have placed the table in the middle of the page, and as you can see, the overall appearance of the table has improved somewhat.

Numerically Aligned Columns

There is something wrong with the examples above. The prices are left-aligned. Prices really should appear with the decimal points aligned vertically. The years appear correct because they are all the same size, so their numerical values are not significant here. But they should really be treated as numbers, because that is what they actually are.

Now we show how to make numeric fields line up properly. We do this by changing the format specification letters for the years and the prices.

We made one important change to the table. The format specification part indicates that the second and third columns are numerically aligned columns. This means that numbers placed in the second and third columns of each line of data will be aligned properly.

```
$ cat cabernet
.TS
center tab (/) ;
l n n .
Sterling Vineyards/1974/20.00
            <etcetera . . .>
Silver Oak/1973/7.50
.TE
$
```

If numbers contain decimal points, as in the example, `tbl` lines them up on the decimal points. When numbers do not contain decimal points, `tbl` lines them up on their units digits. Here is how the table looks when we format it:

Sterling Vineyards	1974	20.00
Joseph Phelps Vineyard	1975	8.75
Carneros Creek Winery	1976	8.50
Chateau Montelena	1973	8.50
Diamond Creek Vineyards	1976	10.00
Dehlinger	1976	5.00
Chateau Chevalier	1976	10.00
Trefethen	1974	6.50
Mayacamas	1974	9.50
Silver Oak	1973	7.50

The table looks better when the numerical data is aligned on the decimal point.

Tables with Headings

Now we show how our example can be expanded to include captions for the individual columns. Here is an improved version of our table:

```
$ cat cabernet
.TS
center tab (/) ;
cfI cfI cfI
l n n .
Establishment/Year/Price
.sp 1
Sterling Vineyards/1974/20.00
            <etcetera . . .>
Silver Oak/1973/7.50
.TE
$
```

The example above now shows an extra line in the format description part, and some extra data in the data part.

The first line of the format descriptions indicates that there are to be three columns of data. There are two items of information for each of the key letters:

- The `c` means that each item of data should be centered within its column.
- The `fI` means that the data in these columns will be printed in the italic font.

This format applies to the very first line of the data.

The second (and last) line of the format description part is the same as before, and it applies to all the remaining data lines in the table.

When we format this new layout, we get something different:

Establishment	*Year*	*Price*
Sterling Vineyards	1974	20.00
Joseph Phelps Vineyard	1975	8.75
Carneros Creek Winery	1976	8.50
Chateau Montelena	1973	8.50
Diamond Creek Vineyards	1976	10.00
Dehlinger	1976	5.00
Chateau Chevalier	1976	10.00
Trefethen	1974	6.50
Mayacamas	1974	9.50
Silver Oak	1973	7.50

As you can see, we have a table with headers for the specific data columns.

You should note that we used an `troff .sp` request to generate a blank line in the table after the header line. In general, `tbl` ignores `troff` commands appearing in table layouts and passes them on through to `troff`. If you use a real blank line, `tbl` interprets it as part of the data, and you don't always get the desired results.

Tables with Spanned Headings

Our next example shows a table with a header for the entire table. There is to be an overall heading line, which is only one column, centered across the whole table. When you describe a table the format description part, part (2) of the table, must always describe the largest number of columns which that table will have. If there are some lines which will have less columns of data, you must indicate what to do with those specific lines. In the example on the next page, we show what is called a 'spanned heading'. This means that a column of data spans across into the next column.

The first line of the format description part now shows a centered, spanned column. A spanned element can span as many or as few columns as you like.

```
$ cat cabernet
.TS
center tab (/) ;
cfI s s
cfI cfI cfI
l n n .
Selected California Cabernet Sauvignon
.sp 1
Establishment/Year/Price
.sp 1
Sterling Vineyards/1974/20.00
            <etcetera . . .>
Silver Oak/1973/7.50
.TE
$
```

Here is the result of formatting the above table:

Selected California Cabernet Sauvignon		
Establishment	*Year*	*Price*
Sterling Vineyards	1974	20.00
Joseph Phelps Vineyard	1975	8.75
Carneros Creek Winery	1976	8.50
Chateau Montelena	1973	8.50
Diamond Creek Vineyards	1976	10.00
Dehlinger	1976	5.00
Chateau Chevalier	1976	10.00
Trefethen	1974	6.50
Mayacamas	1974	9.50
Silver Oak	1973	7.50

The table now has an overall header nicely centered over the other columns.

Tables Enclosed in Boxes

`tbl` can enclose a table in a box. There are three choices for boxing in a table:

- The entire table can be enclosed in a box,
- The entire table can be enclosed in a double box,
- The entire table, and every item in it, can be enclosed within box lines.

Here is our wine information table, with specifications for boxing it:

```
$ cat cabernet
.TS
center box tab (/) ;
cfI s s
cfI cfI cfI
l n n .
Selected California Cabernet Sauvignon
.sp 1
Establishment/Year/Price
.sp 1
Sterling Vineyards/1974/20.00
Joseph Phelps Vineyard/1975/8.75
            <etcetera . . .>
Mayacamas/1974/9.50
Silver Oak/1973/7.50
.TE
```

In the 'options' part, part (1) of the table, we added the `box` keyword, to indicate that the whole table is to be enclosed in a box.

Here is the table after formatting:

Selected California Cabernet Sauvignon		
Establishment	*Year*	*Price*
Sterling Vineyards	1974	20.00
Joseph Phelps Vineyard	1975	8.75
Carneros Creek Winery	1976	8.50
Chateau Montelena	1973	8.50
Diamond Creek Vineyards	1976	10.00
Dehlinger	1976	5.00
Chateau Chevalier	1976	10.00
Trefethen	1974	6.50
Mayacamas	1974	9.50
Silver Oak	1973	7.50

■ *If you happen to be using* `nroff`, *as soon as you start to use boxes, the interface between* `tbl` *and* `nroff` *gets somewhat more complicated. When you ask* `tbl` *to put boxes around tables, it starts generating* `nroff` *requests which produce reverse paper-motions in the output. Most printers cannot handle reverse paper-motions. To handle this case, we must use* `col` *as the final filter in the command line. Also, it is necessary to tell* `nroff` *the specific kind of output device upon which the results will be printed. This means we have to use the* `-T` *option to* `nroff`.

Drawing Lines in Tables

It is also possible to draw horizontal lines in a table. We stick with the same example, but we draw lines after the two headers. Here is how we have to modify the table to do this:

```
$ cat cabernet
.TS
center box tab (/) ;
cfI s s
cfI cfI cfI
l n n .
Selected California Cabernet Sauvignon
_
Establishment/Year/Price
_
Sterling Vineyards/1974/20.00
Joseph Phelps Vineyard/1975/8.75
              <etcetera . . .>
Mayacamas/1974/9.50
Silver Oak/1973/7.50
.TE
```

Instead of the `.sp 1` requests, we have placed an underline character _ which indicates to `tbl` that a horizontal line is to be drawn at this point in the table. When the table is formatted, the results are like this:

Selected California Cabernet Sauvignon		
Establishment	*Year*	*Price*
Sterling Vineyards	1974	20.00
Joseph Phelps Vineyard	1975	8.75
Carneros Creek Winery	1976	8.50
Chateau Montelena	1973	8.50
Diamond Creek Vineyards	1976	10.00
Dehlinger	1976	5.00
Chateau Chevalier	1976	10.00
Trefethen	1974	6.50
Mayacamas	1974	9.50
Silver Oak	1973	7.50

It is possible to draw vertical lines as well, between any selected columns. It is also possible to draw horizontal lines across parts of a table. We do not cover these issues here; they are described in the paper entitled *Tbl — A Program to Format Tables*, by M. E. Lesk.

Enclosing Everything In A Table In Boxes

`tbl` also has the `allbox` capability, which draws lines around every object in the table, as well as drawing a box around the whole table. To get this capability, just change the table header part to include the keyword `allbox` instead of the simple `box` keyword.

```
$ cat cabernet
.TS
center allbox tab (/) ;
cfI s s
cfI cfI cfI
l n n .
Selected California Cabernet Sauvignon
Establishment/Year/Price
Sterling Vineyards/1974/20.00
Joseph Phelps Vineyard/1975/8.75
            <etcetera . . .>
Mayacamas/1974/9.50
Silver Oak/1973/7.50
.TE
```

When we format the table, it has the following effects:

Selected California Cabernet Sauvignon		
Establishment	*Year*	*Price*
Sterling Vineyards	1974	20.00
Joseph Phelps Vineyard	1975	8.75
Carneros Creek Winery	1976	8.50
Chateau Montelena	1973	8.50
Diamond Creek Vineyards	1976	10.00
Dehlinger	1976	5.00
Chateau Chevalier	1976	10.00
Trefethen	1974	6.50
Mayacamas	1974	9.50
Silver Oak	1973	7.50

Flowing Text Blocks in a Column

So far, the data in the columns of the tables have been fixed within certain boundaries. A frequent requirement is to have ordinary flowing text in a specific column of a table. Flowing text is justified between the margins of the specific column in which it appears in the table. In `tbl` parlance, these sections of flowing text are called 'text blocks'. Each block of text is bracketed with the markers `T{` (at the start), and `T}` (at the end). The `T{` marker must be at the end of a line, and the `T}` marker must be at the start of a line. The example below illustrates this feature. We start the discussion with a small table showing the more popular grape varieties grown in the California wine producing regions. Here is what the source text looks like:

```
$ cat winetypes
.TS
center allbox tab (/) ;
cfI s
cfI cfI
a a .
Guide to California Grapes
Grape Type/Comments
Cabernet Sauvignon/T{
Finest of the red wines. Lots of fruit.
Highly perfumed.  Long lasting wine.
T}
Chardonnay/T{
Finest of the white wines.
Perfumed, grape flavor.  Lasts well.
T}
Johannisberg Riesling/T{
Fruity, flower scented white wine.
Often in late-harvest versions with high
quantities of residual sugar.
T}
.TE
$
```

When we format that file, we get the results as shown on the next page.

Guide to California Grapes	
Grape Type	*Comments*
Cabernet Sauvignon	Finest of the red wines. Lots of fruit. Highly perfumed. Long lasting wine.
Chardonnay	Finest of the white wines. Perfumed, grape flavor. Lasts well.
Johannisberg Riesling	Fruity, flower scented white wine. Often in late-harvest versions with high quantities of residual sugar.

Although the text in the second column 'flows' between the margins of the column, it does not do so very well, because the column is too short. To improve on this, we have to tell `tbl` to make the second column of the table wider.

Modifying the Format of Columns

When you describe the layout of a table, `tbl` makes some decisions as to how wide the columns need to be to accommodate the various pieces of data. It often happens that `tbl`'s decisions are not entirely adequate. For example, you might decide that a particular column should be wider, in order to display some text in a more pleasing way. In the previous example, you can see that the flowing text in the right hand column doesn't really look all that good, because the column is too narrow. It would look better if the column were wider. `tbl` provides the ability to specify the width of a column in the format description part of the table.

When you specify the layout of a column in the format description part of the table, each of the format key letters can be followed by further description items, which modify the column layout in some way. There are a number of these modifiers. Some of them concern changing fonts and altering point sizes, those are not covered in this book.

To change the width of a column, you follow the key letter with a letter `w` (width), then enclose the column-width specification in parentheses. The width can be specified as a number, in which case it is taken to be that many n-spaces. Otherwise, you can place a units letter, such as `i` (inches), after the number. The example on the next page shows a table with the second column defined to be 3.0 inches wide.

We made two changes in the table format. Firstly we defined the second data column to be left adjusted instead of alphanumeric. Then we defined the width of the column to be 3.0 inches wide.

```
$ cat winetypes
.TS
center allbox tab (/) ;
cfI s
cfI cfI
a lw(3.0i) .
Guide to California Grapes
Grape Type/Comments
Cabernet Sauvignon;T{
                <etcetera . . .>
Fruity, flower scented white wine.
Often in late-harvest versions with high
quantities of residual sugar.
T}
.TE
$
```

This is what the table looks like now when it is formatted:

Guide to California Grapes	
Grape Type	*Comments*
Cabernet Sauvignon	Finest of the red wines. Lots of fruit. Highly perfumed. Long lasting wine.
Chardonnay	Finest of the white wines. Perfumed, grape flavor. Lasts well.
Johannisberg Riesling	Fruity, flower scented white wine. Often in late-harvest versions with high quantities of residual sugar.

The table is now not only formatted somewhat better, with less gaps between the words, but the table is also shorter because of the wider column. Overall, this second table has a more pleasing appearance than does the first example.

Changing the Format of a Table

It is possible to change the layout of the data columns anywhere in a table. The overall layout of the table cannot be changed, but the format specification part can. To do this, the `.T&` request is used, to indicate a temporary end to the current portion of the table, and to introduce a new format specification part for the table.

To illustrate this capability, we add some Chardonnays to our Cabernet file from earlier in this chapter:

```
$ cat cabandchard
.TS
center box tab (/) ;
cfI s s
cfI cfI cfI
l n n .
Selected California Cabernet Sauvignon
_
Establishment/Year/Price
_
Sterling Vineyards/1974/20.00
Joseph Phelps Vineyard/1975/8.75
            <etcetera . . .>
Mayacamas/1974/9.50
Silver Oak/1973/7.50
_
.sp 1
.T&
cfI s s
cfI cfI cfI
l n n .
Selected California Chardonnay
_
Establishment/Year/Price
_
Caymus Vineyards/1976/12.00
Chateau St. Jean/1976/11.50
Robert Mondavi/1977/9.00
Spring Mountain/1976/10.00
Sterling Vineyards/1976/10.00
Chaparral/1977/8.50
Dry Creek Winery/1977/8.00
St. Clements/1977/10.00
Chateau Montelena/1975/10.00
Mayacamas Vineyards/1976/11.00
.TE
$
```

The `.T&` request states that this is a temporary end to the table, and that a new format specification part is to appear. In this example, we have just inserted a new set of headings for the Chardonnay wines introduced in the latter part of the table. The formatted table produced is shown in figure 10.1 on the next page.

Selected California Cabernet Sauvignon		
Establishment	*Year*	*Price*
Sterling Vineyards	1974	20.00
Joseph Phelps Vineyard	1975	8.75
<*etcetera...*>		
Mayacamas	1974	9.50
Silver Oak	1973	7.50

Selected California Chardonnay		
Establishment	Year	Price
Caymus Vineyards	1976	12.00
Chateau St. Jean	1976	11.50
Robert Mondavi	1977	9.00
Spring Mountain	1976	10.00
Sterling Vineyards	1976	10.00
Chaparral	1977	8.50
Dry Creek Winery	1977	8.00
St. Clements	1977	10.00
Chateau Montelena	1975	10.00
Mayacamas Vineyards	1976	11.00

Figure 10.1 Table with Multiple Sections

The `tbl` program has much more capability than we have described above. However, what we have shown should be sufficient to give you an idea of the kinds of things which can be achieved using `tbl`.

10.2. Mathematical Equations with `eqn`

`eqn` is a preprocessor for `troff` that assists preparation of documents containing mathematical equations.

`eqn` is a preprocessor for `troff`; `neqn` is a preprocessor for `nroff`. For the purposes of the discussion, we assume that you are using the `eqn` and `troff` packages to format equations.

`eqn` turns an English-like description of an equation into formatting requests necessary to generate the mathematical symbols for that equation. In chapter 9 we described briefly the macros that introduce equation displays. Now we get a little further into the capabilities of how you actually specify equations.

Imagine you're 'talking' an equation over the telephone to someone else. There's a well-accepted 'language' of equations so that the person at the other end has a good idea what you have in mind. `eqn` is designed to accept this English-like 'language' into `troff` requests that produce the printed results you want.

Here is a minimal example of an equation formatted using `eqn` and `troff`. On the left is what you type and on the right is what the formatters produce.

What You Type	*Results After Formatting*
`.EQ` *(Start Displayed Equation)* `x = {-b +- sqrt{b sup 2 -4ac}} over 2a` `.EN` *(End Displayed Equation)*	$x=\frac{-b\pm\sqrt{b^2-4ac}}{2a}$

The rest of this section provides a very brief overview of eqn's capabilities.

Getting Started with eqn

There are two main styles of equations:

- *Displayed Equations* — are broken out of the main body of the text like a display. We mentioned the displayed equation capabilities in chapter 9.
- *Inline Equations* — appear right there in the running text like $r=\sqrt{x^2+y^2}$ as you see here.

Equations in your document appear between the `.EQ` and `.EN` macros. Let's suppose you have a manuscript file containing equations and you've called the file *equations*. To use eqn with `troff`, you must type a command line like this:

```
$ eqn equations | troff options | postprocessing software . . .
```

If you want to run the other `troff` preprocessors (`pic` or `tbl`), they should be run in the order:

- `pic` comes first in the pipeline,
- `tbl` comes after `pic`,
- eqn comes after `tbl`.

Input to eqn is essentially free-form. eqn uses spaces and newlines in the input text to recognize parts of an equation and to separate things. These spaces and newlines do not create space in the printed output — eqn applies a well-defined set of rules as to where space should appear, how much space, and where to break long equations.

eqn's rules as to where to inject space in the printed output are largely based on the assumption that `troff` will set the equation in ten-point type in the Times Roman font. If you deviate from this, and sometimes even if you don't, the printed output doesn't always appear as good as it might. In these cases you can get extra space inserted in the printed output by using 'space' characters of various sizes. The tilde character (~) produces a space equal to the normal word-spacing in text. A circumflex character (^) generates a space half the size of that generated by the tilde character. Spaces, tildes, and circumflexes also delimit parts of an equation.

Subscripts and Superscripts

One of eqn's simplest applications is to obtain subscripts and superscripts for equations. The `sup` keyword introduces superscripts, and the `sub` keyword introduces subscripts. For example:

What You Type	*Results After Formatting*
`.EQ` *(Start Displayed Equation)* `x sup 2 + y sup 2 = 1` `.EN` *(End Displayed Equation)*	$x^2+y^2=1$

Fractions

Fractions are introduced with the `over` keyword. The stuff to the left of `over` is placed on the top, and the stuff to the right of `over` appears underneath:

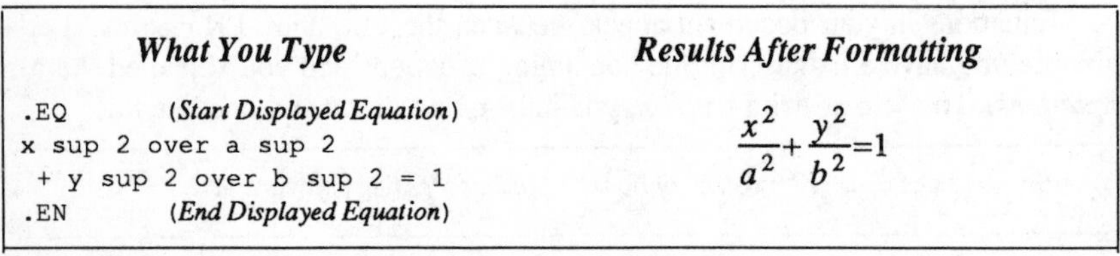

What You Type	*Results After Formatting*

`.EQ` *(Start Displayed Equation)*
`x sup 2 over a sup 2`
`+ y sup 2 over b sup 2 = 1`
`.EN` *(End Displayed Equation)*
	$\frac{x^2}{a^2}+\frac{y^2}{b^2}=1$

Grouping Compound Expressions with Braces

eqn uses braces ({ and }) to group parts of expressions that should be considered as a single unit.

For example, here is an equation using braces to group the things that should be under the square root sign:

What You Type	*Results After Formatting*
`.EQ` *(Start Displayed Equation)* `r = sqrt { x sup 2 + y sup 2 }` `.EN` *(End Displayed Equation)*	$r=\sqrt{x^2+y^2}$

Here is what happens if you omit the braces:

What You Type	*Results After Formatting*
`.EQ` *(Start Displayed Equation)* `r = sqrt x sup 2 + y sup 2` `.EN` *(End Displayed Equation)*	$r=\sqrt{x^2}+y^2$

The square root only gets applied to the x^2 instead of to the entire x^2+y^2.

A string within braces can appear anywhere that a single character can appear. Make sure that you make pairs of braces balance. Braces can also appear within braces.

Square Roots

Square roots are introduced with the `sqrt` keyword:

What You Type		Results After Formatting
`.EQ`	*(Start Displayed Equation)*	$r=\sqrt{x^2+y^2}$
`r = sqrt { x sup 2 + y sup 2 }`		
`.EN`	*(End Displayed Equation)*	

Big Parentheses, Braces and Brackets

Some equations get rather tall and require large parentheses, brackets, or braces to group the parts of the equations. You get these large objects by coding `left` *thing* to get the left-hand *thing*, where *thing* is one of `(` for the left parenthesis, `[` for the left bracket, or `{` for the left brace. Similarly, you code `right` *thing* to get the right-hand *thing*, where *thing* is one of `)` for the right parenthesis, `]` for the right bracket, or `}` for the right brace. Let's look at the Lagrange expansion:

$$g(x)=g(x_0)+\sum_{k=1}^{\infty}\frac{(y-y_0)^k}{k!}\left[\frac{d^{k-1}}{dx^{k-1}}\left(g'(x)\left\{\frac{x-x_0}{f(x)-y_0}\right\}^k\right)\right]_{x=x_0}$$

The input text that produced that equation looks like this:

```
.EQ        (Start Displayed Equation)
g ( x ) = g ( x sub 0 ) + sum from { k = 1 } to
 inf { ( y - y sub 0 ) sup k } over k! left [ d sup { k - 1 } over
 dx sup { k - 1 } left ( g ' ( x ) left { { x - x sub 0 } over
 { f ( x ) - y sub 0 } right } sup k right ) right ] sub { x = x sub 0 }
.EN        (End Displayed Equation)
```

Summations and Integrals

eqn recognizes these constructs:

`sum` meaning the $\sum$ summation sign,

`int` meaning the $\int$ integral sign,

`prod` meaning the $\prod$ product sign,

`union` meaning the $\cup$ union sign,

`inter` meaning the $\cap$ intersection sign.

You would use these signs to construct formulas like this:

What You Type	*Results After Formatting*
`.EQ` *(Start Displayed Equation)* `s = sum from { i = 0 } to { i = inf } x sub i` `.EN` *(End Displayed Equation)*	$s=\sum_{i=0}^{i=\infty} x_i$

Note the `from` and `to` keywords in the formula. The `from` and `to` keywords must appear in that order if they both appear. The braces are necessary around the `i = 0` and the `i = inf` constructs because they contain spaces and so you must indicate where the constructs begin and end.

Mathematical and Greek Characters

`eqn` has knowledge of a complete Mathematical and Greek symbol font.

The Mathematical characters are obtained by writing out their names. You've already seen constructs such as `sqrt` for the $\surd$ sign, as well as for the $\sum$, $\int$, $\prod$, $\cup$, and $\cap$ signs. Refer to the *Mathematics Typesetting Program* in the System V *Document Processing Guide* for the rest of the story.

In addition to the special Mathematical characters, you also get access to the Greek characters by spelling out their names. For example, you write the word `psi` (lower case) to get the ψ character, and you write the word `PSI` (upper case) to get the Ψ character.

In Line Equations

Frequently you would like the equations to appear in-line in the running text instead of being broken out as displays.

To get equations set in-line, you must delimit them in some way. The way to do this is to type an equation that contains only a `delim` statement

```
.EQ
delim @!
.EN
```

In this example, we chose the `@` sign as the starting delimiter and the `!` sign as the ending delimiter. The delimiters can in fact be the same character. To get the delimiters switched off[1] you just code an equation that looks like:

[1] Usually a good idea when you don't need them.

```
.EQ
delim off
.EN
```

For example, if you want to talk about the β-test phase of the γ-ray projection system based on Heisenberg's ψ-functions, you could type some text that looks like this:

```
.EQ         (Start Equation)
delim $$
.EN         (End Equation)
. . . . the $beta$-test phase of the $gamma$-ray
projection system based on Heisenberg's $psi$-functions . . .
```

For a writeup on eqn, with many illustrations of the power and flexibility of this remarkable tool, see *Mathematics Typesetting Program* in the System V *Document Processing Guide*.

10.3. The pic Graphics Description Language

troff and its supporting software have had no adequate drawing facility for many years. If you wanted illustrations in a document, you either didn't do any, or you had an illustrator draw the pictures for you and then you pasted them into the document. The major problems with the manual cut-and-paste process are that cut-and-paste are labor-intensive, error-prone, and non-repeatable.

More modern versions of troff have available yet another preprocessor for describing pictures. pic is a preprocessor and a language for describing diagrams. pic is (fairly well) integrated with troff and the other supporting tools. We feel that pic's life is limited with the availability of visual graphics software, but we give a short run-through of pic in this section. For more details read the pic manual.

Basics of pic

pic has a small number of 'primitives' — basic objects that you can draw and then use to construct more complicated pictures. At first sight, pic is deceptively simple to learn and use. As soon as you go beyond the very simple diagrams, however, pic can get very complicated very fast.

The basic objects available in pic are shown in the diagram on the next page.

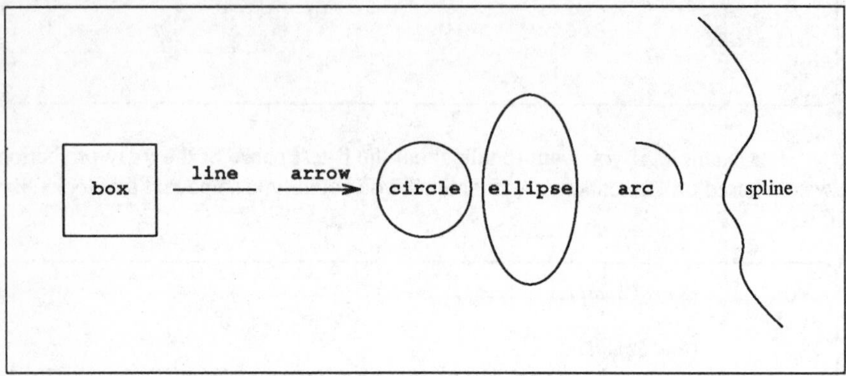

Basic Layout of a Picture Each `pic` diagram begins with a `.PS` macro and ends with a `.PE` macro. In between the macros are the commands for describing the picture. Here is a very simple picture composed of two boxes with an arrow between them:

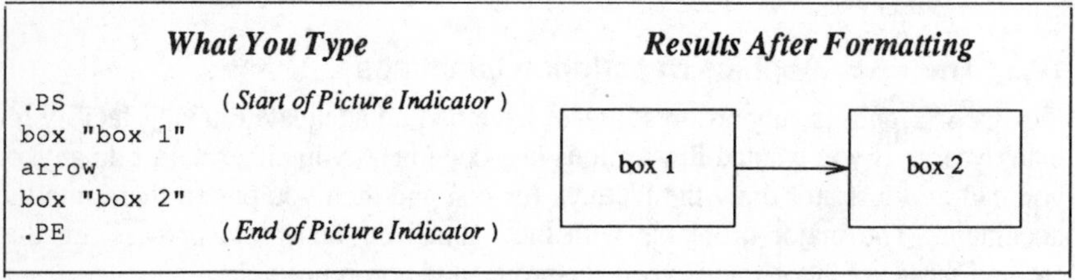

What You Type
Results After Formatting
.PS (*Start of Picture Indicator*)
box "box 1"
arrow
box "box 2"
.PE (*End of Picture Indicator*)
box 1
box 2

You can place *comments* in `pic` diagrams — a comment starts with a # sign and continues to the end of the line.

Long lines can be continued over more than one input line by placing a backslash (\ ) character at the end of the line to be continued.

Objects Available in `pic`

Now we introduce the objects that you can draw using `pic`.

Keyword	*Object*
`box`	draws a box ¾" wide × ½" high
`line`	draws a line ½" long
`arrow`	draws an arrow ½"long
`circle`	draws a ½" diameter circle
`ellipse`	draws an ellipse ¾" wide × ½" high
`arc`	draws an arc of ½" radius
`move`	moves ½" in the current direction

Here is the example from before, but drawing with ellipses and circles instead of boxes:

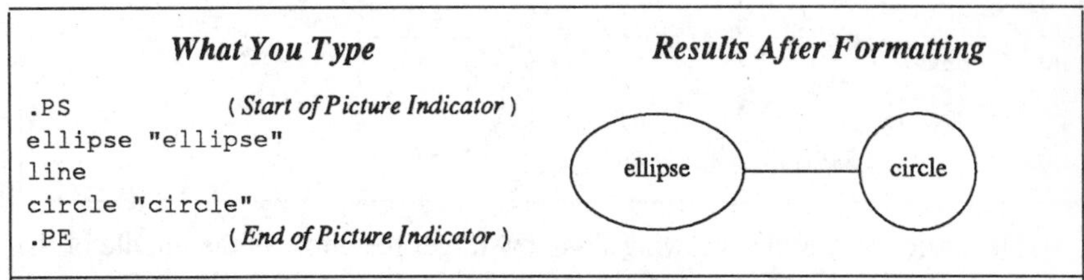
What You Type
Results After Formatting
.PS (Start of Picture Indicator)
ellipse "ellipse"
line
circle "circle"
.PE (End of Picture Indicator)
ellipse
circle

Objects can have *attributes* associated with them that alter their standard appearance. For instance, you can get boxes and lines dotted and dashed by adding `dotted` or `dashed` after the object.

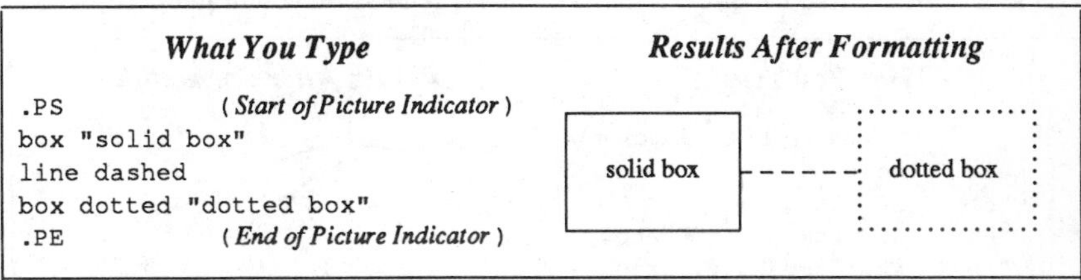
What You Type
Results After Formatting
.PS (Start of Picture Indicator)
box "solid box"
line dashed
box dotted "dotted box"
.PE (End of Picture Indicator)
solid box
dotted box

Text is also an attribute of an object. In general, text is centered within an object. For lines and arrows, text is positioned right on top of the line or arrow, which doesn't look all that good. You have to supply the keyword `above` or `below` to get the text positioned at the correct place.

Positioning Objects Using `pic`

Now we delve into the mysteries of how you position objects. `pic` uses a standard Cartesian coordinate system — you refer to things in *x*,*y* coordinates.

So you can write `pic` sequences like

```
box at (1, 2)
```

or

```
ellipse at (2, 3)
```

to get objects positioned at specific places. Objects are positioned at their geometric centers.

Referencing Objects

Instead of laying out your drawings with every objects positioned at its own absolute coordinates, it's much more convenient to position objects *relative* to other objects. This means that you must be able to attach a *label* (a name) to an object so that you can refer to it later. Here's a short example:

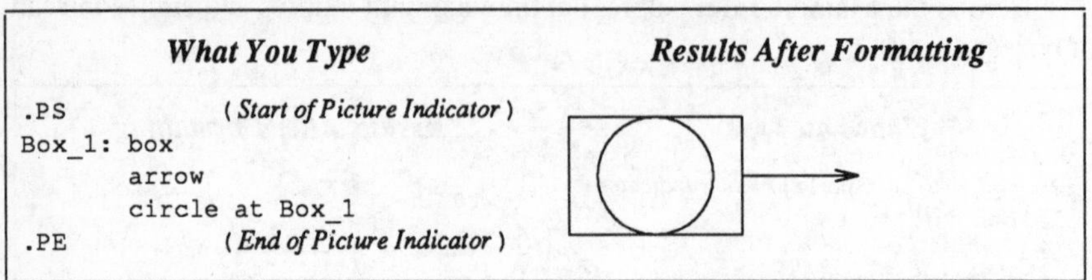

The basic issue in this drawing was how to get the circle in the middle of the box we drew. Well, just give the box a name — this case we called it '`Box_1`'. Then later on, we just asked for a circle `at Box_1` and that's what we got.

There's more to come — most objects have 'corners' which you refer to with the points of the compass. Some objects such as lines have a start and and end as well as a center. Here's a circle with its compass points and center marked:

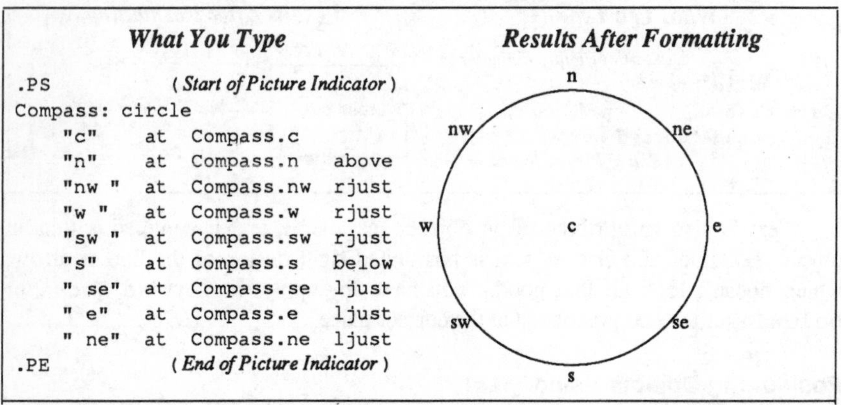

What You Type
Results After Formatting
.PS (Start of Picture Indicator)
Compass: circle
"c" at Compass.c
"n" at Compass.n above
"nw " at Compass.nw rjust
"w " at Compass.w rjust
"sw " at Compass.sw rjust
"s" at Compass.s below
" se" at Compass.se ljust
" e" at Compass.e ljust
" ne" at Compass.ne ljust
.PE (End of Picture Indicator)
n
nw
ne
w
c
e
sw
se
s

Given the capability to refer to corners of objects, you can now position things relative to their corners. You can use the `with` keyword to position things, like:

```
B1: box at (1, 2)
    box with .sw at B1.ne
```

gets you two boxes joined at their corners.

`pic` Macros

`pic` has a capability to define *macros* — predefined sequences of `pic` commands that can be referenced by name. A `pic` macro definition looks like

`define` *macro_name* δ *macro_body* δ

- The `define` keyword tells `pic` that a macro definition is on the way.
- *macro_name* is the name of the macro being defined.
- The δ is any arbitrary *delimiter* character that does not appear in the macro body.
- Finally, the *macro_body* is the text that will be substituted when *macro_name* is referenced (used) later in the `pic` diagram.

  `pic` macros can have up to nine ***arguments.*** You indicate where in the macro body an argument will appear by a $*n* indicator — where *n* is 1 through 9.

For example, here's how we defined the 'fat arrows' you've seen in other parts of the book:

```
.PS
define fat_right_arrow ! box invisible width 3/8 height 2/16 $1
   line from last box.e to last box.n+(0, 0)
.ps 36
   line from last box.e to last box.s+(0, 0)
.ps
   line from last box.w+(0, -1/32) to last box.w+(0, 1/32)
.ps 36
   line from last box.w+(0, -1/32) to last box.s+(0, 1/32)
.ps
   line from last box.w+(0, 1/32) to last box.n+(0, -1/32)
   line from last box.n+(0, -1/32) to last box.n
   line from last box.s+(0, 1/32) to last box.s !
.PE
```

and here's how you would *use* this fat right pointing arrow:

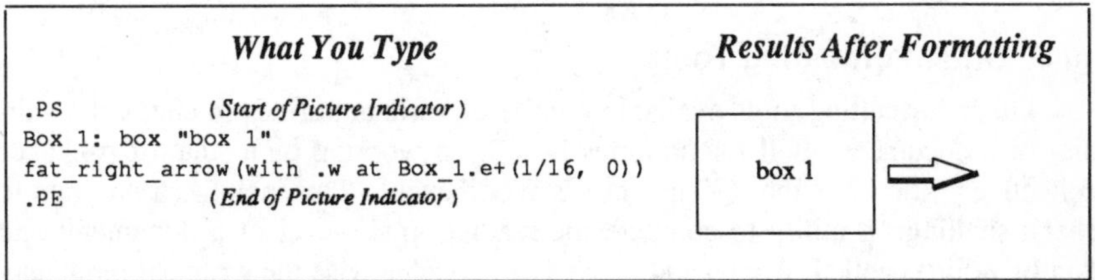
What You Type
Results After Formatting
.PS (Start of Picture Indicator)
Box_1: box "box 1"
fat_right_arrow(with .w at Box_1.e+(1/16, 0))
.PE (End of Picture Indicator)
box 1

Handy Hints for Using `pic`

When we first used `pic`, we found it cumbersome. Here are a few of the things we discovered:

- Use *relative* positioning always. Relative positioning means that you nail down the position of only one object in a picture, and the nail down the positions of everything else relative to the other objects. Then when you move a given object, the other objects follow it around.

- Use `invisible` objects as anchor points to establish the positions of other objects. For instance, here's how to generate this rotated square:

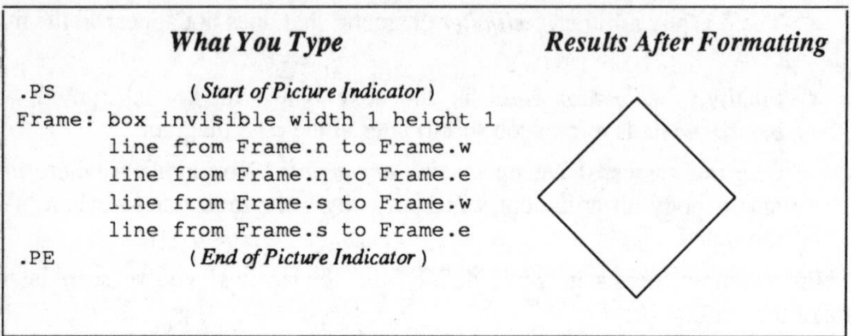

What You Type	*Results After Formatting*
`.PS` (*Start of Picture Indicator*)	
`Frame: box invisible width 1 height 1`	
`line from Frame.n to Frame.w`	
`line from Frame.n to Frame.e`	
`line from Frame.s to Frame.w`	
`line from Frame.s to Frame.e`	
`.PE` (*End of Picture Indicator*)	

- `pic` will often 'crash' when presented with what is apparently good input. The most insidious is the placement of keywords and text. For instance, the statement:

  ```
  line above "text"
  ```

  generates a 'crash' — the statement *should* read:

  ```
  line "text" above
  ```

`pic` is not what people expect from a 'real' graphics language. There is no texturing nor filling for example. You can't draw elliptical arcs. You can't scale and rotate objects arbitrarily. Some of these limitations are understandable when you realize that `pic` is simply a preprocessor for `troff`. Notwithstanding all that, all the diagrams in this book were generated using `pic`, so you *can* get the job done.

10.4. Other Formatting Tools

Other formatting tools available consist of various utilities to check the validity of a document. Bell Laboratories have been working on a suite of packages collectively known as the 'Documentor's Workbench'. This includes a program to check spelling; a utility to compute the reading grade-level of a document; and finally, utilities called `style` and `diction`, which advise the writer of redundant usage, archaic forms, and dubious grammatical constructs.

10.5. Summary

By now you should be saturated with System V's capabilities for handling text and processing documents. It is worth while studying some of the other macro packages available, and comparing their capabilities.

If you have the appropriate output devices, play with `tbl` and `eqn` to see how they function. Experiment with `diffmark` to get revision bars on different versions of your document.

In many ways System V documentation facilities are somewhat cumbersome. The `troff` package, after all, is a lineal descendant of a package developed 20 years ago, under entirely different constraints and assumptions. But, the lesson that these documentation packages teach us is clear: do not put all the eggs in one basket. Instead, separate out the functions (equation processing, table layout, revision bar generation, page layout) into independent packages, instead of making one monster utility which does none of those things very well.

Lastly, on-line documentation has the tremendous advantage that once something is typed, it need never be retyped, it only needs correcting and revising. Parts of documents can be replicated at different places in a manuscript without the need to retype it each time. The idea of computer aided documentation is a fairly new idea in most of the computer industry, but is catching on slowly. The tools are there, you just need to use them.

11 Typesetting with `troff` and `nroff`

In chapter 9 we described the -mm macro package which provides the principal interface to using `troff`. This chapter provides a look at `troff` in the raw, as it were, and goes into more detail on the intricacies of this powerful system.

11.1. Basic Ideas of `troff`

`troff` was originally designed to drive a second-generation typesetter called a C/A/T. Unfortunately much of `troff`'s language and concepts reflect the behavior of this machine. The C/A/T is practically defunct now, and so `troff` has had to be adapted for other kinds of devices such as laser printers.

In addition to `troff` which was geared up specifically for one typesetter, there is a variation called `nroff`, which is oriented towards line-printer devices and letter quality printers such as Diablo printers. `nroff`'s capabilities are more limited than `troff`'s — `nroff` can't change sizes of type for example. There have been two separate lines of development:

- Some people have written postprocessing software that converts `troff`'s C/A/T-oriented output codes into codes suitable for driving other devices.
- Brian Kernighan at Bell Laboratories made extensive revisions to `troff` to create a new version called Device Independent `troff` (*ditroff*).

In this chapter we concentrate on `troff`, and assume that you either have old-style `troff` with either a C/A/T system (unlikely), some software package for driving other devices from `troff`'s output codes (more likely), or that you're using device-independent `troff` as we are.

The `troff` text formatter reads an input file containing unformatted text which is to be formatted so as to produce a neatly laid out document. First you prepare the input file, using the editor of your choice, then you format that text using `troff` as we described back in chapter 9.

The input file might, or might not, contain `troff` 'requests' interspersed with the text to be formatted. In the absence of any formatting requests, `troff`'s basic action is to tidy up the input to produce neatly formatted output. It makes all output lines the same length, as far as possible, and adjusts the spacing so as to make both the left and right margins regular. However, if you leave blank lines in the input they are transferred to the output. If you put leading spaces on a line, they are also transferred to the output. So if you type paragraphs separated by blank lines, with the first line indented five spaces, the output from `troff` is also paragraphs separated by blank lines, with the first line of each paragraph indented five spaces. But the paragraphs produced by `troff` look much neater than those you typed. In chapter 9. we showed an example of input to `troff` without any formatting requests, and the formatted version. That example showed how `troff` tidies up your typing.

There is more to formatting a manuscript than this, however, and `troff` provides very tight control over the final appearance of a document. `troff` lets you select your page size: number of lines on the page, length of the lines, size of margins. You can select your text to be both left and right justified, or some other layout, or you can tell `troff` to leave it exactly as you typed it. You have complete control over indentation, so you can have any style of paragraphing that you require. `troff` can center headings, and emphasize (either by italicizing or underlining) things. With the help of 'macros' you can get footnotes, automatic page numbering and titles, automatic paragraph numbering, and automatic generation of table of contents.

`troff` accepts very low level formatting requests. For example, when you begin a new paragraph you might want to take the following steps:

1. leave one or more blank lines
2. make sure that you don't get an 'orphan' (that is, the first line of the paragraph at the bottom of a page and the rest of it on the next page).
3. indent the first line of the paragraph by 5 spaces

You have to specify each of these steps separately to `troff`, you can't simply say 'start a new paragraph'. However, `troff` does give you the capability to design your own high-level formatting instructions. So you could create for yourself a 'start new paragraph' request, which could be made up of some, or all, of the steps outlined above, plus anything else you wanted to do at each new paragraph. Such a self-made request is called a 'macro'.

Macro definitions can be quite complex. There are available several collections of macros that have already been defined. These are called 'macro packages', and we described one of them — the -mm macro package — in chapter 9. Because fairly important things like page numbering are not automatically done by `troff`, it is usual to use such a macro package which will provide the basics. However, it is still important to know the low-level `troff` requests because you will need to use these in conjunction with the macros.

In this chapter we will show you how to use `troff` to do fairly simple things. We do not go into details of how to design macros for paragraph numbering, footnotes and such, but we show you a fairly simple macro for page numbers. For more details of the formatter, refer to *nroff/troff Formatting Program* in the *System V Document Processing Guide*.

11.2. Format of troff Requests

A `troff` 'request' is embedded in the text of the document to be formatted. Requests control the overall layout of the formatted document, or establish conditions for the formatter itself. Each request to `troff` must appear by itself at the beginning of a line. A request cannot appear on the same line as the text to be formatted (although sometimes part of the text to be formatted can be given as an argument to a request).

A formatting request consists of a basic `troff` instruction, or a call to a `troff` macro, optionally followed by one or more arguments separated by spaces.

A `troff` instruction consists of a period or 'dot' (`.`), followed by one or two characters. There is an alternative form of `troff` instruction that starts with a apostrophe or single quote (`'`), rather than the dot. We explain what this means when we talk about text filling.

Here are some annotated `troff` requests:

Request	***Comment***
`.pl 9.0i`	*Set the length of the page to 9 inches*
`.po 1.0i`	*Set the page offset to 1 inch*
`.bp`	*Start a new page*
`.in 5`	*Indent the left margin by 5 en-spaces*
`.ti -3`	*Temporarily back out the indent of the next line of text by 3 en-spaces*
`.in +5`	*Indent the left margin by 5 en-spaces more than its current value*
`.ce 4`	*Center the next four lines of text*
`'ul`	*Underline (nroff) or italicize (troff) the next line of text*
`.BL`	*Start a bulleted list in the -mm macro package*

The last example is a *macro reference* as described in the `-mm` macro package. The remainder are basic `troff` instructions.

A reference to a `troff` macro looks exactly the same as a regular `troff` instruction. All `troff` instructions consist of lowercase letters. Conventionally, macro packages such as the `-mm` macro package use uppercase letters to distinguish them from the basic `troff` instructions. Note that this is only a convention — some macro packages such as the (now almost defunct) `-me` macro package ignore it and use lowercase letters for the macros.

In all our examples we show a space between the instruction and any numerical value that an argument may take. In practice, it is not necessary to have the space between the request and the first argument. Some of the above examples could have been written as shown below.

```
.pl9.0i
.po1.0i
.ce4
```

These work just as well, but are not so easy to read. We use spaces in our examples for enhanced readability.

The form that the arguments can take depend on the instruction or macro, but in many cases the arguments are numeric. There are three different possible forms of numeric arguments. A number may be given as an unsigned number, this means that it is to be taken as an absolute value. For instance,

```
.in 4
```

means indent the margin four en-spaces in the case of `troff`, or just four plain spaces in the case of `nroff`[1].

An argument may also be a number preceded by a plus sign or a minus sign. This means a change relative to the existing value of whatever it is you're altering. For example

```
.in +0.25i
```

means indent the margin ¼-inch more than what it is now, and similarly

```
.in -0.25i
```

means back off that indent by ¼-inch.

11.3. Specifying Page Layout

The page size that `troff` provides is intended to fit U.S. letter size paper. Such a page is 8½ inches wide and 11 inches long. In general, the macro packages set up default page dimensions for a 6½ inch wide by 9 inch long text block centered in this page size.

Setting the Page Offset

`troff` starts off with the left-hand edge of the printing right up against the left-hand edge of the paper. This is not normally a desirable situation, since you usually want some margin on the left side of the paper. The `.po` request changes the page offset, which is the distance between the left-hand edge of the paper and the left-hand edge of the printing. For instance,

```
.po 1.0i
```

sets the page offset to one inch. This is a reasonable value for the page offset, it gives more or less equal left and right margins with the default line length.

---

1 An en-space is a space about half the width of a letter 'm' in the current size of the text.

The current page offset can be changed by giving a number preceded by a plus sign or a minus sign. For example `.po +0.25i` increases the left margin by ¼ inch, and `.po -0.25i` reduces the left margin by ¼ inch. If you do not supply any argument to the `.po` request the page offset is reset to what it was before you last changed it.

Some macro packages adjust the margins to be different on even and odd pages, so that the resulting document is suitable for double-sided copying.

Once you have set the page offset for a document, you should not change it except under very unusual circumstances. One situation where you might need to adjust the page offset temporarily is if you have a table or diagram which is wider than the normal line length, in that case you may need to ease the left margin a little more leftwards.

Setting the Line Length

The `.ll` request alters the line length. The line length and the page offset together determine the width of the right margin. The length of the lines of text produced by `troff` can be set to a given value:

```
.ll 6.5i
```

sets the length of each line to 6½ inches. Alternatively, the line length can be increased or decreased: `.ll +0.5i` increases the length of each line by ½ inch, and `.ll -1.0i` reduces the line length by one inch.

Omitting the argument to the `.ll` request sets the line length to what it was before you last changed it.

You may wish to change the line length, depending on the layout of the text you are formatting. For example, if you want to shrink both margins, you would use `.ll` and also adjust either the page offset or the indentation depth.

Setting the Page Length

The `.pl` request adjusts the length of the printed page. You can set the page length to 9½ inches, which fits European A4 size paper, by this request:

```
.pl 9.5i
```

The current page length can be changed: `.pl -2.0i` reduces the length of the page by two inches, and `.pl +1.0i` increases the length of the page by one inch.

Omitting the argument to the `.pl` request resets the page length to its standard value of 11 inches (for `troff`), or 66 lines per page (for `nroff`).

You will probably never want to change the page length unless you have to use a different size of paper.

■ *If the size of the page does not match the physical size of the paper you are using, your output will probably be a mess.*

Changing the Page Number

`troff` does not automatically provide page breaks and page numbering. This must be done under control of a macro, either one you have defined yourself (we show you how later), or by using a macro package. However, the current page number is kept in a 'page number register', which is incremented each time a pagefull of formatted text has been created.

The `.pn` request alters the value of the page number held in the page number register:

```
.pn 23
```

sets the value in the register to 23; `.pn +1` adds one to the page number in the register, and `.pn -2` subtracts 2 from the page number register.

If you enter a `.pn` request with no argument `troff` just ignores the request completely, with no effect on the page number register.

When `troff` starts work on a document, the initial value of the page number register is set to 1.

Producing Page Breaks

You can do your own page breaks by inserting the `.bp` request to begin a new page at strategic points in your document:

```
.bp
```

simply starts a new page. `troff` produces enough blank space to fill the current page, and continues the formatted text output on a new page. The page number register is incremented. You will probably want to follow this with some blank lines to form a top margin, unless you have a macro to provide automatic page control. Even when you are using macros to give automatic page breaks, `.bp` can be used to force the start of a new page.

You can specify the page number at which the new page is to start, by giving an argument to the request: `.bp 10` starts a new page and sets the page number register to 10. If the number given to `.bp` is preceded by a plus sign or minus sign, the page number register is incremented or decremented by that amount when the new page is started.

Keeping Blocks of Text Together

Sometimes you have the situation where you want to make sure that some lines will all appear on the same page. A table of figures, for instance, should not start at the bottom of one page and be continued on the next.

The `.ne` request tells `troff` that you need a specified amount of space available so that (for instance) a block of lines will appear all on the same page. So a request like:

```
.ne 1.0i
```

starts a new page if there is less than 1 inch left on the current page.

A `.ne` request with no argument is taken to be `.ne 1`, which has the same action as if the `.ne` request wasn't there.

Most macro packages provide a 'new paragraph' macro which uses the `.ne` request to avoid orphans[2].

11.4. Filling and Adjusting Text Lines

Perhaps the most important reason for using `troff` is to use its filling and adjusting capabilities.

- *Filling* means that `troff` produces output lines that are all as long as they can be without overflowing the line length. Filling continues until something happens to break the filling process, such as a blank line in the text.
- *Adjusting* (also called justification) means that filled lines are then padded with spaces between words so that both the left and the right margins come out straight.

Here is an example of some input text as you might have typed it (on the left), and on the right we show the effect of filling and adjusting the text:

What You Type	***Results After Formatting***

`On the edge of a great forest lived a`
`poor woodcutter with his wife and two`
`children.  The boy's name was Hansel`
`and the girl's name was Gretel.  They`
`had little enough of crust or crumb,`
`and once, when there was great famine`
`in the land, they could not even find`
`their daily bread.`
	On the edge of a great forest lived a poor woodcutter with his wife and two children. The boy's name was Hansel and the girl's name was Gretel. They had little enough of crust or crumb, and once, when there was great famine in the land, they could not even find their daily bread.

Adjusting, in `troff`, usually means justification. The spacing between words in the filled output lines is adjusted to completely fill the line length. This produces straight (flush) margins on both the right and left edges of the printing.

Justification implies filling — it makes no sense to adjust lines without also filling them. Notice that the last line is not justified. Justification stops when a break occurs in the filling process.

In the absence of any other information, `troff`'s standard behavior is to fill lines and adjust for straight left and right margins, so it is quite possible to create a neatly formatted document which only contains lines of text, and no formatting requests.

No Adjusting

If you don't specify otherwise, `troff` justifies your text so that both left and right margins are straight. This can be changed if necessary, and one way is to

---

2 An orphan is the first line of a paragraph at the bottom of the page.

request no adjusting at all, with the `.na` request:

```
.na
```

requests no adjust — adjusting of output lines is turned off.

Output lines will still be filled, providing that filling hasn't also been turned off (see `.nf` below). If filling is still on, `troff` produces flush left, ragged right output.

Specifying Adjusting Styles

You can ask `troff` to adjust the position of your lines in four different ways:

- You can have both margins straight, which we showed in the example above.
- Another way is 'flush left, ragged right', which is what you normally get when you have filling without adjusting. The 'flush left, ragged right' style is usually called 'ragged right'. The left margin is lined up but the right margin is ragged.
- A third way is the reverse of 'flush left, ragged right' — 'flush right, ragged left' — the right margin is lined up but the left margin is ragged.
- The fourth way is to have each line centered to give both left and right ragged margins. This method is an unusual way of formatting text, and you probably won't use it very often. Mostly you use centering only for headings. There is a separate `troff` request for centering, described under *Centering and Emphasizing*.

The `.ad` (adjust) request specifies one of the four different methods just described for adjusting text.

The adjust left

```
.ad l
```

request produces flush left, ragged right output, which is the same as filling with no adjustment. The adjust right

```
.ad r
```

request produces flush right, ragged left output. The adjust center

```
.ad c
```

request centers each output line, giving both left and right ragged margins.

Finally either of the requests:

```
.ad b
```
or
```
.ad n
```

(`b` for both, or `n` for normal) gives complete justification of both left and right margins.

```
.ad
```

on its own simply turns on adjusting of lines in the last mode requested.

It makes no sense to try to adjust lines when they are not being filled, so if filling is off when a `.ad` request is seen, the adjusting is deferred until filling is turned on again.

The examples below illustrate the various kinds of adjusting.

Flush Left Ragged Right Formatting

What You Type	*Results After Formatting*

`.ad l`
`On the edge of a great forest lived a`
`poor woodcutter with his wife and two`
`children.  The boy's name was Hansel`
`and the girl's name was Gretel.  They`
`had little enough of crust or crumb,`
`and once, when there was great famine`
`in the land, they could not even find`
`their daily bread.`
	On the edge of a great forest lived a poor woodcutter
	with his wife and two children. The boy's name was
	Hansel and the girl's name was Gretel. They had little
	enough of crust or crumb, and once, when there was
	great famine in the land, they could not even find their
	daily bread.

Flush Right Ragged Left Formatting

What You Type	*Results After Formatting*

`.ad r`
`On the edge of a great forest lived a`
`poor woodcutter with his wife and two`
`children.  The boy's name was Hansel`
`and the girl's name was Gretel.  They`
`had little enough of crust or crumb,`
`and once, when there was great famine`
`in the land, they could not even find`
`their daily bread.`
	On the edge of a great forest lived a poor woodcutter
	with his wife and two children. The boy's name was
	Hansel and the girl's name was Gretel. They had little
	enough of crust or crumb, and once, when there was
	great famine in the land, they could not even find their
	daily bread.

Centered Formatting

What You Type	*Results After Formatting*

`.ad c`
`On the edge of a great forest lived a`
`poor woodcutter with his wife and two`
`children.  The boy's name was Hansel`
`and the girl's name was Gretel.  They`
`had little enough of crust or crumb,`
`and once, when there was great famine`
`in the land, they could not even find`
`their daily bread.`
	On the edge of a great forest lived a poor woodcutter
	with his wife and two children. The boy's name was
	Hansel and the girl's name was Gretel. They had little
	enough of crust or crumb, and once, when there was
	great famine in the land, they could not even find their
	daily bread.

Figure 11.1 Formatting Styles Using the `.ad` Request

Turning Filling On and Off

The `.nf` (no fill) request turns off filling. Lines in the result are neither filled nor adjusted. The output text appears exactly as it was typed in, this is often called *as-is text*, or *verbatim*.

The `.fi` request turns on filling. If adjusting has not been turned off by a `.na` request, output lines are also adjusted in the prevailing mode set by any previous `.ad` request.

11.5. Hyphenation

When `troff` fills lines, it takes each word in turn from the input text line, and puts it on the output text line, until it finds a word which will not fit on the output line. At this point `troff` tries to hyphenate the word. If it can, the first part of the hyphenated word is put on the output line followed by a '-', and the remainder of the word is put on the next line.

■ *At this point we should emphasize that, although we have been showing the examples both filled and justified, it is during the filling process that* `troff` *hyphenates words, not the process of adjusting.*

If you have in your input text words containing a hyphen (such as jack-in-the-box, or co-worker), `troff` will if necessary split these words over two lines, regardless of whether hyphenation is turned off.

Controlling Hyphenation

Normally, when you invoke `troff`, hyphenation is turned on, but you can change this. The

```
.nh
```

request (no hyphenation) turns off the automatic hyphenation process. The only words that are split over more than one line are those which already contain '-'. Hyphenation can be turned on again with the `.hy` request.

`.hy` can be given an argument to restrict the amount of hyphenation that `troff` does. The argument is numeric

- `.hy 2` stops `troff` from hyphenating the last word on a page.
- `.hy 4` instructs `troff` not to split the last two characters from a word; so, for example, 'repeated' will never be hyphenated 'repeat-ed'.
- `.hy 8` requests the same thing for the first two characters of a word; so, for example, 'repeated' will not be hyphenated 're-peated'.

The values of the arguments are additive: `.hy 12` makes sure that words like 'repeated' will never be hyphenated either as 'repeat-ed' or as 're-peated'. `.hy 14` calls up all three restrictions on hyphenation.

A `.hy 1` request is the same as the simple `.hy` — it turns on hyphenation everywhere. Finally, a `.hy 0` request is the same as the `.nh` request — it turns off automatic hyphenation altogether.

If there are words that you want `troff` to hyphenate in some special way, you can specify them with the `.hw` request (hyphenate words). This request tells `troff` that you have special cases it should know about, for example:

```
.hw pre-empt ant-eater
```

Now, if either of the words 'preempt' or 'anteater' need to by hyphenated, they will appear as specified on the `.hw` request, regardless of what `troff`'s usual hyphenation rules would do. If you use the `.hw` request, be aware that there is a limit of about 128 characters in total, for the list of special words.

Controlling Line Breaks

Earlier we said that when filling is turned on, words of text are taken from input lines and placed on output lines to make them as long as they can be without overflowing the line length, until something happens to break the filling process. When a break occurs, the current output line is printed just as it is, and a new output line is started for the following input text. There are various things that cause a break to occur:

- A `.br` request — a break request can be used to make sure that the following text is started on a new line.
- `troff` requests — many `troff` requests cause a break in the filling process. However, there is an alternate format of these requests which does not cause a break. That is the format where the initial period character (`.`) in the request is replaced by the apostrophe or single quote character (`'`).
- End of file — the filling process stops when the end of the input file is reached.
- Spaces — spaces at the beginning of a line are significant. If there are spaces at the start of a line, `troff` assumes you know what you are doing and that you really want spaces there. Obviously, to achieve this, the current output line must be printed and a new line begun. Avoid using tabs for this purpose, since they do not cause a break.
- Blank line(s) — if your input text contains any completely blank lines, `troff` assumes you mean them. So it prints the current output line, then your blank lines, then starts the following text on a new line.

It is these last two things that enable you to take advantage of the filling and justification features provided by `troff` without having to use any `troff` requests in your text. Figure 9.2 back in chapter 9 showed an example of a memo as it was input to `troff`, and the results of formatting that memo. There were no formatting requests in the document at all.

11.6. Line Spacing

`troff` normally produces its output single spaced, but this can be changed, either by explicit line spacing requests, or by embedded blank lines in the text.

Setting Line Spacing

The `.ls` request adjusts line spacing. If there is an argument of *N* on the request, *N*–1 blank lines appear after each line of text is produced. For example, the request:

```
.ls 2
```

sets double line spacing. There is one blank line following each line of text in the output. Similarly, `.ls 3` sets triple spacing.

A `.ls` request without any argument returns the line spacing to what it was before you last changed it.

The default value when `troff` is invoked is equivalent to `.ls 1`, or single spacing.

Generating Blank Lines

Blank lines can be produced in the output by using the `.sp` request. The appropriate number of blank lines are left in the output text. For example, a `.sp` request like this:

```
.sp 0.25i
```

leaves a quarter of an inch of vertical space. Note that for `troff`, the standard measurement of spacing (in the absence of any dimensions) is the current value of the vertical spacing — described later in this chapter. For `nroff`, the standard measurement of spacing is lines. A `.sp` request with no argument is the same as `.sp 1`, one unit of vertical spacing or one blank line is left in the output.

Blank lines can also be produced by just leaving blank lines in the input text. The advantage to using the `.sp` request, instead of leaving blank lines in the input, is that it is easier to change. For instance, suppose you had left two blank lines before each paragraph, then decided your document would look better with three blank lines. With a text editor it is much easier to change all occurrences of `.sp 2` to `.sp 3`, than it is to find all sequences of two blank lines and add another one.

To illustrate these requests, consider the piece of poetry in the example on the next page.

In double-spacing mode (`.ls 2`) there is one blank line following each line of text. In single spacing, there are no blank lines. To leave a blank line between the second and third stanzas we have to deliberately say `.sp 1`. The second `.ls` request returns the line spacing to its previous value of `.ls 2`.

What You Type	*Results After Formatting*

`.nf`
`.ls 2`
`O what can ail thee, knight-at-arms,`
`Alone and palely loitering?`
`The sedge is wither'd from the Lake,`
`And no birds sing.`
`.ls 1`
`O what can ail thee knight-at-arms,`
`So haggard and so woe-begone?`
`The squirrel's granary is full,`
`And the harvest's done.`
`.sp 1`
`.ls`
`I see a lily on thy brow`
`With anguish moist and fever dew,`
`And on thy cheeks a fading rose`
`Fast withereth too.`
	O what can ail thee, knight-at-arms,
	
	Alone and palely loitering?
	
	The sedge is wither'd from the Lake,
	
	And no birds sing.
	
	O what can ail thee knight-at-arms,
	So haggard and so woe-begone?
	The squirrel's granary is full,
	And the harvest's done.
	
	I see a lily on thy brow
	
	With anguish moist and fever dew,
	
	And on thy cheeks a fading rose
	
	Fast withereth too.

The `.ls` request does not cause a break in the filling process. The previous example doesn't show this, since we requested no filling. You usually only change line spacing for whole paragraphs, so there is no problem for the most part.

11.7. Centering and Emphasizing

The subjects of centering lines of text and emphasizing text are grouped together, because these two ways of dealing with text are frequently used to produce different styles of headings. Apart from that, there is no logical connection between them. In the *Nroff/Troff Formatting Program* in the System V *Document Processing Guide*, centering and emphasizing are described in different sections.

Centering Lines of Text

When we described 'Filling and Adjusting', we showed how the text produced by `troff` could be centered by using the `.ad c` request. Setting text adjustment for centering is a fairly unusual way of getting centered text. When you only want a few lines centered, it is not necessary to change your usual adjusting mode. Instead, you can use the `.ce` request, which centers lines of text.

If you just use a `.ce` request without an argument, one line is centered:

```
.ce
```

centers the following line of text, whereas:

```
.ce 5
```

centers the following five lines of text. Filling is temporarily turned off when lines are centered, so each line in the input appears as a line in the output, centered between the left and right margins. For centering purposes, the left margin includes both the page offset and any indentation that may be in effect.

■ *Note the difference between centered lines using the* `.ce` *request versus centered adjusting using the* `.ad c` *request—if filling is on, the* `.ad c` *request has the lines filled, then centered. The* `.ce` *request implies no filling.*

An argument of zero to the `.ce` request simply stops the process of centering. So, if you don't want to count how many lines you want centered, you can say `.ce 100` (or some large number) before the first, then stop centering by putting a `.ce 0` request after the last line you want centered.

Note that the argument to the `.ce` request only applies to following text lines in the input. Lines containing `troff` requests are not counted.

Here is an example of a three-line centered title:

What You Type	***Results After Formatting***

`.ce 3`
`Courtship Rituals of Old Moldavia`
`A Treatise`
`by Horace Postlethwaite`
	Courtship Rituals of Old Moldavia
	A Treatise
	by Horace Postlethwaite

If you want to space this out a bit, you could change the input text to look like this:

What You Type	***Results After Formatting***

`.ce 3`
`Courtship Rituals of Old Moldavia`
`.sp`
`A Treatise`
`by Horace Postlethwaite`
	Courtship Rituals of Old Moldavia
	
	A Treatise
	by Horace Postlethwaite

The `.sp` does not affect the number you give to the `.ce`; only text lines to be centered are counted.

You can stop the centering process by putting a `.ce 0` request after the `.sp` request, in which case the results look like:

```
        Courtship Rituals of Old Moldavia
A Treatise by Horace Postlethwaite
```

Now, only the first line is centered, and the next two input lines appear on the same output line, because filling is resumed after centering stops.

Emphasizing Text

Sometimes headings are emphasized in some way, rather than centered. The standard way of emphasizing text using `troff` is to set the text in *italic font*.

The `nroff` processor cannot set type in italic and so underlines the text instead.

There are two requests to emphasize text — `.ul` (underline) and `.cu` (continuous underline). Note that the 'underline' requests are a hangover from the days of `nroff` and its predecessors, which underlined stuff instead of italicizing it.

There are two types of emphasizing that `troff` (or `nroff`) can do. The `.ul` request only emphasizes alphanumeric characters. As with the `.ce` request, `.ul` with no argument emphasizes a single line of text, so:

```
.ul
```

simply emphasizes the following line of text. A numeric argument to the `.ul` request specifies the number of text lines you want emphasized, so:

```
.ul 3
```

emphasizes the next 3 lines of text. As with centering, an argument of zero (`.ul 0`) cancels the emphasizing process.

The other form of emphasizing is called up with the `.cu` request, and asks for continuous emphasizing. This is the same as the `.ul` request, except that *all* characters are emphasized. This is not so noticeable with `troff` — it's more noticeable in `nroff` because you get spaces underlined as well as the alphanumeric characters. You'd only notice the continuous italics in `troff` if there were non-alphanumeric characters such as brackets (*[*) in italics and you'd see that they 'leaned' a little.

As with `.ce`, only lines of text to be emphasized are counted in the number given to the emphasize request. `troff` requests interspersed with the text lines are not counted.

The difference between the two types of emphasizing is shown in this diagram of what `nroff` would do to the formatting:

What You Type	***Results After Formatting***

`.cu`
`1.0 General Introduction`
`.sp`
`.ul`
`1.1 Historical Background`
	`1.0 General Introduction` (all characters underlined)
	
	`1.1 Historical Background` (letters and numbers underlined)

In the first call for underlining (the `.cu` request), all characters including spaces are underlined. In the second (the `.ul` request), only letters and numbers are underlined.

On the next page you can see what `troff` does with the same input text.

What You Type	*Results After Formatting*

`.cu`
`1.0 General Introduction`
`.sp`
`.ul`
`1.1 Historical Background`
	1.0 General Introduction
	
	1.1 Historical Background

As you can see, when using `troff` there is not much difference between the two forms. But if you want your document to be portable to `nroff`, use the different forms where you really want them different.

Centering and emphasizing can be combined, and the combination is frequently used to produce headings. Here's what `troff` produces for headings:

What You Type	*Results After Formatting*

`.ce 4`
`.cu 2`
`Courtship Rituals of Old Moldavia`
`.sp`
`A Treatise`
`by`
`.ul`
`Horace Postlethwaite`
	Courtship Rituals of Old Moldavia
	
	A Treatise
	by
	Horace Postlethwaite

Italicizing or underlining is not used just for headings, but is often used in paragraphs of text to add *emphasis* (in `troff`) or emphasis (in `nroff`) to individual words:

What You Type	*Results After Formatting*

`One thing was certain, that the`
`.ul`
`white`
`kitten had had nothing to do with`
`it: it was the`
`.ul`
`black`
`kitten's fault entirely.`
	One thing was certain, that the *white* kitten had had nothing to do with it: it was the *black* kitten's fault entirely.

Notice that we had to arrange our input so that each of the two words we want emphasized appears on a line of its own. This is because the `.ul` request emphasizes all of the following input line.

In some older versions of `troff`, the `.ul` or `.cu` requests cause a break in the filling process. This is one case where you would have to use the alternative form of the request — `'ul` — to indicate that filling is to continue.

Sometimes you may want to emphasize a whole block of text. On the next page there is a fragment of a document with a block of text emphasized.

Notice that although the block of text that is emphasized occupies three lines in the output, it occupies four lines in the input. It is the number of input lines which is the figure given to the `.cu` request. When you think about it, this is a fairly obvious way to do things. Until the text has been formatted, you don't know (and usually don't care) how many lines it will occupy in the output, but you do know how many input lines it occupies.

What You Type	*Results After Formatting*

`Since they only work a six-hour day,`
`you may think there must be a shortage of`
`essential goods.`
`.br`
`.cu 4`
`On the contrary, those six hours are`
`enough, and more than enough,`
`to produce plenty of everything`
`that's needed for a comfortable life.`
	Since they only work a six-hour day, you may think there must be a shortage of essential goods. *On the contrary, those six hours are enough, and more than enough, to produce plenty of everything that's needed for a comfortable life.*

If you don't want to count the number of input lines in the passage to be emphasized, you can specify some number on the `.cu` request which you know is larger than the number of input lines, then stop the emphasizing process with a `.cu 0` request. If we format the following block of text:

What You Type	*Results After Formatting*

`Since they only work a six-hour day,`
`you may think there must be a shortage of`
`essential goods.`
`.br`
`.cu 10`
`On the contrary, those six hours are`
`enough, and more than enough,`
`to produce plenty of everything`
`that's needed for a comfortable life.`
`.cu 0`
	Since they only work a six-hour day, you may think there must be a shortage of essential goods. *On the contrary, those six hours are enough, and more than enough, to produce plenty of everything that's needed for a comfortable life.*

the result is exactly the same as in the example that went before.

11.8. Sizes and Fonts

In chapter 9 we showed you the methods for changing the size of text and also for obtaining different fonts.

When you use raw `troff` or `nroff` there are requests for setting the size of the text and for setting the font.

Setting Point Size

You can set the size of the text (the point size) using the `.ps` request.

You type a

```
.ps 16
```

request to obtain 16-point type. A `.ps` command with no arguments reverts to the previous value of the size.

Note that `nroff` can't change the size of type and so ignores such requests.

Setting Vertical Spacing

You can also change the vertical spacing between the lines (called the 'leading') by using the `.vs` (vertical spacing) request. For regular body type of the kind you're reading right now, you should set the vertical spacing to about two points more than the point size. So, you'd type

```
.vs 18
```

request to obtain 18-point leading. A `.vs` command with no arguments reverts to the previous value of the spacing.

Setting Font

You can also request a specific font using the `.ft` request.
You type a `.ft` request like

`.ft` *fontname*

where *fontname* is the name of a font that `troff` knows about. The selection of fonts is very dependent on your particular installation. `nroff` really only understands that it should use underlining for italic. A `.ft` request typed with no argument reverts to the previous font. The 'standard' fonts that `troff` is normally equipped with are the Times Roman family: `R` (Times Roman), `I` (Times Italic), `B` (Times Bold), and `S` (a Special font containing mathematical and Greek symbols). Use the mnemonic **RIBS** to remember the standard fonts.

Other fonts that may be available are `H` (Helvetica), and possibly `CW` (Constant Width).

Standard `troff` is limited to four fonts at a time, but device-independent `troff` can essentially handle an unlimited number of fonts.

11.9. Paragraphs and Indenting

Paragraphs are the basic elements of manuscripts. Most documents (other than poetry maybe) are built around paragraphs. There are various styles of paragraphing. Some of the styles are illustrated in figure 9.5 back in chapter 9.

The paragraph styles that we address here are:

- First we show simple blocked paragraphs,
- then we show indented paragraphs, where the first line of each paragraph is indented by some amount.
- then there is the layout where a whole paragraph is indented from the surrounding paragraphs; this is called a 'display'. We have shown both the display and the surrounding paragraphs as blocked, but they could also be indented paragraphs. Frequently the display paragraph is non-filled, as are the examples we use throughout this book, for instance.
- a variation of a display is a 'quotation', where the paragraph is indented from the surrounding paragraphs on both left and right margins.
- Finally we show the 'hanging indent' style of layout, where the whole paragraphs are indented, but the first line of each extends to the left a little. This layout is used for producing lists of items.

Blocked paragraphs are easy to achieve using `troff`; you simply insert blank lines where you want to start a new paragraph:

What You Type	*Results After Formatting*

`These people are most excellent`
`mathematicians, and arrived to`
`great perfection in mechanicks,`
`by the countenance and`
`encouragement of the emperor,`
`who is a renowned patron`
`of learning.`
 	
`This prince hath several machines`
`fixed on wheels, for the carriage`
`of trees and other great weights.`
`He often buildeth his largest men`
`of war, whereof some are nine foot`
`long, in the woods where the timber`
`grows, and has them carried on`
`these engines three or four`
`hundred yards to the sea.`
 	
`Five hundred carpenters and engineers`
`were immediately set to work to`
`prepare the greatest engine they had.`
	These people are most excellent mathematicians, and arrived to great perfection in mechanicks, by the countenance and encouragement of the emperor, who is a renowned patron of learning.
	
	This prince hath several machines fixed on wheels, for the carriage of trees and other great weights. He often buildeth his largest men of war, whereof some are nine foot long, in the woods where the timber grows, and has them carried on these engines three or four hundred yards to the sea.
	
	Five hundred carpenters and engineers were immediately set to work to prepare the greatest engine they had.

To achieve the other paragraph styles, we have to use the `troff` indentation requests.

Indenting Lines of Text

There are two ways to indent text. The `.in` (indent) request indents all following lines of text by a specified amount, until another indent request changes it. The `.ti` (temporary indent) request indents only the single line following the request. Both forms indent the text lines relative to the page offset.

The plain `.in` request indents the following lines in the output text by the specified amount:

```
.in 0.25i
```

indents all lines by a quarter inch from the left hand edge of the printing on the page. The argument given to the `.in` request can be relative to the previous indent. For instance `.in +0.25i` indents all lines by a quarter inch to the right of the current indentation depth, and similarly `.in -0.25i` indents all lines by a quarter inch to the left of the current indentation depth.

In common with many similar requests, a `.in` request with no argument makes the indentation depth revert to what it was before it was last changed.

If you type an argument of zero to the `.in` request, `.in 0`, it means that there is no indentation, and so the output text appears on the page at the position of the page offset (specified by a previous `.po` request).*

When `troff` is first invoked, the indentation depth is zero, so all lines are aligned at the page offset. When you use standard `troff`, the page offset starts off at $\frac{26}{27}$ of an inch (honest!). When you use `nroff`, the page offset is zero at the start of a document.

The difference between page offset and indentation is illustrated in figure 11.2 below.

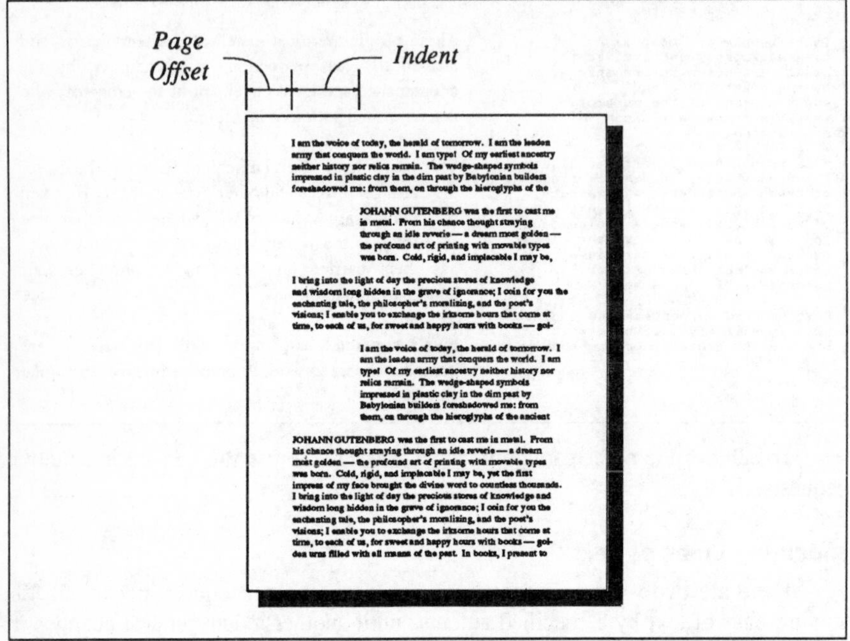

Figure 11.2 Relationships Between Page Offset and Indentation

Temporary Indent of One Line

The `.ti` request differs from the `.in` request in that it requests a temporary indent. Only the first line of output text following the `.ti` request is indented. The remainder of the output text remains at the indentation depth set by the previous `.in` request. The interpretation of arguments to `.ti` is as described for `.in`.

Paragraph Styles

The various styles of paragraphing can be achieved by using combinations of the indent (`.in`) and temporary indent (`.ti`) requests described above.

For instance, indented paragraphs can be produced using temporary indentation as shown on the next page.

What You Type	*Results After Formatting*

`.ti 5`
`These people are most excellent`
`mathematicians, and arrived to`
`great perfection in mechanicks,`
`by the countenance and`
`encouragement of the emperor,`
`who is a renowned patron`
`of learning.`
`.sp 1`
`.ti 5`
`This prince hath several machines`
`fixed on wheels, for the carriage`
`of trees and other great weights.`
`He often buildeth his largest men`
`of war, whereof some are nine foot`
`long, in the woods where the timber`
`grows, and has them carried on`
`these engines three or four`
`hundred yards to the sea.`
`.sp 1`
`.ti 5`
`Five hundred carpenters and`
`engineers were immediately set to`
`work to prepare the greatest`
`engine they had.`
	These people are most excellent mathematicians, and arrived to great perfection in mechanicks, by the countenance and encouragement of the emperor, who is a renowned patron of learning.
	
	This prince hath several machines fixed on wheels, for the carriage of trees and other great weights. He often buildeth his largest men of war, whereof some are nine foot long, in the woods where the timber grows, and has them carried on these engines three or four hundred yards to the sea.
	
	Five hundred carpenters and engineers were immediately set to work to prepare the greatest engine they had.

A display, where an entire paragraph is indented from the surrounding paragraph, is achieved using the `.in` request. Consider the following piece of formatted text:

What You Type	*Results After Formatting*

`In the opening sentence of 'The Vicar`
`of Wakefield', the leading character`
`opines:`
`.sp`
`.in +0.5i`
`''I was ever of the opinion, that the`
`honest man who married and brought up`
`a large family, did more service than`
`he who continued single and only talked`
`of population."`
`.in -0.5i`
`.sp`
`It is not known if Goldsmith was`
`expressing the popular feeling of`
`his time, but if so \(em how things are`
`changed in the 200 or so years since`
`those words were written.`
	In the opening sentence of 'The Vicar of Wakefield', the leading character opines:
	
	"I was ever of the opinion, that the honest man who married and brought up a large family, did more service than he who continued single and only talked of population."
	
	It is not known if Goldsmith was expressing the popular feeling of his time, but if so — how things are changed in the 200 or so years since those words were written.

To indent the middle paragraph we used a `.in +0.5i` request. This takes it ½ inch to the right from the current indentation depth. The current indentation depth was zero, so in this case `.in 0.5i` would have exactly the same effect. However, using the relative form of the request is more flexible. We might decide later that all of the above text should be an insert in an outer surrounding paragraph, to get the effect shown in figure 11.3.

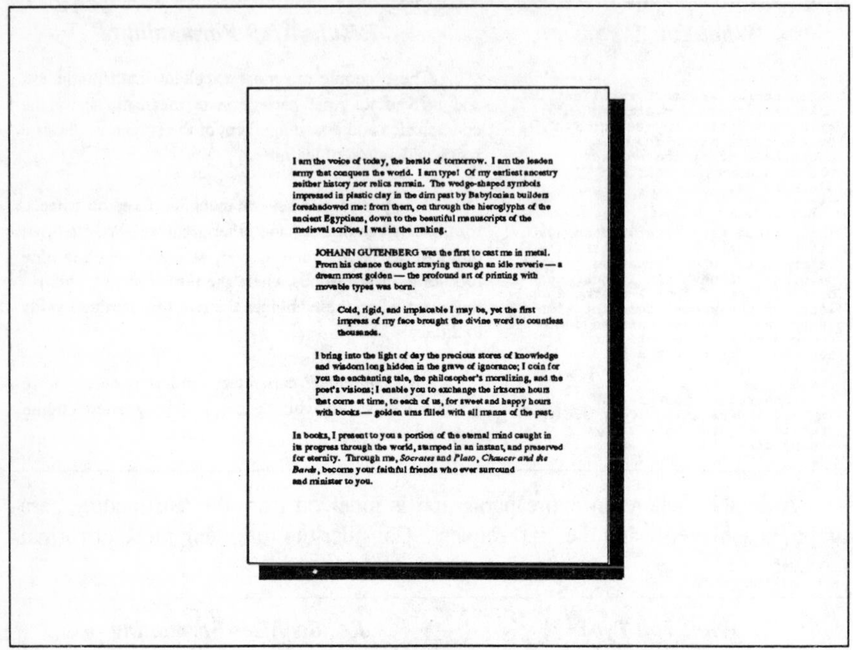

I am the voice of today, the herald of tomorrow. I am the leaden army that conquers the world. I am type! Of my earliest ancestry neither history nor relics remain. The wedge-shaped symbols impressed in plastic clay in the dim past by Babylonian builders foreshadowed me: from them, on through the hieroglyphs of the ancient Egyptians, down to the beautiful manuscripts of the medieval scribes, I was in the making.

> **JOHANN GUTENBERG was the first to cast me in metal. From his chance thought straying through an idle reverie — a dream most golden — the profound art of printing with movable types was born.**
>
> > **Cold, rigid, and implacable I may be, yet the first impress of my face brought the divine word to countless thousands.**
>
> **I bring into the light of day the precious stores of knowledge and wisdom long hidden in the grave of ignorance; I coin for you the enchanting tale, the philosopher's moralizing, and the poet's visions; I enable you to exchange the irksome hours that come at time, to each of us, for sweet and happy hours with books — golden urns filled with all manna of the past.**

In books, I present to you a portion of the eternal mind caught in its progress through the world, stamped in an instant, and preserved for eternity. Through me, *Socrates* and *Plato*, *Chaucer and the Bards*, become your faithful friends who ever surround and minister to you.

Figure 11.3 Nested Indented Paragraphs

Had we used the absolute form of the request in our original text, we would now have to change it to `.in 1.0i`, whereas our relative form of the request requires no change. The same reasoning lies behind the use of `.in -0.5i` to move the left margin back. We could also have used a plain `.in` to make the margin revert to what it was previously.

The display in our previous example is a quotation from a book. Let's reformat the text to produce a 'quotation' style of paragraph, where the text is indented from both left and right margins. We achieve this by a combination of indenting and changing line length. We simply add two `.ll` requests as we show in the example on the next page.

One other small change we made was to insert a

```
.ti -1n
```

to make the initial quote mark of the insert lie outside the indentation depth. This is common practice in manuscript forms, and looks better.

Another thing you might note is that we used the character sequence `\(em` to get the em-dash (—) character in the text. As we discussed back in chapter 9, good typographic form dictates that you use em-dashes as the weak parenthetical construct instead of two hyphens (--) which look terrible.

What You Type

```
In the opening sentence of "The Vicar
of Wakefield", the leading character
opines:
.sp
.ll -0.5i
.in +0.5i
.ti -1n
``I was ever of the opinion, that the
honest man who married and brought up
a large family, did more service than
he who continued single and only talked
of population."
.in -0.5i
.ll
.sp
It is not known if Goldsmith was
expressing the popular feeling of his
time, but if so \(em how things are
changed in the 200 or so years since
those words were written.
```

Results After Formatting

In the opening sentence of 'The Vicar of Wakefield', the leading character opines:

> "I was ever of the opinion, that the honest man who married and brought up a large family, did more service than he who continued single and only talked of population."

It is not known if Goldsmith was expressing the popular feeling of his time, but if so — how things are changed in the 200 or so years since those words were written.

Lists and Descriptions

The *hanging paragraph* style illustrated in figure 9.5 is not often used exactly as shown, except possibly when quoting poetry.

This form of document is produced by using both `.in` and `.ti` requests:

What You Type

```
.in 0.25i
.ti -0.25i
O what can ail thee, knight-at-arms,
Alone and palely loitering?
The sedge is wither'd from the Lake,
And no birds sing.
.sp
.ti -0.25i
O what can ail thee knight-at-arms,
So haggard and so woe-begone?
The squirrel's granary is full,
And the harvest's done.
```

Results After Formatting

O what can ail thee, knight-at-arms, Alone and palely loitering? The sedge is wither'd from the Lake, And no birds sing.

O what can ail thee knight-at-arms, So haggard and so woe-begone? The squirrel's granary is full, And the harvest's done.

However, the general layout has other possibilities.

For instance, hanging indents can be used to produce an indented list of items, each item being marked with a 'bullet'.

A variation of the hanging indent paragraph style is the so-called 'description list', usually used when describing (say) a list of commands.

Now we get to some tricky stuff, which is the reason for using a macro package instead of raw `troff`. You can set an indent where the left margin of the block of text will go. You set a negative temporary indent to get the bullet or description item back into the left margin so that it stands out. The problems arise when you want to get the right amount of space between the bullet and the first line of the block of text. You can't just add spaces — that will only work for `nroff` which uses fixed pitch fonts. Remember that `troff` uses proportional fonts where characters are different widths. What you have to do is some fancy footwork with tabs. The start of your bullet items have to do these steps:

- Set a tab stop to the same distance as the text block indent.
- Make a negative temporary indent to get the bullet or description item back into the left margin.
- Place the item, followed by a tab character, followed by a `\c` escape sequence — this sequence is a *continuation indicator* and is described in more detail later on.

Here's how you make the whole thing work. The *tab* markers in the example are where you'd put real TAB characters in your document:

What You Type	***Results After Formatting***

`Bullet lists are a common form of`
`textual structure found in documents:`
`.sp`
`.in +4n`
`.ta 4n`
`.ti -4n`
`\(sq`***tab***`\c`
`the bullets catch the eye`
`and make the stuff stand out.`
`.sp`
`.ta 4n`
`.ti -4n`
`\(sq`***tab***`\c`
`lists are a short snappy way`
`to present material concisely.`
`.in -4n`
	Bullet lists are a common form of textual structure found in documents:
	
	□ the bullets catch the eye and make the stuff stand out.
	
	□ lists are a short snappy way to present material concisely.

Here's the same process applied to a description list:

What You Type	***Results After Formatting***

`Here are the four styles of`
`adjusting text:`
`.in +8n`
`.sp`
`.ta 8n`
`.ti -8n`
`both`***tab***`\c`
`fills the lines and justifies both margins`
`.sp`
`.ta 8n`
`.ti -8n`
`left`***tab***`\c`
`flush left, ragged right`
`.sp`
`.ta 8n`
`.ti -8n`
`right`***tab***`\c`
`flush right, ragged left`
`.sp`
`.ta 8n`
`.ti -8n`
`centered`***tab***`\c`
`both margins ragged`
`.in -8n`
	Here are the four styles of adjusting text:
	
	both fills the lines and justifies both margins
	
	left flush left, ragged right
	
	right flush right, ragged left
	
	centered both margins ragged

11.10. Simple Macros and Traps

We have said several times that it is possible to define your own troff formatting requests. These special user-defined requests are called macros.

A macro is a shorthand form, wherein one request is a synonym for a number of other requests. You use macros in situations where the same detailed sequence of requests keeps appearing. At the beginning of the chapter we gave an example of the actions you need to take each time you start a new paragraph: leave a blank line, make sure you won't get an orphan, indent the first line. If you define a 'new paragraph' macro, it will save you the tedium of doing these things for each new paragraph. It will also ensure that all you paragraphs look the same: that there is the same vertical space between them, and they are all indented the same amount.

Of course, before you start defining your own macros, you might want to look at some of the macro packages already in existence, since it is highly likely that the macros you want are already defined somewhere.

In addition to seeing if you can use what's already available, you might also try modifying one of the existing macro packages instead of trying to define a completely new one. This book, for example, was formatted using a heavily hacked over version of the -ms macro package.

In this section we show you some very easy macros, just to give you some idea of what they can do for you. We show you how to provide simple page numbering, so that you will be able to get that feature without having to use a macro package.

Defining a Macro

The .de request defines (introduces) a new macro. To define a new macro named XY, you use the request like this:

```
.de XY
```

The end of a macro definition is signalled by two periods at the start of a line, on their own

```
..
```

All input lines, between the .de request and the .. constitute the definition of the macro.

To use the XY macro in troff input text, simply type it like any basic troff request:

```
.XY
```

the body of the macro is substituted in place of the macro call.

Macro names are usually two characters long. By convention people use uppercase letters to distinguish macros from basic troff formatting requests.

A macro must be defined before it can be used. If troff sees a line beginning with a dot '.', but can't identify the following two characters as either a basic request, or as a defined macro, it simply ignores the line.

This example below illustrates a simple `troff` macro to start a new paragraph. We call the new macro NP for New Paragraph:

```
.de NP
.sp 2
.ne 3
.ti +5
..
```

Now, every time you want to start a new paragraph, you just place the .NP macro reference before the paragraph, and `troff` will automatically perform the defined actions.

But just what are these actions? It's not always easy to remember what all the detailed request mean, so let's re-write the NP macro, putting in some comments:

```
.de NP     \"New Paragraph macro
.sp 2      \" leave 2 blank lines
.ne 3      \" make sure 3 lines will fit on page
.ti +5     \" indent first line 5 spaces
..         \"End of New Paragraph macro
```

There are many special character sequences, each one starting with the reverse slash \, which have a special meaning to `troff`. We describe some of the more useful ones later in this chapter.

The special character sequence \" means that the rest of the line is ignored, and does not appear in the `troff` output. The \" sequence can therefore be used to put comments in `troff` input text. Comments are not generally useful in ordinary `troff` requests. Macro definitions, on the other hand, usually contain many ordinary `troff` requests, and often call other macros. It is therefore a good idea to put comments in macro definitions, so that they can be read and understood more easily.

Now let's see an example of using these macros. The example on the following page shows the results of formatting one of our previous examples, using .NP macros instead of regular requests.

Much more complex macros are possible. For example, you might find that you are generating lots of numbered lists. In such a case, you might define a 'start numbered list' macro, a 'finish numbered list' macro, and a 'next item macro'. Then, each time you use the macros, you would be assured that the same sequence of `troff` requests would get generated. The -mm macro package we described in chapter 9 contains macros to define and generate lists for you.

What You Type	*Results After Formatting*

<pre>.de NP   \"New Paragraph macro
.sp 2   \" leave 2 blank lines
<*etcetera*>
..   \"End New Paragraph macro
.NP
These people are most excellent
mathematicians, and arrived to
great perfection in mechanicks,
by the countenance and
encouragement of the emperor,
who is a renowned patron
of learning.
.NP
This prince hath several machines
fixed on wheels, for the carriage
of trees and other great weights.
He often buildeth his largest men
of war, whereof some are nine foot
long, in the woods where the timber
grows, and has them carried on
these engines three or four hundred
yards to the sea.
.NP
Five hundred carpenters and
engineers were immediately set to work
to prepare the greatest engine they had.</pre>
	These people are most excellent mathematicians, and arrived to great perfection in mechanicks, by the countenance and encouragement of the emperor, who is a renowned patron of learning.
	
	This prince hath several machines fixed on wheels, for the carriage of trees and other great weights. He often buildeth his largest men of war, whereof some are nine foot long, in the woods where the timber grows, and has them carried on these engines three or four hundred yards to the sea.
	
	Five hundred carpenters and engineers were immediately set to work to prepare the greatest engine they had.

Setting a Trap

We also said at the beginning of this chapter that `troff` does not automatically handle page control and page numbering. These can only be achieved by using macros and traps.

A trap defines a place on the page at which a macro is to be called up. A trap can be set to invoke a predefined macro at any position on the page. A trap is set by using a `.wh` (when) request, whose general form is:

`.wh` *N xx*

where *N* is the position on the page at which the trap is to take place, and *xx* is the name of the macro to be called at that position.

If the position *N* is a positive number, it means that distance *down* from the top of the page. If the position *N* is negative, it means that distance *up* from the bottom of the page. A position *N* of zero means top of page.

If you set a trap in the form `.wh N`, without a macro name specified, any trap previously set at position *N* is removed.

Let's look an example of some traps:

```
.wh 0  HD      \"invoke macro HD at top of page
.wh -1.0i FT     \"invoke macro FT at foot of page
```

We have called two macros `.HD` and `.FT` at the head and foot of each page. Notice that while `.HD` is called exactly at the top of each page, `.FT` is called a little before the bottom of the page, so that there will be some blank space at the bottom of each page.

The definitions of the macros HD and FT can be as simple as:

```
.de HD          \"Head of page macro
.sp 0.5i           \"   leave some blank space at top of page
..

.de FT          \"Foot of page macro
.bp             \"    start a new page
..
```

Note that these macro definitions must be defined before the trap `.wh` is activated. In practice it is usual to define the macros before setting the trap with the `.wh` request.

When a point ½ inch from the bottom of a page is reached, the macro `.FT` is called. This immediately starts a new page, so there is ½ inch of blank space at the bottom of the page. But as soon as the new page is started, the macro `.HD` is called, which spaces down ½ inch. So now you have a top and bottom margin of ½ inch each on every page of your document.

More complex macros can be defined to put running titles and folios on a page, and to do automatic numbering of pages.

11.11. Titles and Page Numbers

A nice feature of `troff` is the provision for three part titles. A title line can consist of three fields: left, right and center. Any one of the fields may be left blank. The length of title lines can be set independently of the usual line length, so you can have titles that are longer or shorter than the body of the text.

Setting the Text and Length of a Title

The `.tl` (title line) request defines a title string. The `.tl` request is in the form of:

`.tl` *' left part' center part' right part'*

The title consists of the three parts separated by single quotes. The *left part* is left justified on the line, the *right part* is right justified on the line, and the *center part* is centered in the gap between the left and the right parts. Any of the strings may be blank.

The length of subsequent title lines can be defined with the `.lt` (length of title line) request. The form of the request is:

`.lt` *N*

where *N* is the length required. As with the `.ll` request, preceding the *N* with a plus or minus sign increments or decrements by *N*. The title length is initially set to be the same as the text line length.

Let's take a look at some examples of titles:

```
.tl 'The Vicar of Wakefield'A Novel'Oliver Goldsmith'
.tl 'The Vicar of Wakefield''Oliver Goldsmith'
.tl ''The Vicar of Wakefield'Oliver Goldsmith'
```

These three `.tl` requests show variations on the same title. In the first one we have used all three fields; in the second variation we have left out the center field; in the last we have moved the left field into the center field. When this input is `troff`-ed, the result is:

The Vicar of Wakefield	A Novel	Oliver Goldsmith
The Vicar of Wakefield		Oliver Goldsmith
	The Vicar of Wakefield	Oliver Goldsmith

The next three `.tl` requests define a 3-line title. The first line contains only the left field; the second line only the center field; and the last line only contains the right field:

```
.tl 'Young Courtship Rituals of Old Moldavia'''
.tl ''A Treatise''
.tl '''by Horace Postlethwaite'
```

When `troff` has formatted these three title definitions, the results are like this:

Young Courtship Rituals of Old Moldavia		
	A Treatise	
		by Horace Postlethwaite

Notice that the left field actually overlaps the middle field. `troff` makes no check for overlapping fields, it just goes ahead and prints one on top of the other. Had we tried to put our three line title all on one line, like this:

```
.tl 'Young Courtship Rituals of Old Moldavia'A Treatise'by Horace Postlethwaite'
```

the formatted output would look like this:

Young Courtship Rituals of Old MoldaTreatise by Horace Postlethwaite

You must design your title so that the fields don't overlap within the length of the title line.

Getting Page Numbers In Titles

Within a title defined with `.tl`, the percent sign (`%`) means something special. Everywhere `%` appears inside a `.tl` request, it is replaced by the current value of the page number register. To show an example in this book without taking up a lot of space, we have to pretend we have a very short page (only 2 lines, in fact):

```
.pl 2
.bp 1
.tl 'Courtship Rituals of Old Moldavia''Page %'
.bp
.tl 'Courtship Rituals of Old Moldavia''Page %'
```

when `troff` has processed the above file, it produces this result:

Courtship Rituals of Old Moldavia Page 1

Courtship Rituals of Old Moldavia Page 2

This is how you can get automatic page numbering. Now we can expand the header and footer macros that we defined above:

```
.de HD         \"Head of page macro
.sp 3          \"   leave some blank space at top of page
.tl 'Courtship Rituals of Old Moldavia'''
.sp 2          \"   space between title and text
..

.de FT         \"Foot of page macro
.sp 2          \"   put some blank lines
.tl ''%''      \"   then the page number
.bp            \"   start a new page
..
```

Our document will now have a title at the top of each page and the page number centered at the bottom of each page.

Much more complex macros than this are possible. For instance, it is possible to have page numbers on the right-hand side of the page on odd numbered pages, and on the left for even pages; this makes the document suitable for double-sided copies. However, a detailed description of how to write `troff` macros is beyond the scope of this book.

For the most part, you probably won't want to write your own macros, but will more likely use one of the available macro packages.

11.12. Special Character Sequences

When we introduced macros, we also introduced the special character sequence `\"`, which enabled us to put comments within the macro definition. There are many of these special character sequences, which are also known as 'escape sequences'. We describe some of the more useful ones in the following paragraphs.

Unpaddable Space '\ '

It sometimes happens that you have a sequence of words that you would like to appear all on one line, but which occur in the text in such a way that `troff` splits them over 2 lines. For instance, consider the appearance of this block of formatted text:

> Tucked away behind the busy thoroughfare of St.
> Helens Avenue, we find the bijou restaurant 'Le Coq
> d'Or'. The ambience is very intimate, the menu is *tres*
> French, the food is absolutely divine!!

This schmaltzy restaurant review would look better if the street name, 'St. Helens Avenue', and the name of the restaurant, 'Le Coq d'Or', were not split across lines. We can tell `troff` to keep these words together by using the special character sequence known as the 'unpaddable space'. This sequence is simply the reverse slash \ followed by a space.

If we use this sequence in place of ordinary spaces, `troff` makes sure that the words on either side of the unpaddable spaces are not split over more than one line. `troff` also ensures that each unpaddable space in the input text is replaced by one space in the formatted output, so if you have some special spacing requirements, '`\ `' can be used for this too.

If our example uses '`St.\ Helens\ Avenue`', and `Le\ Coq\ d'Or '` ' everywhere in place of the straightforward '`St. Helens Avenue`', and '`Le Coq d'Or`', our formatted output looks as shown on the following page.

> Tucked away behind the busy thoroughfare of St. Helens Avenue, we find the bijou restaurant 'Le Coq d'Or'. The ambience is very intimate, the menu is tres French, the food is absolutely divine!!

Now at least the appearance of the review is better.

Zero Width Character \&

In the section on 'Paragraphs and Indenting' we gave an example of a description list which itemized directory manipulation commands. Suppose we want to show a similar list which itemizes `troff` requests. One item in the list might be:

> .fi filling is turned on. Output lines are filled. If adjusting has not been turned off by '.na', the output lines are adjusted in the prevailing mode.

We cannot achieve this by the straightforward input text shown here:

```
.in +5n
.ta 5n
.ti -5n
.fitab\c
filling is turned on.  Output lines
are filled. If adjusting has not been
turned off by '.na', the output lines are
adjusted in the prevailing mode.
```

because the `.fi` on the fourth input line is seen as a formatting request. The rest of the line is ignored, and the output text looks like this:

> filling is turned on. Output lines are filled. If adjusting has not been turned off by '.na', the output lines are adjusted in the prevailing mode.

To stop `troff` interpreting the `.fi` as a request, we use the special character sequence `\&`. This is a non-printing zero-width character; nothing appears in its place in the formatted output. The text shown on the following page produces the results we want.

```
.in +5n
.ta 5n
.ti -5n
\&.fi tab \c
filling is turned on.  Output lines
are filled. If adjusting has not been
turned off by '.na', the output lines are
adjusted in the prevailing mode.
```

The line containing `.fi` is now seen as a plain text line, since it doesn't start with a dot.

Preventing Extraneous Line Breaks

In the section on 'Centering and Emphasizing' we showed how you could emphasize individual words in a sentence using `.ul` or `.cu` requests. What if you wish to emphasize only part of a word, for instance:

> The troff request '.ce' produces *ce*ntered output lines from the input text.

If you try to emphasize a part of a word with this simple input:

```
The troff request '.ce' produces
.ul
ce
ntered output lines from the input text.
```

what you actually get is this:

> The troff request '.ce' produces *ce* ntered output lines from the input text.

because `troff` assumes there are full words on the input text lines, and it puts spaces between them in the output text. Worse still, `troff` might even split the word across two lines, so that the resultant output looks like this:

> The troff request '.ce' produces *ce*
> ntered output lines from the input text.

You can stop this behavior by using the special character sequence `\c`, which tells `troff` that the following input line is a continuation of the current input line. The input:

```
The troff request `.ce' produces
.ul
ce\c
ntered output lines from the input text.
```

gives us the result we want.

Half Line Motions with `\u` and `\d`

Two special character sequences worth mentioning are `\d` (down), and `\u` (up). These cause the output to go half a line-space down, and half a line-space up. They give you the (very primitive) capability of doing subscripts and superscripts. Supposing you want an equation formatted like this:

$$y = c_1 x^2 + c_2 x + c_3$$

You can get that result from this `troff` input:

```
y = c\d1\ux\u2\d + c\d2\ux + c\d3\u
```

This is in fact a very primitive and quick and dirty way of formatting an equation — there's a *lot* more to getting good mathematical layout than we just showed here. For instance, the names of the variables should be in italic font, and the subscripts and superscripts should be in a smaller point size than the standard text.

The example shown above is more appropriate for use with the `nroff` formatter.

If you're using `troff`, the `eqn` preprocessor discussed in chapters 10 and 9 should be used when you're doing anything more complex than the simplest equations. For example, here's what you'd get if you used `eqn` to format the above equation:

$$y=c_1x^2+c_2x+c_3$$

and here's what you would have typed to get that result:

```
.EQ
y = c sub 1 x sup 2 + c sub 2 x + c sub 3
.EN
```

■ *If you're using* `nroff`*, you should note that these character sequences can only be used if you have a printer which is capable of vertical motions of less than one line. If your input text contains* `\u` *or* `\d`*, you should use the* `-T` *option to* `nroff` *to specify the type of printer.*

Multi-Line Requests

One last special character sequence to be aware of is \ followed by a newline. This escape sequence is for continuing a `troff` request onto another line, in much the same way as you can type a System V command on more than one line. Since most `troff` requests are short, you don't need to use it very often.

11.13. Running the Formatter

So far, we have shown you the kinds of things you can do with the various `troff` requests, macros, and traps. Now we get to the business of actually using the `troff` utility to format the text, and some of the options which can appear on the command line.

When you have created your file containing text to be formatted interspersed with formatting requests, you produce the formatted output by typing the `troff` command line:

```
$ troff -t options file
```

Standard `troff` attempts to drive the C/A/T typesetter directly. To get the output of `troff` directed to the Standard Output, you must use the `-t` option as shown in the example. The output from standard `troff` is an arcane binary code that will display garbage all over your terminal. If you're using device-independent `troff`, the formatted document is produced on the Standard Output (the terminal screen). The output from device-independent `troff` is in a strange and wonderful intermediate code that's not usually worth looking at. You will normally just want to send the results to the printer:

```
$ troff -t options file | lp
$
```

Throughout the rest of the chapter, we refer to *printer software* on the command lines, because the nature of the printer filters for `troff` varies widely from on installation to another.

The process of formatting text can take some time, so you might want to run `troff` in the background:

```
$ troff -t file | printer software &
2042
$
```

as we described in chapter 4 — *Processes and Standard Files.*

In practice, the `troff` command line might not be quite that simple. The general format of the `troff` command is:

```
$ troff -t  [options]  file ...
```

There are some options you can use if you want, and you can format more than one file at a time.

If you give more than one file to `troff`, all the files are concatenated and the resulting text formatted. This means that it is not a good idea to try to format separate documents with a single `troff` command.

Suppose you have three separate memos called *memo1*, *memo2*, and *memo3*. You should not format these with a single `troff` command:

```
$ troff -t  memo[123] | printer software
$
```

because this could cause problems.

For instance, `troff` automatically starts at the top of the first page, so you do not normally put a `.bp` at the front of each memo. So if you format all three memos in a single `troff` run, *memo2* will follow immediately after *memo1* without starting a new page, and the same for *memo3*. A `.bp` at the front of each memo will avoid this problem, but will produce an extra blank sheet at the start of each memo when it is formatted separately.

Other possible sources of trouble are indentations. You may have used `.in 4.0i` to put the author's name over on the right hand side, just below a space for signature. Since it is at the end of the memo, it is quite common to leave that indentation rather than cancelling it with `.in 0`. Imagine the result of trying to format two such memos together!

All these problems can be avoided with due care and attention, but the general rule is:

■ *If files represent separate documents, they should be formatted separately.*

In our example, we should use the three separate commands:

```
$ troff -t  memo1 | printer software
$ troff -t  memo2 | printer software
$ troff -t  memo3 | printer software
$
```

Sometimes it is desirable to hold a large document in more than one file. It may be just because it's easier to organize things that way; or it might be that if the document was all in one file, that file would be too big for the editor to cope with. For instance, you might have a document consisting of six sections called *section1* through *section6*, and three appendices called *appendixA* through *appendixC*. To format and print the entire document, you type this `troff` command:

```
$ troff -t section[1-6] appendix[A-C] | printer software
$
```

Another reason for using more than one file might be that you have defined your own macros, and you use them in many of your documents. Rather than repeating the macro definitions in each file, you can keep them in a separate file, then use them by:

```
$ troff -t macros memo1 | printer software
$
```

The document in the file *memo1* is formatted using the macro definitions held in file *macros*.

If the '-' character appears in the list of files to be formatted, troff reads the Standard Input at that point:

```
$ troff -t letterhead  - letter | printer software
$
```

This troff command takes the contents of the file *letterhead*, followed by the Standard Input, followed by the contents of the file *letter*, and formats the resulting text. Here, the Standard Input is taken from the terminal keyboard, so troff formats whatever you type, until you type a control-D to end input from the keyboard.

This could be used to create a 'personalized' form letter, by repeating the command for each person to receive it, and entering the name at the appropriate point. However, this sort of thing is much better done with the troff .rd (read) request, described later under '*Switching Input to* **troff**'.

Using '-' to get the Standard Input is more commonly used in conjunction with piping. For instance, suppose you have a list of people that you want printed in alphabetical order, double spaced, and with a nice header on each page. You can keep a file of people in any order, then produce the list you want with the command:

```
$ sort + 1 lotsofpeople | troff peoplehead - | printer software
$
```

The file *peoplehead* should contain macros for pagination and titles, and the line spacing requests.

11.14. Options to the `troff` Command

There are many options that can be specified on the `troff` command line. Some of these are connected with some of the advanced features of `troff` which we haven't described, so we don't describe those options either. If you are interested in the advanced features of `troff`, refer to the various papers in the *System V Document Processing Guide*. Here we discuss some of the more useful `troff` options.

Printing Specific Pages Only

Suppose that you have just printed out a 100-page document, and then you notice a spelling mistake on page 10. The correction of the mistake won't affect any of the other pages, so you really don't want to print the whole thing out again. You can print only the page you want by using the `-o` (output) option:

```
$ troff -t -o10 document | printer software
$
```

There must not be any spaces before the `-o` and the number of the page you want. If there several pages that need reprinting, you can specify them all in the same `-o` option, with the page numbers separated by commas:

```
$ troff -t -o10,19,47,95 document | printer software
$
```

If there are some consecutive pages to be printed, you can specify them as a range by separating the first and last page numbers by a '`-`' character:

```
$ troff -t -o3-6 document | printer software
$
```

which is the same as saying:

```
$ troff -t -o3,4,5,6 document | printer software
$
```

The two different methods of specifying page numbers (lists and ranges) can be combined:

```
$ troff -t -o3-6,10,47-50,95 document | printer software
$
```

to print pages 3 through 6, page 10, pages 47 through 50, and page 95 of the document. If the first page of a range of pages is the very first page of the document, it can be omitted, so that:

```
$ troff -t -o-9 document | printer software
$
```

prints the document from the beginning (page 1) up to and including page 9. In a similar way:

```
$ troff -t -o95- document | printer software
$
```

prints from page 95 through to the last page of the document. In all cases, the entire document is formatted, but only the specified pages are sent to the output. No formatting time is saved, only printing time, and paper.

Specifying the Starting Page Number

By using the `-n` (number) option, you can specify what number you want the first page to be. So if you have a large document held in several files, you can format the files separately and still have continuous page numbering throughout the document.

Suppose the first section of your document takes 15 pages. To preserve the page numbering you can format the second section by:

```
$ troff -t -n16 section2 | printer software
$
```

If you are using the automatic table of contents feature provided by some macro packages, it is not a good idea to format the sections of a document separately in this way, because the table of contents gets clobbered.

Using Macro Packages

The `-m` option to `troff` is used to call up standard packages of predefined macros. The command:

```
$ troff -t -mm document | printer software
$
```

has the same result as if you had said:

```
$ troff -t /usr/lib/tmac/tmac.m document | printer software
$
```

It is the -m option which gives the names by which the macro packages are known (mm, ms, me, and so on).

If you have your own set of macros which you would like to call up in this way, you must put them (or persuade your system administrator to put them) in the system directory */usr/lib/tmac* with a filename which begins with *tmac.*. For example, if the macros were in a file *tmac.blurb* in the */usr/lib/tmac* directory, you could call them up by:

```
$ troff -t  -mblurb  document | printer software
$
```

11.15. Switching Input to troff

We now describe two troff requests that we omitted earlier, because their usefulness is more apparent when you understand the troff command line. Normally troff takes its input from the files given when it is called up. However there are ways in which the formatter can be made to take part of its input from elsewhere, using troff requests embedded in the document text.

One of these is the .so request, which tells troff to switch over and take its source from the named file. For example, suppose you have a set of macros that you have defined, and you have them in a file called macros. We can call them up from the troff command line:

```
$ troff -t macros document
$
```

as we showed earlier, but it's a bit of a nuisance having to do this all the time. Also, if only some of our documents use the macros, and others don't, it can be difficult to remember which is which. An alternative is to make the first line of the *document* file look like this:

```
.so macros
```

Now we can format the document by:

```
$ troff -t document
$
```

The first thing troff sees in the file *document* is the request .so macros which tells it to read input from the file called *macros*. When it finishes taking input from *macros*, troff continues to read the original file *document*.

Another way of using the .so request lets you format a complete document, held in several files, by only giving one filename to the troff command. Let us create a file called *document* containing:

```
.so macros
.so section1
.so section2
.so section3
   <etcetera...>
.so appendixC
```

We can now format it with the `troff` command line:

```
$ troff -t document | printer software
$
```

This is a lot easier than typing all the filenames each time you format the document, and a lot less prone to error.

This technique is especially useful if your filenames reflect the contents of the various sections, rather than the order in which they appear. For instance, look at this file which describes a whole book (something like the one you are reading):

```
$ cat book
.so bookmacros
.so preface
.so intro
.so login     \"Getting Started on the UNIX System
.so filesys   \"Directories and the File System
.so stdio     \"Commands, Processes, and Standard Files
         <etceter...>
.so sysadmin    \"System Administration
$
```

It is obviously much easier to format the whole thing with a `troff` command line like this:

```
$ troff -t book | printer software
$
```

than it would be if you had to supply all the filenames in the right order. Notice that we used the comment feature of `troff` to tie chapter titles to filenames.

Another `troff` request that switches input from the file you specify is `.rd` (read). The `.rd` request reads an insertion from the standard input. When `troff` encounters the `.rd` request, it prompts for input by sounding the terminal bell. A visible prompt can be given by adding an argument to `.rd`, as we show in the example below.

Everything typed up to a blank line (two newline characters in a row) is inserted into the text being formatted at that point. This can be used to 'personalize' form letters. If you have an input file with this text:

```
.nf
.in 20n
14th February
.in 0
Dear \c
.rd who
     Will you be my Valentine?
     If you will, give me a sign
     (I like roses, I like wine).
```

then when you format it, you will be prompted for input:

```
$ troff -t valentine | printer software
who:Peter

$
```

Notice that in the example above, we had to end the line with the word 'Dear' with a `\c` character. That's because we are formatting this short letter in no-fill mode, but we want the line typed from the terminal to be part of the salutation.

After typing the name Peter you have to press the **RETURN** key twice, since `troff` needs a blank line to end input. The results of formatting that file is:

```
                    14th February
Dear Peter
  Will you be my Valentine?
  If you will, give me a sign
  (I like roses, I like wine).
```

To get another copy of this for Bill, you just run the `troff` command again:

```
$ troff -t valentine | printer software
who:Bill

$
```

and again for Joe, and for Manuel, and Louis, and Alphonse, and...

`troff` takes input from the terminal up to a blank line, so you are not limited to a single word, or even a single line of input. You can use this method to insert addresses or anything else into form letters.

11.16. Dimensioned Arguments in troff Requests

What if you just type dimensionless numbers to `troff`, like this?

```
.ll 55
.po 8
.in +5
.sp 3
```

`troff` and `nroff` assume that these numbers have some implicit dimensions. In the case of `nroff`, dimensions are mostly in terms of columns and lines. When you get to using `troff`, however, the story gets more complex. The dimensions (units) that `troff` understands are:

Unit	*Meaning*
i	inch
c	centimeter
m	m-space — a space the width of a letter 'm' in `troff`; the width of a character in `nroff`.
n	n-space — a space the width of a letter 'n' in `troff`; the width of a character in `nroff`.
v	vertical line space (v-space) — the current line-spacing in `troff`; one line in `nroff`.
p	points (approximately $\frac{1}{72}$ inch)
P	Picas ($\frac{1}{6}$ inch)

If you don't put any dimension on your request, the formatter assumes a default dimension of m on horizontal, and v on vertical requests.

The actual distances taken by m-spaces, n-spaces and v-spaces depend on the device that your document will be finally produced on. The distances produced by `troff` are different from those produced by `nroff`. In particular, in `nroff` an m-space is the same as an n-space, while in `troff` an m-space is twice as wide as an n-space.

If you are transporting documents between `troff` and `nroff`, it will pay you to specify your some of your spacing in centimeters or inches. These quantities are the same regardless of the type of output device.

Notice we just said 'some of your spacing'. There are many cases where you need to use ems and ens when using `troff`. This is because `troff` works with proportional fonts that can have different sizes. The ems and ens measures are proportional to the size of the text being used, so it's wise to use them in those cases where you want the spacing to be a function of the size of the type you use.

11.17. Summary

In this chapter we have shown you the basic facilities of the `troff` text formatter, and the ideas of page layout, paragraphing styles, page headers and footers, titles, and page numbers. Read the documentation on `troff` and `nroff`. You should try typing some documents, and formatting them using `troff`'s facilities. Experiment with different paragraph styles, try defining some simple macros.

The adventurous may want to get deeper into macro definitions. Investigate some of the more advanced features such as tab-leaders, number registers, strings, diversions. These facilities mean you can define macros for automatically numbering headings or list items, for producing footnotes, and for generating tables of contents automatically.

For a thorough exposition of `troff` for the serious book designer, read `troff` *Typesetting for UNIX Systems* by Sandra Emerson and Karen Paulsell, published by Prentice-Hall.

12 Advanced Text Manipulation

In this chapter we talk about sed, the non-interactive stream editor, and awk, which is described as a pattern scanning and processing language.

These are similar in flavor to the utilities we introduced earlier in Chapter 6, but there is a wide range of complexity in their use. When used in a simple way they provide alternatives to other commands such as grep, but when their full power is exploited they are capable of complex text manipulations that cannot be achieved by any other single System V command. awk, in particular, can be considered a programming language in its own right.

12.1. The Stream Editor sed

The stream editor, sed, is a non-interactive text editor. Whereas ed copies your original file into a buffer and lets you explore the text in whatever order you want, sed works on your file from beginning to end and allows you no choice of edit commands once you have invoked it.

If you think of ed as performing some changes on a set of data, you should think of sed as passing some data through a set of transformations. This concept is similar to the idea of pipelines that was described in chapter 4 — *Processes and Standard Files*, in that a stream of data is passed through some processes which modify it in some way. In this case, the 'processes' are editor commands.

Because sed does not read the file to be edited into a buffer, it can be used to edit files that are too big for ed.

Because the default mode of sed is to apply edit commands globally on the file, and also because its output is to the Standard Output, sed is ideal for changes which are of a transient nature, rather than permanent modifications to a file. sed can be used to simulate the grep and tr commands, as we will show in the examples which follow.

On the face of things, sed is a relatively simple command, having only three options. However, because sed has regular expression capabilities, and also most of the editing operations provided by ed, using it can be a fairly complicated affair. We make no attempt to explain all the intricacies of the stream editor. Rather, we show you how to perform some useful operations, which will give you sufficient insight to be able to work out more complex operations for yourself. Mostly, we repeat the by now familiar examples introduced in chapter 6 — *Text Manipulation*.

sed has the capability to take its edit operations from either the calling command line, or from a file (called the 'edit script'). For simple use you would use the former method, but when you have many edit operations to perform it is easier to put them in a file and tell sed to work from that script.

Putting Edit Operations on the Command Line

We showed some simple examples of sed, with the edit operations on the command line, in our earlier chapter on *Text Manipulation*, Chapter 6.

We showed how you can change the string 'Smith' to 'White' using this command:

```
$ mv people people.old
$ sed s/Smith/White/ people.old >people
$
```

and we further showed that, in order to restrict this so that only Sally Smith's name was affected, this command should be used:

```
$ sed "s/Sally Smith/Sally White/" people.old >people
$
```

The edit command that you give sed must form a single argument so, because the strings in the argument contain spaces, the quotes surrounding the whole argument are necessary. If you don't put quotes around commands containing spaces, you will get an error message:

```
$ sed s/Sally Smith/Sally White/ people.old
command garbled: s/Sally
$
```

By now you should have realized that the edit command given to sed in the above examples looks like the substitute command in the ed and ex interactive text editors. The edit commands which can given to sed are similar to the edit commands available in ed, but the format of them is slightly different in some cases.

The general format of the commands is the same as ed commands:

[*line* [, *line*]] *operation* [*parameter*]

or to show it pictorially, in the diagram on the following page.

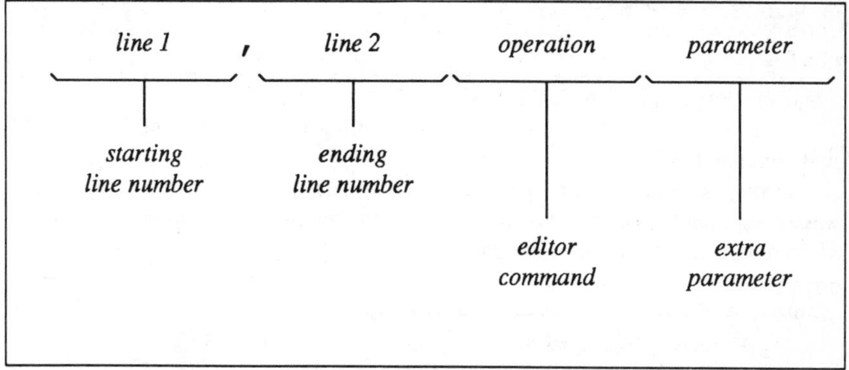

That is, a `sed` command consists of an optional line-address (or two line addresses separated by a comma), then a single letter edit operation, optionally followed by another parameter.

However there are some important differences from `ed`:

- The only operation which can take the optional final parameter is the `s` (substitute) operation.
- If no line numbers are specified, the operation is performed on *all* lines. This is quite different from `ed`, where the default line is usually **dot**.
- Lines can be addressed by number, or by text pattern using fixed character strings, or by regular expressions. Because the default mode of operation is global, there is no concept of 'current line', nor of relative line addresses. Line numbers are absolute in the file.
- Operations that require text input (`a`, `i` and `c`) have a different format from the same operations in `ed`.
- Many `ed` operations have no counterpart in `sed`. In particular, the `m` (move) and `t` (transpose, copy) operations do not exist.
- Contrariwise, there are some operations that are available in `sed` that do not exist in `ed`. One of these is `y` (transform — not too mnemonic).

Our previous examples did not use any line addressing, the commands were applied globally throughout the file. Here is an example of using a text pattern as a line address:

```
$ sed /Sally/s/Smith/White/ people.old >people
$
```

In this case the substitution of the string 'White' for the string 'Smith' is only performed on the line containing the string 'Sally'.

So far we have only shown the substitute operation — this is perhaps the most popular use of `sed`, but you can use any command. For example:

```
$ sed /Henry/d people.old > people
$
```

deletes the line containing Henry from *people*.

You use the `-e` (edit) option to place editing commands right there on the `sed` command line.

In our examples above, however, we didn't use any option at all. If you are only putting one edit command on the `sed` command line, you can omit the `-e`. If we want to be formal about it, we should say:

```
$ sed -e /Henry/d people.old > people
$
```

If you put more than one edit command on the `sed` line, each one must be preceded by `-e`, thus:

```
$ sed -e /Henry/d -e /Sally/s/Smith/White/ people.old
Maryann Clark   101
Sally White     113
Jane Bailey     121
Jack Austen     120
Steve Daniels   111
Sylvia Dawson   110
Hank Parker     114
Charlie Smith   122
Bill Williams   100
$
```

If your edit command contains spaces you must surround it with quotes for `sed` to be able to interpret it poperly, as we showed earlier. You should also use quotes if your edit command contains characters which the Shell treats specially. This will happen when you are using regular expressions. The command:

```
$ sed -e "/^[ ^I]*$/d" somefile > noblanks
$
```

can be used to get rid of blank lines, or apparently blank lines, from a file. As usual, `^I` stands for **CTRL-I**, or **TAB**.

Taking Edit Script From a File

If `sed` is invoked with the `-f` (file) option, the edit commands are taken from a named file:

```
$ sed -f edcomds oldfile > newfile
$
```

The name of the file containing the edit commands must be the very next argument after the `-f` option. The above example shows a command which applies the edit commands contained in *edcomds* to the file *oldfile*. The Standard Output of `sed` is redirected to *newfile*.

Let's take a concrete example, once more using our original *people* file. Among the many changes we have done to this file are:

- delete the line containing Henry Morgan
- add a line containing James Walker at the end of the file
- change Sally Smith's name to Sally White

To make these changes using `sed`, we can first create a file containing the edit commands:

```
$ cat > changes
/Sally/s/Smith/White/
/Henry/d
$a\
James Walker    112
^D
$
```

We use the substitute edit command to change Smith to White on the line containing Sally, the `d` operation to delete the line containing Henry, and `a` to add the line

```
James Walker    112
```

at the end of the file. The dollar sign `$` stands for 'last line' just as it did in `ed`.

The form of the append operation differs from that of `ed`. In `ed`, text input is terminated by a period character `.` on a line of its own, after the last line of text to be input. In `sed`, you place a reverse slash character \ on the end of every line of text *except* the last one. Note that there is a \ character even on the end of the `a` command line.

We can now run `sed` to do the changes, as shown below.

```
$ sed -f changes  people
Maryann Clark   101
Sally White     113
Jane Bailey     121
        <etcetera . . .>
Bill Williams   100
James Walker    112
$
```

sed sends its results to the Standard Output. To capture the changes permanently we have to use redirection:

```
$ mv people people.old
$ sed -f changes people.old > people
$
```

In our *changes* file we gave the edit commands in the order that they would be applied to the file. sed actually goes through a pre-processing stage, where it sorts the commands into an order which it thinks is logical.

For example, deletions take precedence over substitutions. After all, there is no point in doing substitutions on a line which is going to be deleted.

So, we could specify the commands in a different order:

```
$ cat > changes
$a\
James Walker    112
/Henry/d
/Sally/s/Smith/White/
^D
$ sed -f changes people
Maryann Clark   101
Sally White     113
       <etcetera . . .>
Bill Williams   100
James Walker    112
$
```

Either way gives the same results.

To show the global nature of sed, here is an example of how to make a file double-spaced by adding a blank line after each line in the file. Here is a sed script that we'll use for this operation:

```
$ cat > putblank
a\

^D
$
```

and the example below shows what happens when we apply this script using sed on our *people* file.

```
$ sed -f putblank people
Maryann Clark   101

Sally Smith     113

Jane Bailey     121

       <etcetera . . .>
Charlie Smith   122

Bill Williams   100

$
```

Because we didn't specify any line address for the a (add text) operation, the text (our blank line) is added after every line.

We could put a box around our file like this:

```
$ cat > dobox
s/^/| /
s/ [1-9]/|&/
s/$/ |/
1i\
\ ______________________
a\
|________________|_____|
^D
$ sed -f dobox people
 ______________________
| Maryann Clark  | 101 |
|________________|_____|
| Sally Smith    | 113 |
|________________|_____|
      <etcetera . . .>
|________________|_____|
| Hank Parker    | 114 |
|________________|_____|
| Charlie Smith  | 122 |
|________________|_____|
| Bill Williams  | 100 |
|________________|_____|
$
```

The three substitute commands draw the vertical lines. The insert command draws the top line of the box, and the append command draws all the other lines. To get a space in the first column of the line forming the top of the box, we had to escape that space with the reverse slash character, \. sed strips leading spaces and tabs from the beginning of edit commands, so to insert text with leading spaces and tabs we have to escape them in this way.

You can use both `-e` and `-f` options together. To make the required changes to our *people* file, and draw a box round the result:

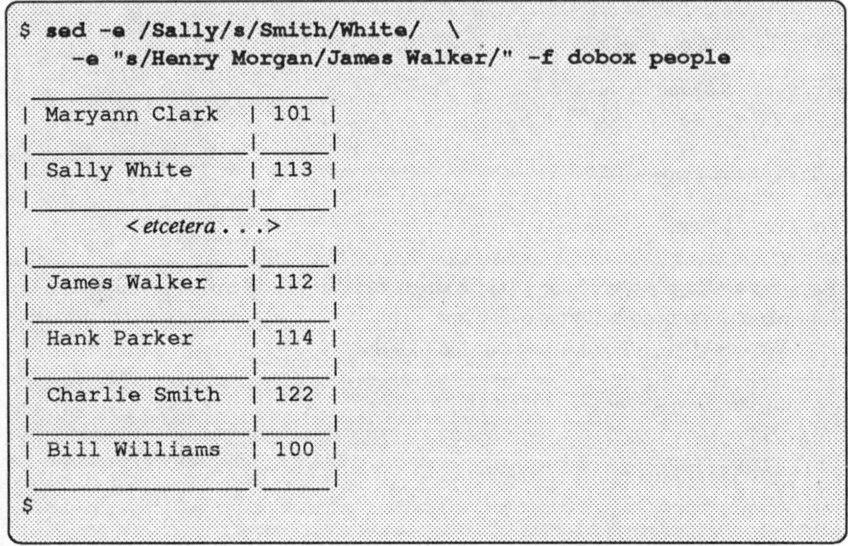

```
$ sed -e /Sally/s/Smith/White/  \
    -e "s/Henry Morgan/James Walker/" -f dobox people
 ________________________
| Maryann Clark  | 101  |
|________________|______|
| Sally White    | 113  |
|________________|______|
        <etcetera . . .>
|________________|______|
| James Walker   | 112  |
|________________|______|
| Hank Parker    | 114  |
|________________|______|
| Charlie Smith  | 122  |
|________________|______|
| Bill Williams  | 100  |
|________________|______|
$
```

When you are using both edit operations on the command line and edit script taken from a file, you *must* use the `-e` option for the command line operations, even if there is only one.

Suppressing Normal Output

As you can see in the above examples, `sed` normally copies all input lines to the output, transformed by the edit operations performed on them. The `-n` option suppresses this normal output, and only lines specially requested with the `p` (print) edit operation appear on the output. For example, the command:

```
$ sed -n /Smith/p people
Sally Smith     113
Charlie Smith   122
$
```

gives output similar to `grep`. Only those lines containing the string `Smith` appear. Because we only have one edit command on the line, we didn't bother to use the `-e` option. If we had used the edit command `/Smith/p` without giving the `-n` option, we would have got the result:

```
$ sed /Smith/p people
Maryann Clark   101
Sally Smith     113
Sally Smith     113
Jane Bailey     121
Jack Austen     120
Steve Daniels   111
Sylvia Dawson   110
James Walker    112
Hank Parker     114
Charlie Smith   122
Charlie Smith   122
Bill Williams   100
$
```

The Smiths appear twice, because we see the normal output as well as the specially requested output.

The -n option is useful for selectively displaying parts of a file. For example, to display only the first 4 lines of a file:

```
$ sed -n 1,4p people
Maryann Clark   101
Sally Smith     113
Jane Bailey     121
Jack Austen     120
$
```

You can also use it for context displays:

```
$ sed -n 1,/Smith/p people
Maryann Clark   101
Sally Smith     113
$ sed -n /Sally/,/Steve/p people
Sally Smith     113
Jane Bailey     121
Jack Austen     120
Steve Daniels   111
$
```

Displaying only the first part of a file can also be achieved by using the q (quit) operation, described in the examples below.

sed usually performs its operations on all lines selected by the addresses. This can be inverted by preceding the operation with an exclamation mark, !. In this case, the operation is performed on all lines that are not matched by the addresses. For instance, the command:

```
$ sed -n /Smith/p
Sally Smith     113
Charlie Smith   122
$
```

produces output similar to that produced by `grep`. We can invert the selection, to give output similar to `grep -v`, using this `sed` command:

```
$ sed -n /Smith/!p
Maryann Clark   101
Jane Bailey     121
Jack Austen     120
Steve Daniels   111
Sylvia Dawson   110
Henry Morgan    112
Hank Parker     114
Bill Williams   100
$
```

Multiple Filenames

`sed` can be given more than one file to edit at a time. The edit commands are applied to all files. Line numbers increment through all files, and `$` means the last line of the last file. Suppose we had people in three separate files, as we did in some text manipulation examples. Here's the *adminpeople* file:

```
$ cat adminpeople
Maryann Clark   101
Bill Williams   100
$
```

And here's the *hardpeople* file:

```
$ cat hardpeople
Jane Bailey     121
Jack Austen     120
Charlie Smith   122
$
```

And finally, here's the *softpeople* file:

```
$ cat softpeople
Sally Smith     113
Steve Daniels   111
Sylvia Dawson   110
Henry Morgan    112
Hank Parker     114
$
```

Now let's use `sed` to print lines 4 through 7:

```
$ sed -n 4,7p adminpeople hardpeople softpeople
Jack Austen     120
Charlie Smith   122
Sally Smith     113
Steve Daniels   111
$
```

you can see that as far as `sed` is concerned, line 4 is the second line of the second file, because the first file contained only two lines.

If no file is specified to `sed`, the Standard Input is used. `sed` is a popular filter used in pipelines. For example, to apply a command to every file in a directory:

```
$ ls | sed "s/^/command /" | sh
$
```

The output of `sed` is a series of lines of the form

command file

These command lines are then executed by piping them to the Shell command `sh`. Using `sed` in this manner is a useful technique when for executing a command on each separate file (or subdirectory) in a directory.

Examples of `sed`

In this section we give examples of ways in which some of the edit operations can be used, where they haven't already been covered in the previous paragraphs.

We have already seen examples of the `s` (substitute) operation. The general format is the same as the `ed` substitute command:

`s/`*string1*`/`*string2*`/`

The first occurrence of *string1* is replaced by *string2* on each of the addressed lines (remember that in `sed` the default is every line). *string1* need not be a fixed character string, it can be a regular expression. In all our previous examples, we have shown the strings separated by the slash character /, but in fact we can use any character that doesn't form part of either the search string or the replacement string. So we can change Sally's name from Smith to White by:

```
$ sed /Sally/s-Smith-White- people > newpeople
$
```

You can use any character to surround the arguments to the substitute command (here we used -). But the string which actually addresses the line you want must be surrounded by / characters — no other character will do.

As in `ed`, to substitute *all* occurrences of the string on the same line, we need a `g` (global) flag on the end of the substitute command. The command:

```
$ sed "s,[0-9],,g" people
Maryann Clark
Sally Smith
     <etcetera . . .>
Bill Williams
$
```

deletes the phone numbers from the file. But there are still spaces at the end of the line. To get rid of the spaces as well, we need a more precise regular expression:

```
$ sed "s, *[0-9]*$,," people
Maryann Clark
     <etcetera . . .>
Charlie Smith
Bill Williams
$
```

A `sed` operation which has no counterpart in `ed` is `y` (transform). This works in a way similar to the `tr` command. Two strings are given, each character in the first string is replaced by the equivalent character in the second string. So we can reverse the alphabet for lowercase characters by:

```
$ sed y/abcdefghijklmnopqrstuvwxyz/zyxwvutsrqponmlkjihgfedcba/ people
  Mzibzmm Cozip   101
  Szoob Snrgs     113
       <etcetera . . .>
  Hzmp Pzipvi     114
  Csziorv Snrgs   122
  Broo Wroorznh   100
$
```

The two strings must be of the same length, there is no padding out as there is in the `tr` command. Neither can you use ranges, so if you try to shorten the first string, you get an error message:

```
$ sed  y/[a-z]/zyxwvutsrqponmlkjihgfedcba/  people
command garbled: y/[a-z]/zyxwvutsrqponmlkjihgfedcba/
$
```

The message arises because the first string `[a-z]` is taken to be 5 characters long, whereas the second string `zyxw....dcba` is 26 characters long. Both strings must be the same length.

You can use a character other than / to separate the strings, so long as the character you use is not contained in the strings:

```
$ sed y,0123456789,9876543210, people
Maryann Clark   898
Sally Smith     886
     <etcetera . . .>
Charlie Smith   877
Bill Williams   899
$
```

We can add blank lines to a file by using a combination of `sed` and `tr`.

First we add some character, not normally found in the file, to the end of every line. Here we have used the sharp, or hash, or octothorpe, character #.

Then we use `tr` to replace # with the newline character, which is the value 012 in octal notation. We have to use `tr` to do this. We can't use the `y` edit operation because none of the `sed` operations will accept characters by their octal values.

```
$ sed "s:$:#:" people | tr "#" "\012"
Maryann Clark   101

Sally Smith     113

     <etcetera . . .>
Bill Williams   100

$
```

If the file you want to be double spaced could contain any characters, you can use a non-printing character, say **CTRL-A**:

```
$ sed "s:$:^A:" file | tr "\001" "\012" > newfile
$
```

The `^A` indicates where you type **CTRL-A** in `sed`; 001 is the octal value of **CTRL-A** — we use this in `tr`.

Another way to get double spacing is to use the `r` (read) command, to read a file containing only a blank line into the text you want spaced out:

```
$ cat > blankline

^D
$ sed "r blankline" people
Maryann Clark   101

Sally Smith     113

      <etcetera . . .>
Bill Williams   100

$
```

If there is no file of the specified name you give on the `r` command, you don't get an error message. `sed` just carries on, and nothing gets read into your file.

The `w` (write) operation can be used to selectively extract lines from the original file and write them into another file. The example below shows all lines containing the word 'Smith' written to a file called *smiths*:

```
$ sed "/Smith/w smiths" people
Maryann Clark   100
Sally Smith     113
      <etcetera . . .>
Charlie Smith   122
Bill Williams   100
$ cat smiths
Sally Smith     113
Charlie Smith   122
$
```

The `w` operation can be appended to an `s` operation. Then the substitutions are done before the lines are written to the file, as in the next example.

```
$ sed "s/Smith/White/w smiths" people
Maryann Clark   100
Sally White     113
     <etcetera . . .>
Charlie White   122
Bill Williams   100
$ cat  smiths
Sally White     113
Charlie White   122
$
```

The next example shows how we can split up our *people* file into the three separate files we showed in an earlier example. To do this, we use the knowledge that all administrative people have phone numbers 10-something, software people have 11-something and hardware people have 12-something.

```
$ sed -n -e "/10.$/w adminpeople" \
         -e "/12.$/w hardpeople" \
         -e "/11.$/w softpeople" people
$
```

We still have our original *people* file, besides the new ones we have created.

As we said earlier, the `q` (quit) operator can be used to display the head of a file. The command shown in the next example stops producing output (quits) after line number 4.

```
$ sed 4q people
Maryann Clark   100
Sally Smith     113
Jane Bailey     121
Jack Austen     120
$
```

When given a search pattern, `sed` quits after the first occurrence of a line containing that pattern. For instance:

```
$ sed /Steve/q people
Maryann Clark   100
Sally Smith     113
Jane Bailey     121
Jack Austen     120
Steve Daniels   111
$
```

stops after the line containing Steve.

The Pattern and Hold Spaces in sed

If you look at the writeup for sed in the *System V User's Manual*, the operations sound more complicated that they are. This is because they are described in terms of something called a 'pattern space', with occasional references to a 'hold space'. Probably the easiest way of describing these 'spaces' is by comparison with the interactive text editors ed and ex.

You will recall that these editors do not work on the file *in situ*, they copy the file into an edit buffer and do the work there. A very loose equivalent of this edit buffer in sed is the 'pattern space'. If you consider that sed has an 'edit buffer' that's one line long, that is the pattern space. All the examples we have shown so far work entirely in the pattern space, before the results are displayed on the Standard Output.

Also remember that ex has other buffers, which hold text that has been deleted or yanked from the main edit buffer. sed's 'hold space' is analogous to these buffers. You can use the hold space to keep a copy of something that was in the pattern space.

From the above analogy you can deduce that we can use the hold space to achieve cut and paste operations using sed, in a similar way to using the yank and put operations in the interactive editors.

The hold space is initially empty. A easy way to make a file double-spaced is to use the G operation to append the hold space after every line in the pattern space:

```
$ sed G people
Maryann Clark    101

Sally Smith      113

      <etcetera . . .>

Bill Williams    100

$
```

Since there was only one sed operation, we didn't bother to use the -e option.

If you use the g operation, which replaces the pattern space with the hold space, instead of G you get a very different result — the output is a series of blank lines, as many as there are lines in the *people* file.

The above examples show how you can access the hold space, but how do you get anything in there in the first place? There are two operations, h and H that put the pattern space into the hold space. When you use h the new text replaces whatever was previously in the hold space, H appends the pattern space to the stuff currently in the hold space. In neither case is the text deleted from the pattern space — it's still there too. There is also an operation x, which exchanges the contents of the pattern and hold spaces.

We will illustrate some simple ways of using the hold space by rearranging our favorite file, the *people* file. Lines can be copied (transposed) at another place in the file like this:

```
$ sed -e 1h -e 4H -e '$G' people
Maryann Clark   101
Sally Smith     113
Jane Bailey     121
Jack Austen     120
Steve Daniels   111
Sylvia Dawson   110
Henry Morgan    112
Hank Parker     114
Charlie Smith   122
Bill Williams   100
Maryann Clark   101
Jack Austen     120
$
```

First we put line 1 into the hold space, then we append line 4 to it. We then copy the hold space after the last line. Notice that lines 1 and 4 are unchanged in the output.

Notice also that in order to get the lines copied after the last line in the file, we enclosed the $G operation in single quotes. This is a case where double quotes won't do, if you try to use them nothing happens to your file. This is because, within double quotes, the Shell is trying to substitute a value for the Shell Variable named 'G'.[1] If this variable is undefined (and this is the most likely case) a null string is substituted for it, the result being that sed doesn't receive your $G operation at all.

The above example used line numbers, and copied some lines of text at a different place in the file. The next example uses text patterns, and *moves* lines rather than copying them.

We move the line containing Maryann from being first in the file to being the penultimate line of the file. We achieve this in three stages: first we copy the line containing Maryann to the hold space and then we delete that line from the pattern space. This illustrates that the h operation does not affect the pattern space itself; finally we append the hold space after the line containing Charlie.

---

[1] Shell Variables are described in Chapter 13 — *Using the Shell as a Programming Language.*

```
$ sed -e /Maryann/h -e /Maryann/d -e /Charlie/G people
Sally Smith     113
Jane Bailey     121
Jack Austen     120
Steve Daniels   111
Sylvia Dawson   110
Henry Morgan    112
Hank Parker     114
Charlie Smith   122
Maryann Clark   101
Bill Williams   100
$
```

Our final example duplicates one we gave in the description of the ed interactive text editor. Remember we showed you how the transpose command made life easier for us when creating this file:

```
$ cat song
My bonny lies over the ocean,
My bonny lies over the sea,
My bonny lies over the ocean,
O bring back my bonny to me!
$
```

because we didn't have to type similar lines over and over again. Here's how to do the same thing with sed. First we create a file containing part of the song:

```
$ cat >song.part
My bonny lies over the ocean,
O bring back my bonny to me!
$
```

and then we give this command to get the full song:

```
$ sed -e 1h -e 1G -e 1s/ocean/sea/ -e 1H -e 1g \
                                  song.part > song
$
```

Using sed does not make life easier for us. Figuring out the exact command to give, not to mention typing it, took a lot longer that typing the whole thing out in full would have. Deciding which operations to use was not hard, but working out the exact order in which they should be applied took several attempts before we hit on the right combination. One of our abortive attempts went like this:

```
$ sed -e 1h -e 1G -e 2s/ocean/sea/ -e 2G song.part
My bonny lies over the ocean,
My bonny lies over the ocean,
O bring back my bonny to me!
My bonny lies over the ocean,
$
```

This failed because the line numbers refer to lines in the pattern space, which are unaffected by lines appended from the hold space.

Mostly you are probably not going to use these features of sed for 'one off' jobs like this. They will be of most use embedded in an often-used shell script, to process a file having a particular layout. You can do all the experimentation you want when designing that script, once you have found a combination that works, it will always be right — until someone changes the format of the file you are processing.

12.2. Introduction to awk

awk is another text selection and alteration tool in the same family as grep and sed. In addition to providing a means to search for text patterns, awk extends the capabilities to selecting specific fields from lines and testing relationships between those fields.

awk can be thought of as a programmable report-generator — if you have a file (or some files) of data held in the form of text strings, you can process them to change the layout, performing comparisons and calculations on the data at the same time. But awk can also be used to filter out unwanted lines in a file, or to check that a file conforms to a particular layout specification.

A full writeup on awk can be found in the paper called: *Awk — A Pattern Scanning and Text Processing Language* (Second Edition), by A. V. Aho, B. W. Kernighan, and P. J. Weinberger. By the way, awk is not an acronym for anything. As far as we can see, it is the initials of the three authors listed in the reference above.

At its simplest, what awk does is to select a line (from a file) according to some *selection criteria.* The selection criteria can be text patterns (regular expressions) as in grep and egrep and other utilities. Having found lines of interest, awk can then perform some actions on the line, or portions of the line.

This selection-action process is represented in awk notation by:

pattern { *action* }

and means, for every record (line) which matches the specified *pattern*, perform the specified *action*. A selection-action specification for awk is called an *instruction*, and a whole list of such instructions is called a *program*.

Both the pattern and the action are optional. A pattern with no corresponding action simply selects the matched record for display on the Standard Output. An action with no associated pattern is performed on all records in the file. In other words, a missing pattern matches all lines in the file.

Use of the word 'pattern' is a little misleading, an awk pattern can be one of many things. But one of the things it can be is a text pattern, or search string as it is sometimes called — in this case you must tell awk that that is what you intend by enclosing the pattern in slashes:

/ pattern /

The pattern can be a regular expression as described for grep and other other commands. awk has the extended pattern matching capabilities, such as alternation, described in egrep.

With this basic knowledge of awk, let's show a few examples. First let's try to mimic the action of grep to find the Smith's in our *people* file:

```
$ awk Smith people
awk: syntax error near line 1
awk: bailing out near line 1
$
```

This went wrong because we forgot to tell awk that we wanted to use 'Smith' as a text string for selection. Let's do it again, remembering to put in the slashes:

```
$ awk /Smith/ people
Sally Smith     113
Charlie Smith   122
$
```

In this example we made use of the fact that the default action is to print the selected lines, so we didn't bother to specify any action ourselves.

If you don't specify any pattern, awk will perform the specified action on all lines in the file. In this case you *must* specify an action, even if what you want is to print the lines. For instance:

```
$ awk {print} people
Maryann Clark   101
Sally Smith     113
Jane Bailey     121
Jack Austen     120
Steve Daniels   111
Sylvia Dawson   110
Henry Morgan    112
Hank Parker     114
Charlie Smith   122
Bill Williams   100
$
```

provides the same output as cat.

From the above examples you can see that the awk program must be the first argument to the command, the remaining arguments are the files that are to be processed. So far we have only asked to process one file, and the program has been very simple. As we expand on awk's capabilities the programs will become more complex, and we will start using characters that mean something special to awk. Most of these characters can also be treated in a special way by the Shell, so to make sure that awk sees them we will be surrounding the program part of the command line with quotes. In most cases double quotes will not do, it is a good idea to get into the habit of always putting your awk programs inside single quotes.

If you have a long complex program (and awk programs can be very long and complex), it would be inconvenient to put it on the calling command line. So awk has an option to take the program from a file:

```
$ awk -f make.list adminpeople hardpeople softpeole
```

In this example awk will take the instructions held in *make.list* and apply them to the data files *adminpeople*, *hardpeople*, and *softpeople*. We will show some examples of this later.

If the program is specified wrongly, the program file can be modified using a text editor, then awk can be re-run. For complex manipulations, this is much easier than having to type the program on the awk command line each time.

Even if your program is fairly simple, if it is one that will be used frequently it is worth putting it into a file — that way you don't have to remember what to type each time you run it.

Referencing Fields in a Line

The examples we have shown so far are not very impressive, we have simply come up with a more complicated way to achieve things that grep and cat are capable of. We now start showing awk manipulations that cannot be done with the simpler commands.

One of the things that awk can do is operate on individual fields within a line, or record[2]. awk considers every record in a file to be composed of *fields*. Fields are separated by *field separators*, which are normally spaces or tabs, but can be changed to whatever you like. Fields are accessed by the notation $*n* where *n* is the number of the field you want, the first field on the line being $1. The field reference $0 is special: it refers to the whole record (line).

Let us demonstrate a very simple example. Suppose that we want to find the Smiths in the *people* file, but we only want to see the first name and the phone number. We use this awk program:

---

2 In this brief description of awk we are considering a line and a record to be the same thing, though in fact they can be different.

```
$ awk '/Smith/ {print $1 " - " $3}' people
Sally - 113
Charlie - 122
$
```

Notice that we had to specifically insert space characters in the output by enclosing them in quoted strings in the print statement. If you just typed the field references one after the other (even with spaces between them) the resultant output would appear all scrunched together. The print statement in the above example could also be written like this:

```
print $1, $3
```

in which case the fields would appear on the output with a single space between them.

We can use this way of referencing fields on a line to rearrange those fields. Assume that the bureaucracy has finally dictated that the people must appear in the *people* file in order of last name, followed by first name. This can be achieved with this `awk` program:

```
$ awk '{print $2 ", " $1 "^I"  $3}' people
Clark, Maryann  101
White, Sally    113
Bailey, Jane    121
Austen, Jack    120
Daniels, Steve  111
Dawson, Sylvia  110
Parker, Hank    114
Smith, Charlie  122
Williams, Bill  100
Walker, James   112
$
```

which has an action but no pattern. In this case, the missing pattern selects every record in the file. The action part specifies that `awk` is to print the fields in the new order.

The above examples simply show selective display and rearrangement of the fields in a line. It is possible, however, to use `awk` to perform complex selection and computations on the elements of lines.

In the case where we arranged the fields on the line, there could be many files that require such processing. So it might pay us to put the `awk` program into a file and use the `-f` option, as in the example below. Instead of placing the name swapping program on the `awk` command line we create a file, called *swap*, containing the `awk` program:

```
$ cat swap
{print $2 ", " $1 "^I"  $3}
$
```

The awk program is now simply a line in a file. The apostrophes (single quotes) have gone away.

Now we can run awk with this program on any file that needs rearranging:

```
$ awk -f swap adminpeople  >adminpeople.new
$ awk -f swap hardpeople  >hardpeople.new
$ awk -f swap softpeople  >softpeople.new
$
```

Built In Patterns

awk has two special 'built-in' patterns, called BEGIN and END. If BEGIN appears as a pattern, it matches the beginning of file, so that you can gain control before any other processing is done. Similarly, the pattern END matches the end of the file so you can gain control when you get to the end of the file.

You could use these to put a header and a trailer on a report you are producing. As a simple example, let's produce a distribution list from our short files of people, *adminpeople*, *hardpeople*, and *softpeople*. We will put a header at the top, and at the bottom we will put a count of the number of people on the list.

First we construct a file, called *make.list*, containing this awk program:

```
BEGIN { print "";
        print "Widget Distribution List" ;
        print ""
}
{ print $1, $2 }
END { print "";
      print "Number of people = " NR
}
```

Now this is beginning to look more like a 'real' program. Notice that it is in 3 distinct sections.

First there is a BEGIN section, all the actions between the opening { and the closing } are performed before the data file is processed. Since there is more than one action to be done, the individual actions are separated from each other by a semicolon. There is no semicolon after the last action before the closing }.

Next follows the body of the program, which in this case is a lot smaller than either the BEGIN or END sections. It consists of only one action, to print the first two fields of each line. Since we want this action on all lines, no pattern is specified.

The last section is the END section, which will be executed after all of the file (or files) has been processed. Again we have a list of actions, each one being separated from the rest by a semicolon.

Here is what we get when we run this awk program:

```
$ awk -f make.list adminpeople hardpeople softpeople

Widget Distribution List

Maryann Clark
Bill Williams
Jane Bailey
Jack Austen
Charlie Smith
Sally Smith
Steve Daniels
Sylvia Dawson
Henry Morgan
Hank Parker

Number of people = 10
$
```

In the last line of the program we made reference to a mysterious entity called 'NR'. This is a built-in awk variable which contains the number of records processed. We describe built-in variables in the next section.

One feature of awk which is worth mentioning at this point is the printf action, which can be used in place of a simple print. When you use printf you have more control over the final output of your program. One of the things that printf provides is a set of special character sequences, each such sequence being introduced by a reverse slash character. For instance, if you put \t into the specification of the string to be printed, printf will put a TAB character in its place when placing the string on the output. Similarly, \n is replaced by a newline character. By using printf instead of print, we could shorten our *make.list* program to:

```
BEGIN { printf "\nWidget Distribution list\n\n" }
{ print $1, $2 }
END { printf "\nNumber of people = " NR "\n" }
```

When you use printf, the output contains newline characters only where you specially request them — that is why there are two \n sequences in the BEGIN section, and there is also a \n at the end of the END section.

`printf` has many features other than these special sequences. For instance, if you want to print out a number, you can specify how many digits before the decimal point, how many after, and `printf` will also do any necessary conversion for you. We are not going into details of `printf` in this book, but we want you to be aware of its availability. The `printf` action in `awk` works in exactly the same way as does the `printf` statement in the C programming language. So, for more details, refer to any of the books on C that are currently available.

Built In Variables

`awk` allows for variables within its programs. Variables can be defined by the user, but there are also some 'built-in', or predefined, variables that the user can reference.

We saw one of these in the last section — NR is a predefined variable that contains the number of the record (line) currently being processed. In our previous example we referred to NR in the END section of the program. At that point the variable contained the number of the last line that was dealt with, and so could be used as a count of the total number of lines. Using NR as a count is not always the best thing to do — it assumes that every line in the file has been processed, which need not always be the case.

To emphasis that NR contains the current line number we will again use `awk` to simulate the action of `grep`, this time with `grep`'s `-n` (display line number) option:

```
$ awk '/Smith/ {print NR ": " $0}' people
2: Sally Smith     113
9: Charlie Smith   122
$
```

The action in this program prints the current line number, then a colon as a separator, and then prints the entire line.

Another predefined variable is NF, which contains the number of fields on the current line or record. This could be used to check the syntax of a file. When showed how to use the `sort` command back in Chapter 6, we explained that our examples would not work if someone had a middle initial that they insisted on using. Suppose our *people* file contains a line such as

```
Hank J. Parker   114
```

which would prevent the file being sorted properly. The following `awk` program can tell us about this:

```
$ awk 'NF > 3 {print "Too many fields on line " NR}' people
Too many fields on line 8
$
```

Here we use a conditional selection expression (on which, more later) to find those lines that have more than 3 fields. When we find such a line, the action is to print a message giving the line number.

Another interesting pre-defined variable is called `FILENAME`, it is set equal to the name of the file currently being processed by `awk`. You will recall that when we use `grep` to search for a string in several files, the output shows the name of the file in addition to the text on the line that matched the pattern. We can make `awk` do the same thing by using the `FILENAME` variable:

```
$ awk '/Smith/ {print FILENAME ":" $0}' *people
hardpeople:Charlie Smith    122
softpeople:Sally Smith      113
$
```

When processing several files with `awk`, an important point to remember is that the `NR` variable gets incremented for each record that is read sequentially through all the files. It does not get reset to 1 when the `FILENAME` variable changes.

By default `awk` assumes fields in a record are separated by 'white space' (spaces or TABs), but this is governed by a variable called `FS`. If the file you want to process has some other field separator, you should set the `FS` variable equal to that separator (probably in the BEGIN section of your program). Alternatively, you could use the `-F` (that's uppercase F) on the `awk` command line to specify the field separator in the input file.

Similarly, output produced by the `print` statement has a default field separator of one space. If you want a different separator you should change the value of the output field separator variable, `OFS`.

There are two other built-in variables similar to `FS` and `OFS`, these are `RS` (input record separator) and `ORS` (output record separator). By default these are set to newline characters, so that records and lines are the same thing on input, and `print` statements write a line of output. If your requirements are different, you can change the values of the variables in the BEGIN section of your `awk` program.

User Defined Variables

You can define your own variables for use in an `awk` program. A variable is defined the first time it is mentioned, and `awk` initializes it to zero, or to a null string. You don't have to specify what type of variable it is, `awk` figures it out from the context. Where necessary, `awk` also does automatic conversion between strings and numerical values.

The next example shows how we use a variable to calculate the average score in our tennis league. First of all, we create an `awk` program in a file called *average*:

```
{total = total + $3}
END  {print  "Average score is ", total / NR}
```

Then we compute the average with awk, like this:

```
$ awk -f average tennis
Average score is 8.9
$
```

This is a very simple awk program. Because variables are automatically initialized we don't need a BEGIN section. The first line of the program adds the value of the third field of each record (line) of the data file to the variable called total. This is the first example we have given that has an action other than print.

But, because a program isn't much use unless it produces some output, the second line contains a print statement. This is in the END section, so it is done after all the lines in the input (data) file have been processed. First we print a message Average score is , then on the same line we print the value of total divided by NR to get show the average score.

In this program we have assumed that the input file has the correct layout: that there are no blank lines, and that each line does have a tennis score in its third field. This is a very sloppy program, we should have checked for such things. Had we made syntax checks like that, it is unlikely that we would have been able to use NR as the divisor in the calculation of the the average score — we would probably have needed to keep a count of the 'good' lines in another variable.

Operations and Functions

Our last example showed some actions that were not simply print statements — they actually performed some arithmetic operations. There are a wide range of arithmetic operations available in awk, so that you can add, subtract, multiply, divide numerical values. There are also some built-in functions to compute square roots, exponentials, integer parts, and natural logarithms.

The syntax of the arithmetic operators is similar to that provided in the C programming language, so you should gain some familiarity with that language before using awk. Or, alternatively, you can consider using awk as appropriate training prior to learning C programming. In either case, go read a good book on C.

awk also provides various ways of dealing with character strings. There are various string-handling functions like length, which returns a numerical value equal to the length of a string, and substr, which extracts a part of a character string. Refer to the writeup on awk in your *System V User's Manual*, for more detail consult the paper on the awk programming language in your *System V Support Tools Guide*.

Conditional Pattern Selection

An awk pattern can in fact be a *conditional expression*, not just a simple character string. We saw an example earlier, when we used the expression

```
NF > 3
```

to select those lines having more than three fields.

We further illustrate conditional expressions by selecting, from our list of tennis players, those whose scores are 10 or more. We can achieve this by the following awk program:

```
$ awk '$3 >= 10 {print $0}' tennis
Maryann Clark     18
Sally Smith       14
Steve Daniels     11
Hank Parker       18
$
```

This awk program introduces the idea of conditional selection based on properties of the individual fields in the record. In this case, the pattern part is the conditional expression which selects all records whose third field is 10 or more. The action part is simply to print the entire line.

The symbol >= means 'greater than or equal to'. The construct:

```
$3 >= 10
```

is a conditional expression.

awk has a complete set of facilities for testing conditions and performing actions depending on the truth or falsity of those tests.

The next example shows how we use awk to select wines from a list of wines, vineyards, years, and prices. We have a directory called *wine*, in which there live files called *chardonnay*, *cabernet*, and so on:

```
$ cd wine
$ ls -x
cabernet  chardonnay  cheninblanc  pinotnoir  zinfandel
$
```

Now we can use awk to answer questions like: "find me a Chardonnay, somewhere in the years 1976 to 1980 at less than $5.50 per bottle"[3].

Here are the contents of our *chardonnay* file:

---

3 If you find one, please write to the authors.

```
$ cat chardonnay
1976  12.00  Caymus Vineyards
1976  18.00  Mount Veeder
1976  11.50  Chateau St. Jean
1977   9.00  Robert Mondavi
1976   7.75  Chateau St. Jean
1976  10.00  Spring Mountain
1977   6.99  Franciscan
1976   7.50  Chateau St. Jean
1976  10.00  Sterling Vineyards
1977   8.50  Chaparral
1977   6.75  Alexander Valley Vineyards
1977   8.00  Dry Creek Winery
1977  10.00  St. Clements
1975  10.00  Chateau Montelena
1976  11.00  Mayacamas Vineyards
1977   7.50  Raymond Vineyards
1977   8.00  Conn Creek Vineyards
1977   7.50  Chalone
1977   9.00  Carneros Creek Winery
1977   5.99  Charles Krug
1977  10.00  Sonoma Vineyards
$
```

The first field in the file is the year, the second field is the price, and the third field is the vineyard which produced the wine.

Now let us use awk to select something good to go with our veal piccata:

```
$ awk '$1 ~ /197[5678]/ && $2 <= 8.00' chardonnay
1976   7.75  Chateau St. Jean
1977   6.99  Franciscan
1976   7.50  Chateau St. Jean
1977   6.75  Alexander Valley Vineyards
1977   8.00  Dry Creek Winery
1977   7.50  Raymond Vineyards
1977   8.00  Conn Creek Vineyards
1977   7.50  Chalone
1977   5.99  Charles Krug
$
```

This awk pattern selects only those entries whose first field lies in the years 1975 through 1978 (using the character class text pattern), *and* whose second field (the price) is $8.00 or under. The tilde ~ means 'match' — that is, test if field 1 matches the pattern shown enclosed in slashes.

The double ampersand && indicate that both conditions must be met for the action to be taken. The operators used in awk programs are similar to those of the C programming language. A detailed list of these operators can be found in the document referred to at the start of this section.

The result is a reasonably short list of Chardonnays for our enjoyment. It would be nice if awk could then advise as to the quality, but there are some things we must do for ourselves.

Note that the second field in each line (the price) has a decimal point. awk performs all its computations in floating point notation, so it doesn't matter whether numbers are entered as integers or fractions.

There are many ways to use awk's capabilities. It is a matter of personal choice and experience whether to use string matching, relational expressions, or other forms.

For instance, the awk command in the example above could have been written in two other equally good ways. One way is like this:

```
awk '/^197[5678]/ {if ($2 <= 8.00) print $0}' chardonnay
```

which first selects lines beginning with the selected pattern (note the ^ sign to indicate a match anchored to the start of the line), then performs a conditional statement to print all lines whose second field is in the price range.

This second example:

```
awk  '$1 >= 1974 && $1 <= 1978 && $2 <= 8.00' chardonnay
```

uses a relational expression to isolate the range of years that were required.

We leave it as an exercise for the reader to look up the awk documentation and analyze these selection expressions.

Pattern Ranges

An awk pattern can reference a range of lines, for example:

```
/1976/, /1977/
```

is a pattern range. There are two patterns here, separated by a comma. awk selects all lines (inclusive) starting at the first line in which the first field is 1976 or more, and ending the first time a line is found where the first field is 1977.

We would like to apply this to our *chardonnay* file, but that file is not sorted properly for the job, since the years are all out of order. First we sort the file so that it ends up with the lines in order by year:

```
$ sort -n -o chard.sort chardonnay
$
```

and then we use awk to select our wines for us.

```
$ awk '/1976/, /1977/ {if ($2 <= 8.00) print $0}' chard.sort
    1976   7.50  Chateau St. Jean
    1976   7.75  Chateau St. Jean
    1977   5.99  Charles Krug
$
```

Note that the pattern range as we gave it above stops at the first occurrence of 1977, not the last.

Further reading on awk

The complete range of applications of awk are far beyond the scope of this book, to fully describe all of awk's features would take a book in itself. We have tried to give you some of the flavor of awk so that you can explore further.

Some features that you might want to experiment with are: associative arrays, the while and for statements for performing instruction loops, the if statement (which we showed, but didn't explain, in our last example) for conditional execution. You might also want to investigate awk's interaction with the Shell: other System V utilities can be called from within awk programs, output can be placed into files using the > and >> redirection indicators, output can even be piped to another System V command.

For further exploration, read the paper referred to at the start of this section: *Awk — A Pattern Scanning and Text Processing Language* (Second Edition), by A. V. Aho, B. W. Kernighan, and P. J. Weinberger, and the section entitled *Awk: Programming Language* which is to be found in the *System V Support Tools Guide*. Mark Sobell, in his book *A Practical Guide to UNIX System V*, gives a comprehensive and cohesive set of sample awk programs — it is worth studying.

12.3. Summary

In this chapter we have described two of UNIX System V's most powerful and flexible utilities. They are not, perhaps because of their power and flexibility, easy to use — but we feel that the sophisticated user will find the effort of learning about them well worth-while.

The stream editor, sed, finds many applications when used within Shell scripts. But beware, using sed can become addictive. Since you can use it to do almost anything you want, you might find yourself trying to a job with sed when there is a much easier way using a different command. Nevertheless, knowledge of sed is a 'must' for the professional Shell script writer.

awk is such a complex command that it hardly deserves the description 'utility program'. It is much more than that, it is can be considered a programming language in its own right. A user desirous of learning to program using the C language should seriously consider gaining an intimate knowledge of awk as a first step. The languages are similar, but with awk you are protected from some of the pettyfogging details, like whether a variable is an integer or a character array (string).

Neither should the experienced C programmer neglect awk. A potential C program could be first cast in the awk programming language. Development would evolve more quickly, because there isn't the necessity to recompile the program before running it after each change. Unfortunately, awk programs are slow in execution, so a final transcription into C would probably be necessary for often-used, or time critical, programs.

The Shell script writer should also consider using awk. Although mathematical processing can be done using Shell scripts, as we shall show in the next chapter, they can be rather cumbersome and an awk program might achieve the same effect with less effort.

13 Using the Shell as a Programming Language

We have mentioned the Shell frequently in many of the previous chapters, but just what is the Shell? Consider the diagram representing a computer system as shown in figure 13.1 below.

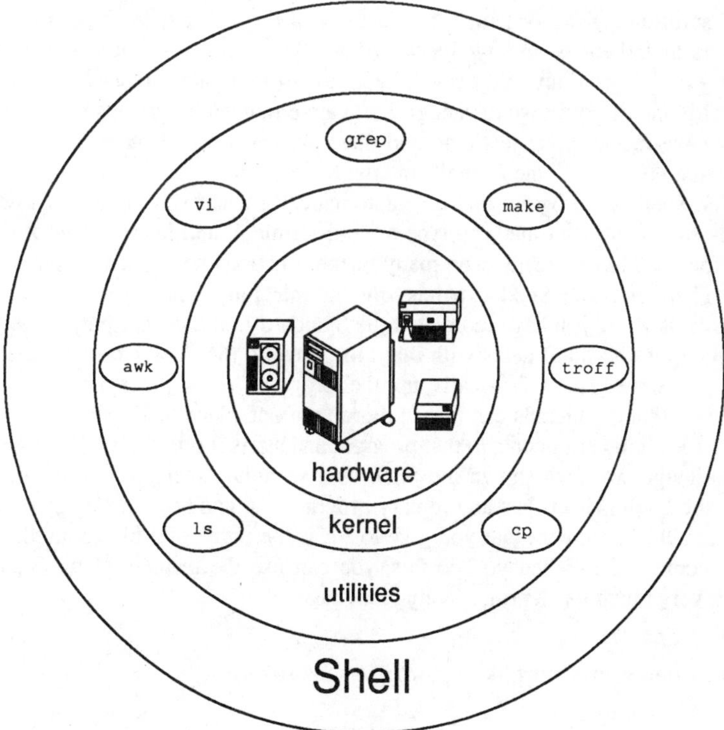

Figure 13.1 Diagram of the Shell

Here's a brief summary of what the diagram represents:

- Right in the very center is the computer and associated equipment — disks, tapes, printers, and so on. This is what is called the *hardware* of the system.

- Surrounding the hardware are some programs that handle details such as talking to disks, managing the computer's resources, organizing the file system, and all sorts of detailed work that users don't really want to know about. This layer of software is the *kernel* of System V.
- The kernel provides a layer of support — independent of the hardware — for the *utility programs* like `sort`, `grep`, the editors, `troff`, and various compilers. These utilities are represented by the next layer outside the kernel.
- The outermost layer represents the *Shell*. The Shell forms the interface between users and the rest of the system.

In fact figure 13.1 above is somewhat misleading — we showed the Shell as a 'layer' surrounding the system, but in fact one of the major strengths of UNIX System V is that *there is nothing special about the Shell*! The Shell is in fact just another[1] utility program. You can (if you are so motivated) replace the standard Shell with one of your own devising. Software engineers in various research institutions have in fact done just that, and there are a variety of other Shells, among them being the C Shell, the B Shell, and the Korn Shell.

The Shell is a program that runs automatically when you log in to System V. It reads each command that you type at your terminal, and interprets what you've asked for. We have already seen many of the functions performed by the Shell in earlier chapters. The Shell expands any file-matching wild-card characters you may have used. If you have redirected the Standard Input and Output, or the Diagnostic Output, the Shell deals with that too. Finally, the Shell examines the command you have asked for, calls up the program from the appropriate place (remember that commands can live in more than one place, like */bin* and */usr/bin*), then passes all the arguments to that program and starts it up.

Although we have shown the Shell as a separate outer layer in the diagram above, the Shell is itself just an ordinary program and can be called up by the command `sh`. The argument that you give to `sh` is the name of a file containing System V commands. When you do this, you can use the features of the Shell that make it very much like a programming language:

- Variables
- Control structures like `if`, `while`, and so on
- Subroutines
- Parameter passing
- Interrupt handling

These features provide you with the capability to design your own tools. We go into this in some detail later in this chapter. Files of commands are called 'shell

[1] albeit a lot more complex than the average utility program.

procedures', or 'shell files', or 'shell scripts', or simply 'shells'. We distinguish between 'a shell' (with a lowercase s) meaning a file of Shell commands, and 'the Shell', or even 'a Shell' (with an uppercase S), which means the program which runs those commands.

Since the Shell is simply a program called upon to interpret commands typed by users, and not an integral part of the kernel, it is easy to have different versions of it. There are several popular Shells, and on some installations more than one Shell could be available for your use. In this book we describe only the Shell that is standard on System V. This is known as the Bourne Shell.[2]

13.1. Login Profile

When you first log in to System V, the Shell is called up to deal with your session. The first thing it does is look for your login profile. This is a file having the specific name *.profile*, in your 'home' directory. If this file exists, then any commands in it are executed by the Shell before it gives you the system prompt. So if there are things you always want to do at the beginning of each login session you should create such a file containing the commands.

Way back in the beginning of the book, we discussed what to do when you make a typing mistake, and we talked about the erase and kill characters. We showed you how to use `stty` to change the erase and kill characters from their default values. `stty` is a command that could be put in your login profile, since you want to do it each time you log in.

You can put any System V commands you like into your login profile. For instance, when you log on you might like to know who else is logged on, what the time is, and what the latest news items are. Your profile will look like:

```
stty erase '^H' kill '^U'
who
news -n
date
```

Another thing that you might want to do in your profile is change the prompt from the usual `$` sign. The prompt is defined by a Shell variable. It is possible to change the value assigned to this variable, which in turn causes the prompt to be different. We show you how to do this later in this chapter.

Another Shell Variable tells the system where to look for commands. These are usually the system directories */bin* and */usr/bin*, but if you want to set up your own cache of private commands you can tell the system to look in other directories too. This should also be in your login profile.

---

2 After S. R. Bourne of Bell Laboratories

13.2. Shell Procedures

As we said at the beginning of this chapter, a shell procedure is a file which contains commands. For instance, suppose you have a file called *dothat* which contains System V commands. There are two ways we can get the system to obey these commands. One is by giving the filename as an argument to the `sh` command:

```
$ sh dothat
```

The other way is to use the `chmod` command to change the mode of the file so that it is executable. When you do this you have effectively made your own command. You can then just type the name of the file just like a command:

```
$ chmod 755 dothat
$ dothat
```

The `chmod` command makes the file executable (`rwxr-xr-x` permissions) — the shell file can now be called up like any other command.

Be careful how you name your shell files; if you duplicate the name of an existing command (one that lives in */bin* or */usr/bin*, for instance), you lose access to that command and can only use your own version. This is not completely true; you can of course access the original command by giving the full pathname to it, but that's cumbersome.

Some Simple Shell Procedures

A very simple procedure can be made using the `echo` command. `echo` writes its arguments to the Standard Output. So the very first shell procedure to write is one which just greets you at your terminal:

```
$ cat > greetings
echo  Hi there
^D
$ chmod 755 greetings
$
```

We have created the shell file *greetings* and made it executable, now when we type the command `greetings` we get:

```
$ greetings
Hi there
$
```

If you would like System V to give you this friendly message every time you log in, you can put the `greetings` command in your login profile.

Let's look at a more useful example. When we discussed the text manipulation utility programs, we took an example of a file containing a list of people and their phone numbers. Suppose we now want to use that file to print out a distribution list, with a heading, and without phone numbers. We can use this pipeline of commands:

```
$ sort +1 -2 people | tr -d "[0-9]" | pr -h Distribution | lp
$
```

This is a long command to type and it is easy to make a mistake. Also, if the distribution list is produced seldom, it is easy to forget what you have to do to get one. The solution to both these problems is to make a shell file:

```
$ cat > makelist
sort +1 -2 people | tr -d "[0-9]" | pr -h Distribution | lp
^D
$
```

and make it executable with a `chmod` command:

```
$ chmod 755 makelist
$
```

Now we can make our distribution list by the simple command:

```
$ makelist
$
```

There is no response other than the prompt because we have routed the output to the printer from inside the shell file itself. If we wanted to check the output of `makelist` before it was printed, we would leave off the final `lp` from the pipeline:

```
$ cat >makelist
sort +1 -2 people | tr -d 0-9 | pr -h Distribution
^D
$ chmod 755 makelist
$
```

The output of this version of `makelist` appears on the terminal screen. To send the output to the printer you have to use the command in a pipeline:

```
$ makelist | lp
$
```

Naming Shell Procedures

Let us examine a not-so-simple shell procedure, which illustrates both how to use the Shell effectively, and also demonstrates some of the potential pitfalls. Suppose that whenever you use `ls` you always use the `-x` and `-F` options to get a multi-columnar listing with directories and executable files marked appropriately. You get tired of typing `ls -x -F` all the time, so you make a shell file called `di` (directory listing).

```
$ cat >di
ls -x -F
^D
$ chmod 755 di
$ di
adminpeople   di*          docs/        hardpeople   people
progs/        softpeople
$
```

This looks OK, but suppose the habit of using `ls` is so strong that you forget about `di` until after you've typed `ls`. You might be tempted to make a copy of `di`, and call the new command `ls`:

```
$ cp di ls
$ ls
```

Now you have your own special version of `ls`, but when you try to use it the system doesn't respond at all! You have to interrupt the command (with **BREAK**, or **RUBOUT**, or **DEL**, or **CTRL-C**) to get the prompt again. This is because your version of `ls` is trying to call `ls` (that is it is trying to call itself), which is trying to call itself, which is trying to call itself, and so on — you see the problem? The way out of this is to use the full pathname to the real `ls`:

```
$ cat >ls
/bin/ls -x -F
^D
$
```

and make it executable using `chmod` as before:

```
$ chmod 755 ls
$ ls
adminpeople    di*          docs/        hardpeople    ls*
people         progs/       softpeople
$
```

This illustrates that you have to be careful when naming your shell files, especially when you are creating one to produce a modified version of an existing command.

So far we have only used this special version of `ls` to list the current directory, let's see what happens when you try to list some other directory:

```
$ ls /etc
adminpeople    di*          docs/        hardpeople    ls*
people         progs/       softpeople
$
```

You still get a listing of the current directory, because your version of `ls` completely ignores any arguments you give it. Later in this chapter we explain how shell procedures can recognize arguments on the calling command line. In the meantime, we can try working around this by changing directory before using your own special variation of `ls`:

```
$ cd /usr
$ ls
bin
dict
games
include
lib
mail
man
news
pub
$
```

Now you are back to using the system version of the `ls` command. If you try to use the one you originally made, `di`, we are even worse off:

```
$ cd /usr
$ di
di: not found
$
```

The system doesn't even recognize your command.

This is because the Shell looks for commands in various directories in a fixed order, the default order being:

- the current directory,
- the system directory */bin*,
- the system directory */usr/bin*.

If the command isn't in any of those directories, you get the 'not found' error message. If a file of the same name as the command lives in one of the directories, but you don't have execute permission on it, you get a different message — 'cannot execute'. The system executes (or tries to) the first version of the command that it finds, so if a command lives in both */bin* and */usr/bin*, it is the version in */bin* which is usually run. This is why you can have a command of the same name as one of the commands in */bin*, and yours takes precedence.

However, if the name of the command you type contains a / (a pathname rather than a simple command name) the system doesn't search the directories, it uses the command specified by the pathname. So you could have said:

```
$ cd /usr
$ /aa/widget/maryann/di
bin/          dict/         games/          include/          lib/
mail/         man/          news/            pub/
$
```

The directories that the system looks at to find commands, and the order in which it looks at them, is called the 'command search path'. The search path is set up as a Shell variable, and it can be changed. So you can designate one of your directories to hold all your special commands, then change the command search path by altering the value of the Shell variable that defines it. If you don't want to change this Shell variable every time you log on, you can define it in your login profile.

Let's first make a directory containing your special commands:

```
$ mkdir bin
$ mv di ls bin
$
```

If you look at things with `ls`:

```
$ ls
adminpeople
bin
docs
hardpeople
people
progs
softpeople
$ ls  bin
di
ls
$
```

you can see that, now that you have moved the files `di` and `ls` into a different directory, you have reverted to using the real `ls`, because you haven't yet set up your command search path to look in your own private directory.

Notice that you now have an entry called *bin* in the `ls` output. This *bin* is the directory where you will keep all your own commands. It is normal practice, and consistent with the naming of the system directories, to call the directory containing your private commands *bin*. But it doesn't have to be called that, you can call it *mycmds*, or whatever you wish.

The next section discusses *Shell Variables* — in it we show you how to change your command search path to include your own private commands.

13.3. Shell Variables

The Shell gives you the capability to define a named variable and assign a value to it. The simplest way of setting a shell variable is via an assignment statement:

variable=value

The value assigned to the variable can then be retrieved by preceding the name of the variable with a dollar sign:

$*variable*

For example, see what happens when we use these commands:

```
$ fruit=apple
$ cheese=cheddar
$ wine=chardonnay
$ echo $fruit, $cheese, $wine ....Mmmm!
apple, cheddar, chardonnay ....Mmmm!
$
```

The value assigned to a variable can be defined in terms of another shell variable, or even defined in terms of itself:

```
$ wine=$fruit-jack
$ fruit=pine$fruit
$ echo $wine and $fruit
apple-jack and pineapple
$
```

Had we wanted 'applejack' without the hyphen, we could not do it with `wine=$fruitjack`. The Shell would look for a variable called 'fruitjack', which doesn't exist. The result is that `$wine` would be assigned a null (empty) string. If we really want the string 'applejack' to be defined in terms of the `$fruit` variable, we must delimit that variable with braces when we use it:

```
$ fruit=apple
$ wine=${fruit}jack
$ echo $wine
applejack
$
```

The curly braces must be used whenever a variable needs to be combined with another string, and there is no other way of distinguishing the end of the variable name and the beginning of the following string.

Although Shell variables are mostly used inside shell procedures, they can also be used from the terminal. They are usually used in this way when you want to use a shorthand notation. For instance, suppose that there is a directory with a long pathname that you are continually accessing. You might set up a shell variable `dir` to the pathname, then access files in that directory by `$dir/file`. This can save a lot of typing, and the frustration of mistyping the pathname again and again.

As another example, if there is a command which you are using frequently, and you have to specify many options, you might want to set it up as a shell variable:

```
$ s="sort +2n +1 -2"
$ $s  tennis | lp
$ $s  racquetball | lp
$ $s  squash | lp
$ $s  pingpong | lp
$
```

Notice the use of quotes to preserve spaces in the variable definition. If you set up a shell variable as an abbreviation of a command line, the command must not contain pipe symbols (|), redirection (< or >), or the background processing symbol (`&`).

Predefined Shell Variables

The Shell *predefines* several variables. Some predefined variables can be modified. Others are read-only — they can be used, but not modified. The most interesting predefined variables are:

- `HOME` is set to be the user's home directory — that is, the default argument to the `cd` command.
- `PATH` is the set of directories that the system searches in order to find commands.
- `PS1` is the primary prompt string. That is the system prompt, which on UNIX System V is the dollar sign, `$`.

From these we can see how we can do two of the things we mentioned might be done in your login profile.

Changing the UNIX System Prompt The system prompt can be changed by redefining the Shell variable which contains the prompt character string.

If you want a reasonably simple prompt, you can include in your login profile the statement:

```
PS1=?
```

Now, instead of the usual `$` prompt you will get `?`. Be careful with this one — some interactive commands (such as `mail`) also have a `?` prompt and you could get confused.

In practice, you will find the system easier to use if there is a space following your prompt. To make sure you get that space you must use quotes:

```
PS1="? "
```

You must also use quotes if you want a more complicated prompt:

```
PS1="whaddya want, OK?"
```

If you always want to use this prompt, you should put the command that sets the Shell variable in your login profile.

Changing the System Command Search Path The usual order in which the system searches directories to find commands is: the current directory, then the */bin* directory, and finally the */usr/bin* directory. The search path variable is called `PATH`:

```
$ echo $PATH
:/bin:/usr/bin
$
```

The full pathnames of the different directories that are searched are separated by colons :, with the current directory implied by the initial :.

If you want to tell the system to look for commands in your own private *bin* directory, you simply change the value of the Shell PATH variable:

```
$ echo $HOME
/aa/widget/maryann
$ PATH=:$HOME/bin$PATH
$ echo  $PATH
:/aa/widget/maryann/bin:/bin:/usr/bin
```

to put your directory in the search path between the current directory and *bin*. This is the usual place, but if you have different requirements you can put them in a different order.

The command to set the search path should be placed in your login profile, otherwise you have to set PATH every time you log in.

Setting a Shell Variable from Command Output

You can set a shell variable to the output of a command by:

```
$ now=`date`
$ echo $now
Sat May 17 14:34:58 PDT 1986
$
```

The characters surrounding the command in the above example are the *grave accent* (`) character, not the apostrophe. The grave accent is found in many different places on a terminal keyboard, usually either above the @ sign, or above the tilde ~ sign.

If you want to set a Shell variable equal to a value contained in a file, you can do it by:

```
menu=`cat food`
```

That is the command cat with an argument *food*, not kitty fodder. If the file *food* contains:

```
apples
cheddar
chardonnay
```

the resulting value of menu is:

```
$ echo $menu
apples cheddar chardonnay
$
```

As you can see from the example, newline characters are transformed into spaces.

13.4. Arguments to Shell Procedures

A different type of Shell Variable is one which is passed to the shell procedure when it is called. This is an argument to the procedure. These are sometimes called positional parameters, because they are accessed by the number of their position in the list of arguments. For example, if we have a procedure which is called by the command:

```
$ dothis grapes apples pears
```

then 'grapes', 'apples' and 'pears' are positional parameters, and are accessed by `$1`, `$2`, and `$3` respectively.

If the command is called:

```
$ dothis gouda brie cheddar
```

then `$1` is 'gouda', `$2` is 'brie', and `$3` is 'cheddar'.

A simple example of this is given by the following shell procedure:

```
$ cat reverse
echo  $5 $4 $3 $2 $1
$
```

which takes up to five arguments and echoes them onto the Standard Output in reverse order:

```
$ reverse fee fie fo fum fiddledee
fiddledee fum fo fie fee
$
```

If the procedure is called with fewer than five arguments:

```
$ reverse tic tac toe
toe tac tic
$
```

null strings are substituted for the missing arguments. If it is called with more than five arguments, all except the first five are ignored.

To give an example of where arguments can be useful, let's go back to our `makelist` procedure:

```
$ cat  makelist
sort +1 -2 people | tr -d "[0-9]" | pr -h Distribution | lp
$
```

This works on one file, and one file only, namely the *people* file. If we put `$1` in place of *people*, we can use it on any file we care to name:

```
$ cat makelist
sort  +1 -2   $1 | tr  -d  "[0-9]" | pr  -h Distribution | lp
$ makelist  adminpeople
$ makelist  hardpeople
$ makelist  softpeople
$
```

There is a limit of nine arguments that can be addressed, `$1` through `$9`. However, there is a '`shift`' command to the Shell that discards the first argument, and renumbers the remainder. In this way it is possible to write a shell procedure which can deal with more than nine arguments.

Another way of accessing all the arguments, even if more than nine are given, is by the notation `$*`. This expands to all the arguments that were given when the shell procedure was invoked. `$*` is the equivalent of

```
$1 $2 $3.........
```

for all arguments.

The parameter `$#` is set to the total number of arguments specified when the shell procedure was called up. For example, if we have a procedure 'count':

```
$ cat count
echo $# items
$ count grapes apples oranges pears
4 items
$ count belpaese gruyere fontina
3 items
$
```

it simply tells you how many items have been listed on the command line.

This is useful when you want to check that the shell procedure has been called with the correct number of arguments.

The name of the shell procedure itself is considered the zero'th argument, and can be addressed by the notation `$0`. The name does not get counted in `$#`, as we saw in the above examples.

13.5. The echo command revisited

Many of the examples we have shown use the echo command, which writes its arguments to the Standard Output. This command is very useful when writing shell procedures. It can be used to give the user progress reports, or error messages, or results; it can be used to prompt the user for input to an interactive procedure — it can even be a useful tool when debugging shell procedures.

In practice your shell procedures will be easier to read if you enclose the message in quotes so that the message forms only one argument to echo. Mostly you will want to use double quotes so that you can get at the values of Shell variables:

```
$ echo "Hi there $LOGNAME"
Hi there maryann
$
```

LOGNAME is one of the special Shell variables. The Shell sets up LOGNAME equal to the user name of the person logged in.

If you use single quotes the values of Shell Variables are not substituted:

```
$ echo 'Hi there $LOGNAME'
Hi there $LOGNAME
$
```

but there could be situations where this is what you want. For instance:

```
$ echo 'You owe me $10' |mail sylvia
$
```

If you need to use a $-sign but you also want to use variables, you can escape the 'real' $ with a reverse slash:

```
$ amount=10
$ echo "You owe me \$$amount" | mail sylvia
$
```

When using echo there are some special character sequences that can be used to affect the layout of the output. These special character sequences consist of a reverse slash followed by a letter — for example, \n. The sequences are listed in the echo writeup in the *System V User's Manual*, the following paragraphs give examples of some of them.

Normally, echo follows its output with a newline. The \c sequence can be used to stop this:

```
$ echo "Hi there $LOGNAME \c"
Hi there maryann $
```

In this case the system prompt appears on the same line as the message. The `\c` sequence is useful when writing interactive shell procedures.

The sequence `\n` can be used to put additional newlines in the output, the sequence `\t` will put tabs in the output. If we send mail giving birthday greetings:

```
$ echo "Happy Birthday Steve, Maryann" | mail steve
$
```

its appearance can be much improved by using these sequences.

```
$ echo "\tHappy Birthday Steve\n\t\t\tMaryann" | mail steve
$
```

Within shell procedures these sequences can save you some typing, and some execution time, since we can use one `echo` command in place of many. Suppose that from within a shell procedure we want to produce a heading for a report. We could use several `echo` commands like this:

```
now=`date`
echo "" >reportfile
echo "" >>reportfile
echo "Widget Project: PR Statistics                $now" >>reportfile
echo "" >>reportfile
echo "" >>reportfile
```

or we could use a single command:

```
now=`date`
echo "\f\n\nWidget Project: PR Statistics\t\t$now\n\n" >reportfile
```

In this last example we have also used the `\f` sequence, which puts a form feed character in the output. This will ensure that the report starts at the top of a page when printed.

In the examples in the rest of this chapter you will see many uses of the `echo` command although we don't, in general, use the special character sequences very often.

13.6. Shell Programming

Within shell procedures you can use several commands which control the action taken by the procedure, depending on some internal or external condition. Programmers will recognize the constructs **if...else**, **while...do**, and other similar statements. In this section we don't go into all the details of what can be done in shell procedures, but we show some examples of how these flow control commands are used, and some instances of where you might want to use them.

When you are creating a new utility or command it is often a good idea to write it first as a shell procedure. The advantage to shell procedures is that they are easy to change. You don't have to re-compile, re-link and reload every time you make a change. They are also easy to debug, since there are options to the `sh` command which provide a trace facility. When you are sure that it does what you want, and you have the user interface set up correctly, you can proceed to code it in C, or any other programming language you choose. Compiled programs execute faster than do shell procedures. If the command is not used very often it may be unnecessary to do such a recasting.

For non-programmers, writing shell procedures can be a good introduction to the underlying principles of programming.

To illustrate the use of the flow control commands, we take the simple `makelist` shell that we introduced in the early paragraphs of this chapter, and refine and expand it. Although the single line:

```
sort +1 -2 people | tr -d "[0-9]" | pr -h Distribution | lp
```

is the heart of the procedure, it is largely irrelevant to the point of illustrating the commands, so for the most part we simply show it as `sort...etc`.

This example is not always sufficient to show all the points we want to cover, so occasionally we will also introduce other, unrelated, examples.

Looping with the `for` statement

Our very first attempt at making our own `makelist` command looked like:

```
$ cat makelist
sort +1 -2 people | tr  ..... etc
$
```

As we have already pointed out this deals with only one file, *people*. Suppose that we had three files — *adminpeople*, *hardpeople*, and *softpeople* — and we want to be able to make a list from any one of them. One possibility is that we have three different procedures, one for each file, called `makalist`, `makhlist` and `makslist`, say.

This is rather cumbersome, a better solution is to arrange for the same procedure to deal with all three files. We can do this by using the `for` statement.

The general layout of the `for` statement is:

> **`for`** *variable* **`in`** *this list of values*
> **`do`** *all these following*
> *commands up until the*
> **'`done`'** *statement.*
> **`done`**

The `for` statement defines a variable to take on various values in turn. For each of these values, the sequence of commands between the `do` and `done` keywords is executed. When there are no more values for the variable to take, the commands following `done` are executed. When we use `for` in our `makelist` command, we get:

```
for file in adminpeople hardpeople softpeople
do
sort +1 -2 $file | tr  ...... etc
done
```

The first line defines a shell variable `file`, which takes on the values 'admin-people', 'hardpeople' and 'softpeople' in turn. The variable is used in the `sort` command line, the value that it currently has is the name of the file that gets processed. In our case we only had one command line, the pipeline beginning with `sort` and ending with `lp`. The output of this version of `makelist` is three lists, one for each of the files given following the `in` keyword.

You can use the Shell's metacharacters in the list following the `in` keyword. We could, for example, have written our procedure thus:

```
for file in *people
do
sort +1 -2 $file | tr  ....... etc
done
```

This generates a list for every file in the current directory that ends with the string 'people'.

We can leave out the keyword `in`; the list then defaults to the arguments that are given when the shell is called up. For example, the shell file:

```
for file
do
sort +1 -2 $file | tr  ....... etc
done
```

generates three lists if called by the command:

```
$ makelist  adminpeople hardpeople softpeople
$
```

but generates only one list if called by:

```
$ makelist  softpeople
$
```

This is a more general and more useful form of the procedure.

Details of the `for` statement are documented under the entry for the `sh` command in the *System V User's Manual.*

Conditional Execution with `if`

Let us revisit our original shell file:

```
sort +1 -2 people | tr -d "[0-9]" | pr -h Distribution | lp
```

We have already shown that we can make this apply to files generally by putting `$1` in place of the file word 'people':

```
sort +1 -2 $1| tr -d 0-9 | pr -h Distribution | lp
```

Now we generate a list for whichever file we specify when we execute `makelist`. However, if we don't specify any filename:

```
$ makelist
```

nothing happens.

This is because, when the Shell tries to substitute a value for `$1`, there isn't anything to substitute, so the command we are trying to execute is:

```
sort +1 -2  | tr  ....... etc
```

When the `sort` command isn't given any filenames, it expects to sort the Standard Input. The net result is that our own special `makelist` command is waiting for us to type in the names that we want to put on the distribution list. This may be a good idea, but if this is what you want, you should arrange to prompt for input in some way.

Let's assume that we only want `makelist` to work on files that have been prepared previously. In order to avoid the situation outlined above, we must put into the procedure a check that a filename has been specified:

```
if test $# -eq 0
then echo "you must give a filename"
     exit 1
fi
sort  +1 -2  $1 | tr  ....... etc
```

The first line in the example tests whether the number of arguments to `makelist` is zero.

We have introduced three new things in the example: an `if` statement, a `test` command, and an `exit` statement. We describe these in a bit more detail in the following paragraphs.

The `if` Statement The keywords connected with this statement are `if` itself, `then`, and `fi`. The general meaning goes like this:

> **`if`** *this command is successful*
> **`then`** *execute all*
> *these commands up to*
> *the following* '**`fi`**'
> **`fi`**

To make the 'program' easier to read, it is usual to indent the commands between `then` and `fi`, as we've shown.

When a command is successful, it is said to 'return a true value'. A true value is the value zero. If the command fails, a non-zero value is returned. In our example we have used the `test` command to check if the number of arguments is zero. If that is true, obviously no filename was specified when the procedure was called up. `test` returns a value of zero if the answer to the test is 'yes', otherwise it returns a non-zero value.

Each of the keywords must be the first word on a line to be recognized by the Shell. If you put them anywhere else they cause trouble. For example, if you try to execute this file:

```
if test $# -eq 0 then
   echo "you must give a filename"
   exit 1
fi
sort +1 -2 $1 | tr  ..... etc
```

which has the `then` keyword at the end of the line, we get this result:

```
$ makelist people
makelist: syntax error at line 5: 'fi' unexpected
$
```

The test command (described below) is probably the most useful one to use with the if statement, but you can use any command. For example:

```
if  cd /aa/widget/steve/docs
then echo thingspec
     cat thingspec
fi
```

If the cd command is successful, then the file *thingspec* is displayed. However, if the attempt to change directory fails for any reason, nothing happens.

The exit statement In our example, if there is no filename given, we want to print an error message and terminate the procedure without executing the sort command. Normally the shell procedure terminates when the end of the file is reached. If you want to finish sooner than that, you must use an exit statement.

The statement that we actually used in the example says **exit 1**. This means that the value returned by 'makelist' is 1 (that is, non-zero) when we have the error condition that no file has been given.

We should properly have put another exit statement at the end of the file:

```
if  test $# -eq 0
then echo "you must give a filename" >&2
     exit 1
fi
sort  +1 -2  $1 | tr  ..... etc
exit 0
```

This ensures that our procedure returns a zero value when it has executed correctly. So we can use makelist in an if statement of another shell file:

```
if  makelist adminpeople
then echo list made OK
fi
```

We sneaked in another little change above. We changed the echo command line to print the error message on the Diagnostic Output, where it belongs, instead of on the Standard Output. In our example it doesn't matter too much that the message goes to the Standard Output. Because we route the required output to the line printer within the shell procedure, the only thing that appears on the terminal screen is the error message. However, if we had arranged that makelist would produce the distribution list on the Standard Output, then if we piped the output of makelist to lp on the command line, the error message would get printed too! By writing error messages to the Diagnostic Output we avoid this annoying situation.

For any shell procedure where it is likely that the normal output will be piped to another command, or redirected to a file, it is important that error messages be written on the Diagnostic Output.

The value on the exit statement is optional; you can simply say `exit`. In this case, the value returned by the procedure is the same as the value returned by the last command that was executed, before the procedure was terminated.

Our example command `makelist` is unlikely to be called from within another procedure, so we are not really concerned what values it returns. In all the following extensions to the example we don't bother to set return values.

The `else` statement This is really part of the `if` statement. The action goes like this:

> **`if`** *this command is successful*
> **`then`** *execute all*
> *these commands up to*
> *the following* '**`else`**'.
> **`else`** *execute this*
> *set of commands up to*
> *the following* '**`fi`**'.
> **`fi`**

So we could have expressed our example:

```
if  test $# -eq 0
then  echo "you must give a filename" >&2
else  sort  +1 -2  $1 | tr  .... etc
fi
```

This time we don't need to use an `exit` statement because the `sort` command follows the `else`, and will only get executed if the number of arguments is greater than zero.

Like the `if`, `then` and `fi` keywords, `else` must appear at the start of a line.

The `elif` statement This is a combination of `else` and `if`. To illustrate, let's first see what happens if we call up our shell with the name of a file that doesn't exist:

```
$ makelist  nopeople
sort: can't open nopeople
pr: -- empty file
$
```

If someone was using your `makelist` command, and didn't know that `sort` and pr were involved, this message could confuse them. It would be better to check for the existence of the file before calling the sort utility.

To do this we need another if to test for presence of the file:

```
if   test $# -eq 0
then  echo "you must give a filename" >&2
elif  test ! -s $1
then  echo "no file $1" >&2
else  sort  +1 -2  $1 | tr  ..... etc
fi
```

The second test command checks that there is a file of the given name. So now we only execute the sort command if a filename is given, and if the file exists.

We could achieve the same thing by using a second if statement following the else:

```
if test $# -eq 0
then echo "you must give a filename" >&2
else if test ! -s $1
     then echo "no file $1" >&2
     else sort +1 -2 $1 | tr ...... etc
     fi
fi
```

This time we have two separate if statements, one nested inside the other. Each if has its closing fi statement. This is different from elif, which forms part of the original if statement, so there is only one fi. There are occasions when you cannot use elif to achieve the results you want, and you must use a separate nested if statement.

In the above example, the second if was not the first thing on the line, which seems to be breaking the rules. But the rule is really that the keywords have to be the first in the command. Normally this would mean first on the line, but if a command follows a keyword you will get two keywords one after the other, and that is OK.

The if, elif and else statements, along with the attendant then and fi are documented under the sh command in the *System V User's Manual.*

The test command

The test command is not part of the Shell, but it is intended for use inside shell procedures. We have already seen some examples of test in action.

Basically, the arguments to test form an expression. If the expression is true, test returns a zero value (the test was successful). If the test fails, the command returns a non-zero value.

There are three main sorts of test that can be performed:

- tests on numerical values
- tests on file types
- tests on character strings

For each type of test, there are a set of *primitives* which construct the expression that `test` evaluates. These primitives describe the properties to be tested. There are also operators which can be used to invert the meaning of the expression, and to combine expressions.

Tests on numerical values These test the relationship between two numbers, which may be represented by shell variables. The general form of the expression tested is:

N <primitive> *M*

The primitives that can be used in the expression tested are:

`-eq`	the values of *N* and *M* are equal
`-ne`	the values of *N* and *M* are not equal
`-gt`	*N* is greater than *M*
`-lt`	*N* is less than *M*
`-ge`	*N* is greater than or equal to *M*
`-le`	*N* is less than or equal to *M*

Here are some examples of using these primitives:

```
users=`who | wc -l`
if test $users -gt 8
then echo "more than 8 people logged on"
fi
```

The first line of the file sets the shell variable `users` equal to the value produced by the pipeline of commands **`who|wc -l`**. This is in fact a count of the number of users currently logged on to the system. This value is then compared with the number 8, and if it is greater the message is printed.

The following example assumes that the procedure requires one argument, and that the argument is a directory:

```
this=`ls | wc -l`
that=`ls $1 | wc -l`
if test $this -ne $that
then echo "current directory and $1 do not match"
fi
```

We again use a pipeline involving the wc command; this time to count the number of files in the current directory, and again to count the number of files in the given directory. We then compare the two values and print an appropriate message.

The last example:

```
if  test $# -eq 0
then  echo "you must give a filename" >&2
else  sort  +1 -2  $1 | tr  ...... etc
fi
```

is one we have already seen. $# is the total number of arguments given when the shell procedure was called up. We check to see if that number is zero, and if it is we print an error message.

In performing the tests numerical values are taken, so if we define three shell variables:

```
number=1
nombre='    1'
numero=00001
```

they will all compare equal with -eq. Any leading zeroes or spaces used in defining the values are ignored.

The Shell only deals with integers — if you try to give it

```
numone=1.0
numtwo=1.3
```

these will also compare equal to each other, and they will be equal to the three numbers above.

Negative values are accommodated. Suppose we have a shell file:

```
$ cat  posneg
if test $1 -ge 0
then echo "argument is positive"
else echo "argument is negative"
fi
$ posneg  2300
argument is positive
$ posneg -871
argument is negative
$
```

Negative values are frequently obtained after performing arithmetic on shell variables using the expr command, described later in this chapter.

Tests on File Types These tests are concerned with the existence or otherwise of files, and the properties of files. The general layout of the expression to test these things is:

<primitive> *filename*

The most common primitives which are used in this type of test are:

- `-s` check that the file exists and is not empty
- `-f` check that the file is an ordinary file (not a directory)
- `-d` check whether the file is really a directory
- `-w` check that the file is writeable
- `-r` check that the file is readable

In an example in the previous paragraph, we compared the number of files in the current directory against the number of files in a specified directory. Suppose that the name we were given was not a directory? We would get an incorrect answer, since the output of `wc` would be one line, an error message. But we're only counting lines, not reading them. So we should check that the name we are given is that of a directory:

```
this=`ls | wc -l`
if test -d $1
then that=`ls $1 | wc -l`
else echo "$1: not a directory"
fi
if test $this -ne $that
then echo "current directory and $1 do not match"
fi
```

The check for a name being a directory implies that it exists. If there is nothing existing with the specified name, then it cannot be a directory. Although we have the appropriate test in the procedure, we still go ahead and assign values of the shell variables. Really, we need to reorganize the file:

```
if test -d $1
then that=`ls $1 | wc -l`
     this=`ls | wc -l`
     if test $this -ne $that
     then echo "current directory and $1 do not match"
     fi
else echo "$1: not a directory"
fi
```

This is another example of one `if` statement nested within another `if` statement. Notice that each `if` has its corresponding `fi`.

In practice, it is often easier to deal with all the error (or abnormal) conditions first, then proceed to the details of what to do if all is well. Here, this means testing to see whether the argument given is *not* a directory. To do this you use the exclamation mark (!) which is the *unary negation operator*:

```
if test ! -d $1
then echo "$1: not a directory"
else that=`ls $1 | wc -l`
     this=`ls | wc -l`
     if test $this -ne $that
     then echo "current directory and $1 do not match"
     fi
fi
```

The ! operator inverts the sense of the `-d` primitive; the value returned by the `test` command is zero (true) if the specified name is not a directory. The operator ! and the primitive `-d` are separate arguments to the `test` command, so there are spaces between them.

Perhaps the most useful thing to test about a file is its mere existence. The `-s` primitive checks this, and it even checks that the file has something in it, that it is not a zero-length file. We have used `-s` in our `makelist` command:

```
if   test $# -eq 0
then  echo "you must give a filename" >&2
elif  test ! -s $1
then  echo "no file $1" >&2
else  sort  +1 -2  $1 | tr  ..... etc
fi
```

We have used `-s` in conjunction with the ! operator. What this means is NOT(the file exists AND has non-zero length), which translates to 'if the file does not exist, or has zero length'. We used this rather awkward construct in order to be able to deal with all error conditions first.

Tests on Character Strings These tests operate on character strings, they can be subdivided into tests which compare character strings, and tests for the existence of a character string.

For character string comparisons, the form of the expression is:

S <primitive> *R*

and there are two primitives that can be used:

= test that the strings are equal

!= test that the strings are not equal

The primitive != is a single argument to the `test` command — there is no space between the ! and the = signs.

Because we are comparing character strings, not numerical values, two variables defined like this:

```
number=1
numero=00001
```

will not compare equal. If we have another variable defined:

```
nombre='     1'
```

it will never compare equal with '00001'. Whether or not it compares with '1' depends on how the test is set up. If you just say:

```
test  $number = $nombre
```

the strings will compare equal, because the spaces in the variable `nombre` get absorbed into the spaces between the arguments of `test`. If you want to preserve spaces in the strings, you must surround the strings in quotes:

```
test  "$number" = "$nombre"
```

In this case the strings will not be equal.

Here are a couple of examples of using these:

```
if test "$1" = ""
then echo "you must give a filename"
else sort ..... etc
fi
```

This is a different way to check for the presence of an argument. We test to see if the argument compares with the null string.

The next example shows how you can restrict a shell file so that only one particular user can execute it, regardless of whether other people have execute permission on the shell file.

```
if test $LOGNAME != maryann
then echo this command is restricted to maryann
     exit
else ........
fi
```

The `test` command has other expressions to test for the presence or absence of a string. The format of these expressions is:

<primitive> *S*

and the primitives available are:

-z check if the string *S* has zero length

-n check if the string *S* has non-zero length

The presence of a string can also be tested by the simple command:

```
test S
```

So now we have several more ways to test for the presence of an argument:

```
if test -z "$1"
then echo "you must give a filename"
else .......
fi
```

checks whether the (presumed) first argument is a zero length string,

```
if test ! -n "$1"
then echo "you must give a filename"
else .......
fi
```

checks for NOT (non-zero length) string, and

```
if test ! "$1"
then echo "you must give a filename"
else .......
fi
```

tests for NOT (string is present).

In general, when dealing with character strings, it is best to enclose the strings in quotes. It is especially important to do so in the case where you are using a shell variable which might be a null string. If you leave out the quotes you get an error message from the Shell:

```
$ cat testarg
if test ! -n $1
then echo no argument
else echo argument is $1
fi
$ testarg
testarg: test: argument expected
```

This is because, after the value of the first argument has been substituted for `$1`, the `test` command reads:

```
test ! -n
```

which is an incomplete command.

For the most part, you will probably need double quotes, rather than apostrophes. This is because substitution for shell variables doesn't take place inside single quotes. So if you have two variables:

```
fruit=apple
pie=apple
```

the command

```
test "$fruit" = "$pie"
```

will compare the strings 'apple' and 'apple', which are equal, whereas

```
test '$fruit' = '$pie'
```

compares the strings '$fruit' and '$pie', which are not equal.

Combining tests, the Operators -a and -o There are two operators, `-o` and `-a`, for combining several test expressions on a single `test` command. The `-a` stands for a logical 'and', the result of the test is true only if both expressions are true. The `-o` stands for logical 'or'; the result of the test is true if either expression is true.

For example, suppose we have a shell procedure `append`, which is invoked:

```
$ append thisfile thatfile
$
```

and has the effect of adding *thisfile* onto the end of *thatfile*. We can combine suitable checks for read and write permissions in one `if` statement:

```
if test -w $2 -a -r $1
then cat $1 >> $2
else echo cannot append
fi
```

From the user's point of view, this is not so good as doing the tests separately. We only produce one error message for two different conditions. By doing testing each condition on its own, like this:

```
if test ! -w $2
then echo $2 not writable
else if test ! -r $1
     then echo $1 not readable
     else cat $1 >> $2
     fi
fi
```

we can give the user explicit reasons why something isn't working

Combining if and for Statements

Our makelist shell procedure, with all the checks for arguments and existence of files, still only copes with a single file. What we really need to do is put these tests into the version that loops around, doing its thing for each given argument.

The check for existence of the file can be put inside the for loop:

```
for file
do if test ! -s $file
   then echo "no file $file" >&2
   else sort +1 -2 $file .......
   fi
done
```

This illustrates another exception to the rule that if must be the first thing on a line: if is recognized following do.

Now that we can deal with more than one file, it is important that we are using the else statement, and not using exit when we find that there is no file of the given name. Consider a shell file that looks like this:

```
for file
do if test ! -s $file
   then echo "no file $file" >&2
        exit
   fi
sort $file ......
done
```

If we gave it ten filenames, and the third one was wrong, the remaining seven would be ignored. By using else and leaving out the exit, we make our command do as much work as it can.

If we call up this shell file without giving it any filenames, it does nothing, and you just get your prompt back straight away. If we had arranged that the output of the command was to the Standard Output, it would be obvious that something was wrong. But we have piped the output to the line printer from within the shell, so we have no indication that anything is amiss. We still need a check for the presence of an argument:

```
if test $# -eq 0
then echo "Usage: $0 file ....." >&2
     exit
fi
for file
do if test !-s $file
   then echo "no file $file" >&2
   else sort $file ......
   fi
done
```

This test goes before the `for` loop, and if there are no arguments we exit the procedure immediately.

Notice that we have changed the error message from what it was when we could only cope with one file. The new message gives a synopsis of how the command should be used, just as it would appear in an entry of the *System V User's Manual* under the SYNOPSIS heading. Notice too that we have used `$0` for the command name. If we decide to call our shell file something else, we don't have to change the text of that message.

Looping with the `while` statement

We have used the `for` statement to make our shell procedure `makelist` work on more than one file. There is another way we could do this, and that is by using the `while` statement.

`while` provides another method of looping around, executing various commands. The difference between it and `for` is that whereas you give `for` a list of things that have to have certain actions performed on them, `while` performs certain actions while a specified condition pertains:

> **`while`** *this command is successful*
> **`do`** *all these*
> *commands up to*
> *the following* '**`done`**'.
> **`done`**

As is the case with the `if` statement, the most common command to use with `while` is `test`, but it could be any command.

Another statement often used in conjunction with `while` is `shift`. Effectively what this does is throw away the first argument `$1`, and renumber all the following arguments. So what was `$2` now becomes `$1`, what was `$3` gets to be `$2`, and so on down the line. The total number of arguments, `$#`, is reduced by one.

So we can rewrite our shell file using these two statements:

```
if test $# -eq 0
then echo "Usage: $0 file ....." >&2
     exit
fi
while test $# -gt 0
do  if test ! -s $1
    then echo "no file $1" >&2
    else sort +1 -2 $1 | tr -d  ......
    fi
    shift
done
```

As long as there are some arguments, as tested by `$#` being greater than zero, the commands between `do` and `done` are executed. One of those commands is `shift`, which renumbers the arguments, and decrements `$#`. When `$#` gets down to zero, the loop terminates and we carry on executing the commands after `done`. In this case there aren't any, and the end of the loop is also the end of the procedure.

Altering loop execution with `break` and `continue`

The `break` and `continue` statements can be used to break out of a `while` or `for` loop unconditionally.

Strictly speaking, `continue` does not break out of the loop — it causes the rest of the commands in the loop to be ignored for this iteration, and starts back at the beginning of the loop for another iteration.

As an example of using this, remember our shell procedure that looks like this:

```
for file
do if test ! -s $file
   then echo "no file $file" >&2
        exit
   fi
sort $file .......
done
```

We noted that if we gave it ten filenames, and the third one was wrong, the remaining seven would be ignored. We got round this by using `else` and leaving out the `exit`. We could have used `continue` instead as we show in the next example.

If there is no file of a given name, we ignore the rest of the `for` loop for this iteration, and continue with the next iteration.

```
for file
do if test ! -s $file
   then echo "no file $file" >&2
        continue
   fi
sort $file .......
done
```

`continue` could also be used in our `while` loop:

```
if test $# -eq 0
then echo "Usage: $0 file ......" >&2
     exit
fi
while test $# -gt 0
do   if test ! -s $1
     then echo "no file $1" >&2
          shift
          continue
     fi
     sort +1 -2 $1 | tr  ..........
     shift
done
```

This time we shift the arguments before continuing, to move on to the next file.

The `break` statement breaks out of the loop entirely. In all our examples we have only had one loop, so a `break` would take us right out of the procedure in the same way as `exit` does.

But if you have a situation where you have one loop inside another, break can be useful:

```
while test1
do
     <some commands>
     while test2
     do
          <some commands>
          break
          <more commands>
     done
     <more commands>
done
```

The `break` statement breaks out of the loop `while test2` and resumes iteration of the loop `while test1`

The `until` statement

`until` is very much like `while`, but it inverts the test of loop termination. Whereas `while` keeps going until the test returns a false answer (that is, it loops while the condition is true), `until` finishes looping as soon as it gets a true value.

So we could invert the loop in our `makelist` command:

```
if test $# -eq 0
then echo "Usage: $0 file ....." >&2
     exit
fi
until test $# -eq 0
do   if test ! -s $1
     then echo "no file $1" >&2
     else sort +1 -2 $1 | tr -d .........
     fi
     shift
done
```

By using `until` instead of `while` we change the test condition from 'still some arguments left' to 'no more arguments left'.

The `true` and `false` commands

Two simple commands that can sometimes be useful are `true` and `false`. As their names imply, `true` always returns a true (zero) value, and `false` always returns a false (non-zero) value.

They can be used to make 'do forever' loops. For instance, the procedure:

```
while true
do
    sleep 300
    lpstat
done
```

will execute, displaying the line printer status every 5 minutes, for ever — or until it is interrupted by the user hitting the **BREAK** key, or the system crashes.

We could also have used `until`:

```
until false
do
    sleep 300
    lpstat
done
```

The sleep command that we used in the above examples provides a way of marking time. It simply does nothing for the specified period of time, which is expressed in seconds.

Selective Execution using the case statement

Let's get fancy and expand our command to include some options. Let's introduce one option -t (together), such that if we use this option all the files we specify are sorted and merged together to produce a single distribution list. If we don't use the -t option each file is printed as a separate list. The -t option must be specified before any file names, as is usual on System V commands.

Obviously, we now have to examine the first argument to makelist to see whether it is '-t' or not. We could do this with an if statement, but a more general way to match patterns like this is using the case statement:

```
if test $# -eq 0
then echo "Usage: $0 [-t] file ....." >&2
     exit
fi
together=no
case $1 in
    -t) together=yes
        shift;;
    -?) echo "$0: no option $1"
        exit;;
esac
if test $together = yes
then sort -u +1 -2 $* | tr .......
else while test $# -gt 0
     do   if test ! -s $1
          then echo "no file $1" >&2
          else sort +1 -2 $1 | tr ......
          fi
          shift
     done
fi
```

We start off in the usual fashion, with a test for no arguments. Then we have a shell variable called together, which is used as a flag to indicate what to do when we get to the sort. If the together variable is set to 'yes' all files will be sorted and merged together to produce the list, otherwise they will be listed separately. So we first set the together variable to its default value of 'no'.

Then we have the case statement. The general layout of a case statement is:

```
case string in
string_1) if 'string' is the same as 'string_1'
        then execute all these commands up until
        ';;', ignore the rest of the cases ;;
string_2) if 'string' is the same as 'string_2'
        then execute all these commands up until
        ';;', ignore the rest of the cases ;;

string_3)  ...... etc....

esac
```

Basically, we have a list of strings that we want to check against, and a list of actions to be performed if we find a match. The end of each string to be checked is indicated by `)`, and the end of each action to be taken, or set of commands to be executed, is indicated by double semicolons `;;`. The end of all the strings is indicated by the keyword `esac`. You can make use of the Shell's pattern-matching capabilities using the metacharacters `?`, `*`, and `[-]`.

In our case, we want to check the string that is the first argument to the call on `makelist` to see if it matches '`-t`'. If it does we set the shell variable `together` to 'yes'.

If the first argument is a minus sign followed by any single character other than the letter '`t`', it matches the the '`-?`' pattern, in which case we give an error message, and exit from the procedure.

The order in which we give the patterns that we want to match is important. The first pattern in the list that matches the string governs the action to be taken. If we had put the '`-?`' pattern before the '`-t`', we would always produce the error message, since '`-t`' matches the specification of minus sign followed by any other character.

After we have decided whether we have the `-t` option and set the flag accordingly, we then examine that flag. If it is set to 'yes', we simply use the notation `$*` to pass all the remaining arguments to a single `sort` command. We add the `-u` option to `sort` to make sure that the same name doesn't appear on the list twice. If the flag is set to 'no' we process each file separately in the usual fashion.

This may seem a clumsy way of doing things. We could have checked for the first argument being '`-t`' in the `if` statement, instead of going through all the palaver of setting flags. The reason for using `case` is that we have built a framework in which it is easy to add other options simply by adding another pattern to the list.

Let's add a `-m` (multi-column) option to our shell file.. If the `-m` option is used, instead of the names being listed in a single column, they will be listed in three columns. So we have to add an option to `pr` to produce multi-column output. We will define another shell variable, `cols` which is set to a null string by default, or is set to '`-3`' if `makelist` is called with the `-m` option.

Actually, going from one option to more than one is not quite so simple. Unless we constrain the options to be in a certain order, which would be very awkward for the user, we have to bring our `case` statement inside the `while` loop:

```
if test $# -eq 0
then echo "Usage: $0 [-t] [-m] file ....." >&2
     exit
fi
together=no
cols=""
while test $# -gt 0
do case $1 in
     -t) together=yes
         shift;;
     -m) cols="-3"
         shift;;
     -?) echo "$0: no option $1"
         exit;;
      *) if test $together = yes
         then sort -u +1 -2 $* | tr -d "[0-9]" | pr $cols -h .....
              exit
         else if test ! -s $1
              then echo "no file $1" >&2
              else sort +1 -2 $1 | tr -d "[0-9]" | pr $cols -h .....
              fi
              shift
         fi;;
   esac
done
```

We have four cases. The first two are the options `-t` and `-m`; the next is any other (unknown) option; the last case is anything else (indicated by the `*` pattern), which is taken to be a filename and treated accordingly.

Because the `sort` command that sorts and merges all files together is inside the while loop now, we have to add an `exit` statement to prevent that command being done over and over again.

Using */tmp* Space

The shell file is now arranged such that it is very easy to add more options, simply by adding them to the list of patterns in the `case` statement.

For instance, we could change the command to produce its output on the Standard Output, unless the `-p` (print) option was given. In order to do this, instead of having the `lp` command as the last command on our `sort` pipeline, we put the output into a temporary file. If `-p` is specified we route the file to the printer, otherwise we simply display the file on the Standard Output.

We could use a temporary file in the current directory, but there is nothing so far in `makelist` that implies the user needs write permission on the current directory. It would be a pity to spoil this state of affairs. There is a special directory, */tmp*, that is available for creating temporary files. The */tmp* directory is writeable by everybody.

The new version of `makelist` is shown in figure 13.2 on the next page.

We set up another shell variable, `print`, as a flag with a default value of 'no'. We add another case to change this value to 'yes' if `makelist` is called with the `-p` option.

The biggest change is in the area of the `sort` command pipeline. Instead of finishing up the pipeline with `lp`, we leave the `pr` command as the last one in the pipe, and redirect the output of the line to the temporary file '*$0$$*' in the directory */tmp*. There is good reason for this apparently obscure filename. Since the */tmp* directory is open for everybody to create files, it is a good idea if each file has a unique name, otherwise users could overwrite each other's files. The Shell variable `$$` translates into the process identity number of the current command, which number is unique to that process. So we could have two different users executing `makelist` without them overwriting each other's temporary files, because the filenames are different. Of course, eventually the same process ID number will be allocated to another process, but by that time you will have finished with your files.

To further identify the file we have also used the command name `$0`, so the names of the files that are actually created in */tmp* are something like *makelist1354*. It is not really necessary to use the name of the command as part of the name of the temporary file. However, it is sometimes useful to be able to connect */tmp* files with the commands that create them. For example, when debugging the shell procedure you might want to examine the files created. You don't always know the process ID number, but you do know the name of the command you are debugging, so you can find the relevant files from it.

After executing the `sort` command pipeline we examine the `print` flag, and either `cat` the temporary file, or route it to the line printer. Then we *remove the temporary file*. This is important. There is usually not much space allocated for */tmp*, and there may be lots of users creating lots of files in the directory. If these files are not removed as soon as they are done with, it is very easy to gobble up the entire */tmp* space allocation, and then commands won't work properly because they can't create the files they want. Although the System Administrator can run a program which removes all old temporary files, and probably does on a regular basis, it is much better to keep */tmp* space clean.

However, we will be in trouble if we remove the file before it has been printed. So that we can remove the */tmp* file with impunity, we use the `-c` option on `lp`, so that the line printer spooler makes its own copy of the file, which it removes when it has finished.

```
# this command takes file(s) containing names and phone numbers
# the numbers are removed and the names are printed with a heading
# Options are:
# -t  sort and merge all files together
# -p  route file to printer
# -m  print names in multi-column (3 columns)

if test $# -eq 0
then echo "Usage: $0 [-t] [-m] [-p] file ....." >&2
     exit
fi
together=no
cols=""
print=no
while test $# -gt 0
do case $1 in
     -t) together=yes
         shift;;
     -m) cols="-3"
         shift;;
     -p) print=yes
         shift;;
     -?) echo "$0: no option $1"
         exit;;
      *) if test $together = yes
         then sort -u +1 -2 $* | tr ......... > /tmp/$0$$
              if test $print = no
              then cat /tmp/$0$$
              else lp -c /tmp/$0$$
              fi
              rm /tmp/$0$$
              exit
         else if test ! -s $1
              then echo "no file $1" >&2
              else sort +1 -2 $1 | tr .......... > /tmp/$0$$
                   if test $print = no
                   then cat /tmp/$0$$
                   else lp -c /tmp/$0$$
                   fi
                   rm /tmp/$0$$
              fi
              shift
         fi;;
    esac
done
```

Figure 13.2 Final Version of `makelist`

Comments in Shell Programs

In our last example, you will notice that we have added some lines at the front explaining what the command does. This sort of commentary is very useful for someone who has to read the shell file and figure out what it does.

The # character is used to introduce comments. Although we have used comments that occupy an entire line, it doesn't have to be that way. A comment can also be put at the end of a line of commands. However, a comment can't be put at the beginning, or in the middle, of a command line. This is because the Shell, when it sees a # following a space, throws it away, and also throws away all following characters up to the next newline.

Dealing with Interrupts

Suppose you give the `makelist` command, then change your mind for some reason, and interrupt it by hitting **BREAK** or **RUBOUT** or **DEL**. An interrupt signal is sent to the process (that is, the `makelist` command) and it just stops whatever it was doing and terminates immediately. Now if it had already created some temporary files, but not yet removed them, those temporary files are going to be left lying around forever more (or until the System Administrator cleans up */tmp* space). It would be nice if we could make the procedure tidy up after itself, even if it was interrupted.

There is a `trap` statement which helps you do this. You specify a command that is to be executed when a given signal is received. The layout of the statement is:

`trap` *'command arguments' signal* .....

The command and its arguments must form a single argument to `trap`, hence the quotes. If you want to execute more than one command, they can be separated by *;* characters.

The signal is specified in terms of a number, and more than one can be given. For the most part you are only likely to be concerned with signal number 2, which is what you get when you interrupt a process, or signal number 1, which you get if you hang up (disconnect from the system) while you are in the middle of a process.

To give an example of `trap`, let's arrange that `makelist` will clear out any temporary files that it has created if it gets interrupted. Figure 13.3 on the next page shows an example.

As soon as we get into the loop where we are creating temporary files, we put in a `trap` statement which catches interrupts and hangups. If either of these occur, we remove all temporary files and exit.

```
if test $# -eq 0
then echo "Usage: $0 [-t] [-m] [-p] file ....." >&2
     exit
fi
together=no
cols=""
print=no
while test $# -gt 0
do case $1 in
    -t) together=yes
        shift;;
    -m) cols="-3"
        shift;;
    -p) print=yes
        shift;;
    -?) echo "$0: no option $1
        exit;;
     *) trap 'rm /tmp/$0$$; exit' 2 1
        if test $together = yes
             <etcetera . . .>
```

Figure 13.3 Clearing Temporary Files Using `trap`

Because there is a possibility that there might not actually be any temporary file in existence at the moment we receive the signal, the `trap` statement should really look like this:

```
trap 'rm /tmp/$0$$ 2>/dev/null; exit' 2 1
```

If `rm` produces an error message saying that the file we are trying to remove does not exist, we don't really want to see it. `rm` writes that message to the Diagnostic Output, so we can get rid of it by redirecting the Diagnostic Output to the special device file */dev/null*. */dev/null* is the null device — anything written to it disappears completely.

Doing Arithmetic with `expr`

The `expr` command evaluates its arguments as an expression and writes the result on the Standard Output. There are various ways of using this command, but one of the more interesting ways is to perform arithmetic on shell variables. Here is a very simple example:

```
$ cat sum3
expr $1 + $2 + $3
$ chmod 755  sum3
$ sum3  13 49 2
64
$
```

We have a command which prints the sum of three numbers.

If you give it more than three numbers, all except the first three are ignored; if you give it fewer than three numbers, that is an error condition:

```
$ sum3  13 49 2 64 1
64
$ sum3 13 49
expr: syntax error
$
```

This is a pretty useless shell procedure, you would probably be better off using `expr` directly at your terminal:

```
$ expr 13 + 49 + 2 + 64 + 1
129
$ expr 13 + 49
62
$
```

The arithmetic operators that you can specify to `expr` are:

+	addition
-	subtraction
*	multiplication
/	division
%	remainder

Each operator, and each value to be operated on, forms a separate argument to `expr` so there are spaces between everything.

Let's look at a more complex example. In chapter 12 we showed how to use `awk` to calculate the average score of the players in the tennis league, from the file *tennis*. Here is a shell procedure that calculates the average using `expr`:

```
$ cat avscore
num=`wc -l < $1`
tot=0
count=$num
while test $count -gt 0
do score=`sed -n ${count}p $1 | tr -dc '[0-9]'`
   tot=`expr $tot + $score`
   count=`expr $count - 1`
done
avint=`expr $tot / $num`
avdec=`expr $tot % $num \* 100`
echo Average score is $avint.$avdec
$ avscore tennis
Average score is 8.900
$
```

This example uses all the operators. The first thing we do is count the number of lines in the file, and allocate this number to the variable `num`. In counting the lines, we have to use the standard input to get only a numerical value. If we simply said '`wc -l $1`' the value allocated to `num` would be the string '`10 tennis`' because `wc` repeats the filename. Then we define two more variables: `tot` is to hold the total of all scores, it is initialized to zero; `count` will count round the loop that follows, it starts off equal to the number of lines.

Then we have a loop which, for each line in the file, sets the variable `score` equal to the output of the command pipeline:

```
sed -n ${count}p $1 | tr -dc '[0-9]'
```

The output of the stream editor `sed` is the `count`'th line, and only that line. The `tr` command takes that line and deletes everything except digits. The value of `score` is then added to the total `tot`, and `count` is decremented. The loop is repeated until all lines in the file have been processed.

The final stage is to divide the total score by the number of lines, giving `avint`. Shell variables can only deal with integers, so the result is rounded down to the nearest whole number. In order to get some decimal places, we use the remainder operator, `%`, and the multiply operator `*`.

The important thing about the multiply operator is that the character `*` has a special meaning to the Shell. So when you use it, you get an error message:

```
$ expr 2 * 3
syntax error
$
```

When you use * as an argument to expr you must escape it, to prevent the Shell trying to expand it to match all file names. There are several ways we can escape *:

```
$ expr 2 \* 3
6
$ expr 2 "*" 3
6
$ expr 2 '*' 3
6
$
```

In the avscore shell procedure we used the first of the above methods.

There are other things you can do with the expr command. You can compare numeric values; you can also compare character strings, or see if a character string matches a regular expression. All these things produce output on the Standard Output, so they can be used to set shell variables which are to be used as flags. If expr is used in conjunction with the if statement, you will probably want to throw away the normal output of expr. For example:

```
if expr "$1" : "-."  >/dev/null
then echo argument is an option
else echo argument is not an option
fi
```

finds out whether the first argument is a character preceded with a minus sign. If it does it is assumed to be an option on the command. If we didn't redirect the output to */dev/null* in the expr command, then 0 or 1 (or whatever value is returned by expr) would appear on the output, as well as the message.

Note that for matching character strings, expr uses regular expressions like ed, grep, *et al*, instead of the Shell's pattern-matching metacharacters.

Details of the these expressions are documented under the expr command, in the *System V User's Manual*.

Here Documents

Very early in this chapter we showed a simple shell file, the original version of makelist:

```
sort +1 -2 people | tr -d "[0-9]" | pr -h Distribution | lp
```

and we pointed out that this would only work on one specific file of names.

When we have more than one *people* file to make lists for, one way of doing it is to have a shell file for each file of names. This doubles the number of files you require because for each file of names (data file), you have an equivalent command file: *adminpeople* and `makealist`, and so on. An alternative solution is to combine the commands and the data into a single file. If we combine the *softpeople* file together with the commands necessary to print it as a distribution list, the resulting file looks like this:

```
sort +1 -2 << ! | tr -d "[0-9]" | pr -h Distribution | lp
Sylvia Dawson    110
Sally Smith      113
Steve Daniels    111
Henry Morgan     112
Hank Parker      114
!
```

The notation **<< !** is the important part of the example. The << says 'take all the rest of this file, up to a line consisting of the argument following <<, to be the input of this command'. In our case, the argument following << is the single character `!`. So all lines, up to the line `!`, become the input to the `sort` command.

This feature, where the data can be held along with the commands, is called a *here document*.

There are several different reasons why you might want to use a 'here document'. One is that you might have a very long message to give the user, so instead of using several `echo` commands:

```
if test ! -s $1
then cat << end
     You nincompoop !! You have given an invalid filename.
     Check the spelling of the files in your directory.
     Then check that you are in the correct directory.
     When you know what you are doing, try again!!
end
else cat $1
```

In this case, all of the lines of the shell file, up to the line consisting of the word 'end', form the input to the `cat` command, and thus are displayed on the Standard Output.

The word 'end' must be at the start of the line, even if you indent the text that forms the here document. You would normally indent this text for clarity of reading your shell file, unfortunately the tabs you use to indent are copied to the output. You can stop tabs in the here document being processed by using the notation

```
cat <<- end
```

In this case the word 'end' can also be indented.

You could also use a here document to call up an inte
within a shell procedure. Suppose we have a shell file:

```
troff -mm $1 | lp
mail $LOGNAME << +
Your format of $1 is complete.
It has been routed to the printer.
+
```

You can put this command in the background to format you
you will get mail. Substitution of shell variables takes place
document. If you don't want values substituted, you can p
reverse slash (\ ) between the << and the following character.

13.7. User Input to Shell Procedures

In this section discuss two situations. One is where you are calling up an interactive program, such as a text editor, from within a shell procedure. In this case you want to ensure that the user input to the shell procedure gets passed on to the program you are calling.

The other situation is where you are writing a shell procedure which is itself an interactive process. You want to prompt the user for some input, then read that input for processing.

Passing the Standard Input

The Standard Input can be passed on to an interactive program called up in a shell procedure by using the notation `<&0`. For example, back in chapter 8 — *The* **ex** *and* **ed** *Line Editors* — we talked about making a shell procedure to call the `ed` editor with a prompt. Such a shell procedure might look like this:

```
$ cat myed
ed -p '*' $* <&0
$
```

The `$*` passes all the arguments to `myed` on to `ed`. Since `ed` only takes one filename, we could in this case have just said `$1`. The `<&0` ensures that user input to `myed` also gets passed on to `ed`.

Mostly this isn't necessary, the Standard Input gets passed on to the called program without specifying the `<&0`. But, even with System V, there are different versions around and some older ones don't behave very nicely. If you leave the `<&0` out of your shell file:

```
$ cat myed
ed -p '*' $1
$
```

and you get this response when you try to use it:

```
$ myed somefile
1439
* 1,$p
```

where your input is totally ignored, then you probably need to change your `myed` procedure to look like the one we showed in the first example.

We also talked earlier, in chapter 6, about writing a shell procedure to display a file one screen-full at a time using the `pr` command. Although `pr` is not usually an interactive command, when you use the `-p` option it waits for you to type RETURN before proceeding.

A shell procedure to use this feature would look something like this:

```
$ cat pag
pr -tpl21 $* <&0
$
```

Remember that these commands should be placed in a directory that is in your command search path as defined by the $PATH variable.

Writing interactive shell procedures with `read`

Sometimes you want to write a shell procedure that can take some input from the user, and act upon it. This can be achieved using the `read` statement, which takes in one line of user input and assigns that value to a variable.

A simple, but not very useful example would be:

```
$ cat parrot
echo "You say: \c"
read what
echo "I repeat: $what"
$
```

The variable `what` is defined by its presence on the `read` statement, the value it is assigned is determined by what the user types in.

When this procedure was called you would see:

```
$ parrot
You say: have a nice day
I repeat: have a nice day
$
```

More than one variable can be defined one the `read` statement. In this case the first variable is assigned the value of the first word of the input, the second variable is assigned the value of the second word, and so on. A word is any string of character surrounded by spaces or tabs. For example, suppose we have a shell procedure, called `newhire`, that adds a line to a list of employees:

```
echo "Enter department extension lastname firstname"
read dept ext last first
echo "First name: $first\nLast name: $last"
echo "$last, $first\t$dept\t$ext" >> employees
echo "Employee added to list"
```

When you use the procedure, the 'conversation' would look like this:

```
$ newhire
Enter department extension lastname firstname
widget 115 Chan Philip
First name: Philip
Last name: Chan
Employee added to list
$
```

If there are more words on the input line that there are variables defined, then all the leftover words are assigned to the last defined variable. This is illustrated by another call to our `newhire` procedure:

```
$ newhire
Enter department extension lastname firstname
blivet 153 Campbell Bruce Hamish Alexander
First name: Bruce Hamish Alexander
Last name: Campbell
Employee added to list
$
```

The above are really 'toy' examples, let's see how this feature of the Shell can be put to a more practical purpose. In chapter 14 — *Programming Tools in System V* — you will see that to put several programs under SCCS takes a lot of typing.

Each admin command line is quite long, the only thing that is different is the filename, and that has to be typed twice in each line.

We could design a shell procedure, called say putwidget, that would be used to put source code (or documents) into the widget project's library of SCCS files. The *putwidget* shell file could look like this:

```
echo "Enter filenames, one per line\n"
while true
do
     echo "? \c"
     read line                          # get another filename
     if test "$line" = ""
     then exit                          # finish if blank line
     fi
     if test ! -s $line                 # check if file exists
     then echo no file $line
     else admin -fi -i$line /aa/widget/srclib/s.$line
     fi
done
```

First we tell people that they are to enter each filename on a separate line. Then we prompt them for input using the question mark, ?. Whatever they type, presumably a filename, is the value assigned to the line variable.

Then we check to see if the line was empty, and if it was we exit from the procedure. Otherwise we check that the file exist and, if it does, we use the admin command to put it in the SCCS library.

So this procedure takes filenames, one per line, and for each valid file puts it in the library. When a blank line is typed you exit form the procedure.

In practice it is not a good idea to use a blank line as the criterion for termination of the procedure. It is too easy to type a **RETURN** twice by accident, and it can be frustrating for the user to have to re-enter the command. Our next version of putwidget ignores blank lines — if you type one you simply get re-prompted. We use the fairly common convention of a **dot** on a line of its own as the indication that the user is finished.

The new version of putwidget appears on the next page.

```
echo "Enter filenames, one per line\n"
while true
do
     echo "? \c"
     read line                          # get another filename
     if test "$line" = "."
     then exit                          # finish if dot
     fi
     if test "$line" != ""              # ignore blank lines
     then if test ! -s $line            # check if file exists
          then echo no file $line
          else admin -fi -i$line /aa/widget/srclib/s.$line
          fi
     fi
done
```

What if the user doesn't follow the rules, and enters more than one filename per line? Well, we could put in a test for that and reprimand her:

```
echo "Enter filenames, one per line\n"
while true
do
     echo "? \c"
     read line                          # get another filename
     if test "$line" = "."
     then exit                          # finish if dot
     fi
     if test "$line" = ""               # ignore blank lines
     then continue
     fi
     if echo $line | grep " " >/dev/null  # see if any spaces
     then echo "only one filename per line, please"
          continue
     else if test ! -s $line            # check if file exists
          then echo no file $line
          else admin -fi -i$line /aa/widget/srclib/s.$line
          fi
     fi
done
```

This makes use of the fact that `grep` returns a true (zero) value if it finds a match, and a false (non-zero) value if no matches are found. In our case a match is an error, so we use `continue` to bypass the `admin` command and re-prompt for a filename.

It really would be better if our command could accept multiple filenames on a line, and process them properly. At this point it is tempting to define several variables (`file1`, ,`file2`.... *etcetera*) on the `read` statement. But the question is — how many files should you allow for? If we think about using a `for` loop to process the filenames it turns out to be unnecessary, we can write our shell procedure like this:

```
echo "Enter filenames\n"
while true
do
     echo "? \c"
     read line                              # get more filenames
     if test "$line" = "."
     then break                             # finish if dot
     fi
     if test "$line" = ""                   # ignore blank lines
     then continue
     fi
     for file in $line
     do
         if test ! -s $file                # check if file exists
             then echo no file $file
             else admin -fi -i$line /aa/widget/srclib/s.$file
         fi
     done
done
```

There are many improvements we could make to this procedure. For instance — we have assumed that all files will be in the working directory when the procedure is called, but what if the user enters a relative (or even a full) pathname? We need to use this pathname following the `-i` option, but when we create the SCCS file we only need the actual filename. There are several ways we can separate the filename from the rest of the path. One is using the `expr` command, or you could use `sed`, but probably the easiest way is to use the `basename` command — refer to your *System V User's Manual* for details.

Another sophistication we could add is to display the `help` message if the `admin` command fails for some reason. To do this we must find out if `admin` produces its error messages on the Standard Output or the Diagnostic Output. Then we must capture that output and extract the error code so that we can give it as an argument to `help`.

None of these possible improvements are concerned with the `read` statement that we are trying to illustrate in this section, so we leave it as an exercise for the reader to enhance our embryo 'front end' for the SCCS system.

13.8. Shell Functions

A function is similar in effect to a shell procedure — that is, you designate a set of System V commands to be executed when called up by a single name on a command line. But, whereas a shell procedure must be contained in a file having the name that you wish to use, a function can be simply defined to the Shell.

Use of functions instead of procedures is not really suitable for long lists of UNIX System V commands, but a function can be easily used in place of a simple shell procedure.

At the beginning of this chapter we talked about designing your own special version of `ls`, to always use the `-x` and `-F` options. This could have been defined with a function:

```
ls ()
{
/bin/ls -x -F $*
}
```

The first line shows the *name* of the function, followed by parenthesis, `()`. The lines between the curly braces, { and }, constitute the *body* of the function — the System V commands that are to be executed when the function is invoked. The opening curly brace, and the closing brace, must each be the first thing on a line to be recognized by the Shell as defining the body of the function.

We also talked about designing your own special version of the `ed` line editor, which always invoked the editor with a prompt. This could have been defined with a function:

```
ed()
{
ed -p '*' $* <&0
}
$
```

You can type these function definitions at your terminal, in response to the system prompt `$`. If you do this, you will get be prompted with the *secondary prompt string* — usually the symbol >. The conversation would look like this:

```
$ ed()
> {
> ed -p '*' $* <&0
> }
$
```

You automatically revert to the usual primary prompt string, `$`, after you have typed the closing } to terminate the definition of your function.

If you do it this way, the definitions of these functions only last for your login session, they disappear when you log out. So if you want to use these specialized commands on a permanent basis, the function definitions should be put in your login profile.

You can also use a shell function within a shell procedure. To give an example, let's look at a different version of the putwidget procedure that we introduced in the previous section:

```
nextfile()  # extract the next filename and remove from line
{
file=`echo $1`
shift
line=`echo $*`
}

echo "Enter filenames\n"
while true
do
     echo "? \c"
     read line                          # get more filenames
     if test "$line" = "."
     then break                         # finish if dot
     fi
     while test "$line" != ""
     do
          nextfile $line
          if test ! -s $file            # check if file exists
               then echo no file $file
               else admin -fi -i$file /aa/widget/srclib/s.$file
          fi
     done
done
```

The first thing we do is define a function, `nextfile`, which simply extracts the next filename from the line. The main body of the procedure starts, as previously, with a `while true` statement. Within this loop we have a second loop that calls the `nextfile` function until the line is empty.

13.9. Debugging Shell Procedures

As we saw in an earlier example of an improper `if` statement, the error messages produced by the `sh` command are very explicit, and are a great help in determining syntactical errors in a shell procedure.

However, there are other aids to help you check out shell procedures. One is a 'self-help' technique, where you use the `echo` command to print out messages to trace the path through the procedure. When the procedure is known to be correct, the `echo` commands are removed.

There are also arguments to the `sh` command that are helpful when you are checking out shell procedures.

The `-v` (verbose) option tells the Shell to print the commands before executing them. So if we use it on our shell file to compute the average score, what we see is:

```
$ sh -v avscore tennis
num=`wc -l < $1`
tot=0
count=$num
while test $count -gt 0
do score=`sed -n ${count}p $1 | tr -dc '[0-9]'`
   tot=`expr $tot + $score`
   count=`expr $count - 1`
done
avint=`expr $tot / $num`
avdec=`expr $tot % $num  100`
echo Average score is $avint.$avdec
8.900
$
```

This is just a listing of the shell file. Everything up until the `done` statement is printed, then there is a pause while the total is computed. Then the remainder of the shell file is printed, followed by the result.

An even better trace facility is the `-x` (execute) option. When this option is used each command is printed, with all variable substitution shown, as it is executed. The output of the trace through our command is shown in figure 13.4 on the next page.

Each command appears on a line flagged with a + at the beginning. The values of any variables used in the command are shown. After the command has been executed, the values of any variables affected are printed. This feature really lets you see what's going on in your procedure.

If there is the possibility that you could do some damage (destroy some important files, for instance) while you are debugging your shell procedure, you might want to use the `-n` option. The Shell reads the commands in the shell file, but does not execute them. You can use this in conjunction with the `-x` option.

```
$ sh -x avscore tennis
+ wc -l
num=     10
tot=0
count=     10
+ test 10 -gt 0
+ tr -dc [0-9]
+ sed -n 10p tennis
score=2
+ expr 0 + 2
tot=2
+ expr 10 - 1
count=9
+ test 9 -gt 0
      .
      .
< and so on round the loop >
      .
+ test 1 -gt 0
+ tr -dc [0-9]
+ sed -n 1p tennis
score=18
+ expr 71 + 18
tot=89
+ expr 1 - 1
count=0
+ test 0 -gt 0
+ expr 89 / 10
avint=8
+ expr 89 % 10 * 100
avdec=900
+ echo Average score is 8.900
$
```

Figure 13.4 Tracing A Shell Procedure

13.10. Summary

This chapter has shown you the most useful of the features provided by the System V Shell. There are many more things you can do with the Shell, but some of them are fairly obscure, and hard to see an application for. Try making up your own shell procedures for tasks that you routinely perform. Experiment with the different checks that can be made using the `test` command.

Most users are unlikely to write shell procedures as complex as the ones we have shown. But you can see that it is possible to design sophisticated tools for specialized tasks. People who are in the position of toolsmiths for particular projects need to be aware of all the Shell's capabilities.

Above all, the important thing when writing shell procedures is to be aware of the power of UNIX System V as a whole. Know what commands are available, and what they can be made to do for you.

Browse through the *System V User's Manual*, paying attention to the options available for each command. Many commands and options seem, when considered in terms of interacting with the system from a terminal, either useless or too complicated to use. But, when you look at these commands in terms of writing Shell procedures, they become transformed into wonderful tools. The stream editor, `sed`, is a good example of this transformation — for the 'professional' Shell script writer, a thorough knowledge of `sed` is a must.

Make good use of shell variables and pipelines; above all — use you ingenuity and don't forget to build on (and improve on) the work of others.

14 Programming Tools in System V

This chapter is an overview for those who need to write computer programs on UNIX System V. Here we discuss some of the tools that help in the task of developing software.

Because System V evolved (and is still evolving) in the environment of computer software development, many of the tools that form part of the system go towards assisting the program development process. System V provides a particularly rich environment for the development of computer programs and their associated documentation.

This chapter is not intended as a detailed coverage of all available programming tools and languages. But our experience has been that many people have trouble finding out just what is available on the system. So this chapter covers the major programming tools that are present on UNIX System V.

Topics discussed in this chapter are some of the programming languages available, the link-editor facilities for binding many object code files together into an executable program, and the archive utility for building libraries. We also talk about SCCS, the Source Code Control System.

14.1. The C Programming Language

When talking about programming on System V, C is the programming language that comes to mind most readily. The history of C and that of the UNIX system (any version) itself are intertwined to such a degree that you might almost say that C was invented for the purpose of writing UNIX.

There are of course languages other than C on System V. There is a FORTRAN 77 compiler called `f77`. There is also a Rational FORTRAN compiler, called `ratfor`.

Running the C Compiler

This is not intended as a tutorial on the C programming language. For an excellent introduction to C, read *The C Programming Language*, by Brian Kernighan and Dennis Ritchie. What we are trying to convey here is the environment in which you must work when using System V to write programs.

To write a C program you create a file, using your favorite text editor, into which you place the source code of the C program that you want to try out. Files containing C source text should have a suffix of *.c*.

In figure 14.1 we show an example of a small C program. It is called *roman.c*, and its purpose is to convert decimal numbers into Roman numerals. The decimal argument(s) must lie in the range between 1 and 9999. This example is not necessarily representative of optimum C programming style.

We don't show the actual process by which the file called *roman.c* was created. By now you should be familiar with at least one of the text editors. We just show the finished result.

To compile this C program, use the `cc` (C Compiler) command:

```
$ cc roman.c
$
```

If there are no errors in your program, the various phases of the compilation proceed without gratuitous chatter from the system.

Eventually, an executable version of this program appears in a file called *a.out* (assembler output).

In general, the executable version of a program always appears in a file called *a.out*. If you want the name to be different, you must indicate that fact to the compiler or link-editor. The compilation process makes the *a.out* file executable, so to run the program, it is sufficient to just type that filename:

```
$ a.out
Usage: roman decimal_number
$
```

In the examples to follow, however, we wish to show the runnable version of the program appearing in a file which has the same name as the source file, but minus the suffix.

To get your program into a file other than *a.out*, you can do one of two things. You can either change the name of the output file from *a.out* to *roman* (in this case) by using the `mv` command:

```
$ cc roman.c
$ mv a.out roman
$ ls -x
roman        roman.c
$
```

or you can use the `-o` (for output) option to the C compiler. Note that the option is a lowercase 'o' (the uppercase 'O' calls up the Optimizer).

```
#include  <stdio.h>
                        /*  Roman numeral conversion program  */
#define  ROWS         4
#define  COLS         4
int  pows [ROWS] [COLS] = { {1000, 1000, 1000, 1000},
                            { 900,  500,  400,  100},
                            {  90,   50,   40,   10},
                            {   9,    5,    4,    1} };
char  *roms [ROWS] [COLS] = { { "m", "m",  "m", "m"},
                            {"cm", "d", "cd", "c"},
                            {"xc", "l", "xl", "x"},
                            {"ix", "v", "iv", "i"} };
main (argc, argv)
    int  argc;          /*  Number of command line arguments  */
    char  *argv [];     /*  Pointers to command line arguments  */
{
    int  low;           /*  Starting number from command line  */
    int  high;          /*  Ending number from command line  */
    char  roman [25];   /*  Converted Roman number  */

    if (argc < 2) {
        fprintf (stderr, "Usage: roman  decimal_number\n");
        exit (0);
    }
    high = low = atoi (argv [1]);
    cheknum (low);
    if (argc > 2)  {
        high = atoi (argv [2]);
        cheknum (high);
        if (low  > high)  {
            fprintf (stderr, "low must be less than high\n");
            exit (0);
        }
    }  else
        low = 1;        /*  low side is 1 if only one argument  */
    for (;  low <= high;  low++)  {
        to_roman (low, roman);
        printf ("%d %s\n", low, roman);
    }
}
cheknum (value)
    int  value;
{
    if (value < 1 || value > 9999) {
        fprintf (stderr, "Use numbers in range 1 .. 9999\n");
        exit (0);
    }
}
to_roman (decimal, roman)
  int  decimal;
  char  roman [];
{
  int  rom_pos = 0;     /*  Current character position  */
  int  power;           /*  Current power of 10  */
  int  indx;            /*  Indexes through values to subtract  */
  roman [0] = '\0';
      for (power = 0;  power < ROWS;  power++)
          for (indx = 0;  indx < COLS;  indx++)
              while (decimal >= pows [power] [indx])  {
                  strcat (roman, roms [power] [indx]);
                  decimal -= pows [power] [indx];
              }
}
```

Figure 14.1 Roman Number Conversion Program

This example runs the C compiler just as before, but places the output code in a file called *roman*, and makes that file executable:

```
$ cc -o roman roman.c
$ ls -x
roman        roman.c
$
```

Now, to run this program, you can just use the file name as the command name, `roman`:

```
$ roman
Usage: roman  decimal_number
$ roman 0
Use numbers in the range 1 .. 9999
$ roman 100 10
low must be less than or equal to high
$ roman 10
1 i
2 ii
3 iii
4 iv
5 v
6 vi
7 vii
8 viii
9 ix
10 x
$ roman  7654  7664
7654 mmmmmmmdcliv
7655 mmmmmmmdclv
7656 mmmmmmmdclvi
7657 mmmmmmmdclvii
7658 mmmmmmmdclviii
7659 mmmmmmmdclix
7660 mmmmmmmdclx
7661 mmmmmmmdclxi
7662 mmmmmmmdclxii
7663 mmmmmmmdclxiii
7664 mmmmmmmdclxiv
$
```

These examples show a program that compiles without any errors. In reality, the first time you try to compile a new program you will probably get some error messages from the compiler. Unlike many compilers, the System V C compiler does not stop at the first error, it keeps going as long as it can. To illustrate this we will do something drastic:

```
$ sed "s/;//g" roman.c >dudprog.c
$ cc dudprog.c
"dudprog.c", line 12: syntax error
"dudprog.c", line 12: warning: old-fashioned initialization: use =
"dudprog.c", line 12: warning: undeclared initializer name roms
"dudprog.c", line 12: illegal indirection
"dudprog.c", line 12: illegal indirection
"dudprog.c", line 12: illegal indirection
"dudprog.c", line 12: syntax error
"dudprog.c", line 12: warning: old-fashioned initialization: use =
"dudprog.c", line 12: illegal lhs of assignment operator
"dudprog.c", line 12: warning: illegal pointer combination, op =
"dudprog.c", line 12: cannot recover from earlier errors: goodbye!
$
```

The `sed` command removes all semicolons from our program. When we try to compile the resultant program we get all sorts of error messages from the compiler, all about the same line. But the C compiler shows as many errors as it can, until it gets hopelessly lost and gives up. So a point to note is that all your messages might not be separate errors, they might be the result of a single syntax error. When you get error messages from the compiler, try clearing the obvious ones and recompiling — the other 'errors' might disappear automatically.

The simple program in the above examples was self-contained, and so the process of generating an executable version of it was also simple. In practice things can get more complex than that. If a program is made up of several parts (modules) which are separately compiled, you should know how to use the link-editor to combine those parts into a composite whole.

Linking Multiple Object Files

The example of using the C compiler above really deals with a 'toy' program. In practice any reasonable sized project will have many separately compiled modules, each in a separate file. Each of the modules is separately compiled so as to generate a relocatable object file, and then the final program is generated by linking all the separate bits together.

The `ld` command is the link-editor, sometimes called the linking loader. Its job is to link, or bind, multiple object-code files into a single executable file.

Even though the `roman` program above is a small program, and is really better left in one piece, it does have three parts, and can thus serve as a simple example of using the link-editor.

We cut our Roman program into three separate files, called *roman.c*, *cheknum.c*, and *toroman.c*. It is not simply enough to chop the original file into three parts, just containing the three functions. We now have to add declarations to two of them. Here are the three separate files:

```
$ cat roman.c
#include  <stdio.h>
                      /*  Roman numeral conversion program  */

#define  ROWS        4
#define  COLS        4
         <etcetera . . .>
           <etcetera . . .>
$
```

```
$ cat cheknum.c
#include  <stdio.h>
cheknum (value)
    int  value;
   <etcetera . . .>
     <etcetera . . .>
$
```

```
$ cat toroman.c
#define  ROWS        4
#define  ROWS        4
int  pows [ROWS] [COLS];
char  *roms [ROWS] [COLS];

to_roman (decimal, roman)
   <etcetera . . .>
     <etcetera . . .>
$
```

In the *cheknum.c* file we had to add an #include statement, because the function uses the standard I/O library. In the *toroman.c* file we had to add declarations of the two arrays that are also declared and initialized in the main program.

We can now compile those three programs separately, but first we look at what files we have, so that we can do a before and after comparison:

```
$ ls -x
cheknum.c       roman.c       toroman.c
$
```

Now we will compile those files:

```
$ cc -c roman.c
$ cc -c cheknum.c
$ cc -c toroman.c
```

and when we take another look at what files we have, here's what we get:

```
$ ls -x
cheknum.c     cheknum.o     roman.c     roman.o     toroman.c
toroman.o
$
```

The `-c` option to the `cc` command is an instruction that the corresponding *.o* file should be created, and the compilation finish there instead of going the full course of trying to link the (incomplete) program. At the end of the three compiles, there is a *.o* file corresponding to each *.c* file, as the `ls` command illustrates.

If you do not use the `-c` option the C compiler tries to call up the link-editor after the compilation has completed and, because the program is unfinished, there will be error messages from the loader. For example, if we compile the *toroman.c* file on its own, without the `-c` option to the C compiler, we get:

```
$ cc toroman.c
ld: Undefined -
_main
$
```

It is not necessary to compile all the *.c* files separately. They can all be compiled at the same time by typing all the filenames on the `cc` command line:

```
$ cc -c roman.c cheknum.c toroman.c
roman.c:
cheknum.c:
toroman.c:
$
```

As you can see, the compiler prints the name of each file as it processes it, so you can see how far it has got.

No matter how the object files (the *.o* files) get generated, the next thing is to use the `ld` command to produce a runnable version of the file. The example on the following page illustrates using `ld`.

```
$ ld /lib/crt0.o *.o -lc
$ ls
a.out       cheknum.c     cheknum.o     roman.c     roman.o
toroman.c   toroman.o
$
```

As you can see, the `ld` command generates the file called *a.out*. You can now run the resulting file, just as when it was compiled from a single file containing the entire program.

There are a number of points to note about the `ld` command line above. The first is that we added a filename called */lib/crt0.o* as the first file in the link sequence. */lib/crt0.o* is the run-time startup for C programs. The `ld` command uses the first file in the sequence as the entry point for the linked program, and in this case, the run-time startup routines must appear first in the sequence.

Try linking the files in some other order. You get odd results, ranging from a program which doesn't generate any sensible results to one that gives a core dump.

There are different run-time startup files for different applications. For example, the file */lib/fcrt0.o* must be used for FORTRAN programs. The file */lib/mcrt0.o* must be used for programs using the floating point library.

The other point of note is that the last entry on the line is the `-lc` field. This is an abbreviation for

```
/lib/libc.a
```

and in general, any field on the `ld` command line of the form

```
-lx
```

is an abbreviation for

```
/lib/libx.a
```

The `-lx` fields must appear at the correct place in the sequence of files. The reason is that the link-editor searches the libraries for external references after all the external references have been seen. If you were to place the `-lc` field first, for instance, there would have been no unsatisfied external references at that time, and so the library would never get searched. At the end of the link there would still be a bunch of unsatisfied references, which would give rise to some messages from the link-editor.

If a `-lx` field appears on the `ld` command line, the link-editor first searches the */lib* directory for the files and then looks in */usr/lib*.

The linking loader has various options. As usual on System V, these options are introduced by a - sign. Beware of confusing the options with the library specifications; the options must precede the names of the programs to be linked, the library specifications follow. A command such as the one shown on the next page will result in error messages about undefined variables or procedures.

```
$ ld -s -lc /lib/crt0.o program.o
ld: Undefined -
      _exit
      __iob
      __atoi
$
```

The correct order is:

```
$ ld -s /lib/crt0.o program.o -lc
$
```

The -s option to the loader, which we showed in the above examples, stands for 'strip'. Usually the loader generates a lot of stuff other than the executable code in the output file — this is used by the various System V debuggers. When your program is fully debugged, or if you are not going to use the debuggers, you might want to save space by stripping out this unnecessary stuff. There is command called strip which does the same thing.

As we mentioned earlier, the **C** compiler command knows enough to call the link editor after the compile process. In fact you can call cc just for the purpose of using the link editor, in this case you put the names of the object files you wish to link on the command line:

```
$ cc -o roman roman.o cheknum.o toroman.o
$
```

This is easier than calling up ld — you don't have to remember about */lib/crt0.o* — cc remembers it for you.

Also, in this case, you don't have to remember to use -lc, the cc command knows about that library too. But this only applies to the standard C library; if you are using any other library (for instance the math library which lives in */lib/libm.a*), you must specify it on the command line:

```
$ cc -o program program.c -lm
$
```

The cc command is not as fussy as the link editor — the library specification can also appear before the program name.

14.2. The Standard I/O Library

The examples before used the printf function to do formatted printing to the Standard Output. The printf function is a part of what is called the

'Standard I/O Library'.

For programmers coding in the C programming language, System V provides a powerful and flexible library of I/O routines called the 'Standard I/O Library' or sometimes the 'Buffered I/O Library'. The Standard I/O library traces its ancestry from a library of I/O routines created in the 1970's and called 'The Portable C Library'.

Programmers who are new to System V often have trouble deciding which sets of functions to use to do I/O and other interactions with the environment. "Should I use `open` or `fopen`?" is a common cry. In general, the average simple program should use the facilities of the Standard I/O Library. Resist the temptation to use the `open`, `close`, `read`, and `write` functions of the System V kernel, but rather use the Standard I/O Library functions that do much of the setup and control for you.

Routines in the Standard I/O library work on the notion of *streams*. The routines can be broadly classified into two major categories:

- *Control* — set up and tear down stream I/O, positioning, error control, and status enquiries.
- *Data transfer* — obtain data from a stream, send data to a stream. This category includes functions for conversion of numbers to strings and vice versa, and operations for formatted conversion of strings to numbers — *formatted scanning*.

Control Functions in the Standard I/O Library

The picture on the next page describes the standard I/O library control functions.

Here is a *very* brief description of what the functions listed do:

- `fopen` opens a file and associates a stream with that file. `freopen` is typically used to attach already opened streams, such as the standard input and output, to files. `fdopen` is used in cases where a file has already been opened using `open`, it attaches a stream to the opened file.
- `popen` opens a stream as a *pipe* — that is, the stream is used for direct communication with another process, not with a file. `pclose` closes the stream associated with a pipe.
- `fseek`, `ftell`, and `rewind` are for setting the position of a stream and for interrogating the position of a stream. `fseek` positions the stream pointer to an arbitrary byte offset in the stream. `ftell` obtains information as to the current position of the stream pointer. `rewind` resets the stream pointer to the beginning of the stream.
- `fflush` flushes any buffered data to the specified stream. `fclose` closes the stream and removes its stream number from the list of active streams.

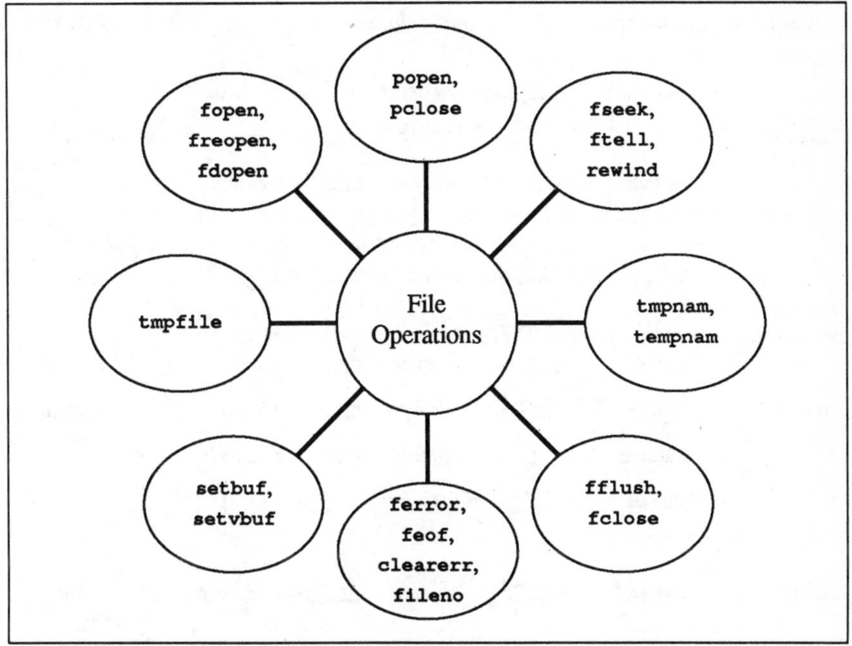

- `ferror` checks whether an error has occurred while reading from or writing to a stream. `feof` checks if an END-OF-FILE (EOF) indicator has been detected while reading the input stream. `clearerr` resets the error and EOF indicators for a stream. `fileno` returns the integer file descriptor associated with a stream.
- `setbuf` can be used after a stream has been opened, but before it is used for reading or writing. It causes a user-defined buffer to be used instead of an automatically allocated buffer. `setvbuf` is similar, you can also specify the type of buffering to be full, line buffering, or completely unbuffered.
- `tmpfile` creates a temporary file and opens it, the file is automatically deleted when the process using it terminates.
- `tmpnam` and `tempnam` generate filenames that are unique, and can therefore be safely used to create temporary files. The caller must open the files, and remove them when their usefulness is done.

Data Transfer Functions in the Standard I/O Library

The picture on the next page describes the standard I/O library data transfer functions.

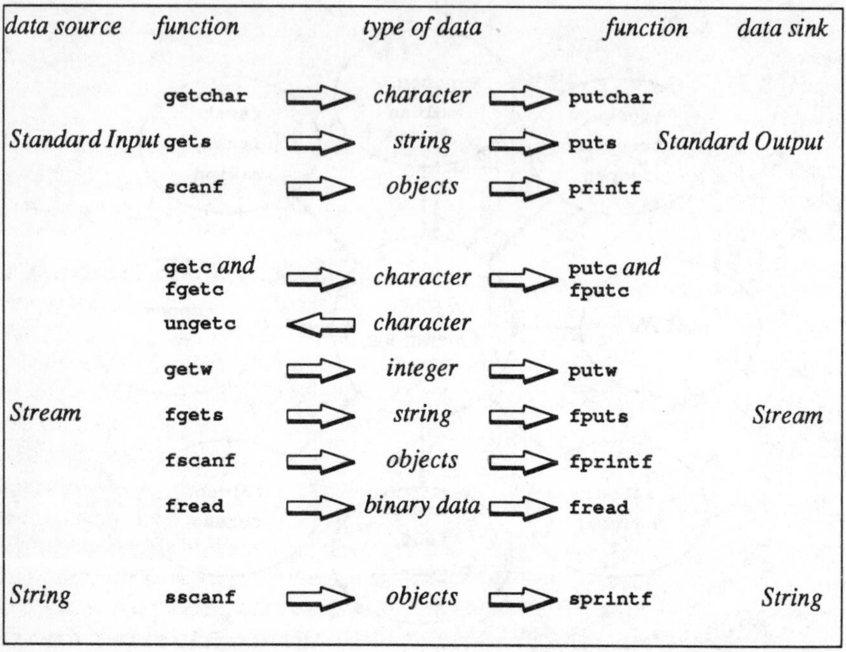

data source	*function*		*type of data*		*function*	*data sink*
	`getchar`	⇨	*character*	⇨	`putchar`	
Standard Input	`gets`	⇨	*string*	⇨	`puts`	*Standard Output*
	`scanf`	⇨	*objects*	⇨	`printf`	
	`getc` *and* `fgetc`	⇨	*character*	⇨	`putc` *and* `fputc`	
	`ungetc`	⇦	*character*			
	`getw`	⇨	*integer*	⇨	`putw`	
Stream	`fgets`	⇨	*string*	⇨	`fputs`	*Stream*
	`fscanf`	⇨	*objects*	⇨	`fprintf`	
	`fread`	⇨	*binary data*	⇨	`fread`	
String	`sscanf`	⇨	*objects*	⇨	`sprintf`	*String*

The diagram shows a remarkable degree of symmetry between the two sides of obtaining data (reading) and sending data (writing). The Standard I/O Library functions obtain their data from and send their data to one of three different places:

- Standard Input and Standard Output — no stream is specified.
- Specified stream.
- Character string residing in memory.

Notice there is one function that is asymmetric — `ungetc` 'pushes back' one character to a specified stream. It is frequently used in parsing routines that read one character too far in an input stream.

On the next page, figure 14.2 shows an example of one of the simplest possible programs using functions from the Standard I/O Library — this program copies its Standard Input to its Standard Output.

```
#include <stdio.h>

main()
{
        int     c;

        while ((c = getchar()) != EOF)
                putchar(c);

        exit (0);
}
```

Figure 14.2 Simple Copy Program

Formatted Conversion Functions in the Standard I/O Library

Of special mention are the routines for formatted conversion. These routines bear much resemblance to the formatted I/O functions familiar to FORTRAN programmers.

`printf` performs formatted printing — it converts numbers ready for printing on the Standard Output. `fprintf` is exactly the same except that you can name the stream to which the formatted data will be sent. `sprintf` performs just like `printf` and `fprintf` but its destination is a character string in memory. `sprintf` is thus useful for building up formatted strings piecemeal.

Each of these routines accepts a *formatting template* that controls how the remainder of its arguments will be converted.

The analogous functions for reading data are `scanf`, `fscanf`, and `sscanf`.

14.3. Maintaining Libraries with `ar`

In this section we talk about `ar`, the file archive utility. One of `ar`'s major functions (but by no means the only one) is maintaining the libraries which the various compilers and the loader use.

In the previous section, where we showed how to use the `ld` command to link the parts of our roman conversion program, we illustrated that all the *.o* filenames must be specified on the `ld` command line. Obviously, if you were working on any substantial project, the number of files required would rapidly get out of hand, and typing them all would be a very tiresome (not to mention error-prone) job.

Using the link-editor's capabilities, in conjunction with the `ar` utility, you can keep those subroutine files in a library and refer to that library on the `ld` command line.

Let us make a library file out of the two subroutines as we show below.

```
$ ar rcv roman.a cheknum.o toroman.o
a - cheknum.o
a - toroman.o
$
```

In this example, we assume that this is a new library. The file *roman.a* is the name of the new library. Archive files, in general, have a suffix of *.a*. The two *.o* files are the new files to be placed into the library.

The first argument to `ar` is the options which you want to specify. `ar` basically accepts a *key letter*, which tells it what operation you want to perform. The key letter can then be combined with *options*, which modify the behavior in one way or another.

In this example, the key letter is `r`, which means replace files in the library. When creating the library for the first time, the replace option simply adds new members to the library.

The options we specified here are `c` (for create), and `v` (for verbose). `ar` will normally create the library file anyway, if it does not already exist.

We used the `v` option just to show what is going on in library creation. The `ar` utility displays each member as it is added to the archive.

Use of the `v` option is a personal choice. Some users get impatient with all the verbiage, and never use the option. In general, if a command takes a long time to run, it's nice to use any verbose option it might have. That way you have the reassurance that the command is still working and the system hasn't crashed while you weren't looking. The `ar` command usually goes fairly quickly, so using the `v` option for that purpose is not necessary. However, it does give confirmation that the right things are being added to the archive. If you had some old *.o* files lying around and gave the argument `*.o` to `ar`, you wouldn't see that they were also being archived unless you used the verbose option.

You can see what is in the archive by using the `t` (table of contents) key to `ar`:

```
$ ar t roman.a
cheknum.o
toroman.o
$
```

Now, you can link the `roman` program with a `ld` command like this:

```
$ ld -o roman /lib/crt0.o roman.o roman.a -lc
$
```

or compile and link *roman.c* with a `cc` command like this:

```
$ cc -o roman roman.c roman.a
$
```

When creating a library archive of subroutines the order of the files in the archive can be important. For instance, if you have a subroutine `jabber` which calls another subroutine `jab`, then *jabber.o* must precede *jab.o* in the archive. There is a command, `lorder`, which searches a library archive for such dependencies and prints them.

These are toy examples; the principle of splitting things into manageable-sized pieces applies more strongly as the size of a project increases. Later in this chapter there is a short discussion on the `make` utility, which is intended for automating much of the book-keeping chores associated with complex projects.

14.4. Performance Monitoring Aids

System V has a number of useful tools to aid the programmer in monitoring the performance of programs. These tools can be used to determine how much time a program takes to run, enabling comparisons to be made between different programs, and different implementations of the same program.

There are profiling tools which can be used to find out where a program spends its time, and thus suggest areas where algorithms can be improved.

Monitoring Execution Time with `time`

One of the valuable tools provided on System V gives the facility to find out how much time a program uses. The arguments to the `time` command are the name of a program and its arguments. The output is a display of the time taken to run that program.

To time our Roman numerals conversion program, we give it the largest possible number of values to convert. We throw away the results by redirecting them to */dev/null* (the bit-bucket) to avoid confusing the printout of the time taken with printing of the results. `time` produces its output on the Diagnostic Output, so the times show up on the terminal screen even with the standard output redirected.

```
$ time roman 9999 >/dev/null

real        47.9
user        47.5
sys          0.2
$
```

The three lines of data here indicate the following:

`real` is the so-called 'wall-clock' time. This is the actual number of seconds that the program takes, and should be the same as if you timed it with a stopwatch. Obviously, in a time-sharing system, the wall-clock time can vary depending on the number of people using the system, and what they are doing.

`user` is the amount of time actually spent obeying the instructions in the user's program.

`sys` is the time that was spent inside System V itself, doing work on behalf of the user's program.

This particular example was run on a DUAL SYSTEMS 83/80 when there were no other users logged on at the time, and there were no background processes running. The results show that the user time and the wall-clock time were very close.

If we have something running in the background, the results are different:

```
$ troff -mm bigdoc >bigdoc.fmt &
231
$ time roman 9999 >/dev/null

real     1:06.7
user       47.4
sys         0.3
$
```

You can see that, although the time the system spent executing the `roman` program is much the same as before, the 'wall clock' time has increased. This is because the system is now sharing its time between the background job (the `troff` program) and the foreground job of running `roman`.

Don't worry if the times don't add up exactly. System V timing capability has a certain 'granularity', so that results of timing tests might vary a little on different runs of the program.

Finding the Size of a Program with `size`

The `size` utility displays the size of the different sections of a program. Each program consists of three parts:

- the executable code (called 'text' everywhere).
- the initialized data portions of the program. In the `roman` program, these are the arrays of numbers and strings that you see defined, plus the strings that occur inside the various `print` statements.
- the uninitialized data areas.

```
$ size roman
11288+1260+2752 = 153000b
$
```

The `size` program displays the sizes of the three parts of the `roman` program, and then displays the total. The sizes are given in bytes, as indicated by the 'b' at the end of the total.[1]

If no filename argument is given to `size`, it displays the statistics for the file *a.out* by default.

Since the compiler translates your source code into low-level instructions, the size of a program depends on the central processing unit used in your computer hardware. For instance, the above sizes for the `roman` program are for a System V running on a DUAL SYSTEMS 83/80. The identical source code, when compiled on a System V installation using a different processing unit, has a different size:

```
$ size roman
17000+1296+8736 = 27032b
$
```

Another thing that can affect the size of your executable file is the options that were used when the program was compiled. For instance, if we call up the optimizer when compiling, the result is a little different:

```
$ cc -o roman -O roman.c
$ size roman
11192+1260+2752 = 15204b
$
```

You can see that the executable code ('text') has gone down from the original example, though the data portions are unchanged.

The sizes displayed by `size` are in decimal. If you would prefer to see them in hexadecimal you should use the `-x` option:

```
$ size roman
2C18+4EC+AC0 = 0X3BC4b
$
```

There is also a `-o` option that displays the sizes in octal.

---

1 If you are reading this chapter we assume you have some programming knowledge, and therefore know what a byte is.

Making a Profile of a Program

System V provides some tools to generate what is called a profile of a program. A profile generates a list of how much time is spent in various parts of the program. By examining the results of a profile, time-critical or inefficient parts of the program can be identified. The organization of data or the algorithms involved can then be changed to improve the performance, if that is in fact desired.

Let us show the use of the profile capability on our original version of the `roman` program. First we have to re-compile the program, using the `-p` option to the C compiler:

```
$ cc -p roman.c
$ mv a.out roman
$
```

This results in a specially modified form of the executable program, which includes some extra code. This is illustrated by using `size` on the compiler output:

```
$ size roman
12500+3776+2768 = 19044b
$
```

Basically, the profile facility inserts code that generates calls to a system routine called `monitor`. This routine keeps track of where the running program spends its time. At the end of the program the profile data is written into a file called *mon.out*. The `prof` utility is then used to interpret the results found in the *mon.out* file.

We run the `roman` program, then look at the files that got generated. We send the results of the run to */dev/null*, so as to not perturb the results too much with file access:

```
$ roman  9999 >/dev/null
$ ls -x
mon.out        roman        roman.c
$
```

Then we run the profiler to interpret the results for us, as we show on the next page.

This is a shortened form of the full output of the profile run. Such a tool can tell you a lot of things about your program. For example, the display indicates that the `_to_roma` (truncated form of the `to_roman` function) was called 9999 times. This is as it should be, because that is what we typed on the command line when we ran the program. If the number of calls was different, it might indicate something wrong with the logic of the program.

```
$ prof  roman
name      %time  cumsecs      #call      ms/call
_to_roma 25.67% 15.05sec       9999        1.50ms
__doprnt 20.15% 11.81sec       9999        1.18ms
_strcat   9.54%   5.59sec     99000        0.06ms
              <etcetera . . .>
_strlen   1.87%   1.09sec      9999        0.11ms
   lmul   1.60%   0.94sec
_printf   0.99%   0.58sec      9999        0.06ms
  _main   0.88%   0.52sec         1      515.63ms
              <etcetera . . .>
_monitor  0.00%   0.00sec         2        0.00ms
_cheknum  0.00%   0.00sec         1        0.00ms
              <etcetera . . .>
$
```

Similarly, the `cheknum` function was called once. That is also what we should expect, because only one number was typed on the command line.

The columns in the profile display have these meanings:

`name` is the name of the symbol which was monitored.

`%time` is the percentage of the total program's run time that was spent in a particular function.

`cumsecs`
is the cumulative seconds spent in the various parts of the program.

`#call` is the number of times that the specific function was called during execution of the program.

`ms/call`
is the number of milliseconds per call of the specific function.

If you have written a program that has several different options, and hence several different execution paths, you will probably need to run `prof` many times to fully check out where time is being spent.

Remember to run your program before calling up `prof` to analyze the *mon.out* file. If there is no *mon.out* file you will get the usual 'file not found' type of message, but if there is an old *mon.out* file lying around in your directory, you could be in trouble.

If the file is for some completely different program you will probably realize this when you are trying to interpret the results. But if the old *mon.out* file is left from running a previous version of your program, or from running your program with a different set of options than you think, you could use wrong data to try and improve your program. It is a good idea to run your program immediately before calling up `prof`.

Only with tools such as profilers can real quantitative measurements be taken, and steps taken to improve things if possible. For example, the roman program spends 26% of the time in the function that actually performs the conversion. However, notice that about 30% of the time is spent in the C language string routines. If we 'improved' the run time of the to_roman function so that it took no time at all, the overall run time of the program would decrease by 15.33 seconds. This represents a 26% speed up. The remainder of the time is still spent moving strings.

14.5. Other Software Development Tools

This section provides a quick overview of some of the other tools which are available to System V programmers. It has been our experience that even relatively skilled software people are often unaware of just what is available (probably because there is so much available). Since this book is addressed to the relative newcomer to the system, we supply a rundown of what's there to assist you in your search for the right tools.

Checking C Programs with `lint`

The lint utility is intended to verify some facets of a C program, such as its potential portability. lint derives from the notion of picking the fluff out of a C program. lint advises on C constructs and usages which might turn out to be 'bugs', portability problems, or dead code.

Let us apply lint to the *roman.c* source file from earlier in this chapter:

```
$ lint  roman.c

roman.c
==============
(63)  warning: rom_pos unused in function to_roman



==============
value type declared inconsistently
    exit        llib-lc(51) :: roman.c(54)
    strcat      llib-lc(403) :: roman.c(71)
function returns value which is always ignored
    fprintf         printf          strcat
$
```

If you look at the *roman.c* file — sure enough, there is an unused variable. This variable was actually there in an earlier version of the program, and got left in during the evolution to the current state.

And it is true that, in this program, we are not interested in the values returned by the `printf`, `fprintf`, and `strcat` functions — so we ignore them.

The other things that `lint` complains about are not so easy to interpret. Since our program is running quite well on the current system, we won't worry about them until we have to consider transporting the program onto some other installation.

There are various options to `lint`, to restrict or extend the extent of the checks performed. Refer to your *System V User's Manual* for details of these options.

Beautiful Listings using cb

One of the factors that contributes to a 'readable' program is the layout of the code. It is usual to indent the list of statements following branching and looping statements `if`, `while`, *etc*., and to position the enclosing braces { and } such that they obviously relate to the conditional expressions. But some people cannot be bothered with these niceties.

If you are one of these people, or if you are stuck with the problem of maintaining code written by one of these people, you might consider using the C Beautifier command, `cb`.

`cb` reads C programs and reformats them to introduce spacing and indentation that reflects the structure of the code. It produces its output on the Standard Output, so to capture that output you have to use it like this:

```
$ cb ugly_prog.c >beaut_prog.c
$
```

In all things "beauty is in the eye of the beholder", and the layout of C code is no exception. So be aware that you might not like the output of `cb`. For one thing, it indents by increments of TAB, which some people think is more than necessary. Also the positioning of {'s and }'s to enclose statement lists might not agree with your philosophy. Nevertheless, when faced with a horrendous piece of code, using `cb` might be a useful first step. It probably won't solve the worst of your problems but it will help some, with little effort on your behalf.

Be aware that this program should only be used on programs which compile correctly, if there are syntax errors in the code `cb` can't cope with them.

If you are managing a large software project where the individual pieces of code are being written by several programmers, you might consider enforcing the use of `cb` before code is put into the 'library' for the project — this will ensure that code layout is consistent across the project.

Cross Referencing with `cxref`

In any large project comprising many pieces of code that are developed, compiled, and debugged separately, there comes a time when someone asks the question "just where is that variable defined?", or "who else uses this procedure?". A tool that can help answer these questions is the C cross reference utility, `cxref`.

This program analyzes a collection of files containing C code and builds a cross-reference table which it writes onto the Standard Output. It will do this for each individual file or, if the `-c` option is used, for the combination of files. For instance, to create a cross-reference table for our chopped up version of the `roman` program, we would say:

```
$ cxref *.c > roman.xref
cheknum.c:
roman.c:
toroman.c:
$
```

assuming that the only files in the current directory are related to that program.

A very small part of the result would look like this:

```
SYMBOL          FILE              FUNCTION      LINE

argc            roman.c              --           16
                roman.c             main         *17   24   30
argv            roman.c              --           16
                roman.c             main         *18   28   31
atoi            roman.c             main          28   31
cheknum()
                cheknum.c            --          *6
                roman.c             main          29   32
```

The output shows the variable name, or the procedure name followed by parentheses. The next column shows the file in which the references occur. Then comes the name of the procedure within that file, and all the lines in the file that reference the variable or procedure. A line number preceded by an asterisk, *, indicates a declaration — all other line numbers indicate a usage of the variable or procedure.

`cxref` has other options to control the amount of information shown — refer to your *System V User's Manual* for details.

Analyzing Flow Control with `cflow`

Within a large project another question that comes up is "which other procedures does this one call?". A System V utility that helps answer this question is `cflow`, which generates a flow graph for C programs.

If we invoke `cflow` to generate a graph for our `roman` program, we get this result:

```
$ cflow *.[ch]
1       main: int(), <roman.c 19>
2               fprintf: <>
3               exit: <>
4               atoi: <>
5               cheknum: int(), <cheknum.c 8>
6                       fprintf: 2
7                       exit: 3
8               to_roman: int(), <toroman.c 10>
9                       strcat: <>
10              printf: <>
$
```

If we reverse the question — "which procedures call this one?", we must use the `-r` option to obtain the answer:

```
$ clfow -r *.[ch]
1       atoi: <>
2               main : <>
3       cheknum: int(), <cheknum.c 8>
4              main : 2
5       exit: <>
6               cheknum : <>
7               main : 2
8       fprintf: <>
9               cheknum : 6
10              main : 2
11      main: int(), <roman.c 19>
12      printf: <>
13              main : 2
14      strcat: <>
15              to_roman : <>
16      to_roman: int(), <toroman.c 10>
17              main : 2
$
```

Other Programming Languages

In addition to C, System V also supports the FORTRAN 77 language through the `f77` compiler.

Had we written the Roman numerals conversion in FORTRAN 77, we would call it *roman.f*. FORTRAN 77 programs have a suffix of *.f* in System V conventions. We do not go into any details of this program, since the mechanics are much the same for all the programming languages. We only show the compilation process.

To compile a FORTRAN 77 program, use the `f77` command:

```
$ f77 roman.f
$
```

At the end of the compilation, there is an *a.out* file, just as for a C program. While the diagnostics could be improved somewhat, the `f77` language can be valuable for certain types of scientific programming, and can be a useful tool.

The `ratfor` language stands for 'Rational FORTRAN', and was developed as a preprocessor for FORTRAN. `ratfor` imposes 'structured programming' constructs on top of FORTRAN. The constructs emulate the C programming language to a large extent. In addition, `ratfor` supplies some 'syntactic sugar', making FORTRAN's syntactic constructs easier to cope with.

`ratfor` is a preprocessor that converts Rational FORTRAN programs into ordinary irrational FORTRAN. It is used like this:

```
$ ratfor roman.r > roman.f
$
```

By convention, files containing `ratfor` source have the suffix *.r*.

The `efl` (Extended FORTRAN Language) command is used in a similar way:

```
$ efl roman.e > roman.f
$
```

Files containing `efl` source conventionally have a *.e* suffix. `efl` is another preprocessor for FORTRAN, it provides much the same capabilities as does `ratfor`.

System V also has a SNOBOL interpreter, the command to use this is `sno`. SNOBOL is a world famous language for processing strings. It was originally developed at Bell Laboratories for linguistics research, and has been transported to dozens of different systems.

Since Pascal is a popular programming language, many installations have tools to support this language. However, Pascal is not part of the basic System V. There are various Pascal compilers available, your local System Administrator can tell which, if any, are available on your installation. The same remarks apply for the LISP List Processing Language.

Language Development Aids

Here are a few of the more advanced tools available on System V for assisting in the program generation process. The philosophy behind many of these tools is one of getting things working quickly so that they may be tried out in a real environment and, most importantly, junking them if they don't work out.

The `lex` utility is one of a family of text-processing tools. `lex` is intended mainly for generating the lexical scan parts of compilers and other language processors.

`yacc` is a tool for generating language parsers. `yacc` stands for Yet Another Compiler-Compiler. `yacc` and `lex` can work together quite happily. The choice of which constructs to place in `lex` and which to handle with `yacc` are purely a matter of the designer's choice.

Technically speaking, `yacc` converts a context-free grammar into a set of tables that drive a LR(1) parsing automaton. It is possible to handle an ambiguous grammar with a `yacc` generated parser, by giving precedence rules which resolve the ambiguous situations.

The `m4` macro processor can be used as a pre-processor for languages such as `f77`, `Ratfor` or **C**. Macro processors can be a valuable aid to mechanizing the generation of things such as tables, where there is a lot of repetitive text with only a few differences between occurrences of distinct items. Macro processors are often used in conjunction with programming languages to define names like `EOF` (end-of-file), in place of 'magic numbers' such as `-1`.

`m4` derives from various efforts to generate 'general purpose' macro processors which are not limited to any particular kind of code. They differ from the macros which a typical 'macro-assembler' will handle.

Debugging Programs

Unfortunately, producing good-looking code that compiles correctly is only a small part of the programming process — you still have to make the program produce the correct results. Very few programs so this the first time they are run, they need to be debugged.

In our experience, most System V programmers don't use the debugging utilities provided. They prefer to add `printf` statements into their code to trace program execution, then recompile and rerun the program.

However, there are debugging utilities available on System V. Depending on your installation you will have available either a debugger called `adb`, or the symbolic debugger `sdb`, or both. Both are similar: they work on object files so you don't have to do a special compilation to use them, they can be used for both C and FORTRAN 77 programs. They provide facilities for looking at code and data, setting breakpoints, modifying variables, and all the good things usually found in debugging utilities. We're not going into details in this book, we refer you to another book — *The UNIX System* by S.R. Bourne.

If your code is written in C, you might want to try using the `ctrace` utility. This is actually a preprocessor for C code, it inserts more code to print the text of executable statements and the values of all variables as they are referenced or modified, so to use it you must do a compilation first:

```
$ ctrace roman.c >Troman.c
$ cc -o roman Troman.c
$
```

Now when you run the `roman` program you will get, on the standard output, a trace of what the program is doing. Here is an example of a very short path through our program:

```
$ roman
 17 main (argc, argv)
 25      if (argc < 2)
         /* argc == 1 */  {
 26           fprintf (stderr, "Usage: roman  decimal_number0);
 27           exit (0);
$
```

`ctrace` produces a tremendous amount of output. A simple call to our `roman` program, to translate just four numbers, produced a trace printout that was twelve pages long! There are various options that can be used to reduce the amount of trace information — for instance it is possible to specify that only certain functions are to be traced. As usual, we refer you to your *System V User's Manual* for details.

14.6. Maintaining Computer Programs with `make`

Managing large amounts of computer software is a task that can be overwhelming without some tools to help the process. But this is true of any other process as well. For instance, if you have the job of looking after a large documentation project, the sheer size of the thing could soon get out of hand.

`make` is a utility oriented towards easy maintenance of computer programs. `make`'s job is to ease the process of going from the original source text of a computer program to the final executable form of that program. It does this by using built-in rules to decide what commands to run in order to get to the final desired form.

`make` was originally designed for maintaining computer programs, and we talk about it in that context because it is easier to describe. Bear in mind though, that if your application is, say, managing some huge documentation project such as the Golden Gate Bridge internal guidebook, `make` can certainly ease the burden.

`make` constructs a program (or some programs) according to a set of criteria held in a description file, which is usually referred to as a 'makefile'. A makefile contains three items of information that `make` looks for. Briefly, the three items can be considered *what*, *how*, and *why*.

- The *what* is the name(s) of what you are trying to construct. In `make` terminology, the *what* is called a *target*.
- The *how* is the system commands that `make` should call on to construct the targets from the sources. In `make` terminology, the *how* is called a *rule*.
- The *why* is the tricky part of using `make`. You tell `make` the reason that a given target should be constructed from a given set of component pieces. In general, you reconstruct a target from its components when the target gets out of date with respect to the components it depends on. Thus the *why* information is called a *dependency*.

Figure 14.3 below shows the process.

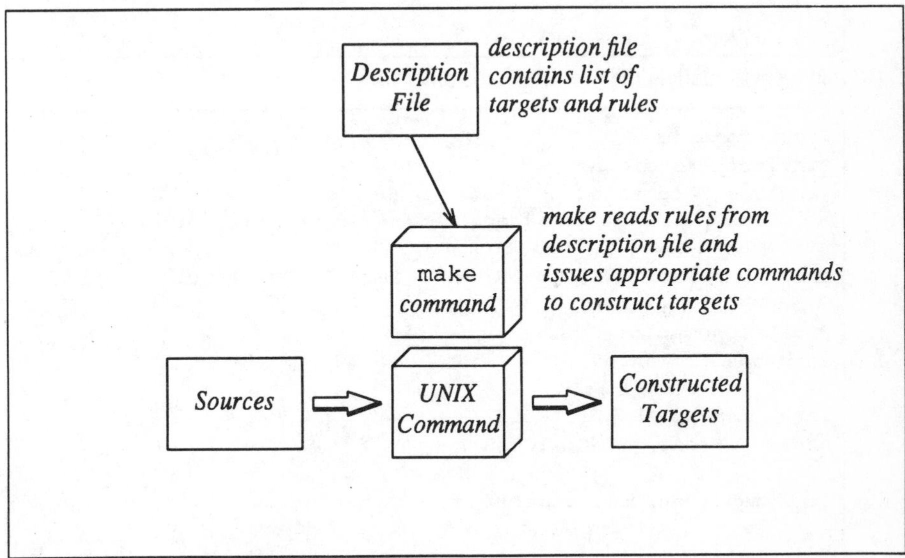

Figure 14.3 Flow of Control in `make`

If you call `make` on its own, without any arguments:

```
$ make
```

it will expect to find the dependencies and rules defined in a file called either *makefile* or *Makefile*. It is this default action on `make`'s part that leads to the description file being commonly referred to as a makefile.

However, if you want to call your description file something else, you can tell `make` its name by using the `-f` option:

```
$ make -f prog.def
```

In the discussion that follows we always use the default names for the description files.

In this section, we use our chopped up `roman` program as a small example of how `make` can be used to automate the software process, but we will first chop it up some more. You will recall that some of the data definitions in *roman.c* were repeated in *toroman.c*. We will create an include file containing these data definitions:

```
$ cat roman.h
#define  ROWS        4
#define  COLS        4
$
```

and we will include the new file in the other files:

```
$ cat roman.c
#include  <stdio.h>
#include  "roman.h"
                  /*  Roman numeral conversion program  */

int      pows [ROWS] [COLS] = { {1000, 1000, 1000, 1000},
          <etcetera . . .>
$ cat toroman.c
#include "roman.h"

int      pows [ROWS] [COLS];
char     *roms [ROWS] [COLS];

to_roman (decimal, roman)
          <etcetera . . .>
$
```

This is for the purpose of illustrating dependencies.

To put our program together using `make`, we first create a description file called *Makefile*, containing the information shown in the box on the next page.

It is common practice to call the file *Makefile*, with a capital 'M', because it then appears close to the beginning of the list of files in a directory listing.

```
#
#  Description file for roman number conversion program
#
roman:   roman.o cheknum.o toroman.o
         cc -o roman roman.o cheknum.o toroman.o

roman.o: roman.c roman.h
         cc -c roman.c

cheknum.o: cheknum.c
         cc -c cheknum.c

toroman.o: toroman.c roman.h
         cc -c toroman.c
$
```

make ignores any lines starting with the # character, so the first few lines of our makefile are comments. The next line is a *dependency* definition. The first thing on the line is the *target*, our roman program. It it separated from the things it depends on, called its *prerequisites*, by a colon (:). The prerequisites for the program are all the individual object files. The next line contains the System V commands that must be executed to construct the target from its prerequisites — these are the *rules*. In our example there is only one such command, a call to the link editor, ld. If there were more commands to be executed we would have additional lines stating the commands.

■ *All lines in the rules must start with a* TAB *character — spaces will not do the job. This is a subtlety of* make *that has confused many a beginning makefile maker.*

Following this, we have defined three other targets: each of the object files depends on its corresponding source file and, except for *checknum.o*, a common include file. The rules for constructing the object files are simply calls to the C compiler.

Now we can use make to construct the entire roman program just by typing this command:

```
$ make
     cc  -c roman.c
     cc  -c cheknum.c
     cc  -c toroman.c
     cc -o roman roman.o cheknum.o toroman.o
$
```

The make process tells you what is going on while it is processing. At the end you have a runnable version of the roman program.

To emphasize that you must have tabs in your *Makefile*, here's what happens if you have spaces there instead:

```
$ make
Make: Must be a separator on rules line 7. Stop.
$
```

We don't have to construct the entire program each time — we can tell make to just make a part of the program:

```
$ make toroman.o
     cc  -c toroman.c
$
```

This might seem like a lot of fuss and bother just to compile a program, but the advantage of using make is that you do the minimum amount of work necessary. For instance, if we update the *cheknum.c* file, and then call make:

```
$ make
     cc  -c cheknum.c
     cc -o roman roman.o cheknum.o toroman.o
$
```

only that file gets recompiled before calling ld to link the objects together. If you call make without having changed any of the files, you get this message:

```
$ make
'roman' is up to date
$
```

and make doesn't do any work.

make decides what to do from the modification dates of the files. If a target file is older than any of the files it depends on, then that target is re-made according to its rules. If the target file is newer than the files it depends on, make takes no action.

Often, when dealing with a large project, we want to re-compile everything in sight, just to assuage our feelings of unease that we might have missed something. In this case, we can use the touch command before using make

```
$ touch *.[ch]
$
```

touch simply updates the modification date of each file in its argument list. A following call to make will rebuild everything defined in the makefile.

Built-In Dependencies and Rules

The version of *Makefile* that we showed earlier is more detailed than it needs to be. This is because make is an 'intelligent' program, it has some built-in knowledge of dependencies. For instance, it knows that a *.o* file will depend on a *.c* source file of the same name, so it will look for that source file and check whether the object file needs to be re-made. make even knows enough to call up the C compiler to produce the object file. In fact, make knows about other programming languages too. If it finds a *.f* file rather than a *.c* file, it will call up the FORTRAN compiler to produce the object. It also knows about efl, ratfor, yacc, lex, and assembler source files.

With this knowledge of make's intelligence, we can shorten our *Makefile:*

```
#
#  Description file for roman number conversion program
#
roman:   roman.o cheknum.o toroman.o
         cc -o roman roman.o cheknum.o toroman.o

roman.o: roman.c roman.h
         cc -c roman.c

toroman.o: toroman.c roman.h
         cc -c toroman.c
$
```

by removing the dependency statement for *cheknum.o*. We can't do the same thing for the other two object files, because they depend on include files. Because there is no correspondence between included and including filenames, make doesn't know about include files.

If you are sure that you are never, ever, going to change your include file you can shorten *Makefile* still further:

```
#
#  Description file for roman number conversion program
#
roman:   roman.o cheknum.o toroman.o
         cc -o roman roman.o cheknum.o toroman.o
$
```

Since include files are usually data definitions, which change rarely, we can probably get away with this. If we do need to change *roman.h*, we can always force make to rebuild everything by using touch first.

Macros in Makefiles

Our *Makefile*, short though it is, contains a certain amount of repetition. We can ease the task of creating it by using macros, as follows:

```
#
#  Description file for roman number conversion program
#
OBJECTS= roman.o checknum.o toroman.o
roman:   $(OBJECTS)
         cc -o roman $(OBJECTS)
$
```

The first line (after the comments) defines a macro called OBJECTS. The name of the macro is on the left hand side of the = character, the definition of the macro is on the right hand side of the =. A macro is referenced by preceding its name with a `$` sign and, if there is more than one character in the name, enclosing the name either in parentheses as we have shown, or curly braces

In our small example using a macro doesn't save much typing but, in a long and complex makefile, using macros can save much work. Perhaps the best reason for using macros is the fact that, if you change their definition, you only have one line to change. You only need to change the definition, without it you would have to change every line where that string was used.

If we now use `make` to completely rebuild the `roman` program, we see this:

```
$ touch *.[ch]
$ make
     cc -O -c roman.c
     cc -O -c cheknum.c
     cc -O -c toroman.c
     cc -o roman roman.o cheknum.o toroman.o
$
```

You can see that when using `make`'s built-in rules, the compiler is called up using the Optimizer. If you don't like the built-in rules provided by `make`, you must always put your own rules in the makefile.

Like many utilities on System V, `make` can be tailored to fit the needs of any particular installation. So the rules and dependency criteria on your system might be different from those we have described here. An interesting exercise is to use the `-p` option to find out just what the rules are. The command:

```
$ make -p -f - </dev/null 2>/dev/null >makerules
$
```

will put the rules into the file *makerules*. Study this, in conjunction with the papers *Make — A Program for Maintaining Computer Programs* by S. I. Feldman, and *An*

Augmented Version of Make by E. G. Bradford.

The example we have used throughout this discussion is short and simple. In practice, makefiles can be long and complex. For instance, a makefile for a UNIX System V command could include, not only rules for compiling it, but also rules for installing it in the proper system directory, and for installing that manual page in a place suitable for viewing with the `man` command.

A useful option to `make` is the `-n` option. This does not actually execute the commands in the makefile, but just shows you what it would do. This is a valuable feature for checking out complex make files. It can also be useful to see just how much work `make` has to do to rebuild (or partially rebuild) some software — this in turn can help you figure out how long it will take.

As we said at the beginning of this section, although `make` is primarily intended for building programs, it can also be used for documentation. An interesting use of `make` in this context is to provide insulation between the user and the processing necessary to produce a document. Consider the following makefile:

```
#
#  Print out project documentation
#
block.diagram:
        lp blkdiag

glossary:
        pr -o5 -h "Glossary of Terms" glossfile | lp

thingspec: spec.thing.fmt
        lsr spec.thing.fmt

spec.thing.fmt: spec.thing spec.macros
        troff spec.macros spec.thing >spec.thing.fmt
```

which defines the rules necessary for obtaining a hard-copy printout of three documents. *block.diagram* simply needs routing to the line printer, *glossary* needs to be processed by `pr` before it is routed to the printer. The document *thingspec* needs to be routed to a laser printer (we have assumed a mythical `lsr` command to do that); but if the formatted file is not up to date, or if the macros used to format it have changed, then `troff` must be called first. By using a makefile, any user wanting a printout of one of these documents need not be aware of all this. She can get a copy simply by saying, for example:

```
$ make glossary
```

14.7. Maintaining Revision History with SCCS

The Source Code Control System (SCCS) is a collection of UNIX System V utilities that assist in managing software when there are many files and many people working on the same files. SCCS does two major functions:

- Maintains *history* or version control for modules.
- Provides locks so that only one person can work on a file at one time.

With these two functions in mind, we will again use the Roman numeral conversion program as an example of how to use SCCS.

When using SCCS it's worth while having the components of your program in a single directory. Let's see what we have so far:

```
$ ls -x
Makefile    cheknum.c   roman.c     roman.h     toroman.c
$
```

One of the main functions of SCCS is version, or revision, control. To take full advantage of this, you should arrange your files so they contain revision control statements. These statements will include some SCCS 'Identification keywords', each of which consists of an uppercase letter surrounded by percent signs — for example, `%M%`.

We explain more about the ID keywords later in the section, for now here is an example of what you could put at the start of each *.c* file before placing it under SCCS:

```
#ifndef lint
static  char sccsid[] = "%Z%%M% %I% %E%";
#endif
```

And here's what you can add to the *.h* files:

```
/*      %Z%%M% %I% %E%    */
```

SCCS will work without these statements, but the next few examples assume you have them in your files. So if they are not there, the results of the SCCS commands will not be as we show.

Creating Initial Versions with `admin`

Now you're almost ready to place these files under SCCS's control. SCCS tends to create other files gratuitously and we find that we can work better if we aren't distracted by the clutter of a lot of extraneous files lying around. For this reason, we place the SCCS database files in a subdirectory. We call the subdirectory *srclib*, for 'source library'. Here's what you do to get your files into the SCCS format. You use the `admin` command to create the initial version of your SCCS file, which is called an *s-file*:

```
$ mkdir srclib
$ chmod 775 srclib
$ admin -icheknum.c srclib/s.cheknum.c
$ admin -iroman.c srclib/s.roman.c
$ admin -iroman.h srclib/s.roman.h
$ admin -itoroman.c srclib/s.toroman.c
```

First you create the *srclib* subdirectory, then change its permissions so that other members of your group can access the files in there as well as you. Then you just type a bunch of `admin` commands. `admin` can only create one *s-file* at a time so you have to repeat the process. If you had a really huge number of files you could create a shell procedure to process the files one by one — we show an example of such a procedure in chapter 13 — *Using the Shell as a Programming Language*.

The function of the `admin` command is shown pictorially here.

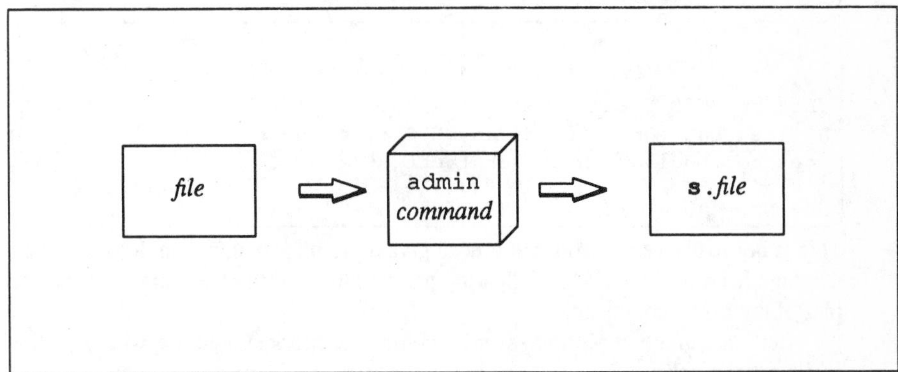

Now you've created the initial *s-file*'s using the `admin` command. SCCS *s-files* are always created read-only (mode 444), regardless of the value of `umask`.

Although SCCS requires that its *s-files* start with *s.*, it's not clever enough to put the *s.* there automatically. If you forget to put it, you will get this response:

```
$  admin -icheknum.c srclib/cheknum.c
ERROR [srclib/cheknum.c]: not an SCCS file (co1)
$
```

and there will be an empty file called *cheknum.c* left in the *srclib* directory.

At this point let's take time out to explain about the `help` command. From the name of the command you might think that `help` would give help in using any System V command, but this is not the case. The command is only concerned with SCCS. You can call the command with two different sorts of arguments. One is to give the name of the SCCS command you want help with, like this:

```
$ help admin

admin:
  admin [-n] [-i<name>] [-r<rel>] [-t<name>]
        [-f<add-flag<flag-val>>] ...  [-d<del-flag>] ...
        [-a<add-login>] ... [-e<erase-login>] ...  [-m<mrlist>]
        [-y<comment>] [-h] [-z] file ...
$
```

This is pretty heavy stuff, but if you look closely you will see that it corresponds to the SYNOPSIS heading of the command writeup in the *System V User's Manual.*

A more common way of using `help` is to find out more about a particular error message from an SCCS command. Whenever you get such an error message there is a code, displayed in parentheses, that you can use as an argument to help. In the example of mis-using `admin` that we gave above, the code was `co1`. If we give this to the `help` command, we see this message:

```
$ help co1
co1:
"not an SCCS file"
A file that you think is an SCCS file
does not begin with the characters "s.".
$
```

This is not really very useful, but it does give more information than does the error message from `admin`. In the following paragraphs we will give some more examples of the `help` command.

Let's assume that all your `admin` commands worked, and see what's in the *srclib* subdirectory:

```
$ ls -x srclib
s.cheknum.c  s.roman.c     s.roman.h     s.toroman.c
$
```

There are a bunch of files there all with the *s.* prefix. Now what have you in your program directory?

```
$ ls -x
Makefile    srclib    cheknum.c    roman.c    roman.h    toroman.c
$
```

Now here's the important part: *the files in your program directory should be removed — the s-files in the srclib subdirectory are the definitive copies!* So go ahead and remove those files. If you don't, `get` will complain later on and refuse to do anything.

```
$ rm *.[ch]
$ ls -x
Makefile    srclib
$
```

Now that you've created the initial *s-file*'s using the `admin` command as described above, there are two basic paths you can take from the *s-file* as shown in the picture below. Note that both paths involve the `get` command.

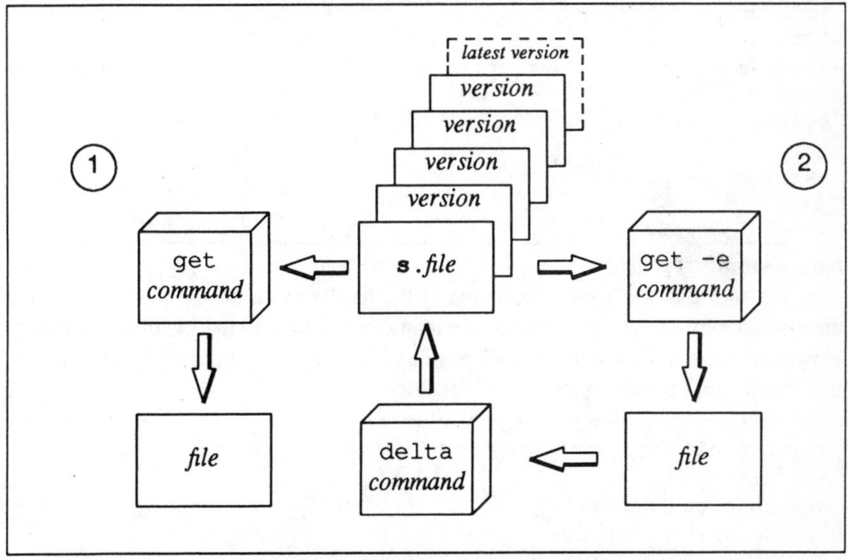

Path 1 uses the `get` command to retrieve a *read-only* version of the file. This is the version that you compile, or perform any other operation that does not change the file. SCCS jargon refers to this file you just got as the *g-file*.

Path 2 uses the `get` command with the `-e` (for editing) option to retrieve a *writeable* version of the file. Now you can edit the file. The general process in this path is to make your changes and check them. When you are satisfied that the changes you made are correct, you then use the `delta` command to create a new version (delta) of the *s-file*. Note that the `delta` command removes the *g-file*, so you must do another `get` to obtain it again.

Getting a Version with `get`

Now what? Well, you want to extract the files from the *srclib* subdirectory so that you can compile the program. You do this with the `get` command. Here's the hard way to do the job:

```
$ get srclib/s.cheknum.c srclib/s.roman.c \
           srclib/s.roman.h srclib/s.toroman.c

srclib/s.cheknum.c:
1.1
13 lines

srclib/s.roman.c:
1.1
48 lines

srclib/s.roman.h:
1.1
4 lines

srclib/s.toroman.c:
1.1
25 lines
$
```

Notice that SCCS is chatty.

We said that the above command is the hard way to do the job. You would have to do a lot of typing if there were many, many files in the *srclib* subdirectory. However, there's a shorter way. If you name a directory as the argument to `get`, then SCCS extracts all *s.* files in that directory:

```
$ get srclib

srclib/s.cheknum.c:
        <etcetera>
$
```

Now you've extracted the files from the SCCS database, you can use `make` to create the program again:

```
$ make
make
cc  -c roman.c
cc  -c cheknum.c
cc  -c toroman.c
cc -o roman roman.o cheknum.o toroman.o
$
```

Now notice that the files that the `get` commands extracted in the examples above are *read-only* copies of the *s.* files. Under no circumstances should you change the permissions on these copies and edit them. If you do, SCCS gets confused. To edit these files you must explicitly `get` them for editing. You do this by using the `get` command with the `-e` (editing) option. Let's suppose that you just want to make a small change to one of those files. The `to_roman` function in *toroman.c* happens to have a variable that is declared but never used. We discovered this earlier by using `lint`. So, let's get *toroman.c* out so you can edit it:

```
$ get -e srclib/s.toroman.c
1.1
new delta 1.2
25 lines
$
```

What is SCCS telling you here? It's telling you that you just extracted version (delta) 1.1. It's also saying that the next version that you create will be called version 1.2.

Remember earlier we said that after you'd created the *s-file* using `admin` you should remove the originals? Here's what happens if you didn't remove them:

```
$ get -e srclib/s.toroman.c
ERROR [s.cheknum.c]: writable 'toroman.c' exists (ge4)
$
```

and a call to `help` will give you more information:

```
$ help ge4
ge4:
"writable '...' exists"
For safety's sake, SCCS won't overwrite an existing g-file if it's writable.
If you don't need the g-file, remove it and rerun the get command.
```

`get` complains and refuses to do anything. This is a safety feature so that only one person can be editing a 'writable' (*sic*) copy of the file at a time.

Preventing two people editing the same file at the same time doesn't rely solely on the presence of a writeable file. After all, if all the SCCS files are in a common directory, someone else would probably try to do their `get`'s to a different directory. What happens is that SCCS creates a *p-file* (so called because it starts with the characters *p.*) in the directory containing the *s.* file. This file remains in existence until the current set of changes is complete and a `delta` has been done. If anyone else tries the do a `get -e` before then, they will get an error message. Even if you try to do one yourself, from a different directory, you will get the error message:

```
$ cd ../temp
$ get -e ../progs/srclib/s.toroman.c
ERROR [../progs/srclib/s.toroman.c]: being edited:
 '1.1 1.2 james 86/05/23 14:52:36' (ge17)
$
```

As you can see, the message tells you who is editing the file, when they got the file, and what version is being created. If we use `help` we get a bit more information, and some suggested actions to take:

```
$ help ge17
ge17:
"being edited: '...'"
You can't do a get with an -e argument because someone else already
did and hasn't made a delta yet.  If that someone else is really you,
you can regenerate a new file to be edited, if necessary, by using
the -k argument.  If you want to cancel the reservation entirely, see
your SCCS administrator, and tell him/her you want the p-file edited.

The data in quotes is from the p-file.
$
```

Making a New Version with `delta`

Having made the changes and tested them, you can now create the new version using the `delta` command, as shown in the following example.

`delta` prompts you for comments. Your response should be a brief summary of what you changed in the program, and why. The comments are terminated by typing **RETURN**; if you have done extensive changes, one line of comments might not be sufficient. If you have a lot of comments, you can make your comments span more than one line by using \ to escape each **RETURN** except the last.

```
$ delta srclib/s.toroman.c
comments? Removed unused rom_pos variable.
1.2
0 inserted
1 deleted
24 unchanged
$
```

`delta` also gives you messages telling you what changed — how many lines have been inserted or deleted, and how many remain unchanged.

When `delta` has done its work, it *removes* the writeable copy of the *g-file* that you obtained, so before you make the program again, you must extract a read-only copy of the file using `get` as shown previously.

SCCS History Display with `prs`

The `prs` command can be used to display all the changes that have been made to an SCCS file. Here's an example for the *toroman.c* file:

```
$ prs srclib/s.toroman.c
srclib/s.toroman.c:

D 1.2 86/05/23 15:15:35 james 2 1        00000/00001/00024
MRs:
COMMENTS:
Removed unused rom_pos variable.

D 1.1 86/05/23 14:35:45 henry 1 0        00025/00000/00000
MRs:
COMMENTS:
date and time created 86/05/23 14:35:45 by henry
$
```

You can see that `prs` tells you who created each version of the program, and when, and what they did — this last information is obtained from the comments that were supplied when the `delta` was done.

Getting a Previous Version with `get`

SCCS is a complex (and complicated) system; most of the commands have numerous options to specify various things, and `get` is no exception.

In general you won't need to use any of the options except `-e`, but an option that can sometimes be useful is the `-r` option.

When you use this option you can tell `get` which version (or revision) of the file you want. So if you want a copy of version 1.1 of the *toroman.c* file, you would use this command:

```
$ get -r1.1 srclib/s.toroman.c
1.1
25 lines
$
```

Printing an SCCS file

Quite often, the reason for getting a file is simply to look at it. If you don't want to compile the file, or change it, it would be nice to just see what is in the *s-file* itself.

If you try to look at an SCCS file with `cat`, you will see that it is not a straightforward text file. This is because SCCS holds in the *s-file* the original version, plus all the changes (deltas) that have been made to it. Trying to interpret this can be quite a job.

You can use the `-p` option to `get` to 'view' any version of the `s-file`. When the `-p` option is used, no *g-file* is created. Instead the information is printed on the standard output, from there it can be routed to the line printer, or redirected to a file for viewing. For instance, to get a printout of the latest version of *toroman.c:*

```
$ get -p -s srclib/s.toroman.c | pr -h toroman | lp
$
```

In this example we also used the `-s` option, which suppresses `get`'s usual messages about version number and number of lines.

SCCS with `make`

When using `make` to construct a program where the individual pieces are under SCCS, we should really ensure that we have the latest versions by doing a `get` on each piece to before compiling. We could achieve this by adding lines like:

```
cheknum.c: srclib/s.cheknum.c
        get srclib/s.cheknum.c
```

into the makefile.

However, we don't need to do this, because System V's `make` command is geared up to be aware of SCCS conventions. For instance, `make` knows to look for a *s.cheknum.c* file if it doesn't find *cheknum.c*. So you could shortcut some of the processes shown above. For example, after you'd made a delta of `toroman.c` you don't have to `get` it again — you can get `make` to do it for you.

Unfortunately, make only looks in the current directory. But you could make your program in the *srclib* directory by using the command:

```
$ cd srclib
$ get s.roman.h
1.1
4 lines
$ make -f ../Makefile
        get -p s.roman.c >roman.c
1.1
48 lines
        cc -O -c roman.c
        rm -f roman.c
        get -p s.cheknum.c
          <etcetera>
        cc -o roman roman.o cheknum.o toroman.o
$
```

As you can see, make uses the -p option to get and puts the output into a file, which is removed after compiling. Because we have taken out the lines showing the dependency on the *roman.h* include file, make won't know to look for that. We had to do our own get before issuing the make command.

In fact, make knows about SCCS even to the extent that, if it can't find either of the files *makefile* or *Makefile*, it will look for *s.makefile* and *s.Makefile*. So we could put our makefile under SCCS, but first we'll change it to look like this:

```
#
#  %Z%%M% %I% %E% for roman program
#
OBJECTS= roman.o cheknum.o toroman.o

roman: $(OBJECTS)
        cc -o roman $(OBJECTS)
```

and then we put it under control of SCCS:

```
$ admin -iMakefile srclib/s.Makefile
$
```

Now we can make the complete program by:

```
$ cd srclib
$ make
+ get s.Makefile
1.1
8 lines
        get -p s.roman.c >roman.c
        <etcetera>
        cc -o roman roman.o cheknum.o toroman.o
$
```

The makefile obtained by the `get` command is held in `make`'s internal program space, so that only the SCCS *s-file* exists in the *srclib* directory after `make` has completed its job.

Identification Keywords in SCCS Files

At the start of this discussion we showed you some extra lines you need to add to your *.c* and *.h* files to keep SCCS happy. Now we explain what they're for. Here again is what you added to your *.c* files:

```
#ifndef lint
static  char sccsid[] = "%Z%%M% %I% %E%";
#endif
```

This defines a character array (a string), which is normally never used by the program. The `#ifndef` and `#endif` statements are to stop `lint` complaining about this. If you are not intending to use `lint` on your program you can leave these out.

The capital letters surrounded by `%` signs are called 'ID keywords', for Identification keywords. When the `get` command extracts a read-only copy of the file, it replaces these keywords by various information. Let's look at the head of one of the files in the program directory. The funny line from above now looks even funnier:

```
#ifndef lint
static  char sccsid[] = "@(#)cheknum.c 1.1 86/05/23";
#endif
```

Here's an explanation of the four keywords above:

- The `%Z%` keyword gets replaced by a special string that the `what` command uses. In the standard system, the special string is '`@(#)`'.
- The `%M%` keyword gets replaced by the name of the module (file).

- The `%I%` keyword gets replaced by the delta (version) of this file.
- The `%E%` keyword gets replaced by the date that the latest delta was created.

There are a host more of these keywords, many of dubious benefit. All the keywords are listed under the entry for `get` in the *System V User's Manual*.

Not having the keywords at all is OK, except that SCCS complains about it all the time. `admin` complains when you create the file:

```
$ admin -icheknum.c s.cheknum.c
No id keywords (cm7)
$
```

`get` complains when you extract a copy of the file:

```
$ get s.cheknum.c
1.1
9 lines
No id keywords (cm7)
$
```

and `delta` complains when you make a new version:

```
$ delta s.cheknum.c
        <etcetera>
No id keywords (cm7)
        <etcetera>
$
```

A call for `help` gives you the explanation shown in the example on the following page.

As you can see, absence of ID keywords is not a real error, and all the SCCS commands work (albeit grudgingly) without them. The `admin` command will create the *s-file* even if you don't have keywords. But by not using the keywords you miss the full advantage of using SCCS.

If you want to have keywords, but are inclined to forget to put them in your original file, you can use the `-fi` flag on the `admin` command. This means that the absence of keywords will be treated as a fatal error, and `admin` will not create a *s-file* unless they are present. Of course, you might forget to use the flag too — this is another good reason to write a shell procedure as a 'front end' for `admin`.

```
$ help cm7
cm7:
"No id keywords"
No SCCS identification keywords were substituted for.
You may not have any keywords in the file,
in which case you can ignore this warning.
If this message came from delta then you just made a
delta without any keywords.
If this message came from get then
the last time you made a delta you changed the lines
on which they appeared.
It's a little late to be
telling you that you messed up the last time you made a delta,
but this is the best we can do for now,
and it's better than nothing.

This isn't an error, only a warning.
$
```

Determining a Version with `what`

Now that we've explained the ID keywords, you may very well be asking yourself "But what good are they?". The answer is, simply, `what`.

`what` is an SCCS command that searches files for all occurrences of a special pattern (the pattern that the `%Z%` keyword expands to), and displays what follows it. The extra lines that we put in our **C** program files are such that they expand to 'executable code' — that is, they will also appear in the object files, and in the final runnable program. Here's an example of `what` in action against one of the object files in your program directory:

```
$ what toroman.o
toroman.o
        toroman.c 1.2 86/05/23
$
```

When used on the final executable version of the program, `what` shows the versions of all the component pieces:

```
$ what roman
roman:
        roman.c 1.1 86/05/20
        cheknum.c 1.1 86/05/20
        toroman.c 1.2 86/05/23
$
```

This feature of SCCS can be very useful for making sure that the code that is being executed is, indeed, the latest version. In general, you won't want to do this for *.h* include files, which is why we only put a comment containing the ID keywords. Bear in mind that include files don't change very often if they are simply data definitions, and that by including a statement that translates to executable code you pay a penalty by increasing the size of your program.

You can also use `what` to list the version numbers on all the source files that go into making up a program — this can be useful in defining the components of any particular software release.

Tracking Line Numbers in SCCS

Most of the ID keywords are concerned with versions, names, and dates for source code. But there is one keyword that is a little different. The %C% keyword expands to the line number on which it appears.

This is *not* intended to get line numbers into a file, but it can be useful when printing error messages from within a program. If your C program contains statements like:

```
printf ("File not found at %M%, line %C%");
printf ("Impossible error at %M%, line %C%");
```

then, if one of these should happen unexpectedly, you can immediately identify the part of code where the error occurs. This can be particularly useful when you are debugging your program.

Summary of Other SCCS Commands

Now you have seen the three commands that account for most use of SCCS — `admin` to create the initial *s-file*, `get` to obtain versions of the *g-file* that you can work with, and `delta` to create a new version of the *s-file*. And we've shown you a few other useful SCCS goodies.

There are many other SCCS commands available. Most of them you use once in a blue moon. Here is a quick summary of the remaining SCCS commands.

`cdc` — Changes the commentary associated with a delta. You would use this if you realized, after doing your `delta`, that you hadn't commented on all the changes. `cdc` doesn't modify the existing comment, it adds another comment to it, so you shouldn't use it to correct minor spelling mistakes in your `delta` comment.

`comb` — Combines two or more consecutive deltas of an *s-file* into a single delta. Could be useful if your first attempt at a functional change to a program didn't work, and you had to do one or more additional `delta`'s to fix bugs. Realistically, all these changes belong in one chunk, and they should be combined into a single delta.

`rmdel` Removes a delta from an *s-file*. Useful for removing deltas that were created by mistake, or for backing out a functional change to a program.

`sccsdiff` Shows the differences between any two versions of an *s-file*.

`unget` Removes the *p-file* created as a locking mechanism when a `get -e` is done. Useful if you change your mind and decide the file does not need changing after all.

`val` Validates an *s-file*. This command can be used to find SCCS files that have certain characteristics, like version numbers, names, types.

This has been a brief walk-through of the most often used SCCS command. In fact, there is a lot more to SCCS than we have room to present in this book, and there are many features that we haven't covered.

For instance, it is possible to restrict changes to an *s-file* to a particular user, or users. There is the capability to prevent changes being made to old versions of a file. You can cause a branch in the changes made, so that one version of a file can be the 'parent' of two different development streams. There is the capability to define different 'types' of *s-file*s, according to the needs of your software development project.

Unfortunately, all these features make for commands that are not always easy to use — they have many, many options and arguments. For this reason, if you are making extensive use of the sophisticated SCCS features, you will probably want to create a set of shell procedures as a 'front end' for the commands. This can achieve two things: an easier user interface, and enforcement of standards (such as presence of keywords). It can also help if you want your SCCS files to be in a completely separate 'project' directory, each individual user need not be aware of the location of that directory.

A final word on SCCS — although the acronym stands for Source Code Control System, the emphasis should be on 'Source' rather than on 'Code'. Too often people use the system for their programs only; but documentation is source too, the 'object' in this case being the formatted document. And so are shell procedures, `awk` programs, and makefiles, even though there is no corresponding 'object'.

14.8. Summary

This then, was a brief 'show and tell' of the programming tools available on UNIX System V. If your application is developing new software, System V is rich in tools to aid this process. In addition, the system is built around the philosophy of sharing information, re-using existing kits of parts, getting things running quickly and trying them out, and rebuilding them if they don't work out.

Although System V provides a multitude of aids for the software developer, before you decide to rush off and write a program to do a particular job, always ask yourself these questions:

- Can you avoid doing the job in the first place? Not doing a job is often cheaper.
- Can the job be done by using existing utilities in a pipeline? System V's capabilities in this area are often more powerful than you think.
- Can the job be done using the Shell's capabilities that we described in chapter 13?

If the answer to all these questions is 'no', you might then start looking into writing a program to do it. If you do have to write programs, we urge you to write them in the philosophy of so much of System V. Five small programs, that do one job each and can work together, are easier to use and more reliable than one large program that does five functions.

15 System Administration

System administration is concerned with the day-to-day aspects of looking after UNIX System V: assigning new login names, managing the file system, and a host of other duties.

Under normal circumstances, system administration is an area with which the average user doesn't need to be concerned. However, with the spread of UNIX System V to small computers such as the Motorola MC68000, any given System V installation is no longer a large installation in a company or a laboratory, but may exist in a small business office or even in the home. In these latter cases, the owner of the system will also have to be the System Administrator.

Because UNIX System V comes in many guises, and is implemented on many different processors, it is impossible to be specific about the details necessary for administration of any one installation. In this chapter we give an overview of the major aspects of caring for and feeding System V. It is hoped that your particular supplier will have provided adequate documentation — this chapter should be considered a supplement to that documentation, not a replacement for it.

In this chapter we describe a number of commands which are specially oriented towards system administration. These commands (such as `fsck`, `mount`, `mknod`, and so on) are usually found in the */etc* directory. They are placed in */etc* instead of */bin* so that users other than the administrator won't inadvertently use them.

Just about all of the discussions in this chapter assume that you are the super-user. In fact, only the super-user can type some of these commands. The super-user gets a different system prompt, namely a # sign instead of a $ sign. Throughout the examples in this chapter, we show the prompt as the # sign, to remind you that you are the super-user.

15.1. Special Users

In addition to the hordes of 'normal' users, there are a number of 'special' users who can use commands, and do things on the system, which are unavailable to the normal user.

In this section, we only talk in detail about the so-called super-user, whose login (user) name is 'root'. The other special users are given an honorable mention, but not discussed further, because every System V installation has a different complement of these special users.

'root' is the super-user, who has Olympian powers over the running (and the possible destruction) of the system. The super-user is unconstrained by any protections that the system has: she can get at any file, can kill any process.

There are some system operations which only the super-user can do. Setting the date with the `date` command is one example. Mounting a file system with the `mount` command, and making special files with the `mknod` command are others.

There are a number of ways in which you can become the super-user. The first of these is to bring the system up in single-user state. This situation occurs when the system is booted up (see the discussion below on booting the system). At boot-up time, the initial Shell runs with all the super-user privileges. On a multi-user system, you can either log out and log in again as the super-user, or you can use the `su` command to gain access as the super-user.

Another of the special users is 'bin'. The user 'bin' is in charge of commands which live in the */bin* and */usr/bin* directories, and is also responsible for libraries which live in */lib* and *usr/lib*.

Whenever possible, you should log in as 'bin' if your duties do not require you to be 'root'. There are valid reasons for this. Apart from the ability to kill the system, the super-user's powers override all permissions in the system. Thus many times you can set up files and assign permissions, only to find that as a regular user you cannot access these things, nor do anything useful.

15.2. Starting Up and Shutting Down the System

'Booting' is the process you must apply to get the system running when the computer is initially switched on, or when the computer is restarted after a halt.

Booting derives from the notion of 'lifting yourself by your bootstraps'. A small stupid program loads in a medium sized smart program which knows enough to load, configure, and start entire wizard systems such as UNIX System V.

Now it may turn out that you are running System V on a small (cabinet-sized, or table-top) computer, in which case the boot process might very well turn out to involve floppy disks. Such systems require some form of 'stand-alone restoration' capability, such that the entire system can be regenerated on a blank slate.

We cannot, obviously, tell you exactly how to boot the particular UNIX System V that you happen to have. We don't know whose system it is. If you are on a PDP-11, for example, booting involves setting console switches, and loading a particular disk. On other systems, you might just insert a floppy disk, then press some reset switch. You will have to consult the documentation for your very own System V for details of how to boot up.

The initial boot program often lives in the magical 'block zero' of the device (most likely a disk) which must be located onto the boot device. When the boot program runs, you usually have a dialog which might look something like this:

```
boot device ? dw(0,0)unix
Loading at 0x1000: 68492+3820+3616
Welcome to Wonderful Widgets Co. UNIX System
#
```

In the example, the 'dw(0,0)' refers to the device called *dw*. The (0,0) refers to the device number and block offset to use. The name *unix* is the name of the file in which you can find the kernel. The first 0 in this case, refers to device *dw0*. That is, major device *dw* and minor device 0 (we discuss these topics later on in this chapter). The second 0 in the parentheses above refers to the block offset where the root file system is to be found on that device.

It is possible to start a file system at some block other than the very first, in which case the dialog might look like this:

```
boot device ? dw(0,60)unix
Loading at 0x1000: 68492+3820+3616
Welcome to Wonderful Widgets Co. UNIX System
#
```

The numbers displayed indicate the sizes of the various parts of System V, namely the text (executable code), the initialized data area, and the uninitialized data area.

The initial program does not have to be called `unix`. The boot program understands the structure of the file system. It might be that you wish to load up some form of stand-alone diagnostic. For example, all the diagnostics might live in the */tests* directory under the root. In that case, the boot up sequence might well look like this:

```
boot device ? dw(0,0)/tests/memory
. . . . . messages from the memory test program . . .
```

In this example, we are loading up a memory test program called `memory` from the */tests* directory.

Many System V installations have a 'stand-alone' boot program, which doesn't require you to specify any device. This program lives directly under the root file system, in the file called */unix*. If you have this situation, your start-up procedure might well look like this:

```
Standalone Boot Version 2.3
Loading at 0x1000: 68492+3820+3616

Dual 83/80 68000 System V UNIX

INIT: SINGLE USER STATE
```

When the system first boots up, you are up in 'single-user' state. This means that the system is only running one user at this time, and the multi-user capability (if any) is not yet enabled. When a single-user system is running, there are only a Shell and the system initialization processes active. The person at the console (who should be the super-user) is the only person who can do anything.

After an initial boot-up, one of the first things you should do is set the date.

Setting the Date with `date`

The `date` command, when typed without arguments, displays the date. The other variation on `date`, namely setting the date, is only available to the super-user.

```
# date  8608100834
#
```

The argument you give to the `date` command is in the form

yymmddhhmm

where *yy* is a two-digit year, the first *mm* is a two-digit month, *dd* is the two-digit day of the month, *hh* is the two-digit hour of the day (24-hour clock), and the last *mm* is the two-digit minutes in the hour field. Each of the fields must be two digits in length, so you might have to pad out a field with a zero to make it two digits long.

The example above sets the time and date to 8:34 in the morning of 10th August, 1986.

It is possible to omit leading fields in the date. If (say) the year and month are the same as they were the last time you set the date, you don't have to type them:

```
# date  100834
#
```

sets the date the same as in the previous example.

Having set the date you are now ready to bring up the system in multi-user state.

Entering Multi-User State

To go from single-user state to multi-user state, you use a program called `init`. This program provides for various levels, the number of users and devices available at each level is controlled by information in a file called */etc/inittab*, which also specifies what action is to be taken when a level is initialized.

`init` provides for 6 levels, numbered 1-6, there is also a S (or s) level for returning to the single-user state. A new level is entered by specifying the level number on the `init` command line. A detailed description of `init` is given in the man-pages in the *System V Administrator's Manual*, the *inittab* file is described in the section 4 man-pages, which are in the *System V Programmer's Manual*.

Which `init` level you need to specify to bring the system up in multi-user state is going to vary from one installation to another, but the most common is:

```
# init 2
```

Depending on what actions are specified in */etc/inittab*, there might be various messages displayed on the console terminal to indicate what is happening during the initialization process. When initialization is complete you see the regular request for login:

```
Wonderful Widgets Co. UNIX System
;login: maryann
Password: wizard
$
```

Usually, you would log in as a normal user unless you absolutely must be the super-user. The dialog here shows Maryann, having booted the system, bringing it up in multi-user state, and then logging in as her normal unprivileged self.

There are other things you might have to do to make the system fully operational, such as mounting file systems. We cover this topic later, under the `mount` command.

The System Initialization Script

Upon startup, the system initialization process looks for a file called */etc/rc*. This file is simply a Shell script, and can contain any commands you like. It typically contains commands to clean out the */tmp* directories and others, and to start up some of the daemons. Here is a typical */etc/rc* file:

```
# cat /etc/rc
PATH=/bin:/usr/bin
rm  /etc/mtab
cat  /dev/null  >/etc/utmp
/etc/mount  /dev/rm1  /usr
rm  -rf  /usr/tmp/*
rm  -rf  /tmp/*
/etc/update
/etc/cron
date  >/dev/console
#
```

The steps that this script goes through are:

- remove the */etc/mtab* file, used later by `mount`,
- empty out the record of logged in users held in the file */etc/utmp*,
- mount the */usr* directory,
- clean out the temporary space directories,
- start up the `update` and `cron` processes,
- display the date on the console.

Shutting Down the System

In a large multi-user system it might be necessary to shut down the machine now and again. The exact procedure will differ depending on the configuration. A typical procedure might be something like this:

- Send out warning messages to everyone logged in that the system is coming off the air in five minutes, four minutes, ...right now! This can be done using the `wall` command, which is similar to `write`, but writes to *all* users.
- `kill` all running processes except the console process,
- Demount file systems as required,
- Perform any backup dump procedures which might be required,
- Use the `sync` command to make sure that all file system input-output activity has stopped,
- Power down the system, if required.

Most System V installations provide a shell script, */etc/shutdown*, which performs all these functions in turn, except for the backup procedures — they must be done separately.

15.3. Accounts, Users, and Groups

Every user who has an account on System V has an entry in the password file. In addition, it is possible that there is a 'group' file, where the information about which users live in what groups is recorded.

The password file is called *passwd*, and lives in the */etc* directory. Similarly, the group file is called *group*; it also lives in the */etc* directory.

The Password File

There is nothing magic about the password file. It is just a regular ASCII text file which you can change with a text editor. If you look in the password file you see something like this:

```
# cat  /etc/passwd
root:kWFpmBP9vvKr2:0:1:The Superuser:/:/bin/sh
daemon:1fOk6tjt9Wn5a:1:1::/:/bin/sh
sys:8VMat0UUSkz41:2:2::/:/bin/sh
bin:Par19UAYok4R1:3:3::/bin:/bin/sh
maryann:KmHuRTfMVK1hE:201:10:Maryann Clark:/aa/widget/maryann:/bin/sh
sally:rDG6OoXq32m17:202:10:Sally Smith:/aa/widget/sally:/bin/sh
jane:GXkGUFA1NofyM:203:10:Jane Bailey:/aa/widget/jane:/bin/sh
jack:Koris34zpim3m:204:10:Jack Austen:/aa/widget/jack:/bin/sh
steve:oPUUJ3YLgN2Zc:204:10:Steve Daniels:/aa/widget/steve:/bin/sh
sylvia:kxUUskz41mqu5:206:10:Sylvia Dawson:/aa/widget/sylvia:/bin/sh
henry:Nz1gLj157en8c:207:10:Henry Morgan:/aa/widget/henry:/bin/sh
hank:79NiJVTuyF3ts:208:10:Hank Parker:/aa/widget/hank:/bin/sh
charlie:yLKXK5936GyIw:209:10:Charlie Smith:/aa/widget/charlie:/bin/sh
bill:86mZodBsaCk4d:210:10:Bill Williams:/aa/widget/bill:/bin/sh
joe:jRXtm96jotPc7:210:20:Joe Mugg:/aa/blivet/joe:/bin/sh
fred:tBnFQs45kph99:210:20:Fred Basset:/aa/blivet/fred:/bin/sh
patty:H0eay7Zf0x:210:20:Pat Manders:/aa/blivet/patty:/bin/sh
```

This is not the most lucid display in the world, but each of the fields on each line in the password file does in fact have some rational meaning. The entries in the password file are mostly intelligible, but the second field on each line is the encrypted form of the user's password. The entries from a typical line in the password file are pointed out in figure 15.1 below.

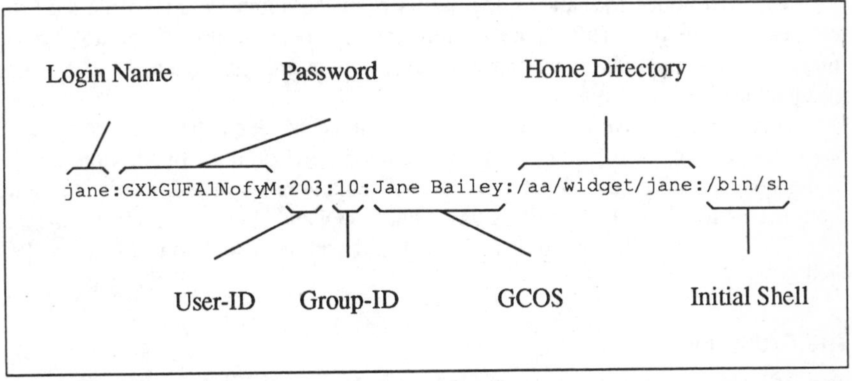

Figure 15.1 Typical Password File Entry

The fields in the line have these meanings:

Login name
: login name for that user. Note that 'root' and 'bin' are not special in any way.

Encrypted password

This field is set when the user's password is assigned via the `passwd` command.

User Identity

numerical user id. This is a unique number given to a user.

Group Identity

numerical group id. You can see that we have two main groups. The people in the 'widget' project have all been placed in group 10, and the members of the 'blivet' project are all in group 20. The numbers are purely arbitrary. Choose something that is easy to deal with.

GCOS field

this is a 'free' field that can be used for any purpose you want. It is called the GCOS field for historical reasons — Bell Laboratories uses this field on the GE (GCOS) timesharing system. The most common use is to hold the full name of the user, as we have shown, but it could also be used for accounting purposes.

Home Directory

this is the directory in which the user finds himself after logging in.

Initial Shell

name of the program to use as a Shell, for use on those systems where there is a choice of Shells available.

At this point we wish to highlight some of the features of the way in which user numbers are allocated in the system.

You will notice that all the regular users in the above password file start at number 101 and 201. This choice of numbers to allocate to users is entirely arbitrary. Also note that all the users are in the two main groups. Again, the choice of group number is arbitrary.

There are, however, some numbers that must be fixed. 'root' must always have user-id zero. Many of the system utilities depend on this. In addition, many of the system utilities also depend on the root actually being called 'root'. It might seem reasonable to call yourself by any name you want, even if you are the super-user. Unfortunately, if you do that you will find you have shut yourself out of the system.

The Group File

As stated previously, the group file lives in */etc/group*. Here is a typical group file for our system:

```
# cat /etc/group
root::1:root,shutup,daemon
sys::2:bin,sys
widget::10:maryann,sally,jane,jack,steve,sylvia,henry,hank,
charlie,bill
blivet::20:joe,fred,patty
#
```

and here is a picture describing the various fields:

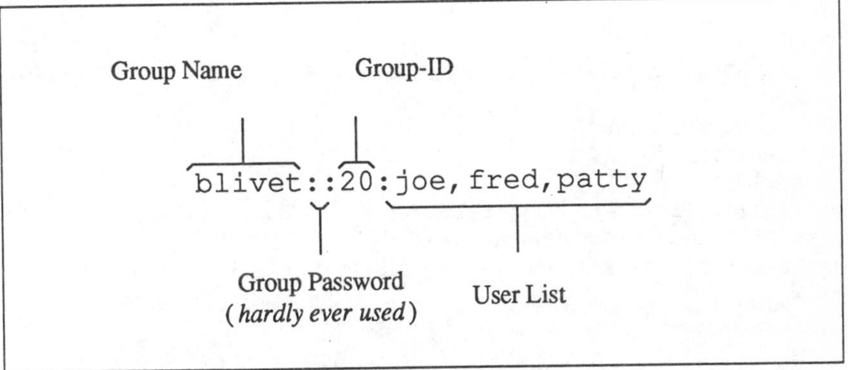

The first field in a group entry is the group name. The second field is the group password. All our groups here are without a password, this is the normal case since group passwords are not very useful. The third field is the group ID, this is the number that utilities look for when any work has to be done on groups.

The last field in a group entry is a comma-separated list of the people who belong in that group. In our case all the 'widget' project are in group 10, and all the 'blivet' project in group 20.

Adding A New User to the System

If you have to add new users to the system there are three things which must be done:

1. The new user's name and other information must be placed in the password file.
2. The new user must have a home directory allocated for them. The ownership of that directory must reflect that user's ID.
3. That user must be placed in the group file if necessary.

On some installations there is a specially built Shell script, called `adduser`, which allocates new users. In fact, some systems have a special 'adduser' administrator whose sole duties are to add new users, and that is all that can be done from the 'adduser' account.

In this discussion, we go the simple route of adding a new user by hacking the password file with the editor. This seems to be the way most administrators do the job. The easiest way to do it is simply to replicate a line in the password file, then change the user-id, name, home directory, and initial Shell as required.

Here, we have to add a new account to the system for Roxanne, who is going to work in the 'blivet' project. Here is how we can use the ed editor to add a new user called 'roxanne' to the password file:

```
# cd  /etc
# ed  passwd
705
* $
patty:H0eay7Zf0x:210:20:Pat Manders:/aa/blivet/patty:/bin/sh
* t.
* s/patty/roxanne/g
* s/H0.*0x//
* s/210/211/p
roxanne::211:20:Pat Manders:/aa/blivet/roxanne:/bin/sh
* s/Pat Manders/Roxanne Romero/p
roxanne::211:20:Roxanne Romero:/aa/blivet/roxanne:/bin/sh
* w
742
* q
#
```

In practice you might prefer to use the vi display editor.

What we did was to replicate the last line of the password file, whose entry is for Patty, then change 'patty' to 'roxanne', change the user-id from 210 to 211, and wipe out the encrypted password field. Roxanne now has no password until she decides to create one for herself.

Now we have to create a home directory for Roxanne, with the appropriate ownership:

```
# cd /aa/blivet
# mkdir roxanne
# ls -ld roxanne
drwxr-xr-x   2 root    root           32 Aug 11 09:07 roxanne
# /etc/chown roxanne roxanne
# /etc/chgrp blivet roxanne
# ls -ld roxanne
drwxr-xr-x   2 roxanne blivet         32 Aug 11 09:08 roxanne
#
```

The other thing left to do is to add Roxanne to the list of people in the 'blivet' project in the group file. You might also want to provide her with a default login profile, and create a *.profile* file in her home directory.

Changing Ownership with `chown` and `chgrp`

The `chown` (change owner) command is used to change the ownership of a directory or file, that is, to 'give' the directory or file to someone else. We saw one use of `chown`, above, when we created a new account for Roxanne. The directory that we created as her home directory must belong to her, else she will find it hard to work on the system.

The `chgrp` (change group) command changes the group ownership of directories or files. In other words, those directories or files are assigned to a different group in the system.

Any user can use `chown` and `chgrp` to give a file to someone else, provided that he owns the file to start with. However, mostly these commands are only used by the super-user.

Changing A User's Password with `passwd`

As you know, you can change your own password with the `passwd` command. If you are the super-user, you can change anybody's password. Newcomers to a site often forget their password. In that case, they will come to the super-user with their tale of woe. What you do as a super-user is to assign them a known password with the `passwd` command:

Let us assume that Roxanne has forgotten whatever password she chose. You log in as the super-user, and use `passwd` like this:

```
# passwd  roxanne
New password: stoopid
Retype new password: stoopid
#
```

We have shown the password you type enclosed in a lozenge — this is to remind you that, in reality, the password is not echoed as you type it.

Setting Special File Modes with `chmod`

In addition to the nine protection modes that a file or directory normally has, there are three more special modes that affect the way that the file is used as an executable program.

These modes only apply to executable files, and only the super-user can set them. These extra modes correspond to octal values 4000, 2000, and 1000, and have the following meanings in the system:

mode 4000
: is called the 'set user ID' bit, and indicates that when the program executes the user-ID is set to that of the owner of the actual file.

mode 2000

is called the 'set group ID' bit, and indicates that when the program executes the group-ID is set to that of the group ownership of the actual file.

Both the set user ID and the set group ID bits are there for the purposes of programs such as `mail`, which must create files in directories not necessarily owned by the person running the program. Under normal circumstances, a person running `mail` could not create the mail information file in the */usr/mail* directory, because they don't own that directory. The owner of the `mail` program, however, is usually 'root', and so the set user ID bit for `mail` means that for the duration of its execution, the effective owner is 'root', who can create files anywhere.

mode 1000

is called the 'sticky-bit', and applies to programs whose executable text is sharable by many users. The sticky-bit implies that the swap-space for that program is not abandoned even when there is no-one using it. The sticky bit is usually only set for heavily used programs. It improves overall response time for use of that program.

15.4. Becoming the Super-User with `su`

Frequently, you will find that you are logged in as a regular (non-super) user, and you suddenly have to do something that requires your super-user powers. Instead of logging out and logging in again, you simply use the `su` (for switch user) command:

```
$ su
Password: genghis
#
```

Now you can do whatever it is that is required. When you have finished, you revert to your old user status by typing a **CTRL-D**, just as if you were logging out.

In fact, you can use `su` to switch to be any other user, providing you know the password. For instance, if Joe Mugg is logged in as 'joe', and wishes to do something under the 'payroll' account, he can change over by:

```
$ su payroll
Password: sheckels
$
```

To revert to being 'joe' he must type **CTRL-D**.

15.5. File Systems

A System V file system is a complete directory structure, including a root directory, and all the directories which live under the root.

We cannot talk about file systems in any constructive way without also discussing devices. A device (on which you put a file system) is usually some form of magnetic disk.

A file system can correspond to a physical device, or more than one file system can live on a device. If a disk is a small one (in the region of 5000 blocks), the entire disk can be devoted to a single file system. It is in fact possible to place a file system on a floppy disk, which might have a capacity of between 500 and 1000 blocks. If a disk is large, it is possible to split it into several 'logical' disks, each of which occupies some portion of the physical disk. It is then possible to put several file systems on it. Each file system then occupies one of the logical disks.

When a file system is first brought on-line, it must be 'mounted' so that the kernel is aware of its existence. The notion of mounting a file system corresponds very well to the idea of mounting a physical disk pack. This notion is carried over even to the situation where there are several file systems on the same disk. Each one of the file systems still must be mounted separately.

Every file system has the same basic layout as shown in figure 15.2, and has four fundamental parts:

The boot block
: The very first block (block zero) on every file system, is reserved for a bootstrap program. It can, of course, contain anything you want to place there. Block zero does not have any meaning in the file system. All file system information really starts in block one of the device.

The Super-block
: The first block (block one) of every file system is called the 'super-block'. It contains the major pieces of information about the file system, such as its size in blocks, the file system name, number of blocks reserved for i-nodes, the free i-node list, and the start of the chain of free blocks. All these topics are expanded upon in the sections to follow.

i-nodes
: Following the super-block come a number of blocks containing i-nodes. The number of blocks of i-nodes varies depending on the number of blocks in the file system. The number of i-nodes is specified in the super-block. There is one i-node for every directory and file in the file system. If an i-node is allocated, it contains a description of a directory or file somewhere in the file system.

Data Blocks
: The rest of the logical device is full of data blocks. Data blocks contain the actual data stored in the directories and files. There are also data blocks which serve as indirect blocks, containing block-numbers of large files.

A file in System V is described by an object called an 'i-node'. For every file there is a single i-node that describes that file, and contains pointers to the blocks that comprise that file.

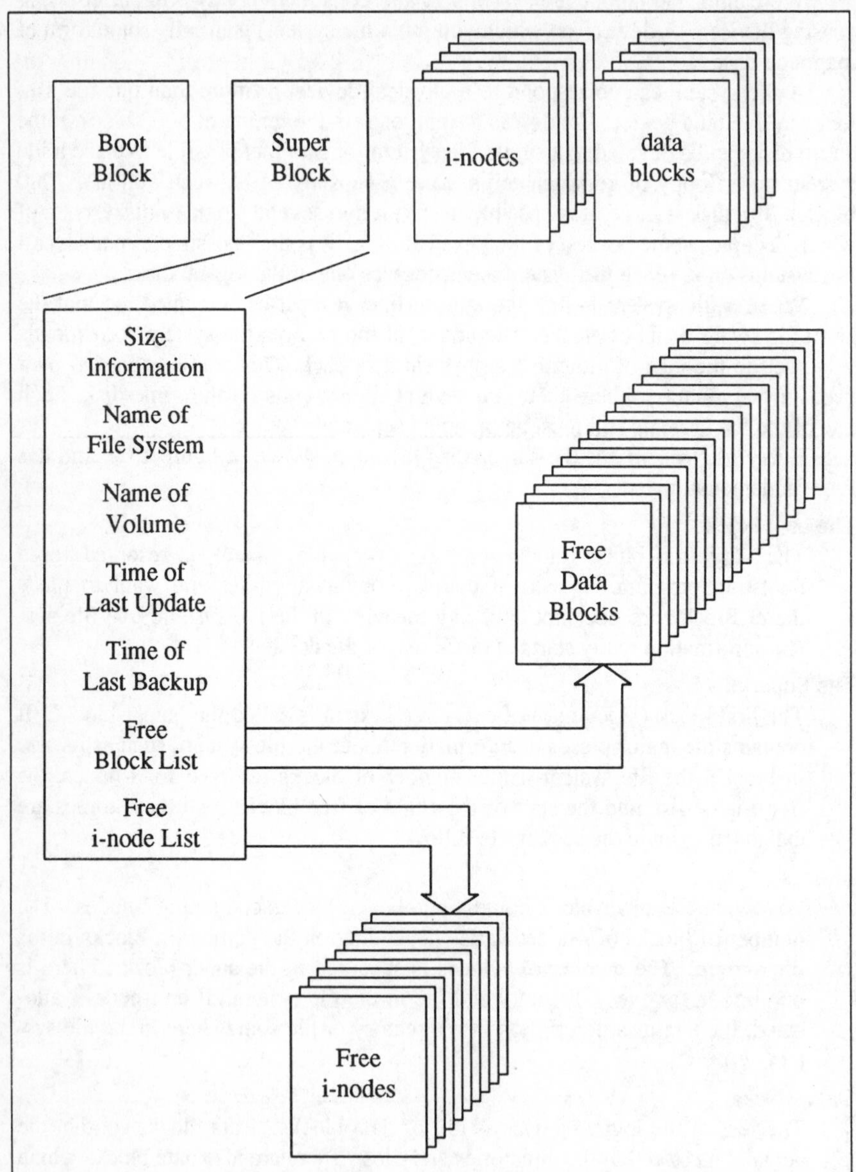

Figure 15.2 Layout of A System V File System

The i-node contains information about the access rights (permissions) on the file, number of links, and some other information. Then there appear the block numbers. The first ten block number entries directly refer to blocks containing the actual data in the file. In UNIX System V each block is 1024 bytes, although the system can also support blocks of 512 bytes.
So the direct blocks can handle a file up to 1024×10=10,240 bytes.

If the file is larger than ten blocks, the eleventh pointer refers to a block that contains 256 pointers to other data blocks. This is called an 'indirect block'. Using one indirect block means that the file can be up to 1024×(10+256)=272,384 bytes.

If there are more than 266 blocks in the file, the twelfth pointer refers to a block that contains pointers to 256 indirect blocks. These second level of blocks are known as 'double-indirect blocks'. Such a file, using double-indirect blocks, can now contain up to $1024\times(10+256+256^2)$=67,381,248 bytes.

If the file is still bigger than can be accommodated in 65802 blocks, the thirteenth and last pointer in the i-node refers to a 'triple-indirect block'. This is a block that contains pointers to 256 double-indirect blocks. This block extends the size of the file by another 16,777,216 blocks.

Thus the maximum size of a file in the System V is:

$$1024 \times (10 + 256 + 256^2 + 256^3) = 17{,}247{,}250{,}432 \text{ bytes}$$

This is bigger than will fit on your disk!

The Root File System

When the system is booted up there is always one predetermined file system on a well-known device, which is the root file system. In the root file system can be found all the important directories such as */dev*, */etc*, */bin*, and so on. It is from this root file system that all the important system programs, such as the Shell, and the system initialization program, can be found.

Making A File System with `mkfs`

The `mkfs` command creates a new file system. The basic form of the `mkfs` command is like this:

```
# /etc/mkfs name size
#
```

Notice that the `mkfs` command lives in the */etc* directory. It is there so that users won't inadvertently start creating file systems all over the place by executing the command out of */bin* or */usr/bin*.

When you make a new file system, you must specify the number of blocks that the file system contains. The `mkfs` command uses that number to determine, by some rules of thumb, the number of blocks it will set aside for i-nodes.

Let us assume that there is a device out there on a floppy disk, and it is called */dev/fl0*. Let us further assume that there are maximum of 2000 blocks that can fit on this floppy. You make a file system on this device like this:

```
# /etc/mkfs /dev/fl0 2000
isize = 230
m/n = 3 500
#
```

The mkfs command responds with two messages. The first is the number of blocks it has reserved for i-nodes.

The second is an interleave factor and a cycle number. Only those who are deep into the theory of rotating disks need bother with that second message.

As it stands, all you have now is a file system created on a device. There still remains the need to make this file system known to the rest of System V. This is done with the mount command, described next.

Mounting a File System with mount

Having made a file system on a device, it is just sitting out there, and only you know it is there. System V is quite indifferent to all the work you just did to create the file system.

The way to get a file system on a device attached to the rest of the file system is to create a directory entry in the root of the file system, then mount the device under that directory.

The mount command is what actually mounts a file system so that the kernel is aware that the file system is there. Even if the device which contains the specified file system also contains other file systems, each file system must be mounted separately. This associates a file system with a logical device, quite independently of other file systems on the same physical device. Therefore any given file system can be moved to a different logical device with no trouble.

The mount command is used like this:

```
# /etc/mount device dirname
#
```

where *device* is the name of the device on which the file system is to be mounted, and *dirname* is the name of the directory under which that file system is to be mounted. *dirname* must already exist — it is usually created by a prior mkdir command.

Let us use our prior example of the file system we just created on the floppy disk. We will create a new directory under the root, and mount the file system on the floppy under that directory.

```
# cd /
# mkdir /supergiz
# /etc/mount /dev/f10 /supergiz
#
```

Now you have a file system, which is just another directory under the root file system. You can change directory into the new file system, make directories, create files, and so on. There is no special magic about it.

At any time, you can find out what file systems are mounted by just giving a `mount` command on its own, without arguments:

```
# /etc/mount
/dev/f10 on /supergiz
#
```

The information as to what is mounted is kept in a file called */etc/mtab*. Every time you mount a file system, the `mount` command updates that file to reflect the new mounted file system. Every time you unmount a file system, the specific entry in the */etc/mtab* file is removed. You should be aware, however, that the `mount` and `umount` commands update the */etc/mtab* file purely for the convenience of the users. This file is not used in any other way. In particular, the table is not used as any form of validity check as to what is already mounted, since the system keeps its own mount table in memory.

■ *Make sure that the permissions on the root directory of a mounted file system match those of the directory under which it is mounted. Strange and wonderful things happen when the permissions don't match, especially when the underlying file system is less privileged than the directory under which it is mounted.*

Eventually, you will probably want to take the removable device off the system, and store it away somewhere safe, perhaps in the cellar with your champagne. Demounting (or 'unmounting') a device is our next topic of discussion.

Demounting a File System with `umount`

Given that you have one or more file systems on a removable device, you cannot just simply walk up and remove it. After all, there might be people using it. Even if there is nobody using that particular file system at the moment, someone might decide to use it later, and if the operating system couldn't find it, there could be problems.

The `umount` command is used to 'unmount' (demount) a file system or device. Note that the command is spelled '`umount`'. There is only one 'n' in the word.

The umount command is used like this:

```
# /etc/umount device
#
```

where *device* is the name of the file system which is to be demounted. Let us assume that the file system on the */dev/fl0* floppy disk is to be removed. You would go through the following sequence of commands:

```
# cd /
# /etc/umount /dev/fl0
#
```

First of all, we changed our current working directory to the root of the file system. Then we gave the umount command, as shown. This now results in a disassociation of the specific device with the directory it was attached to. The device can now be removed safely, and stored away somewhere.

Note that the */supergiz* directory is still there. It has not gone away, but an ls command typed on */supergiz* would not show anything — there is nobody home. It is perfectly feasible, now, to mount an entirely different file system under the */supergiz* directory, or to use */supergiz* as a normal directory and create subdirectories under it.

What kinds of problems and responses can you get from umount? Well, one very common problem is that you are not back at the root of the file system when you try to unmount the device, but instead you are (or someone else is) positioned in a directory somewhere in the file system you are trying to unmount. In this case, you get this response:

```
# /etc/umount /dev/fl0
umount: device busy
#
```

A 'device busy' response gives you a clue that your working directory is somewhere in the file system you are trying to unmount. Corrective action could be:

```
# pwd
/supergiz/frammis
# cd /
# /etc/umount /dev/fl0
#
```

In this example, we used the pwd command to discover that we are positioned somewhere down the */supergiz* hierarchy. We then changed directory back up to the root and typed the umount command again, this time all went well.

Another fairly common mistake is to try to unmount the directory which the device was associated with:

```
# cd /
# /etc/umount /supergiz
umount: Block device required
#
```

This is a fairly easy mistake to make. Remember, you unmount the device containing the file system, not the directory which is associated with that file system.

Lastly, if you try to unmount a non existent device (that is, one which has no entry in */dev*) you get the following rather cryptic results:

```
# /etc/umount /dev/f10
umount: Invalid argument
#
```

Synchronizing Input Output with `sync`

System V is a multi-tasking system. Because of this, you cannot just shut down the system at any time — data which is destined to be written to the disk devices might still be lying around in memory.

In particular, the system maintains an in-memory cache of blocks, which could be data blocks, directory blocks, or most important of all, the super-block. Any of these could contain information which needs to be written to disk. If you were to just walk up and shut down the system, the state of the file systems would be horribly corrupted.

During normal operation, the system sweeps through all the disk buffers on a periodic basis and 'flushes' the buffers (ensures they are written to the disk devices). This regular visitation is called *synchronization*.

Therefore, if at any time you wish to shut the system down or, as we described above in the discussion on the `umount` command, you want to remove a device which has a file system on it, you must ensure that all the disk buffers have been flushed. To do this you use the `sync` command:

```
# /etc/sync
#
```

`sync` does not display any messages when operating.

You should also be aware that when you see the system prompt # after the `sync` command is complete, that does not mean that the buffers have all been written out; it means that the flushing process has started. For this reason, you often see people typing two `sync` commands, one after the other.

15.6. Devices and Special Files

System V knows about certain kinds of peripheral devices on the system. These take the form of magnetic disks, magnetic tapes, terminals, communication lines, and all sorts of other things. Every different kind of device has a piece of System V called a 'driver' which is responsible for communicating with that device. Somewhere deep inside the system there is a table that points to the different device drivers. All devices are treated just like files. The physical bridge between the device name (filename) and the table of drivers is to be found in the */dev* directory, that lives just under the root of the file system.

Adding a Device to the System with `mknod`

When a new device is added to the system, it is necessary to add a new device name in the */dev* directory. This is called 'making a node', and is done with the `mknod` command. Let us look in the */dev* directory of a typical system. We only show parts of */dev*, since a lot of it is repetitive:

```
# ls -l /dev
Total 3
crw--w--w-   2 root    root      0,  0 Aug 10 15:39 console
               < etcetera . . . >
crw--w--w-   1 root    root      1,  0 Aug  8 14:33 lp
brw-rw-rw-   1 root    root      2,  2 Aug  9 08:24 null
brw-rw-rw-   1 root    root      5,  0 Jul 21 21:17 rm0
               < etcetera . . . >
crw-r--r--   1 root    root      5,  8 Jul 11 20:44 rrm0
brw-rw-rw-   1 root    root      5,  5 Jul 21 21:16 mt0
               < etcetera . . . >
crw--w--w-   1 root    root     18,  0 Aug  4 16:11 tty00
crw--w--w-   1 maryann widget   18,  1 Aug 10 08:15 tty01
crw--w--w-   1 root    root     18,  2 Aug 10 20:44 tty02
crw--w--w-   1 jack    widget   18,  3 Aug 10 13:55 tty03
               < etcetera . . . >
#
```

This list of a */dev* directory is taken from a fairly typical large System V timesharing system.

When you want to create an entry for a new device, say *tty16*, you do it with `mknod`:

```
# /etc/mknod /dev/tty16 c 18 16
#
```

The first argument is the name of the device you are making, in this case it is */dev/tty16*.

The second argument (`c` in this case) indicates whether this device is a character (`c`) oriented device such as a terminal, or a block (`b`) oriented device like a disk.

The third and fourth arguments are the major and minor device numbers for that device. Each device in System V has some driver software buried deep in the system, which handles the interactions of that device. In general, the major device number indicates a class of devices that can all be handled by the same driver. The driver uses the minor device number to determine which actual device it is that it is talking to.

The list of devices is something which varies the most from one system to another, so your supplier had better have that information for you.

15.7. The `find` command

`find` is a command that will search recursively through a directory structure and find files matching certain criteria. Among the most commonly used criteria are: the name of the file, its owner, its size, the time it was last accessed, and the time it was last modified. In addition to giving criteria for finding files, you can also specify an action to be taken on the found files — the simplest action is to print the names of the files on the Standard Output.

A complete list of the criteria for finding files, and the actions that can be done on the found files, is documented under the `find` writeup in the *System V User's Manual*. The `find` command is not restricted to the super-user, it is described in this section because it finds most use in administrative procedures.

Our first example searches through a user filesystem for files called *core*. These are files that are left when a program crashes. When the crashed program is one that is under development, the *core* file can give possibly useful information, although few programmers find it worth the trouble to interpret it and usually simply ignore it. When the crashed program is a system command, the user might not even be aware of the file's existence. Since *core* files are of a size that is not trivial, it is a good idea to be aware of their existence. This command uses the `name` criterion to find such files:

```
# find /aa /ab -name core
#
```

Unfortunately, this simple `find` command doesn't tell us about the files. `find` normally does its work silently, if we want to get a list of the files we must explicitly tell it to print out the names using the `print` action:

```
# find /aa /ab -name core -print
/aa/widget/maryann/progs/core
/aa/blivet/patty/ccode/src/core
/ab/payroll/test/core
#
```

In practice, we will not always know the exact name of the file. For instance, suppose users are in the habit of creating backup files that end in *.old* — we don't know the exact filename. `find` uses the same wildcard characters for filename matching as does the Shell. However, we must ensure that the wildcard characters are not interpreted by the Shell, but are passed on to `find`. We can do this by giving quoted arguments:

```
# find /aa -name "*.old" -print
/aa/widget/maryann/docs/people.old
/aa/widget/maryann/docs/softpeople.old
#
```

In practice, all files that end in *.old* are not necessarily really old because 'old' is a relative term. To be sure these are really old files we might also want to see when they were last looked at. We can do this by including the `atime` (time of last access) in the criteria:

```
# find /aa -name "*.old" -atime +7 -print
/aa/widget/maryann/docs/people.old
#
```

The number following the `atime` criterion represents a number of days. If the number is preceded by a plus sign, as in the example, then files older than that number of days are found. If the number is preceded by a minus sign, files younger (newer) than that number of days are found.

In the above example, we have used two separate criteria for finding the files, there is an implicit logical AND between the criteria. To be more formal, we could include the AND in the command line:

```
# find /aa -name "*.old" -a -atime +7 -a -print
/aa/widget/maryann/docs/people.old
#
```

If we want a logical OR between the criteria we must explicitly say so by using a `-o` between the separate criteria. The following example finds both *core* files and files ending in *.old*:

```
# find /aa -name core -o -name "*.old" -print
/aa/widget/maryann/docs/people.old
/aa/widget/maryann/docs/softpeople.old
#
```

Only the *.old* files are printed, although we know from a previous example that there is a *core* file.

This is because `find` evaluates the criteria and actions from left to right, unless you group them using escaped parentheses, `\(` and `\)`. The correct version of the above example looks like this:

```
# find /aa \( -name core -o -name "*.old" \) -print
/aa/widget/maryann/progs/core
/aa/widget/maryann/docs/people.old
/aa/widget/maryann/docs/softpeople.old
/aa/blivet/patty/ccode/src/core
#
```

Notice that the escaped parentheses each form a separate argument to `find`, so there are spaces on either side of them. If you leave out some of the spaces you will get an error message:

```
# find /aa \(-name core -o -name "*.old"\) -print
find: bad option -o
#
```

So far we have used `find` to simply print out a list of the files found, but there are other actions that can be performed on the found files. The `exec` action runs a specified System V command on each file that is found. For example, to remove all */tmp* files that have not been modified for 2 days:

```
# find /tmp -mtime +2 -exec rm {} \;
#
```

we ask `find` to execute the remove files command, `rm`. The notation `{}` means that the name of the file currently being checked against the criteria is to be substituted at this point in the command. The command to be executed must be terminated by an escaped semicolon, `\;` which must form a separate argument to `find` — this means there must be a space in front of it. If you don't put that space, you will get an error message:

```
# find /tmp -mtime +2 -exec rm {}\;
find: incomplete statement
#
```

Another action, which is similar to `exec`, is `ok`. This also performs a System V command but, before doing it, you are prompted for input. If you enter anything other than `y` (yes), the command is not executed. The following command finds all news items that haven't been read for a month, but checks with you first before removing them:

```
# find /usr/news -atime +30 -ok rm {} \;
< rm ... /usr/news >?
< rm ... /usr/news/printer >? y
< rm ... /usr/news/picnic >?
< rm ... /usr/news/leaving >? y
#
```

In this case we removed the items 'printer' and 'leaving', but left the news about 'picnic'.

If you don't give any criteria to `find`, it will find all files. For instance:

```
# find /aa/widget/maryann -print | lp
#
```

will produce a list of all Maryann's files and subdirectories.

15.8. Backups and Restores

Whether your System V system is a huge overloaded installation with 100 users, or just a table-top system with only one user (yourself), it is important to back up the files on a regular basis, to ensure that if anything happens (a 'crash') only a small amount of work needs to be redone.

There are various ways to perform backup operations in a system. The most useful is to take a full dump once a week, then do an incremental dump daily. This means that every day you dump, to some backup device, those files which have changed since the last dump, and every week you dump the entire file system whether it has changed or not.

Backup devices are usually magnetic tape, but in small systems, floppy disks can serve just as well.

Backup and Restores using `cpio`

The utility program most commonly used for performing backups on System V is `cpio` (copy input/output), although partial backups of selected files can also be done using the tape archive program, `tar` (described in the next section).

`cpio` has three main modes, specified by the options:

- `-o`, output,
- `-i`, input,
- `-p`, pass.

There are further subsidiary options that give variations of `cpio`'s actions on any one of its modes.

Dumping Files using `cpio` In the output mode, using the `-o` option, `cpio` takes a list of filenames from the Standard Input; it then combines these files (together with header information) and writes a single file to the Standard Output. Typically, the list of filenames is obtained from the `find` command so, for output, `cpio` is normally used at the end of a pipeline that starts with `find`. In order to get the output to a magnetic tape, or a floppy disk, the Standard Output must be redirected to the appropriate device file.

The following example assumes you have a magnetic tape device, called */dev/rmt0*, and that you wish to backup the entire */aa* filesystem onto it:

```
# find /aa -print | cpio -o > /dev/rmt0
2317 blocks
#
```

Remember that `find`, if given no criteria, finds all files.

A common mistake when using `cpio` is to forget to redirect the output and type this:

```
# find /aa -print | cpio -o /dev/rmt0
```

If you see the file contents appearing on your screen, mixed up with some apparent garbage (the header information), then it means you have probably forgotten the all-important > character to redirect the output to the backup device.

A useful option to use when writing files to a tape archive is the `-v` (verbose) option. `cpio` displays the names of the files as they are being written — this can serve as reassurance that the dump to tape is still working. It can also be used to provide a log of what files have been dumped. Since the Standard Output is what is dumped, the `-v` option writes the filenames on the Diagnostic Output. They can be captured in a file like this:

```
# find /aa -print | cpio -ov >/dev/rmt0 2>/usr/dumplog/aa.log
#
```

The log file can then be printed as a hard-copy record of what is on the tape. If that is all we wanted we could have used the */tmp* directory to hold the log file, but the log file can serve another purpose, as we show below.

To do an incremental dump, we only wish to dump those files that have been modified since we last did a full backup. If our last backup was two days ago, we can achieve this by the command pipeline:

```
# find /aa -mtime +2 -print | cpio -o >/dev/rmt0
#
```

A possibly safer method is to use the `newer` criterion for finding files, like this:

```
# find /aa -newer /usr/dumplog/aa.log -print | cpio -o >/dev/rmt0
#
```

Now, all files that are newer than the log file (created on the last full dump) are written to the incremental backup tape.

The use of `cpio` in conjunction with `find` is so common that there is a special `cpio` action available in the `find` command. This means that you don't need a pipeline, you can do everything using `find` on its own. The syntax for a full backup of a filesystem is:

```
# find /aa -cpio /dev/rmt0 -print >/usr/dumplog/aa.log
#
```

the `-cpio` action writes the files to the device */dev/rmt0*. In this case you don't need the redirection indicator because the output is written to the file specified immediately following the `-cpio`. However we do use redirection to put the output of the `-print` action into the log file. A partial backup can be done using this command:

```
# find /aa -newer /usr/dumplog/aa.log -cpio /dev/rmt0
#
```

In all our examples so far, files have been dumped to tape with their full pathnames. This means they will normally be restored using their full pathnames. If you are using `cpio` to dump files belonging to a single user, you might prefer to dump the files using relative pathnames so that they can be restored anywhere in the filesystem:

```
# cd /aa/widget/maryann
# find . -cpio /dev/fl0
#
```

This time we have done the dump to a floppy disk, the device */dev/fl0*. Notice the use of **dot** to specify the current directory as the base for finding files.

Restoring Files using `cpio` When used in the input mode, that is using the main option `-i`, `cpio` reads the list of files (previously created with a `cpio -o` command) from the standard input, then restores those files to the place they were dumped from. For instance:

```
#  cpio -i </dev/rmt0
#
```

will restore the entire */aa* file system, assuming the tape mounted on the tape unit is the same one that was mounted for the dump process we showed in the earlier examples. There is a subsidiary verbose option, so if you use `cpio -iv` you will see a list of files as they are restored.

Again, a common mistake is to forget the redirection indicator. If, after typing the command, all you get is a glassy-eyed stare from your terminal then you probably typed this:

```
#  cpio -iv /dev/rmt0
```

which doesn't have the < character to redirect the Standard Input. You can type CTRL-D to get out of this situation.

If you want to see what is on the tape before restoring files, you can use the `-t` (table of contents) option, in conjunction with `-i`; that is, say `cpio -it`. Using both the `-t` and `-v` options will give more information in the table of contents.

When you do a global restore like this, `cpio` looks at the modification dates of any files on the tape that have the same pathname as existing files — if the existing file is newer than the copy on tape, that file will not be restored from tape. If you want to force the file to be restored from tape, then you must use the `-u` (unconditional) option.

When restoring files `cpio` expects all subdirectories to exist, you get an error message if it tries to put a file in a non-existent directory. If you had wiped out an entire filesystem, and were trying to restore it from scratch onto a clean slate, creating all the subdirectories manually would be an awesome task. So `cpio` has a `-d` option which creates subdirectories automatically as they are needed.

You don't have to restore all the files that were dumped. `cpio` takes an optional argument which is a pattern specifying which files are to be read. The pattern could be the name of a file, or it could contain wildcard characters to specify several files. `cpio` uses the same wildcard characters as does the Shell, when using them you must use quotes to ensure that they are interpreted by `cpio`, and not by the Shell. The command:

```
# cd /tmp
# cpio -id "*.c" </dev/fl0
#
```

shows all Maryann's C language source files being restored into the */tmp* directory (assuming the floppy disk in the drive */dev/fl0* is the one that was written to in the dump examples above). When restoring only a few files for a user, it sometimes pays to put them in */tmp* space, then ask the user to copy them to their own directories. This is especially true when the user wants to see an old copy of a file that has been modified since the last dump. The file can be removed from */tmp* space later.

In the above example we could restore files to a place other than the one they were dumped from because we had done the initial dump using relative pathnames instead of full pathnames. However, even if you dump using full pathnames, you can still restore the file into another place by using the `-r` (rename) option. When using this option, before it reads a file, `cpio` prompts you for the name of the file. If you type a new name the file will be read in with that name, if you simply type RETURN the file will not be read in. The prompt is given for every file that is to be read, so this option is only recommended when you are using a pattern to restore a few files. For instance, it would not be a good way of trying to restore every file dumped (using a full pathname) from the filesystem */aa* to the filesystem */ac*.

Copying Directories using `cpio` The third mode, pass, of `cpio` provides a convenient way of copying directory structures. The `-p` option basically tells `cpio` that you are bypassing the input/output part of the copy, in this case `cpio` doesn't bother to write the header information usually written to mag tape or floppy disk. In this usage, `cpio` expects the name of the target directory as an argument, so you don't need to use the redirection indicator.

The command:

```
# cd /aa/blivet
# find . -print | cpio -pd /ac/blivet
#
```

copies all the files and subdirectories under */aa/blivet* to the equivalent place in a new filesystem */ac*. The files can then be removed from */aa/blivet*. Moving stuff from one filesystem to another like this is sometimes necessary when the filesystems get full.

The Tape Archive program `tar`

Another useful command for dumping files to tape is the `tar` (tape archive) command. At first sight, `tar` looks like the `ar` archive program, but `tar` knows about directories and links and so on. `tar` dumps files onto a specified device in a special format, with headers and checksums. `tar` writes out a faithful representation of directory structures, files, permissions and stuff, such that a subsequent `tar` run can recover all or part of the dumped files. It is not necessary to place files on a tape with `tar`. You can if you wish just make a tape archive on another disk.

Although we have included `tar` in this section on system administration, any user can in fact use `tar` at any time.

You use `tar` with a command line that looks like this:

`tar` *options files*

In common with most other commands on System V, `tar` does its work quietly with no extraneous chatter, unless you use the `v` (verbose) option.

Dumping Files to Tape with `tar` Let us assume that you have a floppy disk device called */dev/fl0*. Here is a typical `tar` run to dump all the files in a directory to that floppy:

```
# tar cf /dev/fl0  *
#
```

Here we have given two options to `tar`. The `c` (create) option tells `tar` that this is a new archive. In the absence of the `c` option, `tar` assumes that you are adding to an existing archive.

The `f` (file) option tells `tar` that the very next argument on the command line is the name of a file on which the archive is to be placed. In the absence of the `f` option, `tar` places the archive on some default device. The name of this default device varies from one installation to another. The easiest way to find out what it is on your System V, is to type a `tar` command without specifying a filename, and see where it tries to write the archive.

Now, if you want to, you can look at what we placed in the archive, using the `t` (for table of contents) option:

```
# tar tf /dev/fl0
<list
  of
   files
     on
      the
        tape>
#
```

Reading Files from Tape with `tar` Having made a tape archive, how do you get stuff back off the archive? This is easy, you just use the x (for extract) option to `tar`:

```
# tar xf /dev/f10 *people
#
```

The x option tells `tar` to extract the specified files from the archive. Again, `tar` does this work silently.

There is a hidden flaw in the use of the extract option to `tar`, that is not evident from the above example. It is the Shell that expands the shorthand notation of `*people`, and not the `tar` command. So, in order for `tar` to get a correct list of *people* files, they must already exist in the directory in which you want them. If the files do not already exist in the directory, the Shell will not supply the list of filenames to `tar` (because no names were matched), and so `tar` will (silently) do nothing. In such a case, you have to spell out the list of names explicitly. `tar` does not itself have the same pattern-matching capability as does `cpio`, so putting quotes in the command won't help.

There are a few subtleties in the use of `tar` which can help overcome the problems noted just above. One way to get `tar` to restore everything is to tell it a directory name:

```
# tar xf /dev/f10 maryann
#
```

where *maryann* is the name of a directory. Now `tar` will restore all files from */dev/fl0* to that directory and its subdirectories.

Another feature is that files placed implicitly on a `tar` archive from a directory just go on the archive with their names; the pathname is not included. Such files can be restored to any other directory. But, if you explicitly spell out a pathname, such as */aa/widget/maryann/myfile*, that file goes on the archive with the full pathname included, and must be extracted with that name.

15.9. Maintaining File Systems with `fsck`

The file systems are wonderfully organized things. Unfortunately, there are many non-wonderful things that can go amiss with a file system if the wrong things happen at the wrong time. This section is a guide to the sorts of things that can go wrong in a file system, we introduce the `fsck` command which can tell you what problems have arisen, and what you can do to repair those problem areas.

Back in the main discussion on file systems, earlier, we described the layout of a file system, with its i-nodes, blocks, indirect-blocks, the super-block, and so on.

This elegant structure is, unfortunately, subject to disruption due to many causes. For example, consider what happens to a large file if the triple-indirect block gets clobbered in some way. Some of the more prevalent problems that arise are these:

- A given block might be missing from the system. That is, it is not part of a file, nor is it in the free list.
- There might be duplicate i-nodes. That is, i-nodes that seem to describe the same thing twice.
- A block might appear both in a file, and in the free list. This is one of the more serious problems that can arise. If, for example, the block in question is an indirect block, its erroneous presence in the free list might cause it to be reallocated to another file, and so two entirely different files will end up as a badly formed amalgam.
- A file can exist, but is not linked to any directory anywhere.

In the midst of all this gloom, it is fortunate that the organization of the file system brings with it a certain degree of redundancy. Some of the redundant information comes from these situations:

- a data-block which happens to be a directory contains filenames (and /or directory names) and i-numbers. But somewhere, there is an i-node which corresponds to that directory, and that i-node should be marked as a directory, not an ordinary file.
- a block which is part of the free-list should not, in theory, be part of a file anywhere. It is easy to scan through all the i-nodes looking for blocks which are allocated to files as well as the free-list.
- similarly, a block which belongs to a file should belong only to one file. It is easy to check for this.

There are many other redundancies which enable a cleverly constructed program to verify the correctness of the file system, and to make a creditable attempt at fixing up any problems which are found.

The serious user or administrator should read the paper *FSCK — The UNIX File System Check Program*, by T. J. Kowalski. This paper contains an excellent discussion of the file system, the things that can go wrong with it, and the things that a clever program (such as `fsck`) can do to help.

Checking the Integrity of a File System with `fsck`

The `fsck` command is used to perform a file system check. Here is a typical `fsck` run:

```
# /etc/fsck
** Phase 1 - Check Blocks and Sizes
** Phase 2 - Check Pathnames
** Phase 3 - Check Connectivity
** Phase 4 - Check Reference Counts
** Phase 5 - Check Free List
#
```

As you can see from the example run above, `fsck` does its work in several phases. Contrary to most commands on System V, `fsck` is chatty and tells you what it is doing, so that you can respond intelligently. The separate phases do the following work:

Phase	*Description*
1	checks the consistency of i-nodes, such as link counts, i-node types, and i-node formats.
2	checks for directories which point to i-nodes previously found to be in error.
3	determines errors resulting from unreferenced directories.
4	checks the consistency of the link counts in directories and files.
5	checks for bad blocks in the free list, duplicate blocks in the free list, unused blocks which should be in the free list but aren't, and the total free block count.

In addition to the phases described above, there are some subsidiary phases (phase 1b for example) that are only called into play when a prior phase finds some error.

The `fsck` command checks several file systems by default. It always checks the root file system. You can tell it which other file systems to check by placing their names in the file */etc/checklist*.

In the example above, we showed a perfect `fsck` run, where it did not discover any problems. Now we are about to show the kinds of things that `fsck` can discover, what you can do about them, and what they mean.

The example on the next page was taken from a real system under development, where there were often bugs introduced, mangling the file system.

In the example below, `fsck` has discovered a duplicate i-node for a file called *unix* in the directory */usr/src/sys*. This happened to be where the development work was being done. In this case, the super-user decided that that copy of *unix* was of no use, and told `fsck` to go ahead and clear the problem (the '`y`' responses in the dialog).

```
# /etc/fsck
** Phase 1 - Check Blocks and Sizes
528627 BAD I=66
** Phase 2 - Check Pathnames
DUP/BAD  I=66  OWNER=root MODE=100755
SIZE=78409 MTIME=Feb 24 16:45 1982
FILE=/usr/src/sys/unix
REMOVE? y

** Phase 3 - Check Connectivity
** Phase 4 - Check Reference Counts
BAD/DUP  I=66  OWNER=root MODE=100755
SIZE=78409 MTIME=Feb 24 16:45 1982
FILE=/usr/src/sys/unix
CLEAR? y

UNREF FILE  I=361  OWNER=root MODE=100600
SIZE=0 MTIME=Feb 25 09:40 1982
RECONNECT? y
** Phase 5 - Check Free List
157 BLK(S) MISSING
BAD FREE LIST
SALVAGE? y
** Phase 6 - Salvage Free List
302 files 5833 blocks 371 free
#
```

At the end of the run `fsck` decides that there are blocks missing from the free-list. It asks if the free-list is to be salvaged. Upon a positive response to this question, `fsck` goes ahead and salvages the free list. Note that there is then a Phase 6, which did not appear in a normal run of `fsck`.

At the end of an `fsck` run, there may be some messages which indicate the state of things. After a successful run (in which no errors were found), `fsck` prints a message to the effect:

N `files` *B* `blocks` *F* `free`

meaning that there were *N* files in a file system of *B* blocks, leaving *F* blocks free.

After a run of `fsck` where the file system had major surgery done, the message

```
***** BOOT UNIX (NO SYNC!) *****
```

may appear. This message means that the root file system or a mounted file system has been modified in some way. If the system is not immediately rebooted, the salvage job just done will be undone because of the in-memory copies of tables that the system keeps. In that case, you must reboot the system, *without* doing a `sync` command first (else the sync causes all the salvaged information to be overwritten).

The lost+found Directory

The *lost+found* directory is an integral part of using the fsck program. There must be a *lost+found* directory in the root directory of each file system.

When fsck finds directories which are not linked into the file system in a sane way, it links them into the *lost+found* directory instead.

15.10. Other Administrative Topics

This section covers a few topics which do not fit in anywhere else.

Changing Terminal Characteristics

All the terminals which can log in to System V are described in the */etc/inittab* file, which we discussed earlier as being important to the system initialization process. Here is part of a typical */etc/inittab* file taken from a small System V installation.

```
# tail -4 /etc/inittab
co::respawn:/etc/getty console co_9600  #Console Port
lp::off:/etc/getty tty01 tt_9600        #Line Printer
02::respawn:/etc/getty tty02 tt_9600    #Port tty02
03::respawn:/etc/getty tty03 tt_9600    #Port tty03
#
```

We don't have space to go into all the details of what this means, we again refer you to the man-pages for the init command and the *inittab* file. We'll just say that this represents four I/O ports which are configured such that one is the system console, another is a printer, and the remaining two are ordinary user terminals (ttys).

Suppose we wanted to change the port *tty03* so that users can dial into the system at a baud rate of 1200, we would change the last line of the */etc/inittab* file to look like this:

```
# tail -1 /etc/inittab
03::respawn:/etc/getty tty03 du_1200    #dialup
#
```

If we wanted the line to be one you could dial out on, for instance to be able to access another System V installation, the line should be changed to:

```
# tail -1 /etc/inittab
03::off:/etc/getty tty03 du_1200          #dialout
#
```

Running Periodic Jobs with `cron`

System V provides for running tasks on a periodic basis. Way back in the start of this chapter, we showed a typical */etc/rc* file which the `init` process executes. One of the commands started at that time was `/etc/cron`. It is `cron` which performs tasks on a periodic basis.

The `cron` utility is a permanent process that wakes up once every minute. `cron` consults files in a directory called */usr/spool/crontab* to find out what tasks are to be done, and when those tasks are to be done. If the time is right, as specified in the files, `cron` starts the indicated task.

The files in */usr/spool/crontab* are commonly referred to as 'crontab' files. There is typically one file for each user that requires periodic jobs to be run. Mostly these users are the special users: 'root', 'bin' and so on. However, an ordinary user can put a crontab file in the directory using the `crontab` command — this command checks the syntax of the file before placing it in */usr/spool/crontab*.[1]

Here is a typical crontab file:

```
# cat  /usr/lib/crontab
0     *    *    *    *   /bin/date > /dev/console
20    1    *    *    *   /bin/calendar -
0,10,20,30,40,50 * * * * /etc/syslog
#
```

Each line in the file consists of six fields. The last field is simple, being the command which is to be run. In the example above, you can see that the `date` command displays the date on the system console every now and again. The `calendar` command is run periodically, and we have a `syslog` Shell script which is also run on a periodic basis.

The fields are separated by spaces or tabs, this is common practice on System V. The other five fields on each line indicate when the jobs are to be done:

- The first field is a minutes field. It can take on values in the range 0 through 59.
- The second field is an hours field, which can have values in the range 0 through 23.

---

[1] Some older System V installations have a simpler version of `cron`, where there is only one crontab file called */usr/lib/crontab*, and periodic jobs are restricted to the super-user 'root'.

- The third field is a day of the month, in the range 1 through 31.
- The fourth field is the month of the year, in the range 1 through 12.
- The fifth field is a day of the week, in the range 1 through 7. Monday is day 1 in this scheme of things.

Any one of those fields can be a whole list of values, as shown in line 3 of the crontab file above. If the field contains an asterisk character * it means that the job is done for all possible values of the field. Finally, a value in a field can be a pair of numbers separated by a hyphen, which indicates that the job is to be done for all the times in the specified range.

Let us interpret the crontab file from the example above. The first line says that the `date` command displays the current date and time on the console at minute 0 of every hour of every day of every month. In other words, once every hour, on the hour, the date is printed on the console.

The second line runs the `calendar` command on behalf of the users at 20 minutes past one o'clock in the morning, on every day.

The third line says that the `syslog` command is to be run every ten minutes.

If your system has any monitoring processes to do on a periodic basis, it is in */usr/spool/crontab* that the relevant conditions are set up. For example, you might have a program which runs once a day to find out how much storage all the users are using, so you can publish a 'hog' list. You might place a file in */usr/spool/crontab* containing a line that looks like this:

```
0       18      *       *       *       /etc/hogs
```

15.11. Looking After the UNIX System Manuals

As a system administrator, one of your duties might well be to keep the manuals up to date, and to add new entries as users add new tools and facilities to the system. This is a very important part of the administrator's job, since a system without documentation is a poor system indeed.

In general, all the System V Manuals live on-line. Only on very small systems do the manuals have to be off-line on some backup storage device.

The source text for the manuals live on-line in various subdirectories of the */usr/man* directory. The exact layout of the directory structure varies from one installation to another but, usually, there is a subdirectory for each section in the *User's Manual*. Each subdirectory contains the source for the manual pages in that section. You will need to do some exploration to find out what the setup is on your installation.

Some systems keep the formatted, ready-to-print, form of the manuals on-line as well as the source. If the formatted versions are on-line, they are usually found in the various subdirectories of the */usr/catman* directory, but again the exact layout varies from one installation to another.

When a user calls up the man command, it first looks in the appropriate place for the formatted version of the required manual entry. If it is not found there, man then looks in the appropriate */usr/man* subdirectory for the source. Having found the source of the manual entry, man then calls up nroff to format the manual on the fly.

The manual entries for the *System V User's Manual* are, with very few exceptions, formatted in conjunction with the -man macro package. The man macro package is described (tersely) in the section 7 man-pages, which are in the *System V Administrator's Manual*. When you have to add new manual entries to the system, it is much easier to make a copy of an existing entry and hack it about, rather than trying to understand the man macro package from a cold start.

15.12. Concluding Remarks on Administration

This chapter was intended to give you a feel for the kinds of things you need to know about managing a System V installation. You should at least be aware that even when the system is running on a computer which fits on a desktop, it is not a simple system where you can just remove the floppy disks and turn off the power.

Obviously, we could not be specific in this chapter. We have given you enough information to be a menace to yourself and to others. If you have the job of system management, we recommend that you read the relevant sections of the *System V User's Manual*, and the *System V Administrator's Guide*. There is lots of helpful information in there. Make a special effort to absorb the sections called 'init' (the system initialization process) and 'crash' (what to do after a crash). Although these sections are often written for DEC PDP-11's), the generic information is useful.

Above all, have lots of fun with System V (we do!).

Index

There are some special conventions in this index that you should note:

- Page numbers in **bold face** indicate the pages where the topic is defined. Other pages may mention that topic but don't necessarily contain the most definitive version.
- A page range in the form 55 *thru* 59 indicates where the topic covers many pages — the range serves as an aid to quick location of the topic area.